CW00553067

SONS OF JOHN COMPANY

The Indian and Pakistan Armies 1903–91

In the Spellmount/Nutshell Military list::

The Territorial Battalions – A pictorial history
The Yeomanry Regiments – A pictorial History
Over the Rhine – The Last Days of War in Europe
History of the Cambridge University OTC
Yeoman Service
The Fighting Troops of the Austro-Hungarian Army
Intelligence Officer in the Peninsula
The Scottish Regiments – A pictorial history
The Royal Marines – A pictorial history
The Royal Tank Regiment – A pictorial history
The Irish Regiments – A pictorial history
British Sieges of the Peninsula War
Victoria's Victories
Heaven and Hell – German paratroop war diary
Rorke's Drift
Came the Dawn – Fifty years an Army Officer
Kitchener's Army – A pictorial history
On the Word of Command – A pictorial history of the Regimental Sergeant Major
Marlborough – as Military Commander
The Art of Warfare in the Age of Marlborough
Epilogue in Burma 1945–48
Scandinavian Misadventure
The Fall of France
The First Victory – O'Connor's Desert Triumph Dec 1940–Feb 1941
Blitz Over Britain
Deceivers Ever – Memoirs of a Camouflage Officer
Indian Army of the Empress 1861–1903
Waters of Oblivion – The British Invasion of the River Plate 1806–07
The French are Coming – The Invasion Scare 1803–05
Heroes for Victoria 1837–1901
Commando Diary
Craufurds Light Division
Military Marching
British Military Band Uniforms – Vol 1 the Cavalry
British Military Band Uniforms – Vol 2 The Household Regiments

In the Military Machine list:

Napoleon's Military Machine
Falklands Military Machine
Wellington's Military Machine

In the Nautical List:

Sea of Memories
Evolution of Engineering in the Royal Navy Vol I 1827–1939
In Perilous Seas

In the Aviation list:

Diary of a Bomber Aimer
Operation 'Brograt' – From France to Burma – Memoirs of a Fighter Pilot
A Medal for Life – Capt Leefe Robinson VC
Three Decades as Pilot – The Third Generation
Bob Doe – Fighter Pilot
The Allied Bomber War 1939–45

SONS OF JOHN COMPANY

The Indian and Pakistan Armies 1903–91

John Gaylor

Forward by
Field Marshal Sir John Chapple GCB, CBE

SPELLMOUNT LTD.
TUNBRIDGE WELLS, KENT

First published in the UK in 1992 by
Spellmount Ltd
12 Dene Way, Speldhurst
Tunbridge Wells, Kent TN3 0NX

British Library Cataloguing in Publication Data

Gaylor, John
Sons of John Company: Indian and Pakistan Armies, 1903–91. – (Military Pictorial History Series)
I Title II. Series
355.00954

ISBN 0-946771-98-7

Printed and bound in Great Britain by
Biddles Ltd, Guildford and King's Lynn

CONTENTS

FOREWORD
Field Marshal Sir John Chapple GCB CBE

I am delighted to introduce this book by John Gaylor who has for many years been Honorary Secretary of the Military Historical Society and whose interest in and love of the old Indian Army is so manifest in this work. It is a work founded on good research but illuminated by good feelings.

This book is essentially about the individual regiments of the old Indian Army and what has happened to them in the past 40 years or so since they moved, without a break, to the Armies of India and Pakistan.

There have been a number of books published in recent years about the pre 1947 Indian Army. All have something interesting to say and many have added to our sum of knowledge. Many have also been full of fascinating illustrations. However welcome these works have been they share one failing which is that they tend to stop tantalisingly short of the Second World War and the period of Partition. This is partly because the source material is so scarce, and even secondary sources such as regimental histories are much rarer than for earlier periods; it is also partly because events between 1945 and 1947 moved so fast that no-one had much time to record anything – indeed no-one stayed in any job very long either during this period of turmoil.

As a record of the services of Indian Regiments during the Second World War and subsequently, this book serves a most useful purpose and fills a long-felt gap. It will serve as a companion volume to Major Donovan Jackson's India's Army which was published just before the last war. In a sense it brings that work, invaluable as it has been, up to date and to quote from Field Marshal Lord Birdwood's foreword to that book it has 'been wanted for a long time'.

As a work of reference it contains lineages, class composition, battle honours and a brief record of services. It also gives details and dates of the units raised during the Second World War and since 1947 in India and Pakistan. The battle honours granted by these two nations are particularly interesting since they are based on the common Commonwealth list but were awarded on much different criteria from those used for the United Kingdom regiments. The partition and dispersal of the class companies to new regiments in 1947 is also a valuable record, as is the absorption of the Indian State Forces regiments into the new Indian regiments.

All in all this book will be in great demand as a reference work and I am confident of its success.

PREFACE

It is hard to know precisely what prompted this book. Perhaps it was that I grew up in the 1930s when much of the literature for boys had an Indian setting. The perennial unrest on The Frontier continued up to and, indeed, after 1939 and must have made some sort of impression.

I reached India as a colonial soldier of The Royal West African Frontier Force, to join the 82nd (West African) Division then serving in Burma. In early 1946, the Africans returned home whilst those Europeans with high Age and Service Group numbers (which governed demobilisation) remained behind. I was transferred to the Indian Army and made the acquaintance of those Indian battalions still in Burma. Whilst there, I encountered Compton Mackenzie who had come out to write his history of the Indian Army in the Second World War. Sadly, only the first volume of 'Eastern Epic' was ever finished and I devoured that when it appeared.

In 1977, I took a party from the Military Historical Society to India where we visited several regimental centres and, in 1980, we undertook a similar visit to Pakistan. During these visits and others more recently, we were all impressed with the regard for tradition which existed in both countries. It seemed to me then that there was a case for the British to be made aware of their bequests to India and Pakistan and for the recipients of these legacies to have a better idea of the depth of history behind them.

I am indebted to the late Chief of General Staff, Field Marshal Sir John Chapple, himself a 2nd Goorkha, for the foreword and also for contributing a number of suggestions. In quantitative terms, I am grateful to Richard Head for allowing me access to his extensive Indian Army genealogical records and for his constant readiness to answer questions at almost any hour of the day, whenever official records were either lacking or short on detail. Ashok Nath, an ex-Armoured Corps Officer from India and Pushpindar Singh Chopra (son of the late Major-General Mohinder Singh Chopra) have provided valuable photographs of contemporary Indian soldiers, whilst Brigadier Saeed Ismat, the recent Pakistan Military Adviser in London, has done much to resolve my problems with the scant published information on his own country's army.

For permission to use the painting of India's President's Bodyguard I am indebted to the artist, originally Colonel P Giannatassio, now lieutenant general and Italy's Minister of Defence.

Mr J. Enoch Powell, then Brigadier Powell and a member of the Willcox Indian Army Reorganisation Committee convened by the then General Sir Claude Auchinleck in 1944, offered me his hospitality to consult an original copy of the Committee's Report and later made a copy available. This was invaluable in both answering some questions and posing others.

Major General Chand Narain Das OBE, commissioned into the 6th Rajputana Rifles in 1933 has offered great encouragement, as has Lieutenant General S.C. Menezes, late the 4th Bombay Grenadiers whilst several British officers of the Indian Army Association have read their own regiments' entries.

Finally, my thanks must go to my friends Colin and Sue Storton for their unequalled contribution to the labour of typing and correcting my manuscript on their word-processor. My neighbours, they would drop completed work through my letter-box whilst I would return the corrections the next day the same way. As an occasional author, I can recommend no better system.

INTRODUCTION

Britain's legacy to India and Pakistan when Independence and Partition took place in August 1947 was much the same as was given to other overseas territories in the next two decades, but India had been under British influence, both mercantile and military, for three centuries, longer by far than almost all other possessions of the island-race and the two inheritor-nations were well-fitted to lead their own lives in the mould left by their old mentors. The Indian Civil Service did not recruit Britons after 1939 and, in any case, when Partition came, the entire ICS numbered scarcely 1,000, half of that number Indians.

The far larger, subordinate provincial civil service, was wholly Indian and, thus, future administration was in experienced hands, familiar with the labryinthine local legislation which had evolved as a working compromise between indigenous customs and British justice. There were more than 90,000 doctors, trained in western medical skills and as many university professors and lecturers. The law, of course, might well have been thought to be overstocked. The railways were well established, with almost a century of service behind them and, lest all the foregoing be thought too turgid a legacy, cricket was bequeathed to the two new nations for their amusement. Today, in both India and Pakistan, enthusiasm for the game is, if anything, stronger than ever it was before Independence.

To make the entire legacy workable, the British left the English language which was, in India, at least, programmed to last for just a few years, until such time as Hindi could be promoted to take its place. However, Hindi is not a pan-Indian language and South Indian legislators have repeatedly declared their inability to read edicts from New Delhi in Hindi. If Tamil were not used, then they would settle for English.

Now, after almost a half-century of independence, perhaps the most visible evidence of the British legacy apart from English-language advertisment-hoardings and road-signs, is the two armies.

In both India and Pakistan, regiments with British origins and British titles, cherished by their officers and soldiers, continue to wear uniforms and to carry colours, all based on the British pattern. Regimental centres, outdoing Colchester and Aldershot, rejoice in white-painted brickwork behind immaculate quarter-guards whilst paragons of military turn-out direct the traffic in the old cantonments. Some sensitive battle-honours have, perhaps understandably, been overlooked but the classes traditionally enlisted by the British are still heavily recruited in India whilst Baluch soldiers, regarded latterly as unacceptable by Britain, are hardly more numerous now in the Baluch Regiment in Pakistan.

The military legacy has not been entirely one-sided. In the British Army, officers and soldiers with Indian experience have long since retired but much of the Indian influence remains. Colours bear Indian battle-honours, a score of brass gongs on guard-room verandahs betoken Indian service, whilst, in Northern Ireland, the chai-wallah – colloquially rendered as charwallah –

survives. The old, free-enterprise seller of tea and cakes who served British soldiers for a dozen generations moved, after Partition, to Egypt until the Canal Zone was vacated more than thirty years ago: he moved on to Cyprus and now serves in the corrugated-iron sangars of the Six Counties where patrols keep odd hours and welcome hot tea and egg-banjos at 0300 hrs.

Old soldiers of 123 Field Regiment Royal Artillery who meet regularly in Sheffield remember their days in India during the 1939–45 war when they became airborne gunners. They habitually refer to their old unit, not as 'One Two Three Field' but as 'Ek Doh Teen'.

Early last year, during the brief campaign in the Gulf, 40 Field Regiment Royal Artillery deployed four batteries: 10 (Assaye) Battery earned their battle-honour in South India in 1803 as No. 3 Company Bombay Artillery, 38 (Seringapatam) Battery earned theirs, also in South India in 1799 as No. 4 Company Bombay Artillery, 129 (China) Battery won the honour in 1840 as C Company, 2 Bn Madras Artillery whilst the fourth, 137 (Java) Battery formed in 1778, qualified for the honour-title in 1811 as No. 1 Company, 2 Bn Bengal Artillery. An elephant badge is now worn on the upper arm by 10 and 137 Batteries, a tiger by 38 Battery and a China Dragon by 129 Battery.

All four were units of the Army of the Honourable East India Company, known to its servants, British and Indian, as 'John Company'.

India still haunts not only British history but also British social life. It was a relationship which has never been parallelled by any other country and which can never happen again.

1. THE EVOLUTION OF THE INDIAN ARMY

No study of the Indian Army can be undertaken without an awareness of the circumstances which brought about and attended its birth.

It was always customary to claim that the development of the British Empire was the result of trade following the flag. In India, the reverse was true and the flag followed 'The Company of merchants of London trading unto the East Indies' and which became the Honourable East India Company, certainly one of the greatest commercial enterprises ever, where fortunes were made by its employees both for John Company and for themselves.

Trading initially in three of the principal port areas, Bombay, Madras and Calcutta, the Company rapidly spread inland and effectively created areas of influence later to become formalised as the presidencies of Bombay, Madras and Bengal. The factory – as trading stations were first styled – at Surat, north of Bombay, was fully established by 1619 and its first guards were English soldiers as were those at Madras in 1640 who, in fact, were furnished from Surat. In turn, when the factories in Bengal were opened later that century, their guards were sent to Calcutta from Madras. Thus, the first armed forces of the Company were English.

In 1662, the Portuguese presented Bombay to King Charles II of England as part of the dowry from his wife and the king sent a regiment of about 400 men as a garrison but the local Portuguese authorities would not permit them to occupy Bombay until 1665 by which time many of the men had died. Numbers were brought up to strength by the enlistment of other European nationals and some 200 Deccanis, locally recruited. Shortly afterwards, the king handed Bombay over to the Company and the regiment was invited in 1668 to enter Company service and most of the men elected to do so; these, thus, became the first Indian soldiers to be inducted into the Company.

In 1685, John Child, the chief of the Bombay Establishments was appointed Governor and General of all the Company's forces in India but this grandiose title had little real significance.

Other European nations had probed Indian trade possibilities but few as effectively as the French and Portuguese and whilst the latter were prepared to maintain a low profile, the French had established extensive trading factories of their own as well as good relations with powerful local rulers. They recruited local forces and were strong enough in 1746 to take Madras. Major Stringer Lawrence, fresh from England, brought together the Madras European Companies into a battalion in 1748 and this may be considered to be the date of formation of the Madras Presidency Army. Command of Madras was once again restored, aided by troops from Bombay, the first such instance of inter-Presidency help. Subsequently, Stringer Lawrence was appointed Commander of all the Company's forces in India but this also seemed a somewhat empty style since he never visited, nor controlled any of the forces outside Madras. In 1753, HM's 39th Foot arrived in Madras, the first posting of a British Army unit to

India; in 1881, the 39th became the 1st Bn The Dorsetshire Regiment and bore the honour 'Primus in Indis' (First in India) as a unique distinction until 1958 when they were amalgamated with The Devonshire Regiment, the new combined regiment continuing to carry this motto on its cap-badge.

In 1756, Calcutta was taken by the Nawab of Bengal and it was Robert Clive, once a writer in the offices of the Company in that city, who retook it with forces, both European and local from Madras and Bombay and a detachment from HM's 39th Foot. In 1758, Clive formed the Bengal European Regiment and he also inspired the creation of sepoy battalions, with European officers. Hitherto, locally-raised companies had been Indian-officered. That same year, similar battalions were formed in Madras but a further ten years were to elapse before the first sepoy battalions were formed in Bombay.

Although Stringer Lawrence was appointed Commander of all the Company's forces in India, there was not a regular succession in this post until the Government of India Act in 1773 established control by central government over the presidencies and created the appointment of a Commander-in-Chief in India. That said, much freedom of action was enjoyed by the provincial governors and the local commanders.

Then, as ever, came into being those exceptions to the accepted rules which have made the study of the Indian Army such a specialised and complex subject.

In 1843, the conquest of Sind by Sir Charles Napier resulted in the formation in the new province of local regiments which remained under the control of the Bombay Government and its Commander-in-Chief. In the same way, the addition of the Punjab to the Company's possessions in 1849 brought about the formation of the Punjab Frontier Force which was under the orders of the local Punjab Government although, in military matters, it was controlled by the Bengal Army 1200 miles away in Calcutta.

The Devil's Wind blew across Northern and Central India in 1857. The Great Mutiny of the Bengal Army began in Meerut in May and was not finally quelled until the end of the following year. Bombay was hardly affected and Madras not at all but the Bengal Army was scarcely recognisable in the aftermath. By proclamation on the 1st November 1858, the whole army of the Honourable East India Company came under the Crown.

The Company's European infantry, nine battalions, was transferred to the British Line as the 101st to 109th Regiments of Foot, several later to be translated into Irish regiments. The Bengal, Madras and Bombay European artillery was merged into the Royal Artillery. The most newly-created Company units, three regiments of light cavalry, were added to the end of HM's cavalry of the line as the 19th, 20th and 21st Light Dragoons.

The presidential armies continued under their respective commanders-in-chief with the Punjab Frontier Force still under the provincial government but regarded as part of the Bengal Army. The Hyderabad Contingent and other local corps outside the presidencies remained under direct governmental control.

Gradually, steps were taken to unify the army. The three Presidential Staff Corps were merged in 1891 into one Indian Staff Corps which embraced all officers of the Indian Army, a term not generally used previously. Two years later, Madras and Bombay Presidencies lost their posts of Commander-in-Chief and, two years after that, in 1895, the Army was divided into four commands - Bengal, Madras, Bombay and Punjab, a logical development since, over the years, the Bengal area of influence had stretched further and further west from Calcutta; the Grand Trunk Road extended through Delhi and beyond to meet the army's needs but creating a vast, unwieldy military machine.

The table below indicates the then strength of the Army in India:

Command	*Indian Troops*			
	Cav Regts	*Arty Bns*	*Sapper & Miner Corps*	*Inf Bns (ie Regts)*
Punjab	15	5	–	37
Bengal	9	2	1	22
Madras	3	–	1 plus 1 Coy	32
Bombay	7	2	1	26
TOTAL	34	9	3 plus 1 Coy	117

In 1902, Lord Kitchener became Commander-in-Chief, India and, despite conflict with the viceroy, Lord Curzon, began to effect a series of far-reaching military reforms. His objective was to complete the unification of the Indian Army which had begun in 1895 and he abolished the Indian Staff Corps with its suggestion that officers were staff and not regimental officers. Henceforth, all officers were to be gazetted direct to regiments. All cavalry and infantry regiments of the three old presidencies were formed into overall Indian Army cavalry and infantry lines, the Bengal units taking the first numbers, a galling assumption of seniority and much resented by many of the old Bombay and Madras officers who not only knew that the old coast armies were of older lineage but felt affronted that the army which had mutinied should be accorded precedence.

In the new numbering sequence, all reference to the regiments' previous presidency affiliations was omitted from the new titles.

Following the regimental renumbering came the reorganisation of the army into tactical formations for the first time. By 1908, India was divided into two armies:

Northern Army

1st (Peshawar) Division
2nd (Rawalpindi) Division
3rd (Lahore) Division
7th (Meerut) Division
8th (Lucknow) Division
Kohat, Bannu and Derajat Brigades

Southern Army

4th (Quetta) Division
5th (Mhow) Division
6th (Poona) Division
9th (Secunderabad) Division
Burma Division
Aden Brigade

On the outbreak of war in August 1914, the total fighting strength of the Indian Army was approximately 150,000 all ranks. Four years later, in November 1918, this had risen to more than one and a half million.

Following the war came the inevitable reorganization. Problems of reinforcement and supply meant extensive change in the fighting arms. Cavalry, as in the British Army, was in more abundant supply than was needed and the strength was halved by amalgamations. Infantry, the Queen of Battles, as every commander knows, is never in surplus but it was thought more expedient to form twenty regiments, each having an average of four battalions and it was, broadly, in this form that the Indian Army entered the Second World War in September 1939. Its strength was 189,000 then and, at the war's end in August 1945, it numbered two and half millions.

Partition followed in August 1947 so that there was no time for the normal crop of reforms which follows a major war. Division of the army followed on the basis of one third for Pakistan and two thirds for India. The story of subsequent developments will be told later but the old Indian Army still lives on throughout the sub-continent no matter where one looks – regiments, titles, traditions, ranks and uniforms remain firmly based on the British model bequeathed in 1947.

2. THE 1903-23 PERIOD

The decision to unify the armies of the three Presidencies was first made in 1880 after the Second Afghan War but fifteen years were to elapse before the 'Army of India', divided into four Commands – Punjab (including the North-West Frontier and the Punjab Frontier Force), Bengal, Madras (including Burma) and Bombay (including Sind, Quetta and Aden) – was formally established, each Command under a lieutenant-general directly responsible to the Commander-in-Chief, India.

It remained then for Lord Kitchener, appointed C-in-C on 28 Nov 02, to renumber the cavalry and infantry regiments, creating a visibly unified Indian Army. The result is shown in Appendix C but some few comments may be helpful. Numerical preference was given to the Bengal Army which, although the largest, was not the oldest, followed by the Punjab Frontier Force, then the old Coast Army of Madras, then the Hyderabad Contingent and, finally, the old Bombay Army. Although the pre-1903 titles are not, in themselves, relevant to this work, I have included them in Appendix C to illustrate the old titles, with their reference to previous Presidency affiliations. All such references were to be removed, Emphasis was given to subsidiary titles based on historical events or on the names of officers responsible for raising them.

The Cavalry

The Cavalry of the Line received the numbers 1–39, the only vacant number being 24. An attempt was made to retain, wherever possible, a significant digit in the new number. Thus the 1st Punjab Cavalry became the 21st, the 2nd became the 22nd, etc. The 4th Punjab Cavalry was reduced after the Afghan War: otherwise, they would have been the 24th. In this way, the 1st Bombay Lancers were enabled to become the 31st Lancers. The 1st, 2nd and 3rd Madras Lancers were not able to retain their numbers, even in part, but became the 26th, 27th and 28th Light Cavalry. But then, the Madras regiments were always a little different. They were the only ones to ride Government horses in the same way that British cavalry did. The rest of the Indian cavalry was silladar. This was a yeomanry system whereby the individual soldier supplied and maintained his horse, clothing, equipment, arms (not his rifle) and quarters, receiving in return a higher rate of pay than the non-silladar soldier whose needs were met by the Government. If a recruit presented himself for enlistment without the necessary finance, one of his more wealthy fellow tribesmen could offer help. The man so enlisted was known as a Bargir and a recognized portion of his pay was drawn by his fortunate sponsor.

Later, the increasing standard of performance demanded of the Indian cavalry decreed a horse and equipment of better quality than would usually have been obtainable by the silladar. The system was therefore modified; the recruit no longer brought a horse and equipment. These were supplied by the regiment, but a sum of money, known as his assami, was to be paid by the man. A monthly deduction was then made from his pay to provide for the replacement of horse and equipment which became unserviceable. The new system was popular because not only was the soldier protected against the untimely death of his mount, but, on discharge at the end of his service, he would receive the value of his assami in cash, the horse and the equipment then being leased to the next man to join.

Whilst the cost of the silladar regiment was clearly substantially less to Government in peacetime, active service, especially of the kind experienced in the Great War, brought manifest problems. Never before had the cavalry been employed in such large numbers, for so long and so far from home. Reinforcements sent from India to France and Egypt had to be pooled before posting to units often not their own. This involved service among strangers to which the Indian soldier of the time held strong objection.

In peacetime, silladar regiments chose their own pattern dress, equipment and saddlery. It was impossible for the ordnance services to maintain stocks of special-to-regiment stores. Heavy demands for recruits meant that regiments could no longer be expected to insist on payment of assamis in cash. If this had been advanced out of regimental funds and the trained soldier were drafted to the front, it was by no means certain that he would reach his own regiment there. No assamis were levied and then the further complication arose that such a man would be receiving the more advantageous rates of pay of a silladar without having first laid down his initial cash commitment.

All these considerations and others, led to the early abandonment of the silladar-system after the Great War.

The Infantry

As with the cavalry, it was the Bengal element which took precedence in the all-Indian Infantry of the Line constituted in 1903. The first forty-eight were direct title changes as can be seen in the Table in Appendix C: the numbers were unaltered. The left hand column gives the immediate pre-1903 title but many of them were of no great antiquity. The 46th Punjab Infantry was raised in 1900 followed in 1901 by the 47th Sikhs and the 48th Pioneers. The 39th (Garhwali) Regiment of Bengal Infantry came into being in 1891 taking the number surrendered the year before by the 39th Native Infantry. In 1888, at the Rawalpindi Review, where the salute was taken by Lord Dufferin, the then Viceroy, the day dawned fine and troops took up their positions, ready to march past. Then, the rain began to fall in torrents. After the artillery and the cavalry had ridden past, the elephant-batteries completed the task of turning the parade-ground into a morass and even the booted British battalions found it hard to keep their footing, much less keep step. In those days, many of the Indian regiments wore shoes and, after marching past and losing their shoes in the mud, many of the sepoys of the 39th Bengal Infantry fell out to retrieve their footwear. It was said, indeed, that the native officer bearing the Queen's Colour was able to retrieve his shoes with the top of the pole. The regiment was disgraced, and, shortly afterwards, disbanded. Several years later, the 2/3rd Gurkhas, largely made up of Garhwalis, became the 39th (the Garhwali) regiment of Bengal Infantry, a choice of number by no means welcomed by the new regiment in the light of its earlier associations.

Nos 49 and 50 were left blank. As with the cavalry, the Punjab Frontier Force followed: its infantry element consisted of four battalions of Sikh Infantry formed originally from Sikhs of the defeated Sikh army in 1847 and five of Punjab infantry. The Sikh Infantry, previously numbered 1st to 4th was listed as the 51st to 54th, preserving the significant digit as did the cavalry. Nos 55 to 59 took care of the Punjab Infantry and No 60 was left blank.

The Madras Infantry followed, adding sixty to their numbers. Thus the 1st Madras Pioneers became the 61st Pioneers omitting reference to their regional origin and so on. However, a growing trend was formalized in 1903. It was the opinion of General Sir Frederick Roberts that the Southern races did not make good infantry soldiers. The South had long been at peace and its soldiers had lost their keen edge. It was time to run down the Madras elements of the Indian Army's infantry and replace them with the hard men of the North – Sikhs, Rajputs, Dogras, and Punjabi Mussalmans. As early as 1890 the change had begun and the 1902 Indian Army List shows that the then composition of the 2nd Madras Infantry was four companies Punjabi Mussalmans, two companies Jat Sikhs and two companies Rajputs. The next year's change of title was to the 62nd Punjabis, a more apt designation.

It was after the Third Burma War in 1885–87 that six battalions of the Madras Line were designated Burma Battalions, intended for permanent security duty within Burma and it was these which led the way to 'Punjabisation'.

The battalions affected were as follows –

12th Madras Infantry became 2nd Burma Bn
29th Madras Infantry became 7th Burma Bn
30th Madras Infantry became 5th Burma Bn
31st Madras Infantry became 6th Burma Bn
32nd Madras Infantry became 4th Burma Bn
33rd Madras Infantry became 3rd Burma Bn

The 1st Burma Bn, of course, was the old 10th Madras Infantry but they were Gurkhas and so did not need to be 'Punjabised'. The actual cessation of hostilities did not coincide with King Thibaw's exile; for the next few years, the Burma Battalions of the Madras Line continued to earn further clasps to their India General Service Medal 1854.

By a curious paradox, it was the Madras Army which remained totally loyal during the Great Mutiny which lost more of its infantry strength in the period immediately prior to 1903. Madras regiments numbered from 1st to 52nd in the post-Mutiny realignment but, by 1903, the highest-numbered was the 33rd. By then they had come to be known as the 33rd Burma Infantry before adding the 60 to become the 93rd Burma Infantry in that year.

Before proceeding to the Bombay Line whose regiments were made to add one hundred to their unit number, it was found convenient to slip in after the 93rd the six infantry battalions of the Hyderabad Contingent who took the numbers 94 to 99. This contingent actually consisted of four cavalry regiments, six infantry battalions and four field batteries, all intended initially for the protection of the Nizam of Hyderabad but later inducted into the 'new' Indian Army having been maintained, economically enough, by His Exalted Highness. The 'Russell' of the 94th and 95th Infantry was the British Resident in Hyderabad.

The proud 1st Bombay Grenadiers became the 101st Grenadiers, the 2nd (Prince of Wales's Own) Bombay Grenadiers became the 102nd Prince of Wales's Own Grenadiers and so on. There being no sixth Bombay Infantry, a new 106th was created, the 106th Hazara Pioneers.

It should be stressed that references to Bengal, Madras or Bombay Armies should not be regarded as in any way related to those geographical areas which we recognise today. The Bengal Army, commanded from Calcutta, stretched across Northern India to the Punjab, Bombay troops served routinely as far from home as Aden, Karachi, and Quetta whilst Madras embraced all southern India and Burma.

The new Line consisted of battalions numbered from 1 to 130 with nine vacant numbers. The 39th Garhwal Rifles had two battalions and the Guides Infantry remained unnumbered but took precedence after the 54th Sikhs (Frontier Force). Of these Infantry battalions, twelve were pioneers with special training in road and rail making and rough engineering work; they were appropriately equipped but were also trained as infantry. Such a role may not have qualified them to be regarded as elite or socially desirable but they were, in fact, popular postings for British officers who found that the Pioneers tended to see more active service than did many of the more conventional infantry. The Pioneers were unique in the armies of the British Empire since only India apparently expected its soldiers to fight on near-perpendicular slopes by way of goat-tracks and seasonal water-courses.

In 1886, a change in organisation had taken place in that the Infantry regiments (in effect, battalions) were linked together in groups of two or three and were given permanent regimental centres at which one battalion of the group would always be located. Recruits were then enlisted for a group and might be called upon to serve in any of the battalions in that group. This meant that one battalion could only be reinforced at the expense of another. These groups of linked battalions were in no sense regiments but shared a centre. It was, in fact, a foretaste of what was to come in 1923.

The Indian Army List for October 1914 shows the centres and groupings as follows: –

Allahabad	1st Brahmans	3rd Brahmans	
Agra	2nd Rajputs	4th Rajputs	13th Rajputs
	16th Rajputs		
Benares	5th Light Infantry	17th Infantry	18th Infantry
Meerut	6th Jats	10th Jats	
Lucknow	7th Rajputs	8th Rajputs	11th Rajputs
Bareilly	12th Pioneers	48th Pioneers	
Mooltan	14th Sikhs	15th Sikhs	45th Sikhs
Jhelum	19th Punjabis	22nd Punjabis	24th Punjabis
Lahore	20th Punjabis	21st Punjabis	26th Punjabis
Ambala	23rd Pioneers	32nd Pioneers	34th Pioneers
Ferozepore	25th Punjabis	27th Punjabis	28th Punjabis
Peshawar	29th Punjabis	30th Punjabis	31st Punjabis
Sialkot	33rd Punjabis	40th Pathans	46th Punjabis
Rawalpindi	35th Sikhs	36th Sikhs	47th Sikhs
	37th Dogras	38th Dogras	41st Dogras
Lansdowne	1/39th Garwhalis	2/39th Garhwalis	
Bannu	51st Sikhs	53rd Sikhs	54th Sikhs
Kohat	52nd Sikhs	56th Rifles	59th Rifles
Dera Ismail Khan	55th Rifles	57th Rifles	58th Rifles
Hoti Mardan	Guides		
Trichinopoly	61st Pioneers	64th Pioneers	81st Pioneers
	63rd Light Infantry		83rd Light Infantry
Secunderabad	62nd Punjabis	66th Punjabis	84th Punjabis
	75th Carnatic	79th Carnatic	86th Carnatic
	76th Punjabis	82nd Punjabis	87th Punjabis

Bangalore	67th Punjabis	69th Punjabis	74th Punjabis
Mandalay	72nd Punjabis	92nd Punjabis	93rd Burma Infantry
St. Thomas's Mount	73rd Carnatic	80th Carnatic	88th Carnatic
Meiktila	89th Punjabis	90th Punjabis	91st Punjabis
Ahmednagar	101st Grenadiers	108th Infantry	109th Infantry
Dusa	102nd Grenadiers	112th Infantry	113th Infantry
Satara	103rd Mahratta LI	105th Mahratta LI	110th Mahratta LI
Nasirabad	104th Rifles	123rd Rifles	125th Rifles
Kirkee	107th Pioneers	121st Pioneers	128th Pioneers
Poona	114th Mahrattas	116th Mahrattas	117th Mahrattas
Mhow	119th Infantry	120th Rajputana	122nd Rajputana
Quetta	106th Pioneers	124th Baluch	126th Baluch
Karachi	127th Baluch	129th Baluch	130th Baluch

In the decade following the Kitchener reforms several disbandments left gaps in the infantry line, many of which were to be promptly filled during the First World War.

The 65th Carnatic Infantry was disbanded in 1904 as was the 71st Coorg Rifles, the latter because of insufficient recruits. The 77th and 78th Moplah Rifles were disbanded in 1907 after a brief existence. The Moplahs were a race of Dravidians from the Malabar coast with claims to Arab ancestry. They were fanatical Muslims who, on more than one occasion, opposed Police and European troops with a fervour which it was felt might be profitably harnessed in the Government's cause. One of the two battalions raised was subsequently sent to the Frontier, wearing the tarbush, a military novelty for the Indian Army but their showing was not impressive and as the potential recruitment pool was not too large the experiment was terminated. They were known, rather flippantly, as the Moppity-Pops.

In 1917 a Bengali unit was formed and they were conveniently allocated the number 49 which was vacant in the 'Bengal block'. The Kumaon Rifles, a successful recruiting experiment, became the 50th, also just in the 'Bengal block'.

In 1917, the 70th Burma Rifles was raised, filling an appropriate space in the 'Madras block'.

In place of the 71st Coorgs, 1917 saw the raising of the 71st Punjabis, recruited from Punjabi Christians.

The post-war army took on the 70th but the 71st vanished in 1919 into the 111th Mahars, themselves only raised in 1917 and fated to disappear in 1922.

Another Burma unit raised in 1917 became the 85th Burman Rifles in 1918.

During the Great War, many battalions raised duplicate units and some triplicate as can be seen in Appendix C but a series of battalions beginning at No 131 and extending, with gaps, to number 156 was recruited quickly, some from battalions in the Middle East, some from armed police forces and others from the princely states. Some of these saw service in Mesopotamia but all were disbanded by 1921.

The immediate post-Mutiny decision concerning Gurkhas was to keep them within the Bengal Line, but later in 1858 they were separated with their own numbered sequence. It was in 1815 that the Gurkhas were first recruited to the British Crown and the 1st Nasiri Battalion came to be designated the 66th Bengal Native Infantry in 1850; in 1861, they became the 1st Gurkha Regiment. The Sirmoor Battalion was designated the 17th Bengal Native Infantry in 1861, to become later that year, the 2nd Gurkha Regiment. The Kamaon Battalion was briefly the 18th Bengal Native Infantry but became the 3rd Gurkha

Regiment in 1861 whilst the Extra Gurkha Regiment, raised in 1857, became, in 1861, firstly the 19th Bengal Native Infantry and then, the 4th Gurkha Regiment.

The 42nd (Assam) Regiment of the Bengal Infantry became officially Gurkha in 1886 as the 42nd Regiment Gurkha Light Infantry but did not join the separately-numbered Gurkha series until 1903 when they became the 6th Gurkha Rifles. Similarly, the 43rd Regiment Bengal Light Infantry, another Assam corps, became the 43rd Regiment Gurkha Light Infantry in 1886, going on to become the 7th Gurkha Rifles in 1903 and, later, in 1907, the 2/8th Gurkha Rifles.

The 44th Regiment Bengal Native Infantry, from Sylhet was restyled the 44th Regiment Gurkha (Light) Infantry and, finally, the 8th Gurkha Rifles in 1903 (subsequently 1/8th).

Thus, with the creation of the Gurkha Line, the numbers 42, 43 and 44 became free to be allocated to the Deoli Irregular Force, the Erinpura Irregular Force and the Merwara Battalion, all three local units from Rajputana.

The Fatehgarh Levy, raised in 1817, became the 63rd Bengal Native Infantry in 1824, surviving the Mutiny to emerge as the 9th Regiment of Bengal Native Infantry in 1861 and being formally recognised as Gurkhas in 1894 on redesignation as the 9th (Gurkha Rifle) Regiment Bengal Infantry. In 1903, of course, they became the 9th Gurkha Rifles.

The only Gurkha regiments not to be embraced by the Bengal Line were the 5th and the 10th. The former was raised in 1858 as the 25th Punjab Infantry or Hazara Gurkha Battalion and went on to become the 5th Gurkha Rifles in 1901. The 10th was created in 1887 as the Kubo Valley Military Police Battalion, to become the 10th Regiment (1st Burma Battalion) Madras Infantry in 1890 and the 10th Gurkha Rifles in 1901.

An 11th Gurkha Rifles, four battalions strong, was formed in Mesopotamia and Egypt in 1918 but it was completely disbanded by mid-1922.

3. AFTER THE GREAT WAR

The Great War ended in November 1918 and plans were already well in hand to implement certain changes in the Indian Army's regimental structures. It would not be scrupulously correct to classify all these as based on pure considerations of military efficiency. Economy also played its part.

Cavalry

Cavalry was in surfeit, as indeed, it was in the British Army. In France, both British and Indian cavalry divisions had fed and tended their horses, cleaned and polished harness and weapons, awaiting their call to mount and ride through the gap punched in the German line by long-suffering infantry and to spread out once through, create havoc in the enemy's rear-areas and bring the war to a speedy conclusion. The call never came. But the tank did and the writing on the wall was even legible from India. Only twenty-one regiments of cavalry were to be retained in the post-war Indian Army. This involved the loss of eighteen regular regiments but, rather than disband them, it was resolved to follow the British Army practice at that time and to amalgamate them in pairs. The thirty-nine regiments were re-formed as eighteen linked pairs and three which were retained as separate entities. These privileged last three were the 27th and the 28th Light Cavalry, the two oldest in the service and the Guides Cavalry which was separated from the Guides Infantry in the Corps of Guides. The latter had previously incorporated elements of both arms in what, nowadays, might be described as a battalion-group. In addition to the effective loss of eighteen regiments, there was also a 56% loss of the pre-war personnel establishment. Details of the amalgamations into regiments, numbered 1–21 are shown in Appendix 'C' with the titles eventually agreed. Initially, linked old numbers were used as in the British Army but the new numbering was accepted with rather ill grace in many cases. The 31st Duke of Connaught's Own Bombay Lancers were the last of the legions to return to India in November 1923, and, by that time, the silladar-system had been abolished. Every sowar now wore Government equipment, rode a Government horse and ate Government rations.

To overcome the problem of the supply of reinforcements experienced during the Great War, seven cavalry groups were designated, each of three regiments and class compositions were adjusted so that all regiments in a group were similarly composed. There were, at this time, three 'class' regiments - 1st Skinner's Horse, composed of Hindustani Mussalmans 14th Murray's Jat Lancers composed of four squadrons of Jats and the 15th Cureton's Multanis, all Multani Pathans. Seven stations were selected to form suitable permanent locations based on internal security duties and one of the three regiments in each group would always be there in a permanent regimental centre. On mobilisation, a group depot would be formed in each station, responsible for the training and reinforcements of the whole group. Personnel surplus to the war establishments of the regiments of the group plus all the reservists would make up the depot, all now of the correct classes. Another change was in the regimental establishment. This was now to consist of three sabre squadrons and a headquarter wing, this latter holding specialists such as signallers, machine-gunners, etc. Previously, four sabre squadrons had each contributed a quota of such specialists when required. This was in line with British cavalry practice at the time.

The seven cavalry groups were as follows, with details of the relevant classes recruited:

1st Poona	1st Skinner's Horse 2nd Lancers (Gardner's Horse) 3rd Cavalry

(One squadron of Hindustani Mussalmans and Mussalman Rajputs (Ranghars), one of Rajputs (United Provinces) and one of Jats).

2nd Lahore	4th Hodson's Horse 5th Probyn's Horse 6th DCO Lancers

(One squadron of Punjabi Mussalmans, one of Sikhs and one of Dogras)

3rd Secunderabad	7th Light Cavalry 8th KGO Light Cavalry 9th Royal Deccan Horse

(One squadron of Deccani Mussalmans, one of Sikhs and one of Jats)

4th Rawalpindi	10th Guides Cavalry (FF) 11th PAVO Cavalry (FF) 12th Cavalry (FF)

(One squadron of Dogras, one of Sikhs and one of Punjabi Mussalmans)

5th Jubbulpore	13th DCO Lancers 14th Scinde Horse 15th Lancers

(One squadron of Pathans, one of Sikhs and one of Mussalman Rajputs)

6th Jhansi	16th Light Cavalry 17th Poona Horse 18th KEO Cavalry

(One squadron of Jats, one of Kaimkhanis and one of Rajputs (Rajputana))

7th Delhi	19th KGO Lancers 20th Lancers 21st KGO Central India Horse

(One squadron of Sikhs, one of Jats and one of Punjabi Mussalmans)

During the war six additional cavalry regiments had been created. The 40th, 41st and 42nd Cavalry were raised in India between April and July 1918 whilst the 43rd, 44th and 45th Cavalry were raised in Egypt in August 1918 from personnel rendered surplus to the immediate requirements of their regiments in consequence of the transfer of the Indian cavalry divisions from France to Palestine. The 43rd, 44th and 45th were sent back to India and brought up to establishment, only to be disbanded in January 1919. The 40th, 41st and 42nd survived rather longer and saw service in Baluchistan and the East Persia Cordon before disbandment in 1921. The 46th Cavalry was the 1st Alwar Lancers, regularised in 1918 'for the duration'.

The peace establishment of an Indian Cavalry regiment at this time was:

14 British Officers
18 Indian Officers
504 Indian NCOs and men

The system of seven cavalry stations continued until 1936 when mechanisation began to be actively considered. Three regiments were selected to be permanent training regiments and the remaining eighteen regiments were regrouped around them in three locations:

1st Group – Jhansi	1st Skinner's Horse 2nd Royal Lancers (Gardner's Horse) 3rd Cavalry 16th Light Cavalry 17th Poona Horse 18th KEO Cavalry 15th Lancers (Training regiment)
2nd Group – Ferozepore	4th Hodson's Horse 5th Probyn's Horse 10th Guides Cavalry (FF) 11th PAVO Cavalry (FF) 13th DCO Lancers 14th Scinde Horse 12th Sam Browne's Cavalry (FF) (Training regiment)
3rd Group – Lucknow	6th DCO Lancers 7th Light Cavalry 8th KGO Light Cavalry 9th Royal Deccan Horse 19th KGO Lancers 21st Central India Horse 20th Lancers (Training regiment)

The three regiments which had effectively been removed from active service and were destined to be permanent training units were not pleased with their new role but, by then, events were moving faster than such military readjustments usually moved in India.

Mechanisation began in 1938 and the decision was made to convert an Indian cavalry brigade consisting of the 3rd Carabiniers (British) the 13th DCO Lancers and the Scinde Horse. The two Indian regiments received armoured cars and 'The Carbs' had light tanks. The Scinde Horse paraded with their horses for the last time on 14 Apr 39.

The following year, Skinner's Horse, the 2nd Royal Lancers and the Central India Horse were unhorsed and became motorised regiments, equipped with 15 cwt trucks. Skinner's Horse's last mounted parade was at Rawalpindi on 28 Oct 39. By the end of 1940, all the Indian cavalry had been mechanised, the last being 19th KGO Lancers whose final horsed parade was in November 1940.

Regiments received light tanks, armoured cars or 15cwt trucks. The last were 'soft-skinned' vehicles and simply conferred improved speed and mobility. They were not indicative of a revolutionary new and proved tactical doctrine but simply of a shortage of armoured vehicles. However, as the supply situation improved, more armour became available and Skinner's Horse which had served in Gazelle Force in East Africa in 1941 in open trucks, found themselves with Humber armoured cars and American White scoutcars in Italy three years later.

In 1940, plans were made for the raising of an armoured divisional HQ, two armoured brigade HQ and one motor brigade HQ. 3rd Motor Brigade HQ was formed in July 1940 and the divisional HQ in September 1940. Immediate orders were issued for the raising of seven new Indian armoured regiments and two British. The latter were the 25th Dragoons and the 26th Hussars whilst the 42nd to 48th Cavalry were some of the born-again Indian regiments which had existed twenty years earlier.

The raisings began in April 1941 by large-scale milking of officers and men from the existing eighteen regiments. The 42nd Cavalry was formed on a British commanding officer and two other British officers, a risaldar-major and 200 men from the 3rd Cavalry. The regiment moved to Ranchi and, in February 1942, became a training unit for VCOs and NCOs of the Indian Armoured Corps, formally created on 1 May 41. The 42nd was disbanded in December 1943 handing over its Daimler and Humber armoured cars to the 8th King George V's Own Light Cavalry.

The 43rd had a longer existence. Converted to an armoured delivery regiment in December 1943, it was responsible for the delivery of fully kitted and crewed tanks to armoured units in Burma. Its strength was doubled when, in 1945, a second such regiment was raised and the two became the 3rd and 4th Armoured Delivery Regiments (43rd Cavalry). Both were disbanded in December 1946.

Risalpur, in the North West Frontier Province saw the raising of the 44th Cavalry in April 1941 on a cadre of a squadron of Jats from the 8th Light Cavalry (later detached to form the 100th Independent Light Tank Squadron which, under the command of an 8th Light Cavalry officer, was sent to Malaya, falling into Japanese hands alongside the 3rd Cavalry). It was turned into a frontier armoured regiment in September 1941 stationed at Peshawar for convoy protection and other frontier tasks. Disbandment followed in March 1943.

The 45th Cavalry was raised under Lieut. Colonel C.P.J. Prioleau, Guides Cavalry, at Meerut in April 1941 with Sikhs, Pathans and Dogras. The Guides Cavalry, 13th DCO Lancers and the Scinde Horse provided the Sikhs and Pathans whilst the Dogras came from Probyn's Horse. Equipped with American Stuart tanks, the 45th served in Burma, returning to India in March 1945 to be refitted with Sherman tanks which, on disbandment in April 1946 at Risalpur, were handed over to the 18th KEO Cavalry.

The 16th Light Cavalry provided the commanding officer and a Ranghar squadron for the formation of the 46th Cavalry whilst other personnel came from the 6th DCO Lancers and the Scinde Horse. Despite joining 254 Indian Tank Brigade in Risalpur in late 1941, the 46th was disbanded in November 1942.

Both 47th and 48th Cavalry were short-lived. The Poona Horse provided men for the 47th and 6th DCO Lancers for the 48th. Both were disbanded in August 1943.

Rather longer-lived and certainly having had a more interesting life was the Indian Long Range Squadron formed by the Ninth Army on Christmas Day 1941 from volunteers from 3 Indian Motor Brigade – 2 Royal Lancers, PAVO Cavalry and 18 KEO Cavalry. It had Squadron HQ and four patrols – J(Jat), M(Mussalman), R(Rajput) and S(Sikh) and was intended to harry the Germans in Iraq, Syria and Persia if the enemy should have successfully attacked through the Balkans. This thrust never occurred and J and R Patrols were sent to Egypt and attached to the Long Range Desert Group where they served on the open desert flank of the Eighth Army, searching for the route to outflank Rommel at Mareth. When the desert war ended, the ILRS was returned to India, expecting to be used in Burma but Wingate had already cornered the market in long range penetration and was not very keen on Indian troops, anyway. This Squadron finally found itself in Baluchistan patrolling the Persian-Afghan-Russian border in an attempt to discourage Soviet attempts to infiltrate clandestine parties into that strategically significant territory. The ILRS returned to India on Partition for disbandment. Its badge was crossed lances with a tablet 'LR' on the intersection.

The early reduction of the newly-raised Indian armoured regiments was simply attributable to the shortage of tanks. British tanks were not available in sufficient numbers to supply needs in India and America's interest in India did not extend any further than it's potential as a base for supplies to its large but unpredictable Chinese ally. However, finally, sufficient Sherman tanks were made available to fit out three British and three Indian armoured regiments for the re-conquest of Burma.

Mention has been made of frontier armoured regiments. In the decade before the Second World War, companies of the Royal Tank Corps, equipped with Vickers Mk II, IV and VI light tanks and Crossley armoured cars, had soldiered to uphold the frontier law. In 1938, the 13th DCO Lancers and Scinde Horse were mechanized to take over their duties and their vehicles. The armoured fighting vehicles (AFVs) were about fifteen years old, no longer fit for war service but good enough to keep the tribesmen in line. The Crossley armoured cars were actually old bodies mounted on Chevrolet chassis and these old monsters, weighing more than five tons each and mounting just two .303″ Vickers machine-guns, trundled along the roads, incapable of cross-country movement. The establishment of a frontier armoured regiment was one light tank squadron, two armoured car squadrons, regimental HQ and the LAD (light aid detachment). Each squadron had nine AFVs deployed in three troops. This particular variant of the cavalry arm was not long-lived. The 13th DCO Lancers were sent to Iraq in some haste in May 1941 and the Scinde Horse was relieved later that year by the 8th KGO Light Cavalry and the 44th Cavalry. In March 1943, the latter regiment was disbanded and the 8th Light Cavalry became a light armoured reconnaisance regiment in which role it later served in Burma in 19th Indian Division. Tanks remained on the Frontier until September 1943 in service with 101 Light Tank Squadron, the personnel of which then rejoined 8th Light Cavalry from which they had earlier been seconded.

The findings of the Willcox Reorganization Committee on the Indian cavalry were that three regiments should be disbanded. The three proposed were the 3rd Cavalry which was, in early 1945, still in Japanese hands and the two junior regiments, the 19th King George V's Own Lancers and the Central India Horse. The latter had suffered a partial mutiny in July 1940 when its Sikh squadron refused to embark at Bombay. This incident apart, the CIH has performed creditably in Egypt, East Africa, Persia and Italy. Only its position at the foot of the seniority ladder qualified it for disbandment.

However, as with so many of the Committee's recommendations, there was no time for their implementation with Partition looming so large after the end of the war and, in the event, as we shall see, Indian armour, far from contracting, was later to increase three-fold.

Pioneers

Pioneers referred to in the armies fighting the eighteenth century battles of Hindustan actually became the parent units of the three latter day Corps of Sappers and Miners and most of the twentieth century pioneers started as line infantry battalions.

The Concise Oxford Dictionary defines a pioneer as 'Member of infantry group serving to prepare road for main body of troops' but as Kipling, the Soldier's Poet, said of another regiment – 'an' when you've found out all it means, I'll tell you 'alf the rest'. In twenty years be-striding the turn of the century, the Bombay Corps was engaged in railway-construction, irrigation projects, barrack-building, dam and dock-work, as well as the expected roads and tracks wherever the Widow at Windsor ordered her sons, both white and brown, to march.

In 1864, there were two native Pioneer battalions, by 1890 there were six and, in 1904, there had become twelve. Pioneers were found to be so useful that existing infantry battalions were converted and new battalions raised as such. Moreover, service with them was popular with young British officers as the Pioneers saw frequent active service and enjoyed a high reputation.

Recruits for the ranks of the Pioneer battalions were not hard to find either. The Indian peasant was not slow to recognise the advantages in having such skills offered to him as could be put to good advantage on long leaves and after discharge.

Section 5 of Field Service Regulations, Part I, Operations 1909, said 'In battle, however, pioneers, being primarily fighting troops, will normally be used as such.'

Pioneers were organized initially, trained and armed as infantry but they were trained additionally in Field Engineering and carried 'Pioneer Equipment' to enable them to do their special tasks.

Every sepoy carried on his back in a leather case secured by straps, either a light pick-axe or a hoe-like tool called a 'mamootee'. NCOs and buglers did not carry these but had other tools, such as billhooks, saws, felling-axes, etc. carried in suitable cases. The remainder of the Pioneer Equipment – shovels, crowbars, carpenters' and blacksmiths' tools, guncotton and its accessories, crosscut saws – was carried on mules.

To compensate for his specialist load, the Pioneer sepoy carried only seventy rounds of ammunition, as against the one hundred carried by normal infantry.

In France, in 1914, it was found that the mamootee was not very useful in digging trenches and the leather equipment was converted to carry a shovel.

On mobilisation in 1914, each Indian division had one Pioneer battalion as part of its divisional troops and their usefulness was soon so apparent in France that British Pioneer battalions were initiated and, eventually, every British division also had a Pioneer battalion on its establishment. These were all disbanded at the end of the war.

The Indian Pioneers came to be used more for field engineering work and less as infantry. An order was published later in France that they were not to be used as infantry but, in Mesopotamia, they continued to serve as such.

By the end of the war, the pre-1914 principle that Pioneers were primarily infantry but might be used for field engineering when required had been overturned. More attention was being given to technical work although, on exercises in India, the Pioneers still often worked as infantrymen.

In the post-Great War reforms. the Pioneer battalions were taken out of the Infantry Line and concentrated into four separate Corps albeit three of them were still to be organised along the same lines as the new infantry regiments viz several active battalions and a training battalion functioning as a regimental centre.

In 1922, each Pioneer battalion, except the Training Battalions, was reorganized, the four Vickers machine-guns taken away and only six of the sixteen Lewis guns left. Tools were all to be carried either in carts or on transport mules and the leather Pioneer equipment was replaced by standard web equipment.

The next year, when 1/2 Bombay Pioneers went to Iraq, it seemed likely that hostilities against the Turks might be resumed and the battalion was, at once, re-equipped with the full, infantry quota of Lewis guns.

Indian Army Order No. 345 of 1927 defined the role of the Pioneers: 'Pioneers are primarily technical and are maintained and trained in peace for their technical duties in war. Pioneer battalions are organised into three companies to suit technical requirements primarily. Consequently, they will only be employed as infantry in an emergency or as a secondary role.'

Two years later, this 'sapperisation' of Pioneers, as it came to be called went further when the six remaining Lewis guns were withdrawn, together with all signalling equipment, thereby making it impossible for the Pioneers to serve as infantry. They became, in effect, marginally-less-effective field companies of Sappers and Miners – but too technically accomplished to be squandered as line infantry.

The writing was on the wall and, in July 1932, the Commander-in-Chief in India, General Sir Philip Chetwode Bart GCB KCMG DSO, announced that all Pioneers were to be disbanded, the official reasons for the decision being:

(a) The changed policy on the Frontier under which local civilian labour is now employed for road construction.
(b) At present, there are two types of field engineering units, one of which, i.e. Pioneers, cannot assume the role of the other, i.e. Sappers and Miners.
(c) Engineering troops of a division must be homogeneous and organized on lines suitable for their general role. The Sapper and Miner organization is that most suited to the tasks of a division and, moreover, the work of Field Companies embodies everything now done by Pioneers.
(d) By concentration of work in one organization, greater efficiency will be obtained in respect of direction, control and output and an unnecessary link in the chain of administration will be eliminated.
(e) The retention of an organization which is not fully suited to our needs cannot be justified'

On 10 Feb 33, all Pioneer battalions were struck off strength and disbandment was completed.

Infantry

On the outbreak of war in August 1914, the Indian Infantry and Pioneers consisted of 129 battalions. These were made up of 107 one-battalion regiments and eleven two-battalion regiments – the 39th Garhwal Rifles and the ten Gurkha regiments.

Under the 1886 arrangement, regiments (battalions) were linked together in groups of from two to five units and each group was allotted a centre. All recruits enlisting in any one of the regiments in a group were liable to serve in any other unit of that group if the need arose. One of the constituent units was always required to remain at the group centre as a potential reinforcement pool for the other units in the group.

There were 43 such centres so that, in an emergency situation, the system would either have to be abandoned or forty three battalions – one third of the Indian Army strength – would not be available for an active service role. In fact, linked battalions were independent of each other and when one of them went overseas, it left behind a depot made up of one or two British officers, some clerical and administrative personnel, sick men and other surplus to establishment. Each such depot enlisted and trained its own recruits and acted as record office to the mobilised battalions, the officer-in-charge of the depot keeping in close touch with the commanding-officer in the field.

During the Great War the system broke down, not surprisingly, perhaps, given the statistics. By the end of the war, the Indian Army had 280 battalions, with 115 of them serving overseas. This meant that there were 115 infantry depots in India, each in close touch with its active parent, each seeking recruits and training them and each indenting separately for arms, clothing, etc.

In an attempt to improve on this situation in 1921, a training battalion system was introduced and applied to all infantry and pioneers except for the Gurkhas and the 106th Hazara Pioneers. All battalions were henceforth to be linked together in numbered groups of an average of four with one training battalion in each group. The training battalion was to be a permanent depot for all its active battalions in both peace and war and was to be made up of one training company for each of the battalions in the group. Each active battalion was to supply the commander and administrative and instructional staff of its training company whilst the training battalion was to furnish clerical staff and both to enlist and train recruits on behalf of the active battalion. All recruits would be liable to serve in any battalion of that group and this became a real commitment. Each active battalion could look now for reinforcement not only from its own training company but from the training battalion as a whole.

Once this concept was accepted, it was decided in 1922 to convert the groups into numbered regiments and re-numbering was embarked upon. Twenty infantry regiments were designated, each with four or five active battalions numbered sequentially, 1st, 2nd, 3rd, etc., and one training battalion, numbered the 10th, the last-named consisting of as many companies as there were active battalions. Thus, in the 1926 Indian Army List, the 10/7th Rajput Regiment at Fatehgarh consisted of five companies to service five active battalions whilst the 10/3rd Madras Regt at Trichinopoly had only two companies to service the 1/3rd and 2/3rd, the only two remaining active battalions of a regiment being run down. Numbers up to ten were to be used for active battalions which might be raised, the 10th was always the depot-battalion whilst the 11th was used for the Territorial battalions which had begun to be raised in 1921 and which were now being incorporated into the new regimental families. Some few regiments raised two Territorial battalions, in which case the second one became the 12th Bn.

The 3rd Madras actually raised four which were numbered 11th to 14th and they survived the disbandment of their parent regiment, to be resuscitated in 1942 as the active battalions of the new 3rd Madras Regiment, being re-numbered accordingly.

The pioneer regiments were separated from the line infantry and similarly grouped into large regiments of Madras, Bombay and Sikh Pioneers, each with a 10th Bn as its training-centre plus the single-battalion 4th Hazara Pioneers.

As will be seen, all the Pioneers vanished from the active part of the Indian Army List in early 1933.

The ten two-battalion regiments of the Gurkha Rifles remained unaffected by the post-war changes.

With the redeployment into large regiments came, in 1923, a new infantry battalion establishment. Before 1914, there were five different authorised establishments for Indian infantry battalions, varying in strength between 600 and 912 Indian ranks. The Retrenchment Committee of 1922–23 authorised a standard format on 14 Aug 23 as under:

		British Officers	*Indian Officers*	*Indian Other ranks*	*Total Indian ranks*
Infantry	Active	12	20	742	762
	Gurkhas	13	20	921	941
	Training (Average)	9	14	636	650
Pioneers	Active	12	16	720	736
	Independent (4th (Hazara Prs)	13	18	923	941
	Training (Average)	9	11	469	480

After the allocations had been made to the twenty 'new' large regiments, the following units on the strength of the Indian Army on 1 Aug 14 were disbanded on the dates shown below:

3rd Brahmans	disbanded 6 May 22
5th Light Infantry	disbanded 12 Jan 22
17th Infantry (The Loyal Regiment)	disbanded 20 Dec 21
42nd Deoli Regiment	disbanded 10 Dec 21
43rd Erinpura Regiment	disbanded 15 Oct 21
44th Merwara Regiment	disbanded 22 Jun 21
63rd Palamcottah Light Infantry	disbanded 13 Sep 22
80th Carnatic Infantry	disbanded 10 Sep 21
88th Carnatic Infantry	disbanded 10 Jan 22

In 1937, Burma ceased to be a province of India and the 20th Burma Rifles vanished from the Indian Army List, reappearing in the Burma Army List simply as The Burma Rifles. The number was not re-utilised in India. Subsequent British officer postings to the Burma Rifles were from the British

Service although most Indian Army officers serving with Burma units remained with them to cover the transitional period. Events, however, overtook plans and most of the regular Burma Rifles battalions began the war with Indian Army officers.

When war broke out in 1939, the Indian Territorial Force battalions were mobilised, albeit not all at once and the 1922 system put to the test. The term 'Regimental Centre' came into use and 10th Battalions were dropped. Garrison battalions were raised, beginning at the 25th and these consisted of some reservists, over-age and medically-graded men, the latter usually relegated from the active battalions warned for service overseas. As with the ITF, some regiments raised more than one garrison battalion, a notable one being the 5th Mahratta Light Infantry which formed six, numbered from 25 to 30. One of them, the 27/5th gained a Burma 1942–45 battle-honour.

Also raised during the Second World War were garrison companies, formed for service in India. These were usually serially-numbered and indentifiable; thus, the four garrison companies of the 17th Dogra Regiment were numbered 117, 217, 317 and 417.

The Gurkha regiments during the 1939–45 War were only four or five battalions strong and so could not each have supported a 25th Garrison Battalion. Instead, two new regiments were created – the 25th and the 26th Gurkha Rifles with their own regimental badges – formed from men either over-age or not fit enough for full active service.

In 1939, the realities of war did not immediately reach the Indian Army but thought was given to wider recruitment, spreading the net to induct classes not normally considered for a soldier's life.

Mazhbi and Ramdassia Sikhs were enlisted for what became the Sikh Light Infantry and Mahars for the Mahar Regiment. Chamars were enlisted into 27/2 Punjab, later restyled The Chamar Regiment and the Willcox Committee reported that Chamars also enlisted as Mazhbi and Ramdassia Sikhs after growing beards.

Territorial battalions of the 4th Bombay Grenadiers formed the Ajmer Regiment in 1942, made up of Mussalman Katats and Hindu Rawats and Minas (the latter a criminal tribe), from Ajmer-Merwara and the surrounding states.

The 11/19 Hyderabad was converted to active status in September 1941 and became the 1st Bihar Regiment, half recruited from the aboriginals of South Bihar – Hos, Mundas, Oraons, Santhals – and half of Biharis, partly Hindu (Rajputs or Ahirs) and partly Mussalman.

Men from the hill tribes of the Burma border (Lushais, Kukis and Nagas) and from Central Assam (Garos and Khasis) were formed into the Assam Regiment in 1941 on a cadre from the Assam Rifles.

Afridis were recruited once again for the 1st Afridi Battalion in 1942 after a lapse of 23 years. In 1919, the Khyber Rifles had mutinied and were disbanded, Afridi enlistment being then terminated.

A garrison battalion of Lingayats was raised on the centre of the 5 Mahratta Light Infantry whilst 17 Dogra raised a garrison battalion of Kabirpanthis.

Finally, there was a persistent desire that a combatant unit should be raised in Bengal and a Territorial infantry battalion was formed in 1940 but had to be disbanded in 1942 as they were unwilling to accept general service: the general transport company formed from the remnants was disbanded a few months later for indiscipline. A Bengali coast artillery battery formed in 1940 had a series of problems of discipline resulting in a court-martial in 1943 in which nine death sentences were awarded. The Willcox Committee recognised the desire for combatant service but, in a rare flash of whimsy, concluded that such a desire was not shared by potential recruits.

The fortunes of some of these forays into recruiting minority classes may be traced in the following regimental entries.

In the regimental records of service which follow, I have shown infantry regimental centres for 1923 and also for 1946. The earlier date, of course, indicates the location of the 10th Battalion and its associated regimental and training facilities. The term 'regimental centre' came into use during the Second World War and it has seemed more appropriate to use that in both cases. The class compositions have been extracted from the Indian Army Lists of the period.

In listing the areas of service in the two world wars, I have not stopped abruptly at 1918 but have included service out of India in Turkey, on the East Persia Cordon, etc. since these were war-linked postings. Similarly, after 1945, regiments served in Indo-China, the Dutch East Indies, etc., in some cases not returning to India until after Partition in August 1947.

The books listed against each regiment entry are not necessarily all the known books relating to that particular regiment, but in most cases, the most useful and the most readily available.

Information on the transfers in and out of the various class-squadrons and companies after Partition is very uneven. Some regimental histories offer copious details whilst others barely touch upon the subject.

Indeed, such was the confusion at the time that companies posted in initially were often subsequently passed on to other regiments when establishments were balanced in the following months.

One consistent factor in the reading of the events in August 1947, is that regiments, whether bound for India or Pakistan, took care of the men of the companies being posted out to ensure that they reached the Punjab frontier in safety and were protected from the marauding religious terrorist gangs so far as was possible.

In the regimental entries, mention is made of the badges that were prescribed for wear in Indian Army Dress Regulations. However, these were not necessarily the patterns worn. Many officers contrived to wear the badges of their earlier regiment whilst 15 Punjab had distinctive badges for several of its battalions.

For the most part, the other ranks did not wear a badge in the headdress until the 1939-45 War, when the beret and its illegitimate brother, the cap GS, came into use. This subject is covered more fully in the appendix on badges and insignia.

Finally, whilst the regimental entries for the cavalry are headed by the title borne in 1939, the range of titles used from the turn of the century is given after each entry. Designations had changed to regularise titles in popular useage: in 1922, numbers had been given priority with regional titles or the regimental founder's name in brackets. By 1939, most of these had been reversed, the more commonly used title preceding the number which then appeared in brackets.

4. INDIANISATION

In 1918, after the end of the Great War, some reward was due to India. Her soldiers had held the line in France in 1914 and 1915, fought in Gallipoli, the Middle East and East Africa whilst still garrisoning Hong Kong, Singapore and Malaya and keeping the border-law on the North-West Frontier.

The Montagu-Chelmsford Report was clearly the reward for that service and sacrifice and the right to self-government brought with it the responsibility for self-defence. Whatever the problems, the decision to Indianise the hitherto British-officered Indian Army was to go ahead. Caution, however, was to be the watchword and a guarded programme of ten cadet-places per year was launched. Indian gentlemen-cadets were to be admitted to the Royal Military College at Sandhurst and, on commissioning, were to be referred to as King's Commissioned Indian Officers. These young officers would then be posted in the same way as their British colleagues, their first year in India being spent with a British battalion before joining their eventual Indian regiment.

This programme, not unreasonably, perhaps, was not felt to be an adequate one for Indianisation and the Indian Legislative Assembly demanded some sort of structured future. Lord Rawlinson, the Commander-in-Chief, India, was to chair the Military Requirements Committee 'to frame a progressive policy, working up by degrees to final Indianisation'.

Indian doctors, serving with the Indian Medical Service, of course, had held the King's Commission during the war and several of them received gallantry awards.

In August 1917, seven Indians, already serving in the army, were granted King's Commissions and, in 1918, a programme began at the Indore Cadet School (popularly known as the Daly Military College). The first successful cadets, thirty-nine of them, were commissioned in December, 1919 and the School was closed after that year.

In the meantime, the Military Requirements Committee ruled that the planned process should continue in three stages, each of fourteen years. Initially, seven regiments of cavalry, twenty battalions of infantry and sundry other units would be nominated: this would require 81 Indian commissions per annum and no British officers would then be posted to these units. In Phase 2, after fourteen years, a further seven cavalry regiments and forty battalions of infantry would be inducted into the system and, in Phase 3, all units would be Indianising. By year forty-two of the scheme (1967), every unit of the Indian Army would have Indian officers from top to bottom. The India Office decided to mark time on this plan and suggested that four units should be Indianised at first. It was, they said, only by segregating units in this way that it might be known that an Indian-officered unit could be completely efficient. This, of course, could not be proved until such time as there were Indian lieutenant-colonels, some twenty-six years hence. Rawlinson saw the absurdity of this last suggestion and prevailed upon the India Office to rethink the programme. The announcement was made by him to the Legislative Assembly in February 1923 in the following terms:

'Sir, with your permission I desire to make a statement to the House. Speaking in this Assembly on the 24th January last, I expressed the hope that it would be possible to announce at no very distant date what measures are to be adopted in regard to the Indianisation of the Indian Army. In the short interval that has elapsed, the correspondence, which I then said was proceeding, has been concluded and I am able to announce to the House the following decision. The Government consider that a start should be made at once so as to give Indians a fair opportunity of proving that units officered by Indians will be efficient in every way. Accordingly, it has been decided that eight units of cavalry or infantry be selected to be officered by Indians. This scheme will be put into force immediately. The eight units to be wholly Indianised will be mainly infantry units, but there will be a proportion of cavalry. They will be chosen judiciously so as to include as many representative types as possible of infantry battalions and cavalry regiments of the Indian Army. Indian officers holding commissions in the Indian Army will be gradually transferred to Indianising units so as to fill up the appointments for which they are qualified by their rank and by their length of service, and the process of Indianising these units will then continue uninterruptedly as the officers gain seniority and fitness in other respects which will qualify them for the senior posts. I have given the House these few details because I think they will be of some interest as revealing some of the practical aspects of the change. There is one other point, however, which it is necessary for me to explain. It is that, simultaneously with the Indianisation of these selected eight units, Indians who qualify for King's commissions will continue as at present to be posted to the other units of the Indian Army. The number of Indian cadets now sent to Sandhurst each year, if all pass out successfully, is more than sufficient to replace the normal wastage in the eight units alone. I draw attention to this matter as it has a significance which the House, I am sure, will not fail to appreciate. Once more, before sitting down, I wish to express my gratification that this great step forward has been made. I hope that the people of India will appreciate the importance of the step and will realise also that it now rests with them to justify the decision of the Government. I hope that no effort will be spared to make the measures which has been approved a solid and a conspicuous success. The responsibility which lies before these young men who will officer the Indianised regiments is no light one. They will have in their hands not only the lives of their men but also the task of maintaining untarnished the high and ancient traditions of the regiments to which they are appointed. I can assure them that in the new and in the wider career which will now lie open to them they will have the active and generous support of the Government of India and of their British colleagues in the Army. Their success or their failure will mean much to India. The initiation of this scheme constitutes an entirely new departure which, though limited in its scope is one which may have far-reaching results. I trust that the members of this Legislature and that the people of India as a whole will support the Indian officers of these Indianised regiments with living and practical encouragement, for by this means only can Indianisation hope to deserve and to command success'.

The Units selected for Indianisation were:

7 Light Cavalry	1/7 Rajput
16 Light Cavalry	1/14 Punjab
2/1 Punjab	4/19 Hyderabad
5/5 Mahratta Light Infantry	2/1 Madras Pioneers

The practice of nominating specific units to receive newly-commissioned Indian officers was initially an administrative convenience but it became the target for accusations of segregation. Of the first ten Indians commissioned after the Great War, four refused to transfer from the Indian Army units in which they had become established when the first group of Indianising units was nominated in 1923. Regimental loyalty was, after all, the keystone of both British and Indian Army systems and some of these young Indian officers had, by then, had up to five years service in their original regiments and had no wish to transfer to new 'families'.

The Indian Sandhurst Committee, formed in 1925 to examine the problems of the slow progress in Indianisation, established that the failure rate of Indian cadets at the RMC was 30% whilst that of British cadets was only 3%, not, perhaps, surprising when one considers their respective backgrounds and education. Sandhurst, after all, was not a much harder life than many British public schools from which most of the British cadets had recently come. The only remotely comparable establishment in India was the Prince of Wales's Royal Indian Military College at Dehra Dun. Moreover, the cost to an Indian family of sending a son to the Royal Military College in the UK was substantial. Even after commissioning he would still be a family expense whereas, if he had chosen to go to the Indian Civil Service, medicine or the law, he might reasonably have been found self-sufficient after qualification. Some alternative had to be found and it was recommended that an Indian Military Academy be set up to improve the supply of Indian officers. Dehra Dun, in the foothills of the Himalayas, was the location selected and some disused railway college buildings became the Indian Military Academy, being opened on the 10 Dec 32 by Field Marshal Sir Philip Chetwode. The keynote of his address to the first cadets was inscribed on the walls – *'The safety, honour and welfare of your country come first, always and every time. The honour, welfare and comfort of the men you command come next. Your own ease, comfort and safety come last, always and every time'.*

Those words are still on the walls of the Academy in Dehra Dun.

The initial capacity was one hundred and, by 1938, its output would be 56 officers each year. No Indians would go to Sandhurst any more. The first Commandant was Brigadier LP Collins CB DSO OBE, a 2nd Goorkha and it is on record that Mrs. Collins was to play a significant part in settling the first Indian cadets into their new home.

The new officers were to hold the King's Commission but in His Majesty's Indian Land Forces only – in the same way that Australian and Canadian officers held similarly limited commissions within their own armies. The commissions granted to those from Sandhurst, whether British or Indian, were in HM Land Forces and authorised command over both British and Indian troops.

The newly-commissioned Indian officers were paid on the scale of British officers in the United Kingdom whilst British officers continued to receive an allowance as compensation for serving abroad.

In 1933, a further group of units was nominated for Indianisation as follows:

3 Cavalry	5/10 Baluch
5/2 Punjab	5/11 Sikh
5/6 Rajputana Rifles	4/12 FF Regt
5/8 Punjab	6/13 FF Rifles

These, together with those already Indianising and sundry designated units of the arms and services, would provide the basis for the first planned Indian division.

Three units from the Indian Engineers which had been selected for Indianisation were three field companies – 5 (Bengal), 15 (Madras) and 22 (Bombay). The process began in 1934 and by the outbreak of war in September 1939, 5 (Bengal) Field company had completely Indianised.

Accusations of segregation persisted and a written answer by the India Office in November 1934 to a question on the House of Lords did little to dispel them.

1. *To ensure that the Indian officers should stand on their own merits. Indianisation was an experiment and it was felt that there would be some risk if Indians were distributed throughout the Army with the result that any defects on their part due to inexperience or other causes would be covered by their British colleagues.*
2. *To test not only the merits of individual Indian officers but also the corporate efficiency of the units in which they were to begin to take command.*
3. *To prevent a setback in the recruitment of British officers for the remainder of the Indian Army. There was evidence that candidates were deterred from joining the Indian Army by the fear that their position would be prejudiced if the practice were continued of distributing Indian officers indiscriminately throughout the Army.*

All these reasons are based on the fact that all ranks in an army unit are closely interdependent. If, for instance, a single officer fails in a moment of emergency he may immediately endanger the lives of his brother-officers and of his men.

The first point assumes somehow that an inexperienced Indian might fail in a crisis whereas a British subaltern with the same experience of service would succeed yet both would have had the same demanding Sandhurst/Dehra Dun education and training.

The second point might be accorded some validity when one realises that the only experience which the writer might have had of an all-Indian unit would be the wholly Indian-officered forces of the princely states. These were of an immensely varied standard and seldom high but, then, those officers had not been the product of the British-Indian system.

Point 3 seemed plainly discriminatory but, in fact, except for one year, British officer-recruitment figures did not appear to be affected.

The final point cannot be challenged on an isolated statement but it fails to explain how it should be that the Indian officer might be the weak link in the command-chain when, during the Great War, Indian officers (later VCOs) had proved themselves to be so competent.

Moreover, British commanding officers of Indianising units had reported favourably on the quality of their young Indian officers, rating them as good as,

Uniform—Scarlet. *Facings*—Royal blue.

7th Rajput Regiment.

"Delhi, 1803" "Laswarree" "Deig" "Bhurtpore" "Affghanistan, 1839" "Khelat" "Cabool, 1842," "Maharajpore" "Moodkee" "Ferozeshah" "Aliwal" "Sobraon" "Chillianwallah" "Goojerat" "Punjaub" "Lucknow" (with a Turretted Gateway) "Central India," "China, 1858-59" "Afghanistan 1878-80" "Tel-el-Kebir" "Egypt, 1882" "Burma, 1885-87" "Pekin, 1900" "China, 1900" "Afghanistan, 1919".

The Great War.—**"Macedonia, 1918" "Suez Canal," "Egypt, 1915" "Aden" "Basra" "Kut al Amara, 1915" "Ctesiphon" "Defence of Kut al Amara" "Tigris, 1916" "Mesopotamia, 1914-18" "Persia, 1915-18" "N. W. Frontier, India, 1915, '17."**

COLONEL-IN-CHIEF—Field Marshal *H. R. H. The Duke of* Connaught and Strathearn, K.G., K.P., G.C.B., G.C.S.I., G.C.M.G., G.C.I.E., G.C.V.O., G.B.E., V.D.T.D. (*Personal A. D. C. to the King*).

1st Battalion (Queen Victoria's Own Light Infantry)—(*late 2nd Q. V. O. Rajput Light Infantry*).

THE ROYAL AND IMPERIAL CYPHER OF QUEEN VICTORIA WITHIN THE GARTER.

Carries a third or honorary colour bearing the words "Lake and Victory", granted 1803 for distinguished service.

Class Composition :—Rajputs and Punjabi Musalmans (including Niazi Pathans).

Broon-ki-paltan.—Raised at Sasseram in 1798, by Maj G. S. Browne, as 2 Bn., 15 Regt., Bengal N. I. Became 31 Regt of B. N. I., 1824; 31st Regt. of B. N. (L.) I., 1858; 2 Regt. of B. N. (L.) I., 1861; 2 (The Q. O.) Regt. of B. N. (L.) I., 1876; 2 (The Q. O.) Regt. of B. (L.) I., 1885; 2 (Q. O.) Rajput Regt. of B. (L.) I., 1897; 2 (Q. O.) Rajput L. I., 1901; 2 (Q. O.) Rajput L. I., 1903; 2 Q. V. O. Rajput L. I., 1911; present designation, 1922.

COLONEL—Brig.-Genl. Frederick A. Smith (*Retd.*) 26-8-21.

1st Commn. or Enrolmt.	Names and Rank.	Army rank.	Present appointment in Battn	Remarks.
	Commandant.			
12-9-14	Hawkes, Lt.-Col. L. V. C., *p.s.c.*†	3-5-39	3-5-39	Comdg., Kamptee.
	Second-in-Command.			
	Company Commanders.			
2-6-18	Browning, Maj. J. M.	20-12-36	18-7-38	*Lv. ex. I., 8 m. to 15 Oct. 39.*
16-7-19	3. Norrish, Maj. W. E.	16-7-37	18-7-38	
17-7-20	*Cariappa, Maj. K. M., p.s.c.*†	17-7-38	18-7-38	*Bde. Maj. Khojak Bde.*
17-7-20	Roy, Maj. S. B. S.	17-7-38	11-1-39	
	Company Officers.			
1-2-23	Nathu Singh, Capt. *Thakur, p. s.c.*† ...	1-2-32	20-4-24	
27-8-27	*Afif Khan, Capt.*	27-8-36	5-11-34	*With 10 Bn.*
2-2-28	*Nasir Ali Khan, Capt.*	2-2-37	23-3-29	*11 Bn.*
29-1-27	Raza, Capt. A. M.	18-10-37	...	*Lv. in & ex I., 8 m. to 1 Feb. 40.*
21-1-29	Gurdial Singh, Capt....	31-1-38	25-3-30	
29-8-29	Gohel, Capt. M. B.	1-8-38	1-11-30	Qr. Mr., 16 Feb. 38.
28-8-30	*Paranjpe, Capt Y. S.*	28-8-38	6-7-36	Offg. *Staff Capt., A. G.'s Bch., A. Hdqrs.*
29-1-31	Bilimoria, Capt. N. D.	29-1-39	5-11-32	*Lv. in & ex I., 8 m. to 14 Dec. 39.*
27-8-31	*Sarda Nand Singh, Capt.*	27-8-39	7-3-33	*With 10 Bn.*
1-9-32	Prithvi Jeet Singh, Lt.	1-12-34	5-3-34	
31-8-33	Latif Khan, Lt. M. A.	30-11-35	19-3-35	Offg. Adjt.
2-9-34	*Mohammad Khan Janjua, Lt.*	2-12-36	16-8-36	*Ind. Air Force.*
2-9-34	Moti Sagar, Lt.	2-12-36	10-8-36	S. S. O., Kamptee.
2-9-34	*Kuldip Singh, Lt. B.*	2-12-36	10-8-36	*With 10 Bn.*
3-2-35	Mohammad Said, Lt.	3-5-37	25-2-37	
1-9-35	Raj Bir Chopra, Lt.	1-12-37	10-8-37	
1-9-35	Raja Ghulam Mohammad Khan, Lt. ...	1-12-37	10-8-37	
2-2-36	Nisar Ahmad Qureshi, Lt.	2-5-38	25-2-38	
2-2-36	Ramasami Gurusami Naidu, Lt.	2-5-38	25-2-38	
30-8-36	Rajindar Singh Paintal, Lt.	30-11-38	10-8-38	
30-8-36	Sarin, Lt. R.	30-11-38	10-8-38	
31-1-37	Virendra Singh, Lt.	30-4-39	24-2-39	
31-1-37	Malik, Lt. S. S.	30-4-39	24-2-39	
31-1-37	Fraser, Lt. L. J. D.	30-4-39	24-2-39	
15-7-38	de-Souza, 2nd-Lt. G. F.	15-7-38	...	
	Attached.			
18-6-17	Hayes-Newington, Maj. E. A., O.B.E. ...	30-3-36	...	2-4 Bombay Grs.—Offg. 2nd-in-Comd.
	Subadar-Major.			
		Jemadar.	Subadar.	Sub.-Major.
29-10-15	Nur Khan (23, 26, 33, 36, 120, 163, 201) ...	1-4-22	15-2-31	12-3-38
	Subadars			
7-10-14 / 10-6-22	*Umakant Shukla* (25, 30)		2-1-29	*Instr., Chemical Warfare Schl., India.*
12-8-15	Rahmat Khan, I.D.S.M. (33, 43)	16-8-31	12-3-38	
31-1-18	*Partab Singh* (24, 25, 30, 33)	1-6-34	10-8-38	*With 10 Bn.*
	Jemadars			
8-7-24	Rai Niaz Ali Khan (24, 25, 29, 33, 36) ...	1-6-29		
29-4-15	Musa Khan (33)	1-7-30		*With 10 Bn.*
11-5-15	Rajaram Singh (33)	16-5-33		Jemdr. Adjt.
1-4-12	Shamsher Singh (33)...	1-11-33		
	Warrant Officer, Class I.			
1-11-25	Pindi Das (23, 26)	1-7-36	Head clerk.	

The 1st Bn., 7th Rajput Regt. (Q. V. O. L. I.), has an additional Jemadar for the third colour.

Uniform—Scarlet. *Facings*—Yellow.

7th Rajput Regiment.

2nd Battalion (Prince Albert Victor's)—(*late 4th P. A. V. Rajputs*).

Class Composition: —Rajputs and Punjabi Musalmans (including Niazi Pathans).

Hilliard-ki-paltan.—Raised at Baragaon in 1798, by Lt.-Col. John Hilliard, as the 2nd Battalion, 16th Regiment of Bengal Native Infantry. Became the 33rd Regiment of Bengal Native Infantry, 1824; the 4th Regiment of Bengal Native Infantry, 1861; the 4th Regiment of Bengal Infantry, 1885; the 4th (Prince Albert Victor's) Regiment of Bengal Infantry, 1890; the 4th (Prince Albert Victor's) Rajput Regiment of Bengal Infantry, 1897; the 4th (Prince Albert Victor's) Rajput Infantry, 1901; 4th Prince Albert Victor's Rajputs, 1903; present designation, 1922.

COLONEL—Col. John C. Simpson (*Retd.*) . . . . 18-3-32.

1st Commn. or Enrolmt.	Names and Rank.	Army rank.	Present appointment in Battn.	Remarks.
	Commandant.			
10-12-14	Wood, Lt.-Col. E., M.C., *p.s.c.*†	1-1-35	18-6-38	Secy. to the Govt. of India, Dept. of Supply.
	Second-in-Command.			
15-10-15	Latham, Maj. H. C., *p. s. c.*†	14-7-38	15-10-38	Offg. G. S. O., 2nd gr., A. Hdqrs.
	Company Commanders.			
26-4-17	Marsland, Maj. K. D. [*l*]	4-1-36	1-4-37	Offg. 2nd-in-Comd.
5-5-17	Scott, Maj. R. E.	1-2-36	3-12-37	
29-1-20	Salomons, Maj. J. A., *q*.	29-1-38	18-7-38	Attd. 4 Bn.
14-7-21	*Somers, Maj. R. A. J.*	1-8-38	11-1-39	*Adjt., B. B. & C. I. Ry. R., A. F. I.*
	Company Officers.			
23-12-21	*Ward, Maj. E. C. S.*...	23-12-38	28-10-23	*Adjt., E. B. Ry. Bn., A. F. I.*
29-1-27	Long, Capt. R. H.	29-1-36	4-4-36	Adjt., 5 July 37.
23-9-31	*Pease, Capt. J. W.*	30-3-36	23-9-31	*Tochi Scouts.*
14-11-35	Gillan, Lt. G. M.	14-2-33	12-12-35	Qr. Mr., 15 June 38.
29-1-31	Cable, Lt. G. E. P.	29-4-33	22-6-32	
1-2-34	Bradley, Lt. W. A. McL	1-5-36	1-4-37	*Lv. ex I., 8 m. to 7 Jan. 40.*
1-2-35	*Pollen, Lt. H. C. H.*	1-5-37	5-4-36	*With 10 Bn.*
29-8-35	Kealy, Lt. N. H. B.	29-11-37	17-11-36	*Lv. ex I., 8 m. to 7 Dec. 39.*
27-8-36	Gordon, Lt. D. F.	27-11-38	6-11-37	
28-1-37	Payne, Lt. S. H.	28-4-39	3-4-38	
	Honorary Officer.			
26-3-18	Capt. *Kumar Shri* Himmatsinhji	26-3-24	*I. A., Retd.*	

Subadar-Major.

		Jemadar.	Subadar.	Sub.-Major.	
26-8-18	Ata Muhammad (25, 33)	1-3-26	20-9-31	12-2-36	

Subadars.

23-8-18	Abdul Majid Khan, I.D.S.M. (23, 25, 26, 33)	23-8-18	12-5-21	
27-6-14	Dilawar Ali Khan (25, 42)	1-4-22	2-4-31	
25-7-12	Sunehra Singh (36, 52, 62)	22-12-23	18-6-31	
1-9-14	Jagat Singh (25, 33, 38)	1-11-25	1-3-32	
12-10-12	Ashraf Khan (33)	14-1-28	12-2-36	
29-7-18	Barkat Ali (25, 32)	1-5-28	1-6-37	Edn. Offr., 1 Aug. 38.
19-4-16	*Surajpal Singh* (29, 33, 52, 62)	12-2-31	1-7-38	*With 10 Bn.*
5-4-18	Raghbir Singh (25, 33)	18-6-31	1-11-38	

Jemadars.

12-4-16	Muhammad Khan (25, 29, 33, 36, 62) ...	1-10-28	
12-6-19	Muhammad Hayat Khan (23, 25, 26, 33, 36, 62)	2-4-31	Offg. Ind. Instr., A. Schl. of Edn., Belgaum.
20-11-17	*Ghulam Muhammad* (33, 38)	20-9-31	*With 10 Bn.*
3-10-14	Sriram Singh (25, 29, 33)	1-3-32	
31-12-17	Farzand Ali (33, 38, 49, 52)	19-8-32	Jemdr. Qr.-Mr., 15 June 35.
8-4-17	Habib Khan (33, 36, 62)	1-4-33	
22-10-19	Risal Singh (33, 36, 49, 62)	7-12-33	
31-1-20	*Abdul Majid Khan* (25, 33)	12-2-36	*With 11 Bn.*
3-5-18	Sheodan Singh (23)	1-11-36	Head Clerk.
16-3-25	Mahabir Singh (33, 36)	1-11-36	
7-6-20	*Chhottar Singh* (25, 33)	1-6-37	*With 10 Bn.*
2-6-22	Muhammad Qasim Khan (33, 43)	1-3-38	
26-6-20	Ganga Singh (32, 38)	1-7-38	Jemdr. Adjt., 1 Feb. 39.
14-7-19	Multan Singh (33, 37, 38)	8-8-38	
23-8-20	Madho Singh (25, 29, 33)	1-11-38	
20-2-23	Abdul Aziz Khan (25, 33, 43)	1-7-39	

if not better than their British contemporaries. Of course, there was also the challenge that these units should excel and endeavour not only to shine as an Indianising unit but also to set the pace for the traditional British-officered units.

One of the less appreciated effects of Indianisation was what was introduced in 1936 as 'platoonisation'. Hitherto, squadrons in the cavalry and infantry companies had been commanded by British officers whilst troops and platoons had had VCOs in charge. VCOs, it was said, were necessary to assist the British officer with the problems of the country but, with Indian commissioned officers, this buffer would no longer be essential. Indian officers would command troops and platoons, VCOs would be phased out and warrant-officers would be introduced.

The disappearance of the VCO rank did not please the men in the ranks who had always, in the past, been able to look forward to the prospect of a Viceroy's Commission with its associated privileges. There was also the fact, ignored by the India Office, that the Indian officer might well have as little in common with his men as the newly-commissioned British subaltern and might even have welcomed a VCO's presence.

The copies of the relevant pages of a 1939 Indian Army List on pages 26 and 27 show the differences between two battalions of the same regiment, one Indianising and the other not. The variations in VCO strengths can be clearly seen and, in 1/7 Rajput, the VCO Head Clerk has already been replaced by a warrant-officer. Only the commanding officer and two of the majors are British: it is of passing interest that one of the two Indian majors was KM Cariappa (with a Staff College qualification), who went on to become the first Commander-in-Chief in an Independent India from 1949 to 1953 and who was created India's second field marshal in 1986. He was one of the cadets who graduated from Daly Military College in December 1919.

In Roorkee, in September 1939, the Adjutant of the Bengal Sappers and Miners recorded in his newsletter – *'5 Field Company is now fully Indianised and all the VCOs have now left it'.*

The Second World War wrought many changes in the commissioning of Indians. Platoonisation came to an end, mourned by few and VCOs were reintroduced. By the end of the war in 1945 there were 8,300 Indian officers from a total officer-strength of 41,500.

It was Field Marshal Sir Claude Auchinleck, ever the friend and champion of the Indian Army, who stated in a letter to South East Asia Army Commanders in 1946:

> *'There is little doubt that 'Indianisation' was at its inception looked upon as a political expedient which was bound to fail militarily. There is no doubt also that many senior British officers believed and even hoped that it would fail.*
>
> *The policy of segregation of Indian officers into separate units, the differential treatment in respect of pay and terms of service as compared with the British officer and the prejudice and lack of manners by some – but by no means all – British officers and their wives, all went to produce a very deep and bitter feeling of racial discrimination in the mind of the most intelligent and progressive of the Indian officers . . '*

In the event, both Indian and Pakistan received a sound officer-corps when Partition came in August 1947 but one can be certain that this would not have come about if a world war had not intervened. Indianisation was forced upon the authorities with the massive expansion of the Indian Army.

Despite all the foregoing, there is little evidence that the process of Indianisation was opposed by the younger British officers who would have had to complete their service in a progressively Indianising Army. Major General G.J. Hamilton, a Guides Infantry officer, commissioned in 1932 and with a DSO for a Frontier action as a subaltern said – '. . . *we all knew, even in the twenties, that independence for India could not be long delayed and it was our duty to see that our Indian successors, both in the services and civil administration, were properly trained.*

An interesting footnote is provided by the report of the Willcox Committee published in 1945. This was a study undertaken on the orders of the Commander-in-Chief and it did not, of course, foresee Partition. Its mandate was to make recommendations for the post-war, peacetime Indian Army.

It assumed that there would be a return in broad terms to the same army that had existed before 1939 and it assumed that there would still be a substantial British Army presence in the sub-continent.

Examining the question of future officer-requirements, it was suggested that, for the present, they would be looking for 50% to be British although this figure would be revised if the situation demanded it. Some 7,000 Indian emergency commissions had been awarded during the war to the army and the Committee was concerned at this very low figure. Considerable analysis was obviously done on this question and one of the conclusions reached was that Indian education was committed to 'the purveying of book knowledge with the object of passing examinations. It does nothing either by direct or indirect means towards the training of character, particularly in independence of thought and action, sense of duty and responsibility, or power of leadership. These defects are now widely recognised'. Remedies were put forward but the beneficial effects of these were unlikely to be seen 'until about 1960'.

The report also suggests that the VCO will disappear once more. It is now some 45 years since this particular recommendation was made and the Junior Commissioned Officer as he is now known in both the Indian and Pakistan Armies is still firmly established.

Two of the officers who compiled this report were Brigadiers K.M. Cariappa and J. Enoch Powell.

5. INDIA'S TERRITORIAL SOLDIERS

European Volunteers were first raised from among the merchants of Calcutta and their staff to combat the threat of the Nawab of Bengal in 1756 but it must be confessed that they did not make an impressive showing (Robert Clive was an exception and he went on to become a career soldier) and interest soon waned.

It was, without doubt, the Great Mutiny of the Bengal Army in 1857, which prompted the raising throughout India, of units of European and Anglo-Indian (then usually described as Eurasian) volunteers to combat the contemporary threat and to provide protection for the future if such a situation should arise again. Military volunteering, of course, was then much in vogue in Britain where many local Volunteer units dated their raising from 1858 and 1859.

As in the home country, para-military enthusiasms fluctuated and many units wasted away. However, in India, such units were frequently sustained by the innate insularity of their 'Europeanness' but less-than-dedicated volunteers often did little more than the basic minimal training commitment. It was felt that one did not necessarily expect European plantation-managers or factory-owners to become proficient soldiers but, if the need arose, they would turn out in uniform in a show of strength. In India, a platoon in the right place at the right time was usually better than a battalion twelve hours later.

As with the Volunteers and, later, the Territorial Force in the UK, a regular adjutant would administer the unit with the help of several British regular NCOs.

Although India did not send troops to South Africa at the turn of the century to subdue rebellious Boers, there was a feeling that something should be done by the Europeans. It fell to Lieutenant Colonel Dugald McTavish Lumsden to sound the call; born in Peterhead in 1851, Lumsden had sailed for India in 1873 to the Borelli Tea Estate at Tezpur in Assam. He promptly became a volunteer, serving in the Darrang Mounted Rifles in its brief existence before it was incorporated into the Assam Valley Light Horse. He left India in 1893 but did not lose touch with his old friends, returning every cold weather to visit them. Whilst in Australia in late 1899, depressed with news from the Cape of British reverses, he decided that his Light Horse friends and others could perform useful service against the Boers so he cabled his friend, Sir Patrick Playfair in Calcutta on the 15 Dec 99 – *'Offer Government fifty thousand rupees and my services any capacity towards raising European Mounted Infantry Contingent, India, service Cape. Wire Melbourne Club, Melbourne. Leaving nineteenth due Calcutta January 9. Do not divulge name until my arrival. Lumsden.'*

With almost indecent haste, the War Office seized the offer – *'Her Majesty's Government having accepted the offer of the Government of India to provide a force of Mounted Volunteers for service in South Africa, two companies of Mounted Infantry, to be called the Indian Mounted Infantry Corps (Lumsden's Horse) will be raised immediately at Calcutta under the command of Lieutenant Colonel D.McT. Lumsden, of the Volunteer Force of India, Supernumerary List, Assam Valley Light Horse'.*

Two hundred and fifty volunteers were sought but Lumsden could have had a thousand and the correspondence-columns of the press in Calcutta carried indignant letters from frustrated would-be soldiers, bearing scarcely-veiled hints of bias in the selection. Not all were serving Volunteers and the nominal roll shows a captain and first and second officers of the British India Steam Navigation Company, Calcutta. Regular saddler- and farrier-NCOs were posted in from cavalry regiments in Meerut and Lucknow. The volunteers were engaged to serve for a year and they sailed from Calcutta in February 1900 to a warm welcome in South Africa. Their service there was quite eventful with one officer and six men killed in action, one recommendation for a Victoria Cross (reduced to a Distinguished Conduct Medal), a CB for Lumsden, one CMG, two DSOs and five DCMs. Only 160 returned to Bombay on 31 Dec 00 for onward transit by train to Calcutta for disbandment. Many of those who did not return had been tempted to remain in South Africa in the police service or had been granted British Army commissions.

The undemanding tenor of the Volunteer's life continued until 1917 when the Indian Defence Force Act was passed. By this act, all the units of the Indian Volunteers became units of the Indian Defence Force, service was made compulsory for all Europeans in India between the ages of 18 and 41 and the ranks of some units were opened to accept certain Indians as recruits.

Units were sequentially numbered as follows:

1st Bihar Light Horse
2nd Surma Valley Light Horse
3rd Calcutta Light Horse
4th Bombay Light Horse
5th Punjab Light Horse
6th Assam Valley Light Horse
7th (Southern) United Provinces Light Horse
8th (Northern) United Provinces Light Horse
9th North Bengal Mounted Rifles
10th Southern Provinces Mounted Rifles

With the 1917 Indian Defence Force Act, the word 'Volunteer' had to be removed from the unit titles. The 1918 Indian Army List showed the new listing for infantry as follows, the numbers being incorporated into the full title:

1. Madras Guards
2. Nagpur Rifles
3. Punjab Rifles
4. Simla Rifles
5. Calcutta Battalion
6. Bangalore Coorg & Mysore Battalion
7. East Indian Railway Battalion
8. Allahabad Rifles
9. Mussoorie Battalion
10. Naini Tal Company
12. Eastern Bengal Railway Battalion
13. Great Indian Peninsula Railway Battalion
14. Tenasserim Battalion
15. Bombay Battalion
16. Cawnpore Rifles
17. Bombay, Baroda and Central India Railway Battalion
18. Rangoon Battalion
19. Agra Company
20. Nilgiri Malabar Battalion
21. Burma Railways Battalion
22. Bengal and North West Railway Battalion
23. Sind Battalion
24. North Western Railway Battalion
25. Oudh and Rohilkhand Railway Battalion
26. Hyderabad Rifles
27. Baluchistan Company
28. South Andaman Rifles

29. South Indian Railway Bn
32. Madras and Southern Mahratta Railway Rifles
34. Upper Burma Battalion
35. Poona Battalion
36. Bengal Nagpur Railway Regt
37. Calcutta Presidency Battalion
38. East Coast Battalion
39. Chota Nagpur Regiment
41. East Bengal Company
42. Assam Bengal Railway Bn
43. Kolar Gold Fields Battalion
44. Calcutta Scottish
45. Aden Rifles

The Indian Defence Force was short-lived and, in 1920, the Auxiliary Force, India, was born, bringing with it a further restyling of units, the discarding of the numbers and the end of compulsory service. Basically, units were liable for call-out for local service in an internal security role and terms of service were similar to those of the Territorial Army in the UK.

The great railway companies of India were early in the field to organise volunteer units from among their own employees and the first one was the East Indian Railway Volunteer Corps, raised in 1869. Among their employees were many Anglo-Indians and time-expired British soldiers who had taken their discharge in India and married locally. There were three battalions of the East India Railway Regiment – as it became in 1920 – and several of the other railway corps had two. The railway companies, of course, had ready-made communities and could recruit the entire length of their lines. Notwithstanding their strengths, there was never any large-scale mobilisation or utilisation of these units, or, indeed, any of the others. In times of national emergency, train-crews were too important as train-crews to allow them to act as soldiers and, thus, the AFI railway regiments became little more than local clubs with military associations.

The initial aim of the original Volunteers had been born of the Mutiny, the protection of British families, but they and the successor AFI found themselves used as a ready source of British officers to regular Indian Army units in two world wars. Knowledge of Hindi or Urdu plus, possibly, another local language, plus basic military training, made them welcome officer-reinforcements in both 1914 and 1939. Calcutta units alone furnished almost 600 and Bangalore 300 whilst the Assam Valley Light Horse supplied 377 officers during the Second World War.

Details of the units of the Auxiliary Force, India as at 1945 are as follows together with dates of embodiment:

Present title and date that title assumed	*Former titles*		*Called out/embodied*
ALLAHABAD CONTINGENT			
United Provinces Horse (Southern Regiment) 1920	1. Allahabad Troop Light Horse (formed from Allahabad Volunteer Rifle Corps)	1884	
	2. Allahabad Light Horse	1890	
(See also Cawnpore and Lucknow Contingents	3. United Provinces Light Horse (Cawnpore Light Horse, Ghazipur Light Horse, Gorakhpur Light Horse, Oudh Light Horse were amalgamated)	1904	
	4. 1st United Provinces Horse	1900	
	5. 7th (Southern Regiment) United Provinces Horse	1917	
Allahabad Rifles 1920	1. Allahabad Volunteer Rifle Corps	1871	
	2. 8th Allahabad Rifles	1917	May 30, Ghazipur Dett, called out
BOMBAY CONTINGENT			
Bombay Light Patrol 1922	Formed from Bombay Light Horse and Bombay Light Motor Patrol		15–25 Jan 19 (Strike) 10–17 Feb 29 4–8 May 29 5–6 May 30 31 Dec 30–1 Jan 31 16–21 May 32 15–17 Apr 44 (in aid of civil power – Bombay Docks explosion) After 3 Sept 39 part of unit provided guards, escorts, etc.
	Bombay Light Horse:		
	Troop of mounted rifles of the Bombay Volunteer Rifles	1885	
	Bombay Light Horse	1891	
	Bombay Light Motor Patrol:		
	Raised as the light motor patrol of the Bombay Bn.	1926	
	Bombay Light Motor Patrol	1933	
Bombay Coast Battery RA 1941	1. Bombay Volunteer Artillery	1887	
	2. 4th (Bombay) Group Garrison Artillery	1917	
	3. No.V (Bombay) Field Brigade	1920	
	4. No.10 (Bombay) Battery RA	1933	25 May 40 Embodied
No.3 (Bombay) Fortress Company RE 1933	1. Raised from Bombay Volunteer Artillery	1903	
	2. No.3 Electrical Engineer Coy	1917	
	3. No.3 (Bombay) Field Company	1920	25 May 40 Embodied
Bombay Battalion 1920	1. Bombay Volunteer Rifle Corps	1877	10–17 Feb 29 31 Dec 30 – 1 Jan 31 16–20 May 32 (in aid of civil power)
	2. 15th Bombay Battalion	1917	21 Mar 41 'A' Coy embodied

Present title and date that title asumed	*Former titles*	*Called out/embodied*
CAWNPORE CONTINGENT		
United Provinces Horse (Southern Regiment) 1920	See under Allahabad Contingent	25 Mar–2 Ap 31 (Riots)
No.20 (Cawnpore) Field Battery RA 1920		25 Mar – 2 Ap 31 (Riots)
Cawnpore Rifles 1920	1. Cawnpore Volunteer Rifle Corps 1877 2. 16th Cawnpore Rifles 1917	25 Mar–2 Apr 31 15–18 Feb 39 (Riots)
Ditto Armoured Car Section	Ditto	
Ditto W.T. Section	ditto	
KARACHI CORPS		
No.4 (Karachi) Fortress Company RE 1933	1. Raised from Karachi Artillery Volunteers 1902 2. No.4 Electrical Engineer Coy 1917 3. No.4 (Karachi) Field Coy 1920 4. No.4 (Karachi) Electrical and Mechanical Coy 1925 5. No.4 (Searchlight) Company 1928	3 Sep 39–31 Sep 43 (Manora Fort searchlights) 15 Jan 44 onwards – 1 officer + 15 men – night guard
Sind Rifles	1. Sind Volunteer Rifle Corps 1879 2. 23rd Sind Battalion 1917	8 Jul 42–22 May 43 and 3 Feb 44 onwards – Platoon strength night guards. Minor duties after 3 Sep 39
No.2 (Karachi) Company, MGC 1920	1. Karachi Artillery Volunteers 1892 2. 2nd (Karachi) Brigade Mobile Artillery 1917	

Present title and date that title assumed	*Former titles*	*Called out/embodied*
LUCKNOW CONTINGENT		
United Province Horse (Southern Regiment) 1920	See under Allahabad Contingent	
No. 13 (Lucknow) Field Battery RA 1933	1. Oudh Volunteer Rifle Corps 1865 2. Lucknow Volunteer Rifle Corps 1872 3. Oudh Volunteer Rifle Corps 1884 4. Lucknow Volunteer Rifle Corps 1903 5. 5th (Lucknow Group) Garrison Artillery 1917 6. No. VI (Lucknow) Field Brigade RA 1920 7. Transferred to Lucknow Rifles in 1942 when guns were withdrawn	
Lucknow Rifles 1933	No.7 (Lucknow) Company, Machine Gun Corps 1920	
MADRAS CONTINGENT		
Madras Coast Battery RA 1941	1. Madras Artillery Volunteers (raised from Madras Volunteer Guards 1879 2. 2nd Madras Group Garrison Artillery 1917 3. No. II (Madras) Field Brigade 'The Duke's Own' 1920 4. No.3 (Madras) field Battery 'The Duke's Own' 1933	25 May 40 Embodied
Madras Guards 1920	1. Madras Volunteer Guards 1857 2. 1st Madras Guards 1917	25 May 40 – One Platoon Embodied 10 May 41 – Remainder Embodied
Madras Signal Company 1942	1. No.1 (Madras) Field Company (raised from Madras Artillery Volunteers) 1920 2. No.1 (Madras) Signal Company Royal Corps of Signals 1928	10 May 41 – Fortress Signal Section Madras Embodied 17 Jan 42 – remainder embodied
POONA CONTINGENT		
No.14 (Kirkee) Field Battery RA 1920	'F' (Kirkee) Battery Mobile Artillery 1917	
Poona Rifles 1920	1. Poona Volunteer Rifles 1887 2. 35th Poona Battalion 1917	

Present title and date that title assumed	*Former titles*	*Called out/embodied*
PUNJAB CONTINGENT		
Punjab Light Horse 1895		4–9 May 27 (civil disturbances) 20–23 Jul 85 (in aid of civil power)
Punjab Rifles 1920	1. 1st Punjab Volunteer Rifle Corps 1861 (absorbed the Punjab Light Horse (volunteers) raised in 1867) 1871 2. 3rd Punjab Rifles 1917	5 Apr – 7 Jul 19 (civil disturbances) 20–23 Jul 35 (in aid of civil power)
Assam Valley Light Horse 1896	1. Assam Valley Mounted Rifles amalgamating: 1891 (a) Lakhimpur Mounted Rifles (1888) ex Lakhimpur Volunteer Rifles Corps (1882) (b) Sibsagar Mounted Rifles 1899 *ex* Sibsagar Mounted Infantry (1886) *ex* Sibsagar Mounted Rifles (1884) (c) Darrang Mounted Rifles (1889) ex Darrang Mounted Infantry (1887) (d) Nowgong Mounted Rifles (1888) (e) Gauhati Rifles (1885) absorbed Shillong Volunteer Rifles 1906 2. 6th Assam Valley Light Horse 1917	20–25 Aug 29, one tp called out, Jorhat
Bihar Light Horse 1884	Bihar Mounted Rifle Corps 1868	16 Aug – 9 Oct 42, 2 officers and 49 men, Tirhut 13 Aug – 9 Oct 42, 2 officers and 21 men, Bhagalpur (both in aid of civil power)
Calcutta Light Horse 1887	1. Calcutta Volunteer Lancers 1887 2. Calcutta Mounted Volunteer Rifles 1881 3. Calcutta Mounted Rifles absorbed Central Bengal Light Horse (1884) 1886	1 Aug–30 Sep 40, 3 Nov–24 Dec 40, 27 Dec 40–2 Jan 41, 1 Feb 41–12 Mar 41 9 Dec 41–16 Jan 42, 27 Jan–23 May 42 1, 8, 15 & 29 Oct 44, 5, 12, 19, & 26 Nov 44, 3 Dec 44 and 12–14 Jan 45

Present title and date that title assumed	*Former titles*		*Called out/embodied*
Chota Nagpur Regiment 1917	1. Chota Nagpur Mounted Rifles 2. Chota Nagpur Light Horse	1891 1910	10 Apr 38–3 officers & 60 men communal riots, Jamshedpur May 39 – 1 officer & 15 men – strike Ghatsila Aug–Sep 42 – 5 officers & 27 men – civil disturbances, Dhanbad Sep 42 – 3 officers & 36 men, night patrol, Damodar Bridge
Northern Bengal Mounted Rifles 1889	Northern Bengal Volunteer Rifle Corps (absorbed Darjeeling Volunteer Rifle Corps)	1873 1881	
Southern Provinces Mounted Rifles 1904			Nov 21 – part of unit during Moplah Rebellion
Surma Valley Light Horse 1886	1. Sylhet Volunteer Rifle Corps 2. Cachar and Sylhet Mounted Rifles	1880 1883	20–28 Apr 30 – 3 officers & 17 men – Chittagong 15 Dec 35 – 10 officers & 10 men, Balisera Valley
Bengal Artillery 1925	Formed from amalgamation of: I (Calcutta) Field Brigade IV (Cossipore) Field Brigade	1925	
	I. (Calcutta) Field Brigade (1920):		
	Calcutta Naval Artillery Volunteers Calcutta Port Defence Group Garrison Artillery	1883 1917	3 Sept 39–14 Feb 40– maintained coast def.bty.at Diamond Harbour 19 Feb 41–30 Apr 42– guards provided on 24 occasions at Budge Budge (av. strength 1 officer & 9 men)
	IV (Cossipore) field Brigade (1920): Cossipore Artillery Volunteers I Cossipore Brigade Mobile Artillery	1884 1917	
No.1 (Calcutta) Fortress Company RE 1933	1. Raised from Calcutta Port Defence Volunteers 2. No.1 Electrical Engineering Company 3. No.1 (Calcutta) Field Company	1902 1917 1920	28 Aug 39–13 Feb 40 – Port and coast defence

Present title and date that title assumed	*Former titles*		*Called out/embodied*
AGRA CONTINGENT 1920	1. Agra Volunteer Rifle Corps	1878	
Note: Pre-war composition was No.17 (Agra) Field Battery RA and No. 5 (Agra) Company, Machine Gun Corps, but arms surrendered for war emergency	2. 19th Agra Company	1917	
BANGALORE CONTINGENT 1933	1. Bangalore Rifle Volunteers	1868	9 Jun 43 – 8 officers & 350 men embodied After 22 Jun 40 – minor duties (guards, station dutie Prisoner-of-war camps, etc.
	2. 6th Bangalore,Coorg and Mysore Battalion (amalagamating the Coorg and Mysore Rifles, 1884) *Note:* On formation of Bangalore Contingent, the following units were amalgamated: (a) Bangalore Armoured Car Company (ex 14th (Bangalore) Field Battery RA,) (b) Bangalore Battalion	1917	
Bareilly Corps 1942	1. Naini Tal Volunteer Rifle Corps	1871	
	2. 10th (Naini Tal) Company	1917	
	3. Naini Tal Rifles	1920	
	4. Bareilly Contingent amalgamated Bareilly Detachment, United Provinces Horse, Northern Regiment *Note:* No.18 (Bareilly) Field Brigade RA is included in Bareilly Corps in name only	1925	Aug 42 – two days during civil disturbances
Calcutta and Presidency Battalion 1926	Formed from amalgamation of The Calcutta Battalion The Calcutta Presidency Battalion	1926	12–14 Apri 19, 24 Apr–10 May 26 15 Sep 30, 19–29 Apr 30, 5–6 May 30 (in aid of civil power)
	The Calcutta Battalion (1920):		5–16 Dec 43, 20, 21, 24 Dec 43, 15, 19 Jan 44, 9 May 44, 19 Nov 44 (Air Raid Precautions)
	Calcutta Volunteer Rifle Corps	1863	After 3 Sep 39, part of unit performed various guards & duties)
	1st Battalion Calcutta Volunteer Rifles	1898	
	5th Calcutta Battalion	1917	
	The Calcutta Presidency Battalion (1920):		15 Jan 40 – one company embodied
	Presidency Volunteer Reserve Battalion	1888	
	Presidency Volunteer Rifle Battalion	1891	
	Presidency Battalion Calcutta Volunteer Rifles	1898	
	37th Calcutta Presidency Battalion	1917	

Present title and date that title assumed	*Former titles*	*Called out/embodied*
Calcutta Scottish 1920	1. Calcutta Scottish Volunteers 1911 2. 44th Calcutta Scottish 1917	12–14 Apr 19, 9 May 26 (Riots) 6 May 3 Whole unit. Apr-May 30- av.1 officer & 14 men on 18 occasions in aid of civil power. After 3 Sep 39, part of unit performed various guards & duties
Coorg and Mysore Company 1933	1. Coorg and Mysore Rifles 1884 2. Amalgamated with 6th Bangalore Coorg and Mysore Battalion 1917	
DEHRA DUN CONTINGENT 1925	1. Mussoorie Volunteer Rifle Corps, amalgamating 1871 (a) Thomason College Volunteer Rifle Corps (1872) 1901 (b) Mussoorie Volunteer Reserve Corps (1889) 2. 9th Mussoorie Battalion 1917 3. Mussoorie Battalion 1920 *Note* On formation of Dehra Dun Contingent the following units were amalgamated:- (a) Dehra Dun Detachment, United Provinces Horse, Northern Regiment (b) Meerut Detachment, No.5 company, Machine Gun Corps.	Saharanpur Dett-armoury guard for three months, 1930–31 One motor platoon and one section embodied 5 Apr 45.
DELHI CONTINGENT 1921	Formed from detachments of the Punjab Light Horse and the Punjab Rifles	11–14 Aug 42-patrols sent to Gurgaon in aid of civil power
East Coast Battalion 1920	1. Godavari Rifle Volunteers 1885 2. East Coast Rifle Volunteers 1890 amalgamating Vizagapatam Rifle Volunteers 1885 3. East Coast Volunteer Rifles 1903 4. 38th East Coast Battalion 1917	Between 1920 & 1922 in connection with Narasapatam Road disturbances Between 1929 & 1933 in connection with Chittagong Armoury Raid Embodied 31 May 41
Eastern Bengal Company 1920	1. Dacca Volunteer Rifle Corps 184 2. Eastern Bengal Volunteer Rifles amalgamating: 1900 Chittagong Volunteer Rifle Corps (1885) 3. 41st Eastern Bengal Company 1917	

Present title and date that title assumed	*Former titles*	*Called out/embodied*
Hyderabad Rifles 1920	1. Hyderabad Volunteer Rifle Corps 1882 2. 26th Hyderabad Rifles 1917	After 3 Sep 39 unit performed various guards and duties
Kolar Gold Field Battalion 1920	1. Formed from detachment of Bangalore Rifle Volunteers 1903 2. 43rd Kolar Gold Field Battalion 1917	7–8 Apr 30
Nagpur Rifles 1937	1. Nagpur Volunteer Rifles amalagamated: 1860 Berar Volunteer Rifle Corps (1879) 1904 2. 2nd Nagpur Rifles 1917 3. Nagpur Rifles 1926 4. Nagpur Regiment 1927	6-13 Sep 27,12 Aug-4 Sep 42 30 Oct-3 Nov 42 (internal security duties)
Nilgiri Malabar Battalion 1920	1. Nilgiri Volunteer Rifles 1878 Absorbed Coimbatore Volunteer Corps (1885) 1892 2. 20th Nilgiri Malabar Battalion amalgamating: 1917 Malabar Volunteer Rifles (1885) *ex* Calicut and Tellicherry Volunteer Corps	During Moplah Rebellion 1921–4 officers and 184 men at various centres May 30-Dec 31 – 112 men at various centres (civil disobedience) 31 May 41 – 3 officers & 207 men embodied 4 Feb 42 – 1 officer & 29 men embodied
Simla rifles 1920	1. 2nd Punjab or Simla Volunteer Rifle Corps 1861 2. Simla Volunteer Rifles 1904 3. 4th Simla Rifles 1917	
Assam Bengal Railway Battalion 1920	1. Assam Bengal Railway Volunteer Rifles 1901 2. 42nd Assam Bengal Railway Battalion 1917	1930 – Chittagong Armoury Raid. After this, part of unit performed minor guards and internal security duties
Bengal Nagpur Railway Battalion 1933	1. Bengal Nagpur Railway Volunteer Rifle Corps 1883 absorbed Orissa Volunteer Rifles 1898 2. 36th Bengal Nagpur Railway Regiment 1917 3. Bengal Nagpur Railway Regiment 1920	7-8 Jun 30 Av.daily strength 2 officers and 50 men (civil disturbances) 17 May 42–31 Jul 43, Av.daily strength 4 officers and 128 men (civil disturbances) Minor guards since Dec 41
Bombay Baroda and Central India Railway Regiment 1920	1. Bombay Baroda and Central India Railway Volunteer Corps 1877 absorbed Ghadeshi Volunteer Rifle Corps (1885) 1886 absorbed the Rajputana-Malva Volunteer Rifle Corps (1882) as 2nd Battalion 1887 2. 17th Bombay Baroda and Central India Railway Battalion 1917	25 Apr 30-Oct 31 Minor ordinary guards during civil disturbances After 27 Aug 39 six occasions in strength up to one coy for guards, etc. After 3 Sep 39, minor guards and duties

Present title and date that title assumed	*Former titles*	*Called out/embodied*
Eastern Bengal Railway Battalion 1920	1. Eastern Bengal State Railway Volunteer Rifle Corps 1873 2. Eastern Bengal Railway Volunteer Rifle Corps 1882 amalgamating:- Northern Bengal State Railway Volunteer Rifle Corps (1879) 3. Eastern Bengal State Railway Volunteer Rifle Corps 1884 4. 12th Eastern Bengal Railway Battalion 1917	17 Apri 30–31 Mar 31, 40 men for ordinary guards 5–7 May 30 – 3 officers and 70 men for protection of Sealdah Station After 3 Sep 39, various posts, etc. In 1942 rebellion, 5 officers and 102 men on train patrols
East Indian Railway Regiment 1920	1. East Indian Railway Volunteer Rifle Corps 1869 absorbed Sibpore College Volunteer Rifle corps (1881) 1890 2. 7th East Indian Railway Battalion 1917 amalgamating: St.Michael's School Cadet Corps (1892) 3. 7th East Indian Railway Corps 1918 absorbed Oudh and Rohilkhand Railway Battalion 1926 4. Reorganised as two Battalions 1933	Part of unit called out in aid of civil power during communal disturbances 1933–41 and 1942 rebellion. 2–22 Feb 22 – 11 men – armoury guards (strike) 22 Jul 34 – Cawnpore Dett. (riot) 2 Mar 39 – Moradabad Dett. (in aid of civil power) 13 Aug–5 Nov 42 – 1 officer and 17 men to Moghulsarai 17 Aug–22 Nov 42 – 28 men Cawnpore 22 Aug-22 Sep 42 – 28 men Allahabad 24 Aug-22 Sep 42 – 7 men Mirzapore 28 Aug–18 Oct 42 – 26 men Tundla
Great Indian Peninsula Railway Regiment 1920	1. Great Indian Peninsula Railway Volunteer Corps 1875 absorbed as 2nd Battalion: Midland Railway Volunteer Corps (1890) 1902 2. 1/13th and 2/13th Great Indian Peninsula Railway Battalions 1917 Also administers: Nasik Road company	Jan 30-Nov 31 and in 1942 rebellion railway security duties and armoury guards Apr 30-Apr 31 part of unit carried out armoury guard duties

Present title and date that title assumed	*Former titles*	*Called out/embodied*
Madras and Southern Mahratta Railway Rifles 1920	*1st Battalion* 1. Madras Railway Volunteers 1885 2. 1st Bn.Madras and Southern Mahratta Railway Rifles 1910 3. 1st Bn. 32nd Madras and Southern Mahratta Railway Rifles 1917 *2nd Battalion* 1. Southern Mahratta Railway Rifle Corps 1886 absorbed Bellary Volunteer Rifle Corps (1885) 1898 2. 2nd Battalion Madras and Southern Mahratta Railway Rifles 1910 3. 2nd Battalion 32nd Madras and Southern Mahratta Railway Rifles 1917	Apr 30-Dec 31 – armoury guards 13–16 Apr 42 – 11 officers and 138 men (riots) Aug 42 – 1 officer and 48 men at Nellore, Bezwada and Godavari Bridges Jan–Jul 43 – guards railway vulnerable points
North Western Railway Battalion 1933	1. 3rd or Sind,Punjab and Indus Valley Railways Volunteer Rifle Corps 1880 2. 3rd Punjab (North Western Railway) Volunteer Rifle Corps 1888 3. North Western Railway Volunteer Rifles 1892 4. 24th North Western Railway Battalion 1917	10 Aug–5 Sep 30 – Armoured Train (North-West Frontier operations) 1930 'C' Coy (Sukkur riots) 20–24 Nov 39 'D' Coy (Sukkur Riots)

Present title and date that title assumed	*Former titles*	*Called out/embodied*
Oudh and Tirhut Railway Battalion 1943	1. Tirhut State Railway Volunteer Rifle Corps 1879 2. Bengal and North Western Railway Volunteer Corps 1892 amalgamating Ghazipur Volunteer Rifle Corps (1879) *ex* Ghazipur Volunteer Rifle Battalion (1881) *ex* Ghazipur Volunteer Rifle Corps (1885) 3. 22nd Bengal and North Western Railway Battalion 1917 4. Bengal and North Western Railway Battalion 1920	30 Apr–24 May 30 – Armoury guard 14–15 Aug 42 – Gorakhpur Dett. 13 Aug–8 Sep 42 – Sonepore Dett. 15 Aug–20 Sep 42 – Samastipur Dett.
Southern Indian Railway Battalion 1920	1. Southern Indian Railway Volunteer Rifle Corps 1884 2. 29th Southern Indian Railway Battalion 1917	Moplah Rebellion 1921

In 1937, when Burma ceased to be a province of India, all the local Auxiliary Force, India units became units of the Burma Auxiliary Force. They were as under:

1937 title and date that title assumed	*Former titles*
III (Rangoon) Field Brigade 1920	1. Rangoon Volunteer Artillery 1879 2. Rangoon Port Defence Volunteers 1892 3. Rangoon Port Defence Artillery Volunteers 1906 4. 3rd (Rangoon Port Defence) Group, Garrison Artillery 1917
Burma Railways Battalion 1920	1. Rangoon and Irrawaddy State Railway Volunteer Rifle Corps 1879 2. Burma State Railway Volunteer Corps 1884 3. Burma Railways Volunteer Corps 1899 4. 21st Burma Railway Battalion 1917
Tenasserim Battalion 1920	1. Moulmein Volunteer Rifle Corps 1877 amalgamating:- (a) Moulmein Volunteer Reserve Company (1889) 1901 (b) Moulmein Volunteer Artillery Corps (1885) 1917 2. 14th Tenasserim Battalion 1917
Rangoon Battalion 1920	1. Rangoon Volunteer Rifle Corps 1877 amalgamating: Akyab Volunteer Rifle Corps (1880) 1883 2. 18th Rangoon Battalion 1917
Upper Burma Battalion 1920	1. Upper Burma Volunteer Rifles 1886 2. 34th Upper Burma Battalion 1917

Table 1 Indian Territorial Force Battalions

Date of Raising	*First Title*	*Post 1922 Title*	*Location*	*Regular Unit*	*Employment in 1939–45 War*	*Notes*
11 Mar 22	1(T)Bn Bombay Pioneers	11/2 Bombay Pioneers	Bombay			Disbanded 1 Sep 28
15 Apr 22	2(T)Bn Bombay Pioneers	12/2 Bombay Pioneers	Bombay			Disbanded 15 Oct 27
5 Aug 21	1(T)Bn62 Punjabis	11/1 Punjab Regt.	Jhelum	9/1 Punjab Regt.	Transferred to R.Indian Navy	
5 Aug 21	1(T)Bn73 Carnatic Infantry	11/3 Madras Regt.	Trichinopoly	1/3 Madras Regt.	ALFSEA	
28 Jan 22	1(T)Bn75 Carnatic Infantry	12/3 Madras Regt.	Cannanore	2/3 Madras Regt. (MG)	NW Frontier	
11 Mar 22	1(T)Bn79 Carnatic Infantry	13/3 Madras Regt.	Cannanore	3/3 Madras Regt.	NW Frontier	
11 Mar 22	1(T)Bn 83 Wallajahbad Light Infantry	14/3 Madras Regt.	Mercara, Coorg	1 Coorg Bn	ALFSEA (Garrison Bn)	
14 Nov 39	15(Madras) Bn		Madras	4/3 Madras Regt	ALFSEA	
13 Jun 40	16(Bengal)Bn			76 GT Coy RIASC		Converted to GT Coy 2 Feb 42-Disbanded 5 Sep 42
11 Mar 22	1(T)Bn 44 Merwara Infantry	11/4 Bombay Grenadiers	Ajmer	1 Ajmer Regt	NW Frontier	
5 Aug 21	1(T)Bn 103 Mahratta Light Infantry	11/5 Mahratta Light Infantry	Belgaum	15/5 Mahratta Light Infantry	Training Unit	
14 Nov 39	12/5 Mahratta Light Infantry			16/5 Mahratta Light Infantry	NW Frontier	
11 Mar 22	1(T)Bn 4 Prince Albert Victor's Rajputs	12/7 Rajput Regt	Agra	14/6 Rajputana Rifles	Training Unit	Transferred from 7 Rajput Regt in 1928 to become 11/6 Rajputana Rifles

14 Feb 40	12/6 Rajputana Rifles		Agra	15/6 Rajputana Rifles	NW Frontier	
5 Aug 21	1(T)Bn 2 Queen Victoria's Own Rajput Light Infantry	11/7 Rajput Regt	Fyzabad	9/7 Rajput Regt	Training Unit	
14 Feb 40	12/7 Rajput Regt			14/7 Rajput Regt	NW Frontier	
11 Mar 22	1(T)Bn 6 Royal Jat Light Infantry	11/9 Jat Regt	Meerut	7/9 Jat Regt	Training Unit	
14 Feb 40	12/9 Jat Regt			8/9 Jat Regt	NW Frontier	
11 Mar 22	2(T)Bn 51 (Prince of Wales's Own) Sikhs	11/12 Frontier Force Regt	Nowshera	14/12 Frontier Force Regt	ALFSEA	
11 Mar 22	1(T)Bn 66 Punjabis	11/13 Frontier Force Rifles	Campbellpore	15/13 Frontier Force Rifles	Transferred to R.Indian Navy	
11 Mar 22	1(T)Bn 26 Punjabis	11/14 Punjab Regt	Delhi	9/9 Jat Regt	NW Frontier	
14 Nov 39	12/14 Punjab Regt			14/9 Jat Regt	NW Frontier	
5 Aug 21	1(T)Bn 25 Punjabis	11/15 Punjab Regt	Jullundur	8/15 Punjab Regt	NW Frontier	
14 Nov 39	12/15 Punjab Regt			9/15 Punjab Regt	NW Frontier	
11 Mar 22	1(T)Bn 37 (Prince of Wales's Own Dogras)	11/17 Dogra Regt	Jullundur	6/27 Dogra Regt	NW Frontier	
14 Nov 39	12/17 Dogra Regt			7/17 Dogra Regt	NW Frontier	
10 Mar 22	1(T)Bn 39 Royal Garhwal Rifles	11/18 Royal Garhwal Rifles	Lansdowne	6/18 Royal Garhwal Rifles	NW Frontier	
5 Aug 21	1(T)Bn 94 Russell's Infantry	11/19 Hyderabad Regt	Calcutta and Dinapore	1 Bihar Regt	ALFSEA	
3 Aug 21	1(T)Bn 70 Burma Rifles	11/20 Burma Rifles	Meiktila			Transferred to Burma Army in 1937

All the Burma units, of course, saw some period of embodiment during the Burma Rebellion of 1930–32. In 1942, many of their personnel who withdrew to India were formed into the Burma Intelligence Corps and their local knowledge and linguistic abilities utilised by attachment to British and Indian units returning for the re-conquest of Burma.

The Indian Territorial Force was first constituted in 1920 as part of the Montagu-Chelmsford Reforms. The Force *'was intended to cater, amongst other things, for the military aspirations of those classes of the population to whom military service has not hitherto been a hereditary profession.'* Seven such 'provincial' battalions were created in 1921 and the scheme was extended to twenty the following year. They were normally raised in or near the location of the respective regiments' training battalions and usually from the same classes from which the regular battalions of that regiment were recruited. Not all infantry regiments had a Territorial battalion but the 3rd Madras Regiment had four in 1922 which enabled the parent regiment to be re-raised quickly in 1942 despite its disbandment in the 1930's (the ITF battalions were maintained in the care of other regiments whilst 3 Madras was not in existence). Once the 1922 changes in regimental title and structure had been implemented, the ITF battalion was absorbed into the 'family' as the 11th Bn (in 3 Madras, they were numbered 11th, 12th, 13th, etc). Enlistment was basically for six years, capable of extension on completion of the initial periods. Training was for twenty-eight days each year, generally carried out in the cold weather but, later, this period was extended to two months each year. As a rule, the battalion assembled at the headquarters of the regiment's training battalion. Five regular British Officers were attached to each battalion, the senior acting as commanding officer during annual training. One of the others acted as adjutant and it was he who, as administrative commandant, maintained the ITF battalion throughout the year: the remaining officers – company commanders during training – then returned to the training battalion at the CO's disposal. Other officers were Indians.

Organisation of the ITF battalions was intended to be the same as that of a regular Indian Army battalion but, by 1939, the 11/17 Dogra was still only armed with rifles. It was not until the spring of 1941 that they received their first limited supply of Bren light machine-guns and mortars. However, the intention was, that in the event of war, the ITF battalions should be mobilised and become, to all intents and purposes, standard, all-purpose, infantry battalions. It was, of course, in that respect that the Indian Territorial soldier differed from his British counterpart in India. The Auxiliary Force, India units were never intended to become units of the line in the event of war and, in fact, were never generally mobilised. The AFI was primarily for internal security work, for aid to the civil power. It was never intended to fill a gap in the order of battle. The ITF was expressly excluded from internal security duties in peacetime due to the essentially local nature of its recruitment. After embodiment, of course, and once away from their own localities, battalions could be so employed.

During the Second World War, ITF battalions were mobilised and utilised, for the most part in railway protection, bridge-guards and static duties at first. However, as is shown on Table 1, many of them were converted to fully-active battalions, renumbered, re-armed and sent to active theatres. In many cases, of course, this also involved posting-out of unfit men and reinforcement by new personnel.

It is of interest that 11/17 Dogra, re-designated 6/17 Dogra in Sep 41, became 2/17 Dogra-a regular battalion - in Apr 46 whilst 12/17 Dogra, redesignated 7/17

Table 2

Unit	*Date of Raising*	*Remarks*
1st. Bombay (Parsi) Urban Infantry	2 Sep 28	Disbanded 30 Sep 31
2nd Bombay (Presidency) Urban Infantry	1 Sep 28	—
3rd (Madras) Presidency) Urban Infantry	1 Sep 28	Disbanded 14 Mar 38
4th (United Provinces) Urban Infantry	1 Sep 28	—
5th (Bengal Presidency) Urban Infantry	16 Jan 37	—
6th (Punjab) Urban Infantry	13 Jun 40	Disbanded 30 Sep 42
7th (Central) Provinces) Urban Infantry	25 Jul 40	—

Dogra in Sep 41, became 3/17 Dogra in May 46. Both 2 and 3 regular battalions had been lost in Malaya in February 1942.

After the first experiments in creating the provincial ITF battalions had been put in hand, seven urban battalions were created. Details are shown on Table 2.

Whilst the provincial battalions had been raised to accommodate the military aspirations of the agricultural population, the urban battalions were intended to cater for the townsman who could not be away from his employment for so long. These battalions were not parented to regular infantry regiments and none of them converted to active status during 1939-45 war. In fact, as can be seen, two of them were disbanded before the beginning of the war and one in 1942.

It was not until 1978 that it was revealed that a wartime action in Portuguese Goa in Mar 43 was the work of a party of fourteen men from the Calcutta Light Horse and four from the Calcutta Scottish. A German radio and supply-base in the harbour was put out of action by a coup-de-main party which had sailed from Cochin in an antique hopper-barge which had been sailed, hugging the coast, from Calcutta. The bulk of the boarding-party had taken the train from Calcutta. With Portugal, our oldest ally, still a neutral, the strictest secrecy had to be maintained and those taking part in the raid were warned that if it miscarried they would be disowned by the British authorities. If it succeeded, there would still be no rewards other than, of course, virtue. No medals either, it was emphasized and, this time, the Government kept its word. Not even a 1939–45 Star was awarded although the ticket-collectors at Howrah Station in Calcutta received this because they were AFI men embodied to prevent the risk of any labour dispute slowing the essential flow of rail traffic. The regimental history, published in 1957 carried the single paragraph headed 'The unwritten chapter'. It read: *'this portion of the History is suppressed for reasons of security'*.

The Willcox Committee in 1945, mindful that the role of the Auxiliary Force, India had proved to be principally as a source of officers for the Indian Army, made certain recommendations for its post war future. The following units, all essentially metropolitan, were to be retained in an officer-producing role:

enlistment would be open both to Europeans and Indians:

Bangalore Contingent
Bengal Artillery (one battery)
Bombay Light Patrol (two companies)
Calcutta Light Horse } Amalgamated
Calcutta Scottish }
Madras Guards
Punjab Light Horse
United Provinces Horse

The following units, recruited in outlying districts, would be re-assigned as a voluntary special constabulary, retaining their old titles. Officer-training was not thought possible in the scattered areas. However a majority of the Committee considered that the two Assam units might be officer-producing. Their wartime records in this field would seem to have prompted this recommendation:

Assam	– Assam Valley Light Horse Surma Valley Light Horse
Bengal	– Northern Bengal Mounted Rifles
Bihar	– Bihar Light Horse Chota Nagpur Regiment
Madras	– Southern Provinces Mounted Rifles Nilgiri Malabar Battalion
United Provinces	– Dehra Dun Contingent

Those units not covered above and not recommended for disbandment were to be absorbed into existing ITF battalions with regimental associations as shown below:

1.	Bengal	– Calcutta & Presidency Battalion 5 (Bengal Presidency) Urban Infantry	Amalgamated	7 Rajput
2.	Bombay	– Bombay Contingent (less Bombay Light Patrol) 2 (Bombay Presidency) Urban Infantry	Amalgamated	4 Bombay Grenadiers
3.	Bombay	– Poona Contingent		5 Mahratta Light Infantry
4.	Central Provinces	– Nagpur Rifles 7 (Central Provinces) Urban Infantry	Amalgamated	6 Rajputana Rifles
5.	Madras	– Kolar Goldfield Battalion		3 Madras
6.	Madras	– East Coast Battalion		3 Madras

7. Punjab	– Punjab Rifles	8 Punjab
8. Sind	– Karachi Contingent	10 Baluch
9. United Provinces	– Lucknow Contingent	2 Punjab
10. United Provinces	– 4 (United Provinces) Urban Infantry	2 Punjab
11. Madras	– Madras Signal Company	Indian Corps of Signals

The remaining Auxiliary Force, India units for disbandment were :

Agra Contingent
Bareilly Corps
Calcutta Fortress Company
Coorg & Mysore Company
Delhi Contingent
East Bengal Company
Hyderabad Rifles
Simla Rifles

plus all the railway regiments.

Hitherto, the Indian Territorial Force had been made up of infantry units but the Willcox Committee recommended the formation of thirty anti-aircraft artillery batteries and that three general transport companies be raised on each RIASC training centre.

Partition came in August 1947 and the Auxiliary Force, India was promptly disbanded. By that time, also, all the ITF battalions had been disbanded or, as in the case of the two Dogra battalions, upgraded to regular status.

6. THE PRINCELY STATES

Before Partition in 1947, almost a quarter of the population of the sub-continent (now India, Pakistan and Bangladesh) lived, not in 'British India' but in one of the princely states, controlled by traditional, hereditary rulers. Many of these rulers had contracted into relations with the Honourable East India Company and, subsequently, with the Crown to maintain their own armed forces within their states for which the Company, in the first place, found the officers. In addition, some of the rulers funded elements of the Company's troops for their protection.

For the most part, the latter category vanished in 1857 when the troops mutinied with the rest of the Bengal Army. Two exceptions, however, were Baroda and Hyderabad. In the former state, HM Government was committed to keep, in times of peace, two Indian cavalry regiments, 4,000 Indian infantry and a British artillery battery but this appeared latterly to be something of a notional commitment as, before 1939, there was only one Indian battalion there and, during the Second World War, none at all. In Hyderabad, the Crown was expected to keep one regiment of Indian cavalry, five infantry battalions and a gunner element. Before 1939, these numbers were often exceeded but, during the war, the strength fluctuated from four infantry battalions in 1942 to five regiments of armour, four of artillery and some engineers in 1944.

The state-raised forces maintained by the princes were not limited by treaty but they were not regarded with favour by the Government of India. It was the accelerating technical development of warfare which gradually deprived these forces of any serious military value and rendered them just adequate for ceremony and local security.

The perennial Russian threat brought in 1885 an offer from certain of the rulers to make elements of their states' forces available to the paramount power in time of war or emergency. Such specified troops were to be known as Imperial Service Troops and the Government of India would contribute to their equipment. They would be expected to reach a standard of training which would make them fit to stand in line with the regular Indian troops of the Queen-Empress. Training was supervised by officers on secondment from the Indian Army, schools of instruction were set up to train the new Imperial Service Troops and officers went on attachment to regular Indian Army units.

Kashmir, with a shared Russian frontier, volunteered to furnish two batteries of mountain artillery and it was that state whose Imperial Service Troops were the first to take the field; they formed part of the force engaged in the 1891 campaign in Hunza Nagar and they subsequently fought in the Chitral action in 1895.

In the Frontier War in 1897, contingents from Gwalior, Jaipur, Jind, Kapurthala, Kashmir, Malerlkotla, Nabha, Patiala and Sirmoor all took part. A detachment of 36 men from the Kapurthala Jagatjit Infantry perished to a man when cut off and overrun by tribesmen. It subsequently transpired that the men had never previously served outside their barrack area in the state and they were patently unfit to engage in frontier operations. The subadar in command died fighting but the 36 men surrendered their rifles.

Although not generally known at the time, orders had been issued that Imperial Service Infantry should never be exposed to danger! Furthermore for political reasons, they were to be praised, whatever they did. Colonel Hill, commanding the Kurram Mobile Column, was obliged, therefore to write a fulsome report on the action, stating that, in an excess of zeal, they had engaged a superior force and had died fighting.

Troops from Alwar, Bikanir, Jodhpur and Malerkotla went to China during the Boxer Rising in 1901 where they were accompanied by the Maharajah of Bikanir and Maharajah Sir Pratab Singh of Jodhpur. During this campaign, a daffadar from Jodhpur earned the Indian Order of Merit – then the nearest equivalent to the Victoria Cross open to Indian soldiers – for gallantry in the field.

A contingent from the Bikanir Camel Corps was sent to Somaliland in 1902 to meet an urgent need for mounted troops but Imperial Service Troops reached their peak in the Great War.

Before the outbreak of war in 1914, there were twenty-nine states participating in the Imperial Service Troops scheme and the strengths of the arms represented were as follows:

Cavalry	7,673
Infantry	10,298
Artillery	373
Sappers	741
Signals	34
Camel Corps	637
Transport Corps	2,723
TOTAL	22,479

During the war, some 18,000 served overseas and whilst contingents from some of the smaller states were not large enough to serve abroad, they were utilised in India, either on internal security duties or in training cavalry remounts.

Hyderabad, Mysore and Patiala sent their cavalry regiments to the Middle East to form the Imperial Service Cavalry Brigade where, together with the Bikanir Camel Corps and detachments from several other states, they performed creditably in Egypt and Palestine. In particular, the Jodhpur Lancers captured the fortified town of Haifa. They had already served in France under the personal command once more of His Highness Maharajah Sir Pratab Singh. Also in France were Sappers from Faridkot, Malerkotla and Tehri-Garhwal whilst transport units came from Bharatpur, Gwalior and Indore.

Alwar, Gwalior and Patiala sent infantry to the Middle East and two companies from the last-named were sent as reinforcements to Gallipoli where they suffered heavy casualties. Sirmoor Sappers were also singled out for honourable mention in Mesopotamia.

The campaign in East Africa engaged units from Bharatpur, Faridkot, Gwalior, Jind, Kapurthala, Kashmir and Rampur, the Sappers from Faridkot being particularly commended.

Transport units in the Middle East from Bahawalpur, Bharatpur, Gwalior, Indore, Jaipur, Khairpur and Mysore filled a great need, especially at a time when motor transport in the Indian Army was in its infancy.

Details of the Imperial Service Troops placed at the disposal of the Crown are shown in Table 3

Table 3. Indian States Forces

Name of State (*a*)	*Imperial Service troops placed at disposal of the Crown during the Great War 1914–1918* (*b*)	*ISF units provided for use by the Crown during the 1939–45 war, excluding those recruited in British India* (*c*)	*ISF units recruited in British India* (*d*)	*Units which might be accepted in a future war* (*e*)	*Remarks* (*f*)
1. Alwar	*1 sqn cavalry 2 sqns cavalry *1 bn infantry	1 bn infantry			
2. Bahawalpur	*dets camel corps camel corps *camel tpt	1 bty mtn artillery *2 bns infantry		1 lt bty 1 GT coy	*One lost in Malaya
3. Baroda			1 bn infantry		
4. Bharatpur	*1 bn infantry *1 tpt corps	1 grn coy			
5. Bhopal	1 regt cavalry		2 bns infantry		
6. Bikaner	*1 camel corps	1 camel regt 1 bty mtn artillery 1 bn infantry 1 PW guard bn		1 lt bty 1 bn inf 1 GT coy	
7. Cochin		1 grn coy			
8. Cutch		1 grn coy			
9. Faridkot	*1 coy sappers	2 fd coy			
10. Gwalior	over 1½ regts cavalry *2 bns infantry *det tpt corps	1 recce regt 1 bty fd artillery 2 btys mtn artillery 2 bns infantry 1 AT coy		1 lt bty 1 AT coy	
11. Hyderabad	*1 regt cavalry	2 recce regts 1 bty fd artillery *3 bns infantry		1 lt bty 1 bn inf 1 GT coy	*One lost in Malaya
12. Indore	*1 sqn cavalry *1 tpt corps	½ AT coy	1 bn infantry		*Composite Indore-Rewa AT coy
13. Jaipur	*1 tpt corps	2 bns infantry 1 AT coy		1 bn inf 1 AT coy	
14. Jammu and Kashmir	*dets cavalry *1 bty mtn artillery *3 bns infantry 1 bn infantry	1 sig sec 3 bns infantry		1 lt bty 2 bn inf	
15. Jind	*1 bn infantry	*1 bn infantry		1 bn inf	*Lost in Malaya

16. Jodhpur	*1 regt cavalry	1 recce regt 2 bns infantry	1 bn inf 1 GT coy	
17. Kapurthala	*1 bn infantry	1 bn infantry		
18. Khairpur	*dets infantry *dets tpt corps 1 tpt corps			
19. Kolhapur		1 bn infantry	1 GT coy	
20. Kotah		1 bn infantry		
21. Malerkotla	*over 1 coy sapprs	1 fd coy		
22. Mandi				
23. Mewar (Udaipur)	*det cavalry dets cavalry	1 bn infantry		
24. Mysore	*1 regt cavalry *1 tpt corps	*1 bn infantry 1 grn bn	1 bn inf 1 GT coy	*Lost in Malaya
25. Nabha	*1 bn infantry	1 bn infantry	1 bn inf	
26. Nawanagar	1 sqn cavalry	2 grn coys		
27. Patiala	*1 regt cavalry *1 bn infantry	1 recce regt 1 bty mtn artillery 2 bns infantry	1 lt bty 1 bn inf 1 GT coy	
28. Rajpipla		1 grn coy		
29. Rampur	dets cavalry *1 bn infantry	1 bn inf		
30. Rewa		1 grn coy ½ AT coy	1AT coy	*Composite Indore-Rew AT coy
31. Sirmoor	*2 coys sappers	1 fd coy		
32. Suket		1 br pl		
33. Tehri-Garhwal	*1 coy sappers *det infantry	1 fd coy		
34. Travancore		2 bns infantry	1 bn inf 1 GT coy	
35. Tripura		1 bn infantry		

NOTES

*Units marked with an asterisk were used on active service overseas.

Every war produces reforms and changes and it was realised that although the Imperial Service Troops had contributed greatly to the 1914-18 struggle, differences in establishments, strengths, etc. from those of similar Indian Army units often made for problems.

As a result, 1920 brought about a revision of conditions by which the Crown undertook to arm and equip at full scale a number of State Force units which were styled Field Service Units. They would be unconditionally available to the Crown in the event of need. They were to be organised on Indian Army establishments and armed with the same weapons as their counterparts in the Indian Army. In addition, the Crown would supply arms and equipment at cost price to the states for other units which might be placed at the disposal of the Crown. These became General Service Units if accepted and were then brought up to the scale of Field Service Units at the Crown's expense. A third category was to consist of a type of militia unit, not permanently embodied and with lower standards of training, discipline and weapons. The new system claimed almost 50,000 men, twice the numbers in 1914–18 and forty-nine states were in the scheme, ranging from Gwalior and Hyderabad with divisional strengths down to states with one platoon.

The training of the forces was under the control of military advisers under a general officer designated the Military Adviser-in-Chief. However, progress was slow and when war broke out in September 1939, the changes projected in 1920 had only finally been agreed and implemented.

Thus, with very few exceptions, the Field Service Units needed re-training, re-equipping and often re-officering at the expense of the Indian Army, then itself short of officers. Notwithstanding these strictures, a substantial number of units from the states served with the Indian Army during the Second World War as can be seen in Table 3

Establishments, however, were still often at variance with regular Indian Army units and the history of the Indian Engineers recorded that the five field companies which were made available to the Crown in 1939 varied in strength from 129 to 233 officers and men.

Major units served in East Africa, in the Western Desert, in Paiforce (Persia and Iraq), in Italy and in Burma whilst smaller units served on garrison and internal security duties in India and throughout the Middle East.

Malaya in 1941 did not appear to be destined to be a seat of war and five battalions, one each from Bahawalpur, Hyderabad, Jind, Mysore and Kapurthala were stationed there with regular Indian Army troops, only to be overrun and forced to surrender in Singapore in February 1942.

As will be seen from the table referred to above, three states - Baroda, Bhopal and Indore had raised battalions outside their own boundaries, recruited from British India.

Conversely, recruitment from within the princely states for the Indian Army continued and, during the Second World War, more than 350,000 were enlisted against fewer than 50,000 recruited by the states themselves although certain of the states, Gwalior and Patiala among them, restricted Indian Army recruitment in favour of their own states' forces.

The Willcox Committee, in 1945, felt that there were inherent problems in the Indian State Forces scheme as it existed. Differing standards in training and discipline still meant additional tasks for the Indian Army when units were transferred to Crown service at a time when the army was, itself, under pressure with mobilisation measures. Reinforcement of Indian States Forces units also presented problems whilst subsidisation of the states for raising troops would seem to be misplaced if recruitment for States' units were to be undertaken in British India.

It recommended that the Field Service Units and General Service Units as previously constituted be abolished but suggested that the Crown would provide arms and equipment at cost price for a fixed number of units of agreed types and establishments for the maintenance of internal order including, in the event of war, railway protection and, in the case of Kashmir, frontier defence. The Crown would also furnish pre- and post-commission training for Indian States Forces' officers and offer vacancies at Indian Army schools to States' personnel. In return, the Crown would have the right in an emergency to utilise such units which would be maintained and reinforced thereafter from Indian Army resources.

Table 3 also shows a tentative selection of the units envisaged: the selection, the Committee emphasised, would depend upon the units actually being maintained at the time by the states. However, clearly, there was to be some Crown guidance as to the type of unit likely to be needed.

The Willcox Committee's report, of course, was a wartime forward-look at the post-war Indian Army which did not envisage Partition.

The rulers of the princely states had all contracted agreements with the Crown and it was made clear to them that, after India became independent, the relationship hitherto existing between them and the Crown would lapse. A Union of India was projected in which British India and the states would combine to form the new dominion. Most of the rulers acceded to the suggestion but some of the bigger states like Travancore and Hyderabad made noises of dissent and hinted that they might favour a treaty relationship with India as between sovereign states.

However on the 15 Jun 47, the Congress Party announced that it could not countenance such an arrangement and, shortly afterwards, the Government of India set up a department for dealing with matters between the states and central government. Mountbatten lent his weight to the view that the princes should accede to either India or Pakistan 'as the successor powers to the British Raj'. To Pakistan this was almost academic since most of the princely states were in Rajputana, Central and Southern India.

By the 14 Aug 47, all but three of the states had acceded to one or other of the two dominions. The three in question were Hyderabad, Junagadh and Jammu and Kashmir. All three had, basically, a religious conflict. Jammu and Kashmir had a Hindu ruler of a predominantly Muslim population whilst Hyderabad and Junagadh, with Hindu populations, had Muslim rulers.

Junagadh was a small state of some 5,000 square miles in Gujerat and the Nawab, its Muslim ruler, announced his accession to Pakistan. He promptly sent his troops into the neighbouring state of Mangrol which had acceded to India. Predictably, Indian troops in brigade-strength were sent to restore sovereignty whereupon the Hindu populace of Junagadh arose, rejected the Nawab who fled to Pakistan and the people set up a provisional government which turned its back on Pakistan and opted for India.

Hyderabad was a rather bigger problem. Occupying most of the Decan plateau, almost 83,000 square miles in extent, its army consisted of three armoured-car regiments, a horsed cavalry regiment, eleven infantry battalions and some artillery. Apart from those regular troops, an irregular horsed cavalry regiment, four irregular infantry battalions and a garrison battalion increased the state's forces to divisional strength all under an Arab Commander-in-Chief. The Nizam of Hyderabad had declined to accede to India but had secured a Standstill Agreement pending a final decision. An attempt was made again to secure dominion-status within the Commonwealth but Mountbatten ruled this out. Within the state, a militant Muslim organisation – the Razakars – had sprung up, the senile vacillations of the Nizam making this easy, given the feudal conditions which had prevailed for centuries. Organised militarily, the Razakars began a covert campaign of insurgency, attacking trains and even going so far as to ambush an Indian Army convoy, killing six and wounding five soldiers.

Finally, Prime Minister Nehru announced to the Lok Sabha that since the start of the trouble in Hyderabad, over seventy villages had been attacked, about 150 incursions had been made into Indian territory, twelve trains had been attacked and property worth more than ten million rupees looted. A protest to the Nizam had brought the response that conditions within his state were entirely normal and that his own troops were quite capable of maintaining law and order.

Table 4. States forces' units perpetuated in the Indian Army

	NOW
CAVALRY	
1 Gwalior Lancers 2 Gwalior Lancers Jaipur Kachhawa Horse Jodhpur Lancers Mysore Lancers B Sqn, 2 Patiala Lancers Saurashtra Horsed Cavalry	61 Cavalry
ARTILLERY	
Gwalior Mountain Battery	74 (Gwalior) Mtn Bty
Patiala Mountain Battery	75 (Patiala) Fd Bty.
Jammu & Kashmir Mountain Battery	76 (Jammu & Kashmir) Fd Bty.
Bikanir Bijay Battery	83 (Bikanir) Fd Bty.
Gwalior Scindia's Field Battery	84 (Scindia) Fd Bty.
Patiala Field Battery	85 (Patiala) Fd Bty.
ENGINEERS	
Tehri Garhwal Field Company	84 Fd Coy (Tehri Garhwal), Bengal Group
2 Faridkot Field Company	94 Fd Coy (Faridkot), Bengal Group
Mandi Field Company	95 Fd Coy (Mandi), Bengal Group
Sirmoor Field Company	100 Fd Coy (Sirmoor), Bengal Group
1 Faridkot Field Company	368 Fd Coy (Faridkot), Bengal Group
Malerkotla Field Company	369 Fd Coy (Malerkotla), Bengal Group
Sirmoor Brass Band	Bengal Engineer Group Brass Band
INFANTRY	
Jind Infantry	13 (Jind) Punjab Regt.
Nabha Akal Infantry	14 (Nabha) Punjab Regt.
1 Patiala Infantry	15 (Patiala) Punjab Regt.
2 Patiala Infantry	16 (Patiala) Punjab Regt.
1 Travancore Infantry	9 (Travancore) Madras Regt.
2 Travancore Infantry	16 (Travancore) Madras Regt.
1 Cochin Infantry	17 (Cochin) Madras Regt.
1 Mysore Infantry	18 (Mysore) Madras Regt.
Kutch State Forces	7 Grenadiers
Baria, Idar, Lunawada, Rajpipla State Forces	8 Grenadiers
Mewar Infantry Alwar Jey Paltan Bharatpur Infantry Kotah Umed Infantry	9 (Mewar) Grenadiers
Bikanir Ganga Risala Jaisalmer Camel Corps	13 (Ganga Jaisalmer) Grenadiers
Kolhapur Infantry	19 (Kolhapur) Maratha LI
Baroda Lancers 1 Baroda Infantry 2 Baroda Infantry	20 (Baroda) Maratha LI
2 Hyderabad Infantry	22 (Hyderabad) Maratha LI
Jaipur Sawai Man Guards	17 (Sawai Man) Rajputana Rifles

CAVALRY	NOW
Bhavnagar Lancers Bhavnagar Infantry Dhrangadra Infantry Nawanagar Infantry Porbandar Infantry	18 (Saurashtra) Rajputana Rifles
Bikanir Sadul Light Infantry	19 (Bikanir) Rajput Regt.
Jodhpur Sardar infantry	20 (Jodhpur) Rajput Regt.
Chamba, Mandi, Sirmoor, Suket Infantry	16 Dogra
4 Gwalior Infantry	14 (Gwalior) Kumaon Regt.
1 Indore Infantry	15 (Indore) Kumaon Regt.
1 J & K Infantry	1 J & K Rifles
2 J & K Rifles	2 J & K Rifles
3 J & K Rifles	3 J & K Rifles
4 J & K Infantry	4 J & K Rifles
5 J & K Light Infantry	5 J & K Rifles
6 J & K Infantry	6 J & K Rifles
7 J & K Infantry	7 J & K Rifles
8 J & K Infantry	8 J & K Rifles
9 J & K Infantry	9 J & K Rifles
1 Tripura Manikya Rifles	6 Assam Rifles

TRANSPORT

Gwalior Pony Company	10 Animal Transport Coy ASC

States forces' units perpetuated in the Pakistan Army

ARTILLERY	NOW
Bahawalpur Mountain Battery	14 (Abbas) Fd Regt.
INFANTRY	
1 Bahawalpur Infantry	8 Baluch
2 Bahawalpur Infantry	9 Baluch
3 Bahawalpur Infantry	20 Baluch
4 Bahawalpur Infantry	21 Baluch

Clearly, India would not accept this state of affairs for long and 13 Sep 48 was nominated as D-Day for Operation Caterpillar, the campaign later referred to as the 100-hour War. On the 17 Sep 48 the Nizam announced the cease fire. The Indian Army's casualties were 66 killed/missing and 97 wounded. The Hyderabad Army had 490 killed and 122 wounded whilst the Razakars sustained even heavier losses.

The Indian task-force, at approximately divisional strength, included state forces from Mysore and Jodhpur. With few exceptions, the Hyderabad forces did not put up much resistance although the Razakars are reported as fighting well which probably explains their heavier casualties.

The situation in Jammu and Kashmir concerned a Hindu ruler, Sir Hari Singh, controlling a 77% Muslim population. His initial inclination had been to vacillate, having signed a Standstill Agreement with Pakistan and endeavouring to complete a similar arrangement with India.

However, Mohammed Ali Jinnah, the founder of Pakistan, was not prepared to wait any longer and he launched a propaganda campaign, urging the Muslims within the state to rise and depose their Dogra ruler. This was followed, in early September 1947, by a series of raids by armed civilians from West Pakistan. The raids were stepped up and the Maharajah's forces were unable to cope with the increased activity, orchestrated, it was felt, by the Pakistan Army. Finally, on the 24 Oct 47, the Maharajah sought support from the Indian Government which would not offer troops unless he first agreed to accede to India. The instrument of accession was signed on the 26th October and, on the 27th, the first elements of 1 Sikh were in Kashmir, preparing to defend Srinagar. Another week saw 161 Infantry Brigade in position although it was a very different brigade from the same one a year earlier. The battalions had just shed their Muslim elements to battalions allotted to Pakistan and had not yet had time to absorb the non-Muslim companies which they had received in exchange. Even 1 Sikh, the first battalion on the scene, was short of one company and an infantry company was organised hastily from a Sikh artillery unit in garrison in the Red Fort in Delhi to fill the gap. In the circumstances, some state forces were utilised and the Sawai Man Guards from Jaipur and both artillery and infantry from Patiala found themselves alongside Indian Army regular troops again.

The Muslim soldiers in the Maharajah's army were soon induced to desert to Pakistan whilst the non-Muslims were incorporated into the Indian Army, later to form the Jammu and Kashmir Rifles.

Following the accession of the states to the Union of India, there was, of course, no need for the continued existence of their armies. The Government maintained these forces, however, and after careful screening, opted to retain those which they felt came up to Indian Army standards. The transfer of the selected units took place on the 1 Apr 51 and they were permitted to retain in their titles the relevant links with their past : thus, 1 Patiala Infantry became 15 Punjab (Patiala), 4th Gwalior Infantry became 14 Kumaon (Gwalior) etc., as can be seen in Table 4.

In the case of Pakistan, it was mainly the forces of the state of Bahawalpur which were involved. After Partition, the Bahawalpur Regiment was raised, with four battalions but subsequent changes in the organisation of Pakistan's infantry in 1956 swept these into the Baluch Regiment where the state force is perpetuated in the 8th, 9th, 20th and 21st Battalions.

In 1951, there were still horsed cavalry units in the Indian States and when these were integrated into the Indian Army, they were reconstituted in 1953 to form 61 Cavalry which still functions as a horsed cavalry regiment in the Indian Army today.

7. THE REGIMENTS AND ARMS OF THE BRITISH-INDIAN ARMY

SKINNER'S HORSE (1st DUKE OF YORK'S OWN CAVALRY)

Known to the world as the 1st Bengal Lancers, the only corps in the armies of the British Empire to wear a canary-yellow coat, Skinner's Horse had its origins in the service of Scindia, the Mahratta prince. James Skinner, the son of a Scots officer in the Honourable East India Company's army and a Rajput lady became a soldier of fortune with Scindia. He was unable to secure a Company commission because he was 'country-born' and not British. When war came between the British and his master, he resolved to be faithful to Scindia but was dismissed because he was British! Lord Lake, the then British Commander-in-Chief, invited him to raise a regiment of irregular cavalry but Skinner accepted only with the provision that he should not be required to draw his sword against his late master. The choice of uniform was dictated by Rajput legend. It was recounted that a Rajput prince, riding out to fight, would often vow that if he could not win he would die. His men would accept this commitment, put saffron on their faces and put on a yellow cloak over their armour. These were called the clothes of the dead. they were known as the Yellow Men who would not return from battle unless they were victorious. James Skinner set out to command the finest cavalry regiment in the service of John Company.

Skinner found Lord Lake an appreciative commander who authorised an increase in the unit strength to 3,000 in December 1814. The next year, three corps were formed, each of ten risalas of 100 men each. Robert Skinner, James's younger brother, was to command the 2nd and a Major Fraser the 3rd. Four years later, the 3rd was disbanded. Wherever trouble arose in Company territory, one or other of the Skinners was there: Nepal, the campaign against the Pindaris, as part of the Army of the Indus, to Baluchistan, to Afghanistan for the First Afghan War. The 1st corps became the 1st Bengal Cavalry in 1861 after the Great Mutiny when the irregular cavalry were formally installed as regular regiments and, in 1896 were converted to lancers, becoming the 1st Bengal Lancers.

Three years later, a royal patron brought about a change of title to 1st (Duke of York's Own) Bengal Lancers and it was under this style that they went to China in 1900 to suppress the Boxer Rebellion. The 2nd Corps, in 1861, became the 3rd Bengal Cavalry and, in 1901, the 3rd Bengal Cavalry (Skinner's Horse). They did not wear the canary coats but wore blue instead although their lance-pennons, instead of the customary red-over-white (the national colours of Poland, the traditional home of the lancers), were blue over yellow. The 3rd sent a remount detachment to South Africa at the turn of the century but the British Government did not consider it politic to use Indian troops against the Boers.

When war came in 1914, the 1st were on the North-West Frontier and remained there throughout the war. The 3rd, however, proceeded to France with the Meerut Cavalry Brigade, remaining there until their transfer back to India in 1916 for service in Mesopotamia. However, this did not happen and they served out the rest of the war on the Frontier. Both regiments earned the 1919 honour for service against Afghanistan.

The spring of 1921 saw both regiments at Sialkot for amalgamation into the 1/3rd Skinner's Horse. The badge chosen for the amalgamated regiments was crossed lances with crown above and the White Rose of York on the intersection; below, a scroll reading 'Himmat i mardan madad i Khuda' or 'The bravery of man is by the help of God'.

The 3rd notionally assumed the canary coats worn by the 1st since the earliest days. In fact, of course, full-dress never returned for universal wear after 1914. However, in 1936, Captain C R D Gray went to Rangoon to serve as ADC to the Governor of Burma and became the last British officer to wear 'Old Sikandar's' yellow coat.

The Regiment was mechanised in 1939 as a motor cavalry regiment – equipped with ordinary 'soft-skinned' road-vehicles, affording mobility but no armoured protection. It was as the reconnaissance regiment of the 4th Indian Division that Skinner's found themselves in Italian East Africa as part of Gazelle Force in early 1941. Whilst there they were attacked by a mounted force of Italian-officered local cavalry which they beat off. The many loose horses left after the action were rounded up by jubilant sowars who rode them triumphantly. The Italian officer commanding the local cavalry, the Baron Amedeo Guillet, subsequently became the Italian ambassador to an independent India where he became the lifelong friend of any Indian cavalryman, and an honorary member of 4th Indian Division Association! This incident will probably prove to be the last action by British troops against horsed cavalry. Major C R D Gray whom we last saw in Burma was present during the attack.

Returning to Egypt in September 1941, the regiment spent a few months in Cyprus before being posted to Paiforce. In June 1944, Skinner's Horse sailed for Italy where it joined 10th Indian Division, remaining there for the rest of the campaign.

On Partition in August 1947, Skinner's Horse was allotted to India. The Mussalman squadron went to the 19th King George V's Own Lancers in exchange for their Sikh Squadron.

BATTLE HONOURS

Bhurtpore, Ghuznee 1839, Afghanistan 1839, Khelat, Candahar 1842, Maharajpore, Moodkee, Ferozeshah, Aliwal, Kandahar 1880, Afghanistan 1879–80, Punjab Frontier, Pekin 1900, France & Flanders 1914–16, NW Frontier India 1915, Baluchistan, Afghanistan 1919 Agordat, Keren, Amba Alagi, Abyssinia 1940–41, Senio Floodbank, Italy 1943–45,

BOOKS

'A Short History of the 1st Duke of York's Own Lancers (Skinner's Horse) 1803–1908' by Major H Roberts. (Indian Daily Telegraph Press, Lucknow, 1908).

'Skinner's Horse' by Christopher Rothero. (Almark Publishing Co. Ltd., Malden, Surrey 1979).

'Sworn to Die' by Lieut Col M A R Skinner. (Lancer International, New Delhi 1984).

CHANGES OF TITLE

Pre 1903	1st Duke of York's Own Bengal Lancers (Skinner's Horse)	3rd Bengal Cavalry (Skinner's Horse)
1903	1st Duke of York's Own Lancers (Skinner's Horse)	3rd Skinner's Horse

1921	1/3rd Skinner's Horse
1922	1st Duke of York's Own Skinner's Horse
1927	Skinner's Horse (1st Duke of York's Own Cavalry)

THE 2nd ROYAL LANCERS (GARDNER'S HORSE)

Two of the oldest regiments of the old Bengal Army went to form the 2nd Lancers (Gardner's Horse) in 1922. They were the 2nd Lancers (Gardner's Horse) and the 4th Cavalry.

William Linneaus Gardner, once an officer of the 74th Highlanders, left the Queen's service to pursue a more individual career with one of the Mahratta princes. However, he was threatened with execution when he refused action against Company troops so he escaped to join Lord Lake who authorised him in 1809 to raise a cavalry unit. The corps' first action was in the Nepal War of 1815.

Thereafter, they went to Burma where they qualified for the exclusive honour 'Arracan'. Shortly after their return, Colonel Gardner retired and died in July 1836, having married forty years earlier a thirteen-year-old princess of Cambay. He never once returned to Britain and his family formed a small Christian community on their estate at Khasgunj, near Agra.

As the 2nd Bengal Cavalry after the Mutiny, they served on the Frontier and this was followed by a period of calm until 1882 when the 2nd went off to Egypt to gain two honours. In 1890, newly-issued with the lance, they became the 2nd Bengal Lancers and, in 1903, when previous presidential loyalties were erased from regimental titles, old William Linneaus Gardner was again remembered and their title became 2nd Lancers (Gardner's Horse).

The 4th Cavalry was raised in 1838, under Captain C. Newbury, initially for service with the King of Oudh but two years later, it was taken back into the Company's army, becoming the 6th Regiment of Bengal Irregular Cavalry. They saw service in Sind, not a popular posting at the time and, as a result of this, were granted an honorary standard bearing the device of a lion passant regardant. During their stay in Sind, Prince Waldemar of Prussia was attached to the regiment as he was keen to gain some experience of frontier warfare.

Following this atachment, the King of Prussia asked that all the officers might, in the future, wear the helmet similar to that worn by the Prussian Garde du Corps, a spendid head-dress in polished black leather surmounted by a gilt eagle and, for many years, this continued to be worn. After the Great Mutiny in 1857, the 3rd and 5th Bengal Irregular Cavalry were disbanded and the 6th moved up to become the 4th Bengal Cavalry, and, in 1873 the lion passant regardant from the standard awarded twenty-five years earlier was sanctioned for wear on regimental accoutrements.

Service on the Frontier followed but the 4th's first battle-honour was gained in the Second Afghan War. The lance was issued in 1900, bringing a change of style to 4th Bengal Lancers but this was short-lived and, in 1903, they became simply the 4th Lancers. However, that title too was soon changed and, the following year, they became the 4th Cavalry.

When 1914 came, the 2nd were mobilised in October and sailed for France where they stayed for three years, to gain an enviable reputation.

The 4th, however, had left India in August 1914 as the divisional cavalry of the 7th Meerut Division. At Festubert, they served alongside the 2nd Black Watch, fighting hand-to-hand in the trenches with their lances. In the winter of 1915, they transferred to Mesopotamia and then in late 1917, back to India.

After Cambrai in 1917, the 2nd left France for Egypt and Palestine where, with Allenby's force, they drove the Turks North in the greatest cavalry drive in history. They remained behind after the armistice to pacify Palestine and Syria, only returning to India in 1920.

In April 1922, they merged with the 4th Cavalry at Bombay. Sadly, the 2nd would appear to have swallowed the 4th. Certainly the 4th's title vanished totally after the Regiment's brief life as the 2/4th Cavalry but their lion passant regardant survived. The new badge was crossed lances, a crown on the intersection and the lion above it: below the crown, a figure '2' and, across the lance-butts, a scroll reading 'Scinde'.

In 1935, in the Silver Jubilee honours, the 2nd Lancers became the 2nd Royal Lancers (Gardner's Horse). Their badge changed and the 4th's lion now appeared within the Garter, surmounted by a crown and backed by four crossed lances.

The outbreak of war in September 1939 found the Indian cavalry slowly mechanising and Gardner's Horse was at Sialkot where they became part of the 3rd Indian Motor Brigade with the 11th PAVO Cavalry (Frontier Force) and the 18th King Edward VII's Own Cavalry – all equipped with soft-skinned road vehicles – bound for Egypt in January 1941. In April, they fought a defensive battle at El Mechili where they were forced to surrender only to Rommel's personal demand. Reconstituted in Ferozepore in September, they returned to the Brigade and spent some time in Syria before being returned to Egypt in early 1942, now equipped with tracked carriers. Overrun by three Axis armoured divisions at Point 171 in the Gazala actions in May, the survivors of Gardner's Horse were withdrawn to Haifa, being again reconstituted before being transferred to Paiforce. Returning to India in January 1943, they were to be converted to an armoured car regiment. In October, at Quetta, Lieut. Colonel M. Rajindrasinhji (later General and Chief of Army Staff) took over, the first Indian officer to be given command of an armoured regiment. They spent the remainder of the war on the Frontier but were ordered to Malaya in May 1946, finally sailing in January 1947.

On Partition in August 1947, the regiment was allotted to India. The Hindustani Mussalman squadron sailed direct to Karachi from Malaya and was subsequently replaced by a squadron of Rajputs transferred as surplus from the 18th King Edward VII's Own Cavalry.

BATTLE HONOURS

Arracan, Sobraon, Punjaub, Mooltan 1857–58, Afghanistan 1879–80, Tel-el-Kebir, Egypt 1882, La Bassee 1914, Givenchy 1914, Neuve Chapelle, Festubert 1915, Somme 1916, Morval, Cambrai 1917, France & Flanders 1914–18, Egypt 1915, Megiddo, Sharon, Damascus, Palestine 1918, Tigris 1916, Mesopotamia 1915–16, Afghanistan 1919, El Mechili, Point 171

BOOKS

'A brief history of the 2nd Lancers (Gardner's Horse) 1800–1909' – Anon. (Pub: Pioneer Press, Allahabad 1909)

'A history of the 2nd Lancers (Gardner's Horse) from 1809 to 1922' by Capt. D E Whitworth MC. (Pub: Sifton Praed & Co. Ltd. London 1924)

'A history of the 2nd Royal Lancers (Gardner's Horse)' by Brigadier E W D Vaughan CB DSO MC. (Pub: Sifton Praed & Co. Ltd., London 1951)

'A Squire of Hindoostan' (the life of William Linneaus Gardner) by Narindar Saroop CBE (Pub: Nottingham Court Press, London, 1987)

CHANGES OF TITLE

Pre 1903	2nd Bengal Lancers	4th Bengal Lancers
1903	2nd Lancers (Gardner's Horse)	4th Lancers
1904	2nd Lancers (Gardner's Horse)	4th Cavalry

1921	2/4th Cavalry
1922	2nd Lancers (Gardner's Horse)
1935	2nd Royal Lancers (Gardner's Horse)

3rd CAVALRY

The 3rd Cavalry, Skinner's Horse and the 2nd Royal Lancers (Gardner's Horse) were the only three regiments which could trace their beginnings back to the old Bengal Cavalry of the Company's Army. The two regiments which went to form the 3rd in the merger in 1921 were the 5th and 8th Cavalry.

The 5th were raised at Bareilly in 1841 as the 7th Bengal Irregular Cavalry in consequence of the First Afghan War. Their first battle-honours were 'Mooltan' in the Sikh Wars, gained in an infantry role and 'Punjaub' as a theatre-honour. On the outbreak of the Great Mutiny, the 7th were in Peshawar and helped in disarming dissident infantry battalions but that service did not give them Mutiny honours. The 1861 reorganisation saw them become the 5th Bengal Cavalry following the disbandment of the 3rd and 5th, both senior. After service in the Second Afghan War, the regiment was quartered at Landi Kotal and the Risaldar-Major, Mohammed Aslam Khan, was detailed to raise a body of local irregulars for protection of the Khyber. They later became known as the Khyber Rifles and Mohd Aslam Khan became their commandant in 1897.

The Great War found the 5th engaged in internal security duties within India, only moving to Mesopotamia in October 1918 for occupation duty.

The 8th Cavalry originated in the 18th Bengal Irregular Cavalry, the last regiment to be raised before the Great Mutiny, in 1846. They moved to Mian Mir, near Lahore, where they were responsible for constructing their own lines on the site of the present cantonment.

Like their partners, the 7th, they served in Peshawar, disarming mutinous Sepoys in 1857. In 1861, in the course of the reorganisation, ten regiments of irregular cavalry, all senior, were disbanded which promoted the 18th to become the 8th Bengal Cavalry.

They served in the Second Afghan War and remained to garrison Kabul before moving back to Quetta. Lances were issued in 1890 wereupon they became the 8th Bengal Lancers, changing to the 8th Lancers in 1903 and the 8th Cavalry in 1906.

It fell to the lot of the 8th to spend the whole of the Great War on internal security duty in India, only leaving for Palestine in 1920.

The 8th had left Secunderabad for Palestine and it was to Secunderabad that they returned the next year for amalgamation with the 5th to form what became the 3rd Cavalry. The badge selected was a simple Roman 'III' beneath a crown, above a scroll reading 'Cavalry'. Sadly, the shortage of battle-honours and the lack of a colourful personage in their history would appear to have led to a lack of heraldic inspiration.

In 1932, they were nominated to become one of the second block of regiments for Indianisation. The 1938 Mechanisation Plan had provided for the conversion of the 3rd Cavalry to begin in May 1940 but the regiment was not content to wait and went ahead on its own account. Four lorry chassis were purchased from regimental funds and some NCOs were attached to local garages in Jubbulpore to train as mechanics. The 8th Indian Division was to have the 3rd Cavalry as its reconnaissance regiment and the regiment moved to Meerut. Training was desert-oriented and the vehicles provided were of the soft-skinned variety. Mobilisation orders came in July 1941 but, in March of that year, three officers, a risaldar-major and 200 men were posted out as a cadre for the raising of the 42nd Cavalry. This 'milking' was to have serious consequences before the year was out. Non-desert paint was ordered for the vehicles and it dawned that they were eastward-bound, totally unprepared for service in Malaya, whither they arrived in Penang on the 28 Nov 41, a week before the Japanese invasion. Singapore ordnance depot issued thirty Marmon-Harington armoured cars on the 8th December, the Japanese having landed on the east coast the previous night. Withdrawal down the Malay Peninsula followed and the entire force was captured on Singapore Island in February, 1942.

The Willcox Committee, in 1945, in recommending that the Indian Army's armoured regiments should be cut by three in the post-war army, suggested that the 3rd Cavalry 'be not reformed', doubtless feeling that the regiment, in fact, had already effectively ceased to exist. However, the survivors returned to India and, on 1 Apr 46, they began to re-form as an airborne reconnaissance regiment under its first Indian commanding officer, with a mixed-class recruitment helped by volunteers from other regiments of the Indian Armoured Corps.

On Partition in August 1947, the 3rd Cavalry was allotted to India. A Sikh squadron which the 18th King Edward VII's Own Cavalry had taken from the 11th PAVO Cavalry (Frontier Force) on the latter regiment's posting to Pakistan was posted in after a few months when strength-balances were established.

BATTLE HONOURS

Mooltan, Punjaub, Afghanistan 1878–80, Mesopotamia 1917–18, North Malaya, Central Malaya, Malaya 1941–42.

BOOKS

'Nobody's Own – the history of the 3rd Cavalry and it predecessors 1841–1945' by Brigadier H W Picken. (Pub: privately, Eastbourne 1962).

CHANGES OF TITLE

Pre-1903	5th Bengal Cavalry	8th Bengal Lancers
1903	5th Cavalry	8th Lancers
1906	5th Cavalry	8th Cavalry

1921	5/8th Cavalry
1922	3rd Cavalry

HODSON'S HORSE (4th DUKE OF CAMBRIDGE'S OWN LANCERS)

The two regiments which went to form the 4th Duke of Cambridge's Own Hodson's Horse in 1922 were the 9th Hodson's Horse and the 10th Duke of Cambridge's Own Lancers (Hodson's Horse) although they had been known popularly for years as the 1st and 2nd Hodson's Horse.

William Stephen Raikes Hodson, a student of Rugby School, graduate of Cambridge University, officer in the Bengal Fusiliers and son of a Christian Divine was not a man who shirked his duty.

The first cavalry regiment to be raised from the Punjab during the Great Mutiny was formed from risalahs raised and brought in to Delhi by prominent Sirdars. Sikhs, Muslims and Afghans streamed in, not, it must be confessed, all fired with sympathy for the British cause. Rumours about the rich pickings to be had when Delhi fell were not entirely without substance. Hodson, then on staff duty with the Delhi Field Force was given the task of forming a regiment and, by the time that Delhi had fallen, he had enough men to form three. One of his exploits was the capture of the King of Delhi, bent on escape, and the summary execution of the princes of the royal house.

After Delhi, the force moved to the relief of Lucknow where Hodson met his death. He is buried near where he fell, in the grounds of La Martiniere College.

By 1858, the force had become too large for a single unit and it was split into three but the third was disbanded in 1860, most of the men going to Fane's Horse, then being raised for service in China. The first and second became, in 1861, the 9th and 10th Bengal Cavalry.

The 10th found themselves in Abyssinia in 1871, an expedition consisting mainly of Bombay units with a brigade from Bengal. During the period of the Second Afghan War in 1887–80, both 9th and 10th were out of India. The 9th with a squadron of the 10th was sent to Malta, to join a force ready to act if Russia should extend warlike activities into Asia – she was then at war with Turkey. The balance of what had become, in 1871, the 10th Bengal Lancers, went to Afghanistan. During their stay in Malta, the 10th had been inspected by HRH The Duke of Cambridge who took a proprietorial interest and bestowed his name upon them: they became the 10th Bengal (Duke of Cambridge's Own) Lancers in 1878.

In 1885, the 9th was the only Indian cavalry regiment to join the expedition to the Sudan when they were equipped with the lance, becoming the 9th Bengal Lancers in the following year. The 9th also saw service in Chitral in 1895–97 although, in line with normal mountain warfare practice, it was not as a single unit but in small detachments.

In 1901, their founder's name was restored to both regiments: they became the 9th Bengal Lancers (Hodson's Horse) and the 10th Duke of Cambridge's Own Bengal Lancers (Hodson's Horse), changing in 1903 to the title which both bore when they came to the amalgamation in 1921.

On the outbreak of war in August 1914, the 9th was at Ambala and was promptly mobilised for service in France wih the Ambala Cavalry Brigade. They were destined to remain in Europe until February 1918 when they sailed for what was then called the Near East to join Allenby's great cavalry campaign in Palestine. During their service in France, their medical officer, Captain Som Dutt MC, Indian Medical Service, was presented with the wearer's own Iron Cross by a badly-wounded German colonel whose injuries the MO was treating under heavy German fire.

The 9th had the record for overseas service in the Great War and after. They sailed for France in October 1914 and returned to Ambala on 1 Jan 21.

The 10th were not to serve in France but went to Mesopotamia where they took part in the capture of Baghdad. The two regiments came together at Multan on the 3 Sept 21 as the 9/10th Hodson's Horse. The badge chosen was crossed lances with a crown above the intersection and a scroll across the lance-butts reading 'Hodson Horse'. Although the merger of the '1st and 2nd Hodson's Horse' was not an unhappy one, it meant, as it did for most of the other merged pair of cavalry regiments, a surplus of both officers and men. They mustered out 31 Indian officers and 963 other ranks. British officers numbered some forty to fifty on strength and this figure had to be cut to half within the next year.

Mechanisation to Hodson's Horse meant light tanks but they went to Iraq in October 1941 with carriers and some South African armoured cars. Thereafter, they moved around the Paiforce area, converting to tanks once more the next year. In October 1943, they moved to Egypt, were re-equipped with American Sherman tanks, in high expectation of service in Italy. Hopes faded, however, and the Regiment moved back to Syria until the end of 1945 when they returned to India with four years overseas service and not a battle-honour to show for them.

In August 1947, Partition allotted Hodson's Horse to India. The Guides Cavalry, bound, logically for Pakistan, handed over its Dogra squadron in exchange for Hodson's Punjabi Mussalmans. This left Hodson's with two Dogra squadrons so they passed on the Guides' Dogras to the Scinde Horse in exchange for the Sikh Squadron which the Scinde Horse had received from Probyn's Horse.

BATTLE HONOURS

Delhi 1857, Lucknow, Abyssinia, Afghanistan 1878–80, Suakin 1885, Chitral, Punjab Frontier, Givenchy 1914, Somme 1916, Bazentin, Flers-Courcelettes, Cambrai 1917, France & Flanders 1914–18, Megiddo, Sharon, Damascus, Palestine 1918, Khan Baghdadi, Mesopotamia 1916–18.

BOOKS

'Hodson's Horse' by Major F G Cardew OBE. (Pub: Blackwood, Edinburgh 1928)

'A short history of Hodson's Horse 1857–1940' by Lieut Cdr the Hon Charles Willoughby RN. (Pub: Gale and Polden Ltd., Aldershot)

CHANGES OF TITLE

Pre-1903	9th Bengal Lancers (Hodson's Horse)	10th Duke of Cambridge's Own Bengal Lancers (Hodson's Horse)
1903	9th Hodson's Horse	10th Duke of Cambridge's Own Lancers (Hodson's Horse)

1921	9/10 Hodson's Horse
1922	4th Duke of Cambridge's Own Hodson's Horse
1927	Hodson's Horse (4th Duke of Cambridge's Own Lancers)

PROBYN'S HORSE (5th KING EDWARD VII'S OWN LANCERS)

It is, perhaps, appropriate that the senior cavalry regiment to go to Pakistan in August 1947 had its origins in two regiments raised in Lahore (now in Pakistan) in 1857 by order of Sir John Lawrence, the Chief Commissioner of the Punjab. The 1st and 2nd Sikh Irregular Cavalry came into being with no difficulty: there were plenty of ex–soldiers of the Khalsa's war against the British and the 1st, under Captain Wale of the 18th Bengal Irregular Cavalry were despatched to what became the United Provinces, the then seat of operations against the mutineers. Sadly, Wale was shot by a sniper on the 1 Mar 1858, being replaced by Major Dighton Probyn who had been awarded the Victoria Cross the previous year. The Regiment was to bear his name unofficially until formally granted in 1904.

The 2nd Sikh Irregular Cavalry, raised by Captain Hockin of the 17th Bengal Irregular Cavalry, reached Delhi too late to join in its relief but were employed in Oudh where some sixty sowars charged a formed body of 1,200 mutineers and drove them from the field.

In 1859, the Chinese Imperial Government had seized a Hong Kong ship and an expedition was sent from India to put things right. A cavalry brigade was included. The British regiment was the 1st King's Dragoon Guards whilst the 1st Sikh Irregular Cavalry and Fane's Horse were the two Indian units. Fane's had been raised especially for the task, employing many of the men from the newly–disbanded third regiment of Hodson's Horse. The campaign was good for its cavalrymen and the 1st newly–armed with the lance, won a good reputation.

Returning to India, they found that they had become the 11th Bengal Cavalry whilst the 2nd became the 12th. Neither regiment had been exclusively Sikh but had admitted men of other Punjab martial classes.

The 12th found themselves in 1867 in Abyssinia whence an expedition had been sent against King Theodore III, in an attempt to teach him to respect foreigners. It was not cavalry work but involved road patrols and protection. In 1876, the 11th had been honoured by becoming the 11th Prince of Wales's Own Bengal Lancers.

Both 11th and 12th Bengal Cavalry saw service in the Second Afghan War but, after that, the 12th did not see further active service for forty years.

The 11th, however, took part in the Black Mountains Expedition, went to Chitral and formed part of the Malakand Field Force.

Neither regiment was to see service in France in the Great War but both went to the Middle East.

Major General the Right Honourable Sir Dighton Probyn VC who gave up his command of the 11th in 1866, was appointed their honorary colonel in 1904 when his name was officially restored to their title. He retained this post until his death in 1924 at the age of 92.

The first title of the combined regiment in 1921 was the 11/12th Probyn's Horse, promptly changed the next year to incorporate the 11th's royal style when they became the 5th King Edward's Own Probyn's Horse. The new badge was crossed lances with the Prince of Wales's plumes on the intersection and a scroll across the lance–butts reading 'Probyn's Horse'.

In Risalpur in 1940, the Regiment was mechanised as part of 1 Indian Armoured Brigade, whereupon it moved to Quetta. By mid-1942 it was equipped with one squadron of Stuart tanks and two of Lee tanks. Two years later, now fitted out with Shermans, the move was made to Imphal as part of 255 Indian Tank Brigade. Their part in the reconquest of Burma was significant and they finished the campaign in Rangoon. May 1946 found them back in Secunderabad as part of 1 Indian Armoured Division.

Partition in August 1947 saw Probyn's Horse allotted to Pakistan. Their Dogra squadron was exchanged for the Punjabi Mussalman squadron of the Royal Deccan Horse. The Sikh Squadron went to the Scinde Horse whilst Probyn's received a Kaimkhani squadron from the 18th King Edward VII's Own Cavalry.

BATTLE HONOURS

Lucknow, Taku Forts, Pekin 1860, Abyssinia, Ali Masjid, Peiwar Kotal,

Charasiah, Kabul 1879, Afghanistan 1878–80, Chitral, Malakand, Punjab Frontier, Mesopotamia 1915–18, Meiktila, Capture of Meiktila, Defence of Meiktila, Taungtha, Rangoon Road, Pyawbwe, Pyinmana, Toungoo, Pegu 1945, Burma 1942–45.

BOOKS
'A history of the XI King Edward's Own Lancers (Probyn's Horse) by Capt E L Maxwell. (Pub: A.C. Curtis Ltd. Guildford 1914)
'A history of Probyn's Horse (5th King Edward's Own Lancers)' by Major C A Boyle DSO. (Pub: Gale & Polden Ltd. Aldershot 1929)

CHANGES OF TITLE

pre-1903	11th Prince of Wales's Own Bengal Lancers	12th Bengal Cavalry
1903	11th Prince of Wales's Own Lancers	12th Cavalry
1904	11th Prince of Wales's Own Lancers (Probyn's Horse)	12th Cavalry
1906	11th King Edward's Own Lancers (Probyn's Horse)	12th Cavalry

1921	11/12th Probyn's Horse
1922	5th King Edward's Own Probyn's Horse
1927	Probyn's Horse (5th King Edward's Own Lancers)
1937	Probyn's Horse (5th King Edward VII's Own Lancers)

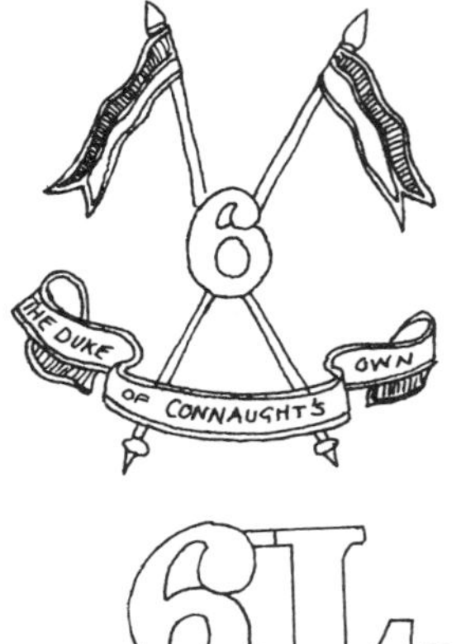

6TH DUKE OF CONNAUGHT'S OWN LANCERS (WATSON'S HORSE)

The two regiments which went to form the 6th Duke of Connaught's Own Lancers (Watson's Horse) were the 13th Duke of Connaught's Lancers (Watson's Horse) and the 16th Cavalry.

The 13th was raised as the 4th Sikh Irregular Cavalry in 1858 but Lieutenant

John Watson VC who had been appointed to its Command did not join until1860. He had been serving with the 1st Punjab Cavalry and recovering from sickness. His command lasted for eleven years but his name was in common use until confirmed officially in 1904. Discounting his Victoria Cross, Watson was, perhaps, best known for his introduction of a change in cavalry riding–practice. It had formerly been customary for the rider to sit in the saddle and bump with – and on – the horse, to the obvious discomfort of both rider and mount. Watson's preference was, on non-ceremonial occasions, for the rider to rise in the stirrups at the trot. This change, however, was not officially introduced until 1875, by which time Watson was commanding the Central India Horse.

The 1861 changes saw the 4th Sikh Irregular Cavalry become the 13th Bengal Cavalry and, in 1864, the 13th Bengal Lancers. Their first battle-honour was awarded for service in the Second Afghan War and, shortly afterwards, they were off to Egypt to earn two more honours and harass Arabi Pasha into surrender. Their performance so impressed the Duke of Connaught that he asked his royal mother if he might become the Colonel of the 13th. Queen Victoria, ever the champion of her Indian soldiers, confirmed the appointment and the Duke's name was added to the regimental title in 1884.

The tribal rising on the North West Frontier in 1897 gave more opportunities for mounted action and was rewarded by the grant of that hard-won honour 'Punjab Frontier'.

In the 1903 changes, the 13th became the 13th Duke of Connaught's Own Lancers and, in 1906, 'Watson's Horse' was added as a subsidiary title.

The Great War did not provide the opportunity for the 13th to distinguish themselves in Europe; their destiny was to remain on the Frontier until July 1916 when they reached Mesopotamia for the relief of Kut-al-Amara.

The 16th originated as the Rohilkand Horse. Notices were posted by the Commissioner of Rohilkand, thus –

> *Whoever is willing to take service in a cavalry regiment under the Sirkar, let him come with his horse to the Pass of Haldwani on the 1st September*

This was, of course, in the year 1857, the year of the Devil's Wind, when traditional loyalties were being challenged and when the men of the north were establishing their ascendancy in the Bengal Army. There was no shortage of volunteers and, on formation, the regiment received a European serjeant from the 4th Hussars who contrived for himself a permanent posting and rose to the rank of risaldar, normally an Indian officer's rank.

The first two years were spent in subjugating Rohilkand and in 1864, being then the 16th Bengal Cavalry, they went off to join the Bhutan Field Force where they suffered not only from the climate but also from the terrain. Disbandment followed in 1882 when three regiments were broken up to provide an additional, fourth squadron for the other regiments. The other two which suffered were the 3rd Scinde Horse from the Bombay Cavalry and the 4th Punjab Irregular Cavalry. However, they were not to remain dormant for long; fears of Russian invasion grew and a strength increase of three cavalry regiments was approved. The 16th was re-raised in 1885 at Ambala. In 1900, as the 16th Bengal Lancers, they went to China to relieve the international legations in Peking which were being besieged by the Boxers. On relieving the American Legation, the 16th were presented with the US flag which had flown over the building and, for many years, the flag hung in the Officers' Mess.

In early 1915, the 16th Cavalry, as they then were, joined Indian Expeditionary Force 'D' as the Mesopotamia Force was styled and served under Townshend. Curiously, before setting out to defend Kut-al-Amara, Townshend sent most of his cavalry away and the Regiment returned to India, much under strength, in October 1916.

Both 13th and 16th were together in Waziristan in 1919, earning a joint honour for Afghanistan service.

Amalgamation took place formally in 1921 as the 13/16th Cavalry but renaming took place the next year when they became the 6th Duke of Connaught's Own Lancers. The new badge was to be crossed lances with a figure '6' on the intersection and a generous scroll across the lance-butts, reading 'The Duke of Connaught's Own'.

Although cavalry was not ideally suited for work in the mountains, there was plenty of the North West Frontier Province in which they could operate very successfully. The 6th, serving in 1 Cavalry Brigade with the Guides Cavalry received commendation for their part in the action of the Khajuri Plain when the Afridi made to advance upon Peshawar in support of the Civil Disobedience movement then fashionable in India.

The outbreak of the Second World War in September 1939 found the Regiment contemplating mechanisation after which they were intended to join 10 Indian Division as its divisional reconnaissance regiment but the Iraq crises in April 1942 changed that. Equipped with South African Morris armoured cars, the 6th DCO Lancers reached Iraq towards the end of the year to join the 8 Indian Division in Tenth Army. In September 1942, they were transferred to 6 Indian Division in Persia to meet a possible German threat through the Caucasus. The following year they were returned to 8 Indian Division for operations in Italy, equipped with tracked carriers. Landing in Italy in October 1943, they fought their way north, all set to race to Venice when they were stopped. The Italian campaign ended on the 2 May 45 and the Regiment returned to India in June.

In August 1947, Partition saw the 6th Duke of Connaught's Own Lancers allotted to Pakistan. Their Jat squadron went to the 7th Light Cavalry in exchange for their Punjabi Mussalman squadron whilst their Sikh Squadron went to the 8th King George V's Own Light Cavalry in change for the 8th's PM squadron.

BATTLE HONOURS

Afghanistan 1878–80, Tel-el-Kebir, Egypt 1882, Punjab Frontier, China 1900, Shaiba, Kut-al-Amara 1915–17, Ctesiphon, Tigris 1916, Baghdad, Sharqat, Mesopotamia 1915–18, North West Frontier, India 1915, Afghanistan 1919, The Trigno, Tufillo, The Sangro, The Moro, Cassino II, Pignataro, Liri Valley, The Senio, Santerno Crossing, Italy 1943–45.

BOOKS

'The 6th Duke of Connaught's Own Lancers in Italy' by Major F. Brock. (Pub: privately 1948)

CHANGES IN TITLE

Pre-1903	13th Duke of Connaught's Own Bengal Lancers	16th Bengal Lancers
1903	13th Duke of Connaught's Own Lancers	16th Lancers

1906 13th Duke of Connaught's Own Lancers (Watson's Horse) — 16th Cavalry
  1921 13/16th Cavalry
  1922 6th Duke of Connaught's Own Lancers

7th LIGHT CAVALRY

One of the oldest Indian cavalry regiments in the service of British India, they began life in the service of the Nawab of Arcot. First styled the 2nd Madras Native Cavalry, they were formed from three regiments later disbanded for mutiny. Subsequently, their number changed, first to the 1st and then to the 3rd, changes made on account of the seniority of their commanding offiers.

It was as the 3rd that they served from 1788 to 1903, first against the French for supremacy in India, and then in the Mysore and Mahratta Wars. During the Great Mutiny, they served in columns operating in the Deccan, but not near enough to the main seat of operations to qualify for Mutiny honours.

In 1903, when a unified army was created in India, the 3rd Madras Cavalry became the 28th Light Cavalry, the title which they bore in 1922.

It was as the 28th Light Cavalry that they gained their most unusual distinction – that of having fought against the Russians, probably the only cavalry in the armies of the British Empire to have so done.

On the outbreak of war in 1914, the 28th were in Quetta and when, in June 1915, mobilisation orders came, they were not for France or Mesopotamia as might have been expected but to East Persia to form a cordon with the Russians to keep unfriendly persons out of Afghanistan.

When the Revolution broke, the Russians quit Persia, leaving a 350 mile gap which the 28th moved to close. With the Russians out of the war, German agents were free to make their way via the Central Asian Railway to the Afghan border and there was a real risk that Turkish troops might also use the same route to encourage the Afghans to march on India at a time when her forces were engaged elsewhere. Accordingly, troops were sent into Russia to deny them this access and the 28th Light Cavalry moved with them to reinforce those engaged against the Bolshevik forces. It was in the advance to Merv that they fought several actions, earning that unusual battle-honour. The end of operations in Russia brought them back in time for an Afghan honour before returning to Lucknow and the post-war reforms.

The 28th were not required to amalgamate but their number changed to the 7th Light Cavalry and, in 1923, the 7th together with the 16th Light Cavalry, another ex-Madras cavalry regiment, were nominated to become Indianising units

The badge chosen was crossed lances with a '7' on the intersection and a crown above. In 1930, the design changed to the pattern at the head of this entry.

Mechanisation was completed at the end of 1940 at Bolaram when they became a motor regiment. As a Stuart-equipped tank regiment, they served in Burma in support of both 19th and 20th Indian Divisions, being withdrawn in May 1945 for conversion in Ahmadnagar to Sherman tanks. This programme was interrupted by orders detailing them for service in Japan with the British Commonwealth Occupation Force whence it proceeded in April 1946.

When Partition came in August 1947, the 7th Light Cavalry was allotted to India. A Jat Squadron from the 6th DCO Lancers bound for Pakistan was taken on strength against the exchange of the 7th's Punjabi Mussalman squadron.

BATTLE HONOURS

Mysore, Seringapatam, Maheidpoor, Merv, Persia 1915–19, Afghanistan 1919, Imphal, Kyaukmyaung, Mandalay, Meiktila, Rangoon Road, Burma 1942–45.

BOOKS

'The 28th Light Cavalry in Persia and Russian Turkistan 1915–20' by Major J C A Kreyer and Capt G Uloth. (Slatter & Rose Ltd., Oxford 1926)

CHANGES OF TITLE

Pre-1903	3rd Madras Lancers
1903	28th Light Cavalry
1921	28th Light Cavalry
1922	7th Light Cavalry

8th KING GEORGE V's OWN LIGHT CAVALRY

The two regiments which went to form the 8th KGO Light Cavalry in 1922 were the 26th King George's Own Light Cavalry and the 30th Lancers (Gordon's Horse).

The 26th dated back to 1787 when they were raised at Arcot by Captain Henry Darley as the 5th Madras Native Cavalry at a time when the Madras Presidency was engaged in a war with neighbouring Mysore. The following year, in a re-numbering of the Madras cavalry, the 5th became the 1st and, in 1790, the now 1st Madras Native Cavalry joined in the operations to defeat Tippu whose father, Hyder Ali, had earlier seized the throne of Mysore. Once he had been pushed back into his fortress of Seringaptam, the force withdrew; it had been a hard campaign, particularly so for the horses.

Subsequently, Tippu became engaged in negotiations with the French, a relationship not to the taste of the Honourable East India Company and hostilities were resumed. Seringapatam was stormed on the 4 May 1799, Tippu killed and peace restored – or, nearly so – and the 1st Madras were kept fully occupied in suppressing the late Tippu's adherents.

In 1826, they went to the First Burma War and, almost sixty years later, to the Third. In between, they had seen service in Afghanistan but not in a serious combatant role.

The 1903 changes saw twenty-five added to the numbers of the Madras cavalry regiments: thus, the 1st Madras Lancers became the 26th Light Cavalry. It was a curiosity of the Madras service that infantry ranks had, until then, been used by the cavalry but, in 1903, subadars became risaldars, havildars became daffadars and all the other ranks were similarly changed, sepoys of course, becoming sowars.

The Prince of Wales was appointed their Colonel-in-Chief in 1906 and so, in 1910, on his accession to the throne, the title changed once more, to become the 26th King George's Own Light Cavalry. In 1911, they marched to Bombay to furnish the escort for the King who landed there before proceeding to Delhi for the Durbar.

When war broke out in August 1914, the 26th were in Bangalore and, the next year, a wing of the Regiment was despatched to Aden. A special service squadron also went to South Persia in June 1918 for a year, ensuring an honour for Afghanistan 1919.

The 30th Lancers were raised in 1826 by Captain Sir John Gordon as the 4th Regiment of Nizam's Cavalry. There was no lack of work for efficient light cavalry in Hyderabad and its environs and the Governor of Madras had cause more than once to congratulate them. In 1854, they became the 4th Cavalry Hyderabad Contingent, and gained a Mutiny honour for service in Central India.

Their first overseas service was to Burma in 1887 where, in common with most units, they suffered more from disease than from the enemy. In 1890, newly-equipped with the lance, they became the 4th Lancers Hyderabad Contingent and, finally, in 1903, the link with Hyderabad was broken. The Contingent became part of the Indian Army: the artillery was disbanded, the infantry went to Madras Command and the cavalry to Bombay Command. The new title for the 4th was to be the 30th Lancers (Gordon's Horse).

When war broke out in 1914, the Ambala Cavalry Brigade, including the 30th Lancers, mobilised at Ambala on 31 Aug and sailed for France on the 17 Oct. The break-up of the Indian Cavalry Corps in France sent them back, not to Mesopotamia as expected but to Peshawar and the Frontier. However, they left India for Iraq, returning once more to Peshawar for amalgamation with the 26th on the 1 Jun 22.

The title allotted in 1921 to the planned merger was the 26/30th King George's Own Light Cavalry but the union was not effected until 1922 by which time, yet another title had been agreed – the 8th King George's Own Light Cavalry. The badge was crossed lances with the figure '8' on the intersection, a crown above and the letters 'KGO' below.

The outbreak of war in September 1939 found the 8th engaged in Waziristan operations, still horsed, but mechanisation began in October 1940, one of the last regiments to convert. The following year, they became a frontier armoured regiment and, in December 1943, were equipped with Daimler and Humber armoured cars from the 42nd Cavalry, then disbanding. Then came a sudden move to the Bay of Bengal coast, near Vizagapatam, on coast-watching patrols against an expected Japanese invasion. finally, in early 1945, the Regiment was detailed to join 19 Indian Division in Burma as its reconnaissance regiment.

On Partition in August 1947, 8th King George V's Own Light Cavalry was allotted to India. They accepted a Sikh squadron from the 6th DCO Lancers in exchange for their Mussalman squadron.

BATTLE HONOURS

Mysore, Seringapatam, Ava, Central India, Afghanistan 1879–80, Burma 1885–87, Givenchy 1914, France & Flanders 1914–18, Aden, Afghanistan 1919, Sittang 1945, Burma 1942–45.

BOOKS

'History of the 30th Lancers (Gordon's Horse)' by Major E A W Stotherd. (Gale & Polden Ltd., Aldershot 1911)

'History of 8th King George V's Own Light Cavalry' by H G Rawlinson CIE (Gale & Polden Ltd., Aldershot 1948)

CHANGES OF TITLE

Pre-1903	1st Madras Lancers	4th Lancers Hyderabad Contingent
1903	26th Light Cavalry	30th Lancers (Gordon's Horse)

1906	26th Prince of Wales's Own Light Cavalry	30th Lancers (Gordon's Horse)
1910	26th King George's Own Light Cavalry	30th Lancers (Gordon's Horse)

1921	26/30th King George's Own Light Cavalry
1922	8th King George's Own Light Cavalry
1937	8th King George V's Own Light Cavalry

THE ROYAL DECCAN HORSE (9th HORSE)

The two regiments which went to form the 9th Royal Deccan Horse in 1922 were two old Hyderabad-raised regiments, the 20th Royal Deccan Horse and the 29th Lancers (Deccan Horse).

The Nizam of Hyderabad had been persuaded to have his army officered by Britons and this decision had not been unpopular with the army – all soldiers enjoy receiving their pay regularly and this had not, unfailingly, been the case before then.

It was in 1816 that Captain Evans Davies arrived in the state and four cavalry regiments were created which became the 1st, 2nd, 3rd and 5th Regiments Nizam's Cavalry. The 4th was to be raised in 1826.

Their being based permanently on the four cavalry stations within the state – Bolarum, Aurangabad, Hingoli and Mominabad – on a rotational basis, did not mean that they were less efficient than others. The Pindaris presented an ongoing threat to peace and good order.

In 1854, the cavalry force was reduced to four regiments and had already won the approval of Lord Gough, then Commander-in-Chief, India who, in 1853, before a House of Commons Committee had called the Nizam's Cavalry 'the finest irregular cavalry in the world'. Their new designation was to be the 1st to 4th Cavalry, Hyberabad Contingent.

The Great Mutiny saw the Contingent on service in Central India. In 1880, they were equipped with the lance but the designation was not changed until 1890 when they became the 1st to 4th Lancers, Hyderabad Contingent.

Until 1903, the four regiments of the Contingent had each had only three squadrons. In that year, they were to become part of the Indian Army and the 3rd Prince of Wales's Own Hyderabad Lancers were broken up to provide an additional squadron for each of the three remaining regiments. The new titles were to be the 20th Deccan Horse (1st) the 29th Lancers (Deccan Horse) (2nd) and the 30th Lancers (Gordon's Horse) (4th). All mention of Hyderabad ceased.

Both the 20th and the 29th served in France in the Great War and then, when the Indian Cavalry Corps moved to Palestine, both regiments served in the Jordan Valley and in Allenby's final victorious campaign.

In 1921, in recognition of the services of the Indian cavalry in the Great War HM The King-Emperor was pleased to confer the title 'Royal' upon the 20th Deccan Horse, the only regiment to be so honoured. On the 16 Jul 21, the two regiments were amalgamated, briefly to be known as 20/29th Horse.

The badge chosen for the new regiment was the Garter, surmounted by a crown and backed by crossed lances. Below was a title-scroll whilst the letters 'RDH' appeared in the centre.

In 1939, when war broke out, four regiments were allocated tanks. Probyn's Horse and the Royal Deccan Horse were the Indian regiments of 251 Indian Tank Brigade. The RDH was issued with three Stuart tanks for training at the end of 1941 but tactical training was done in 15 cwt trucks. Stuart and Lee tanks were supplied at Secunderabad when they moved there for jungle training in mid-1942 but it was with Sherman tanks that they were to go into Burma in 1944 as part of 255 Indian Tank Brigade.

On Partition in August 1947, The Royal Deccan Horse was allotted to India. Their Punjabi Mussalman squadron was posted to the Pakistan-bound Probyn's Horse in exchange for the latter's Dogra squadron.

BATTLE HONOURS

Central India, Givenchy 1914, Somme 1916, Bazentin, Delville Wood, Flers-Courcelettes, Cambrai 1917, France & Flanders 1914–18, Megiddo, Sharon, Damascus, Palestine 1918, Meiktila, Capture of Meiktila, Defence of Meiktila, Rangoon Road, Pyawbwe, Burma 1942–45.

BOOKS

'A history of the Hyderabad Contingent' by Major R G Burton. (Govt printer, Calcutta 1905)

'The Royal Deccan Horse in the Great War' by Lieut. Col E Tennant. (Pub: Gale & Polden Ltd., Aldershot 1939)

CHANGES OF TITLE

Pre-1903	1st Lancers, Hyderabad Contingent	2nd Lancers Hyderabad Contingent
1903	20th Deccan Horse	29th Lancers (Deccan Horse)
1921	20th Royal Deccan Horse	29th Lancers (Deccan Horse)

Jul 21	20/29th Horse
1922	9th Royal Deccan Horse
1927	The Royal Deccan Horse (9th Horse)

THE GUIDES CAVALRY (10th QUEEN VICTORIA'S OWN FRONTIER FORCE)

The Guides Cavalry was one of the three cavalry regiments which found itself little affected by the reorganisation after the Great War. Not having previously borne a number it now found itself with one and a place in the cavalry line whereas, previously, The Corps of Guides had been an independent composite body. The Guides Infantry were now to become part of the 12th Frontier Force Regiment.

It was in December 1846 that Lieut. H.B. Lumsden raised a troop of cavalry and two companies of infantry at Peshawar and from then until 1922, the Guides were one Corps.

Scarlet was clearly unsuited for frontier warfare but tradition died hard and Lumsden was, for many years, a lone exponent of inconspicuous dress for soldiers on service. In the case on the Guides, the new khaki shade was to be worn for both campaign and review order.

Their first battle-honour was gained by the cavalry at Mooltan and others followed for the same campaign. Lumsden was also the Deputy Commissioner of Peshawar so that the Guides Cavalry were constantly engaged on the Frontier. In March 1857, Lumsden, with a small Guides escort, was sent on a special mission to Kandahar and it fell to Henry Daly to march the Guides to Delhi in May of that year to join the Delhi Field Force. The morning of the 9th June saw the Guides march in having covered 500 miles in twenty-two days. Within hours they were in action and every one of their officers was wounded that day.

In 1876, HM Queen Victoria was pleased to make them a Royal regiment. The Royal Cypher was granted for use on their appointments and they became The Queen's Own Corps of Guides.

Service in the Second Afghan War followed and the Guides were back in India. The Amir of Afghanistan signed the Treaty of Gandamak in May 1879 and agreed to accept the British envoy, Sir Louis Cavagnari, who proceeded to Kabul with an escort of one officer. Lieut W.R.P. Hamilton VC, and 76 men from the Guides, 25 of them from the Cavalry. The Afghans resented the British presence and, on the 3rd September, they attacked the Residency in the Bala Hissar. The four Europeans were killed and the Afghans offered quarter to the Guides under a Sikh jemadar, saying that they had no quarrel with the Indians. The Guides chose to fight on and the residency finally fell twelve hours later, its defenders dead, surrounded by 600 dead Afghans. Double pensions were granted to the widows and heirs of the escort.

Throughout the 1890's the Corps was more or less continuously engaged in frontier actions – to Hazara in 1891 and Chitral in 1895, the Malakand Pass and Chakdara in 1897.

The 1903 reorganisation did not affect the Guides as they bore no territorial title but, in 1906, the Cavalry became Queen Victoria's Own Corps of Guides (Frontier Force) (Lumsden's) Cavalry.

The Great War saw the Guides on the Frontier until November 1917 when they left to join 11 Indian Cavalry Brigade in Mesopotamia and actions at Sharqat and Khan Baghdadi. After the armistice, they remained in Persia to counter a Bolshevik threat, returning to India in 1921, some of the first to qualify for the new General Service Medal with clasp for North-West Persia.

On 5 Jan 22, the following correspondence was received at Mardan, the Guides' family home. It was a copy of a letter dated 16 Dec 21 from the Adjutant General, India to Northern Command.

> *'With reference to your No. 6344/1/A/1 dated 16th November 1921, I am directed to inform you that it has been decided that the QVO Corps of Guides will not be reconstituted as a Corps.*
>
> *The Cavalry regiment and Infantry Battalion will be separate units with the normal establishment of officers in each case.'*

Notwithstanding their separate existences, both cavalry and infantry wore the distinctive Guides' badge, the 'VR' Cypher within the Garter, Victorian crown above, surrounded by a ribbon-scroll reading 'Queen Victoria's Own Corps of Guides'.

Barely twenty years after their service in Persia and Mesopotamia, the Guides cavalry were back in Mesopotamia or, rather, Iraq, but this time with wheeled carriers and 15 cwt trucks (The farewell to horses took place on 26 Sep 40). In March 1942, they moved to Egypt and served on the Eighth Army's desert flank during the withdrawal to the El Alamein positions. They returned to Paiforce in September 1942 and thence to India in November 1943 where they converted to an armoured-car role, based at Kohat on the North-West Frontier. Re-equipment with Stuart tanks followed in November 1945 but only briefly since Churchill tanks were issued in early 1946 for service with 2 Armoured Brigade.

On Partition in August 1947, six armoured regiments out of eighteen went to Pakistan, the Guides Cavalry being one of them. Their Dogra squadron went to Hodson's Horse in exchange for the latter's Punjabi Mussalman squadron: the Sikh squadron went to the Poona Horse in exchange for their Kaimkhanis. The Guides also took an additional Ranghar squadron from the Scinde Horse.

BATTLE HONOURS

Mooltan, Goojerat, Punjaub, Delhi 1857, Ali Masjid, Kabul 1879, Afghanistan 1878–80, Chitral, Malakand, Punjab Frontier, Khan Baghdadi, Sharquat, Mesopotamia 1917–18, North West Frontier, India 1915, Bir Hacheim, Minqar Qaim, Deir el Shein, North Africa 1940–43.

BOOKS

'The story of the Guides' by Col G J Younghusband. (MacMillan & Co. Ltd., London, 1908)

'The history of the Guides 1846–1922 Vol I' Anon. (Gale and Polden Ltd., Aldershot, 1938)

'The history of the Guides 1922–1947 Vol II' by Lieut General Sir George MacMunn KCB KCSI DSO. (Gale & Polden Ltd., Aldershot 1950)

CHANGES OF TITLE

Pre-1903	Queen's Own Corps of Guides, Punjab Frontier Force
1904	Queens Own Corps of Guides (Lumsden's)
1911	Queen Victoria's Own Corps of Guides (Frontier Force) (Lumsden's) Cavalry
1921	Queen Victoria's Own Corps of Guides (Frontier Force) (Lumsden's) Cavalry
1922	10th Queen Victoria's Own Corps of Guides Cavalry (Frontier Force)
1927	The Guides Cavalry (10th Queen Victoria's Own Frontier Force)

PRINCE ALBERT VICTOR'S OWN CAVALRY (11th FRONTIER FORCE)

The two regiments which went to form the 11th Prince Albert Victor's Own Cavalry (Frontier Force) in 1922 were the 21st Prince Albert Victor's Own Cavalry (Frontier Force) (Daly's Horse) and the 23rd Cavalry (Frontier Force). Both had been part of the old Punjab Frontier Force which had ceased to exist in 1903.

After the British annexation of the Punjab in 1849, five regiments of Punjab Irregular Cavalry were formed, numbered 1st to 5th to cover the frontier from Hazara to Scinde. The 1st, under Henry Daly of the 1st Bombay Fusiliers, was raised in Lahore from a ready supply of recruits and promptly despatched to the frontier where there was no lack of action. One squadron was sent to Delhi under John Watson who earned a Victoria Cross in subsequent operations. The pacification of Oudh followed and, in the post-Mutiny changes, the 1st was re-styled simply the 1st Punjab Cavalry.

They subsequently saw service in Afghanstan where they were part of the force which took Kandahar and distinguished themselves in the action at Ahmad

Khel in April 1880. In 1890, their title was changed to the 1st Prince Albert Victor's Own Punjab Cavalry when the prince became their honorary colonel. He was, in fact, better known as the Duke of Clarence and Avondale, the eldest son of HM King Edward VII and Queen Alexandra and would have acceded to the throne on this father's death in 1910 had he not pre-deceased the King in 1892.

The 3rd Punjab Irregular Cavalry was raised at Peshawar in the spring of 1849 by Lieut W G Prendergast of the 8th Light Cavalry. They were soon to be usefully employed when they were despatched to Amritsar where they suppressed the mutiny of the 66th Bengal Native Infantry. During the Great Mutiny in 1857, the 3rd remained on the Frontier.

The Second Afghan War found the 3rd Punjab Cavalry, as they became in 1861, with Roberts on his advance to Kandahar.

Both 1st and 3rd were to serve in the Mahsud campaign of 1894–95 and in the major tribal insurrections of 1897–98. The 1st were in Tochi, the 3rd in the Kurram Valley and on the Samana Ridge.

The 1903 changes meant that Lord Kitchener removed the 'Punjab' designation and added twenty to their number. Thus, the 1st became the 21st Prince Albert Victor's Own Cavalry (Frontier Force) and the 3rd was re-designated the 23rd Cavalry (Frontier Force). The next year, Henry Daly was remembered and the 21st added '(Daly's Horse)' to their title.

Both regiments were to serve in Mesopotamia during the Great War, the 21st being present at the recapture of Kut-al-Amara and the 23rd engaged in the protection of the Anglo-Persian Oil Company's pipe-line, then a vital line of supply for the Royal Navy.

The Third Afghan War found both 21st and 23rd back in India to qualify for an Afghan honour without any more significant actions than minor affairs against dissident tribesmen.

On the 6 Jun 21, the amalgamation of the 21st and 23rd took place, to be known briefly as the 21/23rd Cavalry. The following year, Prince Albert Victor's name was restored to the newly-numbered 11th Cavalry. The badge chosen was to be similar to the Kandahar Star, awarded for the famous march, a five-pointed star indicative of the Punjab (Land of Five Rivers): in the centre, a circle inscribed 'Kabul to Kandahar 1880' enclosing the letters 'PAVO' and a crown above. Backing the star were the crossed sabres of the 23rd.

When mechanisation began, early in the Second World War, the PAVO Cavalry was to become a frontier armoured regiment but, in July 1940, its role was changed to a motor regiment and it joined 3 Indian Motor Brigade at Sialkot. The other two regiments in the Brigade were the 2nd Royal Lancers (Gardner's Horse) and 18th King Edward VII's Own Cavalry. Their first service overseas was in the Middle East in the Western Desert, Syria and Iran until the end of 1942. In January 1943, the regiment returned to India and, by March 1944, as reconnaissance regiment to XXXIII Corps, was back in action against the Japanese in the Corps' advance to Imphal. Thereafter, PAVO fought its way down to Rangoon where it was promptly re-routed back to Ahmadnagar for re-equipping and despatch to Singapore and, later, to the Dutch East Indies. May 1946 saw them back once more in India, at Secunderabad, re-equipped with Sherman tanks as part of 1 Armoured Brigade.

Partition in August 1947 allotted the Regiment to Pakistan. Its Sikh squadron was transferred to the 18th King Edward VII's Own Cavalry and later passed on to the 3rd Cavalry but there appears to be no trace of a squadron transferred in.

BATTLE HONOURS

Delhi 1857, Lucknow, Ahmad Khel, Kandahar 1880. Afghanistan 1878–80 Kut-al-Amara 1917, Baghdad, Khan Baghdadi, Sharqat, Mesopotamia 1915–18, Afghanistan 1919, El Mechili, Halfaya 1941, Bir Hacheim, North Africa 1940–43, Relief of Kohima, Monywa 1945, Mandalay, Myinmu Bridgehead, Capture of Meiktila, The Irrawaddy, Rangoon Road, Burma 1942–45.

BOOKS

'History of the 23rd Cavalry (Frontier Force), late 3rd Regiment, Punjab Cavalry' Anon
(Pub. unknown c. 1910)

'Short history of the PAVO Cavalry (11th Frontier Force)' Anon
(Pub. unknown c. 1936)

CHANGES OF TITLE

Pre-1903	1st Punjab Cavalry (Prince Albert Victor's Own)	3rd Punjab Cavalry
1903	21st Prince Albert Victor's Own Cavalry (Frontier Force)	23rd Cavalry (Frontier Force)
1904	21st Prince Albert Victor's Own Cavalry (Frontier Force) (Daly's Horse)	23rd Cavalry (Frontier Force)

1921	21/23rd Cavalry
1922	11th Prince Albert Victor's Own Cavalry (Frontier Force)
1927	Prince Albert Victor's Own Cavalry (11th Frontier Force)

SAM BROWNE'S CAVALRY (12th FRONTIER FORCE)

The regiment which became, in 1922, the 12th Cavalry (Frontier Force) was formed from two regiments of the old Punjab Irregular Force, the 2nd and the 5th which, in 1903, had become the 22nd Cavalry (Frontier Force) and the 25th Cavalry (Frontier Force).

Of the five regiments of Punjab Cavalry, the 1st and the 3rd went to form the 11th Prince Albert Victor's Own Cavalry (Frontier Force) as already narrated; the 4th Regiment, raised in 1849, as were the others, had only a brief existence and was disbanded in 1882.

It was Lieut. Samuel J. Browne of the 36th Bengal Native Infantry who received orders to raise a regiment of Punjab cavalry in Lahore to be designated the 2nd Punjab Irregular Cavalry. The 5th was raised at Mooltan by Captain Robert Fiztpatrick of the 12th Bombay Native Infantry.

Both regiments were promptly engaged in frontier operations.

Both 2nd and 5th went to the seat of action when the Great Mutiny began in 1857 and Captain Dighton Probyn was awarded the Victoria Cross. Browne, now a major, charged and captured a rebel gun, accompanied by only a single sowar. He lost is left arm but earned a Victoria Cross. The decoration had only recently been instituted and there is no doubt that it was awarded rather more liberally than in later years but it is certain that there was no lack of opportunities for young officers with fire in their belly and the need to secure advancement.

The mutiny operations completed, both regiments returned to the Frontier and, in 1861, they were regularised and became the 2nd and the 5th Punjab Cavalry. It was at about this time that the famous Sam Browne belt was to make its appearance, an item of dress to be adopted widely and surely one of the few accoutrements still to be in use 130 years later with little or no change. The colonel, having lost his left arm had difficulty in carrying his sword comfortably, whether mounted or dismounted, leaving his one hand free. Its design was also intended to carry a leather pistol holster whereby the weapon could be safely carried without the risk of accidental discharge – as the pistols of the day were inclined to do. The original belt is now on display in the India Room at the Royal Military Academy Sandhurst.

The Second Afghan War in 1878–80 found the 2nd in the Kandahar Field Force, distinguishing themselves in the cavalry action at Ahmad Khel in April 1880.

In 1903, the regional titles were abolished and the 2nd Punjab Cavalry became the 22nd Cavalry (Frontier Force), changed a year later to the 22nd Sam Browne's Cavalry (Frontier Force). Sadly, General Sir Sam Browne VC, GCB, KCSI had died in 1901.

The 5th, on its return to the Frontier, displayed several times the advantages of shock-action by a small, disciplined body of cavalry over a large but less cohesive force. In March 1860, 150 men under an Indian officer attacked a 3,000 strong lashkar of Mahsud Waziris at Tank, killing 300 and dispersing the others. In January 1867, an Indian officer with 27 sowars charged a body of 1,000 tribesmen, killed 150 and captured most of the rest.

In Afghanistan, the 5th were present at the capture of Charasiah and Roberts ordered that they and HM's 9th Lancers should share the honour of escorting him into Kabul. At the storming of the Asmai Heights in December 1879, near Kabul, Captain William Vousden made repeated charges with a small body of men of the 5th, passing through the ranks of an overwhelming force again and again until the enemy fled. Vousden received a Victoria Cross and his ten surviving men the Indian Order of Merit.

The changes of 1903 saw the 5th become the 25th Cavalry (Frontier Force).

It was 1916 before the 22nd went overseas to Mesopotamia but they remained abroad for four years, returning to India only in 1920.

The 25th went to German East Africa in 1915 and joined in the pursuit of von

Lettow Vorbeck to the Mozambique border before being withdrawn in the face of the depredations of the tsetse fly on cavalry operations. They were back at home in time to gain an honour for the Third Afghan War.

The amalgamation of the 22nd and 25th saw the disappearance of Sam Browne's name: the first title was to be, briefly, the 22/25th Cavalry but this was changed in 1922 to the 12th Cavalry (Frontier Force). However, five years later, they became Sam Browne's Cavalry (12th Frontier Force) but this was shortlived. The new badge showed a mounted figure within a circle carrying the title 'Sam Browne's Cavalry XII FF' with a crown above. The new regiment was destined not to fire a shot in anger.

In line with a new training policy, Sam Browne's dropped out of the order-of-battle in 1937 when they were made the permanent training regiment of the 2nd Indian Cavalry Group stationed at Ferozepore.

BATTLE HONOURS

Delhi 1857, Lucknow, Charasiah, Kabul 1879, Ahmad Khal, Afghanistan 1878–80, Kut-al-Amara 1917, Baghdad, Mesopotamia 1916–18, North West Frontier, India 1914–15, East Africa 1917, Afghanistan 1919.

BOOKS

Very little of substance but the 'Journal of the late General Sir Sam Browne VC, GCB, KCSI 1849–98' was published posthumously on the initiative of his daughter: (Pub. William Blackwood & Sons, Edinburgh, 1937)

CHANGES OF TITLE

Pre-1903	2nd Punjab Cavalry	5th Punjab Cavalry
1903	22nd Cavalry (Frontier Force)	25th Cavalry (Frontier Force)
1904	22nd Sam Browne's Cavalry (Frontier Force)	25th Cavalry (Frontier Force)
1921	22/25th Cavalry	
1927	Sam Browne's Cavalry (12th Frontier Force)	

13th DUKE OF CONNAUGHT'S OWN LANCERS

The union in 1923 of the 31st Duke of Connaught's Own Lancers and the 32nd Lancers to form the 13th Duke of Connaught's Own Lancers should not have been an unhappy one. Both regiments had had a common origin in the old Bombay Squadron of Cavalry, raised for service under Lord Lake with whom it served at the siege of Bhurtpore in 1805.

The Squadron was split in 1817 and, with two troops each as a cadre, the 1st and 2nd Bombay Light Cavalry were formed.

The 1st saw service in the First Afghan War in 1839 when, with a detachment of the 2nd, they were at the capture of Ghuznee and in the march to Kabul returning to India in 1840.

Eight years later, the Second Sikh War saw the 1st in action when they were at the storming of Mooltan where they remained as garrison for the remainder of the campaign.

May 1857, the start of the Great Mutiny, saw the 1st at Nasirabad where they were the only ones to remain loyal. Artillery and infantrymen urged them to go over to them but the sowars refused and, under their officers, charged in an attempt to take the guns. They failed to do so but successfully disengaged and took part in the campaign of pacification in Central India.

In 1862, Mahrattas joined the 1st Bombay Light Cavalry, the only Indian cavalry regiment to enlist the class. It was alleged that the Mahratta was averse to the silladar system then obtaining in the cavalry and so, if he joined the army, he opted for the infantry where he was not required to advance hs own money. The 1st, and, later, the 31st Duke of Connaught's Own Lancers, continued to maintain a Mahratta Squadron until the amalgamation in 1923. Thereafter, the squadron was reduced and the class was not recruited again until some forty years later when Mahrattas were accepted into the armoured cavalry of an independent India.

In 1846, the 1st had formed a mounted band. This was not unique, of course, but most of the other regiments with such bands had had to close them down during the Great War. However, the band of the old 1st continued through with the 13th DCO Lancers until the Second World War.

During the summer of 1878, the 1st were sent to Malta and Cyprus together with a troop of the 2nd. The object of this was to exert gentle pressure on the Russians.

Burma was their next overseas posting in 1885, a campaign no more attractive then than sixty years later.

The Duke of Connaught, then Commander-in-Chief of the Bombay Army, became their colonel-in-chief in 1890. He still held the appointment in the 13th DCO Lancers on his death in January 1942.

Their third spell of service abroad was a brief stay at Suakin on the Red Sea in 1896 when, as the 1st Bombay Lancers – in consequence of the issue of the lance – they formed part of a mixed brigade sent out from India.

The 2nd Bombay Light Cavalry, as already recorded, sent a detachment with the 1st to Afghanistan in 1839.

In 1857, they were stationed at Neemuch and saw service in the pacification of Central India. One of its subalterns, later General Sir James Blair, won a Victoria Cross during these operations.

Afghanistan in 1878–80 found the balance of the 2nd (one troop was in the Mediterranean with the 1st) where they were part of the force under General Phayre which went to relieve Kandahar.

In 1903, Bombay cavalry had thirty added to their numbers and, thus, the 1st (Duke of Connaught's Own) Bombay Lancers became the 31st Duke of Connaught's Own Lancers and the 2nd Bombay Lancers became the 32nd Lancers, the old Presidency designations being abolished.

During the Great War, the 31st remained on the Frontier but the 32nd went to Mesopotamia late in 1916 and were alleged to be first Imperial troops to enter Baghdad.

In April 1917, at the battle of Istabulat, a detachment led by the commanding officer, charged an entrenched Turkish position resulting in all the officers and most of the men becoming casulaties.

Having remained in India throughout the war, the 31st served in the Third Afghan War and then went to perform garrison duties in Palestine, being the last Indian cavalry regiment to serve there, as they did, until 1923 when, on their amalgamation with the 32nd Lancers in September of that year, they were the last two regiments carrying their old titles. This particular merger, of course, was simply a reunion of two regiments separated more than a hundred years before.

The new badge was to be crossed lances with '13' on the intersection and a crown above: across the lancebutts was a scroll reading 'Duke of Connaught's Own'.

The 13th Duke of Connaught's Own Lancers were one of the first two Indian cavalry regiments nominated for mechanisation. Converted at Sialkot following their last horsed parade on 9 Apr 38, one squadron was equipped with Vickers light tanks and two with Chevrolet armoured cars. Thereafter, they took over Frontier duties from companies of the Royal Tank Corps but, in April 1941, they traded their tanks for one squadron of Scinde Horse armoured cars and left for Iraq with 10 Indian Division. The 13th was the only Indian cavalry regiment to receive an honour for Frontier Service during the war. Thereafter, they served against the Vichy French in Syria and then proceeded to see much of Iran and Iraq before joining the Eighth Army. Before the battle of El Alamein in October 1942, however, the 13th were back in Persia. Finally, after a frustrating visit to Egypt where they were re-equipped with Staghound armoured cars in anticipation of going to Italy, they returned to India and prepared to land in Malaya. Despite Japanese surrender, there was still action to be had in South

East Asia and they moved on to Java in support of 5 and 23 Indian Divisions in their holding-action there. In August 1946 the 13th returned to Secunderabad as the reconnaissance regiment of 1 Indian Armoured Division.

On Partition in August 1947, the 13th DCO Lancers were allotted to Pakistan. No details would appear to be available of any squadron transfers.

BATTLE HONOURS

Ghuznee, Afghanistan 1839, Mooltan, Punjaub, Central India, Afghanistan 1878–80, Burma 1885–87, Kut al Amara 1917, Baghdad, Sharqat, Mesopotamia 1916–18, North West Frontier, India 1917, Afghanistan 1919, North West Frontier 1937–40, Damascus, Deir es Zor, Raqaa, Syria 1941, Gazala, Bir Hacheim, El Adem, Gambut, Sidi Rezegh 1942, Tobruk 1942, Fuka, North Africa 1940–43.

BOOKS

'A brief historical sketch of His Majesty's 31st Duke of Connaught's Own Lancers, Indian Army' by Colonel G F Newport-Tinley CB. (Pub. Bombay Gazette Electrical Printing Works, Bombay 1910)

CHANGES OF TITLE

pre 1903	1st (Duke of Connaught's Own) Bombay Lancers	2nd Bombay Lancers
1903	31st Duke of Connaught's Own Lancers	32nd Lancers

1921	31/32nd Lancers
1922	13th Duke of Connaught's Own Bombay Lancers
1927	13th Duke of Connaught's Own Lancers

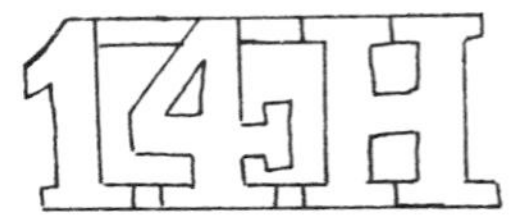

THE SCINDE HORSE (14th PRINCE OF WALES'S OWN CAVALRY)

The regiment born on 1 Jan 22 as the 14th Prince of Wales' Own Scinde Horse was made up of two old and tried regiments raised in the almost literal cauldron of the Sind (or as it was then spelt, the Scinde) Desert in the first half of the nineteenth century. Sind and Baluchistan were in the Bombay area of operations and a detachment of the Poona Horse became the nucleus of the Scinde Irregular Horse in 1838. British reverses in the First Afghan War prompted some local restiveness and a Lieut. John Jacob of the Bombay Artillery was sent to take command. His policy of what was to become known later as aggressive patrolling had the desired effect and British withdrawal from Southern Afghanistan in 1842 was not hampered by local tribesmen. Later that year, the pacification of Scinde began under Sir Charles Napier and the Scinde Irregular Horse earned its first honours. By 1846, they had done so well that authority ordered that another corps be formed and this was done by splitting the original and completing the establishment of the two regiments, principally with Muslim recruits. Jacob did not think highly of Sikhs and, in any case, the better classes of the Punjab did not find service in Scinde attractive.

The 1st Regiment served in Persia in 1857, returning to Central India to help in the suppression of the Great Mutiny whilst the 2nd Regiment remained on the Baluch border. A 3rd Regiment was raised in late 1857 but, was disbanded in 1882 by an ungrateful government after they had gained a hard-won honour in the Second Afghan War. By 1885, the remaining 1st and 2nd Scinde Horse had become the 5th and 6th Bombay Cavalry (Jacob-ka-Risallah) but, three years later, they were designated the 5th Scinde Horse and 6th Jacob's Horse. These titles, in 1903, became the 35th Scinde Horse and 36th Jacob's Horse by the process of adding thirty to the Bombay cavalry regiments' numbers.

Jacob, of course, had long since died but his name lived on outside his regiment in the town of Jacobabad in Scinde (now in Pakistan), one of the hottest stations in India (135°F for nine months of the year).

In the Great War, the 35th Scinde Horse remained in India, training drafts and serving on the Frontier but, in March 1920, they went to Mesopotamia for a stay of eighteen months during which time they saw hard and varied service.

Meanwhile, the 36th Jacob's Horse was early off to France with the Lucknow Brigade of the 1st Indian Cavalry Division to see their first action at Festubert in January 1915, waist deep in water-filled trenches. They served at Second Ypres, the Somme and Cambrai. Moved to Palestine, they joined the 4th Cavalry Division and fought in Allenby's remarkable cavalry campaign. However, the war completed, the Regiment remained on garrison duty in Syria and Palestine, only to return to India in 1921 where they joined the 35th Scinde Horse at Jubbulpore in preparation for the merger.

The badge chosen for the new regiment was an Afghan horsemen above a title scroll, equally applicable to both elements of the merger, but with no mention of the new number.

In 1938, the Scinde Horse became one of the first two Indian cavalry regiments nominated for mechanisation and the last mounted parade took place in April 1939.

During the Second World War, they served as a frontier armoured regiment, based at Dera Ismail Khan for two years before going on to serve in Paiforce, Egypt and Syria. Unfortunately, they were one of several regiments who received no honours for that war.

On Partition in August 1947, the Scinde Horse, despite its title, was allotted to India. They received a Sikh Squadron on transfer from Probyn's Horse and transferred their Ranghar squadron to the Guides Cavalry. This left them with two Sikh squadrons and, in January 1948, they exchanged one of them for Dogras which Hodson's Horse had had from the Guides Cavalry.

BATTLE HONOURS

Meeanee, Hyderabad, Cutchee, Mooltan, Goojerat, Punjaub, Persia, Central India, Afghanistan 1878-80, Somme 1916, Morval, Cambrai 1917, France & Flanders, 1914–18, Megiddo, Sharon, Damascus, Palestine 1918, North West Frontier, India 1914–15, '18.

BOOKS

'Prince of Wales's Own, The Scinde Horse 1839–1922' by Col E B Maunsell. (Butler & Tanner, London, 1926)

'The Scinde Horse, 14th Prince of Wales's Own Cavalry 1922–1947' by Lieut Col K R Brooke. (Deighton's Embassy Press, Haslemere, 1957)

CHANGES OF TITLE

Pre-1903	5th Bombay Cavalry (Scinde Horse)	6th Bombay Cavalry (Jacob's Horse)
1903	35th Scinde Horse	36th Jacob's Horse
1921	35/36th Prince of Wales's Own Cavalry	
1922	14th Prince of Wales's Own Scinde Horse	
1927	The Scinde Horse (14th Prince of Wales's Own Cavalry)	

15th LANCERS

The two regiments which went to form the 15th Lancers at Lucknow on 15 Feb 22 were never employed as regiments in battle. Neither the 17th Cavalry nor the 37th Lancers (Baluch Horse) was engaged in regimental action and thus did not qualify for more than 'theatre honours'.

The original 17th was raised in 1857, partly from the Rohilkand Police and, the following year, became Robart's Horse. Colonel Robart, the first Commandant was one of those larger-than-life characters which the Indian Army had in plenty. He recruited only wild Afghan tribesmen and formal discipline did not appear to be much in evidence. However, in 1861, they became the 17th Bengal Cavalry, seeing action with the Bhutan Field Force in 1866, for which no honours were awarded. In the Second Afghan War they served on the lines-of-communication from Jamrud to Dakka but fought no recorded action. The customary post-war economies meant the disbandment of the 17th in 1881 but, after the Penjdeh Incident in 1885, they were hurriedly re-raised at Mian Mir (Lahore Cantonment) from Punjabi Mussalmans and Pathans.

Bad luck dogged the 17th Cavalry as they became in 1903. They missed out on the Boxer Rising in 1900 in China when, following an outbreak of cholera, their place was taken by the 13th (Duke of Connaught's) Bengal Lancers (Watson's Horse). In 1914, they succumbed to equine infection and they had to yield their place in Indian Expeditionary Force 'A' (the contingent which went to France in 1914) to the 29th Lancers (Deccan Horse).

However, a Pathan Squadron went to East Africa in January 1915 to protect the Uganda Railway and only returned, thirty strong, two years later, but detached squadrons do not collect honours and so the 17th missed out once more. In the Third Afghan War in 1919, the 17th Cavalry served with distinction.

The other partner to the merger began life as the 7th Bombay Cavalry in 1885 in Sind, converting to the 37th Lancers (Baluch Horse) in 1903 and recruiting Baluchis and Pathans from Derajat District. Their only service was in the Third Afghan War.

The badge chosen for the 15th Lancers after the merger in 1922 was crossed lances with a monogram 'XV' on the intersection and a scroll 'Lancers' below.

Following a change in policy in 1937, the 15th Lancers dropped out of the order-of-battle, becoming the permanent training regiment of the 1st Indian Cavalry Group, stationed at Jhansi.

BATTLE HONOURS

Afghanistan 1879–80, Afghanistan 1919.

BOOKS

'The Star and Crescent – 17th Cavalry from 1858–1922' by Major F C C Yeats-Brown (Pioneer Press, Allahabad, c. 1927).

CHANGES OF TITLE

Pre-1903	17th Bengal Lancers	7th Bombay Cavalry (Baluch Horse)
1903	17th Lancers	37th Lancers (Baluch Horse
1921	17/37th Cavalry	
1922	15th Lancers	

16th LIGHT CAVALRY

The oldest cavalry in the Indian service, in spite of its relatively high number, the 16th Light Cavalry assumed its present identity in 1922. It was not the result of an amalgamation but was one of the three regiments which simply changed their numbers.

The precise date of their first raising is unknown but it is believed to be about 1776 when they were formed as the 3rd Regiment of Cavalry in the Carnatic, in the service of the Nawab of Arcot.

The Nawab's four regiments of cavalry were all commanded by officers of the Honourable East India Company but the men were not happy, being in a more or less total state of mutiny owing to the irregularity of their pay. Finally, the Company took them into its own service and they earned their first honour – 'Sholinghur' – when they defeated Hyder Ali in 1780, the only cavalry regiment still to bear that honour.

Between 1784 and 1788, they became first, the 4th and then the 2nd Madras Cavalry, the latter a number which they were to retain until 1903. Serving in South India, they earned honours under Wellesley, moving then to the Deccan for service against the Mahrattas, a protracted campaign for which no honours were granted. A squadron served in Afghanistan in 1880 when it marched on Kandahar but squadron-service was not sufficient to bring a battle honour to the Regiment. Defeat of King Thibaw in the Burma campaign of 1885–87 saw the 2nd Madras Cavalry in action at last in an unpopular theatre of war, a hard-won battle honour.

The abolition of the separate armies in 1903 saw their title changed to the 27th Light Cavalry, their title in 1922.

A world war might have been expected to bring opportunities for foreign service and honours and the 27th sent detachments to Persia but remained to serve in India, unhonoured. Afghanistan 1919 was a well-earned distinction, however, when the Regiment performed with particular elan, at a time when the arme blanche was in its death-throes.

The new title in 1922 when they became the 16th Light Cavalry was easier to accept than it was for regiments which had suffered amalgamation. Moreover, in February 1923, the 16th was nominated to become one of the two cavalry regiments in the Indianisation programme. The other one was the 7th Light Cavalry, once the old 3rd Madras Lancers and another of the three cavalry regiments not to have been merged in the recent reforms. Doubtless, it was felt that the twin traumae of amalgamation and Indianisation might have proved too much.

The badge chosen for the new regiment was crossed lances, with '16' on the intersection, a crown above and scroll 'Light Cavalry' below.

All trace of its Southern origins had long since gone and, in accordance with the 'martial-classes' doctrine, the ranks consisted of Jats, Kaimkhanis and Rajputana Rajputs.

The Regiment was slow to mechanise, only being completed in October 1941. It served as a Frontier armoured regiment before going to Burma under Lieut Colonel J.N. Chaudhuri (later General and Chief of Army Staff in an independent India) where it led the advance on Rangoon. Moving to French Indo-China for occupation duties after VJ-Day, it returned to Lucknow in October 1946. A decision had been made to convert the 16th Light Cavalry, the senior ex-Madras cavalry regiment, to an all South India classes unit once more.

On Partition in August 1947, the 16th Light Cavalry was allotted to India. The changeover to South Indian classes meant that there was no question of squadron-transfers to Pakistan or to Pakistan-bound regiments.

BATTLE HONOURS

Sholinghur, Carnatic, Mysore, Seringapatam, Burma 1885–87, Afghanistan 1919, Meiktila, Capture of Meiktila, Defence of Meiktila, Pegu 1945, Sittang 1945, Rangoon Road, Burma 1942–45.

BOOKS

'Historial Records of the 2nd Madras Lancers, now 27th Light Cavalry' by Col J B Edwards (Christian Mission Press, Jubbulpore 1907)

'History of the 16th Light Cavalry (Armoured Corps)' by Lieut Col C L Proudfoot (Calcutta c. 1976)

CHANGES OF TITLE

Pre 1903	2nd Madras Lancers
1903	27th Light Cavalry
1921	27th Light Cavalry
1922	16th Light Cavalry

THE POONA HORSE (17th QUEEN VICTORIA'S OWN CAVALRY)

The two regiments which went to form the 17th Queen Victoria's Own Poona Horse in 1922 were two old Bombay regiments, each with more than a century of service – the 33rd Queen's Own Light Cavalry and the 34th Prince Albert Victor's Own Poona Horse.

Both had been raised in the same cantonment, Sirrur, and both had shared the same campaigns. The 3rd Bombay Light Cavalry was raised on 4 May 1820 as the third and last regiment of cavalry in the Bombay Army. Their first action was the siege of Kithoor (between Belgaum and Dharwar) in 1824 where the Rajah had died without issue. The Honourable East India Company annexed the principality.

The 34th, although previously the 4th Bombay Cavalry, was not raised as such. Bajee Rao, the Peshwa of Poona had been unable to preserve order and John Company agreed by treaty that a force should be raised, officered by the Company and partly funded by Poona finances. Altruism was seldom the dominant factor in the Company's deliberations and it was doubtless known that the Peshwa was preparing to lead a Mahratta confederacy against it. The cavalry, 5,000 strong, was to be known as the Poona Auxiliary Horse and the Resident at Poona, Mountstuart Elphinstone, ordered troops up to Kirkee and sent 1,000 of the new cavalry to join them. They arrived too late but, by then, the Peshwa had been repulsed.

At Corygaum, on New Year's Day, a small British force of some 850 men, made up of 300 of the Poona Auxiliary Horse, a troop of Madras European Artillery and a very under-strength Bombay Native Infantry regiment (later to become 2/4 Bombay Grenadiers) fought off a Mahratta force of some 30,000 men (the memorial raised to this action refers to it as Koregaon).

On the dissolution of the Mahratta Confederacy in 1819, the strength of the Poona Auxiliary Horse was gradually reduced so that, by 1838, it numbered only about one thousand.

Both the 3rd and the Poona Auxiliary Horse went to Afghanistan in 1839 in the Bombay Cavalry Brigade and both qualified for the Ghuznee honour. Similarly, both were in the campaign in Scinde in 1842–43.

Persia invaded Afghanistan in 1856, capturing Herat. The Shah was asked to withdraw but he refused and an expeditionary force was sent to the Persian Gulf and, once again, both regiments were included. The force landed near Reshire in December 1856, reduced the fortified town of Bushire and then rested, to await the remainder of the force from India. Early in January 1857, it arrived and Sir James Outram, the force commander, decided to attack the 7,000 strong Persian force assembled near Khushab. The 3rd broke a Persian square and two officers were awarded the Victoria Cross, whilst the Poona Irregular Horse – as they became in 1847 – put to flight a Persian regiment, spiked the guns and captured their standard. Surmounting the standard was a silver hand, the palm of which was inscribed in Persian 'The Hand of God is above all things'. In later years, until 1923, the Hand was a part of the 34th Poona Horse's regimental shoulder-title.

Hurrying back to India, both regiments were able to take part in the pacification of Central India and another Victoria Cross was won by an officer of H M's 17th Lancers on secondment to the 3rd Bombay Light Cavalry. In 1861, there was a move to make all the Bombay Cavalry into Silladar regiments and the 3rd became the 3rd Silladar Light Cavalry whilst the Poona Horse (an 1860 change) was brought into line as the 4th Poona Silladar Cavalry.

This status was short-lived and, the following year, the two regiments became respectively the 3rd Bombay Light Cavalry and the 1st Poona Horse.

Abyssinia was next to see the 3rd for a campaign which carried little glamour and few opportunities for glory in 1867–68.

In 1876, the Prince of Wales, later HM King Edward VII, became Colonel of the 3rd who were also styled 'The Queen's Own' whilst, in 1891, the Prince of Wales's son, Prince Albert Victor was appointed Colonel of the 1st Poona Horse. Sadly, the Prince died in 1892 but the Poona Horse continued to bear the subsidiary title 'Prince Albert Victor's Own' until 1921.

It was back to Afghanistan for both regiments in 1878-80 and they were together in Kandahar until relieved by Roberts marching in from Kabul.

The 3rd (Queen's Own) Bombay Light Cavalry went off the China in 1900 for the suppression of the Boxer Rising and the three regiments of Indian cavalry with the force wore khaki on active service for the first time.

The 1903 changes made the 3rd into the 33rd Queen's Own Light Cavalry. The following year, the King became their Colonel-in-Chief and in 1911, the Royal and Imperial Cypher of Queen Victoria was approved as a badge of the Regiment: their title was changed once more and they became 33rd Queen Victoria's Own Light Cavalry.

The 4th (PAVO) Bombay Cavalry (Poona Horse), as they had become in 1890, were restyled in 1903 the 34th Prince Albert Victor's Own Poona Horse.

Aurangabad was the station from which the 33rd set out for Mesopotamia in October 1914. Like most of the cavalry, they avoided capture at Kut but were returned to India to reinforce and refit. Thereafter, they were back to the Frontier and 1 Indian Cavalry Brigade for the Third Afghan War.

The 34th were in France in time for Lieut F A DePass to win a Victoria Cross in November 1914 at Festubert. After Cambrai, they joined 14 Cavalry Brigade of the Desert Mounted Corps in Palestine.

After their return to India, the 33rd and the 34th joined, first as the 33/34th Cavalry and, in 1922, as the 17th Queen Victoria's Own Poona Horse.

The badge chosen was the Royal Cypher of HM Queen Victoria within the Garter, a crown above and a scroll below, reading *'Queen Victoria's Own Poona Horse'*.

The Regiment was mechanised in 1940 and, the next year, joined 6 Indian Division at Bolarum as its reconnaissance regiment. In July 1941 it received South African Mk 3 armoured cars and wheeled carriers. It landed at Basra in November and, in April 1942, it joined 252 Indian Armoured Brigade. In June, it moved to Egypt to become reconnaisance regiment for XXX Corps but no suitable vehicles were available. September found them back in Iran where they rejoined 6 Indian Division. Paiforce was to be their home until September 1944 when the Regiment moved to Cyprus. Italy was expected to be next but Cyprus was destined to be their last foreign station before returning to India in August 1945. Thereafter, they moved to Muttra and to Risalpur in early 1947, newly-equipped with Sherman tanks as part of 3 Independent Armoured Brigade.

At the outbreak of war in September 1939, the Poona Horse had borne more battle-honours than any other cavalry regiment in the King-Emperor's service. Sadly, the Second World War added ony one honour to their earlier impressive list.

Partition in August 1947 allotted the Regiment to India and their Kaimkhani squadron was exchanged for the Sikh Squadron of the Guides Cavalry who were bound for Pakistan. In September, during its move from Nowshera, in North West Frontier Province, to the Indian border, the Poona Horse's train was attacked by mobs en route but they had taken the prudent precaution of posting armed guards in both the engine cab and the guard's van to ensure that no unscheduled stops were made.

BATTLE HONOURS

Corygaum, Ghuznee 1839, Afghanistan 1839, Candahar 1842, Ghuznee 1842, Cabool 1842, Meeanee, Hyderabad, Reshire, Bushire, Kooshab, Persia, Central India, Abyssinia, Kandahar 1880, Afghanistan 1878–80, China 1900, La Bassee 1914, Armentieres 1914, Somme 1916, Bazentin, Flers-Courcelettes, Cambrai 1917, France & Flanders 1914–18, Megiddo, Sharon, Damascus, Palestine 1918, Shaiba, Ctesiphon, Tigris 1916, Mesopotamia 1914-16, Afghanistan 1919, North Africa 1940–43.

BOOKS

'Historical record of the 33rd (Queen Victoria's Own) Light Cavalry' Anon. (Pub: The Orphanage Press, Poona 1913)

'The Poona Horse' (17th Queen Victoria's Own Cavalry) 1817–1931' (Two Volumes) Vol I (1817– 1913 by Major M H Anderson, Lieut Col E S J Anderson and Colonel G M Molloy OBE. Vol II (1914–1931) by Colonel H C Wylly CB. (Pub RUSI, London 1933)

'Indian Cavalry Officer 1914–15: Captain Roly Grimshaw' Ed. Colonel J Wakefield & Lieut Col J M Weippert. (Pub: Costello, Tunbridge Wells, 1986)

CHANGES OF TITLE

Pre 1903	3rd Queen's Own Bombay Light Cavalry	4th (Prince Albert Victor's Own) Bombay Cavalry Poona Horse)
1903	33rd Queen's Own Light Cavalry	34th Prince Albert Victor's Own Poona Horse

1921	33/34th Cavalry
1922	17th Queen Victoria's Own Poona Horse
1937	Poona Horse (17th Queen Victoria's Own)

18th KING EDWARD VII's OWN CAVALRY

When the post-war reforms on cavalry were being implemented, the 6th King Edward's Own Cavalry and the 7th Hariana Lancers amalgamated at Risalpur in November 1921, initially as the 6/7th Cavalry but being restyled the following year as the 18th King Edward's Own Cavalry.

Both 6th and 7th had begun as regiments of Bengal Irregular Cavalry before the Great Mutiny. The 8th Bengal Irregular Cavalry was raised at Fatehgarh in 1842 by Lieut. Ryves and was active the next year in the Gwalior campaign in which they earned 'Punniar' as their first battle-honour.

In 1845, the 8th moved north to become part of the Army of the Sutlej and for the start of the first Sikh War. Three more honours were won in this hard-fought campaign.

Burma was the first opportunity for the 8th to serve abroad and they were there after the period of the Second Burma War, during the years 1853–55.

Bareilly was the station of the 8th in 1857 when the Devil's Wind swept through Central India: the regiment was thought to be dependable and two additional troops were raised to help suppress the revolt. The new recruits were instrumental in convincing the older soldiers of the justice of the cause of the mutineers and the greater number of them deserted, leaving the officers and most of the NCOs standing firm. By February 1858, the Regiment was brought up to full-strength and they served in the subsequent pacification of Oudh. They did not, however, receive any Mutiny honours.

In the 1861 changes, the 8th became the 6th Bengal Cavalry when the 3rd and 5th Bengal Irregular Cavalry were disbanded. The next twenty-one years were years of peace for the 6th but, in 1882, they were in action in Egypt at the battle of Tel-el-Kebir, wearing khaki for the first time. For these services, HRH The Prince of Wales was appointed their Colonel and they became the 6th Prince of Wales's Own Bengal Cavalry in 1883.

In the Tirah campaign, they were in several actions in the Kurram Valley and, in the same campaign, two squadrons were heavily engaged, together with two companies of the 5th Gurkhas, in rescuing men of the 12th Bengal Infantry from a dangerous situation in the foot-soldiers' first campaign in the Frontier.

In the changes of 1903, there was little change in the title; only the word 'Bengal' was discarded.

No active service was then encountered until 1914 but, in 1905, the then Prince of Wales – later HM King George V – visited the Regiment, professed himself pleased with what he saw and, shortly afterwards, the title 'King Edward's Own' was accorded to the 6th.

When war broke out in August 1914, the 6th King Edwards Own Cavalry was in Sialkot as part of 2 (Sialkot) Cavalry Brigade and they sailed for France on 17 Oct 14. From France, after Cambrai in 1917, they went to Palestine to replace British yeomanry regiments bound for France as machine-gun units. After the campaign, they remained in Egypt and Asia Minor, only returning to India in October 1920 after six years' absence.

As mentioned, the 7th Hariana Lancers also originated as a Bengal Irregular Cavalry unit, the 16th raised in Meerut and Cawnpore by Captain Liptrott in February 1846. It was a raising born of the First Sikh War in anticipation of the Second. The following year, they were relegated to become the 17th Bengal Irregular Horse. When the Second Sikh War broke out, they did not become offensively engaged but found themselves in the reserve force, all ranks receiving the Punjab medal.

The outbreak of the Mutiny in May 1857 found the 17th on the Frontier and although recruited from rebel districts, the men remained loyal.

In 1861, when the Bengal Army was being reconstructed, the irregular cavalry regiments numbered from the 8th to the 16th were disbanded and the 17th became the 7th Bengal Cavalry.

They went to Burma in 1886 for the Third Burma War and this was their last action until the Great War.

In 1900, their title changed to the 7th Bengal Lancers and, again in 1903, this time to simply the 7th Lancers. Yet again, in 1904, they suffered another change of title. For no very apparent reason, based on the fact that many of their men came from that particular district, they became the 7th Hariana Lancers. No other regiment was so differentiated.

They arrived in Mesopotamia on 9 Mar 15 and fought in the three-day battle of Shaiba where, on 13 April 15, Major G C M Wheeler received a posthumous Victoria Cross for gallantry in the attack. Subsequently, one squadron was lost in Kut-al-Amara but the rest of the regiment served on and returned to Bolarum in October 1916. In 1920, they returned to Mesopotamia once more but were back in time for the amalgamation at Risalpur in November 1921.

The initial new title was, briefly, the 6/7th Cavalry but that was soon changed to the 18th King Edward's Own Cavalry. The new badge was to be crossed lances with '18' on the intersection and the Prince of Wales's plumes above:

across the lance-butts, the scroll read *'King Edward's Own'*. In 1937, on the occasion of the Coronation of HM King George VI, the title became more specific and they became the 18th King Edward VII's Own Cavalry. An appropriate change was made to the title-scroll of the badge.

Orders were issued in October 1939 for the mechanisation of three regiments – 2nd Royal Lancers (Gardner's Horse), PAVO Cavalry and the 18th Cavalry – as the components of 3 Indian Motor Brigade within 1 Indian Armoured Division. The concept of a motor cavalry regiment was a new one and much regimental initiative and inspiration was displayed. Finally, the entire brigade sailed for Egypt from Bombay on 26 Jan 41.

After a stand by one squadron at El Mechili, the rest of the regiment was besieged in Tobruk for five months until relieved in August 1941. A spell in Syria followed before a return to the desert where, within thirty-six hours of its arrival, three Axis divisions attacked the brigade which responded by destroying sixty enemy tanks. Thereafter, in August 1942, they returned to Iran to join 31 Indian Armoured Division but returned to India when infantry battalions had arrived to replace the motor cavalrymen. Back in Rawalpindi, Stuart tanks were issued and training began for South East Asia Command. However, VJ-Day intervened and, in March 1946, newly-equipped with Sherman tanks, the 18th KEO Cavalry joined 3 Independent Armoured Brigade at Risalpur.

On Partition in August 1947, the 18th King Edward VII's Own Cavalry was allotted to India. Their Kaimkhani squadron was transferred to Probyn's Horse and a Sikh squadron was received from the PAVO Cavalry but that was later passed on to the 3rd Cavalry and the 18th accepted a squadron of Hindustani Mussalmans under raising in the 2nd Royal Lancers.

BATTLE HONOURS

Punniar, Moodkee, Ferozeshah, Sobraon, Punjaub, Tel–el–Kebir, Egypt 1882, Burma 1885–87, Punjab Frontier, Somme 1916, Morval, Cambrai 1917, France & Flanders 1914–18, Megiddo, Sharon, Damascus, Palestine 1918, Shaiba, Kut-al-Amara 1915, Ctesiphon, Tigris 1916, Mesopotamia 1915–16, El Mechili, The Kennels, Defence of Tobruk, North Africa 1940–43.

BOOKS

'Regimental history of the 18th King Edward VII's Own Cavalry' by Lieut. Col L Lawrence-Smith. (Pub. The Station Press, Meerut, 1938)

CHANGES OF TITLE

Pre–1903	6th Prince of Wales's Own Bengal Cavalry	7th Bengal Lancers
1903	6th Prince of Wales's Own Cavalry	7th Lancers
1904	6th Prince of Wales's Own Cavalry	7th Hariana Lancers
1905	6th King Edward's Own Cavalry	7th Hariana Lancers

1921	6/7th Cavalry
1922	18th King Edward's Own Cavalry
1937	18th King Edward VII's Own Cavalry

19th KING GEORGE V's OWN LANCERS

The two regiments which, in 1922, went to form the 19th King George's Own Lancers were 18th King George's Own Lancers and 19th Lancers (Fane's Horse).

The 18th Bengal Cavalry – to use the 1861 title – was raised in 1858 at Gwalior as the Tiwana Horse, in the wake of the Great Mutiny. Joined with the 2nd Mahratta Horse in 1861, the 18th Bengal Cavalry was born. Tiwanas were a Mussalman Rajput class (from Jhelum and Shahpur, both now in Pakistan), with a reputation for sporting and soldierly qualities.

A Lieutenant Fane of the Madras Native Infantry was responsible for the raising of the 19th in 1860 at Cawnpore. It might seem curious that, at a time when cavalry regiments were being disbanded, a new one was being created for service in China. However, the regiment was to cross the sea and so all the sowars were required to be men who would be able to do so by their caste–laws. Queen Victoria had been denied her treaty–rights to have her envoy in Peking and an Anglo-French force was being mustered to re–establish this post. Fane called for volunteers from the disbanded regiments and these were forthcoming largely from the then disbanding 3rd Hodson's Horse – Sikhs, Pathans and Punjabi Mussalmans. Reaching Calcutta, Fane's Horse found itself brigaded with the 1st Sikh Irregular Cavalry (later Probyn's Horse) and HM's 1st King's Dragoon Guards, bound for Hong Kong. They chased off the Tartar cavalry once they reached China and facilitated the taking of the Taku Forts. Five Indians of Fane's Horse won the Indian Order of Merit and, on its return to India, the Regiment found itself the 19th Bengal Cavalry.

In 1847, they became the 19th Bengal Lancers despite having already been lance–armed for ten years.

Both 18th and 19th served in the Second Afghan War, the former in a lines-of-communication protection role. Whilst this might seem to have been something of a backwater, it must be remembered that the supply–route ran through Waziristan and Mahsud territory where the indigenous population was not slow to seize its opportunities for plunder. The 19th were in the Kandahar garrison and went to Kabul to link up with Roberts, taking part in the notable action at Ahmad Khel.

The 18th served in the Tirah expedition of 1897–98, occasioned by the tribal uprising but the 19th was not in action again until 1908 when they were involved in the Zakha Khel and Mohmand operations on the Frontier.

In 1903, the 18th became the 18th Tiwana Lancers, a title that they were not destined to hold for long. HRH The Prince of Wales, during his visit to India in 1906, became their Colonel-in-Chief so that they then became the 18th (Prince of Wales's Own) Tiwana Lancers.

The 19th became the 19th Lancers (Fane's Horse) in 1903 and it was under that title that they came to the merger in 1921.

In the meantime, the Prince of Wales had acceded to the throne as HM King George V and the 18th was the obvious regiment to act as his escort for the state entry into Delhi at the Coronation Durbar in 1912.

One incident connected with the 18th deserving of notice was not linked in any way with enemy action. At the outbreak of the Great War, a detachment of the Regiment was escorting a boundary commission in North Persia and the British Officer was ordered to return alone. The remaining nineteen Indian soldiers under an Indian officer, Jemadar Tiwakli Khan were to follow, bringing the British officer's dog and two Persian chickens. One man died on the way but the party eventually reached India, 1,600 miles later, after travelling through hostile territory; both chickens and the dog were safe but one horse had fallen down a precipice. In due course, the party rejoined their unit in France from where King George V summoned the jemadar to London to decorate him personally with the Order of British India.

By this time, of course, the 18th were already in Europe in December 1914 in 7 (Meerut) Cavalry Brigade of 2 Indian Cavalry Division.

The 19th had already arrived the previous month with 2 (Sialkot) Cavalry Brigade of 1 Indian Cavalry Division. Both regiments were to serve in all the actions of the Indian Cavalry Corps. At the start of 1918, they set off for Palestine, the 19th setting a record in the approach to Damascus – 250 miles in a week. The 18th reached Aleppo on 31 Oct 18, the day of the Turkish Armistice.

November 1920 found the 18th back in India, the 19th following early in 1921 and they amalgamated in New Delhi on 23 Aug 21.

The new badge was to be crossed lances with the Cypher 'GRI' on the intersection. '19' above and a crown above all; across the lance–butts, a title scroll read 'King George's Own'.

When war broke out in 1939, 19th King George V's Own Lancers had, with the Poona Horse, been scheduled to remain horsed. All eighteen cavalry regiments were now to be mechanised and a further eighteen were to be raised to meet India's defence commitments. Notwithstanding, the 19th was the last to mechanise at the end of 1941 when it joined 1 Indian Armoured Division as its reconnaissance regiment. The division, with the 19th, moved to Karachi, equipped with Humber armoured cars but HQ 31 Indian Armoured Division (the re-numbered 1 Indian Armoured Division – to avoid confusion with British formations, in April 1942) moved alone, without its regiments in June 1942. In 1943, the Regiment moved to Madras on coast-watching duties against an anticipated Japanese landing but, the following year it was equipped with Sherman tanks and joined 50 Indian Tank Brigade near Poona. The brigade was to join XV Indian Corps in the Arakan and it fought there from December 1944 until March 1945. After taking part in the capture of Akyab and the Ramree landings the 19th joined 26 Indian Division and landed with it south of Rangoon on 2 May 45. In June, it returned to India and later joined 3 Armoured Brigade at Rislapur before moving to Peshawar.

When Partition came in August 1947, the 19th King George V's Own Lancers were allotted to Pakistan. Their Jat squadron was exchanged with the Punjabi Mussalman squadron of the Central India Horse and their Sikh squadron replaced the Mussalman squadron of Skinner's Horse.

BATTLE HONOURS

Taku Forts, Pekin 1860, Ahmad Khel, Afghanistan 1878–80, Tirah, Punjab Frontier, Somme 1916, Bazentin, Flers-Courcelettes, Morval, Cambrai 1917, France & Flanders 1914–18, Megiddo, Sharon, Damascus, Palestine 1918, Buthidaung, Rangoon Road, Mayu Valley, Myebon, Kangaw, Ru–Ywa, Dalet, Tamandu, Burma 1942–45.

BOOKS

'History of the 19th King George's Own Lancers' by General Sir Havelock Hudson GCB. (Pub: Gale & Polden Ltd Aldershot 1937)

'The Spirit of a Regiment' by Brigadier JG Pocock. (Pub: Gale & Polden Ltd. Aldershot 1962)

CHANGES OF TITLE

Pre-1903	18th Bengal Lancers	19th Bengal Lancers
1903	18th Tiwana Lancers	19th Lancers (Fane's Horse)

1921	18/19th Lancers
1922	19th King George's Own Lancers
1938	19th King George V's Own Lancers

20th LANCERS

Both regiments which went to form the 20th Lancers in the reforms after the Great War were born of the days of the Great Mutiny of the Bengal Army in 1857.

Moreover, both of them were single-class regiments: the 14th Murray's Jat

Lancers consisted of Hindu Jats whilst the 15th Lancers (Cureton's Multanis) was made up of Multani Pathans and related tribes. The Jat Horse Yeomanry under Captain Murray of the disbanded Gwalior Contingent, was the first Jat unit to be raised by the Honourable East India Company and, whilst fighting several containing actions against bodies of rebel troops, did not qualify for Mutiny honours. Subsequently they served in the Bhutan Field Force and in the Second Afghan War where they attracted the favourable notice of Roberts. In May 1902, the then General Sir John Murray KCB died and, the following year, the Regiment became the 14th Murray's Jat Lancers, usually shortened to 'Murray's Jats'.

In the Great War, they served on the North-West Frontier in 1915 before going to Mesopotamia in 1916.

The 15th Lancers were originally raised as The Multanee Regiment of Cavalry from Pathan and Baluch tribesmen of the Derajat District who volunteered to serve against the mutineers in 1857. Captain C. Cureton of the 2nd Irregular Cavalry took command and led them to central India in actions similar to those of Murray's Jats. Later, they gained Afghanistan 1878–80 as an honour but were only employed on the Baluchistan border.

In August 1914, the 15th Lancers, as they had become in 1861, mobilised for service in France with the Lahore Division where, in fact, they were the first Indian cavalry to arrive. Leaving France in December 1915, they went to Persia to patrol the East Persia Cordon, designed to keep enemy propagandists out of Afghanistan.

During the war, the 15th ceased to be a class Mussalman regiment. The heavy demand for recruits to replace war wastage could not be met with Mussalman reinforcements and two squadrons had to be recruited from Jats.

After the Great War, the 14th and 15th Lancers joined to become the 20th Lancers at Sialkot on 21 Sep 20. The badge chosen for the new regiment was crossed lances, a crown on the intersection above 'XX' and a scroll, 'Lancers' below.

In 1937, in line with new plans for the Indian Army's cavalry, the 20th Lancers ceased to be an active regiment, becoming the permanent training regiment for the 3rd Indian Cavalry Group, stationed at Lucknow.

BATTLE HONOURS

Charasiah, Kabul 1879, Afghanistan 1878–80, Neuve Chapelle, France & Flanders 1914–15, Kut-al-Amara 1917, Sharqat, Mesopotamia 1916–18, Persia 1916–19, North-West Frontier, India 1915.

BOOKS

'15th Lancers (Cureton's Multanis) 1858–1908' – Anon
(Supt. of Govt. Printing, Calcutta, 1910)

CHANGES OF TITLE

Pre-1903	14th Bengal Lancers (Murray's Jat Horse)	15th (Cureton's Multani) Bengal Lancers
1903	14th Murray's Jat Lancers	15th Lancers (Cureton's Multanis)

1921	14/15th Lancers
1922	20th Lancers

THE CENTRAL INDIA HORSE (21st KING GEORGE V's OWN HORSE)

Originating as a local corps in Central India and consolidating loyal elements of sundry cavalry units in 1858 under Captain H O Mayne of the Hyderabad Contingent, the predecessors of the Central India Horse underwent several changes of identity. At one time, in 1860, Mayne's Horse consisted of three regiments soon to be reduced to two, primarily for service in Central India but willing to serve anywhere, at home or abroad. Mayne, alas, was not popular with his political masters. He was posted to the Madras Army and his command restyled the 1st and 2nd Central India Horse, destined to serve under a succession of distinguished cavalry leaders – Daly of the Guides, Sam Browne VC, Dighton Probyn VC, and John Watson VC. They marched with 'Bobs' from Kabul to Kandahar in the Second Afghan War, thereby earning their first battle–honour. They went on to serve on the Frontier in 1897, earning another.

The reorganization in 1903 saw the two regiments re–styled the 38th and the 39th Central India Horse and, in 1906, a Royal Colonel–in–Chief HRH The Prince of Wales, was appointed, making both regiments 'Prince of Wales's Own', a title changed a few years later, on the Prince's accession, to 'King George's Own'.

In 1911, the 39th were sent to Persia where they remained for almost two years, protecting the King-Emperor's subjects from the depredations of local dissidents.

The Great War saw the 38th in France in December 1914 as part of the Mhow Brigade of the 2nd Indian Cavalry Division. They moved on to Palestine under Allenby and finally returned to India in February 1921 after further service in Syria, after more than six years abroad.

The 39th Central India Horse remained in India throughout the war.

In 1923, the 38th and 39th with their shared title and common origins enjoyed a virtually painless merger into one regiment as The Central India Horse (21st King George V's Own Horse). The badge was crossed lances with the monogram 'CIH' on the intersection and a crown above.

Mechanization was ordered in September 1939 and the Regiment handed over its horses to Hodson's Horse prior to moving to Secunderabad in November on conversion to a motor cavalry regiment. The first Indian cavalry regiment to serve overseas, the Central India Horse sailed for Egypt in July 1940 without its Sikh Squadron which had mutinied in Bombay and refused to embark. The Dogra squadron of the 11th PAVO Cavalry (Frontier Force) was transferred to take its place. Once in Egypt the CIH went on to serve in the Western Desert, in Italian East Africa, in Paiforce, Italy and Greece.

The Willcox Committee had also recommended that the Central India Horse be disbanded after the war, but, like the 3rd Cavalry and the 19th Lancers, the CIH lived on to see Partition which guaranteed their survival.

On Partition in August 1947, the Regiment was allotted to India. Their Punjabi Mussalman squadron was transferred to the 19th Lancers, who were going to Pakistan, in exchange for the latter's Jat Squadron.

BATTLE HONOURS

Kandahar 1880, Afghanistan 1879–80, Punjab Frontier, Somme 1916, Morval Cambrai 1917, France & Flanders 1914–18, Megiddo, Sharon, Damascus, Palestine 1918, Keren-Asmara Road, Abyssinia 1940–41, Relief of Tobruk 1941, North Africa 1940–43, Gothic Line, Italy 1944–45, Greece 1944–45.

BOOKS

'King George V's Own Central India Horse' by Major General W A Watson CB CMG. CIE (Blackwood, Edinburgh, 1930)

'King George V's Own Central India Horse' by Brig A A Filose (Vol II of the regimental history). (Blackwood, Edinburgh 1950)

CHANGES OF TITLE

Pre-1903	1st Central India Horse	2nd Central India Horse
1903	38th Central India Horse	39th Central India Horse
1906	38th Prince of Wales's Own Central India Horse	39th Prince of Wales's Own Central India Horse
1921	38th/39th Cavalry	
1922	38/39th King George's Own Light Cavalry	
1923	21st King George's Own Central India Horse	
1927	The Central India Horse (21st King George's Own Horse)	
1937	The Central India Horse (21st King George V's Own Horse	

ARTILLERY

The history of the Gun in India dates back to the fifteenth century but it was Babar, the Moghul emperor, who used it so decisively in 1526 at the battle of Panipat. The patent superiority of the new weapon made it essential that successive Moghul emperors should not recruit the subject races of India into the new artillery arm. The Moghul artillery was to be manned at first by Persians and Turks and, later, by Europeans, half-castes and Christian converts. Subsequently, Europeans – British, French, Portugese and Dutch – were recruited not only as gunners but as consultants in gun construction.

The artillery arm developed apace under the Emperor Akbar and new, wheeled carriages, such as had been in use in Europe for years, were adopted, giving a new mobility in battle.

Notwithstanding earlier strictures on their use, Indian gunners proved to be apt pupils and, after the Sikh Wars, many Sikh gunners were enlisted by the British into the Company's artillery.

Regular artillery companies had been approved by the Honourable East India Company in 1748 for the three Presidency armies of Bengal, Madras and Bombay. These were not the first gunners to be mustered but they were the first formal units. Despite the acceptance of Indians in certain gunnery duties, the technicalities of the chemistry behind the art were to be denied them.

Thus, the Court of Directors ruled that–

> *'No foreigner whether in our service or not (except such as hath been admitted into it by the Court of Directors) nor no Indian black or person of mixed breed, nor any Roman Catholic of what nation soever, shall on any pretence be admitted to set foot in the laboratory, or any of the Military Magazines, either out of curiosity, or to be employed in them, or to come near them, nor shall any such person have a copy or sight of any accounts or papers relating to any military stores whatsoever'*

With the conclusion of the Second Sikh War, the British made the acquaintance of the North West Frontier. Some seven hundred miles of mountainous border stretching from Hazara to Sind had to be secured and mountain artillery was to come into prominence. Thus, before the Great Mutiny in 1857, the Company's artillery consisted of the mountain units, the horse artillery and the somewhat curiously–termed 'foot' artillery (Field gunners). The last two were made up of British and Indians but the new mountain trains consisted of Indians only under a British commanding officer.

The Mutiny saw almost the entire Bengal native artillery rise in arms against the British except for the newly-raised mountain trains and the Horse Field batteries employed on the Frontier. After 1858, the task of rebuilding the Bengal Army brought to the fore the question of the artillery's future. Almost unanimous opinion was that there should be no more native artillery: House of Commons paper No. 216 of 1859 recorded the view of the Governor General.

> *'In no way in future should the natives of the country be entrusted with British Artillery, nor should any native in India be instructed in the use of such dangerous weapons. The native drivers are good horsemen, and the gunners most excellent: and in proportion as they are most valuable to the government they serve, so are they more formidable when they choose to be rebellious'.*

The European part of India's artillery was to be handed over to the Royal Artillery. Two mountain trains, the three Piffer batteries and two Bombay Native Artillery companies were to survive plus four field batteries of the Hyderabad Contingent in Madras Presidency. Within the next twenty years, two of the Piffer batteries (the third had been disbanded in 1870) and the Bombay companies had reclassified as mountain batteries. The Piffers became the 1st (Kohat) Mountain Battery FF and the 2nd (Derajat) Mountain Battery FF whilst the Peshawar Mountain Battery became 3rd and the Hazara the 4th. At the same time, the two Bombay batteries were redesignated the 1st and 2nd Bombay Mountain Batteries. The 1st Bombay, with unbroken service since 1827, thus became the oldest Indian unit of artillery and this was recalled in 1990 when India's 57 Mountain Regt celebrated 163 years of history as Artillery Day. Thitherto, the 1935 date of raising of the 1st Indian Field Brigade had been observed as the anniversary for the Regiment of Artillery.

The four Frontier Force batteries and the 2nd (Bombay) were engaged in the Second Afghan War whilst the Hazara Battery and the 1st (Bombay) went on to Burma. Two further mountain batteries were raised for that campaign, the 7th (Bengal) at Rawalpindi and the 8th (Lahore) at Mian Mir. To keep things tidy, the 1st and 2nd (Bombay) were re–numbered the 5th and 6th respectively. After the Punjab Frontier campaign of 1897–98 the 9th (Murree) was raised at Abbottabad in 1890 and the 10th (Abbottabad) raised there in 1900–01.

In 1901, the numbers were dropped and the mountain batteries were known only by their names but the 1903 reforms brought the numbers back and added twenty to each old number. Thus, the Kohat Mountain Battery was restyled the 21st Kohat Mountain Battery FF and so on. After the Great War, in 1920, during the course of which no Indian gunner units went to Europe, authority decreed that heavy artillery was henceforth to be known as medium artillery whilst mountain artillery was to become pack artillery. The next year, numbers were again changed when one hundreed was added to the original battery numbers, changing the old 1st (Kohat) into the 101st (Kohat) Pack Battery, etc.

In 1922, the 101st became the 101st Royal (Kohat) Pack Battery FF as recognition of the services of the mountain batteries during the recent conflict. In 1924, the letters 'RA' were added to battery titles. Finally, on 1 May 27 the designation 'Pack' was discarded and 'Mountain' restored: one hundred was deducted from the battery numbers and the old 1st (Kohat) became the 1st once again as the 1st Royal (Kohat) Mountain Battery RA (FF).

By 1920, fifty mountain batteries had been raised but seventeen of these had been disbanded or dispersed before the 1939–45 war began.

Indian Coast Artillery was a post 1920 creation with companies in Bombay, Calcutta, Karachi and Rangoon, the object being to assist coast defence companies of the Royal Garrison Artillery in non–technical duties.

The decision during the Great War to commission Indians was not immediately implemented in the artillery which had to wait until 1935 for its first Indian officers.

On 15 Jan 35, 'A' Field Brigade (a regiment in today's terms) was formed at Bangalore to take the place of 14 Field Brigade RA on reversion to the United Kingdom establishment. It was made up of RHQ and four field batteries:

1 (Madras) Fd Bty	(Madrassis)
2 Fd Bty	(Cis–Beas Punjabi Mussulmans)
3 Fd Bty	(Rajputana Rajputs)
4 Fd Bty	(Ranghars)

The incorporation of 'Madras' into the title of 1 Fd Bty marked the raising of that unit largely by transfers from 'A' Company of the last remaining unit of the Madras Pioneers. Training of NCOs had begun a year earlier. The first Indian officer was 2/Lt. Prem Singh Gyani (retired as lieutenant general in 1965) to be followed quickly by two others, P.P. Kumaramangalam and A.S. Kalha. Being created on the Royal Artillery model, the regiment had no establishment for VCOs and instead, Warrant Officers I and II were authorised. Armament was 18 pounders in 1 and 2 Batteries and 4.5″ howitzers in 3 and 4 Batteries, a total of eight guns and eight howitzers. Dress was substantially the same as was worn by the European gunners but pagris took the place of the foreign service helmet, being worn in the military styles formalized for their respective classes.

On 1 Aug 39, mountain artillery ceased to be RA and became Indian Artillery but no IA component went to Africa with 4 Indian Division that year.

A second field regiment (the title had now been changed) was authorized on 15 May 40 as 'B' Field Regiment, again at Bangalore. Thereafter, Indian heavy batteries, anti-aircraft regiments and anti-tank regiments were raised, all distinguished by an alphabetical designation but on 2 Apr 41 this changed and thus 'A' Fd Regt became 1 Indian Field Regiment and 'K' Anti-Tank Regt became 1 Indian Anti-Tank Regiment.

Cadres for the new raisings came from 1 Indian Fd Regt and the mountain batteries but these had now been milked almost dry and it was proposed that twelve infantry battalions be converted, with their officers, into gunners. Five were to become anti–tank regiments, four to become light anti–aircraft regiments and three heavy anti-aircraft regiments (details of these are given in the various regimental entries).

Sixty-six regiments were raised during 1939–45: one of these was lost in Malaya and ten were disbanded. One pre-war mountain regiment was lost in Malaya. The years 1943–44 saw the Indian Artillery at peak strength of sixty-four regiments.

During the war, Indian gunners served in East Africa. Malaya, the Middle East, Italy and Burma where their only Victoria Cross was awarded to Havildar Umrao Singh for supreme and sustained gallantry in the Kaladan Valley during a Japanese attack on the 15/16 Dec 44.

His Majesty the King-Emperor was pleased to confer the title 'Royal' on the Regiment in the light of its performance in that war.

The post-war rundown in strength reached a low of twenty-eight regiments, the strength of the Royal Indian Artillery at the time of Partition. Indianization of the officer-cadre was not envisaged for some time; only two Indian officers had reached the rank of lieutenant-colonel – Prem Singh Gyani and P P Kumaramangalam, the latter with a DSO, both original officers from 'A' Field Brigade in 1935.

Following the 2:1 split of the twenty–eight regiments on Partition, India received eighteen and a half whilst Pakistan received nine and a half. The allocation of the regiments was as follows:

INDIA	**PAKISTAN**
1 Fd Regt (SP) RIA	3 Fd Regt (SP) RPA
2 Fd Regt (SP) RIA	4 Fd Regt RPA
7 Fd Regt RIA	5 Fd Regt RPA
8 Fd Regt RIA	
9 Para Fd Regt RIA	
11 Fd Regt RIA	12 Fd Regt RPA
13 Fd Regt RIA	
16 Fd Regt RIA	
17 Para Fd Regt RIA	18 HAA Regt RPA
20 Survey Regt RIA (less one battery)	21 Mountain Regt RPA
22 Mountain Regt RIA	
24 Mountain Regt RIA	25 LAA Regt RPA
26 LAA Regt RIA	
27 LAA Regt RIA	33 A/Tk Regt RPA
34 Mahratta A/Tk Regt (SP) RIA	
35 Lingayat A/Tk Regt RIA	
36 Mahratta A/Tk Regt RIA	
37 Coorg A/Tk Regt RIA	38 Med Regt RPA
40 Med Regt RIA	

The badge chosen for the Regiment of Indian Artillery was the traditional gun of the Royal Artillery but with a five-pointed star in place of the crown: the upper scroll bore the word 'India' whilst the lower scrolls bore 'Izzat o Iqbal', a reasonable Urdu translation of 'Honour and Glory' from the Royal Artillery motto. After Partition, the word 'Sarvatra' (Sanskrit) replaced 'India' on the upper scroll, a translation of the Latin 'Ubique' for 'Everywhere'. The balance of the Urdu motto was retained.

The Royal Pakistan Artillery took the gun–badge of the Royal Artillery, initially retaining even the crown but incorporating the Star and Crescent on the wheel. On the upper scroll was a vernacular rendering of 'Pakistan' whilst the lower scrolls carried the traditional 'Izzat o Iqbal', also in the same script.

After India became a republic in January 1950, the 'Royal' part of the title was dropped. The prefix 'Indian' was felt to be redundant and it became simply The

Regiment of Artillery. Units were to drop the 'RIA' from the end of the designations and substitute the word 'Artillery'.

Pakistan did not claim republican status until 1956 when the 'Royal' part of the title of the Royal Pakistan Artillery was discarded: a flaming grenade replaced the crown but the scrolls remained as before.

Sadly, the two erstwhile parts of the Royal Indian Artillery have spent the greater part of the past four decades in confrontation of each other. They have grown immensely, both in numbers and sophistication of equipment, much of it Russian in India and Chinese in Pakistan. New skills have been taught and military lessons learned. Only the politicians now appear to be in need of training.

Born of the needs of the artillery arm in both countries was an air element, Pakistan was the first to raise an Army Aviation Corps in 1975 which is now well established. India was rather slower and most of the Indian Corps pilots are operating in an Air OP role.

BOOKS

'History of The Regiment of Artillery, Indian Army' by Major General DK Palit VrC. (Pub. Leo Cooper, London 1972)

'Izzat o Iqbal' by Major General Shaukat Riza. (Pub. School of Artillery, Nowshera 1980)

ENGINEERS

The engineer establishment in British India consisted, in broad terms, of two categories. The one, purely military in make–up and function, was the four corps of Sappers and Miners, whilst the other was the Military Works Services, or Military Engineer Services as they later came to be called.

The duties of the latter category were mainly those which would have been handled in the UK by civilian contractors working under War Office control on static locations. The Sappers and Miners were the soldiers and it is with them that this chapter deals.

The first unit of 'Pioneers' was formed of European volunteers during the siege of Madras in 1759. A corps of European officers had infantry troops placed under their command for specific tasks and their training was what would now be described as of the 'hands–on' variety. Once the campaign was over, the units would revert to their normal infantry role or would be disbanded as redundant in the prudent fashion of British governments down the centuries. Cawnpore was the birthplace in 1803 of the Corps of Bengal Pioneers albeit some had served on a temporary basis in 1764. Bombay's 'Pioneer Lascar Company' was authorized in 1777. The three Presidency armies, of course, were effectively autonomous and there was no co-ordination between them in terms of titles or establishments. Not so the Burma unit which sprang, ready made, from the Madras Corps in July 1887, to be born as the Burma Sappers and Miners.

The Bengal Corps became Bengal Sappers and Miners in February 1819 with its headquarters at Allahabad. The following year, the Bombay Sappers and Miners were so designated on the 1st August, but it was not until May 1831 that the Madras Sappers and Miners received their title. Most of the latter were stationed at Bangalore, a pleasant cantonment which was destined to remain their home.

The Bengal Sappers and Miners succeeded in registering one of the few successes of the disastrous First Afghan War when they blew the Kabul Gate of the fort at Ghuznee in July 1839. At the conclusion of that campaign, an ad hoc body known as Broadfoot's Sappers – having been raised by Captain George Broadfoot, 34th MNI, despite the presence of companies from Bombay, Bengal and Madras Corps in the force – put iron into the hearts of the defending force at Jellalabad. In recognition, Broadfoot's command, then three companies strong, was incorporated into the Bengal Corps in early 1843.

At the onset of the Great Mutiny in May 1857, a proportion of the Bengal sappers, based at Roorkee, joined the mutineers in Delhi but the subsequent conduct of the remaining men who took part in the breaching of the Kashmir Gate at Delhi and at the relief of Lucknow did much to erase the stigma of mutiny from the corps.

In the Second Afghan War, all three Corps were present although, not for the first time, they were deprived of adequate transport and suffered from poor equipment. Notably, the 2nd Company of the Bombay Sappers earned martial glory by their stand at Maiwand with the survivors of HM's 66th Foot against thousands of fanatical Ghilzais.

It was during this campaign that the Bengal Sappers received as their commandant Major Bindon Blood RE, an evocative name for an officer destined to reach general officer rank, who was responsible for proposing an all-embracing scheme for the reorganization of the Sappers and Miners in India. This took five years but the Indian Army Order born of this lengthy gestation was the Sappers' guideline until the outbreak of the Great War in 1914.

The campaign in Abyssinia in 1867 was less one for soldiering than it was for engineer work and both the Madras and the Bombay Corps took part. It was to be barely eighty years before Indian troops were to be again in that country in a campaign against the Italians.

Other overseas ventures ranged from Egypt to China via Somaliland. In particular, the Madras Sappers distinguished themselves in the Sudan in 1885 when they helped to avert a major disaster at McNeill's zareba outside Suakin. Hardly had the troops returned to India when all three Corps were called upon to furnish companies for the Third Burmese War in the force's advance up the Irrawaddy to Mandalay under Major General HND Prendergast VC CB. The force was well-provided with engineer companies, not surprising perhaps when the commander-in-chief in the field was himself a sapper. The campaign was brief but the aftermath unpleasant and unhealthy.

The raising of a Burma Company of Sappers and Miners was authorised on 9 Jul 1887, being affilitiated initially to the Madras Corps. Recruiting was slow at first and the company did not reach full-strength until October 1890.

It was in 1885 that the Corps of Sappers and Miners came to be officered exclusively by officers of the Royal Engineers, many of whom, despite their British Service status, spent their entire army life in India after being commissioned.

The North-West Frontier came to be an area of opportunity for what were then called service companies – field companies after 1909 – it provided the chance for improvization which Sapper officers excelled in and in which the Indian other ranks offered such inspired support. In the main, training manuals did not cover the requirements of the harsh frontier terrain with its steep gradients, deep gorges, mountain torrents, all exacerbated by a less than welcoming indigenous population. Bridging became an urgent priority to maintain the impetus of advance of the infantry columns and to ensure their re-supply. The North-East Frontier also saw its share of expeditions, the most significant, perhaps, being that to Tibet in 1904. This was commanded by a Sapper, Major-General J R L Macdonald: the passes rose to as much as 17,000 feet whilst the crossing of the Tsanpo River presented its own problems, resolved by use of locally-extemporised bridging equipment. Both Bengal and Madras Sappers took part in this venture.

The reforms of 1903 brought organisational changes. The Bengal Corps became the 1st Sappers and Miners. In 1906, HRH The Prince of Wales became their Colonel-in-Chief and gave permission for his plumes to be borne on colours and appointments. The new title became the 1st Prince of Wales's Own Sappers and Miners. Republican status notwithstanding, the device is still in daily use at Roorkee although the title was enhanced to the 1st King George's Own Sappers and Miners in 1910. In 1907, class-composition was laid down as:

No. 1 Coy – ½ Sikhs, ½ Punjabi Mussalmans
No. 2 Coy – ½ Sikhs, ½ Punjabi Mussalmans
No. 3 Coy – Hindustanis
No. 4 Coy – ½ Sikhs, ½ Pathans
No. 5 Coy – ½ Sikhs, ½ Punjabi Mussalmans
No. 6 Coy – Hindustanis

Balloon Section (formed in 1901) – Punjabi Mussalmans

'A' and 'B' Coys – Mixed

Mounted detachment Sikhs

The Madras Corps had been made the Queen's Own Corps of Sappers and Miners in 1876 and were made the 2nd QOS & M in 1903.

The class-composition was:

Indian Christians and Pariahs	50%
Tamil Hindus	21%
Telegu Hindus	12½%
Mussalmans	12½%
Other castes	4%

However, the Madras Corps tradition was that caste should not be recognised in service matters.

The Bombay Sappers and Miners became the 3rd Sappers and Miners, recruiting ⅛ Rajputs, ¼ Mahrattas, ¼ Mussalmans, ⅛ Sikhs and ¼ Mixed – the latter to include Brahmins, Ahirs, Telegus, etc.

The Burma Corps was not made the 4th but became the 15th (Burma) Company of the 2nd QO Sappers and Miners.

In 1911, the Madras Corps changed its title yet again, becoming the 2nd Queen Victoria's Own Sappers and Miners.

The various centres had, by now, been firmly established at Roorkee (1st S & M). Bangalore (2nd S & M), Kirkee (3rd S & M) and Mandalay (Burma Coy) and the first three stations remained in Sapper hands in independent India after 1947.

In every theatre of war in the years 1914–19, Indian sappers were deficient in modern weapons, transport and special-to-arm equipment. Despite these shortages, the traditional improvisational skills came to the fore and, not only were engineer tasks accomplished but Bengal and Bombay sappers took over part of the line in France. Losses of officers were such that before New Year's Day 1915, the Bombay companies had lost 300% of their officers.

In Egypt, Palestine and Iraq, railway communications and pipeline construction were the dominant tasks as also was railway work in East Africa which facilitated General Smuts' advance after an initial failure. Work in the Aden Protectorate continued despite heat and lack of water, securing that port on the main communication route to India, Australia and New Zealand. At home, of course, the North-West Frontier had been in almost constant unrest, culminating in the Third Afghan War in 1919, involving the normal tasks of maintaining communications and the water supply to the various expeditions.

Growth in numbers in the war-years had been remarkable. In August 1914, the total Indian strength of the three principal corps was approximately 4.400 and, in November 1918, that figure had grown to some 21,600, an impressive increase in numbers bearing in mind the essentially agrarian nature of the recruitment-pool. As a reward to the Bombay Corps for its wartime services, they were to become, in 1921, the 3rd Royal Bombay Sappers and Miners.

The years 1919 to 1922 saw the rundown in numbers by demobilization and reorganization. The 15th (Burma) Company of the 2nd Queen Victoria's Own Sappers and Miners was briefly brought into line in 1922 as the 4th Burma Sappers and Miners before yet another change in 1923 when numbers were dropped and the four corps were restyled as:

Queen Victoria's Own Madras Sappers and Miners
King George's Own Bengal Sappers and Miners
Royal Bombay Sappers and Miners
Burma Sappers and Miners

Early in the 1920s, the decision was made to build a railway from Peshawar to Landi Kotal, through the Khyber Pass. Although the construction was to be done by contract labour and not by men of the corps, the planning and supervision was carried out by Sapper officers and completed by 1925.

Five railway companies had existed during the war but 27, 28 and 29 Coys were disbanded in 1921 and 25 and 26 Coys a decade later. On the outbreak of war in September 1939, the Army in India had no railway service.

Signal Companies had been part of the Sappers and Miners' structure since

1911 although June 1869 was the earliest record of the Bengal Corps' involvement when the 9th Company was employed on telegraph work. The next year, the 5th Company built a field telegraph line from Rawalpindi to Kohat and, in 1871, the 6th Company erected a line from Dera Ismail Khan to Bannu. Still designated Sappers and Miners throughout the Great War where they served wherever the Indian Army went, they went on to become part of the Indian Signal Corps in December 1925.

Following the abolition of all the Pioneer units in the Indian Army in October 1932, an attempt was made to absorb as many of them into the Corps of Sappers and Miners as possible to minimise the discharges. No problems arose with the transfer of Madras Pioneers to QVO Madras Sappers and Miners but there arose some difficulties in connection with the transfer of some of the Sikhs to the Bengal and Bombay Corps. Details of these are covered in the chapters on Pioneers. The Burma Sappers and Miners were unaffected by these transfers since they were disbanded in April 1929, when the Government of Burma declined to meet the annual financial commitment involved.

It was not until 1937, when Burma was separated from India, that Burmans, Karens, Shans, Kachins and Chins could again be enlisted into an engineer unit.

Indianization, begun after the Great War, did not reach the Sappers and Miners until 1931 when the first Indians commissioned from the Royal Military Academy at Woolwich reached India. These became the first officers in the new Corps of Indian Engineers, to be followed later by officers commissioned from the Indian Military Academy which opened at Dehra Dun in 1932. Other ranks, with effect from 1 Oct 33, also enlisted into the new corps although they joined one of the three Sappers and Miners corps as before. Three field companies were selected for Indianisation (nos 5, 15, and 22); on 1 Apr 39, 22 Fd Coy, then at Kohat, began its life as an Indianised unit.

The outbreak of war in 1939 soon saw three companies, one each from the three Corps, on their way to Egypt. In 1941, six field units of the Bombay Corps were sent to Malaya, two-thirds of its regular units, all to be lost to the Japanese at Singapore. The increasing technicality and sophistication of modern warfare meant the creation of new specialist units and familiarization with jungle warfare. At the start of 1942, the three Corps of Sappers and Miners were renamed 'Groups', a term which embraced the centre and all field units. In 1946, after the war, the Indian Engineers were granted the title 'Royal' and the time-honoured title 'Sappers and Miners' had to be relinquished. Thus, 'QVO Madras Sappers and Miners Group, Indian Engineers' became 'QVO Madras Group, Royal Indian Engineers'.

In 1940, additional Engineer Training Centres were formed at Rawalpindi, Secunderabad, Quetta, Jhansi, Sialkot, Lucknow, Meerut, Nowshera, Dighi (Kirkee) and Kohat for the training of other ranks in all military engineering skills.

During the war, Indian sappers served in Egypt, East Africa, Paiforce, Italy, Greece, Burma, Malaya and the Dutch East Indies. A Madras Field Company went to Japan in 1946 as part of the British Commonwealth Occupation Force, attracting some attention with the 'dupta', the distinctive headdress – rather like a peakless shako – affected by their Corps.

When Partition came in August 1947, there were only some three Mussalman officers with pre-war commissioned service, the most senior Lieutenant Colonel Anwar Khan. Pakistan was to receive 34 engineer units whilst India had 61. India, of course, was to have the traditional three engineer centres in its territory. All units, except for a few overseas, had already been reorganised on a one-class basis. The Madras Engineer Centre at Bangalore was practically unaffected but the Bengal Centre at Roorkee lost its Mussalmans, some 50% of its strength. Similarly, the Bombay Centre at Kirkee lost about 40% of its strength with the removal of its Mussalman personnel. A centre was to be set up at Sialkot for the new Royal Pakistan Engineers and Pakistan's share of equipment and property would be furnished by the centre at Roorkee. The School of Military Engineering was to be at Risalpur in NWFP.

The badge of the Royal Indian Engineers was the five-pointed Star of India within a laurel wreath above a title-scroll. This remained in use notionally in India until January 1950 when a constitutional change to republican status brought a change of badge although the badge was, of course, not changed overnight. The new design incorporated, in the centre, a fort based on the design of the Purana Qila in Delhi within a Sikh chakra: above it the lions of Asoka and, below, a title scroll, reading 'Corps of Engineers', all within a wreath of lotus leaves. The motto 'Sarvatra' ('Everywhere') is to emphasise the link with the Corps of Royal Engineers and its motto 'Ubique'.

The Royal Pakistan Engineers chose to use as a badge the Sapper grenade above a title-scroll. After republican status was declared in 1956, the scroll was amended to read simply 'Corps of Engineers'.

BOOKS

'The Indian Sappers and Miners' by Lieut. Colonel E W C Sandes DSO MC RE. (Pub. Institution of Royal Engineers, Chatham 1948)

'The Indian Engineers' by Lieut. Colonel E W C Sandes DSO MC RE. (Pub. Institution of Military Engineers, Kirkee 1956)

SIGNALS

In April 1920, an Indian Army Order ruled that all Signal units (of the Sappers and Miners) would become a Corps '. . . in the Indian Army Act Rules with the designation Indian Signal Corps'.

Despite this, the signal units continued to be referred to as the Signal Service, Sappers and Miners in Indian Army Orders and in the Indian Army Lists. It was not until 12 Nov 22 that another Indian Army Order drew attention to the Indian Army Act Rules and laid down that the new designation would be taken into general use accordingly.

Somewhat surprisingly, therefore, the Indian Signal Corps had pre-dated the formation of the Corps of Signals in the British Army which took place on 28 Jun 20.

Appreciation of the vastness of its Indian Empire had early compelled Britain to examine the problem of communications and experiments were afoot in 1837 in the science of electric telegraphy in India. Men from the Royal Engineers Depot Battalion were despatched to work with the newly-formed Indian Telegraph Department and work began on the first line in Bengal. By 1856, Peshawar was linked to Calcutta via Agra, Agra via Bombay and Bangalore to Ootacamund and Madras. Further east, Rangoon was connected through Prome to the limit of British Burma. Thus, the service was in operation before the Great Mutiny in 1857 and men of the ITD found themselves indispensable to both the re-establishment of order and the subsequent pacification campaign in Central India. In a letter from Lahore in August 1857, Sir Robert Montgomery, the Judicial Commissioner, wrote 'Under Providence, the Electric Telephone has saved us'.

Army signalling, however, was a military skill exercised in India by British officers and soldiers who pursued their trade with flags, lamps and heliograph.

Some Indian regimental signallers were sent to the School of Army Signalling. Bangalore in 1876 to be instructed and, only a few years later, sepoy-signallers were used in the Second Afghan War. It was, however, not until 1887 that regular training and instruction of Indian ranks in signalling was considered and, in November 1888, complete sets of signalling equipment were sanctioned to a number of Indian cavalry and infantry regiments. Sixteen signallers were to be maintained in each unit, of whom the first eight were to receive an additional annual bonus of five rupees and a badge of crossed flags woven in worsted provided that they had passed the necssary standard and maintained that degree of efficiency. The first 'Manual of Instruction in Army Signalling' for Indian troops was published in 1896 in Urdu, Hindi, and Gurmukhi.

Few, if any, Indian signallers knew any English and the message had no meaning for them. They could, however, recognise block letters but had difficulty sometimes in reading ordinary English handwriting. Despite this, their results were considered creditable and comparable with British other ranks.

Flag-signalling had been developed by the US Army in 1835. In 1871, signalling-flags were authorised to British units in India but opinion of the system was not enthusiastic in the Second AfghanWar. A dark, cloudy day with a clear atmosphere is best for flag-work and, for that reason, it was much favoured in England. Conditions in Afghanistan favoured the heliograph. Signal messages were received over a distance of forty miles. A variant on the heliograph, the heliostat, was also in use and was taken to Egypt in 1882 by Madras Sappers. The heliostat was the invention of Captain E W Begbie, Instructor of Army Signalling at Bangalore. It differed from its parent heliograph in that the solar image was kept constantly and steadily fixed on the distant station being signalled to, whilst the flashes required for formation of the letters were achieved by opening and closing a venetian shutter. The heliograph altered the plane of its mirror to obtain the necessary flashes. On the Mahsud Waziri Expedition of 1881, a range of 67 miles was recorded, for a 12″ mirror, read with field-glasses.

Lamp-signalling was for night-work and the most highly-regarded of these were the Begbie Lamps in various sizes. The principle was a hand-lamp, a kerosene-oil lamp in a metal case, fitted with a noisy shutter-apparatus worked by a lever. Not everyone loved the Begbie Lamps and one officer observed that the 'clankety-clank noise, as the shutter opened and closed' could be heard farther off than the light it gave could be seen. Notwithstanding, the Central School of Signalling at Kasauli claimed a distance of 19 miles for the Begbie BB Lamps and 31 miles for the Begbie CC.

Field telegraphy was jealously guarded by the ITD who took part in operations in Burma (1885–87) Waziristan (1894-95), Chitral (1895), the Tochi Field Force (1897), Malakand (1897), Mohmand Field Force (1897) and the Tirah (1897–98) as well as Tibet in 1903–34. The Sapper Corps were relegated to maintaining instructional squads for duty with the ITD.

Kitchener, as Commander-in-Chief, India, having reorganised cavalry and infantry, turned to signals and proposed the formation of four telegraph companies, each 120 strong. These were approved in 1908 but not implemented. In 1909, a committee was set up in England to co-ordinate methods of communication and a similar committee followed in Simla to report on related requirements in India. It was suggested that four divisional signal companies and a wireless section be raised. The four telegraph companies projected in 1908 could become the divisional companies. The Viceroy advised London in August 1910 what had been agreed, stressing how economically *'the scheme put forward provides this important military service'* and seeking the Secretary of State for India's early sanction 'by telegram'. The Secretary of State for India responded with enviable economy *'Your confidential despatch 87, dated 4th August last. Signal companies I sanction scheme'*.

The units were to be Sappers and Miners units but were not parented to the Corps of Sappers and Miners. There was to be no connection between the signal units and the Corps except that their sepoys were to rank as sappers. In 1911, on formation, Nos 31 and 32 Companies were located at Fatehgarh, 33 and 34 Companies were located at Ahmednagar and 41 Wireless Company at Roorkee. The establishment of the divisional companies was to be 5 British Officers, 2 Indian officers (before 1935, VCOs were referred to as Indian Officers), 44 British and 86 Indian other ranks including eight recruits under training. Class composition was 50% Punjabi or UP Muslims and 50% Dogras and Rajputs in 31 and 32 Companies whilst 33 and 34 Companies were to be 50% Madrassi Muslims and 50% Tamils, Christians and Pariahs. Indian ranks qualifying as second-class visual signallers with knowledge of field cables or as first-class visual signallers or as second-class linemen received extra pay at three annas per day (1 Rupee = 16 Annas).

When war broke out in August 1914, the field army in India consisted nominally of nine divisions and eight cavalry brigades although only seven divisions and five cavalry brigades were fit for service. The four divisional signal companies and 41 Wireless Signal Company were the total signals resources of this army.

The 3rd (Lahore) Division was allocated 32 Coy and a new company, No. 35, was raised for the 7th (Meerut) Division, the two divisions which went to form Indian Expeditionary Force 'A' , bound for Egypt but destined for France. Interestingly, the nine motor-cycle despatch riders authorised on mobilisation joined in Cairo – British volunteers from the Bombay Light Horse and Calcutta Light Horse. They were not the only Volunteers: others who negotiated their way to the seats of war were almost all subsequently commissioned into Indian Army units perpetually short of officers.

Indian Expeditionary Force 'D', destined for Mesopotamia, was to spend four long years out of India, employing more Indian signal units than in any other theatre.

Indian Expeditionary Force 'C' was the brigade sent to Kenya to strengthen the modest force of two King's African Rifles battalions defending the British East Africa colonies.

Meanwhile, Indian Expeditionary Force 'B' was forming in India, a two brigade force – 27 (Bangalore) Brigade and an Imperial Service brigade of state force units – intended to conquer German East Africa.

Every conceivable problem was encountered in East Africa and every signalling medium exploited. Not least of the problems was colonial bureaucracy. The Chief Engineer in Nairobi, appointed Director of Field Telegraphs with accompanying rank of lieutenant-colonel, proposed to follow the advance into German territory, laying a telephone link of bare wire on the ground. It having been pointed out to him that dew and rain would prevent communication, he confessed that he thought this of no consequence just as long as contact was sometimes made. Some idea of the scale of Indian signals strength in East Africa can be gained by the fact that, during 1917, there were more than 750 ITD personnel alone.

Indian Expeditionary Force 'F' consisted of 28, 29 and 30 Indian Infantry Brigades in Egypt and they were followed by Indian Expeditionary Force 'E', another three brigade force. These two were quickly compounded into, respectively, 10th and 11th Indian Divisions and, of course, were in need of signal companies. Expansion was achieved by training local volunteers 'in theatre'. Like the rest of the Indian Army in the Middle East, signals units continued to serve long after the Armistice in November 1918. North Persia 1918–21, Kurdistan 1919, Iraq 1919–22, the East Persia Cordon and the Third Afghan War 1919, all conspired to keep signals busy, now an accepted and essential part of the military family.

Some idea of the scale of the expansions in the signals area can be seen in the following figures:

	BOs	BORs	IOs + IORs	Total
1 Aug 14	22	207	375	604
11 Nov 18	193	2,930	7,120	10,243

The new Signals Depot was to be at Jubbulpore from December 1920 and the wartime expansion embracing all classes within the Indian ranks was checked. In the future, only five classes were to be acceptable – Punjabi Mussalmans, Dogras, Sikhs, Rajputana Rajputs and mixed Madrassis. Men of other classes were permitted to take their discharge or transfer to other arms. Those who did not elect to transfer or accept discharge were allowed to waste out in the normal manner. In 1925, the Rajputana Rajputs were ruled out, reducing the permitted classes to four.

In November 1920, the companies lost their numbers and, thenceforth, were given alphabetical designations. Thus, 31 Coy became 1 (Line) Coy 'A' Corps Signals, 32 Coy became 'A' Divisional Signals, 33 Coy became 'B' Divisional Signals, etc. Three signal groups were established within the Corps: the first was made up of units in Peshawar, Quetta and Meerut (Punjabi Mussalmans and Sikhs), the second of units in Rawalpindi and Kohat (Punjabi Mussalmans and Dogras) and the third, the units in Waziristn and Jubbulpore. Personnel were posted from one signal unit to another within its group.

The North-West Frontier continued to occupy the minds of the Indian Signal Corps as much as the rest of the Indian Army. Wireless had improved and a pigeon-loft with thirty birds was maintained at Razmak, the Frontier's notorious men-only station.

Experiments were carried out with fitting radio telephony sets in ordinary fighting tanks of tank battalions but they were not satisfactory and it was decided that a special signal vehicle was required, to be fitted with wireless telegraphy facilities with a thirtymile range with a radio-telephony attachment working, if possible, off the same station. It was also decided to recommend that all horsed signal units be converted to mechanical transport and, in 1926, the first trials in mechanical cablelaying were carried out.

In 1927, a reorganisation was carried out and the post-war 'alphabetical' companies were redesignated as under:

Old Title	New Title	Location
A Div Signals	Peshawar District Signals	Peshawar
C Div Signals	Waziristan District Signals	Dera Ismail Khan
F Div Signals	Kohat District Signals	Kohat
D Div Signals	1 Div Signals	Rawalpindi
B Div Signals	2 Dv Signals	Quetta
E Div Signals	3 Div Signals	Meerut
G Div Signals	4 Div Signals	Jubbulpore (later Trimulgherry)

The move towards Indianisation of the personnel of the signal companies began in 1928 when British ORs of the line construction and cable sections were replaced by Indian ORs. In April 1933, a Boys Company was formed at the Signal Training Centre, the first of its kind in the Indian Army. The boys were to be trained in the higher technical trades to replace British tradesmen and to qualify for NCO and VCO posts. One of the first boys was Mohammed Suleiman who rose to be a brigadier, Director of Signals in the Pakistan Army.

Officer–Indianisation was slower. Graduates from the Indian Military Academy at Dehra Dun were posted, after commissioning, to the Indian Signal Corps at the rate of one every six months, thus there were only seven Indian commissioned officers in the Corps on the outbreak of war in September 1939 out of a total of 149 officers.

In 1934, buttons and badges were approved for the Indian Signal Corps. The badge was to be the parent corps' Mercury, the messenger of the gods – known as 'Jimmy' to all signalmen – within an oval band bearing the title, surmounted by the Star of India. The Royal Corps of Signals colours were adopted for the new Corps flag, pagri-fringes, etc – green, dark-blue and light-blue signifying the three physical divisions of the universe in which the Corps operates.

The 1930s were busy years for the Indian Signal Corps. Burma, Chitral, East Bengal, the Sino-Burmese Boundary Commission 1935–37, the Mount Everest Expedition 1933, the Frontier in all its sectors and the Quetta earthquake on 31 May 35 all served to engage the attention of signalmen, culminating in August 1939 when 11 Bde Signal Section set sail from Bombay for Alexandria and 12 Bde Signal Section left Madras for Singapore, heralding the largest commitment yet for the Indian Army. The Corps strength then was 142 BOs, 7 IOs, 73 VCOs 1,948 BORs and 4,241 IORs.

During the years 1939–47, officers and men of the Indian Signal Corps served in North and East Africa, in Paiforce, Italy, Greece, Burma, Dutch East Indies, Siam, Japan and wherever else the Indian Army served, fully justifying the traditional 'Ubique' motto of their Sappers and Miners forebears. At the end of the war there were 229 IOs, 825 VCOs and 63,138 IORs plus the British element.

Following Partition, the Corps had to suffer dissection on a 2:1 basis, India:Pakistan. Both the new Corps continued to use Jimmy as their badge. The Royal Corps of Signals had, by this time, removed the constraining oval band, allowing the captive messenger to fly free and the two new Corps followed suit. The Indian Corps' badge shows Jimmy holding the Star of India in his right hand with Hindi scrolls at his feet. The Pakistan Corps badge had Jimmy holding a Star and Crescent with Urdu scrolls at his feet. Sadly, Jimmy was later replaced in Pakistan by a composite device of crossed flags and a lightning flash above a globe, all surmounted by a Star and Crescent.

BOOKS

'History of the Corps of Signals – Vol I'. (Pub: The Corps of Signals Committee, New Delhi 1975)

THE CORPS OF MADRAS PIONEERS

Centre: **BANGALORE**

Class composition: 50% Tamils, 15% Telegus, 35% Adi-Dravidas and Christians (mixed)

The 1st Madras Pioneers, as they were first styled in 1922 when they were formed, were made up of three old Madras Native Infantry regiments of antique lineage.

The 61st King George's Own Pioneers dated their formation from December 1758 when independent companies already in existence were mustered into battalions. Ten such companies became the 1st Battalion of Coast Sepoys at Fort St George, near Madras. In 1769, they became the 1st Carnatic Battalion and, in 1784, when the term 'Carnatic' was discarded, the 1st Madras Battalion.

As the 1/1st Madras Native Infantry, in 1806, they were stationed at Vellore when new regulations were announced concerning new leather hats to be adopted and the prohibition of beards, religious markings on the forehead and the wearing of earrings. The proposed hats were offensive to Hindus and Muslims alike whilst the beard was an outward sign of a Muslim's faith. Similarly, earrings were often linked with family rites in childhood and were worn till death. By an unhappy coincidence, many of the wives and sons of Tippoo Sultan of Mysore were living in the huge palace at Vellore, together with numerous servants. They were more than ready to join any mutinous sepoys, to hold the fort and to enlist support from other troops, to restore the house of Tippoo and to raise the tiger-flag of Mysore. The plot was reported to the colonel of the 1/1st by Mustapha Beg, a private soldier in the battalion but this was disregarded. The mutiny was quickly suppressed and several officers dismissed. Mustapha Beg was given a reward of 2,000 pagodas and pensioned for life on the pay of a subadar.

The 1/1st Madras Native Infantry was struck off the Army's strength on 31 December 1806 as was the 23rd, also involved in the mutiny. Two new regiments were raised – the 24th and 25th. A decade later, after the battle of Seetabuldee, in November 1817, in view of their gallantry there, the old numbers were restored and the 1/1st returned to its place in the Army List in 1818.

It was not until 1883 that they became the 1st Regiment of Madras Native Infantry (Pioneers). Lord Roberts had become Commander-in-Chief of the Madras Army in 1880 and was implementing his views that the southern soldier had grown soft as a result of most of the military action having moved north. He was in no doubt as to the Madras soldier's capabilities in the fields of military engineering and pioneering however and the 1st MNI was lucky to escape disbandment: eight other Madras regiments were removed from the Army List at that time. In 1901, they became the 1st Madras Pioneers and then, two years later, when sixty was added to the numbers of the old Madras units, the 61st Pioneers. Thereafter, they received royal patronage and, at the time of the 1922 changes, were the 61st King George's Own Pioneers, a title granted in 1910.

The 64th Pioneers had as venerable a lineage as the 61st. Consolidated in 1759 in Madras from independent companies then in being, they were designated the 5th Battalion of Coast Sepoys, becoming the 5th Carnatic Battalion in 1769. A year later, they were advanced to become the 4th Carnatic but, like the 1st, lost that title to become the 4th Madras Battalion in 1784. Almost a century later, they escaped extinction by becoming, in 1883, the 4th Regiment of Madras Native Infantry (Pioneers). In 1885, the word 'Native' was dropped from all titles and, in 1901, a further change of style was approved and they became the 4th Madras Pioneers. Two years later, the Kitchener reforms turned them into the 64th Pioneers.

The third component regiment was the 81st Pioneers. They were formed at Chicacole in 1786 by a Captain G. Roberts from the Ganjam Sebundy Corps and drafts from the 11th and 18th Madras Battalions, being designated initially, the 28th Madras Battalion. In 1796, they became the 1/11th Regiment of Madras Native Infantry and, in 1825, the 21st MNI. Pioneer status was awarded in 1891 when they became the 21st Regiment of Madras Infantry (Pioneers). In 1901, they became the 21st Madras Pioneers and, two years later, the 81st Pioneers.

Despite the bias against Madras troops, the 1st, 4th and 21st Madras Pioneers served in Burma, in the 1897 Punjab Frontier actions and in China at the turn of the century.

FIRST WORLD WAR

61st King George's Own Pioneers – India, German East Africa
2/61st (formed in 1918) – India
64th Pioneers – India, Mesopotamia
81st Pioneers – India, Persia
2/81st (formed in 1918) – India

After the war, both second battalions were disbanded. Although they did not serve in France and Flanders where the maximum opportunities existed for the award of decorations, Indian other ranks of the Madras Pioneers received twenty-eight Indian Distinguished Service Medals.

BETWEEN THE WARS
Following the pattern of Line Infantry, the Corps of Pioneers had active battalions for the field and a 10th Battalion as a regimental home. The 61st, 64th and 81st became respectively, in 1922:

1st Bn (King George's Own) 1st Madras Pioneers
2nd Bn 1st Madras Pioneers
10th Bn 1st Madras Pioneers

The first badge chosen was a figure '1' within a circlet bearing the honours 'Seetabuldee' earned by the 1st Battalion and 'Seringapatam' shared by the 1st and 10th: above the circlet was the 2nd Battalion's 'Assaye' Elephant and, below the circlet, a scroll reading 'Madras Pioneers'.

In 1929, certain reductions were made in the ranks of the Indian Army's Pioneers but the 1st Madras did not suffer any disbandments. Notwithstanding, all four Pioneer regiments lost their numbers and became Corps. Thus, the 1st became the Corps of Madras Pioneers and had a change of badge. It featured the 'Assaye' Elephant within a circlet bearing the two honours as before: below the elephant, crossed pick and shovel, all over a scroll reading – 'The Corps of Madras Pioneers'.

However, the new structure was short-lived and, on 10 Feb 33, The Corps of Madras Pioneers was disbanded.

BATTLE HONOURS
Sholinghur, Carnatic, Mysore, Seringapatam, Assaye, Seetabuldee, Nagpore, Ava, Pegu, Central India, Afghanistan 1878–80, Burma 1885–87, Punjab Frontier, Tirah, Afghanistan 1919.

Kut-al-Amara 1917, Baghdad, Mesopotamia 1916–18, Persia 1918, North West Frontier, India 1915, Baluchistan 1918, Kilimanjaro, East Africa 1914–18.

BOOKS
'Records of the IV Madras Pioneers (now 64th Pioneers) 1759–1903' by Major H F Murland (Pub: Higginbothams Ltd., Bangalore, 1922)
'Regimental Records of 2nd Bn 1st Madras Pioneers, 1903–25' Anon (Pub: Regimental Press, Madras, 1926)
'Baillie-ki-Paltan – a history of 2nd Bn Madras Pioneers 1759–1930' by Lieut. Col H F Murland (Pub: Higginbothams Ltd., Madras, 1932)

THE CORPS OF BOMBAY PIONEERS

Centre: **KIRKEE**

Class composition: 1, 2, 3 and 4 Bns – 1 Company Lobana Sikhs, 1 Company Mahrattas and 1 Company Rajputana Mussalmans and Meos from Gurgaon District.
10 Bn – 1½ Companies Lobana Sikhs, 1½ Companies Mahrattas and 1½ Companies Rajputana Mussalmans and Meos from Gurgaon District.

Before 1888, the Bombay Army had no Pioneer units but it had become apparent that no campaign could be satisfactorily prosecuted without having Pioneers in its order-of-battle.

The 28th Bombay Infantry was the first to be converted when, in 1888, they became the 28th (Pioneer) Regiment of Bombay Infantry.

The regiment had been formed on 21 Jan 1846, one of three new regiments formed to garrison the newly-conquered territory of Sind, Bengal troops having refused to serve there without additional allowances.

Twelve years were to pass before another Pioneer unit was created and then it was the 7th Bombay Infantry, raised in 1788 as the 4th Bn of Bombay Sepoys. In 1903, the 21st Bombay Infantry (The Marine Battalion) also became a Pioneer unit, with service dating back to 1777.

These three units were all Bombay regiments and so, in 1903, the Kitchener reforms dictated that they should become the 128th Pioneers, the 107th Pioneers and the 121st Pioneers.

The other two constituents of the Corps actually began as Bengal regiments.

In 1838, the British Government decided that if Afghanistan had a monarch of Britain's choice, India's north-west flank would be secure from both Russian and Persian aspirations. Accordingly, the Amir of Kabul was to be Shuja-al-Mulk, thirty years exiled in Ludhiana. He marched in with his own force, thoughtfully recruited for him in India. One of the six regiments of infantry in the force was the 3rd Regiment of Infantry, Shah Shuja's Contingent. Once the new Amir was installed and his rival, Dost Mohammed, put to flight, some of the troops were sent back to the India. The 3rd Regiment had already attracted favourable comment for its performance in mountain tactics and, in November 1841, they were ordered to occupy the partially ruined fort of Kelat-i-Ghilzie, an unattractive location between Ghuznee and Kandahar. Then followed news of the murder of the British Resident in Kabul and rumours of the fate of the 4,500 strong British force and its 13,000 followers on their march towards Jellalabad.

In April 1842, Shah Shuja was murdered at Kabul and, with the release of Afghan troops and tribesmen following their capture of Ghuznee, the 950 men in Kelat-i-Ghilzie (600 men of the 3rd, 250 men of the 43rd Bengal Native Infantry, 43 European artillerymen and some sappers and other details, all under command of Captain Craigie of the 3rd Regiment) were soon subjected to a close siege lasting several months during which they repulsed attacks by some 6,000 enemy with their only casualties being two sepoys wounded of the 43rd BNI and four sepoys wounded of the 3rd Regiment.

Withdrawal to India followed and celebrations attended the returning force. Similar celebrations were held in Kabul for the returning Dost Mahommed.

When the rest of the late Shah Shuja's force was dispersed, the 3rd Regiment, for its performance in Afghanistan, was to be taken on to the strength of the Bengal Army as an extra regiment, styled The Regiment of Kelat-i-Ghilzie.

In the 1861 reorganization following the Great Mutiny, the Regiment became first the 13th and, later that year, the 12th Regiment of Bengal Native Infantry. It was not until 1864 that '(Kelat-i-Ghilzie)' again appeared after the number.

In March 1903, they changed their role, to become the 12th Bengal Pioneers and, on 31 Jul 03, when Presidency titles were removed, their final title was the 12th Pioneers (The Kelat-i-Ghilzie Regiment).

The other Bengal regiment was the 48th Regiment of Bengal Infantry (Pioneers), raised at Lucknow in March 1901, changing later that year to become the 48th Bengal Pioneers. In 1903, it became simply the 48th Pioneers.

FIRST WORLD WAR

107th Pioneers – India, France, Mesopotamia, Persia
 2/107th (raised in 1917) – India, Egypt.
12th Pioneers (Kelat-i-Ghilzie) – India, Mesopotamia
 2/12th (raised in 1917) – India
128th Pioneers – India, Egypt, Mesopotamia
 2/128th (raised in 1918) – India, Turkey
48th Pioneers – India, Mesopotamia
 2/48th (formed in 1918) – India.
121st Pioneers – India, Mesopotamia, Egypt.

Following the return of Indian troops after the war, all the second battalions were disbanded.

BETWEEN THE WARS

When the four Corps of Pioneers were formed after the Great War, the 2nd Bombay Corps took as its badge crossed axes above the figure '2' whilst, above the inter-section of the axe-hafts was the mural crown awarded to the old 12th Pioneers for its defence of the fortress of Kelat-i-Ghilzie.

107th became the 1st Bn 2nd Bombay Pioneers
12th became the 2nd Bn (Kelat-i-Ghilzie) 2nd Bombay Pioneers
128th became the 3rd Bn 2nd Bombay Pioneers
48th became the 4th Bn 2nd Bombay Pioneers
121st became the 10th Bn 2nd Bombay Pioneers

Additionally, two Indian Territorial Force battalions, the 11th and 12th Bns 2nd Bombay Pioneers, raised in March and April 1922 respectively, were based in Bombay.

In 1926, the 4th Bn was disbanded. It had been serving in Iraq and the British Government was engaged in cutting its overseas garrisons. However, by returning the battalion to India, it then became a charge on the Indian revenues which could not bear the cost. The disbandment was completed at Agra by 20 Dec 26, some personnel being re-mustered into the other battalions.

Little more than two years later, on 1 Apr 29, the four-battalion structure was cut to a Corps Headquarters (in effect, a Training Battalion) and two active battalions – the 1st (Marine) Battalion and the 2nd (Kelat-i-Ghilzie) Battalion. Despite appearances, this did not argue the disbandment of any one battalion but a fusion of all the existing battalions and the reconstitution of the new two-battalion Corps of Bombay Pioneers: each battalion was to provide an equal quota of the classes enlisted. As a result of this contraction, approximately one third of the personnel of all battalions of the 2nd Bombay Pioneers had to be mustered out.

Finally, on 10 Feb 33, the Corps of Bombay Pioneers, together with the other three Corps was struck off strength of the Indian Army.

BATTLE HONOURS

Mysore, Persian Gulf, Seedaseer, Seringapatam, Beni Boo Ali, Burma, Aden, Kelat-i-Ghilzie, Candahar 1842, Ghuznee 1842, Cabool 1842, Maharajpore, Hyderabad, Punjab, Abyssinia, Kandahar 1880, Afghanistan 1878–80, Tofrek, Suakin 1885, Burma 1885–87, Tirah, Punjab Frontier, Afghanistan 1919.

Festubert 1914–15, Givenchy 1914, Neuve Chapelle, Aubers, Loos, France and Flanders 1914–15, Suez Canal, Egypt 1915, Megiddo, Sharon, Palestine 1918, Basra, Shaiba, Kut-al-Amara 1915, 1917, Ctesiphon, Defence of Kut-al-Amara, Tigris 1916, Baghdad, Khan Baghdadi, Mesopotamia 1914–18, Merv, Persia 1918–19, North-West Frontier, India 1916–17, Baluchistan 1918.

BOOKS

'Pioneers on four fronts – being a record of the doings of the 107th Pioneers, now 1/2 Regiment of Pioneers in the Great War' by Edwin Haward (Pub. The Civil and Military Gazette Press, Lahore, 1923)

'History of the Bombay Pioneers 1777–1933' by Lieut Col W B P Tugwell (Pub. The Sydney Press Ltd., Bedford, 1938)

THE CORPS OF SIKH PIONEERS

Centre: **AMBALA**

Class composition: 55% Mazhbi, 30% Ramdassia and 15% Lobana Sikhs

The 3rd Sikh Pioneers, formed in 1922, was made up of four pioneer battalions, all raised as such and including the only wartime-raised pioneer battalion to escape disbandment in the post-war rundown.

The 23rd Sikh Pioneers, the senior regiment, was raised in 1857 at Lahore by Lt R H Shebbeare, initially as the 15th (Pioneer) Regiment of Punjab Infantry. In 1861, during the post-Mutiny realignment, they became the 27th Regiment of Bengal Native Infantry, only to be advanced later the same year to become the 23rd. Three years later, the Pioneer title was restored as the 23rd (Punjab) Regiment of Bengal Native Infantry (Pioneers). In 1885, in common with the rest of the army, the word 'Native' was dropped. Just after the turn of the century, in 1901, they became the 23rd Punjab Pioneers and, finally, in 1903, they were styled the 23rd Sikh Pioneers.

The 32nd Sikh Pioneers were also born of the Great Mutiny in 1857 at Madhopore by a Lt Dyas, being initially known as the 'Punjab Sappers' or the 'Punjab Pioneers'. The following year, they were designated the 24th (Pioneer) Regiment of Punjab Infantry, only to find themselves, themselves, in 1861, the 36th Regiment of Bengal Native Infantry, a title changed a few months later to the 32nd. In 1864, the Pioneer title was restored as the 32nd (Punjab) Regiment of Bengal Native Infantry (Pioneers), dropping the word 'Native' in 1885. Simplified in 1901 to the 32nd Punjab Pioneers and to the 32nd Sikh Pioneers in 1903, it was as the latter that they came to the merger in 1922.

It was not until 1887 that the 34th Sikh Pioneers were formed. This was at Mian Mir (Lahore Cantonment), Colonel A C W Crookshank being the first commandant. Instant pioneers, they were raised as the 34th (Punjab) Regiment of Bengal Infantry (Pioneers), taking the number of the old 34th BN1, disbanded in 1882. Like the 23rd and 32nd, they became the 34th Punjab Pioneers in 1901 and the 34th Sikh Pioneers in 1903.

FIRST WORLD WAR

23rd Sikh Pioneers – India, Aden, Egypt, Turkey
2/23rd (formed in 1917) – India, Egypt
32nd Sikh Pioneers – India, Egypt
2/32nd (formed in 1916) – India, Egypt
3/32nd (formed in 1918) – India
34th Sikh Pioneers – India, France, Egypt, Mesopotamia
2/34th (formed in 1917) – India
3/34th (formed in 1918) – India

Following the return to India after the war, the only wartime-raised battalion to be retained was the 2/23rd Sikh Pioneers which had been formed at Shalluja in Egypt on 3 Feb 17. As a reward for its services in the Great War, the 34th became the 34th Royal Sikh Pioneers in 1922.

BETWEEN THE WARS

The 3rd Sikh Pioneers was to consist of three active battalions and one training battalion and, in 1922, the 23rd, the 32nd, the 34th Royal and the 2/23rd Sikh Pioneers became respectively the 1st, 2nd, 3rd, and 10th Bns 3rd Sikh Pioneers. The new badge was to be the figure '3' within a chakra carrying the words 'Sikh Pioneers', a crown above: below, crossed axes and a scroll bearing the old motto of the 32nd dating from 1877 and now taken into use for the new regiment – '*Aut viam inveniam aut faciam*' (translatable as 'Either find a road or make one').

In 1929, in common with the other Pioneer regiments, the 3rd was to be reduced to two active battalions and a Corps Headquarters in the new Corps of Sikh pioneers. No one battalion was to be positively disbanded but two battalions were to be formed from the three battalions then in being. The new badge was to be similar to the old one but with no numeral in the centre and no crossed axes.

Sadly, the Corps of Sikh Pioneers was to be short-lived. Little more than three years later, on 10 Feb 33, the Corps was finally disbanded. The men, however, had already been dispersed, some 320 Ramdassia and Mazhbi Sikhs going to the Bengal Sappers and Miners and 160 Lobana Sikhs and 320 Ramdassia and Mazhbi Sikhs to the Bombay Sappers and Miners. The historian of the Indian Sappers and Miners commented 'Now, there are Sikhs and Sikhs'. All their Sikhs were Jat Sikhs who did not care to soldier with the lesser breeds. Problems arose and, early in 1933, it was decided that all Jat Sikhs should be concentrated in the Bengal Sappers and Miners whilst Lobanas, Mazhbi and Ramdassia Sikhs were to go to the Bombay Sappers and Miners. Subsequently, the Lobanas were withdrawn and allocated to the Indian Machine Gun Platoons of British infantry battalions.

Unlike the other Corps of Pioneers disbanded in 1933, the Sikh Pioneers were to rise again. In the Second World War, Ramdassia and Mazhbi Sikhs were again recruited as infantry, and, in 1941, the Mazhbi and Ramdassia Sikh Regiment – later to be re-designated The Sikh Light Infantry – was granted the honours and traditions of the old Corps of Sikh Pioneers.

BATTLE HONOURS
Delhi 1857, Lucknow, Taku Forts, Pekin 1860, Abyssinia, Peiwar Kotal, Charasiah, Kabul 1879, Kandahar 1880, Afghanistan 1878–80, Chitral, Punjab Frontier, China 1900, Afghanistan 1919, La Bassee 1914, Armentieres 1914, Festubert 1914, Givenchy 1914, Neuve Chapelle, Ypres 1915, St Julien, France and Flanders 1914–15, Egypt 1916–17, Gazam Megiddo, Sharon, Nablus, Palestine 1917–18. Tigris 1916, Kut-al-Amara 1917, Baghdad, Sharqat, Mesopotamia 1916–18, Aden.

BOOKS
'The history of the Sikh Pioneers (23rd, 32nd, 34th)' by Lieut Gen Sir George MacMunn KCB KCSI DSO (Pub: Purnell and Son Ltd. c. 1936).

THE CORPS OF HAZARA PIONEERS

Centre: **QUETTA**

Class composition: Hazaras

The youngest of the four Corps of Pioneers, the Hazara was to consist of one battalion only.

The 6th Bombay Infantry which would have become the 106th in the 1903 Kitchener reforms was disbanded in 1882. In 1904, Major C W Jacob of the 126th Baluchistan Infantry, until recently commanding the Zhob Levy Corps and, later, to become Field Marshal Sir Claude, raised the 106th Hazara Pioneers with drafts from the 124th Duchess of Connaught's Own Baluchistan Infantry and from his own regiment.

During the Great War, the 106th remained in India until the beginning of 1918 when they went to Mesopotamia. One company went to France where they were attached to the 107th Pioneers. Following the war, the Hazaras fell into no very convenient category and the decision was taken to form them into a fourth Pioneer regiment. The 106th Hazara Pioneers became in 1922, the 1st Bn 4th Hazara Pioneers. Their badge was crossed felling-axes with a crown above the intersection of the axe-hafts, a figure '4' below and a title-scroll below all. Recruitment of Afghan Hazaras became difficult at this point and recourse was had to India-domiciled Hazaras who were not totally satisfactory.

In 1929, as with the other Pioneers, the Hazaras became a Corps – the one-battalion Corps of Hazara Pioneers, their badge simply losing the figure '4'.

Finally, seven weeks after the Madras, Bombay and Sikh Corps of Pioneers, the Hazaras were finally disbanded on 31 Mar 33, their somewhat irregularly recruited Afghan soldiers not acceptable to any of three Corps of Sappers and Miners to which many of the other redundant Pioneers were posted.

BATTLE HONOURS
Mesopotamia 1918, Baluchistan 1915–16.

BOOKS
None published but 'Jawan to General' by General Mohd. Musa H J (Pub. ABC Publishing, New Delhi 1985) gives some details.

1ST PUNJAB REGIMENT

Centre: **1923 JHELUM**
1946 JHELUM

Class composition:	1923	1, 2, 3, and 5 Bns Punjabi Mussalmans, Sikhs and Rajputana Muslims 4 Bn Brahmans (United Provinces), Punjabi Mussalmans and Garhwali Brahmans 10 Bn Punjabi Mussalmans, Brahmans (United Provinces), Sikhs, Rajputana Rajputs and Garhwali Brahmans
	1946	Punjabi Mussalmans from the Punjab (less Ambala Civil Division), including Niazi and other Pathans of the Punjab, Hazarawalas of NWFP and Mussalmans from Jammu and Kashmir State and Gilgit Agency, Sikhs from the Punjab, Rajputs from Ambala Civil Division, United Provinces, Rajputana, Central India states and Bihar

The two senior infantry regiments of the Indian Army bore the territorial title of the area from which the majority of India's soldiers came but the constituent battalions of both the 1st and 2nd Punjab Regiments began life in the old Madras Army and all the eighteenth and nineteenth century battle-honours were gained by the Coast sepoys who had marched and fought under Lake and Wellesley.

However, with the apparent need to remove Madras units from the order of battle and to reinstate them as Punjab regiments, the 2nd, 6th, 16th, 22nd and 24th Madras Infantry were all well on their way to conversion when the official changes of title became effective in 1903. Most of the native officers had already been replaced by Northerners. In 1903, the old Madras regiments, by adding sixty to their numbers, became the 62nd, 66th, 76th, 82nd and 84th Punjabis. Twenty years later, the 1st Punjab Regiment came into being, made up of the 62nd Punjabis (1st Bn), 66th Punjabis (2nd Bn), 76th Punjabis (3rd Bn), 1st Brahmans (4th Bn) – an exception as a Bengal regiment – 82nd Punjabis – (5th Bn) and the 84th Punjabis (10th Bn). An important change was that these previously individual regiments – mostly one-battalion regiments – became battalions of a large regiment. Thus, the old 62nd became the 1st Bn 1st Punjab Regiment, colloquially referred to as First First Punjab and so on.

FIRST WORLD WAR

62nd Punjabis – India, Egypt, Mesopotamia, Aden. Among the regiment's officers was a Captain C J E Auchinleck, later Field Marshal Sir Claude and Colonel-in-Chief of 1st Punjab Regiment.

66th Punjabis – Burma, Mesopotamia. Captured at Kut-al-Amara and spent the rest of the war in Turkish captivity.

2/66th Punjabis (raised in 1918) – India.

76th Punjabis – India, Egypt, Mesopotamia. Captured at Kut-al-Amara and spent the rest of the war in Turkish captivity.

2/76th Punjabis (raised in 1917) – India.

1st Brahmans – India, Aden.

2/1st Brahmans (raised in 1917) – India, Persian Gulf.

82nd Punjabis – India, Mesopotamia.

84th Punjabis – India, Persian Gulf, Mesopotamia, Russia.

Following the return home of Indian troops after the war, all the war-raised battalions were disbanded.

BETWEEN THE WARS

The badge chosen for the 1st Punjab Regiment was basically the Star of India with, superimposed upon it, the Elephant over a tablet 'Assaye', an honour gained by the 1st Bn (62nd Punjabis as the 2nd Madras Native Infantry) and the 10th Bn (84th Punjabis as the 24th Madras Native Infantry): below, a China Dragon gained by both the 1st and 2nd Bn (66th Punjabis as the 6th Madras Native Infantry), all surmounted by a crown.

The new structure for 1 Punjab was to be as follows:

1st Battalion	– 62nd Punjabis
2nd Battalion	– 66th Punjabis
3rd Battalion	– 76th Punjabis
4th Battalion	– 1st Brahmans
5th Battalion	– 82nd Punjabis
10th Battalion	– 84th Punjabis

By this reorganisation and redesignation, the battalions of the Regiment regained their correct seniority in the Indian Infantry, an issue disregarded in 1903.

In February 1923, eight units were selected for Indianisation and the 2nd Bn 1st Punjab Regiment was one of these. The experiment was not universally either popular or successful but several of 2/1 Punjab's young Indian officers ultimately reached general officer rank.

In addition to the six regular battalions, the 11th Bn, formed in 1921 was also based at Jhelum. It was originally the 1st (Territorial) Bn 62nd Punjabis but the title was changed in 1922 to the 11th Bn 1st Punjab Regiment with no reference to its Territorial status. Only Punjabi Mussalmans were enlisted in the 11/1st.

All the regular battalions saw service on the Frontier during the between-wars years and the 4/1st spent a couple of years in China from 1927 in defence of British interests threatened by the Nationalist campaign against the Republicans. In December 1931, after 156 years of honourable existence, the 4/1st – the old 1st Brahmans – was disbanded as a result of retrenchment of the Indian Army. In the Great Mutiny of 1857 it was the only regiment of the old Bengal Line which remained loyal. In 1925 and again in 1928, attempts were made to transfer this battalion with its heavy loading of Garhwali Brahmans to the 18th Royal Garhwal Rifles but the prospective recipients of this windfall battalion declined to accept.

SECOND WORLD WAR

1st Battalion – India, Egypt, Iraq, Burma, Singapore, Dutch East Indies.

2nd Battalion – India, Burma. This battalion received more gallantry awards than any other Indian Army battalion during the war. The list comprised:

VC 1 DSO 4 MC 22 IOM 6 MM 23 GM 1 IDSM 12

3rd Battalion – India, Egypt, Italy. In June 1946, the battalion was nominated for training in a parachute role to join 2nd Indian Airborne Division: training was completed by the end of the year but, early in 1947, 3rd (Para) Bn 1st Punjab Regiment became engaged in operations in aid of the civil power, a situation which all soldiers hate and, in July, was detailed to join the Punjab Boundary Force, formed to keep the peace on the new East-West Punjab border.

5th Battalion – India, Burma, Japan. This battalion was posted after the end of the war to 268 Indian Infantry Brigade which went to Japan as part of the British Commonwealth Occupation Force.

6th Battalion – raised in Benares in August 1940. Captured in Singapore by the Japanese in February 1942.

7th Battalion – raised in Jhelum in April 1941. India, Andamans, Singapore. When Major Budh Singh MC took over command in March 1947, the 7th became the first battalion in the Regiment to have all Indian officers.

8th Battalion – raised in Jhelum in April 1941. In December that year, it was converted to a light anti-aircraft role and its officers mindful of their origins, were permitted to wear a small brass Elephant badge on their khaki helmets. Initially, the 6th (1st Punjab) LAA Regt, they suffered a further change in January 1945 when they began conversion to an airborne role as the 28th (Punjab) Para LAA Regt.

9th Battalion – in September 1939, the Territorial battalion, the 11th, was mobilised and took over railway protection duties from the 2/1st. In June

1941, the 11/1st was disembodied and the 9/1st came into being. In February 1943, after a year on the Frontier, a request was received from the Royal Indian Navy for volunteers to transfer and as seven hundred signified their willingness, the battalion was transferred despite the fact that only very few of the men had ever seen the sea. The only other such transfer was of the 15/13th Frontier Force Rifles, also once a pre-war 11th Bn.

11th Battalion – the pre-war Territorial battalion was converted to active status in June 1941 and redesignated the 9/1st.

14th Battalion – raised in Jhelum in January 1942. India. Disbanded in July 1947.

15th Battalion – raised in Jhelum in July 1942. India. Disbanded in April, 1946.

16th Battalion – raised originally as the 25th Garrison Bn in August 1941, it became a training battalion and, in August 1943 was redesignated the 16/1st. Disbanded in March 1946.

25th Garrison Battalion – raised in Jhelum in August 1942. India. Redesignated the 16/1st in August 1943.

26th Garrison Battalion – raised in Jhelum in March 1942. India. Disbanded in 1943.

PARTITION

In August 1947, the 1st Punjab Regiment went to join the Pakistan Army. It was to be composed henceforth of Punjabi Mussalmans and Pathans from Hazara District. The Sikhs and Rajputs from the various battalions were transferred to units allocated to India whilst 1 Punjab received in their place, Punjabi Mussalmans previously serving in battalions going to India's Army.

Transfers were effected as follows:

	Received	Transferred
1 Bn	PMs from 3/2 Punjab	Sikhs to 1 Sikh Rajputs to 3 Raj Rif
2 Bn	PMs from 2/2 Punjab	Sikhs to 2 Sikh Rajputs to 1 Raj Rif
3 Bn	PMs from 1/2 Punjab	Sikhs to 2 Sikh Rajputs to 4 Raj Rif
5 Bn	PMs from 2 Bn	Sikhs to 3 Sikh Rajputs to Raj Rif
7 Bn	PMs from 1 Bn	Sikhs to Sikh Regt Rajputs to Raj Rif
Regtl Centre	PMs from 2 Punjab Regtl Centre	Sikhs to Sikh Regt Rajputs to Raj Rif

The 5th and 7th Bns did not receive drafts from India-bound units but each received three platoons from the 1st and 2nd Bns.

BATTLE HONOURS

Sholinghur, Carnatic, Seringapatam, Mysore, Assaye, Laswarrie, Bourbon, Nagpore, Arakan, Ava, Bhurtpore, China, Burma 1885–87.

Suez Canal, Egypt 1915, Aden, Shaiba, Kut-al-Amara 1915–17, Defence of Kut-al-Amara, Ctesiphon, Tigris 1916, Baghdad, Mesopotamia 1915–18, NW Frontier India 1915, Afghanistan 1919.

Agordat, Keren, Kissoue, Damascus, Sidi Barrani, Tobruk 1941, Omars, Alem Hamza, Gazala, Carmusa, Defence of Alamein Line, Ruweisat Ridge, El Alamein, Montone, Gothic Line, Lamone Crossing, Pideura, Singapore Island, Pyuntaza-Shwegyin, Yenangyaung 1942, Monywa 1942, Donbaik, Htizwe, North Arakan, Razabil, Mayu Tunnels, Ngakyedauk Pass, Imphal, Litan, Kohima, Defence of Kohima, Kennedy Peak, Meiktila, Taungtha, Rangoon Road, Shwemyo Bluff, Sittang 1945, Arakan Beaches, Ramree, Burma 1942–45.

BOOKS

'A brief history of the 3rd Battalion, 1st Punjab Regiment' (Gale and Polden Ltd. Aldershot, 1927)

'The First Punjabis' by Major Mahommed Ibrahim Qureshi. (Gale and Polden Ltd. Aldershot, 1958)

2nd PUNJAB REGIMENT

Centre: **1923 MOOLTAN**
1946 MEERUT

Class composition:	1923	Punjabi Mussalmans, Sikhs (other than Jat Sikhs), Dogras and Kanets
	1946	Punjabi Mussalmans from the Punjab (less Ambala Civil Division), including Niazi and other Pathans of the Punjab, Hazarawalas of NWFP and Mussalmans from Jammu and Kashmir State and Gilgit Agency, Sikhs from the Punjab, Dogras from the Punjab and Jammu and Kashmir State.

The 2nd Punjab Regiment, created in 1922, was also from old Madras roots, consisting of the 67th Punjabis, 69th Punjabis, 72nd Punjabis, 74th Punjabis, 87th Punjabis and the wartime 2/67th Punjabis. In 1890, the old 12th Madras

Infantry received a new subadar-major, a Sikh, to replace the existing Madrassi and the composition of the Regiment changed to Pathans, Punjabi, Mussalmans and Sikhs. By 1903, the five Madras Infantry regiments – the 7th, 9th, 12th, 14th and 27th – had all effectively become Punjabi in terms of recruitment and, by adding sixty to their numbers, emerged as overt Punjabis.

FIRST WORLD WAR

67th Punjabis – India, Mesopotamia. Part of the regiment was captured at Kut-al-Amara but it was reconstituted on the nucleus of the two remaining companies and went on to serve in Salonika, South Russia and Turkey.

2/67th Punjabis (raised in 1915) – India.

69th Punjabis – India, Aden, Egypt, Gallipoli, France. At Loos, in September 1915, they were in the front line and emerged with fewer than 250 effectives after going into action with 600 officers and men. Subsequently, Loos Day was commemorated each year by a ceremonial parade.

2/69th Punjabis (raised in 1918) – India.

72nd Punjabis – India, Egypt.

2/72nd Punjabis (raised in 1917) – India.

74th Punjabis – Hong Kong, India, Egypt.

87th Punjabis – India, Mesopotamia.

Following the return of troops to India after the war, the 2/69th and the 2/72nd were disbanded.

BETWEEN THE WARS

The formation of the 2nd Punjab Regiment in 1923 necessitated a new regimental badge and the one chosen was the galley of the 69th, a badge awarded to the old 9th Madras Infantry in recognition of their readiness to serve wherever called upon to go. The associated motto was Khushki-wuh-tarri – 'By land and sea'. Notwithstanding, the 4th Bn was reluctant to abandon their own China Dragon awarded to them after the China War and permission was given for this to continue to be worn except by officers attached temporarily to the training battalion, the 10/2nd.

The new structure for 2 Punjab was to be as follows:

1st Battalion	– 67th Punjabis.
2nd Battalion	– 69th Punjabis.
3rd Battalion	– 72nd Punjabis.
4th Battalion	– 74th Punjabis.
5th Battalion	– 87th Punjabis.
10th Battalion	– 2/67th Punjabis.

For most of the regular battalions, service in India was the norm although, in the North West Frontier area this was not necessarily without its dangers and, in the 1930s, all of them qualified for one or other of the 'Frontier medals'. In November 1938, a Punjabi Mussalman sepoy of the 4/2nd stole some rounds of ammunition from some other men in his tent and then ran through the camp, firing at any British or PM officer whom he encountered; in all, four British and three PM officers were killed or subsequently died of wounds. Of the other three British officers present at the time with the battalion, two were wounded, one so seriously that his leg had to be amputated. the sepoy was shot dead whilst attempting to escape. At the court of enquiry, no reason was elicited for the man's actions nor was any collusion or conspiracy suggested with any others in the battalion. Despite the lack of any clear conclusion, it was decided by Army Headquarters that they could no longer retain the services of the PMs of the battalion and they were immediately discharged, reducing the size of the unit by 50%. This decision concided with a move towards effecting a reduction in infantry strength by fourteen battalions and, in January 1939, it was announced that the 4th Bn was to be disbanded, the remaining Sikhs and Dogras being either transferred to other battalions or being discharged. Despite the outbreak of the Second World War a few months later, the 4th was never re-raised and the Indian Government which inherited the 2nd Punjab Regiment in 1947 has also kept that number vacant.

No Territorial battalion was raised for 2 Punjab.

In 1933, 5/2 Punjab was one of the second block of battalions to undergo Indianisation.

SECOND WORLD WAR

1st Battalion – India, Aden, Somaliland, Italian East Africa, Egypt, Italy.

2nd Battalion – India, Ceylon, Burma.

3rd Battalion – India, Italian East Africa, Egypt. Returning to India with 5 Indian Division in 1943, the battalion which had recently been converted to a machine-gun role was changed back to a normal Indian infantry establishment and went on to serve in Burma. Subsequently, they went on to Singapore and the Dutch East Indies.

5th Battalion – Malaya. Captured on Singapore by the Japanese in February 1942. Disbanded on repatriation in 1945.

6th Battalion – raised at Sabathu in October 1940. India. Disbanded in 1946.

7th Battalion – raised in May 1941. India, Burma. The battalion was not disbanded after the war but continued as a regular unit.

8th Battalion – raised at Meerut in January 1942. India. Disbanded in August 1946.

25th Garrison Battalion – raised at Meerut in August 1941. India. Disbanded in 1946.

26th Garrison Battalion – raised at Meerut in March 1942. India. Disbanded in 1946.

27th (The Chamar) Battalion – raised in June 1942 by the enlistment of a never previously recruited class, the Chamars who were workers in leather, not rated very high in the Indian social scale. Officers and NCOs were not Chamars but came from almost every other regiment in the Indian Army List. By mid-1943, the 27/2nd had ceased to exist and The Chamar Regiment, with its badge, a charging bison, had been accepted as a regular unit of the Indian Army. After serving in Burma, they returned to India in December 1946 for disbandment.

PARTITION

In August 1947, the 2nd Punjab remained as part of India's Army whilst the 1st, 8th, 14th, 15th and 16th Punjab regiments went to Pakistan. Half of the strength of the 2nd being Punjabi Mussalmans who opted for Pakistan, the Regiment was left to be made up of 50% Sikhs and 50% Dogras. Partition left the 2nd as the senior infantry regiment in India, a position which it was not destined to occupy for very long as we shall see in a later chapter.

On transfer of power, the regular battalions were the 1st, 2nd, 3rd and 7th.

BATTLE HONOURS

Sholinghur, Carnatic, Mysore, Maheidpoor, Ava, China, Pegu, Lucknow, Burma 1885–87.

Loos, France and Flanders 1915, Helles, Krithia, Gallipoli 1915, Suez Canal, Egypt 1915, Megiddo, Sharon, Nablus, Palestine 1918, Aden, Defence of Kut-al-Amara, Kut-al-Amara 1917, Baghdad, Mesopotamia 1915–18, NW Frontier India 1915, 1916–17, Afghanistan 1919.

Gogni, Agordat, Keren, Ad Teclesan, Berbera, Amba Alagi, Abyssinia 1940–41, British Somaliland 1940, North Africa 1940–43, Pratelle Pass, San Martino-Sogliano, Casa Bettini, Idice Bridgehead, Italy 1943–45, Central Malaya, Ipoh, Singapore Island, Malaya 1941–42, Buthidaung, Point 551, Ngakyedauk Pass, Imphal, Litan, Kanglatongbi, Tengnoupal, Kennedy Peak, Tongzang, Kangaw, Defence of Meiktila, Pyinmana, Burma 1942–45.

BOOKS

'The Golden Galley' by Lieut Col Sir Geoffrey Betham and Major H V R Geary (OUP 1956).

'History of the 1st Bn 2nd Punjab Regiment' by Col H Ogle and Lieut Col H W Johnston (W. Straker, London, c 1923).

'Regimental history of the 3rd Bn 2nd Punjab Regiment' by Col. H C Wylly (Gale and Polden Ltd., Aldershot, 1927).

3rd MADRAS REGIMENT

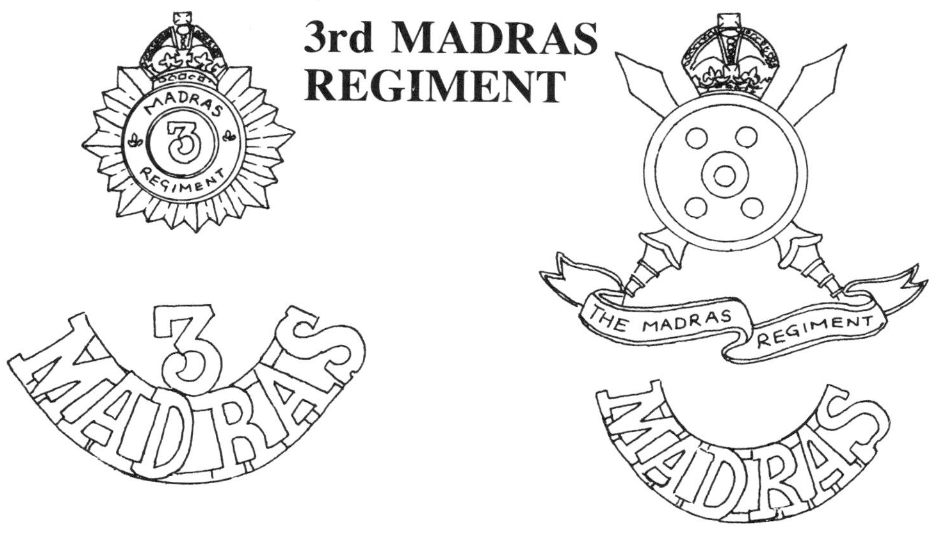

Centre: **1923 MADUKKARAI (COIMBATORE)**
1946 TRICHINOPOLY

Class composition:	1923	Tamils, Madrassi Mussalmans, Paraiyahs and Christians.
	1946	Madrassis from Madras Presidency including Indian states.

As has been seen, the two senior regiments, the 1st and 2nd Punjab Regiments, both began life with reconstituted Madras battalions. In 1922, the 3rd Madras Regiment was formed from five of the old unchanged Carnatic regiments – the 73rd Carnatic Infantry, the 75th Carnatic Infantry, the 79th Carnatic Infantry, the 83rd Wallajahbad Light Infantry, and the 86th Carnatic Infantry.

In 1903, in pursuance of the policy to subordinate the Madras soldier, the establishment of these regiments had been reduced to 600 as they were intended to be used as garrison troops only but this was not made apparent until war broke out in 1914. However, hostilities brought a flood of recruits to the colours and the units were brought up to full strength. In fact, in 1917 and 1918, second battalions were raised by Madras regiments, among them the 2/63rd, the 2/73rd, the 2/75th, the 2/80th and the 2/88th. Also raised was the 1/156th Infantry made up of complete companies from the 73rd, 79th and 80th Carnatic Infantry and the 83rd Wallajahbad Light Infantry. At that time, almost all the Indian infantry battalions in Mesopotamia were greatly over-strength and the decision was made to form a number of new battalions in the 150 numbered series. Turkish intelligence staff were reported to have been perplexed at the overnight appearance of seventeen new battalions springing up ready-armed as in the Greek myth.

FIRST WORLD WAR

During the Great War and in the immediate post-war years all the regiments which went to form the 3rd Madras Regiment saw service in the Middle East, principally in Mesopotamia. Most of this service was on garrison and Lines of Communication duties but a considerable amount of fighting took place after the armistice in Kurdistan and the 73rd served with some distinction in the 3rd Afghan War in 1919.

BETWEEN THE WARS

The structure for the 3rd Madras was as follows:

1st Battalion	– 73rd Carnatic Infantry
2nd Battalion	– 75th Carnatic Infantry
3rd Battalion	– 79th Carnatic Infantry
4th Battalion	– 83rd Wallajahbad Light Infantry
10th Battalion	– 86th Carnatic Infantry.

Hardly had the new regiment been created than, in 1923, the 3/3rd (the old 79th Carnatic Infantry) and the 4/3rd (the old 83rd Wallajahbad Light Infantry) were disbanded. The post-war economy axe cut as deeply in India as it did in Britain. In 1926, the 10/3rd ceased to exist. It is a point of interest that the 10th Bn was to have been raised from the old 80th Carnatic Infantry but, following a clerical error, it was formed from the 86th. It was the old 80th which was the proud possessor of Haider Ali's standard, taken at Sholinghur in 1781 – the Regiment's first battle-honour. In 1926, the 2/3rd Bn (the old 75th Carnatic Infantry) was disbanded, to be followed only two years later by the sole remaining regular battalion, the 1/3rd (the old 73rd Carnatic Infantry). This left only the Territorial battalions with which the 3rd Madras was especially well-endowed – the 11th (Madras), the 12th (Malabar), the 13th (Malabar) and the 14th (Coorg) Bns – all formed in 1921 and 1922. In 1939, the 15th (Madras) Bn was raised.

Briefly, after the disbandment of the last regular battalion, 1/3rd Madras, in 1928, the Territorial battalions were parented to The Madras Pioneers as 11th (Madras) Bn Madras Pioneers, 12th (Malabar) Bn Madras Pioneers, etc. but this did not last for long and they reverted to being Territorial battalions of a regiment in suspended animation. The Madras Pioneers, of course, were soon to suffer disbandment themselves.

SECOND WORLD WAR

It was not until 1941, two years into the war, that it was decided to reconstitute the 3rd Madras Regiment on the prompting of Sir Arthur Hope, the Governor of Madras.

1st Battalion – raised by redesignation of the 11th Bn, pre-war Territorials, India, Burma, Singapore, Dutch East Indies.

2nd Battalion – raised by redesignation of the 12th Bn, pre-war Territorials. India, Malaya. It was from this battalion that the personnel came who were to form the centre at Madukkarai. In January 1947, the battalion was nominated for parachute training prior to joining 2nd Indian Airborne Division.

3rd Battalion – raised by redesignation of the 13th Bn, pre-war Territorials. India. The battalion became a cadre battalion for training VCOs and NCOs whilst batches of recruits to fill the new battalions were sent to every training centre in India for their six months training.

4th Battalion – raised by redesignation of the 15th Bn, pre-war Territorials. India, Burma. The 4/3rd was the first battalion to see action.

5th Battalion – raised in 1943 and granted the traditions of the old 63rd Palamcottah Light Infantry. India.

6th Battalion – raised in 1943 and granted the traditions of the old 80th Carnatic Infantry. India.

7th Battalion – raised in 1943 and granted the traditions of the old 88th Carnatic Infantry. India.

11th (Madras) Battalion – pre-war Territorial battalion redesignated 1/3 Madras when the Regiment was reformed in 1941.

12th (Malabar) Battalion – pre-war Territorial battalion redesignated 2/3 Madras when the Regiment was reformed in 1941.

13th (Malabar) Battalion – pre-war Territorial battalion redesignated 3/3 Madras when the Regiment was reformed in 1941.

14th (Coorg) Battalion – pre-war Territorial battalion redesignated 1st Coorg Bn and became a garrison battalion in 1942.

15th (Madras) Battalion – Territorial battalion formed 14 November 1939 and redesignated 4/3 Madras when the Regiment was reformed in 1941.

25th Garrison Battalion – raised 15 Sep 42. India. Disbanded 1946.

26th Garrison Battalion – raised 15 Sep 42. India. Disbanded 1946.

27th Garrison Battalion – raised in 1943. India. Disbanded 1946.

28th (Coast Defence) Battalion – raised Feb 42. India, Persian Gulf. Disbanded 1946.

HM The King-Emperor approved for the Regiment in 1946, the new badge shown at the right of the head of this section; it was to replace the rather undistinguished-looking star which had previously been worn by and which had come from the old 13th Madras Infantry.

In October 1945, by Special Indian Army Order 134/S/45, the entire Indian Infantry line, with the exception of the Punjab Regiments, lost the number from their regimental designations and, thus, the 3rd Madras Regiment became simply The Madras Regiment.

PARTITION

In August 1947, the Regiment remained as part of India's Army. Being entirely recruited in the South, its battalions were spared the agony of being torn apart to consign Muslim companies to Pakistan. Nor were they required to absorb Hindu companies being shed by Pakistan-bound regiments.

On transfer of power, the battalions were the 1st, 2nd, 3rd and 4th.

BATTLE HONOURS

Amboor, Carnatic, Sholinghur, Mysore, Seringapatam, Assaye, Cochin, Bourbon, Seetabuldee, Nagpore, Maheidpoor, Kemmendine, Ava, China 1840–42, Pegu, Lucknow, Central India, Afghanistan 1879–80, Burma 1885–87, Malakand, Tirah, Punjab, Frontier, China 1900, Afghanistan 1919.

Kut-al-Amara, Baghdad, Mesopotamia 1915–18, Aden, Persia 1918, NW Frontier India 1914–15, 1917, Baluchistan 1918, Kilimanjaro, East Africa 1914–16.

Tamu Road, Ukhrul, Ava, Kama, Burma 1942–45.

BOOKS

History of the 83rd Wallajahbad Light Infantry by Lieut Col J C W Erck (Cannanore 1909).

Madras Infantry 1748–1943 (Government Press, Madras, 1943)

The Madras Soldier 1746–1946 (Government Press, Madras, 1946)

The Madras Regiment 1758–1958 (Defence Services Staff College Press, Wellington, 1958)

All the above three by Lt Col E G Phythian-Adams OBE.

'Now or Never – the story of 4/3 Madras in the Burma Campaign' by Major G D Garforth-Bles and Capt S D Clarke (Thacker's Press, Calcutta, 1945)

'The Black Pom-Poms – History of the Madras Regiment 1941–83)' by Lieut Col J R Daniel (Thomson Press, Coonoor 1986).

4th BOMBAY GRENADIERS/ INDIAN GRENADIERS

Centre: **1923 AJMER**
1946 NASIRABAD

Class Composition:	1923	Rajputana Mussalmans, Rajputana Jats, Mahrattas, Mers and Merats
	1946	Jats from the Punjab, United Provinces, Rajputana and Central India states, Hindustani Mussalmans from Ambala Civil Division, Rajputana, United Provinces, Central India states and the Deccan.

It may be something of a surprise to learn that the oldest regiment of grenadiers in the armies of the Commonwealth is not The Grenadier, or First Regiment of Foot Guards, normally associated with the Royal Household and Buckingham Palace but a Bombay regiment whose right to the title dated from 1779. The First Regiment of Foot Guards did not become grenadiers until after Waterloo. In 1778, a composite battalion, made up of two grenadier companies from each of the 2nd, 3rd, and 5th Bns of Bombay sepoys earned glory for themselves and the Bombay Army against the Mahrattas at Talegaon, near the present Bombay-Poona Road. In 1779, grenadier companies from the six existing sepoy battalions, plus two companies from the Bombay Marine Battalion, were formed into one battalion but, with characteristic lack of imagination, the authorities styled it simply the 8th Bombay Native Infantry. A few years later, the 8th was part of the garrison of Mangalore on the Malabar Coast, then besieged by the army of Tipu Sultan of Mysore and, despite being outnumbered by a force of seventy times its strength, the British-Indian body held out for almost nine months before capitulation with honour. The only other regiment with whom the 8th shared the battle-honour was The Black Watch (Royal Highland Regiment). In November 1784, the 8th was officially awarded the title Bombay Grenadiers and, in 1788, was granted the badge of the White Horse of Hanover. Twelve years later the unnumbered Bombay Grenadiers became the

First of the Bombay Line in the light of their grenadier status. Still fighting the old Mahratta enemy in 1818, the 2nd distinguished itself at Koregaon, near Poona, where the British-officered force of some 850 men put to flight the Peshwa's cavalry force of 25,000, losing a third of its strength in the action. The 2nd then joined the 1st as a two-battalion 1st Grenadier Regiment.

The Bombay Army was always noted for its rather secular attitude to its class composition. The men were more concerned for their regiment than for their caste, a point of view greatly at variance with that of the Bengal sepoy and, to a lesser extent, the Madrassi. This probably accounted for the readiness of the Bombay sepoy to serve abroad, the 2nd Bn being sent to Egypt in 1801 to frustrate French aspirations towards conquest which would have constituted a threat to India. For this venture, the 2nd was joined by a unit subsequently to become the 113th Infantry (and subsequently the 10/4th) and both were granted the award of The Sphinx.

The 1903 changes involved the Bombay regiments in adding one hundred to their numbers and, thus, the 1st Bombay Grenadiers became the 101st Grenadiers and the 2nd (Prince of Wales's Own) Bombay Grenadiers the 102nd Prince of Wales's Own Grenadiers. The 8th, 9th, 12th and 13th Bombay Infantry became respectively the 108th, 109th, 112th and 113th Infantry. These six regiments which had, since 1886, been linked in two groups became the six battalions of the new 4th Bombay Grenadiers in 1923.

In 1904, the 101st Grenadiers had three officers serving who held the Victoria Cross, probably a record unequalled in the armies of the Empire.

FIRST WORLD WAR

101st Grenadiers – German East Africa, Egypt, Palestine, Somaliland.
    2/101st (formed in 1917) – Egypt, India
102nd King Edward's Own Grenadiers – Muscat, Mesopotamia, Aden, India.
    2/102nd (formed in 1918) – India
108th Infantry – Aden, India, Muscat, Mesopotamia.
109th Infantry – Mesopotamia, India.
    2/109th (formed in 1918) – India, Aden, Egypt
112th Infantry – Mesopotamia, India.
    2/112th (formed in 1917) – India
113th Infantry – Mesopotamia, India.
    2/113th (formed in 1916) – India

All second battalions were disbanded by 1921.

BETWEEN THE WARS

The Badge prescribed for the new 4th Bombay Grenadiers was the grenade, fired, in brass with a white-metal figure '4' on the ball. This was to be worn one inch above the inverted 'V' of the pagri in the centre of the forehead. Officers were to wear a white feather hackle in the helmet. However, officers of the 1/4th continued to wear the grenade of the 101st Grenadiers whilst VCOs and other ranks wore a small grenade with a white horse on the ball. The 2/4th, once 102nd King Edward's Own Grenadiers, wore their old badge and the VCOs and other ranks wore the Royal Cypher 'ERI'. Memory is uncertain as to what was worn by the 3/4th, 4/4th and 5/4th but the prescribed pattern was in use during the Second World War until July 1945 when a larger grenade with a White Horse on the ball came into use.

The 1923 consolidation of six regiments into one meant that the 101st became the 1/4th Bombay Grenadiers, the 102nd became the 2/4th whilst the 108th, the

109th, the 112th and the 113th Infantry became instant grenadiers as the 3/4th, the 4/4th, the 5/4th and the 10/4th Bombay Grenadiers respectively. Distinctive coloured cloth backings were authorized in 1925 for wear behind the shoulder-titles – 1st Bn – scarlet, the 2nd Bn – orange, the 3rd Bn – violet, the 4th Bn – grass green and the 5th Bn – navy blue.

The 1/4th went to the Frontier and joined the Mohmand Field Force under Brigadier (later Field Marshal Sir Claude) Auchinleck, an association which contributed to Auchinleck's decision to become Colonel of the Regiment when he became Commander-in-Chief, India.

The 2/4th went briefly to the Afghan War and then to Hong Kong where they were officially re-styled 'King Edward's Own'. The withdrawal of the Indian Army from Iraq meant surplus troops and the 3/4th and the 4/4th were disbanded in March 1930. The 5/4th had a very brief life, indeed, being disbanded in 1923 in the wake of demobilization.

The 10/4th in its role as the Training Battalion found itself with only two active battalions to serve and it was amalgamated with the 10/9th Jat Regiment, moving from Ajmer to Bareilly, to form a joint training depot known as the 10th Bn the 4/9th Regiment. It remained thus from 1930 until 1941.

The 11/4th, as a Territorial battalion, was raised in Ajmer in 1922.

SECOND WORLD WAR

In 1941, a separate battalion, the 10/4th, was again authorised and it was re-formed at Bareilly on 5 Jul 41, moving to Nasirabad on 6 Oct 41 (10/9th Jat Regt. remained at Bareilly).

1st Battalion – India, Iran, Iraq, Egypt, Lebanon, Syria.

2nd Battalion – India, Burma, Malaya, Dutch East Indies.

3rd Battalion – reraised at Nasirabad in November 1940 with drafts from the 1/4th, 2/4th and the 9th Jats. India, Burma.

4th Battalion – reraised at Bareilly in February 1941 with drafts from the 1/4th, 2/4th, 3/4th and the 9th Jats. India, Burma, Iraq.

5th Battalion – reraised as Nasirabad in October 1941. India, Burma. Disbanded September 1946.

6th Battalion – raised at Nasirabad in July 1942. Trained as a motor battalion but was disbanded in April 1943 when there was, apparently, no longer any need for this type of unit. The first six battalions had been nominated by General Auchinleck for a new role, that of support of armour and these six became motor battalions. As the war progressed the need for this type of soldier lapsed, and thus, the 6/4th was disbanded after a life of only ten months.

11th Battalion – the Territorial battalion was embodied on 4 Sep 39 and employed on port-defence duties based on Bombay. In September 1941, they became the 26/4th before being restyled the 1st Bn The Ajmer Regiment in July 1942.

14th Battalion – raised initially as the 34th Training Unit, a shared responsibility with the recently reraised 3rd Madras Regiment. As the latter grew, the Grenadier element became the 14/4th. Disbanded April 1946.

25th Garrison Battalion – raised at Bareilly in August 1941. India.

26th Garrison Battalion – created from the 11/4th, it later became the 1st Ajmer Regt.

27th Garrison Battalion – raised at Santa Cruz on 1 Jan 42 and redesignated the 2nd Bn The Ajmer Regiment on 1 Jul 42.

In October 1945, the Indian infantry regiments, except for the 1st, 2nd, 8th, 14th, 15th and 16th Punjab Regiments lost their numerical designations. At the same time, the Regiment was redesignated The Indian Grenadiers, thereby severing its last link with the old Bombay Army (Special Indian Army Order 132/S/45).

PARTITION

The Indian Grenadiers were logically allotted to India. The active battalions on transfer of power were the 1st, 2nd, 3rd, 4th and 25th. The 1st received Dogras from 5 Baluch as did the 2nd from The Frontier Force Rifles and the 4th from 1/16 Punjab. The Hindustani Mussalmans from these battalions were allotted to Pakistan.

BATTLE HONOURS

Mangalore, Mysore, Seringapatam, Egypt 1801, Kirkee, Corygaum, Beni Boo Ali, Meeanee, Hyderabad, Mooltan, Punjaub, Central India, Abyssinia, Kandahar 1880, Afghanistan 1878–80, Burma 1885–87, Somaliland 1902–04.

Egypt 1916–17, Gaza, Megiddo, Nablus, Palestine 1917–18, Aden, Tigris 1916, Kut-al-Amara 1917, Baghdad, Sharqat, Mesopotamia 1915–18, East Africa 1914–16, Afghanistan 1919.

Kohima, Kalewa, Capture of Meiktila, Defence of Meiktila, Fort Dufferin Taungtha, Pegu 1945, Burma 1942–45.

BOOKS

The Grenadiers: a tradition of valour. Col R D Palsokar MC (Pub Regtl Centre, Jabalpur 1980)

101st Grenadiers Historical Record 1778–1923. Col H S Anderson (Pub Gale and Polden 1885 and 1928)

5th MAHRATTA LIGHT INFANTRY

Centre: **1923 BELGAUM**
1946 BELGAUM

Class composition: 1923 Mahrattas and Deccani Mussalmans
1946 Mahrattas from Bombay Presidencey

During the First World War, some surprise was expressed at the creditable performance in Mesopotamia of the Mahratta soldier but those who voiced these comments should have known better. They might have reflected upon the Mahrattas' record fighting against us in four protracted campaigns and listened to Wellesley – '*Their conduct and success were seldom equalled and never surpassed.*' General Sir Charles Napier, not a man to praise lightly, once said, '*With the Bombay soldiers of Meanee and Hyderabad, I could walk through all lands. They are active, daring, hardy chaps, worthy of Shivaji himself.*'

The first two battalions can claim more than two hundred years of service to the Crown, the foremost in seniority in the old Bombay Army.

The six regiments which went to form the 5th Mahratta Light Infantry in 1923, were the 103rd Mahratta Light Infantry, the 105th Mahratta Light Infantry, the 110th Mahratta Light Infantry, the 116th Mahratta Infantry, the 117th Mahratta Infantry, and the 114th Mahratta Infantry, before 1903, the 3rd, 5th and 10th Bombay Light Infantry and the 16th, 17th and 14th Bombay Infantry.

In the 1923 reforms, the 5th Mahrattas were the only light infantry regiment to be created. In the same way that the title 'grenadier' was awarded for distinguished service, so was the term 'light infantry' although to a slightly lesser degree. Traditionally, in earlier days, the grenadier company of a line regiment held the right flank whilst the left was held by the light company, both posts of honour. The 3rd and 10th Bombay Light Infantry earned their distinction in Abyssinia in 1867–68 whilst the 5th qualified for theirs at Kahun in the First Afghan War in 1840 – an honour unique in the British and Indian Armies.

FIRST WORLD WAR

103rd Mahratta Light Infantry – India, Mesopotamia. Captured at Kut-al-Amara.

2/103rd (formed in 1918) India

3/103rd (formed in 1918) India

105th Mahratta Light Infantry – India, Mesopotamia, Egypt.

2/105th (formed in 1918) India

110th Mahratta Light Infantry – India, Mesopotamia. Captured at Kut-al-Amara.

116th Mahrattas – India, Mesopotamia.

2/116th (formed in 1918) India, Mesopotamia

117th Mahrattas – India, Mesopotamia. Captured at Kut-al-Amara. Reformed from drafts in India and Persia.

2/117th (formed in 1918) India, Mesopotamia.

114th Mahrattas – India, Mesopotamia. After the battle of Sharqat the regiment was awarded 2 DSOs, 4 MCs, 6 IOMs and 15 IDSMs, perhaps the highest number of awards granted to any unit following a single action.

All second battalions were disbanded by 1921.

BETWEEN THE WARS

The badge chosen for the 5th Mahratta Light Infantry was a stringed bugle-horn with a figure '5' between the strings, all surmounted by a crown.

The line-up for the new regiment, the only light infantry regiment then on the Indian establishment, was 1st Bn (late 103rd Mahratta Light Infantry, the 2nd Bn (late 105th Mahratta Light Infantry), the 3rd Bn (late 110th Mahratta Light Infantry, the 4th Bn (late 116th Mahrattas), 5th Royal Bn (late 117th Royal Mahrattas), the 10th Bn (late 114th Mahrattas) and the Territorial battalion, the 11th. A 12th Bn was raised in November 1939. It was only in the Indian Army that the 'Royal' battalion existed. In the other armies under the crown, the creation of a royal battalion justified the redesignation of the entire regiment. In the case of the 5th Royal Bn, the distinction was reflected in dress by the adoption of a blue lanyard, blue hose-tops and a crown above the metal shoulder-title.

In 1923, it was nominated to be one of those infantry battalions for 'Indianisation' whereby all future officers posted to the battalion would be King's Commissioned Indian Officers.

In 1932, the 2nd/5th, known as the Kali Panchwin – the Black Fifth – from the black fringe traditionally worn in the pagri, was in Burma engaged in the suppression of the rebellion. By this time, the decision had been made and implemented to turn the Regiment into a class regiment, composed entirely of Mahrattas except for sundry clerks and bandsmen. Muslims serving were not to be transferred or discharged but to waste out when time-expired.

SECOND WORLD WAR

1st Battalion – India, Iraq, Egypt, Italy. In September 1945, the battalion was warned for service with 268 Indian Infantry Brigade which went to Japan as part of the British Commonwealth Occupation Force.

2nd Battalion – India, Italian East Africa, Egypt. Lost in Tobruk. Reraised in May 1946 by redesignation of the 18th Bn. Served in the Punjab Boundary Force in 1947.

3rd Battalion – India, Italian East Africa, Egypt. In early 1946, the battalion was nominated for conversion to a parachute role as a unit of the 2nd Indian Airborne Division. Training completed, 3rd (Para) Bn The Mahratta Light Infantry moved to Quetta and then to Mooltan where they were engaged in escorting minority communities moving from Pakistan to India.

4th Battalion – India, Burma, Dutch East Indies.

5th Royal Battalion – India, Persia, Egypt. Converted to a machine-gun battalion in January 1943 and reverted to a normal Infantry role in August 1946.

6th Battalion – raised at Mardan in June 1940. India, Burma, Dutch East Indies, Malaya. Disbanded June 1947.

7th Battalion – raised at Fyzabad in August 1940. Redesignated 51st Regt Indian Armoured Corps on 1 Aug 42 but changed again on 1 October to become the 8th (Mahratta) Anti-tank Regt, Indian Artillery.

8th Battalion – raised at Belgaum in February 1941. Redesignated the 5th (Mahratta) Anti-tank Regt, Indian Artillery on 1 Jan 42.

9th Battalion – raised at Belgaum in February 1941. Redesignated the 5th (Mahratta) Anti-tank Regt, Indian Artillery on 1 Jan 42.

11th Battalion – the pre-war Territorial Battalion became an active battalion on 14 Sep 41 and was restyled the 15th Battalion.

12th Battalion – a Territorial battalion raised at Belgaum on 14 Nov 39. Became an active battalion on 16 Sep 41 and was restyled the 16th Battalion.

14th Battalion – raised at Ambala on 1 Feb 41. India, Iraq. Disbanded May 1946.

15th Battalion – the restyled 11th Bn. India. Disbanded March 1946.

16th Battalion – the restyled 12th Bn. India. Disbanded May 1946.

17th Battalion – raised at Belgaum on 15 Oct 41. India, Burma, Malaya. Disbanded January 1947.

18th Battalion – the restyled 25th Garrison Bn. Redesignated the 2nd Bn in May 1946. India. Disbanded 1946.

25th Garrison Battalion – raised at Belgaum on 15 Aug 41. India. Redesignated the 18th Bn in August 1942.

26th Garrison Battalion – raised at Belgaum on 1 Mar 42. India. Disbanded June 1946.

27th Garrison Battalion – raised at Kirkee on 1 Dec 42. India, Burma. The 27th was the only garrison battalion to become engaged in hostile operations and those against the Japanese at Kohima. Disbanded May 1946.

28th Garrison Battalion – raised at Allahabad on 15 May 43. India. Disbanded early in 1946.

29th Garrison Battalion – raised at Khulna on 1 Oct 44 by conversion of the 1st Indian Coast Defence Bn. India. Disbanded June 1946.

30th Garrison Battalion – raised at Comilla in September 1944 by conversion of the 3rd Indian Coast Defence Bn. India. Disbanded in early 1946.

In October 1945, the Indian infantry regiments, with the exception of the Punjab Regiments, lost the number from their regimental title and, thus, the 5th Mahratta Light Infantry became simply The Mahratta Light Infantry.

PARTITION

On partition, the Regiment was allotted to India and, being a one-class regiment, did not have to suffer cross-postings to and from units going to Pakistan.

The battalions on transfer of power were the 1st, 2nd, 3rd, 4th and the 5th Royal.

BATTLE HONOURS

Mysore, Seedaseer, Beni Boo Ali, Seringapatam, Mooltan, Kahun, Gujerat, Punjab, Central India, China 1860–62, Abyssinia, Afghanistan 1879–80.

Burma 1885–87, British East Africa 1901. Basra, Ctesiphon, Kut-al-Amara, Defence of Kut-al-Amara. Baghdad, Sharqat, Mesopotamia 1914–18, Persia 1918, Megiddo, Nablus, Sharon.

Tobruk 1941, Keren, Gobi II, Tobruk 1942, The Sangro, Tengnoupal, Sangshak, Burma 1942–45. Advance to Florence, Gothic Line, Ruywa, The Senio. Italy 1943–45.

BOOKS

A famous Indian regiment – the Kali Panchwin by Sir Reginald Hennell (John Murray 1927)

Historical Record of the 4/5th Mahratta Light Infantry by A R Solly (Thacker and Co 1932)

History of the 1/5th Mahratta Light Infantry by A R Solly (Govt of India Press 1930)

Historical Record of the 110th Mahratta Light Infantry by A R Solly (Govt of India Press 1927)

Historical Records of the 16th Regiment, Bombay Infantry by A R Solly (Govt Press 1897)

5th Royal Battalion – Ki Tawarikh by A R Solly (Army Book Depot 1924)

Chronology of the 114th Mahrattas by A R Solly (Times of India Press 1926)

Valour Enshrined by Lieut Col M G Abhyankar (Orient Longmans 1971)

6th RAJPUTANA RIFLES

Centre: **1923 NASIRABAD**
1946 DELHI

Class composition: 1923 Rajputana Jats, Rajputana Rajputs and Punjabi Mussalmans

1946 Jats from the Punjab, United Provinces, Rajputana and Central India states, Punjabi Mussalmans from the Punjab (less Ambala Civil Division) including Niazi and other Pathans from the Punjab, Hazarawalas of NWFP, Mussalmans of Jammu and Kashmir State and Gilgit Agency, Rajputs from Ambala Civil Division, United Provinces, Rajputana, Central India states and Bihar.

The 6th Rajputana Rifles was India's senior rifle regiment and its first battalion, the 104th, was, as the 4th Bombay Rifles, the senior rifle unit. 'Rifles' always laid claim to superiority over 'redcoat' soldiers even if, with characteristic perversity, the former opted for a position on the left of the line, the flanks being considered the posts of honour. 'Rifles' tactics had been developed in North America and honed to a finer edge in the Peninsula: dressed in dark green, they were admirably suited to move quietly through the woods as huntsmen rather than moving as a scarlet and pipeclayed phalanx with colours flying, drums beating, etc. Riflemen were trained to fire the new rifle and to display a measure of initiative not looked for in soldiers trained to fight in a square in the open.

The 4th Bombay Rifles were designated thus in 1841 although raised in 1775 as the 5th Regiment of Bombay Sepoys. Brigaded for some time with the 60th Rifles (later The King's Royal Rifle Corps), the Regiment felt that the red facings on the green uniforms of the 60th had a distinct appeal. They sought approval for this colourful trim for their own green uniforms and authority smiled upon the idea. Later, all battalions of the new regiment were to have the same distinction. Earlier in the century, service under Wellesley resulted in their being styled 'Wellesley's Rifles' a hundred years later. Both 120th and 122nd

Rajputana Infantry were raised as ordinary line infantry. The 20th Bombay Infantry had the distinction of being the first Indian unit to earn a Victoria Cross – by Captain J.A. Wood in 1856 at Reshire in Persia. The 22nd, on the other hand, was in being for over eighty years before gaining its first battle-honour in China 1900. The 23rd and 25th Bombay Rifles had become Rifles in 1888 and, in 1903, became respectively 123rd Outrams Rifles (from James Outram, their adjutant who went on later to become Sir James, commanding the forces in Persia in 1856) and 125th Napier's Rifles (from Sir Charles Napier, the victor of Sind who asked that his name should be associated with theirs following the campaign). The 10th Bn was not a Bombay regiment but a Bengal one, the 13th (Shekhawati) Rajput Infantry, raised in 1835. Its links with the recruiting areas of the other regiments qualified it for inclusion in the new 6th Rajputana Rifles.

FIRST WORLD WAR

104th Wellesley's Rifles – India, Mesopotamia
120th Rajputana Infantry – India, Mesopotamia
122nd Rajputana Infantry – India, Mesopotamia
123rd Outram's Rifles – India, Mesopotamia, Persia
2/123rd (formed in 1916) – Mesopotamia, Egypt, India
3/123rd (formed in 1917) – India, Persia, Mesopotamia
125th Napier's Rifles – India, France, Egypt, Mesopotamia
2/125th (formed in 1918) – India, Mesopotamia
13th Rajputs – India, East Africa, Mesopotamia

BETWEEN THE WARS

The badge chosen for the new 6th Rajputana Rifles was the black stringed bugle-horn with the letters 'RR' between the strings. The 1st Battalion insisted on a difference and persisted in wearing a badge which carried the old flat-topped Victorian crown in preference to the crown assumed by HM King Edward in 1901 and retained by his son and grandson. The new titles for the battalions were as follows:

104th Wellesley's Rifles – 1st Bn (Wellesley's) 6th Rajputana Rifles
120th Rajputana Infantry – 2nd Bn (Prince of Wales's Own) (the royal association was granted in 1920)
122nd Rajputana Infantry – 3rd Bn
123rd Outram's Rifles – 4th Bn (Outram's)
125th Napier's Rifles – 5th Bn (Napier's)
13th Rajputs – 10th Bn (Shekhawati)

The title 'Prince of Wales's Own' was awarded to the 120th Rajputana Infantry in 1920 in recognition of their services in the Great War and, at the same time, colours were presented. Two years later, these were laid up, together with those of the 122nd when these two redcoat regiments became black-buttoned Rifles battalions.

The 11th Bn, a Territorial unit, was raised in 1921 as the 1st Bn (T) 4th Prince Albert Victor's Rajputs in Agra. Later, it became the 12/7th Rajput Regiment but was transferred in 1928 to the 6th Rajputana Rifles as their 11th Bn.

The 5th Bn (Napier's), when they were the 125th Rifles, were the first to institute pipes and drums and permission was sought for Urquhart tartan to be used for plaids and pipe-ribbons. The reasons for this particular tartan seem to have been lost but it may simply have been that the tartan went particularly well with rifle-green and the red facings. Permission was granted by the Government of India provided that the chief of Clan Urquhart concurred. He did, and permission was confirmed in 1903. In 1924, the 2nd Bn (PWO) formed pipes and drums and adopted Urquhart as being the tartan of the Regiment. Three years later, 1st Bn (Wellesley's) decided to form their own pipes and drums and, in the self-righteous fashion affected by all first battalions, wrote to the Lord Lyon King of Arms in Edinburgh, seeking formal permission to use Urquhart tartan. The Lord Lyon replied that this might not be possible since the clan chieftancy was not certain. However, AI(I)No 1222 of 1924 had given leave for the tartan to be worn by the 5th Bn (Napier's), being again ratified in IAO No 600 of 1926 with the characteristically canny comment that it should 'be only on a no-cost basis'.

Finally, in 1938, the CO of the 10th Bn (Shekhawati) wrote to the Lord Lyon King of Arms to obtain permission for the wearing of Urquhart tartan by his pipers. The letter of reply, still in the Regimental Centre, carried just a hint of exasperation when the Lord Lyon explained that there is no law regarding the use of tartans and, therefore, no reason why the 10/6th should not use it if they so wished. It is still worn today by the Regiment.

In 1933, the 5th Bn (Napier's) was nominated to become an Indianizing battalion.

SECOND WORLD WAR

1st Bn (Wellesley's) – India, Italian East Africa, Egypt, Italy

2nd Bn (Prince of Wales's Own) – India, Iraq, Persia

3rd Bn – India, Burma

4th Bn (Outram's) – India, Italian East Africa, Egypt, Italy. In 1944, the 4/6th was nominated for conversion to an airborne role and, in 1945, to become parachutists as 4 (Para) Bn (Outram's) The Rajputana Rifles, brigaded with 1 FF Regt and 3/16 Punjab.

5th Bn (Napier's) – Hong Kong, India, Burma, Malaya, Dutch East Indies. Allocated to the Punjab Boundary Force in August 1947.

6th Bn – raised in Fyzabad in July 1940. India. Disbanded January 1947.

7th Bn – raised in February 1941. India, Malaya. Captured on Singapore Island in February 1942. Disbanded in May 1946.

8th Bn – raised in February 1941. India. Disbanded 1946.

9th Bn – raised as Nasirabad in February 1941. Redesignated 9th (Rajputana) Light Anti–aircraft Regiment, Indian Artillery.

11th Bn – the pre-war Territorial battalion became an active battalion on 15 Sep 41 when it was restyled the 14/6th Rajputana Rifles.

12th Bn – a Territorial battalion raised on 14 Feb 40. It became an active battalion on 15 Sep 41 when it was redesignated the 15/6th Rajputana Rifles.

14th Bn – raised September 1941 by redesignation of the 11th Bn. India. Disbanded May 1941.

15th Bn – raised September 1941 by redesignation of the 12th Bn. India. Disbanded November 1945.

16th Bn – raised 15 Jul 42. India, Malaya. Disbanded May 1947.

25th Garrison Bn – raised 15 Aug 41. India. Disbanded July 1946.

26th Garrison Bn – raised 1 Jan 42. India. Disbanded July 1946.

27th Garrison Bn – raised 1 Oct 42. India. Disbanded February 1947.

Machine Gun Bn – GHQ had ruled that three regiments would raise MG battalions in line with British Army practice and the 6th Rajputana Rifles was one of the three (the others were the 9th Jats and the 17th Dogras). India, Burma. Disbanded August 1946.

In October 1945, the 6th Rajputana Rifles was deprived of its number and became simply The Rajputana Rifles.

PARTITION

In August 1947, the Regiment was allotted to India. On transfer of power, the regular battalions were the 1st, 2nd, 3rd, 4th and 5th.

The Punjabi Mussalmans serving in the Regiment were transferred to Pakistan units, mainly The Baluch Regiment whilst Rajputs were received from the 1st Punjab Regiment.

BATTLE HONOURS

Mysore, Seringapatam, Bourbon, Kirkee, Beni Boo Ali, Meeanee, Hyderabad, Aliwal, Mooltan, Punjab, Reshire, Bushire, Khooshab, Persia, Central India, Abyssinia, Kandahar 1880, Chitral, Afghanistan 1879–80, Burma, 1885–87, British East Africa 1898, China 1900, Afghanistan 1919, Givenchy 1914, Neuve Chapelle, Aubers, Festubert 1915, France and Flaners 1915–15, Egypt 1915, Gaza, Nebi Samwil, Jerusalem, Tell Asur, Megiddo, Sharon, Sharon, Palestine 1917–18, Basra, Shaiba, Kut-al-Amara 1915–17, Ctesiphon, Defence of Kut-al-Amara, Tigris 1916, Baghdad, Mesopotamia 1914–18, Persia 1918, East Africa 1914, Agordat, Barentu, Keren, Abyssinia 1940–41, Derna, Damascus 1941, Deir-es-Zor, Kissoue, Raqaa, Sidi Barrani, Omars, Gubi II, Alem Hamza, Benghazi, Carmusa, Gazala, The Cauldron, The Kennels, Mersa Matruh, Ruweisat Ridge, Alam el Halfa, El Alamein, Mareth, Djebel el Meida, Djebel Garci, Enfidaville, Tunis, North Africa 1940–43, Cassino I, Monastery Hill, Hangman's Hill, Transimene Line, Montone, Citta di Castello, Pian di Magio, Monte Calvo, Italy 1943–45, Johore, The Muar, Singapore Island, Malaya 1941–42, Rathedaung, Htizwe, Imphal, Shenam Pass, Litan, Ukhrul, Tengnoupal, Kyaukmyaung Bridgehead, Mandalay, Fort Dufferin, Meiktila, Maymyo, Pyinmana, Toungoo, Burma 1942–45.

BOOKS

History of the 1st Bn 6th Rajputana Rifles (Wellesley's) by Lt Col F H James OBE MC (Gale and Polden Ltd, Aldershot 1938)
History of the 2nd Bn 6th Rajputana Rifles (Prince of Wales's Own) by H G Rawlinson (OUP 1936)
Outram's Rifles by H G Rawlinson (OUP 1933)
Napier's Rifles by H G Rawlinson (OUP 1929)
History of the 13th Rajputs by Lt Col W Prior (Traill and Co, Calcutta 1908)
The Rajputana Rifles by Major M G Abhyankar (Orient Longmans 1961)
Traditions of a Regiment by Lieut General A M Sethna PVSM AVSM and Lieut Col V Katju (Lancer 1983)

7th RAJPUT REGIMENT

Centre: **1923 FATEHGARH**
1947: FATEHGARH

Class Composition:

1922:
- 1 Coy Rajputs from Eastern United Provinces
- 1 Coy Rajputs from Western United Provinces
- 1 Coy Hindustani Mussalmans from United Provinces
- 1 Coy Punjabi Mussalmans

1947: Punjabi Mussalmans from the Punjab (less Ambala Civil Division) including Niazi and other Pathans of the Punjab. Hazarawalas of NWFP and Mussalmans from Jammu and Kashmir State and Gilgit Agency. Rajputs from Ambala Civil Division, United Provinces, Rajputana, Central India States and Bihar.

The 7th Rajput Regiment, when created in 1922, consisted of some of the oldest regiments in the old Bengal Army. All the Rajput units with the single exception of the 13th (which went to the 6th Rajputana Rifles) were mustered together to give an impeccable Rajput pedigree to the new Regiment. Of the ten regiments which survived of the Bengal line, six were embodied in the 7th Rajput Regiment.

The 2nd Queen's Own Rajput Light Infantry received their light infantry status following their service in the Great Mutiny when, as the old 31st Bengal Native Infantry, they held the fort at Saugor from July 1857 to January 1858. In the words of the Governor General '*their fidelity was unexampled throughout the regular native army*'. The title 'Queen's Own' was awarded in 1876.

This was, of course, not the 31st's first distinction. Following the campaign under Lord Lake at the beginning of the century which gave them their first battle honours, they received an honorary standard inscribed 'Lake and Victory'. The extra jemadar authorised for the honour of bearing this third colour is shown on the page of the Indian Army List on p. 26.

The 33rd Bengal Native Infantry (later 4th Prince Albert Victor's Rajputs) and the 59th Bengal Native infantry (later the 8th Rajputs) were disarmed initially in 1857 but were duly rearmed and served in the Punjab. The 47th Bengal Native Infantry (later the 7th Duke of Connaughts' Own Rajputs) returned from Burma in 1857 and were promptly sent to China as were the 70th Bengal Native Infantry (later the 11th Rajputs). The famous Bailey Guard Paltan was formed in Cawnpore in 1857 from the loyal remnants of the 13th, 48th and 71st Bengal Native Infantry and was designated The Regiment of Lucknow, receiving in 1861, the title of the 16th Bengal Native Infantry and, in 1903, that of 16th Rajputs (The Lucknow Regiment). Every man in the original garrison at Lucknow received the Indian Order of Merit and two British Officers received the Victoria Cross.

FIRST WORLD WAR

2nd Queens Own Rajput Light Infantry – India, Egypt, Mesopotamia, Salonika, Black Sea.
- 2/2nd (raised in 1917) – India.
- 3/2nd (raised in 1918) – India

4th Prince Albert Victor's Rajputs – India, Mesopotamia
- 2/4th (raised in 1918) – India

7th Duke of Connaught's Own Rajputs – India, Mesopotamia, Aden
- 2/7th (raised in 1918) – India, Mesopotamia

8th Rajputs – India, Mesopotamia
- 2/8th (raised in 1918) – India

11th Rajputs – India, Mesopotamia
- 2/11th (raised in 1918) – India

16th Rajputs (The Lucknow Regiment) – India, Persia

None of the war-raised battalions lived on in the new organisation.

BETWEEN THE WARS

The badge chosen for the 7th Rajput Regiment in 1923 was simply the Roman numeral 'VII' flanked by laurel sprays, surmounted by the Royal Crest above a title scroll. The new regimental line-up was as under:

2nd Queen's Own Rajput Light Infantry – 1st Bn (Queen Victoria's Own Light Infantry) 7th Rajput Regiment.
4th Prince Albert Victor's Own Rajputs – 2nd Bn (Prince Albert Victor's) 7th Rajput Regiment.
7th Duke of Connaught's Own Rajputs – 3rd Bn (Duke of Connaught's Own) 7th Rajput Regiment.
8th Rajputs – 4th Bn 7th Rajput Regiment.
11th Rajputs – 5th Bn 7th Rajput Regiment.
16th Rajputs (The Lucknow Regiment) – 10th Bn (The Lucknow Regiment) 7th Rajput Regiment.

The 11th Bn was a Territorial battalion raised at Fyzabad in 1921. A second Territorial battalion, the 12th was also raised in 1921, but at Agra. Subsequently, it was transferred to the 6th Rajputana Rifles in 1928 as their 11th Bn. In 1924, the 1st Bn was among those selected for Indianisation.

SECOND WORLD WAR

1st Battalion (QVOLI) – India, Burma

2nd Battalion (PAV) – India, Burma

3rd Battalion (DCO) – India, Egypt. In 1946 the 3rd was nominated for conversion to a parachute role and they became 3rd (Para) Bn The Rajput Regt in 77 Indian Parachute Brigade.

4th Battalion – India, Egypt

5th Battalion – India, Hong Kong. Captured December 1941. Captain Ansari of this battalion was awarded a posthumous George Cross for his constant defiance of his captors' propaganda and their attempts to undermine his men's loyalty.

6th Battalion – raised 15 Jul 40. India, Burma. Disbanded January 1947.

7th Battalion – raised India. Redesignated 8th (Rajput) HAA Regt IA 1 Apr 42.

8th Battalion – raised India. Redesignated 7th (Rajput) HAA Regt IA 1 Feb 42.

9th Battalion – formed 15 Sept 41 by redesignation of the 11th Bn, the pre-war Territorial battalion, on conversion to an active battalion. (Converted to Artillery.)

11th Battalion – the pre-war Territorial battalion on conversion to active status, was redesignated the 9th Battalion.

12th Battalion – a Territorial battalion raised 14 Feb 40. On conversion to active status on 15 Sep 41 was redesignated the 14th Battalion.

14th Battalion – formed 15 Sep 41 by redesignation of the 12th Bn, a Territorial battalion converted to active status. India. Disbanded 1946.

15th Battalion – raised 15 Oct 41. India. Disbanded 15 Sep 46.

16th Battalion – raised 15 Apr 42. India. Disbanded 10 Jul 46.

17th Battalion – raised Sept 42 by redesignation of 52 Regt IAC, India, Burma.

18th Battalion – raised 15 Aug 41 on conversion of 25th Garrison Bn to active status. India.

25th Garrison Bn – converted to active status on 15 Aug 41 and redesignated 18 Bn.

26th Garrison Bn – raised 1 Mar 41. India. Disbanded 1946.

Machine Gun Battalion – redesignated 52 Regt IAC. August 1942. Redesignated 17 Bn September 1942.

In October 1945 the 7th Rajput Regiment lost the number in its title, becoming simply The Rajput Regiment.

PARTITION

In August 1947, the Regiment was allotted to India. On transfer of power, the battalions were the 1st, 2nd, 3rd, 4th and 14th.

BATTLE HONOURS

Delhi 1803, Leswarree, Deig, Bhurtpore, Afghanistan 1839, Khelat, Cabool 1842, Maharajpore, Moodkee, Ferozeshah, Aliwal, Sobraon, Chillianwallah, Goojerat, Punjaub, Lucknow, Central India, China 1858–59, Afghanistan 1878–80, Tel-el-Kebir, Egypt 1882, Burma 1885–87, Pekin 1900, China 1900, Macedonia 1918, Suez Canal, Egypt 1915, Aden, Basra, Kut-al-Amara 1915, Ctesiphon, Defence of Kut-al-Amara, Tigris 1916, Mesopotamia 1914–18, Persia 1915–18, NW Frontier India 1915, 1917, Afghanistan 1919, Hong Kong, South East Asia 1941–42, El Alamein, North Africa 1940–41, Donbaik, Razabil, Point 551, Ngakyedauk Pass, Imphal, Tiddim Road, Kohima, Relief of Kohima, Meiktila, Capture of Meiktila, Defence of Meiktila, Taungtha, Rangoon Road, Sittang 1945, Burma 1942–45

BOOKS

3/7th Rajput Regiment (DCO) by H G Rawlinson (OUP 1941).

Heritage: the History of The Rajput Regiment 1778–1947 by Mustasad Ahmad (Pub: Regimental Centre 1989).

8th PUNJAB REGIMENT

Centre: **1923 LAHORE**
1946 LAHORE

Class composition:		
	1923	Punjabi Mussalmans, Sikhs, Rajputana Hindus (other than Rajputs, Jats and Mers)
	1946	Punjabi Mussalmans from the Punjab (less Ambala Civil Division) including Niazi and other Pathans of the Punjab, Hazarawalas of NWFP and Mussalmans from Jammu and Kashmir State and Gilgit Agency, Gujars from the Punjab, United provinces and Rajputana, Sikhs from the Punjab.

Despte its title, the 8th Punjab Regiment was another of those which owed its origins to the old Madras Army. The 29th Madras Infantry was mustered out on 15 Oct 1893 and was reconstituted the next day at Meiktila in Central Burma as the 29th (7th Burma Bn) Madras Infantry, made up of Punjabis and Sikhs. Similarly, the 30th Madras Infantry became the 30th (5th Burma Bn) Madras Infantry, the 31st became the 31st (6th Burma Bn) Madras Infantry, the 32nd became the 32nd (4th Burma Bn) Madras Infantry and the 33rd the 33rd (3rd Burma Bn) Madras Infantry. In 1901, all these titles were simplified by removal of all mention of Madras and the five regiments were styled 29th Burma Infantry, 30th Burma Infantry, 31st Burma Light Infantry, 32nd Burma Infantry and 33rd Burma Infantry. These Burma battalions were to police the troublesome new territories acquired in the Third Burma War. In 1903, when all Madras regiments had sixty added to their numbers, the 29th and 30th became 89th and 90th Punjabis, the 31st became the 91st Punjabis (Light Infantry), the 32nd became the 92nd Punjabis whilst the 33rd only performed a half-change, entering the new Line as the 93rd Burma Infantry. It may be said that it was the Afghan Campaign of 1878–80 which set the seal on the future of the Madras soldier. The 30th Madras Native Infantry served in the Khyber Pass but suffered so much from extremes of cold that it put into doubt the suitability of the Southern soldier for service in what was clearly to be a recurring trouble spot.

FIRST WORLD WAR

89th Punjabis – India, Aden, Egypt, Gallipoli, France, Mesopotamia, Greece, Russia.

2/89th Punjabis (raised in 1917) – India, Mesopotamia

90th Punjabis – India, Mesopotamia

2/90th Punjabis (raised in 1918) – India

91st Punjabis – India, Mesopotamia, Egypt

2/91st Punjabis (raised in 1918) – India, Egypt

92nd Punjabis – India, Mesopotamia, Egypt

93rd Burma Infantry – India, Egypt, France, Mesopotamia, Burma

Following the return of Indian troops after the war, all the second battalions were disbanded with the exception of the 2/89th Punjabis.

BETWEEN THE WARS

The badge chosen for the 8th Punjab Regiment on its creation in 1923 was probably one of the most interesting and heraldically appealing. In the light of the former history of the constituent regiments, it was appropriate that the new regiment should adopt the Chinthe, the mythical lion-dragon, the guardian of Buddhist pagodas, above the numeral '8' and the title scroll.

The new line-up was as follows:

89th Punjabis became 1st Bn 8th Punjab Regiment
90th Punjabis became 2nd Bn 8th Punjab Regiment
91st Punjabis (Light Infantry) became 3rd Bn 8th Punjab Regiment
92nd (Prince of Wales's Own) Punjabis became 4th Bn 8th Punjab Regiment (Prince of Wales's Own)
93rd Burma Infantry became 5th Bn 8th Punjab Regiment (Burma)
2/89th Punjabis became 10th Bn 8th Punjab Regiment

The 92nd had been made 'Prince of Wales's Own' in 1921 for their services during the war. The 5th Bn of the new regiment was nominated in the early 1930s as one of the battalions chosen for Indianization.

There was no Territorial battalion raised for the 8th Punjab Regiment.

SECOND WORLD WAR

1st Battalion – India, Malaya. Captured on Singapore Island in February 1942. Reformed in 1946 by redesignation of 9/8 Punjab.

2nd Battalion – India, Burma.

3rd Battalion – India, Persia, Egypt, Italy.

4th Battalion – India, Iraq, Iran.

5th Battalion – India, Burma, Malaya, Dutch East Indies.

6th Battalion (Machine Gun) – raised in August 1940. India, Burma, Malaya, Dutch East Indies.
7th Battalion – raised in August 1940. India, Malaya. Captured on Singapore Island in February 1942.
8th Battalion – raised in May 1941. India, Burma.
9th Battalion – raised in May 1941. Joined 6/15 Punjab and 6/16 Punjab in 39 Indian Infantry Brigade, the only all-Punjab brigade in the Indian Army. India, Ceylon, Cyprus. Redesignated 1/8 Punjab in 1946.
14th Battalion – redesignated 9th (Punjab) HAA Regt Indian Artillery in June 1942.
15th Battalion – Raised in January 1942. India. Became a training battalion for VCOs and NCOs.
16th Battalion – Raised in August 1943. India.
25th Garrison Battalion – raised in April 1941. India.
26th Garrison Battalion – raised in March 1942. India.

The Regiment's pipes and drums went to London in 1946 to march in the Victory parade, their claim being that they were the best in the Indian Army.

PARTITION

The 8th Punjab Regiment was allocated to Pakistan and the Sikh companies returned to India, principally to replace Punjabi Mussalman companies in battalions of The Sikh Regiment and to help in creation of new Sikh battalions.

The regular battalions on transfer of power were the 1st, 2nd, 3rd and 4th.

BATTLE HONOURS

Cochin, Maheidpore, Ava, Afghanistan 1878–80, Burma 1885–87, China 1900. Loos, France and Flanders 1915, Macedonia 1918, Helles, Krithia, Gallipoli 1915, Suez Canal, Egypt 1915, Megiddo, Sharon, Palestine 1918, Tigris 1916, Kut-al-Amara 1917, Baghdad, Khan Baghdadi, Mesopotamia 1915–18, Afghanistan 1919.

North Malaya, Jitra, Gurun, Malaya 1941–42, The Trigno, Perano, The Sangro, Villa Grande, Gustav Line, Monte Grande, The Senio, Italy 1943–45, Donbaik, North Arakan, The Shweli, Myitson, Kama, Burma 1942–45.

BOOKS

None known.

9th JAT REGIMENT

Centre: **1923 BAREILLY**
1946 BAREILLY

Class composition:	1923	1st, 2nd, 3rd and 4th Bns Jats from the Punjab and Delhi, Punjabi Mussalmans and Mussalman Rajputs
		10th Bn Jats from the Punjab and Delhi, Punjabi Mussalmans and Mussalman Rajputs
	1946	Jats from the Punjab, United Provinces, Rajputans and Central India states, Hindustani Mussalmans from Ambala Civil Division, Rajputana, United Provinces, Central India states and the Deccan. Punjabi Mussalmans from the Punjab (less Ambala Civil Division) including Niazi and other Pathans of the Punjab, Hazarawalas of NWFP and Mussalmans of Jammu and Kashmir State and Gilgit Agency.

Despite an impressive reputation as soldiers, not least in the defence of Bhurtpore against Lord Lake, Jats were not extensively recruited into the Bengal Army before the Great Mutiny. However, towards the end of the last century, there began a policy to enlist these yeoman peasants from the south-east Punjab and two Bengal regiments, the 6th Jat Light Infantry and the 10th Jat Infantry became Jat class regiments. The 19th Bombay Infantry, despatched from Sind in 1849, stormed Mooltan and, after 1903, as the 119th Regiment, bore the subsidiary title '(The Mooltan Regiment)'.

They brought Rajputs, Gujars and Mers to the union as well as Hindustani Mussalmans. The fourth constituent was the 18th Infantry, formerly known as the 18th Mussalman Rajput Infantry which meant that, although styled the 9th

Jat Regiment, Jats were outnumbered. The 18th had, in fact, been born in 1795 as the Calcutta Native Militia which made it the oldest of the four regiments but they were late in being taken into the regular line.

FIRST WORLD WAR

6th Jat Light Infantry – India, France, Egypt, Mesopotamia
2/6th (formed in 1917) – India, Mesopotamia
119th Infantry – India, Mesopotamia
2/119th (formed in 1917) – India, Mesopotamia
10th Jat Infantry – India, Mesopotamia
2/10th (formed in 1917) – India, Egypt
18th Infantry – India, Hong Kong, China
2/18th (formed in 1917) – India, Egypt

All four regiments raised second battalions during the war but the only one to live on after the post-war reforms was the 2/6th Jat Light Infantry.

BETWEEN THE WARS

The badge chosen for the new 9th Jat Regiment was not an inspired choice – the Roman 'IX' with crown above and title scroll below. The line-up for the new regiment was the 1st Royal Bn (6th Royal Jat Light Infantry), an honour granted in 1921 for services in the Great War, the 2nd (Mooltan) Bn (late 119th Infantry), the 3rd Bn (late 10th Jat Infantry), the 4th Bn (late 18th Infantry) and the 10th Bn (late 2/6th Royal Jat Light Infantry) plus the 11th, the Territorial battalion, raised at Meerut. Almost immediately, the 4/9th was disbanded.

The customary 10th Bn, in its training role, abandoned its perpetuation of the 2/6th Royal Jat Light Infantry and assumed the identity of the old 18th Infantry, predecessors of the vanished 4/9th. The decision was taken to merge the training resources of the Regiment with those of the 4th Bombay Grenadiers. The latter had only two active battalions and the Jats three so the linked training unit was known as the 10th Bn 4/9th Regiment and it continued thus until 1941 when wartime expansion demanded separate facilities once more. As a result, the re-raised 10/4th Bombay Grenadiers left to set up a centre at Nasirabad.

SECOND WORLD WAR

1st Royal Bn – India, Burma, Thailand, Malaya
2nd (Mooltan) Bn – India, Malaya. Captured in Singapore February 1942. Re-raised in July 1946 by redesignation of the 15th Bn.
3rd Bn – India, Iraq, Syria, Egypt, Burma, Dutch East Indies.
4th Bn – re-raised at Jhelum on 15 Jul 40. India, Malaya. Captured in Singapore February 1942.
5th Bn – raised at Benares on 1 Feb 41. India, Burma, Dutch East Indies.
6th Bn – raised at Bareilly on 1 Feb 41. India, Burma.
7th Bn – on 15 Sep 41, the Territorial battalion, the 11/9th, was converted to an active battalion and redesignated the 7th Bn. India, Burma. Disbanded on 30 Mar 46.
8th Bn – on 15 Sep 41, the Regiment's second Territorial battalion, the 12/9th, was converted to an active battalion and redesignated the 8th Bn. India. Disbanded 30 Nov 46.
9th Bn – on 15 Sep 41, the 11/14th Punjab Regiment, a Territorial battalion, was converted to an active battalion and redesignated the 9/9th Jat Regiment (the seemingly odd policy of converting a unit of the 14th Punjab Regiment

into a Jat battalion was due to the 11/4th having a high proportion of Jats). India. Disbanded 30 Dec 46.

11th Bn – the Regiment's pre-war Territorial battalion was converted to active status and redesignated the 7th Bn on 15 Sep 41.

12th Bn – the second Territorial batalion, raised at Fyzabad on 5 Jul 40 was converted to active status and redesignated the 8th Bn.

14th Bn – on 15 Sep 41, the 12/14th Punjab Regiment, a Territorial Battalion, was converted to an active battalion and redesignated the 14/9th Jat Regiment (see note against the 9/9th above). India. Disbanded 30 Apr 47.

15th Bn – the restyled 25th Garrison Bn. India. Redesignated the 2nd (Mooltan) Bn on 1 Jul 46.

25th Garrison Bn – raised at Bareilly on 15 Aug 41. Redesignated the 15th Bn on 15 Aug 43.

26th Garrison Bn – raised at Bareilly on 1 Mar 1942. India. Disbanded 15 Aug 46.

27th Garrison Bn – raised at Jubbulpore on 15 Oct 42 from the 17th and 40th Garrison Companies. India. Disbanded 30 May 46.

Machine Gun Battalion – raised on 15 Oct 41. GHQ had ruled that the three regiments should raise MG Bns in line with British Army practice and the 9th Jat Regiment was one of the three (the others were the 6th Rajputana Rifles and the 17th Dogra Regiment). Personnel to form the battalion were found from the four units of the Regiment having support platoons. India, Burma, French Indo-China. Disbanded 15 Aug 46.

In October 1945, the 9th Jat Regiment, in line with the majority of the Indian infantry, lost the number from its regimental designation and became known simply as The Jat Regiment.

PARTITION

On partition, the Regiment was allotted to India. Battalions on transfer of power were the 1st, 2nd, 3rd, 5th and 6th. Details of known incoming and outgoing drafts are as under.

Incoming		*Nos*	*From*	
	Jats	1 Royal Bn (LI)	139	1/15 Punjab
		2 (Mooltan) Bn	124	4/15 Punjab
		3 Bn	156	6/15 Punjab
		5 Bn	99	2/15 Punjab
		6 Bn	196	3/15 Punjab
		Regtl Centre	187	15 Punjab Centre
			901	
Outgoing				
	Punjabi Mussalmans	1 Royal Bn (LI)	216	4 FFRif
		2 (Mooltan) Bn	263	2 FFRif
		3 Bn	222	1/16 Punjab
		5 Bn	242	2 FFRif
		6 Bn	266	3/8 Punjab
		Regtl Centre	238	16 Punjab Centre
			1447	

Outgoing		*From*	*Nos*	*To*
	Hindustani	1 Royal Bn (LI)	153	1/16 Punjab
	Mussalmans	2 (Mooltan) Bn	173	5/8 Punjab
		3 Bn	155	8 Punjab
	(Previously known	5 Bn	173	1/8 Punjab
	as Mussalman	Regtl Centre	158	8 Punjab Centre
	Rajputs)			
			996	

Miscellaneous	Total Strength	Opted for Pakistan Army
Military Band	27	19
Pipes and Drums	20	14
Bugle Band	7	4
Boys' Company	114	34
Jat War Memorial School	Not known	15

The battalions on transfer of power were the 1st, 2nd, 3rd and 5th

BATTLE HONOURS

Nagpur, Afghanistan 1839, Ghuznee 1839, Candahar 1842, Ghuznee 1842, Cabool 1842, Maharajpore, Sobraon, Mooltan, Goojerat, Punjab, Ali Masjid, China 1858–62, Kandahar 1880, Afghanistan 1879–80, Burma 1885–87, China 1900 La Bassee 1914, Festubert 1914–15, Neuve Chapelle, France and Flanders 1914–15, Shaiba, Defence of Kut-al-Amara Ctesiphon, Tigris 1916, Khan Baghdadi, Mesopotamia 1914–18, Kut-al-Amara 1915, NW Frontier, India 1914–15, 1917, Afghanistan 1919, Razabil, Kanglatongbi, Kampar, Malaya 1941–42, Burma 1942–45, Nungshigum, Jitra, The Muar, North Africa 1940–43

BOOKS

War services of the 9th Jat Regiment (Vols I and II) by Lieut Col W Hailes MC and Major J Ross (Pub London 1961)

A brief history of the MG Battalion, The Jat Regiment 1941–46 by Lieut Col E Johnson (Higginbothams, Bangalore 1947)

10th BALUCH REGIMENT

Centre: **1923 RAJKOT**
1946 KARACHI

Class Composition: 1923 Punjabi Mussalmans, Pathans, Baluchis and Brahuis

1946 Punjabi Mussalmans from the Punjab (less Ambala Civil Division) including Niazi and other Pathans from the Punjab. Hazarawalas of NWFP and Mussalmans of Jammu and Kashmir State and Gilgit Agency, Dogras from the Punjab and Jammu and Kashmir State. From within the administrative borders of the NWFP of British India. NWFP states and Tribal Territory.

Perhaps surprisingly, the 10th Baluch Regiment sprang from the old Bombay Army and its predecessors were freely used to sort out India's problems in and around the Persian Gulf and the Arabian Sea. Appropriately, the senior battalion originated in the 2nd (Marine) Bn of the 12th Regiment of Bombay Native Infantry raised in 1820. In 1838, as the 24th Regiment of Bombay Native Infantry, they stormed Aden, bringing that hotbed of pirates under the British flag. The 26th Bombay Native Infantry was raised in 1825 as the 2nd Extra Bn of Bombay Native Infantry, changing its name a year later. Sir Charles Napier raised two regiments in Karachi – the 1st and 2nd Belooch Regiments – for local service within Sind in 1844 and 1846 respectively. The term 'local' was interpreted fairly loosely when it became necessary to send the 2nd Belooch to the Persian War in 1856–57, a campaign frequently overshadowed by the events of the Great Mutiny in 1857. The 1st was in Karachi when the news of the insurrection reached the Commissioner. Sir Bartle Frere despatched them with all haste, on foot across the Sind desert in May to join the siege artillery train on its way to Delhi, the only Bombay unit to join the Delhi Field Force. The regiment was brought into the regular line for its services in Central India and it became the 27th Regiment of Bombay Native Infantry in the post-Mutiny realignment. The 2nd Belooch, in the meantime, had qualified for a similar change in status for their work on the NW Frontier and became the 29th Regiment of Bombay Native Infantry. In 1858, Major John Jacob raised a local battalion, soon to be known as Jacob's Rifles and they made such a reputation in and around Jacobabad that they, too, were accorded regular status, becoming the 30th Regiment of Bombay Native Infantry or Jacob's Rifles in 1861. In the years which followed, the subsidiary title lapsed and does not appear to have been officially revived until 1910, by which time, the 24th, the 26th, the 27th, the 29th, and the 30th had all had one hundred added to their numbers in 1903, emerging as the 124th, the 126th, the 127th, the 129th and the 130th.

A distinction shared by no other regiment was a spell in Japan by the 29th in 1864. They were summoned from Shanghai to Yokohama in September to protect Queen Victoria's British and Indian subjects. The British force remained in Japan until September the following year.

FIRST WORLD WAR

124th Duchess of Connaught's Baluchistan Infantry – India, Mesopotamia, Persia.
2/124th (formed in 1916) – Persia, Mesopotamia,Egypt, India.
3/124th (formed in 1917) – India, Persia, Mesopotamia.
126th Baluchistan Infantry – India, Egypt, Muscat, Aden, Moseopotamia.
2/126th (formed in 1918) – India.
127th Queen Mary's Own Baluch Light Infantry – India, East Africa, Persia.
2/127th (formed in 1918) – India, Egypt.
129th Duke of Connaught's Own Baluchis – India, France, East Africa.
2/129th (formed in 1917) – India, Mesopotamia.
130th King George's Own Baluchis (Jacob's Rifles) – India, East Africa.
2/130th (formed in 1918) – India.

Only the 2nd Bn of the 124th of the wartime raisings was retained after the post-war reforms.

The 129th in the 3rd (Lahore) Division, was the only battalion of the regiment to serve on the Western Front, the first Indian regiment to attack the Germans, the first also on two other counts – to lose the first British officer and to earn the first Victoria Cross, this by Sepoy Khudadad Khan at Hollebeke. Wounded, he recovered to enjoy the distinction of being the first Indian soldier to receive the King Emperor's most coveted gift. Prior to 1911, Indian soldiers had not been eligible to receive the Cross.

BETWEEN THE WARS

The badge chosen for the 10th Baluch Regiment in 1923 was a Roman 'Ten' within a crescent moon, a crown above and title scroll below.

The line-up of battalions for the new regiment was as under:

124th Duchess of Connaught's Own Baluchistan Infantry – 1st Bn 10th Baluch Regiment.
126th Baluchistan Infantry – 2nd Bn 10th Baluch Regiment.
127th Queen Mary's Own Baluch Light Infantry – 3rd Bn (Queen Mary's Own) 10th Baluch Regiment.

129th Duke of Connaught's Own Baluchis – 4th Bn (Duke of Connaught's Own) 10th Baluch Regiment.
130th King George's Own Baluchis – 5th Bn (King George's Own) (Jacobs Rifles) 10th Baluch Regiment.
2/124th Duchess of Connaught's Own Baluchistan Infantry – 10th Bn 10th Baluch Regiment.

There was no Territorial battalion but the 5/10th was selected for Indianisation. It was not among the initial six infantry battalions nominated in 1923, but it featured in a supplementary list in 1933.

SECOND WORLD WAR

1st Battalion – India, Iraq, Iran, Syria, Egypt.
2nd Battalion – India, Malaya. Captured in Singapore in February 1942. Reformed in April 1946 from cadre of 9/10 Baluch.
3rd Battalion – India, Iran, Iraq, Egypt, Sicily, Italy. On return to India the battalion was nominated for conversion to a parachute role to join 2 Indian Airborne Division.
4th Battalion – India, East Africa, Egypt, Cyprus, Italy.
5th Battalion – India, Burma.
6th Battalion – raised in Karachi on 1 Jan 40. India. Disbanded 1 Feb 47.
7th Battalion – raised in Benares on 10 Oct 40. India. Burma.
8th Battalion – raised in Karachi on 1 Feb 41. India, Burma. Disbanded 22 Decr 46.
9th Battalion – raised in Nasirabad on 1 Feb 41. India. Disbanded 25 Apr 46 but almost 500 went to reform the regular 2nd Bn.
14th Battalion – raised in Karachi on 1 Feb 41. India, Burma, Malaya, Siam. Disbanded 15 Sep 46.
16th Battalion – raised in Karachi on 15 Oct 41. India, Burma, Malaya. Disbanded March 1946.
17th Battalion – raised Novovember 1942 by conversion of 53 Regt IAC, India, Iraq, Palestine, Greece, Libya.
18th Battalion – raised originally as 25 Garrison Bn, it became an active battalion and was redesignated 18/10th. India. Disbanded May 1944.
25th Garrison Battalion – raised in Karachi in July 1941. On conversion to active status, it was redesignated the 18/10th.
26th Garrison Battalion – raised in Karachi in March 1942. India. Disbanded 1946.

Machine Gn Battalion – raised in Karachi on 15 Apr 42. Converted to 53 Regt IAC August 1942. Redesignated 17/10th November 1942.

In common with many other Indian Infantry regiments, the 10th Baluch Regiment lost its number and, at the end of 1945, became The Baluch Regiment.

PARTITION

In August 1947, The Baluch Regiment was allotted to Pakistan, the Dogra companies remaining in India and transferring to, among other regiments, The Indian Grenadiers.

On transfer of power, the active battalions were the 1st, 2nd, 3rd, 4th, 5th and 7th.

BATTLE HONOURS

Aden, Reshire, Bushire, Koosh-ab, Persia. Delhi 1857, Central India, Abyssinia, Kandahar 1880, Afghanistan 1878–80, Egypt 1882, Tel-el-Kebir, Burmah 1885–87, British East Africa 1896, British East Africa 1897–99, China 1900, Messines 1914, Armentieres 1914, Ypres 1914–15, Gheluvelt, Festubert 1914, Givenchy 1914, Neuve Chapelle, St Julien, France and Flanders 1914–15, Egypt 1915, Megiddo, Sharon, Palestine 1918, Aden, Kut-al-Amara 1917, Baghdad, Mesopotamia 1916–18, Persia 1915–18, NW Frontier, India 1917, Kilimanjaro, Behobeho, East Africa 1915–18, Afghanistan 1919.

Gallabat, Barentu, Massawa, The Cauldron, Ruweisat Ridge, El Alamein, North Africa 1940–43, Landing in Sicily, Sicily 1943, Castel Frentano, Orsogna, Arezzo, Monte Cedrone, Citta di Castello, Monte Calvo, Gothic Line, Plan di Castello, Croce, Gemmano Ridge, San Marino, San Paulo-Monte Spacata, Monte Cavallo, Cesena, Savio Bridgehead, Casa Bettini, Idice Bridgehead, Italy 1943–45, Athens, Greece 1944–45, North Malaya, Machang, Singapore Island, Malaya 1941–42, Kuzeik, North Ařkan, Point 551, Maungdaw, Shwebo, Kyaukmyaung Bridgehead, Mandalay, Capture of Meiktila, Defence of Meiktila, The Irrawaddy, Pegu 1945, Sittang 1945, Burma 1942–45.

BOOKS

'Historical Records of the 127th Baluch Light Infantry 1845–1905' (Wm Clowes, London, 1905)

'The 10th Baluch Regiment – the 1st and 10th Battalions' by O A Chaldecott (Times of india Press, Bombay c. 1935)

'Capital Campaigners' (3/10th Baluch) by Lieut Col W E Maxwell (Gale and Polden Ltd. Aldershot, 1948)

'The Tenth Baluch Regiment in the Second World War' by W S Thatcher (Baluch Regimental Centre, Abbottabad 1980)

11th SIKH REGIMENT

Regimental Centre:	**1923 – NOWSHERA** **1947 – NOWSHERA**	
Class Composition:	1923	1, 2 and 3 Bns – Jat Sikhs 4, 5 and 10 Bns – Jat Sikhs and Punjabi Mussalmans
	1947	Sikhs from the Punjab, Punjabi Mussalmans from the Punjab (less Ambala Civil Division), including Niazi and other Pathans of the Punjab. Hazarawalas of NWFP and Mussalmans of Jammu and Kashmir State and Gilgit Agency.

History recalls more than one instance when a victorious British force has scarcely completed negotiations for peace when it has begun to enlist ex-enemy soldiers for local service. Thus it was in 1816 with the Gurkhas and also in 1846 after the fiercely fought Sikh Wars. Two regiments were formed – the Regiment of Ferozepore and the Regiment of Ludhiana – albeit not entirely Sikh in composition. The regular Bengal Line supplied a number of Oudh Rajputs as the framework and the now ubiquitous Punjabi Mussalman made up a leavening. Those were the days before the class structure of regiments which developed only fifty years later. During the Great Mutiny, the Regiment of Ferozepore fought it's way with Havelock into the beleaguered garrison of Lucknow and awaited the second relief led by Sir Colin Campbell. The colour-staff borne in that action, chipped and splintered by rebel fire, was still in use well into the twentieth century, although the attached colour had long since been replaced by another, carrying the honour scrolls which offered testimony. At the end of the campaign, the Regiment was granted the right to wear a red pagri, a distinction later extended to the 11th Sikh Regiment. In the post-Mutiny realignment in 1861, they became the 15th Bengal Native Infantry briefly but, later that year, changed to the 14th. The Regiment of Ludhiana was relied upon to hold Benares throughout the period of the Mutiny. In 1861 they became the

16th Bengal Native Infantry, being changed shortly afterwards to the 15th. The Bengal Military Police Battalion was raised by Captain T. Rattray in 1856. Normally known as Rattray's Sikhs, they were serving in Bihar in May 1857. When the Dinapore Brigade mutinied, Rattray's were the only loyal troops, apart from HM's 10th Foot (later The Lincolnshire Regiment) between Calcutta and Benares. Eventually, they were to become a regiment of the Bengal Line with the number 45. In 1887, one of the periodic Russian scares prompted the raising of two more Sikh regiments, the 35th and the 36th. These numbers had previously been borne by the old Mynpoorie and Bareilly Levies of the Mutiny which had both been disbanded in 1882. The 36th earned the distinction of a unique battle-honour in 1897 when the regiment was in the Samana Range, near Fort Lockhart. Saragarhi was a small mud fort on a knife-edged ridge and, there, nineteen Jat Sikh sepoys and two cookboys defended their post for over six hours against an estimated seven thousand Orakzais. They died to a man and the Government of India raised a memorial to them in the Sikh city of Amritsar. In 1901, the 47th (Sikhs) Bengal Infantry was raised to be renamed, in 1903, the 47th Sikhs.

FIRST WORLD WAR

14th King George's Own Ferozepore Sikhs – India, Egypt, Gallipoli, Mesopotamia.

15th Ludhiana Sikhs – India, France, Egypt.

2/15th (raised in 1918) – India.

45th Rattray's Sikhs – India, Mesopotamia.

36th Sikhs – China, India, Mesopotamia

47th Sikhs – India, France, Mesopotamia, Egypt.

35th Sikhs – India.

2/35th (raised in 1917) – India.

In the light of the services performed in the Great War, it seems invidious, perhaps, to single out one regiment but the 14th, in the Gallipoli campaign, suffered 264 killed and 840 wounded. The 47th, in 1921, were accorded the title of the Duke of Connaught's Own. Neither of the second battalions survived the post-war changes.

BETWEEN THE WARS

The badge chosen for the 11th Sikh Regiment on its formation in 1922 was the simple silver quoit but the variations worn by the various battalions were almost infinite.

The 1st, 2nd and 3rd Bns were to be all Jat Sikhs, the 4th and 5th were to be 50% each Jat Sikhs and Punjabi Mussalmans, whilst the 10th Bn would have four Sikh companies and one PM company. There was no Territorial battalion raised for the 11th Sikhs.

The new line-up was as follows:

14th King George's Own Ferozepore Sikhs became 1st Bn (King George's Own) (Ferozepore Sikhs) 11th Sikh Regiment

15th Ludhiana Sikhs became 2nd Bn (Ludhiana Sikhs) 11th Sikh Regiment

45th Rattray's Sikhs became 3rd Bn (Rattray's Sikhs) 11th Sikh Regiment

36th Sikhs became 4th Bn 11th Sikh Regiment

47th Duke of Connaught's Own Sikhs became 5th Bn (Duke of Connaught's Own) 11th Sikh Regiment

35th Sikhs became 10th Bn 11th Sikh Regiment

SECOND WORLD WAR

1st Battalion – India, Burma

2nd Battalion – India, Iraq, Persia, Egypt, Cyprus, Italy, Greece

3rd Battalion – India, Iraq, Persia, Lebanon

4th Battalion – India, Egypt, Italian East Africa, Libya, Iraq, Palestine, Lebanon, Syria, Italy

5th Battalion – India, Malaya, captured in Singapore February 1942. Not re-formed on repatriation

6th Battalion – raised 7 Aug 40. India, Burma. Disbanded 5 Aug 46.

7th Battalion – raised 7 Aug 40. India, Egypt, Syria, Palestine. The battalion was not disbanded after the war but continued as a regular unit.

8th Battalion – raised 1 May 41. Became 8 LAA Regt IA 31 Mar 42

9th Battalion – raised 1 May 41. Became 7 LAA Regt IA 31 Mar 42

14th Battalion – raised 14 Mar 42. India. Disbanded 31 Mar 46

15th Battalion – raised as 25th Garrison Bn 1 Apr 41. Converted to active status August 1942. India. Disbanded 7 Nov 44.

25th Garrison – raised 1 Ap 41. Redesignated 15/11 Sikh August 1942

26th Garrison Battalion – raised 1 Mar 42. India, Disbanded May 1946.

Machine Gun Battalion – raised 15 Jan 42. India, Burma. Disbanded November 1947

In October 1945, in common with most of the Indian Infantry, the 11th Sikh Regiment lost its number and became simply The Sikh Regiment.

PARTITION

In August 1947, The Sikh Regiment was allotted to India and the Punjabi Mussalman companies left for Pakistan. In exchange, the Regiment received Sikh companies from the 8th Punjab Regiment.

On transfer of power, the active battalions were the 1st, 2nd, 3rd, 4th and 7th.

BATTLE HONOURS

Defence of Arrah, Lucknow, Behar, China 1860–62, Ali Masjid, Ahmed Khel, Kandahar 1880, Afghanistan 1878–80, Tofrek, Suakin 1885, Defence of Chitral, Chitral, Malakand, Punjab Fontier, Samana, Tirah, China 1900.

La Bassee 1914, Armentieres 1914, Givenchy 1914, Neuve Chapelle, Ypres 1915, St Julien, Aubers, Festubert 1915, France and Flanders 1914–15, Helles, Krithia, Suvla, Sari Bair, Gallipoli 1915, Suez Canal, Egypt 1915–16, Megiddo, Sharon, Palestine 1918, Tigris 1916, Kut-al-Amara 1917, Baghdad, Sharqat, Mesopotamia 1916–18, Persia 1918, NW Frontier, India 1914, 1915, 1916–17, Tsingtao, Afghanistan 1919.

Agordat, Keren, Abyssinia 1940–41, Iraq 1941, Omars, Mersa Matruh, Deir el Shein, North Africa 1940–43, Gothic Line, Monte Calvo, Coriano, Poggio San Giovanni, San Marino, Italy 1943–45, Greece 1944–45, Kuantan, Niyor, Malaya 1941–42, North Arakan, Buthidaung, Kanglatongbi, Nyaungu Bridgehead, The Irrawaddy 1945, Shandatgyi, Kama, Sittang 1945, Burma 1942–45.

BOOKS

'Regimental History of the 45th Rattray's Sikhs during the Great War and after – 1914–21' by Lieut Col R H Anderson (Sifton Praed and Co. London 1925)

'History of the 45th Rattray's Sikhs – Vol I – 1856–1914' by Col H St G M McRae (Robert Maclehose Co Ltd., Glasgow 1933)

'The 14th King George's Own Sikhs 1846–1933 by Col F E G Talbot (Butler and Tanner Ltd., London 1937)

1st King George V's Own Battalion. The Sikh Regiment' by Lieut Col P G Bamford DSO (Gale and Polden Ltd, Aldershot 1948)
'The Sikh Regiment in the Second World War' by Col F T Birdwood OBE (Jarrold and Sons, Norwich)
'Saragarhi Battalion – Ashes to Glory, The history of the 4th Bn The Sikh Regiment (XXXVI)' by Col Kanwaljit Singh and Major H S Ahluwalia (Lancer International Publishing, New Delhi 1987)

12th FRONTIER FORCE REGIMENT

Centre: **1923 MARDAN**
1947 SIALKOT

Class Composition	1923	Punjabi Mussalmans, Sikhs, Dogras and Pathans.
	1947	Dogras from the Punjab and Jammu and Kashmir State, Pathans from within the administrative borders of the North-West Frontier Province of British India. NWFP States and Tribal Territory, Punjabi Mussalmans from the Punjab (less Ambala Civil Division), including Niazi and other Pathans of the Punjab, Hazarawalas of NWFP and Mussalmans of Jammu and Kashmir State and Gilgit Agency, Sikhs from the Punjab.

Both the 12th Frontier Force Regiment and the 13th Frontier Force Rifles shared a common origin in recruiting veterans of the Sikh Wars. The 12th sprang from the infantry element of the Frontier Brigade authorised in 1846 after the First Sikh War, consisting of a company of artillery and four regiments of Infantry. Colonel Henry Lawrence, the Agent to the Governor-General on the Frontier asked if he might also raise a small irregular body of men – one troop mounted and two companies of infantry – to be called 'Guides'. The term Frontier Brigade was dropped in 1847 and the four regiments became the 1st, 2nd (or Hill Corps), 3rd and 4th Regiments of Sikh Local Infantry. Together with the Corps of Guides, these four regiments went to form the 12th Frontier Force Regiment in 1923.

Despite their title, the regiments were never wholly Sikh, not even when first raised but they fought their way through the next century as the 1st, 2nd, 3rd and 4th Sikhs since they had been raised principally from disbanded regiments of the Sikh Army. The 2nd Sikhs, in fact, was first composed almost entirely of Dogras, enlisted for the first time in the Army of the Honourable East India Company, together with a few Pathans and Gurkhas and it was this make-up which prompted its title of Hill Corps.

In 1851, the four regiments of Sikh Infantry became part of the Punjab Irregular Force and the letters 'PIF' entered Indian and, indeed, British military history. The 'Piffers' they became and the nickname lives on. Despite their mandate to serve in the Frontier areas, there was great keenness to follow the drum wherever it might lead and, at that time, there was no shortage of drums in our Indian territories. The 4th Sikhs volunteered for Burma in 1852 as did the 3rd, but the 4th was accepted and served there for two years. All four regiments went to Central India at the time of the Great Mutiny but the 4th, again, made the headlines even by the exacting military standards of the times.

They marched from Abbottabad to Delhi, 560 miles in thirty days in an Indian June, going into action on their arrival. The Guides beat this with their march from Mardan, a distance of 580 miles in twenty-two marching days but they were a combined cavalry-infantry corps and the infantry element had camels provided, one to every two foot-soldiers.

In 1876, Queen Victoria conferred on the Corps of Guides, the style of 'Queen's Own' making them one of the first units of the Indian Army to become a Royal regiment.

The Second Afghan War involved the Corps of Guides and the 1st, 2nd and 3rd Sikhs and gave the Guides their first two Victoria Crosses.

In 1903, the re-numbering was significant. The 'Bengal block' ended with the 48th Pioneers and the four regiments of Sikh Infantry became respectively the 51st, 52nd, 53rd and 54th Sikhs (Frontier Force). The Guides Infantry became, in 1911, Queen Victoria's Own Corps of Guides (Frontier Force) (Lumsden's) Infantry.

FIRST WORLD WAR

Guides Infantry – India, Mesopotamia, Egypt, Palestine (one company to France in 1914, attached to 57th Wilde's Rifles)
2nd Guides – (raised in 1917) – India, Egypt, Palestine, Syria
3rd Guides – (raised in 1917) India
51st Sikhs – India, Aden, Egypt, Mesopotamia
52nd Sikhs – India, Mesopotamia
53rd Sikhs – India, Aden, Egypt, Mesopotamia
54th Sikhs – India, Egypt, Turkey
2/54th – (raised in 1917) India

Immediately after the war, the 2/54th Sikhs was disbanded as was the 3rd Guides. As a reward for their services in what was later called the Middle East, the 51st became the 51st The Prince of Wales's Own Sikhs (Frontier Force).

BETWEEN THE WARS

The formation of the 12th Frontier Force Regiment in 1922 did not present too much of a problem in re-numbering its battalions. The change was facilitated by the Guides Infantry who, although senior to the Sikh battalions, volunteered to become the 5th Battalion of the new regiment leaving the 51st The Prince of Wales's Own Sikhs (FF), the 52nd Sikhs, 53rd Sikhs and 54th Sikhs to become, once again, the 1st, 2nd, 3rd and 4th Battalions. The 2nd Guides had been retained after the war to become the Training Battalion. Thus, the new line-up was as under but the Guides still took precedence on parade.

51st The Prince of Wales's Own Sikhs (Frontier Force) – 1st Bn (Prince of Wales's Own) (Sikhs) 12th Frontier Force Regt
52nd Sikhs (Frontier Force) – 2nd Bn (Sikhs) 12th Frontier Force Regt
53rd Sikhs (Frontier Force) – 3rd Bn (Sikhs) 12th Frontier Force Regt
54th Sikhs (Frontier Force) – 4th Bn (Sikhs) 12th Frontier Force Regt
1st Bn QVO Corps of Guides (Frontier Force) (Lumsden's) Infantry – 5th Bn (QVO Corps of Guides) 12th Frontier Force Regt
2nd Bn QVO Corps of Guides (Frontier Force) (Lumsden's) Infantry – 10th Bn (QVO Corps of Guides) 12th Frontier Force Regt

The badge chosen for the new regiment was a stringed bugle-horn with '12' between the strings, a crown above and title-scrolls flanking the bugle-horn.

The Territorial battalion, raised on 11 Mar 22 as the 1st (Territorial) Bn 51st (The Prince of Wales's Own) Sikhs in Nowshera, became the 11/12th but wore its own badge, crossed Khyber knives, points down, a crown above and title-scroll below. It recruited only Pathans and, on mobilisation on 4 Sep 39, was the only all-Pathan battalion in the army.

In 1933, the 4/12th was one of the battalions nominated for Indianisation.

Most regiments saw service on the North West Frontier in the between-wars years but few had the experience of the Guides Infantry.

In an action in September 1935, the under-strength battalion, barely 370 all ranks, faced an overwhelmingly superior force of Mohmands, an action in which all the British and most of the Indian officers were killed or wounded. Captain Godfrey Meynell MC, the adjutant, went forward to encourage his men and was over-run with them. His action inflicted heavy losses on the tribesmen and gained him a posthumous Victoria Cross.

Also in 1935, in the Silver Jubilee honours, the 3/12th was made a Royal battalion.

SECOND WORLD WAR

1st Battalion – India, Iraq, Syria, Italy. In late 1946, the battalion was nominated for parachute training to join 2nd Indian Airborne Division.
2nd Battalion – India, Malaya. Captured on Singapore Island by the Japanese in February 1942. Reconstituted 30 Apr 46 on a cadre of 9/12th.
3rd Battalion – India, Italian East Africa, Egypt, Iraq, Cyprus, Sicily, Italy, Greece.
4th Battalion – India, Burma.
5th Battalion (Guides) – India, Iraq, Iran.
6th Battalion – raised 8 Aug 40 at Sabathu. India. Disbanded 5 Jul 44.
7th Battalion – raised 7 Aug 40 at Shillong. India. Became a unit of 39 Training Division. Disbanded February 1946.
8th Battalion – raised 1 Apr 41 at Bareilly. India, Burma. The battalion was not disbanded after the war but continued as a regular unit.
9th Battalion – raised 1 Apr 41 at Jhansi. India, Ceylon, Burma. Indo-China. Reconstituted as 2/12th on 30 Apr 46.
11th Battalion – the pre-war Territorial battalion was mobilised on 4 Sep 39. Converted to active battalion 15 Sep 41 and redesignated 14th (Suba Sarhad) Bn.

14th Battalion – formed 15 Sep 41 on conversion of 11th Battalion to active status. India, Burma, Iran, Greece. Disbanded September 1946.
1st Afridi Battalion – raised 1 Apr 42 at Sialkot. India, Iran, Iraq, Syria. Disbanded January 1946 but re-raised as Khyber Rifles.
Machine-Gun Battalion – raised 15 Jan 42 at Sialkot. India, Burma, Dutch East Indies. Disbanded December 1946.
25th Garrison Battalion – raised 1 Apr 41 at Sialkot. India. Disbanded 20 May 46.
26th Garrison Battalion – raised 1 Mar 42 at Sialkot. India. Iraq. Disbanded February 1946.

PARTITION

On Partition, in August 1947, The Frontier Force Regiment as it had now become since most of the infantry regiments had lost their numbers, was logically assigned to Pakistan. Pathans and Punjabi Mussalmans were retained whilst Dogras and Sikhs were routed to India.

The regular battalions on transfer of power were the 1st, 2nd, 3rd, 4th, 5th and 8th.

BATTLE HONOURS

Pegu, Mooltan, Goojerat, Punjaub, Delhi 1857, Ali Masjid, Kabul 1879, Ahmed Khel, Kandahar 1880, Afghanistan 1878–80, Chitral, Malakand, Punjab Frontier, Tirah, Pekin 1900, Somaliland 1901–04.

Suez Canal, Egypt 1915, Megiddo, Sharon, Nablus, Palestine 1918, Aden, Tigris 1916, Kut-al-Amara 1917, Baghdad, Sharqat, Mesopotamia 1915–18, NW Frontier, India 1914, 1915, 1916–17, Afghanistan 1919.

Gallabat, Tehamiyam Wells, Agordat, Barentu, Keren, Amba Alagi, Abyssinia 1940–41, Gazala, Bir Hacheim, El Adem, North Africa 1940–43, Landing in Sicily, Sicily 1943, Landing at Reggio, The Sangro, Mozzagrogna, Romagnoli, The Moro, Impossible Bridge, Cassino II, Pignataro, Advance to Florence, Campriano, Gothic Line, Coriano, The Senio, Santerno Crossing, Italy 1943–45, Athens, Greece 1944–45, North Malaya, Kota Bharu, Central Malaya, Kuantan, Machang, Singapore Island, Malaya 1941–42, Moulmein, Sittang 1942, 1945, Pegu 1942, 1945, Taukkyan, Shwegyin, North Arakan, Buthidaung, Maungdaw, Ngakyedauk Pass, Imphal, Tamu Road, Shenam Pass, Bishenpur, Kyaukmyaung Bridgehead, Arakan Beaches, Ramree, Taungup, Mandalay, Myinmu, Fort Dufferin, Kyaukse 1945, Meiktila, Nyaungu Bridgehead, Capture of Meiktila, Defence of Meiktila, The Irrawaddy, Rangoon Road,Pyawbwe, Toungoo, Burma 1942–45.

BOOKS

History of the 2nd Sikhs, 12th Frontier Force Regt 1846–1933 by Capt C W May (Mission Press, Jubbulpore 1933)
Historical Records of the 3rd Sikhs 1847–1930 by Lieut Col C I Shepherd (Pardy and Son Bournemouth 1931)
History of the 54th Sikhs, Frontier Force Regiment 1846–1914 by Capt S R Shirley (Gale and Plden Ltd, Aldershot 1915)
The Frontier Force Regiment by Brig W E H Condon OBE (Gale and Polden Ltd, Aldershot 1962)

13th FRONTIER FORCE RIFLES

Centre: **1923 ABBOTTABAD**
1947 ABBOTTABAD

Class Composition:		
	1923	Punjabi Mussalmans, Sikhs, Dogras and Pathans
	1947	Dogras from the Punjab and Jammu and Kashmir, Pathans from within the administrative borders of the North-West Frontier Province of British India, NWFP States and Tribal Territory, Punjabi Mussalmans from the Punjab (less Ambala Civil Division), including Niazi and other Pathans of the Punjab. Hazarawalas of NWFP and Mussalmans of Jammu and Kashmir State and Gilgit Agency, Sikhs from the Punjab.

Like the 12th Frontier Force Regiment, the 13th Frontier Force Rifles recruited the ready and willing veterans of the Sikh Wars. Whilst the battalions of the 12th were styled 'Sikhs', those of the 13th were to be Punjab Infantry. Five battalions were raised in 1849 by Sir Henry Lawrence to form part of the Trans-Frontier Brigade (it also included three light field batteries and five regiments of Punjab Cavalry) and most of the personnel were from the disbanded Sikh armies after the Second Sikh War of 1848.

Two years later, the Punjab Irregular Force combined the five Punjab Cavalry regiments, four mountain batteries, one garrison battery, four regiments of Sikh Infantry, six regiments of Punjab Infantry (the Scinde Camel Corps raised in 1843, was found to be an expensive unit to maintain in the cost-conscious times of peace, so it was restyled the Scinde Rifle Corps in 1853 and became the 6th Punjab Infantry) and one regiment of Gurkha Infantry (later the 5th Gurkha Rifles (FF)).

When the Devil's Wind blew through North India in 1857, the men of the PIF marched from the Frontier to Delhi at the height of an Indian summer. The 4th actually marched 1,000 miles from Bannu. Three battalions of Punjab Infantry were present at the fall of Delhi and two of them went on to Lucknow where, in the storming of the Sikandarabagh with the 93rd Highlanders, Subadar Mukarrab Khan of the 4th, earned immortality by thrusting his left arm through the gap between the closing gates. When the mutineers hacked at it he withdrew it and promptly replaced it with his right arm which was severed at the wrist. The gates remained open and the troops swarmed through. Following the programme of pacification after the Great Mutiny, the regiments of the PIF marched back to the Frontier to maintain and build upon their reputation of total loyalty, instant readiness to take the field and the establishment of law and order.

In 1863, all battalions except the 2nd were engaged in a border campaign at Ambala during which Lieutenant H W Pitcher earned a Victoria Cross for gallantry and leadership.

Two years later, in September 1865 the PIF became the Punjab Frontier Force, the title under which it was to become best known.

The Second Afghan War saw all regiments of Punjab Infantry except the 6th engaged and then a period of relative peace descended on the Frontier until the general rising on the border in 1897. In the economies following the Afghan War in 1882, the 3rd Punjab Infantry was disbanded, never to be raised again. That is not to say that the units of the PFF were left polishing their weapons. Local expeditions were launched to subdue the Orakzai in 1891 whilst the 2nd, 4th and 6th were despatched into Waziristan in 1894 as part of a punitive force sent to avenge an unprovoked attack on the boundary commission fulfilling treaty obligations with Afghanistan. The medal-clasp awarded for this expedition 'Waziristan 1894–95' – was the twenty-first and last to be issued for wear on the 1854 India General Service ribbon.

The Regiment's first overseas battle-honour was earned by the 4th Punjab Infantry which went to China in 1900 to subdue the Boxers.

When the re-numbering took place in 1903, the Punjab Infantry followed on after the Sikh Infantry, being given 'Rifles' status, a tribute to their past services. At the same time three of the five had the names of earlier commandants added to the new number; thus, the 1st Punjab Infantry became 55th Coke's Rifles (Frontier Force), the 2nd became 56th Punjabi Rifles (Frontier Force), the 4th became 57th Wilde's Rifles (Frontier Force), the 5th became 58th Vaughan's Rifles (Frontier Force) and the 6th became 59th Scinde Rifles (Frontier Force). Also in 1903 came the abolition of the Punjab Frontier Force: all units were now to be part of an all-India army and private, local armies had to be seen to exist no longer. Tradition, of course, survives and Pakistan's Army boasts Piffers and retired officers in Britain still use the PFF monogram on Christmas cards.

FIRST WORLD WAR

It is a measure of the 'ever-readiness' of the old Punjab Infantry that, when war broke out in August 1914, four of their battalions were included in the Lahore and Meerut Divisions bound for the front. The 55th Coke's Rifles, universally known as 'Cookies', was to remain on the Frontier but sent almost half its strength to France as reinforcements. Among the latter was Jemadar Mir Dast who earned a Victoria Cross whilst serving with the 58th Vaughan's Rifles in April 1915 during Second Ypres. Coincidentally, his brother, Mir Mast, an Indian officer in the 58th, deserted to the Germans in March 1915 with a small party of Pathans and was said to have been awarded an Iron Cross by the Kaiser.

55th Coke's Rifles – India, German East Africa, Persia
    2/55th (raised in 1918) – India, China
56th Punjabi Rifles – India, Egypt, Mesopotamia
    2/56th (raised in 1917) – India, Egypt
57th Wilde's Rifles – India, France, Egypt, German East Africa
    2/57th (raised in 1918) – India
58th Vaughan's Rifles – India, France, Egypt
59th Scinde Rifles – India, France, Mesopotamia, Egypt

After the war, the 2/55th and the 2/57th were disbanded but the 2/56th remained in service. The 59th Scinde Rifles (FF) became, in 1921, the 59th Royal Scinde Rifles (FF). This was in recognition of their services during the Great War: at Neuve Chapelle, all the British officers had been either killed or wounded and the subadar-major, Perbhat Chand, less than thirty years old, took command and later brought the battalion out of action. Earlier, Lieutenant W A McC Bruce had earned a posthumous Victoria Cross at Givenchy. This particular action had taken place in December 1914 but the award was not gazetted until 1919 after returning prisoners-of-war had told the full story.

BETWEEN THE WARS

When the 13th Frontier Force Rifles was formed in 1922, there was, effectively, a reversion to the earlier, pre-1903 numbers. The old 1st Punjab Infantry had become the 55th Coke's Rifles in 1903 and now was to become the first battalion of the new regiment, as will be seen below. To facilitate the re-numbering, the previous 3rd Punjab Infantry, disbanded in 1882 following the Second Afghan War was remembered and no 3rd Bn was formed for the new regiment. The new line-up is shown below:

55th Coke's Rifles (Frontier Force) – 1st Bn (Coke's) 13th Frontier Force Rifles
56th Punjabi Rifles (Frontier Force) – 2nd Bn 13th Frontier Force Rifles
57th Wilde's Rifles (Frontier Force) – 4th Bn (Wilde's) 13th Frontier Force Rifles
58th Vaughan's Rifles (Frontier Force) – 5th Bn 13th Frontier Force Rifles
59th Royal Scinde Rifles (Frontier Force) – 6th Royal Bn (Scinde) 13th Frontier Force Rifles
2/56th Punjabi Rifles (Frontier Force) – 10th Bn 13th Frontier Force Rifles

The badge chosen for the new regiment was a stringed bugle-horn with crown above: within the strings, the figurtes '13' above 'FFR'.

The Territorial battalion authorised on 11 Mar 22 as the 1st (Territorial) Bn 66th Punjabis was actually raised on 1 Aug 22 as the 1st (Territorial) Bn 55th Coke's Rifles (Frontier Force) based in Campbellpore, changing its title yet again later that year to the 11/13th Frontier Force Rifles. It was entirely Mussalman in composition.

In 1933, The Royal battalion, the 6/13th was one of the battalions selected for Indianisation.

SECOND WORLD WAR

1st Battalion – India, Malaya. Captured on Singapore Island by the Japanese in February 1942. Reconstituted 15 Apr 46 by re-designation of the 14/13th.
2nd Battalion – India, Burma, Dutch East Indies.
4th Battalion – India, Syria, Persia, Egypt, Italy
5th Battalion – India, Iraq, Syria, Italy
6th Battalion – India, Italian East Africa, Persia, Iraq, Syria, Palestine, Italy
7th Battalion – raised 7 Aug 40. India. Disbanded April 1946.
8th Battalion – raised at Solan in the Simla Hills 7 Aug 40. India, Burma, Dutch East Indies. Disbanded September 1946.
9th Battalion – raised 1 Apr 41. Converted to 54 Regt, Indian Armoured Corps August 1942. Re-converted to infantry October 1942 as 9/13th. India, Burma. Disbanded May 1947.

11th Battalion – the pre-war Territorial battalion was mobilized on the outbreak of war in 1939. Converted to an active battalion in September 1941 and redesignated the 15/13th.

14th Battalion – raised at Jhansi on 1 Apr 41. India, Ceylon, Burma, French Indo-China. Redesignated 1/13th 15 Apr 46.

15th Battalion – raised September 1941 by redesignation of the 11th, the pre-war Territorial battalion. After service in Waziristan, a request was received from the Royal Indian Navy for volunteers to transfer and, as more than 600 expressed their willingness to do so, the battalion was disbanded in February 1943, the men going on to serve in Greece and Burma.

16th Battalion – raised 15 Jul 42. India. Disbanded April 1946.

17th Battalion – raised 1 Jul 41 from over-age ex-servicemen. India. Converted to active status but disbanded 14 Dec 44

26th Garrison Battalion – raised 1 Mar 42. India, Maldives. Disbanded 10 Sept 46

27th Garrison Battalion – raised Aug 42. India. Disbanded April 1946.

Machine-Gun Battalion – raised at Abbottabad. January 1942. India, Burma, Siam. Disbanded 15 Dec 46.

PARTITION

The Frontier Force Rifles – as they had now become, following the decision to remove the numbers from the titles of most of the infantry regiments – was allotted to Pakistan. All the remaining Sikhs and Dogras were sent to India, whilst the Pathans and Punjabi Mussalmans were retained.

The regular battalions on transfer of power were the 1st, 2nd, 4th, 5th and 6th.

BATTLE HONOURS

Delhi 1857, Lucknow, Peiwar Kotal, Charasiah, Kabul 1879, Afghanistan 1878–80, Tirah, Punjab Frontier, China 1900, La Bassee 1914, Messines 1914, Armentieres 1914, Festbubert 1914, 1915, Givenchy 1914, Neuve Chapelle, Ypres 1915, St Julien, Aubers, Loos, France and Flanders 1914–15, Suez Canal, Egypt 1915–17, Gaza, El Mughar, Nebi Samwil, Jerusalem, Megiddo, Sharon, Palestine 1917–18, Aden, Tigris 1917, Kut-al-Amara 1917, Baghdad, Mesopotamia 1916–18, Persia 1918–19, North-West Frontier, India 1917, Baluchistan 1918, East Africa 1916–18, Afghanistan 1919.

Gash Delta, Barentu, Keren, Ad Teclesan, Amba Alagi, Abyssinia 1940–41, Deir ez Zor, Raqaa, Syria 1941, Gazala, Sidi Rezegh 1942, Gambut, Mersa Matruh, North Africa 1940–43, The Trigno, Tufillo, The Sangro, Impossible Bridge, Villa Grande, Cassino II, Gustav Line, Pignataro, Advance to Florence, Gothic Line, Monte Grande, The Senio, Bologna, Monte Sole, Italy 1943–45, North Malaya, Kota Bharu, Johore, Gemas, The Muar, Singapore Island, Malaya 1941–42, Pegu 1942 Taukkyan, Monywa 1942, Shwegyin, North Arakan, Point 551, Mayu Tunnels, Maungdaw, Ngakyedauk Pass, Imphal, Litan, Arakan Beaches, Myebon, Ramree, Mandalay, Myinmu, Meiktila, Nyaungu Bridgehead, Capture of Meiktila, Defence of Meiktila, Taungtha, Myingyan, The Irrawaddy, Yenangyaung 1945, Magwe, Rangoon Road, Pegu 1945, Sittang 1945, Burma 1942–45.

BOOKS

'The History of Coke's Rifles' by Colonel H C Wylly (Pub. Gale and Polden, Aldershot, 1930)

'History of the 2nd Bn Frontier Force Rifles' by Anon (Pub. Groom and Son Ltd, Bury St Edmunds 1933)

'History of the 4th Bn 13th Frontier Force Rifles (Wilde's)' by Anon (Pub. Butler and Tanner, London c. 1930)
'History of the 5th Bn 13th Frontier Force Rifles 1849–1926' by Colonel H C Wylly CB (Pub. Gale and Polden, Aldershot 1929)
'Regimental history of the 6th Royal Bn 13th Frontier Force Rifles (Scinde) 1843–1923' by Capt D M Lindsey (Pub Gale and Plden, Aldershot 1926)
'The Frontier Force Rifles' by Brigadier W E H Condon OBE (Pub Gale and Polden, Aldershot 1953)

14th PUNJAB REGIMENT

Centre: **1923 FEROZEPORE**
1946 JHELUM

Class Composition:	1923	Punjabi Mussalmans, Sikhs, Dogras, Pathans
	1946	Dogras from the Punjab and Jammu and Kashmir State. Pathans from within the administrative borders of the NWFP of British India, NWFP states and Tribal Territory. Punjabi Mussalmans from the Punjab (less Ambala Civil Division) including Niazi and other Pathans of the Punjab, Hazarawalas of NWFP and Mussalmans of Jammu and Kashmir State and Gilgit Agency. Sikhs from the Punjab.

The 14th Punjab Regiment, created in 1922, was made up of infantry regiments born of the years of the Great Mutiny. The six in question were, in 1903, the 19th, 20th, 22nd and 24th Punjabis, the 40th Pathans and the 21st Punjabis. The Punjabis had all been raised by John Lawrence's Punjab Administration whilst the 40th Pathans began life as the Shahjehanpur Levy in 1858. Despite service in

Mutiny operations, the new regiment's first battle-honours were won by the 20th and 22nd Punjabis in China in 1860. The 40th Pathans were the only Pathan regiment and the combination of its number and the reputed proclivities of the Pathan resulted in the inevitable nickname of the Forty Thieves; equally inevitable was the unenviable label of Ali Baba for their colonel. Their first active service was in the expedition to Tibet in 1903–04 by which time its exclusive character had been diluted by the Punjabi Mussalmans and Dogras brought in by the linked-battalion system in 1901.

FIRST WORLD WAR

19th Punjabis – India, Persia, Russia

2/19th Punjabis (raised in 1917) – India, Egypt

20th Duke of Cambridge's Own Punjabis (a title awarded after service in Egypt in 1882) – Mesopotamia, Egypt.

22nd Punjabis – India, Mesopotamia, Persia

2/22nd Punjabis (raised in 1917) – India, Hong Kong

24th Punjabis – India, Mesopotamia, Russia, Greece

40th Pathans – Hong Kong, France, German East Africa, India

2/40th Pathans (raised in 1918) – India

21st Punjabis – India, Egypt, Palestine, Russia

2/21st Punjabis (raised in 1917) – India

Following the return of Indian troops after the war, all the war-raised battalions were disbanded.

BETWEEN THE WARS

When the 14th Punjab Regiment was created in 1922, their new badge was a five-pointed star, representative of the five rivers of the Punjab, with the numeral '14' in the centre, a crown above and a scroll below, reading 'Punjab Regiment'.

The battalions of the new regiment were listed as follows – 1st Bn (the old 19th Punjabis), 2nd Bn (the old 20th Punjabis), 3rd Bn (the old 22nd Punjabis), 4th Bn (the old 24th Punjabis), 5th Bn (the old 40th Pathans) and the 10th Bn (the old 21st Punjabis). To these was added the Territorial battalion, the 11th, based in Delhi, originally raised early in 1922 as the 1st (Territorial) Bn, 26th Punjabis.

In 1923, the 1st Bn was among the first units selected for Indianisation. By this process, all future King's Commissioned Officers posted to the battalion would be Indians trained at Sandhurst. By 1938, all officers below field-rank (captains and subalterns) were Indian.

It may well be that the 5/14th Punjab can lay claim to have erected the first 1914–18 war memorial within the British Empire. A huge stone .303 inch rifle-cartridge stands at Attock, overlooking the Indus River and this was dedicated in April 1919.

In August 1935, the Sikh Company of the 5th Bn was sent to Addis Ababa to guard the British Legation during the Italian campaign in Ethiopia. The British Minister's cavalry escort from the 8th Light Cavalry was made up of Sikhs and it was felt that a composite Sikh body would create the right impression. They remained there on detachment for fourteen months.

SECOND WORLD WAR

1st Battalion – India, Malaya. Captured in Singapore in February 1942 by the Japanese.

2nd Battalion (Duke of Cambridge's) – India, Hong Kong. Captured in Hong Kong in December 1941 by the Japanese. Reconstituted in April 1946 by amalgamation with the 8th Bn.
3rd Battalion – India, Egypt, Aden, Italian East Africa, Burma.
4th Battalion – India, Burma, Siam.
5th Battalion (Pathans) – India, Malaya. Captured in Singapore in February 1942 by the Japanese. After the war, the survivors were posted to the 1st Bn. The 5th was not reconstituted before Partition.
6th Battalion – raised in Baroda in October 1940. India, Singapore. Captured in Singapore in February 1942 by the Japanese.
7th Battalion – raised in Kakul in March 1941. India, Burma. Disbanded in May 1946.
8th Battalion – raised in Bareilly in April 1941. India. Redesignated 2/14 Punjab in May 1946.
9th Battalion – raised in Jhansi in April 1941. India, Ceylon, Burma, French Indo-China. Disbanded in July 1947.
11th Battalion – this pre-war Territorial battalion was mobilised in September 1939. Subsequently, it was transferred to the 9th Jats, becoming the 9/9th Jat Regiment in September 1941. This transfer arose because of the large number of Jats in the battalion.
12th Battalion – raised in November 1939 as a second Territorial battalion but it was transferred in September 1941 to become the 14/9th Jat Regiment, again because of the large Jat element.
14th Battalion – raised in Ferozepore in January 1942. India. Disbanded in October 1945.
15th Battalion – formed at Ferozepore in July 1942 by redesignation of the Machine-Gun Battalion. Converted to a normal infantry role in August 1942 and served as a jungle-training unit. India. Disbanded in April 1946.
16th Battalion – redesignation of the 25th Garrison Bn in July 1942 on conversion to active status. India. Disbanded in July 1944.
25th Garrison Battalion – raised in Ferozepore in August 1941. On conversion to active status in July 1942, it was redesignated the 16/14th.
26th Garrison Battalion – raised in Ferozepore in March 1942. Converted to active status in January 1945 but not renumbered. India, Cocos Islands. Disbanded late 1945.
Machine-Gun Battalion – raised in January 1942. Redesignated the 15/14th in July 1942.

Towards the end of the war, the Centre experienced some difficulty in securing recruits. 14 Punjab, with four battalions in Japanese hands, three of them regular, had acquired an unfortunate reputation.

PARTITION

The Regiment was allocated to Pakistan on Partition. On transfer of power, the regular battalions were the 1st, 2nd, 3rd and 4th.

Dogras and Sikhs were posted to India's new army whilst 14 Punjab received Muslim drafts from units routed to India.

BATTLE HONOURS

Taku Forts, China 1860–62, Pekin 1860, Abyssinia, Ali Masjid, Ahmed Khel, Kandahar 1880, Afghanistan 1878–80, Tel-el-Kebir, Egypt 1882, Punjab Frontier, Malakand, Pekin 1900, China 1900.
Ypres 1915, St Julien, Aubers, France and Flanders 1915, Macedonia 1918, Suez

Indian officers 101st Grenadiers c1910.
Lt Col N Poulsom

Risaldar Major Abdul Gaffar Khan, 1st Skinner's Horse, Peshawar 1903.
Lt Col CRD Gray

Skinner's Horse guard-of-honour (Nov 1936) Delhi, showing uniforms of 1st Skinner's Horse (front rank) and 3rd Skinner's Horse (rear rank) on the occasion of the 100th anniversary of the founding of the regimental church by Col James Skinner CB. *Lt Col CRD Gray*

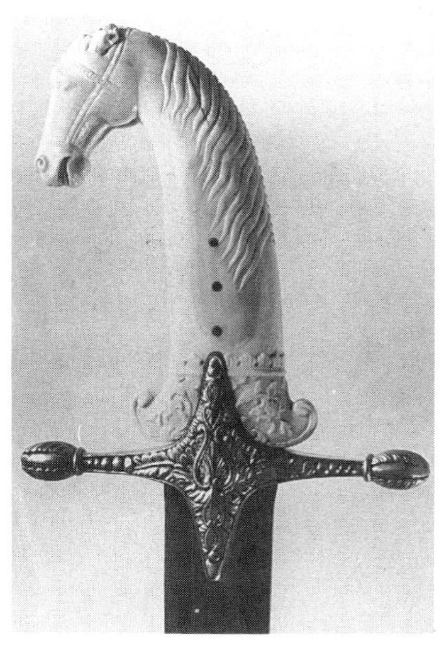

Right: Sword of Robert Skinner on which recruits used to swear on enlistment, presented to the Regiment by Col James Skinner. After being handed to a British officer at Partition, it was later found in the store at the National Army Museum in London by Lt Col CRD Gray who arranged for its return to the Regiment in India. *Lt Col CRD Gray*
Above: Colour-party 1 Sikh with the old colours of the 14th Ferozepore Sikhs.
Top right: Memorial stone to Major SJ Waudby, raised in Bombay 1880. *BP India Ltd*
Far right: 1914-18 war memorial to the 40th Pathans erected April 1919 near Attock in Pakistan.

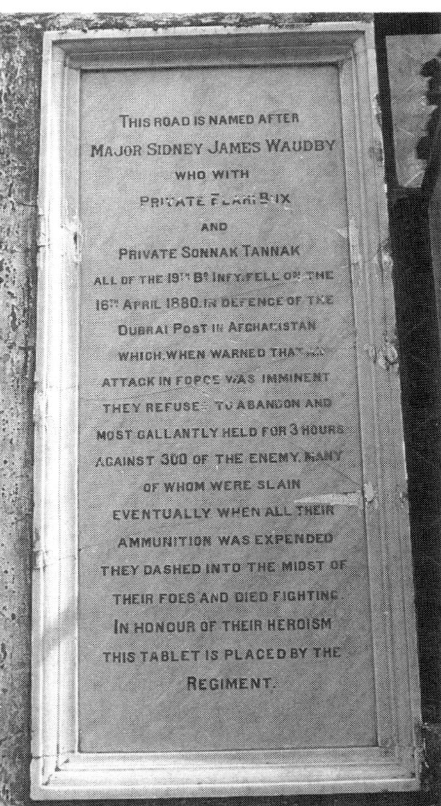
This road is named after
Major Sidney James Waudby
who with
Private
and
Private Sonnak Tannak
all of the 19th Bn Infy. fell on the
16th April 1880. in defence of the
Dubrai Post in Afghanistan
which, when warned that
attack in force was imminent
they refused to abandon and
most gallantly held for 3 hours
against 300 of the enemy. many
of whom were slain
eventually when all their
ammunition was expended
they dashed into the midst of
their foes and died fighting.
In honour of their heroism
this tablet is placed by the
Regiment.

Above: VCOs in London after receiving their Coronation medals 1937.

Right: Guard 1/13 Frontier Force Rifles (Coke's) c1936, showing (from left to right) Pathan VCO, Dogra VCO, Sikh, Pathan and Punjabi Mussalman sepoys.
Lt Col M Wilcox

Left: Pipe-major 1/13 Frontier Force Rifles (Coke's) c1936.
Lt Col M Wilcox

INDIAN

KLB 159

Top left: Rajputana Rifles recruit for CMP(1) on motor-cycle training 1942.
Top centre: Captain P Emerson, preparing to join BCOF in Japan 1946, showing the new badge and shoulder-title with the distinctive black cloth grenade, the Union flag and the Brindiv flash.
Lt Col P Emerson
Left: Part of the Pakistan contingent for the Coronation in London 1953. *Brian Davis*
Top: Copper memorial screen-panels of the 34th Sikh Pioneers returned to The Sikh Light Infantry by HM Queen Elizabeth II. *Regtl Centre Sikh LI*
Right: Major Ayaz Khan, Khyber Rifles in Khyber Pass 1980.
Andrew Gaylor

MP
SSG

Above: Trumpeter, President's Bodyguard, India. *Lt Gen P Giannatassio*

Opposite page
Far left: Regtl policeman, Armoured Corps Centre, Nowshera, Pakistan 1986. *Barbu Alim*
Top left: Regtl policeman, Punjab Regiment, Mardan, NWFP, Pakistan 1986 *Barbu Alim*
Bottom left: NCO Special Service Group, Rawalpindi, Pakistan 1986. *Barbu Alim*

Left: Centre Commandant's orderly, The Rajput Regiment, Fatehgarh, 1986 *Barbu Alim*
Right: Rifleman of 5/5 Gorkha Rifles (Frontier Force) Chindits, in ceremonial dress 1991. *Pushpindar Singh Chopra*

Right: Quarter-guard Sikh LI Regtl Centre, 1991 *Pushpindar Singh Chopra*
Below: Provost havildar, Sikh LI Regtl Centre, Fatehgarh, 1991, showing old British Pioneer badges. *Pushpindar Singh Chopra*

Opposite page
Top left: Madras Sappers in their distinctive doopta 1990. *Ashok Nath*
Top right: NCOs Rajputana Rifles, Delhi 1990. *Ashok Nath*
Far left: NCOs Madras Regiment, Delhi 1990. *Ashok Nath*
Left: NCO Jammu and Kashmir Rifles, Delhi 1990. *Ashok Nath*

This page
Top left: NCOs Punjab Regiment, Delhi 1990. *Ashok Nath*
Top right: Havildar Sikh Regiment, Delhi 1990. *Ashok Nath*
Right: Sepoys Jat Regiment, Delhi 1990. *Ashok Nath*

Colour of 1st Bn Indian Parachute Regiment presented in 1946 by Lt Gen Sir Frederick Browning and returned to the Parachute Regiment in Agra, October 1991 on the 50th anniversary of the raising of airborne forces in India. *British Airborne Forces Museum, Aldershot*

NCO 8 Gorkha Rifles, Delhi 1990. *Ashok Nath*

Canal, Egypt 1915, Megiddo, Sharon, Nablus, Palestine 1918, Basra, Shaiba, Kut-al-Amara 1915, 1917, Ctesiphon, Defence of Kut-al-Amara, Baghdad, Khan Baghdadi, Mesopotamia 1914–18, Merv, Persia 1915–19, NW Frontier, India 1915–17, Narungombe, East Africa 1916–18, Afghanistan 1919.

Agordat, Keren, Abyssinia 1940–41, Alam el Halfa, Defence of Alamein Line, North Africa 1940–43, Kampar, Singapore Island, Malaya 1941–42, Hong Kong, South East Asia 1941–42, The Yu, North Arakan, Buthidaung, Razabil, Maungdaw, Ngakyedauk Pass, Imphal, Shenam Pass, Nungshigum, Bishenpur, Kanglatongbi, Jessami, Naga Village, Mao Songsang, Monywa 1945, Kyaukse 1945, Nyaungu Bridgehead, Letse, Magwe, Rangoon Road, Pegu 1945, Sittang 1945, Burma 1942–45.

BOOKS

'History of the 20th (DCO) Infantry, Brownlow's Punjabis 1857 to 1907' (Swiss and Co. Devonport 1910)

'Historical Records of the 20th (DCO) Infantry, Brownlow's Punjabis Vol II 1909–1922) (Butler and Tanner, Frome and London 1923)

'Records of the 1/XXI Punjabis' by Major P Murray (Gale and Polden Ltd, Aldershot 1919)

'The 40th Pathans in the Great War' (The Civil and Military Gazette Press, Lahore 1921)

'Fourteenth Punjab Regiment 1939–1945' (Lund Humphries, London n.d.)

15th PUNJAB REGIMENT

Centre: **1923 SIALKOT**
1946 SIALKOT

Class composition: 1923 Punjabi Mussalmans, Sikhs, Jats of the Punjab
1946 Jats from the Punjab, United Provinces, Rajputana and Central India states. Pathans from within the administrative borders of the NWFP of British India, NWFP states and Tribal Territory, Punjabi Mussalmans from the Punjab (less Ambala Civil Division) including Niazi and other Pathans of the Punjab, Hazarawalas of NWFP and Mussalmans of Jammu and Kashmir State and Gilgit Agency. Sikhs from the Punjab.

The 15th Punjab Regiment, formed in 1922, was another made up of Lawrence's Punjabi originals, recruited from police and tribal levies and armed with muskets taken from disbanded mutinous regiments. The Lahore, Peshawar, Rawalpindi, Ferozepore and Jullundur Battalions, subsequently to become the 17th, 18th, 19th, 20th and 21st Bengal Native infantry in 1861 were confirmed as the 25th, 26th, 27th, 28th and 29th Punjabis in the new all-India Line in 1903. Although embodied in 1857 to fight the mutineers, they did not receive any Mutiny honours but one regiment, later the 3/15th, won their first battle-honour in China in 1860. On their return to Lahore, they volunteered to care for British troops there who had been stricken by cholera of greater than usual virulence. The subsequent use by the 3rd Battalion of the Royal Imperial cypher within the Garter on its appointments is said to have been a gesture of royal approval for this gesture. It was this same regiment which won the honour 'Somaliland 1901–04'.

FIRST WORLD WAR
25th Punjabis – India, Hong Kong, Mesopotamia, Salonika, Russia and Turkey
2/25th Punjabis (raised in 1917) – India

26th Punjabis – India, Hong Kong, Mesopotamia
2/26th Punjabis (raised in 1918) – India, Mesopotamia
27th Punjabis – India, Egypt, France, Mesopotamia
2/27th Punjabis (raised in 1918) – India
28th Punjabis – India, Ceylon, Mejsopotamia, Egypt
2/28th Punjabis (raised in 1918) – India
29th Punjabis – India, German East Africa, Palestine, Egypt

Following the return home of Indian troops after the war, all the second battalions raised were disbanded.

BETWEEN THE WARS

The badge of the newly-created 15th Punjab Regiment in 1922 embodied a Sikh quoit and linked Muslim crescent with crown above and title scroll below. The five regiments of Punjabis converted easily to their new titles, becoming the 1st, 2nd, 3rd, 4th and 10th Bns of the 15th Punjab Regiment, whilst the 11th a Territorial battalion, formed in 1921 as the 1st (Territorial) Bn, 25th Punjabis, was based at Ambala.

Shortly after the war, the 28th Punjabis, not yet the 4/15th Punjab, were serving in Waziristan in 1921 when Sepoy Ishar Singh earned a 'peacetime' Victoria Cross, making him an even more exclusive soldier than his peers who earned theirs in the heat of a sustained overseas campaign.

SECOND WORLD WAR

1st Battalion – India, Burma
2nd Battalion – India, Singapore, Borneo, Netherlands East Indies. Captured by the Japanese. Reformed in June 1946 by redesignation of 16/15 Punjab.
3rd Battalion – India, Somaliland, Aden, Persia, Iraq, Syria, Italy. Converted to Machine-gun role in 1946.
4th Battalion – India, Burma, Siam, Malaya
5th Battalion – raised in Dehra Dun in August 1940. India. Disbanded in September 1946.
6th Battalion – raised in Lucknow in April 1941 and joined 9/8 Punjab and 6/16 Punjab in 39 Indian Infantry Brigade, the only all-Punjab brigade in the Indian Army. India, Ceylon, Burma
7th Battalion – raised in Ambala in April 1941. India, Burma. Became a training unit. Disbanded March 1946.
8th Battalion – formed in September 1941 by redesignation of the 11th Bn, a Territorial unit, on conversion to an active role. India. Disbanded mid-1946.
9th Battalion – formed in April 1941 by redesignation of the 12th Bn, a Territorial unit, on conversion to an active role. India. Disbanded 8 Jul 47.
11th Battalion – this pre-war Territorial battalion was mobilised on the outbreak of war and, in 1941, was redesignated 8/15 Punjab on conversion to active status.
12th Battalion – this Territorial battalion, raised in Ambala in November 1939, was redesignated 9/15 Punjab on conversion to active status.
14th Battalion – raised in Ambala in January 1942. India. Disbanded in September 1943 and certain personnel were absorbed into the Corps of Military Police (India).
15th Battalion – raised in Ambala in October 1942. Served in a garrison role and broken up into four garrison companies at the end of August 1944. India.

16th Battalion – formed by redesignation of 25th Garrison Bn on conversion to active status in August 1943. India. Reformed in June 1946 as the 2nd Battalion.

25th Garrison Battalion – raised in Ambala in July 1941. Redesignated 16/15 Punjab on conversion to active status in August 1943.

26th Garrison Battalion – raised in Ambala in January 1942. India. Disbanded in April 1946.

27th (Jind) Garrison Battalion – raised in Jind State in September 1943 by amalgamation of 65, 67 and 92 Garrison Companies with reinforcements from the Jind Infantry Training Centre. India. Disbanded August 1946.

Machine-Gun Battalion – raised in Ambala in July 1942. In August 1942, all personnel were transferred to the Indian Artillery to form the 15 Punjab A/Tk Regt.

Indian Christians were recruited for 8/15 Punjab.

All battalions of 15 Punjab were to be converted to a MG role at the end of 1945.

PARTITION

The Regiment was allocated to Pakistan on Partition. On transfer of power, the regular battalions were the 1st, 2nd, 3rd, 4th and 6th.

Jats, Sikhs and Dogras were posted to India and 15 Punjab became a 50% Punjabi Mussalman and 50% Pathan regiment.

BATTLE HONOURS

China 1860–62, Ali Masjid, Peiwar Kotal, Charasiah, Ahmed Khel, Kabul 1879, Kandahar 1880, Afghanistan 1878–80, Burma 1885–87, Chitral, Somaliland 1901–04.

Loos, France and Flanders 1915, Suez Canal, Egypt 1915, Megiddo, Sharon, Palestine 1918, Tigris 1916, Kut-al-Amara 1917, Baghdad, Mesopotamia 1915–18, Persia 1918, NW Frontier India 1917, Kilimanjaro, East Africa 1914–17

Berbera, Abyssinia 1940–41, Tug Argan, British Somaliland 1940, West Borneo 1941–42, South East Asia 1941–42, The Sangro, The Moro, Cassino II, Gothic Line, The Senio, Italy 1943–45, Rathedaung, North Arakan, Kohima, Jail Hill, Naga Village, Kyaukmyaung Bridgehead, Mandalay, Fort Dufferin, Meiktila, Nyaungu Bridgehead, Taungtha, The Irrawaddy, Yenaungyaung 1945, Kama, Toungoo, Sittang 1945, Burma 1942–45

BOOKS

'History of the 1st Bn 15th Punjab Regiment 1857–1937' by Lieut Col J E Shearer MC (Gale and Polden Ltd, Aldershot 1937)

16th PUNJAB REGIMENT

Centre: **1923 MOOLTAN**
1946 SIALKOT

Class Composition:		
	1923	Punjabi Mussalmans, Jat Sikhs, Dogras from Sialkot District and Jammu
	1946	Punjabi Mussalmans from the Punjab (less Ambala Civil Division) including Niazi and other Pathans of the Punjab, Hazarawalas of the NWFP and Mussalmans of Jammu and Kashmir State and the Gilgit Agency, Dogras from the Punjab and Jammu and Kashmir State, Sikhs from the Punjab

The 16th Punjab Regiment, created in 1922, was the last one to be made up of Lawrence's Punjab levies and, like the 14th and 15th Punjab Regiments, although its constituent elements were raised for service in the Great Mutiny, they did not receive honours for that campaign.

The 22nd Punjab Infantry began life in Ludhiana in 1857 and was regularized in 1861 as the 30th Punjab Infantry. The 31st Punjab Infantry was also raised in 1857, in Ferozepore, being known as Bloomfield's Sikhs, a name derived from Captain C G Bloomfield, their first Commandant. In 1878, the 31st served in Malta and Cyprus, both new stations for Indian troops.

The Allahabad Levy was formed from men of more lowly social strata desirous of showing their loyalty to authority at a time when many of their social superiors were less scrupulous. In 1861, they became the 33rd Punjab Infantry and, a few years later, recruitment of the menial classes ceased and, by 1890, the regiment was entirely Punjabi Mussalman in its composition.

The Bhopal Battalion was made up of the loyal remnants of the disaffected Bhopal, Gwalior and Malwa contingents raised for local service in Central India. They remained localized until the Second Afghan War when they were to man the North-West Frontier. In 1903, they were brought into the Line as the 9th Bhopal Infantry.

Raised in 1900, was the old 46th Punjab Infantry who were later to become the 10th Bn 16th Punjab Regiment.

FIRST WORLD WAR

30th Punjabis – India, German East Africa, Egypt

2/30th Punjabis (raised in 1917) – India, Egypt

3/30th Punjabis (raised in 1918) – India

4/30th Punjabis (raised in 1918) – India

31st Punjabis – India, Mesopotamia, Russia

33rd Punjabis – India, Egypt, France, Aden, German East Africa

2/33rd Punjabis (raised in 1917) – India

9th Bhopal Infantry – India, France, Egypt, Mesopotamia

2/9th Bhopal Infantry (The Delhi Regiment) (raised in 1917) – India, Mesopotamia

3/9th Bhopal Infantry (raised in 1917) – India, Mesopotamia

4/9th Bhopal Infantry (raised in 1918) – India

46th Punjabis – India, Egypt

After the return home of all Indian troops after the war, all the war-raised battalions were disbanded.

If one of the component regiments of the 16th Punjab can be singled out for comment, it must surely be the 9th Bhopal – usually referred to as the Bo-Peeps – in Flanders in October 1914. In the late afternoon of a cold, wet, late autumn day, the Bhopals went to the aid of the remnants of a British battalion near Neuve Chapelle. Still in cotton-drill, they had their first encounter with trenches and barbed wire and stayed, locked in battle for three days without food. Their losses were eleven officers and 262 men. Three days later, at Festubert, they lost a further 200. Remaining in France until May 1915, they then went on to Mesopotamia where a sepoy, Chattar Singh, earned a Victoria Cross. On return to India, there remained only fifteen of the originals who had sailed for France in 1914.

The Bhopals did not have linked battalions so that they suffered immediate problems when they sustained the heavy casualties of Flanders in 1914 and 1915. Unknown officers were posted in and whole platoons of reinforcements arrived, made up of differing tribal origins. Notwithstanding, the Bo-Peeps' reputation stood high but they constituted a potent argument in favour of the reforms planned for after the war.

BETWEEN THE WARS

The badge chosen for the new 16th Punjab Regiment in 1922 also incorporated the Sikh quoit and the Muslim crescent with a Maltese cross, a crown above and a title scroll below.

The battalions of the new Regiment became – 1st Bn (the old 30th Punjabis), 2nd Bn (the old 31st Punjabis), 3rd Bn (the old 33rd Punjabis), 4th Bn (the old 9th Bhopal Infantry) and the 10th Bn (the old 46th Punjabis). No Territorial battalion was raised for the 16th Punjab Regiment.

Despite the changes in title in 1922, most officers continued to claim allegiance to, say, the 33rd Punjabis for years afterwards and it took the Second World War to establish the 1922 titles in the minds of the older Indian Army officers.

SECOND WORLD WAR

1st Battalion – India, Burma, Dutch East Indies.

2nd Battalion – India, Malaya. Captured by the Japanese in February 1942. Reconstituted in May 1946 by amalgamation with 5/16 Punjab.
3rd Battalion – India, Malaya, Singapore. Captured by the Japanese in February 1942. Reconstituted in May 1946 by amalgamation with 6/16 Punjab.
4th Battalion – India, Egypt, Italian East Africa, Italy, Palestine
5th Battalion – raised in Dehra Dun in August 1940. India, Burma. Redesignated 2/16 Punjab in May 1946.
6th Battalion – raised in Lucknow in April 1941. Joined 9/8 Punjab and 6/15 Punjab in 39 Indian Infantry Brigade, the only all-Punjab brigade in the Indian Army. India, Ceylon. In January 1945 became Airborne as part of 14 Air-landing Brigade of 44 Indian Airborne Division. Redesignated 3/16 Punjab in May 1946.
7th Battalion – raised in Sialkot in May 1941. India, Burma, Malaya.
9th Battalion – formed by redesignation of the 25th Garrison Bn. India.
25th Garrison Battalion – raised in Sialkot in mid-1941. India. Redesignated 9/16 Punjab in October 1943 on conversion to active status.
26th Garrison Battalion – raised in Sialkot in March 1942. India. Disbanded May 1946.
Machine-Gun Battalion – raised in July 1942. In August 1942, transferred to the Indian Artillery as the 16th Punjab A/Tk Regt.

Despite the grievous loss of two of its regular battalions, Solah (Sixteen) Punjab, as it was known, had a creditable war record.

PARTITION

The Regiment was allocated to Pakistan on Partition. On transfer of power, the regular battalions were the 1st, 2nd, 3rd, 4th – all pre-war battalions – plus the 7th, universally known as Sath Solah and probably rewarded for its notable service in Burma during the war.

The Willcox Committee Report on the future of the Indian Army after the war had recommended the disbandment of the 16th Punjab Regiment but Partition overtook almost everything and Solah Punjab passed to Pakistan to suffer extinction by merger nine years later.

BATTLE HONOURS

Afghanistan 1878–80, Burma 1885–87, Chitral, Tirah, Punjab Frontier, Malakand.

La Bassee 1914, Messines 1914, Armentieres 1914, Festubert 1914, Givenchy 1914, Ypres 1915, St Julien, Aubers, Loos, France and Flanders 1914–15, Macedonia 1918, Suez Canal, Egypt 1915–16, Megiddo, Nablus, Palestine 1918, Aden, Tigris 1916, Kut-al-Amara 1917, Baghdad, Mesopotamia 1915–18. NW Frontier India 1915, 1916–17, Behobeho, Narungombe, Nyangao, East Africa 1917–18, Afghanistan 1919.

Mescelit Pass, Mt Engiahat, Massawa, Abyssinia 1940–41, Jitra, Ipoh, Kampar, The Muar, Singapore Island, Malaya 1941–42, Sidi Barrani, Omars, Benghazi, El Alamein, Mareth, Akarit, Djebel Garci, Tunis, North Africa 1940–43, Cassino I, Kaladan, Imphal, Tamu Road, Litan, Arakan Beaches, Burma 1942–45.

BOOKS

'Solah Punjab' by Lieut Col J P Lawford MC and Major W E Catto (Gale and Polden Ltd, Aldershot 1967)
'Historical Records of the 4th Bn, 16th Punjab Regiment' (Gale and Polden, Aldershot, 1931)

17th DOGRA REGIMENT

Centre: **1923 JULLUNDUR**
1946 JULLUNDUR

Class Composition:	1923	Dogras and Punjabi Mussalmans
	1946	Dogras from the Punjab and from Jammu and Kashmir State

The 17th Dogra Regiment, created in 1922, consisted of four infantry regiments, of no great antiquity – the 37th Dogras, the 38th Dogras, the 41st Dogras and the 2/41st, a creation of the Great War. These became respectively, the 1st, 2nd, 3rd and 10th Bns of the 17th Dogra Regiment.

The British had recruited Dogras as far back as 1840 but the Dogra Paltan, raised in 1846, did not survive as an exclusively Dogra unit and ultimately became a Frontier Force battalion, going eventually to Pakistan.

Dogras, from the Punjab Hills and Jammu and Kashmir, were rated most valuable soldiers. They are Hindus of Rajput origin, traditional soldiers with a record of centuries of service, courageous and with great powers of physical endurance.

The 37th Regiment of the Bengal Line (the Meerut Levy), had been disbanded for five years when, in 1887, it was re-born as the 37th (Dogra) Regiment of Bengal Infantry. The 38th, (previously the Agra Levy), was simply restyled the 38th (Dogra) Regiment of Bengal Infantry in 1890, the low-caste men mustered out and trained men from other Bengal and Punjab regiments drafted in. One NCO and seven sepoys only came from the old 38th as did a few of the officers. It will be seen that, in terms of unbroken service, the 38th was the senior. In 1891, their titles became simply the 37th and 38th Dogra Infantry. The 41st Dogra Infantry came into being in 1900, taking a number in the old Bengal line which had been vacant since 1882. The 2/41st was raised in 1917 at Jubbulpore.

Shortly after its raising, the 37th took part in the Black Mountain Expedition in 1891 and, later, joined the Chitral Relief Force. Together with the 38th, they spent most of the decade in the extreme North-West, the 37th in the Relief

Force and both regiments in the area of the Malakand Pass. The operations of the 38th evoked the admiration of Winston Churchill who had contrived to be present as a war-correspondent in the guise of an officer of the 4th Queen's Own Hussars.

The 41st went to China in 1904 to join an international force and they remained there until 1908.

FIRST WORLD WAR

37th Dogras – India, Mesopotamia
38th Dogras – India, Aden, Egypt
41st Dogras – India, France, Mesopotamia, Egypt
2/41st Dogras (raised in 1917) – India

BETWEEN THE WARS

The badge chosen for the 17th Dogra Regiment was simply the figures '17' beneath a crown and above a scroll reading 'Dogra Regiment'. However, on the 1 Jan 22, the King had appointed the Prince of Wales as Colonel-in-Chief of the 37th and it was to bear the title 'Prince of Wales's Own'. After 11 Dec 22, the 37th became the 1st Bn (Prince of Wales's Own) 17th Dogra Regiment and wore, as a badge, the silver plumes with the word 'Dogras' beneath. The first King's Commissioned Indian Officer to be posted to the 1st Bn – from 123rd Outram's Rifles – was Lieut (later Field Marshal) K M Cariappa; the following year, he was posted to 1/7 Rajput. The 38th Dogras became the 2nd Bn, the 41st Dogras became the 3rd Bn whilst the war-raised 2/41st Dogras were made the 10th Bn.

In late 1925, the 1st Bn's Punjabi Mussalmans were transferred to 15 Punjab from whom they received Dogras in exchange. The 2nd Bn also exchanged PMs for Dogras with 15 Punjab and transferred its Dogra Brahmans to 10 Baluch. Thus, the 17th Dogra Regiment became a purely 'class' regiment, Dogras only.

The 1st Bn went to Burma in May 1930 to help put down the Burma Rebellion and remained in that country until 1936.

In addition to the four existing regular battalions, an Indian Territorial Force battalion was formed in early 1922 at Jullundur as the 1st (Territorial) Bn, 37th (The Prince of Wales's Own) Dogras but it dropped into line the following year as the 11th Bn 17th Dogra Regiment.

The pipers of the 1st Bn were authorised to wear Mackenzie tartan whilst those of the 2nd Bn wore Sutherland tartan.

A little-known responsibility of 10/17 Dogra was its function also as the centre of the Machine Gun Drivers' Training Company. In 1921, when the Machine Gun Corps was disbanded, eight machine guns were included in the equipment of a British infantry battalion. In India, these guns were carried on mules driven, looked after and taken into action by Indian combatant personnel. The latter – one Indian officer and 40 Indian other ranks – were transferred en bloc to another British battalion when 'their' battalion left for the UK on relief. In many instances, these Indian platoons identified themselves totally with their British regiment, often wearing the regiment's badge. Men for these sub-units were recruited and trained by 10/17 Dogra of Jullundur. Campaign medals awarded bore the soldier's name and the British regiment on the rim.

During the hot weather of 1931, it was decided that the 3rd Bn should be disbanded. When the pensioners heard about this a deputation of senior Indian officers went to Simla to protest. The Adjutant-General was not sympathetic but the old soldiers persisted and got to meet the Commander-in-Chief who listened patiently. They challenged him to quote a single instance of political sedition in their community or failure in the field; if such were found he would be justified, they said, in disbanding the entire 17th Dogra Regiment. Orders for the disbandment of the 3/17 Dogra were rescinded.

SECOND WORLD WAR

1st Bn (Prince of Wales's Own) – India, Burma, Malaya, Java

2nd Bn – Malaya. Captured at Singapore February 1942. Reformed on 15 Apr 46 by redesignation of 6/17 Dogra.

3rd Bn – Malaya. Captured at Singapore February 1942. Reformed in May 1946 by redesignation of 7/17 Dogra.

4th Bn – raised at Peshawar on 1 Oct 40. Burma.

5th Bn – raised at Jullundur on 1 Feb 41. Burma. Disbanded 15 Aug 42.

6th Bn – in September 1939, the Territorial battalion, the 11th was mobilised. In September 1941, it was converted to a regular battalion and redesignated 6/17 Dogra. On 15 Apr 46, the battalion again changed its number and, accepting the surviving cadre of the old 2/17 Dogra, assumed that battalion's precedence.

7th Bn – the 12th Bn, the Regiment's second Territorial battalion, was formed on 1 Jan 40 with two companies of Dogras, one company of PMs and one company of Sikhs (Mazhbis and Ramdassias). It was embodied in November 1940 and, on 14 Sep 41, was converted to a regular battalion, renumbered 7/17 Dogra. The Sikhs were mustered out and the battalion became 75% Dogra and 25% PM. India. In May 1946, the battalion again changed its number and, accepting the surviving cadre of the old 3/17 Dogra, assumed that battalion's precedence.

11th Bn – the pre-war Territorial battalion was converted to regular status in September 1941 and redesignated the 6/17 Dogra.

12th Bn – the second Territorial battalion, formed only on 1 Jan 40, was converted to regular status on 15 September 1941 and redesignated the 7/17 Dogra.

25th Garrison Bn – raised at Jullundur on 15 Aug 41. India, Burma. Disbanded 31 May 46.

26th Garrison Bn – raised at Jullundur on 1 Jan 46. India, Ceylon. Disbanded 30 Jun 46.

Machine-Gun Bn – raised at Jullundur on 15 Oct 41. Middle East, Burma, Malaya, Java. Disbanded 8 Jun 47.

It is of interest that 17 Dogra's two Territorial battalions, the 11th and 12th, eventually became 2/17 and 3/17 Dogra respectively, a unique example of two Territorial units qualifying as regular battalions of their regiment.

In common with the rest of the Indian Line, in October 1945, the Regiment lost its number and became simply The Dogra Regiment.

PARTITION

In August 1947, The Dogra Regiment joined India's Army. The Punjabi Mussalmans were posted to units going to Pakistan whilst Dogra companies were transferred in from The Baluch Regiment and from The Frontier Force Rifles. On transfer of power, the battalions were the 1st, 2nd, 3rd and 4th.

BATTLE HONOURS

Chitral, Malakand, Punjab Frontier, La Bassee 1914, Festubert 1914, 1915, Givenchy 1914, Neuve Chapelle, Aubers, France and Flanders 1914–15, Egypt

1915, Megiddo, Nablus, Palestine 1918, Tigris 1916, Kut-al-Amara 1917, Baghdad, Mesopotamia 1915–18, North-West Frontier, India 1915–17, Afghanistan 1919, Kota Bharu, Malaya 1941–42, Donbaik, Nungshigum, Kennedy Peak, Magwe, Burma 1942–45.

BOOKS

'A History of the 1st (PWO) Bn, The Dogra Regiment 1887–1947' by C T Atkinson (pub. Camelot Press, Southampton 1950)

'History, 2nd Bn The Dogra Regiment, 1891–1942' by Lieut Col W B Cunningham and Lieut Col J N Phelps (pub. Krishan Sudama Press, Ferozepore, 1958)

'Memories of the British Raj: a Soldier in India' by Brigadier R C B Bristow (pub. Johnson, London 1974)

'The Dogra Regiment – a saga of gallantry and valour' by Col R D Palsokar MC (pub. Regtl Centre, 1982)

18th ROYAL GARHWAL RIFLES

Centre: **1923 LANSDOWNE**
1946 LANSDOWNE

Class Composition: 1923 Garhwalis
1946 Garhwalis from the United Provinces and Tehri-Garhwal State

Garhwalis spring from the Himalayas to the West of Nepal and they were initially recruited into the Gurkha regiments as early as 1815. It was not until 1887 that orders were issued that the 2nd Bn of the 3rd Gurkha Rifles should be made up entirely of Garhwalis. It was the declared view of General Sir Frederick (later Lord) Roberts that many of the 'Gurkhas' decorated for gallantry were, in fact, Garhwalis. Recruiting at first was slow and, when ordered to Burma in 1890, six Garhwali companies of the 2/3rd Gurkhas sailed from Calcutta, the intention being to complete the battalion with two Gurkha companies.

The decision was then taken to use these two companies to form a new 2/3rd regiment, the 39th (The Garhwali) Regiment of Bengal Infantry. This took effect in January 1891 but it did not meet with unreserved acclaim as the previous 39th – the old Aligarh Levy – had been disbanded for unsoldierly conduct in the incident recounted earlier. The following year, the 39th became 'Rifles'. In 1901, another regiment was raised at Lansdowne, styled at first the 49th (Garhwal Rifles) Regiment of Bengal Infantry but, shortly afterwards, they became the 2nd Bn of the 39th Garhwal Rifles, making the Regiment, apart from the Gurkhas, the only two-battalion one in the Indian Army.

FIRST WORLD WAR

The outbreak of war in 1914 found both battalions in the Meerut Division, in 20 Brigade – one of the old 'square' four-battalion brigades – with 2 Leicesters and 2/3 Gurkha Rifles. They were in Flanders by the end of October and suffered heavy casualties. The next year, the Indian Corps was withdrawn from France and the two battalions of the 39th, now combined at one-battalion strength, found themselves back in Lansdowne to be reformed as two units once more. Thereafter, both went to Mesopotamia, the 2/39th going on to Salonika and Turkey.

3rd Battalion – raised in August 1917 and used largely as drafts for the two battalions in the Middle East. It also provided the nucleus for the 4th Battalion in October 1917, raised mainly from men from Kumaon District. Their designation was soon changed to the 4/39th Kumaon Rifles and, on 30 Apr 18, to the 1st Bn 50th Kumaon Rifles whereupon they ceased to be a Garhwali dependent.

4th Battalion – the 'genuine' version, was raised at Dehra Dun in October 1918 and was promptly sent to the Frontier for the Third Afghan War.

BETWEEN THE WARS

Unlike the other regiments created in 1922, formed in some cases from a handful of disparate regiments from the 1903 Line, The 39th Royal Garhwal Rifles as they became in 1921, were already a family. They did not, as the other regiments, have to adjust to new partners, new title, new badges, etc. The title was in recognition of their performance in the Great War and they were a single-class regiment. The 1st, 2nd and 3rd remained as duty battalions whilst the 4th, in its new role as training battalion, was renumbered the 10th. The Territorial battalion, the 11th was also based at Lansdowne.

In 1924, the Duke of Argyll gave permission for the 42nd (or Government) tartan to be used by the regimental pipes and drums (Indian Army Order No. 600/26 gave official consent).

In 1925, it was suggested that 4/1st Punjab Regiment (late 1st Brahmans) be transferred to the Regiment as a class battalion of Garhwali Brahmans but there was some opposition. The same suggestion in 1928 was similarly received and, as we know, the 4/1st Punjab was disbanded in December 1923 after 156 years of honourable service to the British Crown, never to be reraised.

SECOND WORLD WAR

1st Battalion – India, Burma, Dutch East Indies.

2nd Battalion – India, Singapore. Captured in February 1942 by the Japanese. Reformed in May 1946 by redesignation of 4/18th.

3rd Battalion – India, Italian East Africa, Iraq, Egypt, Cyprus, Syria, Palestine, Italy.

4th Battalion – raised at Lansdowne in June 1940. India, Burma, Malaya. Redesignated 2/18th in May 1946.

5th Battalion – raised at Lansdowne in February 1941. India, Singapore. Captured in February 1942 by the Japanese. Combined survivors of the fighting from 2 Bn and 5 Bn formed The Royal Garhwal Rifles (Malaya).

6th Battalion – the pre-war Territorial battalion, the 11th, was converted to active status in September 1941 and renumbered the 6/18th. India.

7th Battalion – raised at Lansdowne in July 1942 to replace the two battalions – the 2nd and the 5th – lost in Singapore. However, it was not destined to have a long life. In October 1943, the battalion ceased to exist and personnel joined with men of the 17th Dogra Regiment to form a composite training establishment, styled the 1718 Training Unit, intended to give instruction in jungle warfare.

11th Battalion – the pre-war Territorial battalion was converted to active status in September 1941 and renumbered the 6/18th.

25th Garrison Battalion – raised at Lansdowne in August 1941. India.

PARTITION

In August 1947, The Royal Garhwal Rifles which, in common with most of the other infantry regiments, had lost its number after the war, was allocated to India. Having no Muslim element to transfer, its experience during the handover of power was relatively trouble-free.

The regular battalions were the 1st, 2nd and 3rd.

BATTLE HONOURS

La Bassee 1914, Armentieres 1914, Festubert 1914, Neuve Chapelle, Aubers, Egypt 1915–16, Khan Baghdadi, Sharquat, Mesopotamia 1917–18, Macedonia 1918, Afghanistan 1919.

Gallabat, Barentu, Keren, Massawa, Amba Alagi, North Africa 1940–43, Kuantan, Malaya 1941–42, Citta di Castello, Italy 1943–45, Yenangyaung 1942, Monywa 1942, North Arakan, Ngakyedauk Pass, Ramree, Taungup, Burma 1942–45.

BOOKS

Historical Records of the 39th Garhwal Rifles 1887–1922 by Brigadier General J Evatt DSO

Historical Records of the 18th Royal Garhwal Rifles 1923–47 by Lieut General Sir Ralph Deedes OBE MC

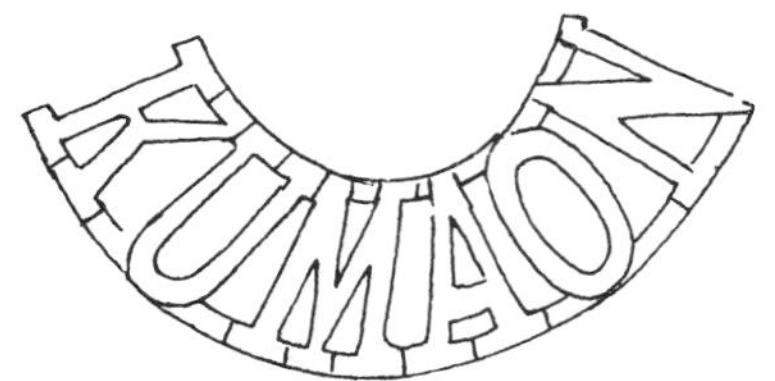

19th HYDERABAD REGIMENT/KUMAON REGIMENT

Centre: **1923 BENARES**
1946 AGRA

Class Composition:	1923	Rajputs from UP, Jats from UP, Ahirs from the Eastern Punjab, Kumaonis.
	1946	Kumaonis from the Kumaon Civil Division, Ahirs from the Punjab, UP and Rajputana, Jats from the Punjab, UP, Rajputana and Central India States

---

By 1903, the six battalions which, in 1923, went to form the 19th Hyderabad Regiment had lost contact with their origins although they and three regiments of cavalry had long been known as the Hyderabad Contingent.

It was in 1812 that Henry Russell (later Sir Henry), the then British Resident in Hyderabad, prevailed upon the Nizam to raise and equip two battalions of infantry upon the British-Indian model. These became known as the Russell Brigade. That done, he turned his attention to Berar. Berar was a territory made over to the Nizam of Hyderabad for his services in the Mysore War and it maintained levies. To bolster Hyderabad's strength and not without a glance at the French, still angling for power in the Deccan, Russell reformed Berar's troops into four battalions, the 1st to 4th Berar Infantry. Russell's men were chiefly Hindus, recruited from Oudh and the area later known as the United Provinces (or, later still, Uttar Pradesh). They did no duty in Hyderabad where they were stationed or with any of the Nizam's other troops. In a report to the Commander-in-Chief of the Madras Army in 1817, Russell claimed: 'In fact, they belong to the Nizam's Army in name only; they consider themselves as Company's troops and, for all practical purposes, they are as much so as those in our immediate establishment'.

In addition to the four Berar battalions, two others belonging to Muhammad Salabat Khan, the Subadar of Berar and commanded by Englishmen, were incorporated into the Nizam's Contingent, making a total of eight battalions, renumbered in 1826 as follows:

Old name	New name
1st Bn Russell Bde	1st Regt Nizam's Infantry
2nd Bn Russell Bde	2nd Regt Nizam's Infantry
1st Berar Infantry	3rd Regt Nizam's Infantry
2nd Berar Infantry	4th Regt Nizam's Infantry
3rd Berar Infantry	5th Regt Nizam's Infantry
4th Berar Infantry	6th Regt Nizam's Infantry
1st Regt Salabat Khan's	7th Regt Nizam's Infantry
2nd Regt Salabat Khan's	8th Regt Nizam's Infantry

It was not until 1853 that, following a certain financial stringency on the part of the Nizam, the Hyderabad Contingent was so styled and transferred to the forces of John Company at the same time being reduced to six battalions. Despite the heavy loading within the Contingent of those classes most to the fore in the ranks of the mutineers, the Great Mutiny did not find the Hyderabad Contingent lacking in zeal in its suppression.

Before the Mutiny, regiments had no structured class composition and 'men stood by chance in the ranks, Hindu and Mussalman, Poorbeah and Punjabi, cheek by jowl'. After 1858, class-companies were established in most regiments but not in the Hyderabad Contingent. In 1879, it was laid down that only 25% of the Contingent's recruits might be enlisted from North India. Subsequently, a shortage of good local recruits led the government in 1894 to accept 50% North Indians. The Hindu:Mussalman ratio was fixed then at 60:40. Finally, the class-company system was adopted by the contingent in 1897 and its units were composed as under:

	1st Inf.	2nd Inf.	3rd Inf.	4th Inf.	5th Inf.	6th Inf.
Rajputs	37.5%	37.5%	37.5%	37.5%	37.5%	37.5%
Jats	25%		25%	25%		25%
Ahirs		25%			25%	
Deccani Muslims	37.5%			37.5%		
UP Mussalmans		37.5%	37.5%		37.5%	37.5%

In the 1903 reorganisation, Kitchener assigned new titles to the six regiments. The Hyderabad Contingent was no more and its infantry was renumbered as shown:

1st Infantry became 94th Russell's Infantry
2nd Infantry became 95th Russell's Infantry
3rd Infantry became 96th Berar Infantry
4th Infantry became 97th Deccan Infantry
5th Infantry became 98th Infantry
6th Infantry became 99th Deccan Infantry

FIRST WORLD WAR

94th Russell's – India, Persia, Mesopotamia
  2/94th – (raised in 1917) – India
95th Russell's – India, Persia, Mesopotamia, Turkey
  2/95th – (raised in 1918) – India
96th Berar – India, Persia, Mesopotamia, Burma
  2/96th – (raised in 1918) – India, Mesopotamia
97th Deccan – India, Mesopotamia
  2/97th – (raised in 1917) – India, Egypt, Palestine
98th Infantry – India, German East Africa, Persia
  2/98th – (raised in 1918) – India, Persia
99th Deccan – India, Persia
  2/99th – (raised in 1918) – India

After the war, all the second battalions were disbanded. However, although clearly not a part of the old Hyderabad Contingent, a battalion of Kumanonis was raised at Ranikhet in October 1917 as the 4/39th Garhwal Rifles, changing its name the next month to the 4/39th Kumaon Rifles. Kumaonis were not new to military service having previously taken employment in the Gurkha regiments, the Garhwal Rifles and the Burma Military Police. In April 1918, the battalion title changed yet again, to become the 1/50th Kumaon Rifles and, in May, they sailed for Egypt where they joined the 60th London Division to serve with distinction in Palestine, alongside the 2/97th. After the end of the war the 1/50th went to Istanbul to join the Army of the Black Sea. On 1 Jun 18, whilst the 1/50th was in action in Palestine, a 2/50th was being formed at Bareilly made up of two companies of Kumaoni Rajputs and one company each of Kumaoni Brahmins and Garhwali Brahmins, the last-named being largely transferred from the 38th Dogras. Warned to proceed to Salonika, the 2/50th was disappointed when the armistice consigned them instead to the North West Frontier. In March 1923, the 2/50th Kumaon Rifles was disbanded.

BETWEEN THE WARS

The immediate post-Great War changes meant the grouping of the old Hyderabad Contingent's six battalions into the 19th Infantry Group but, on 1 Dec 22, the 19th Hyderabad Regiment was formed with its battalions having the following designations:

94th Russell's Infantry became 1st Bn (Russell's) 19th Hyderabad Regt
96th Berar Infantry became 2nd Bn (Berar) 19th Hyderabad Regt
97th Deccan Infantry became 3rd Bn 19th Hyderabad Regt
98th Infantry became 4th Bn 19th Hyderabad Regt
99th Deccan Infantry became 5th Bn 19th Hyderabad Regt
95th Russell's Infantry became 10th Bn (Russell's) 19th Hyderabad Regt

Initially, the 1/50th Kumaon Rifles had gone to the 9th Infantry Group (presumably due to the proximity of the Jat Training Centre at Bareilly to the Kumaoni recruiting areas) but 15 Mar 23 saw the battalion in the 19th Hyderabad Regiment as the 1st Kumaon Rifles, a one-class battalion.

On 5 Aug 21, the 1st (Territorial) Bn 94th Russell's Infantry was raised and joined the 19th Hyderabad Regiment the following year as the 11/19th, based at Dinapore.

As part of the programme of Indianisation, 4/19 Hyderabad was nominated in 1923 to be one of the first battalions for conversion and, in February 1928, Lieutenant Thimayya, destined to be the Colonel of the Regiment and Chief of Army Staff, joined the 4/19th.

The badge chosen for the 19th Hyderabad was not an inspired choice, the Roman numerals 'XIX', a crown above and a title-scroll below. The badge chosen for 1 Kumaon Rif was a stringed bugle-horn with the letters 'KR' above.

Changes in class composition followed for all battalions except 1 Kumaon Rif. Deccani Muslims were an early casualty and the Hindustani Muslims were mustered out in 1923 to be replaced by a company of Kumaonis. Battalions were now constituted with one company each of UP Rajputs, the UP Jats, Ahirs from the Eastern Punjab and Kumaonis. Further changes in 1930 meant that composition henceforth was to be one company each Kumaonis, Jats, Ahirs and mixed.

The Regiment was one of those to suffer the economy-axe and the 5/19th was disbanded in 1924. Seven years later, 3/19th met the same fate. One assumes that 4/19th was inviolate in its status as an Indianising unit.

SECOND WORLD WAR

1st Battalion (Russell's) – Iraq, Palestine, Egypt, Iran, India, Burma, Indo-China, Dutch East Indies.
In mid-1946, the 1st Battalion was nominated to become a parachute battalion to serve in the 2nd Indian Airborne Division. It was redesignated 1st (Parachute) Bn The Kumaon Regiment (Russell's).

2nd Battalion (Berar) – India, Burma, Malaya, Dutch East Indies.

4th Battalion – India, Malaya, Singapore. Captured on Singapore Island February 1942. Reformed on 1 Jun 46 by redesignation of the 8/19th.

5th Battalion – re-raised at Jubbulpore on 15 Jun 40. India. In August 1943, became a jungle warfare training battalion. Disbanded 7 Mar 46.

6th Battalion – raised at Agra on 1 Feb 41. India, Burma.

7th Battalion – raised at Agra on 1 Feb 41. India. Disbanded 20 Dec 46.

8th Battalion – raised at Agra on 15 Aug 41. India, Burma, Malaya. Reformed 1 Jun 46 as 4/19th.

9th Battalion – raised at Agra on 15 Apr 42 as a machine-gun battalion but reverted to normal infantry role shortly afterwards due to the shortage of machine-guns. India. Disbanded 16 Jul 46.

11th Battalion – this was the pre-war Territorial battalion embodied at Dinapore on the outbreak of war. Re-styled the 1st Bn The Bihar Regiment on 15 Sep 41 with its own badge – the Lions of Ashoka.

25th Garrison Battalion – raised at Agra on 1 Jul 41. India. Disbanded 15 May 46.

26th Garrison Battalion – raised at Agra on 1 Mar 42. India. Disbanded 25 Mar 51.

1st Kumaon Rifles – Iran, Persia, Malaya.

As far back as 1935, there had been lobbying within the Regiment for a change of name. It was agreed that there was no longer any connection with Hyderabad and that others tended to look upon it as a 'downcountry regiment'. Moreover, when stationed near Hyderabad State Infantry units there was confusion and that was an argument which probably had most support. Kumaonis, ran the argument, had performed well, had no regiment of their own and, besides, recruitment of Jats had dropped because they were going, increasingly to the Indian Armoured Corps and the Royal Indian Artillery. The Government of India finally yielded: the Jats were transferred to the 4th

Bombay Grenadiers and the 9th Jat Regiment. The future composition of the Regiment was to be 75% Kumaonis and 25% Ahirs. At the same time, on 27 Oct 45, the 19th Hyderabad became The Kumaon Regiment (Special Indian Army Order 132/S/45). The change of badge became necessary and an inspired choice was the demi-rampant lion from the arms of the Russell family above a scroll reading 'Kumaon'.

PARTITION

In August 1947, the Regiment was allotted to India and, as an all-Hindu unit, did not require either to accept or post out Muslims.

The battalions on transfer of power were the 1st, 2nd, 4th, 6th and 26th, and the 1st Kumaon Rifles.

BATTLE HONOURS

Nagpore, Meheidpoor, Nowah, Central India, Burma 1885–87, China 1900, Megiddo, Sharon, Palestine 1918, Tigris 1916, Khan Baghdadi, Mesopotamia 1915–18, Persia 1915–18, North West Frontier, India 1914–15, 1916–17, East Africa 1914–16, Afghanistan 1919, North Africa 1940–43, Slim River, Malaya 1941–42, Bishenpur, Kangaw, The Shweli, Magwe, Kama, Sittang 1945, Burma 1942–45.

BOOKS

History of the 1st Bn 19th Hyderabad Regt (Russell's) (Gale and Polden, Aldershot 1928)

Regimental history of the 2/19th Hyderabad Regt (Berar) by Lieut Col J de L Conry (Gale and Polden, Aldershot 1927)

A history of the 4th Bn 19th Hyderabad Regt by G G C Bull (Gale and Polden, Aldershot 1933)

Valour Triumphs by K C Praval (Thompson Press (India) Faridabad 1976)

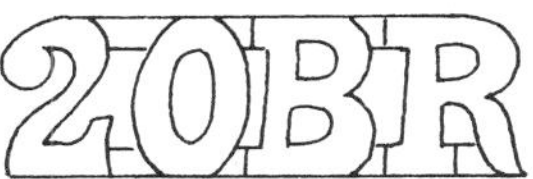

20th BURMA RIFLES

Centre: **1923 MAYMYO**
1937 MAYMYO

Class Composition: 1923 1 Bn – Burmans, Shans, Kachins and Chins
2 Bn – Burmans and Karens
3 Bn – Kachins
10 Bn – Burmans, Karens, Shans, Kachins and Chins
1937 – Kachins, Chins and Karens

It took three wars over a period of more than sixty years to conquer Burma yet it is questionable whether it was the country or the Burmese soldier who was the more formidable enemy. However, after the final campaign in 1885–87, King Thibaw departed to terminal exile in India and his troops melted into the jungle, there to indulge in the type of warfare which they knew best.

Upper Burma was pacified first by the Madrassi sepoy until 1895 when, in pursuance of the policy of running down the Madras Army, seven battalions were raised in northern India from Sikhs and Punjabi Mussalmans, nominated as Madras Battalions, later to be re-numbered as Punjabis and, subsequently, as Burma Infantry. The indigenous population was not initially recruited but they came gradually to be accepted into the Burma Military Police (not a provost organisation but rather a sort of gendarmerie) and these were Karens and not Burmans.

The growth of the Indian Army prompted the raising of two companies of Burma Pioneers in Mandalay in November 1916 and these accepted all Burma's races. Increased to four companies, the Pioneers were converted to the 70th Burma Rifles in September 1917. In the meantime, the 85th Burman Rifles had been raised in July 1917 from the Burma Military Police. The 2/70th Burma Rifles was raised in January 1918 and both 1/70th and 2/70th served in the Middle East, the 1/70th returning to Burma in 1920, only to be shipped to the Straits Settlement (Malaya). The 3/70th, formed in April 1918, went to Southern India to suppress the Moplah Rising whilst the 4/70th raised in May 1918, remained in Burma. A 5/70th was also raised but saw no overseas service.

After the war, the 3/70th and 4/70th were disbanded and the 85th Burman Rifles was reconstituted with three companies of Kachins and one of Chins, becoming in November 1921, the 3/70th (Kachin) Rifles.

On the creation of the 20th Burma Rifles in 1923, the 1/70th Burma Rifles, the 2/70th Burma Rifles and the 3/70th (Kachin) Rifles became the 1/20th, 2/20th and 3/20th Burma Rifles whilst the 5/70th Burma Rifles became the 10/20th Burma Rifles, their training battalion. The 1st (Territorial) Bn 70th Burma Rifles was raised on 3 Aug 21 in Mandalay and became 11/20 Burma Rifles in 1922. The new uniform was to be rifle-green with scarlet facings and the regimental badge a Burmese peacock over a title-scroll, all in white metal.

Burmans, however, were not to remain in favour for long and, within a couple of years, had been mustered out of all save the 2nd Battalion. Finally, in 1927, at a conference of Indian Army officers, none of whom had ever served with a Burma unit, the decision was taken to exclude them from the regular battalions although they were still to be accepted by the Burma Military Police.

In 1937, Burma was formally separated from India and the one foreign-service station garrisoned by the 20th Burma Rifles, Taiping, in Malaya, ceased. The '20th' was removed from the title and the 10/20th Burma Rifles became 4th Bn The Burma Rifles, abandoning its training role as all battalions were now to train their own recruits. Those officers serving in the Regiment were cross-posted to other Indian Army regiments but most chose to remain with the Burma Rifles on secondment. New officer-recruitment was to be from the British Army but, on the outbreak of war in September 1939, there were still more than ninety Indian Army officers on Burma service.

On moving out from under the Indian umbrella, the term Viceroy's Commissioned Officer became no longer applicable, of course, and VCOs became GCOs (Governor's Commissioned Officers).

The make-up of the Regiment in 1939 was 50% Karen and 25% each Kachin and Chin but the decision was taken in 1940 to recruit Burmans once more.

In the newly-raised 5th and 6th Battalions, one company each was Burmese. To form these battalions, cadres were taken from the four regular battalions with resultant reduction of efficiency all round. The 7th Battalion was raised from the Burma Police and the BMP whilst the 8th Battalion came from the Burma Frontier Force (a 1937 creation, five battalions strong, largely Indian, with a strong mounted infantry element). The 9th Battalion was raised in 1941 to train reinforcements and hold drafts whilst the 10th was re-raised as the Centre. The 11th and 12th Battalions were Territorials, the 11th dating back to 1922 and the 13th and 14th Battalions were raised hastily in the Shan States in late 1941.

Following the Japanese attack in 1942, only the 2nd Battalion reached India in recognisable form. The 13th and 14th collapsed as hastily as they had been raised and those battalions which survived the first weeks of the campaign finally foundered in the oilfields of Central Burma at the hottest time of the year.

The 2nd Bn Burma Rifles marched back into Burma in 1945, one-third each Karen, Kachin and Chin. They had served Wingate in his two Long Range Penetration operations in 1943 and 1944. In the first expedition, eleven officers and twenty-one other ranks were decorated whilst, in the second, ten Military Crosses were awarded. By that time, of course, most of the original Indian Army officers were no longer serving with the Regiment.

Independence came in January 1948 and, moving out of the British Commonwealth, Burma Army units were not eligible to receive the accepted battle-honours. Moreover, the hill-tribes, the backbone of the Burma Rifles, were no longer militarily acceptable to the new government and, in most cases, were actually under arms against it.

THE INDIAN PARACHUTE REGIMENT

It was in June 1940 that parachute troops were first formed in Britain and India was not far behind. At least, the intention was there. General Sir Robert Cassels, then Commander-in-Chief in India authorised the formation of a cadre of parachute troops in October that year and sent the commander-designate, Lieutenant Colonel W H G Gough to the UK to attend a course at the Central Landing Establishment, Ringway (now the airport for Manchester). Two other Indian Army officers, Captain P Hopkinson and Captain B E Abbott, then on a staff course, also completed the course at Ringway and all three were back in India by September 1941. The intention was that experiments should be carried out with the RAF and that a mixed brigade of British, Indian and Gurkha parachute troops might be formed.

On 2 Dec 40, the Commander-in-Chief authorised the formation of these battalions and sought War Office approval. Response from London was not enthusiastic and on 30 Jan 41, a signal was sent to GHQ from the War Office suggesting that these raisings be deferred pending a policy-review. However, Cassels was not disposed to accept this delay and set up an Airborne Troops Committee to produce a feasibility-study and on 15 May 41, decided to go ahead with raising the parachute brigade. Approval was given by London in June, subject to one battalion being British and the Secretary of State for India, Mr L S Amery, gave it his blessing.

October 1941 saw the raising of 50 Indian Parachute Brigade at Delhi and Air HQ authorised the setting-up of the Air-Landing School. The Brigade, under Brigadier W H G Gough, consisted of the following:

Brigade HQ
50 Indian Parachute Brigade Signal Section
151 British Parachute Battalion
152 Indian Parachute Battalion
153 Gurkha Parachute Battalion
411 (Royal Bombay) Parachute Section, Indian Engineers

There were no problems in recruitment. The twenty-three British infantry battalions in India provided a ready source for 151 Bn. Most of the volunteers were pre-war regular officers and soldiers who could only, at that time, see India as a permanent garrison-posting with The Frontier begin their only chance of excitement. Japan was not yet in the war and the Germans offered no threat to India. Indian volunteers were accepted for 152 Bn from all the Indian infantry regiments with the excception of 11 Sikh. The inability of the Sikh soldier to wear the parachutist's helmet precluded the acceptance of Sikhs at this stage although, later in the war, the RAF agreed a compromise when Sikh parachutists undertook to wear a protective pad around their pagri. Nine regiments of the Gurkha Brigade furnished the volunteers for 153 Bn. Only the 9th Gurkhas were not acceptable: the 9th recruited high-caste soldiers and they could not have lived and eaten with men from the other Gurkha regiments.

Captain B E Abbott, now a lieutenant colonel was to command 152 Indian Para Bn whilst Captain P Hopkinson was promoted to become Brigade Major. Brigadier Gough, however, was thought to be too old at forty-three and made way for M R J Hope Thompson MC, direct from commanding 4 Para in the UK, at thirty-one, the youngest brigade commander in India Command.

The 152nd Indian Parachute Battalion was a new experiment. It had no class composition, the companies being mixed. Its only communal concession was that separate cookhouses were set up for Hindus and Moslems.

Basic parachute training began in November 1941 but the shortage of equipment meant slow progress. Even the entry of Japan into the war the following month and the subsequent boost to India's importance in the priority of supplies could not meet the needs of 50 Indian Parachute Brigade. Aircraft were in short supply and those that were available were not the most suitable. By mid-1942 parachutes were being made in India in substantial numbers but air-training was not freely available: however, with its increased ground training, 50 Bde was probably the fittest in India.

Parachute training had, hitherto, been in Delhi but this was not the ideal location although it was a useful public-relations spot. In India in 1942, parachuting was still a military novelty but security was impossible. It was decided to move the brigade to Campbellpore and the Air-Landing School to Chaklala (now the airport for Rawalpindi in Pakistan).

For some time, it had been under consideration that 151 British Parachute Battalion might be moved to the Middle East and, on 4 Nov 1942, they sailed from Bombay under the disguise of 20 Bn Queen's which deceived almost nobody. Shortly after their arrival in Egypt, for no apparent reason, the number was changed from 151 to 156. Later, the battalion fought at Arnhem.

To replace 151 in the brigade, 3/7 Gurkha Rifles was posted in as 154 Gurkha Parachute Battalion. After the retreat from Burma, 3/7 GR numbered six officers and about 300 men. By November 1942, after reforming and reinforcement, the battalion was again fit for service and it was suggested that it might be converted to a parachute role if sufficient men volunteered. They did and it was.

March 1944 saw the Brigade's greatest contribution to the campaign in Burma albeit not in a parachute role. It had been sent to the Imphal area for a month's training in January with 23 Indian Division commanded by Major General Ouvry Roberts DSO but suddenly, 152 and 153 Bns (154 Bn was still completing parachute training) found themselves, with 4/5 Mahratta LI under command, facing the Japanese drive north in the area of Sangshak in Northern Burma. An account of the battle published in 1989, written by one of 153 Bn's company commanders, described it as a 'scenario for suicide'. From a strength of 2,000, losses were about 900, of whom about 100 were prisoners of war, later released. The delay imposed upon the Japanese advance on Dimapur by 50 Bde's five-day stand at Sangshak earned the Fourteenth Army a week to prepare and reorganise its defences for a counter-offensive in the Imphal Plain. The Mahratta Light Infantry was granted the honour 'Sangshak' when battle-

ANNEX 1 to LPP/BP 1C of 11 MAY 88

SPECIAL ORDER OF THE DAY

BY

Lt-General W. J. SLIM, C.B., C.B.E., D.S.O., M.C.,

General Officer Commanding-in-Chief, Fourteenth Army.

—Addressed to The 50th Parachute Brigade

IN my last Order of the Day I told you that you had defeated the Jap armies opposing you and that it remained to destroy them. The extent to which you have done that is shown by the fifty thousand Japanese left dead on the soil of India and Northern Burma, the great quantities of guns and equipment you have captured, the prisoners you have taken, the advance you have made, and the flight of the remnants you are still pursuing. To the 15th Corps in the Arakan fell the unique honour of being the first British-Indian formation to hold, break and decisively hurl back a major Japanese offensive.

Theirs was an example of tenacity and courage which inspired the whole Army. The 4th Corps met the main weight of the Japanese Assam offensive, and, in one of the hardest fought and longest battles of the war, shattered it. 33rd Corps in their brilliant offensive from the North not only drove a large Japanese force from what should have been an impregnable position, but destroyed it. Together the 4th and 33rd Corps have swept the enemy out of India.

The troops of 202 and 404 L of C Areas, not only by their gallantry and steadfastness in action, but by their tireless devotion behind the immediate front, have made a contribution essential to victory What you owe to our comrades in the Allied Air Forces I need not remind you. Our whole plan of battle was based on their support. There would have been no success had they failed us. Their share in our combined victory was magnificent and historic.

There is not a division or brigade in the Fourteenth Army which has not proved its superiority over the enemy and knows it. Your Parachute Brigade bore the first brunt of the enemy's powerful flanking attack, and by their staunchness gave the garrison of Imphal the vital time required to adjust their defences.

To the officers and men of the 50th Parachute Brigade I send my congratulations. The Fourteenth Army has inflicted on the Japanese the greatest defeat his Army has yet suffered. He is busily trying to build up again and reinforce his broken divisions. He will fight again and viciously, but we have paid him something of what we owe. There still remains the interest. He will get it.

Field
31 August 44.

W. J. Slim

Lieut-General.
General Officer Commanding-inChief.

honours were awarded in the 1960s. No other regiment in the armies of the Commonwealth has the honour. A Special Order of the Day (reproduced on p. 203) from Lieutenant General Slim shows what he thought of 50 Indian Parachute Brigade.

The intention to form an Indian airborne division had been made known in September 1943 and it had been provisionally numbered the 9th. After Sangshak, the situation in Burma improved and 44 Indian Armoured Division was withdrawn to become 44 Indian Airborne Division, the restyled 9th. South India was chosen as the concentration area for the new division. It was customary at the time for an airborne division to be made up of two parachute brigades and one air-landing (glider-borne) brigade. By chance, 14 (Long Range Penetration) Brigade, withdrawn from its Chindit role in Burma, was recuperating in Bangalore, having already had active air-landing experience. It was made up of:

2 King's Own (later replaced by 6/16 Punjab)
2 Black Watch
4/6 Raj Rif

Secunderabad was housing 50 Para Bde, now complete with 154 Bn. The third brigade in the division was to be 77 Indian Parachute Brigade, the number taken from another Special Force brigade. To meet the then normal brigade structure of two Indian/Gurkha battalions and one British battalion, two new British battalions would be required. The 1st Queen's and the 1st Essex were initially nominated but it was found that these had too many men due for repatriation and 1st King's and 1st South Staffords were substituted. These latter two were reduced to cadre and the volunteers from them became the 15th and 16th British Para Bns. Their strength was made up by volunteers from other British units in India and drafts from the UK.

On 1 Mar 45 the planned Indian Parachute Regiment came into being, consisting initially of four battalions and four independent companies. The Hindu personnel of 152 Indian Bn became the 1st Battalion, the 153 and 154 Gurkha Bns became the 2nd and 3rd Bns respectively whilst the Muslim element of 152 Bn made up the 4th. This was a complete reversal of the previous policy of a mixed Hindu-Muslim battalion and it produced an Indian Army phenomenon, an all-Muslim infantry battalion. The four companies, numbered 14th, 44th, 50th and 77th, were brigade and divisional headquarters defence units. Nos 14 and 50 Companies were Hindu, 44 Company Gurkha and 77 Company Muslim. The Commander-in-Chief ordered that class composition within the Regiment would be:

Hindus	*Muslims*	*Gurkhas*
Mahrattas	Pathans	All classes
Rajputs	Punjabi Mussjalmans	
Dogras*	Rajputana Mussalmans	
Kumaonis*	Mohammedan Rajputs	
Garhwalis*		

* excl. Brahmins

In July 1945, the infantry elements of 44 Indian Airborne Division were as follows:

50 Ind Para Bde	77 Ind Para Bde	14 Air-landing Bde
16 Para (British)	15 Para (British)	2 Black Watch
1 Ind Para Bn	2 Gurkha Para Bn	4/6 Raj Rif
3 Gurkha Para Bn	4 Ind Para Bn	6/16 Punjab
	44 British Indep Pathfinder Coy	

It was at this stage that the maroon beret worn by The Parachute Regiment and Airborne Forces in the UK was taken into use in India. Hitherto, parachute units in India had worn the felt bush-hat with cloth battalion badge on the side but this was replaced by the maroon beret with a new, metal badge – the normal Parachute Regiment pattern but with a tablet 'INDIA' across the rigging-lines. The discarded cloth badges were: for 153 Bn, a pale blue rectangle with an open parachute above crossed kukris, cutting-edges downwards, embroidered in white; for 154 Bn, a rifle-green rectangle with an open parachute above crossed kukris, cutting-edge inwards, 7GR fashion, also in white. Pegasus had already been in use for some time as a formation sign on the upper arm. In the matter of buttons, 152 Bn wore plain 'silver' buttons (as worn by 10 Baluch) whilst 153 wore 2GR buttons and 154 wore those of 7GR. Interestingly, in the early days, officers off-duty had worn a maroon side-cap with bullion-embroidered parachute badge. Shoulder-titles were not worn by 152 Bn but 153 and 154 Gurkha Bns wore blackened numerals. The standard parachute-qualification wings, worn initially above the right breast-pocket, were moved to the right shoulder in 1945.

In May 1945, a composite Gurkha parachute battalion from 2 and 3 Bns landed at Elephant Point, the very mouth of Rangoon River to silence Japanese guns, thereby facilitating the entry of minesweepers into the port and moving north to make contact with ground forces. This was the Regiment's last action and it's only one in a parachute role.

Nationalisation – or Indianisation – had long been the avowed intention of the British Government and one of the earliest post-war changes was the decision to have a completely Indian airborne division. In November 1945, 44th Indian Airborne Division changed to become the 2nd Indian Airborne Division. Other changes were:

(i) All British troops were to be withdrawn
(ii) The Indian Parachute Regiment was to be disbanded and all ranks, except the Gurkhas, transferred to other para units
(iii) All Gurkhas were to be withdrawn from the division (this was probably due to uncertainty as to the plans for them in post-war India)
(iv) All British staff officers were to be replaced by Indians, working from junior ranks upwards
(v) The division to consist of three parachute brigades, the air landing brigade being re-mustered in a parachute role
(vi) Parachute battalions henceforth would be from existing Indian Army regiments

This involved a complete restructuring of the division, the only battalion unaffected being 4/6 Raj Rif although they would have to be converted to parachutists. Traditional regimental distinctions would be retained but all would wear the maroon beret or maroon pagri. To distinguish them from other battalions in their regiment, the word 'Parachute' was inserted after the numeral and before the regimental title – thus 1 (Para) Bn Kumaon Regt.

The Indian Parachute Regiment was formally disbanded on 26 Oct 46, the parade being under the command of Brigadier Paul Hopkinson who had been in at the start of Indian Army parachuting.

In January 1947, the infantry elements of 2nd Indian Airborne Division were as follows:

Divisional HQ. – 1 (Para) Bn Kumaon (Defence Bn)
3 (Para) Bn 15 Punjab (MG)

14 Para Bde	*50 Para Bde*	*77 Para Bde*
4 (Para) Bn Raj Rif	3 (Para) Bn 1 Punjab	1 (Para) Bn 2 Punjab
1 (Para) Bn FF Regt	3 (Para) Bn Baluch	3 (Para) Bn Mahratta L1
3 (Para) Bn 16 Punjab	2 (Para) Bn Madras	3 (Para) Bn Rajput

Before the 2nd Indian Airborne Division could do more than start its specialist training there came the news of impending Partition. The 14 Para Bde went to Pakistan whilst 50 and 77 Para Bdes remained in India: the constituent battalions, of course, went with their regiments. Thus, 4 (Para) Bn Rajputana Rifles went to India whilst 1 (Para) Bn FF Regt and 3 (Para) Bn 16 Punjab went to Pakistan. In 50 Para Bde, 3 (Para) Bn 1 Punjab and 3 (Para) Bn Baluch went to Pakistan whilst 2 (Para) Bn Madras stayed in India. All three of 77 Para Bde's battalions remained in India. Of the divisional troops, 1 (Para) Bn Kumaon stayed in India whilst 3 (Para) Bn 15 Punjab went to Pakistan.

With the exception of the Madras, Mahratta and Kumaon Para Bns, all the others had mixed Hindu-Muslim recruitment. The 3/15 Punjab and 3/16 Punjab had Jats and Sikhs, 3 Baluch had Dogras and 1 FF Regt had Dogras and Sikhs. The problem was to ensure an exchange of these with the Pathans and Punjabi Mussalmans who were to go to Pakistan. For the most part, they parted as friends and reached their new units safely. Despite the communal mayhem, the army generally looked after its own.

Only the Gurkhas were left without a parachuting future. It would be five years before India would form its own Parachute Regiment and accept the now Gorkhas into its ranks.

BATTLE HONOURS

No honours were awarded to the Indian Parachute Regiment. Honours were granted by the Indian Government in 1963–64 and they held that their Parachute Regiment, formed in 1952, could not be considered the successor to the British-raised regiment. Despite this stricture, their present Parachute Regiment carries honours gained a decade before its formation by subsequently converted battalions of line-infantry regiments.

Surviving British officers of 50 Indian Parachute Brigade have petitioned the Government of India for the grant of the honour 'Sangshak' for the action in Upper Burma in March 1944. The honour has already been granted to the Maratha Light Infantry for the part played by 4/5 Mahratta LI whilst under command of 50 Indian Parachute Brigade.

The grant of Sangshak would surely also grant the Indian Parachute Regiment the theatre honour of Burma 1942–45.

BOOKS
'Airborne Forces' (The War Office 1951)
'India's Paratroopers' by K C Praval (Leo Cooper, London 1975)
'The Battle of Sangshak' by Harry Seaman (Leo Cooper, London 1989)
'Pegasus in India' by Col F G Neild (Jay Birch Co (Pte) Ltd. Singapore c. 1970).

THE BIHAR REGIMENT

Centre: 1941 AGRA (shared with the 19th Hyderabad Regiment)
1946 RANCHI

Class Composition: Adibasis from Bihar, Orissa, Bengal and eastern states (including aboriginal tribes of Hos, Oraons, Mundas, Santals and Kharias), Ahirs from Bihar, Rajputs from Bihar and Mussalmans from Bihar.

The Bihar Regiment began life in 1922 as one of the earliest formed battalions of the Indian Territorial Force, the 1st (Territorial) Bn 94th Russell's Infantry, becoming, later that year, the 11/19th Hyderabad Regiment. Based on Dinapore, it was mobilised in 1939 and, on 15 Sep 41, when most Territorial battalions were being converted to regular status, the 11/19th went one step further and became a regiment of its own: the 11/19th became the 1st Bn The Bihar Regiment, its badge the lions of Ashoka over a scroll 'Bihar'. India, Burma

2nd Battalion – raised 1 Dec 41. India
3rd Battalion – raised 1 Nov 45. India
25th Battalion – raised by conversion of the 2nd Indian Coast Defence Battalion. India. Disbanded 1946.

Only the 1st Bn saw action during the Second World War and it served in Burma as part of the Lushai Brigade. The Willcox Committee in 1945 recorded that the battalion's action in the 1944 operations in Manipur had been well reported on but it did not recommend the regiment's retention in the post-war Indian Army: the aboriginal tribes would not appear to offer an adequate recruiting-pool whilst the terms Hindustani Mussalman and eastern Rajput who were already provided for militarily could be extended to include Bihar. Thus, there was no justification for a permanent Bihar Regiment. Notwithstanding, in November 1945, they formed their own regimental centre which moved to Ranchi in March

1946. The Kumaon Regiment – the successors to 19th Hyderabad – continued to provide subadar-majors to the Biharis until 1952.

PARTITION
In 1947, the Regiment was allotted to India and the Muslim companies mustered out for posting to Pakistan.

The battalions on transfer of power were the 1st, 2nd and 3rd.

BATTLE HONOURS
Haka, Gangaw, Burma 1942–45

BOOKS
'The Bihar Warriors' a history of The Bihar Regiment 1758–1986 by Colonel RD Palsokar MC
(Pub: Bihar Regimental Centre 1986)

THE ASSAM REGIMENT

Centre: **1941 SHILLONG, ASSAM**
1946 SHILLONG, ASSAM

Class composition: Assamese from Assam (including all Hindus, Christians and tribesmen but excluding Mussalmans)

In response to a request from the Assam Government in 1941, with a cadre from the Assam Rifles, the new Assam Regiment was created at Shillong. Its badge was a rhinoceros over a scroll bearing the title. The local tribesmen were no strangers to military service; they had served in the Assam Rifles and its myriad predecessors for more than a century. VCOs and NCOs from the Assam Rifles volunteered to form the 1st Battalion which was the only one to see action.

An irregular force, the Lushai Scouts, raised in 1942, was attached to the Regiment and distinguished itself in the Manipur operations in 1944.

The Willcox Committee's report suggested that the men would probably not take to general service away from Assam and felt that there were serious difficulties in combining into a regiment on normal lines tribes speaking numerous mutually unintelligible languages. For the same reason, it would not be possible to combine them with classes from other parts of India. The report, therefore, recommended that the Assam Regiment be not retained on return to a post-war army.

1st Battalion – raised 15 Jun 41
2nd Battalion – raised 15 Apr 42
3rd Battalion – raised 1 Nov 45

PARTITION
On Partition, in August 1947, the Regiment was allotted to India and, since there were no Muslim elements, no postings, in or out were required.
The regular battalions on transfer of power were the 1st, 2nd, and 3rd.

BATTLE HONOURS
Defence of Kohima, Jessami, Mawlaik, Kyaukmyaung Bridgehead, Toungoo, Aradura, Burma 1942–45.

BOOKS
'History of The Assam Regiment Vol I 1941–47' by Capt. Peter Steyn MC (Pub. Orient Longmans, Calcutta, 1959)

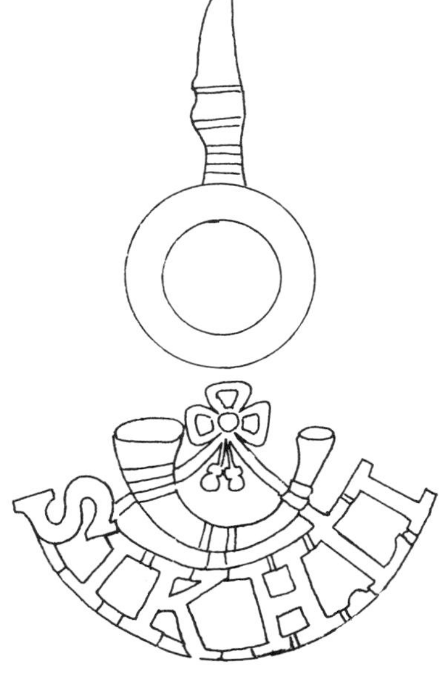

THE SIKH LIGHT INFANTRY

Centre: **1941 BAREILLY** (shared with 9th Jat Regiment)
1946 LAHORE

Class composition: Mazhbi and Ramdassia Sikhs

On the 1st October 1941 at Jullundur, the 1st Bn The Mazhbi and Ramdassia Sikh Regiment was raised. It recruited the scheduled-class Sikh not regarded as acceptable by the 11th Sikh Regiment with its preference for Jat Sikhs and kindred higher-caste co-religionists.

These Mazhbi and Ramdassia soldiers, drawn mainly from the Punjab and adjacent Rajputana were initially recruited by the Honourable East India Company in 1857 to form a regiment of Sikh Pioneers (see p. 127). Subsequently, the successor to these pioneers, the 3rd Sikh Pioneers, was formed from three regiments, the 23rd, the 32nd and the 34th Sikh Pioneers.

When created in 1941, the new regiment assumed the history and traditions of the old Sikh Pioneers although that particular Indian military speciality had disappeared from the Indian Army List eight years earlier.

The somewhat uninspiring and unwieldy title was commented upon adversely by the then Commander-in-Chief, Sir Claude Auchinleck which, in the nature of armies, meant an early adjustment of priorities to find a new name. The Director of Infantry, Sir Reginald Savory, himself an 11th Sikh Regt officer, convened a committee and it reviewed the possibilities of alternatives such as the Sikh Fusiliers and the Sikh Rifles. Sir Reginald felt that the fusil was an ancient and very short-lived weapon and so was not very applicable. Somewhat flippantly, he subsequently confessed, he put forward the suggestion that as the contemporary soldier trained with the Bren light machine-gun, it might be more logical to call the new regiment The Sikh Brenadiers. Predictably, this did not find favour with the committee. He went on to suggest The Sikh Light Infantry. He felt that his idea of modern light infantry was of *'stalwart men, capable of carrying heavy loads, living off the country as far as possible and supplied by air. This was the real light infantry of the present day'*. The new title became effective on the 23 Jun 44.

The badge chosen was the Sikh chakra surmounted by the kirpan, two traditional Sikh edged weapons. The service pagri was, of course, green but the dress-pagri was something of a problem. The regimental flag of the 32nd Sikh Pioneers had been dark-blue, red and gold.

The 11th Sikhs had a red pagri and, no doubt, the blue was felt to be a little too discreet and low-key for a new regiment with a name to make so the decision was made to opt for the old gold. To the uninformed, this may look uncommonly like orange, but it cannot be denied that it is exceptionally distinctive. On appropriate occasions, the steel chakra is worn around the old gold pagri.

On first raising, the Regiment's training element shared that of the 9th Jat Regiment at Bareilly but it moved to Lahore on the 15 Oct 45.

WAR SERVICE

1st Battalion – raised 1 Oct 41. India, Burma
2nd Battalion – raised 1 Jul 42. India
3rd Battalion – raised 15 Aug 42. India
25th Garrison Battalion – raised 1 Jul 42. India. Disbanded 10 May 46.
26th Garrison Battalion – raised 1 Oct 42. India. Disbanded 15 Jul 46.

PARTITION

The Regiment was allotted to India and had, of course, no problems of postings in or out.

On transfer of power, the battalions were the 1st, the 2nd and the 3rd.

BATTLE HONOURS

Taku Forts, Pekin 1860, Abyssinia, Peiwar Kotal, Charasiah, Kabul 1879, Kandahar 1880, Afghanistan 1878–80, Chitral

Egypt 1915–17, Gaza, Megiddo, Sharon, Nablus, Palestine 1917–18, Aden Defence of Meiktila, Rangoon Road, Pyawbwe, Sittang 1945, Burma 1942–45

BOOKS
None known.

THE MAHAR REGIMENT

Centre: **1941 KAMPTEE**
1947 ARANGAON

Class Composition: Mahars from Bombay Presidency

The Mahar Regiment was authorised in September 1941. However, a forebear had existed in the First World War when, in July 1917, the 111th Mahars was raised. The Mahar came traditionally from Bombay and Central Provinces (Madhya Pradesh) and served the Mahratta rulers. He also served in the ranks of the Company's Bombay Army despite his untouchable status: the Bombay Brahmin Sepoy was notably more liberal on this score than his brother in Bengal. During the Second Mahratta War in January 1818, a small force of five British Officers, 500 rank and file of the 2 Bn 1st Bombay Native Infantry, 300 irregular horse and 24 British gunners with two six-pounder guns under Captain Francis Staunton was faced by the army of the Peshwa, some 25,000 horse and 5,000 foot. Captain Staunton moved his force into the small, mud walled village of Koregaon where they held out against repeated attacks by an enemy superior in numbers by forty to one. Of the 834 defenders of Koregaon 275 were killed or wounded and three officers were killed and two wounded. The attackers lost about six hundred. At least half of the defending force were Mahars. In 1822, a polished stone obelisk was erected near the village, listing the names of the fallen in English and Marathi, together with the citation –

THIS COLUMN

> 'Is erected to commemorate the defence of Koregaon by a Detachment commanded by Captain STAUNTON of the Bombay Establishment which was surrounded on the 1st of January 1818 by the Peshwa's whole army under his personal command, and withstood throughout the day a series of the most obstinate and

sanguinary assaults of his best troops. Captain STAUNTON, under the most appalling circumstances persevered in his desperate resistance, and seconded by the unconquerable spirit of his Detachment, at length achieved the signal discomfiture of the enemy and accomplished one of the proudest triumphs of the British Army in the East.

TO PERPETUATE

The memory of the brave troops to whose heroic firmness and devotion it owes the glory of that day, the British Government has directed the names of their Corps and of the killed and wounded to be inscribed on this monument'
MD CCC XXII

For its conduct at Koregaon, the 2/1st was created a grenadier regiment. To maintain their new status, taller men from the North were recruited to enhance the appearance on parade and Mahars ceased to be enlisted. They were victims of their own success.

It was in the 2nd Afghan War of 1880 that specific mention of the MAHARS is found. There was in Bombay a tablet in Waudby Road, the inscription on which is as follows:–

'This road is named after Major SIDNEY JAMES WAUDBY, who, with Private ELAHI BUX and Private SONNAK TANNAK all of the 19th Bo. Infantry, fell on the 16th Apr 1880, in defence of DUBRAI post in AFGHANISTAN which, when warned that an attack in force was imminent, they refused to abandon and most gallantly held for three hours against three hundred of the enemy, many of whom were slain. Eventually when all their ammunition was expended they dashed into the midst of their foes and died fighting. In honour of their heroism this tablet is placed by the Regiment.'

(the tablet was removed from its original place at the corner of Waudby Road and Elphinstone Road and is now cemented on the outer wall of The Alexandra Girls English Institution in Waudby Road. The latter has since been renamed Hazarimal Somani Marg whilst Elphinstone Road has become Mahatma Gandhi Road).

The odds were even greater than at Koregaon and the heroes were of the same classes, a European, a Muslim and a Mahar who had made up the Bombay regiments from the start.

With the abolition of the Presidency Armies and the institution of class companies and battalions, the Mahar was ousted by caste-conscious Mahrattas and not recruited for combatant duties again until 1917 when the 111th Mahars was raised. They served on the Frontier for six months in 1920, absorbed the 71st Punjabis and then moved to Aden, returning to India for disbandment in 1922, there being no room for a single-class battalion in the new organisation.

Two years after the beginning of the Second World War the Mahar Regiment was authorised and the 1st Bn was raised at Belgaum in October 1941, recruited from Mahars serving in the 11th and 12th Bns Mahratta Light Infantry, the two Territorial battalions. The 2nd Bn was raised at Kamptee in June 1942 and the 3rd Bn at Nowshera in November 1942. A 25th Garrison Bn also existed. The badge chosen included the obelisk at Koregaon with a ribbon scroll carrying the battle-honour, over the word 'MAHAR'. None of the battalions saw active service, although one served in North-West Frontier Province. In March 1946, the Regiment learned that it had been designated for conversion to a machine-guns role: the badge was changed to incorporate crossed Vickers machine guns and 'MG' on the title scrolls. The Willcox Committee, the previous year, had recommended that the Regiment should not be retained as part of the post-war army.

PARTITION

In August 1947, the Mahars remained as part of India's Army, with no requirement either to accept or transfer Muslim personnel.

On transfer of power, the regular battalions were the 1st, 2nd, and 3rd.

BOOKS

'The regimental history of The Mahar Machine Gun Regiment' The Army Press, Dehra Dun 1954.

1st AFRIDI BATTALION

Representations were made in 1940 to the Governor of the North West Frontier Province for Afridi enlistment to be reopened into the Indian Army. This had been stopped in 1919 when the Khyber Rifles had mutinied and all the Afridi sepoys had been mustered out.

In early 1942, recruitment began for the 1st Afridi Bn at Sialkot, the location of 10/12th Frontier Force Regiment under Lieut. Colonel G. Brown of the 14th Punjab Regiment. Most of the VCOs were NCOs of the Frontier Corps and the Frontier Constabulary, commissioned on transfer.

The badge chosen was the gateway to a Khyber fort with a title-scroll below, in whitemetal. The battalion was to be part of the 12th Frontier Force Regiment.

Training went ahead during the hot weather and in, August 1942, six British officers, 28 VCOs and 712 Indian other ranks sailed for Suez.

They moved promptly to Aleppo in Syria to replace an Australian battalion bound for El Alamein and then began a move to Paiforce (Persia and Iraq Force) where the battalion was to spend most of the rest of the war. In February

1943, spirits rose when it was reorganised as a Commando unit with a view to undertaking offensive operations if the Germans should advance on Persia through the Caucasus. By July 1943, the threat was thought to have lapsed and the 1st Afridi Bn reverted to a normal infantry role.

At this time, the battalion was so short of British officers able to speak Pushtu that VCOs were commanding companies.

The battalion continued to tour the Middle East, engaged in guard duties and railway protection until late 1945 when it returned to India for disbandment, to be promptly born again as the resuscitated Khyber Rifles.

THE AJMER REGIMENT

Centre: **1941 AJMER**
1946 NASIRABAD

Class composition: Rawats, Katats and Minas

The Ajmer Regiment was born of the 4th Bombay Grenadiers. On 11 Mar 22, the 1st (Territorial) Bn Merwara Infantry was raised, a title to be changed later that year to the 11/4th Bombay Grenadiers.

It was embodied on 4 Sep 39 and employed on port-defence duties in the Bombay area. On 15 Sep 41, it became the 26/4th Bombay Grenadiers as a garrison battalion but, shortly afterwards, on 1 Jul 42, it was restyled 1st Bn The Ajmer Regiment. The new regimental badge was a castellated tower above a scroll 'The Ajmer Regiment'. India. The battalion was disbanded on 30 Aug 46.

2nd Battalion – formed 1 Jul 42 by redisignation of the 27/4th Bombay Grenadiers. India, Burma. Disbanded 20 Jun 46.

3rd Battalion – raised 1 Mar 43. India. Disbanded 15 Jan 46.

25th Garrison Battalion – raised 1 Nov 43. India. Disbanded 20 Sep 46.

Made up of Mussalman Katats and Hindu Rawats and Minas (the latter a criminal tribe) who live in Ajmer-Merwara and the surrounding states, the one battalion which saw action was reported on badly according to the Willcox Committee's report. This was 'chiefly because of faulty junior leaders, from which the rest of the regiment also suffers and which was the reason for the mustering out of these classes from the Army in 1927'. The Committee did not recommend that all classes be further recruited for infantry: the Katats would be acceptable as Rajputana Mussalmans but the Rawats and Minas might be considered for the RIASC.

THE CHAMAR REGIMENT

Centre: **MEERUT**

Class composition: Chamars

In its search during the Second World War for new classes to swell the Army, Chamars were recruited for the 2nd Punjab Regiment's 27th Battalion. They had never previously been selected for military service and, as workers in leather, they did not rate very high in India's stratified society.

The 27/2nd Punjab was raised in June 1942 and officers, VCOs and NCOs, came from most other Indian Army regiments. Employed first on railway protection duties, they later found themselves involved in the war in Assam and, subsequently, in Burma. By the middle of 1943, the battalion had become a regiment, The Chamar Regiment, with its own badge, a charging bison above a title scroll. Not surprisingly perhaps, the history of the 2nd Punjab Regiment speaks very highly of The Chamars but the Willcox Committee's report is less enthusiastic, commenting that it had 'not been very favourably appraised'. It was not recommended that they be retained as infantry but they were warmly commended for their work in animal transport and other branches of the RIASC. Conversely, it seems, the report also mentioned that, after growing beards, some Chamars had enlisted as Mazhbi and Ramdassia Sikhs.

1 Chamar continued to serve on in Burma after the campaign and returned to India in December 1946 for disbandment.

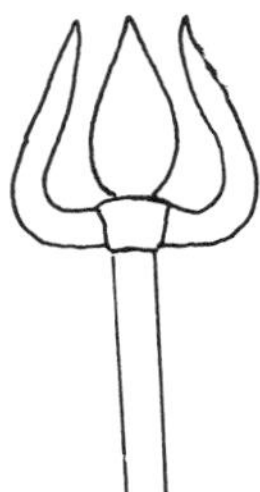

1st LINGAYAT BATTALION

Centre: **1941 BELGAUM**
1946 BELGAUM

Class Composition: Lingayats

The Second World War prompted the authorities to examine once again the military potential of many tribes and classes which had not been enlisted into the peacetime Indian Army. Twenty-five years earlier, they had been through a similar exercise and Lingayats, from the Bombay Presidency had been enlisted into the 103rd Mahratta Light Infantry.

In 1941, the decision was made once again to enlist Lingayats and the 5th Mahratta Light Infantry was authorised to raise a trial battalion at the 10/5th centre at Belgaum.

Unusually, the badge chosen for the new raising was Shiva's trident, a unique example of a device from the Hindu pantheon being used by a unit in the service of the Crown.

The battalion was not considered an infantry success but it was converted in early 1946 to a Gunner role as 6 Indian Anti-Tank Regt RIA, being redesignated 35 (Lingayat) Anti-Tank Regt RIA wef 25 Jan 47 and retained by India after Partition.

1st COORG BATTALION

Centre: **1923 MERCARA, COORG**
1946 TRICHINOPOLY

Class composition: Coorgs

The battalion, formally created in 1942, was not, in fact, a new one, having been raised initially in March 1922 as the 1st (Territorial) Bn 83rd Wallajahbad Light Infantry. On the formation of the 3rd Madras Regiment later that year, it was designated the 14th Bn 3rd Madras Regiment, based in Mercara in Coorg. With the disbandment of the regular regiment in 1928, only its four Territorial battalions remained and a problem arose as to where they should be parented. It seemed logical to attach them to the 1st Madras Pioneers and so the 14th became the 14th Bn 1st Madras Pioneers but not for long since the 1st Madras Pioneers were, themselves, to be reorganised in 1929. Thereafter, the Madras Territorial battalions were to stand on their own, the 14th being re-styled the 14th Coorg Battalion. With the re-formation of the 3rd Madras Regiment in 1941, the 11th, 12th, 13th and 15th Battalions were converted to regular battalions but the 14th Coorg Bn became a garrison battalion in 1942 with its own entity as the 1st Coorg Battalion.

The new badge was crossed Coorg knives above a title scroll 'Coorg', below a letter 'T'.

Coorgs had, of course, been recruited earlier in the century when the 11th regiment of the Madras Line was designated 11th Coorg Infantry in 1902. After the 1903 reforms and the addition of sixty to their number, they emerged as the 71st Coorg Rifles, only to be disbanded in 1904.

In early 1946, the battalion was converted to a gunner role as 10 Anti-Tank Regt RIA, being redesignated 37 (Coorg) Anti-Tank Regt RIA wef 25 Jan 47 and retained by India after Partition.

8. THE GURKHA BRIGADE

The recruitment of the subjects of the sovereign State of Nepal into the armies of the Honourable East India Company began in 1815 during the Second Nepal War.

The Capitulation Act permitted the Company to recruit such Gurkha soldiers as might wish to serve, with the exception of Nepal's household troops. However, the success of such recruitment in the past 175 years has been based upon the admiration of the Gurkha soldier for troops who could beat him on his own ground.

It all began in the early years of the last century when the Nepalese war-machine began the process of empire-building. It took the state of Sikkim, Darjeeling and parts of Tibet in the east and Kumaon and Garhwal in the west as well as making incursions into Dogra country.

A confrontation with the Company became inevitable. Bhim Sen Thapa, the then prime minister of Nepal was convinced that the British would be easy meat and suggested to his young rajah that if a man-made fortress, as at Bhurtpore, could confound the Company's forces, then the hill-country of Nepal would be impregnable. By this time, British rule had reached the Nepalese border and Bhim Sen prompted a gradual programme of infiltration into the Terai, the narrow strip of plain on the Indian border. This forward policy of annexation of villages under British rule was not universally popular in Kathmandu and Amarsing Thapa, one of the Rajah's more rational generals, counselled against it, dismissing the prime minister as a courtier, unfamiliar with soldiering and unaware of the power of the Company. This warning fell on deaf ears: the revenue from the villages seized had been going to Bhim Sen's family.

Finally, in May 1814, eighteen policemen were killed when Gurkha soldiers fell upon three frontier police posts in the Butwal district, in the Terai, south-west from Kathmandu. Lord Moira (perhaps better known by his later title, the Marquess of Hastings), the Viceroy of India, issued an ultimatum to Nepal which was dismissed by Bhim Sen. The 1 Nov 1814 saw the formal declaration of war in Lucknow and four columns began assembling to push the Gurkhas back within their frontiers. The main force, of 8,000 men, under Major General Marley, based on Patna, was to advance by the line of the Bhagmati, against Kathmandu. Another column, of 4,000 men, under Major General J S Wood was to leave Gorakhpur, to attack Butwal and then, to cut the line of communication between Kathmandu and the west. The third column, of some 4,000 men, was under the command of Major General Rollo Gillespie, concentrating in Saharanpur, to strike through Dehra Dun and to seize the fort at Kalunga. The fourth and final column, based on Ludhiana, was under the command of Colonel David Ochterlony, some 4,000 strong, set to advance upon Amarsing's main body. The two-front attack was intended to take out the most formidable part of the Nepalese forces and, then, to march rapidly on Kathmandu. Generals Marley and Wood were not equal to the occasion and failed to reach the ramparts of Nepal. Major General Marley deserted his post but, remarkably, was not dismissed the service, surviving to die, a full general in 1842. He was replaced by Major General George Wood but neither his, nor his namesake's column, was any more successful. Rollo Gillepsie died with a bullet in his heart at Kalunga and only Ochterlony's force was making progress. The

British Government called off the campaign and withdrew to cantonments in India. A second campaign in 1815 was no more successful but, in 1816, a force of 17,000, under Ochterlony, now a general and well-experienced in the ways of the Gurkha enemy, brought Amarsing to surrender in the fort of Malaun.

One of the first Gurkha battalions in the Company's service was authorised on the 24 April 1815 when Lieutenant Frederick Young was sent to the prisoner-of-war camps for the initial batch of recruits. From these he raised the Sirmoor Battalion, eventually to become the 2nd King Edward VII's Own Gurkha Rifles, still in the British service. Young, then thirty years old, had been commissioned in 1800: appearing before the board in London, he was asked his age and whether he was prepared to die for King and country. He confirmed that he was fifteen years old and gave an affirmative reply to the second question. He was granted a commission: psychology did not play a significant part in officer-selection in those days. He remained commandant of the Sirmoor Battalion for twenty-eight years.

Two more battalions, called the Nasiri, or Friendly battalions were raised at Subathu, near Simla, and they subsequently became the 1st King George V's Own Gurkha Rifles (The Malaun Regiment). The Kumaon Battalion was raised in 1815 at Almora in Kumaon and it eventually became 3rd Queen Alexandra's Own Gurkha Rifles. There were no further Gurkha units raised for a further forty years but the existing ones justified themselves in that time. After the battle of Bhurtpore in 1826, a Gurkha was said to have remarked 'The English are as brave as lions; they are splendid sepoys, very nearly equal to us'.

The testing time for Anglo-Nepalese relations came in 1857. Jung Bahadur Rana had taken power in Kathmandu in 1843, relegating the King to the status of a religious figure-head, and he pledged his country's support. India was in turmoil and many of the Indian princes doubted Britain's ability to recover control. Jung Bahadur did not share their doubts. He had been to London and seen that Britain's resources were more than sufficient to suppress the mutiny. He authorised the raising of more Gurkha regiments by the Company and so were born the 4th and 5th Gurkha Rifles. As will be seen, some of today's Gurkha regiments had non-Gurkha origins but, by the outbreak of the Great War in 1914 the Gurkha Brigade was ten regiments strong, each of two battalions, an independent, green-clad, non-tactical grouping, proud of its Rifles traditions, in the Indian Army, yet not of it. They also cherished the privilege of using British troops' canteens, a right denied to Indian soldiers normally. Despite this apparent homogeneity, the ten regiments were different in that they did not all recruit from the same tribes and inter-regimental rivalry was intense. John Masters, a 4th Gurkha, listed the characteristics of the others – the 1st Gurkhas were earnest, the 2nd idle, the 3rd illiterate, the 5th narrow-minded, the 6th downtrodden, the 7th unshaven, the 8th exhibitionists, the 9th Brahminical – they enlisted high-caste Gurkhas - and the 10th alcoholic. The 4th? – they were witty, happy, carefree, tough, efficient, wise . . . .

Between the wars, the Gurkha regiments had each consisted of two battalions only and the Indian infantry training format of a 10th Battalion existing solely as a training centre for each regiment was not practicable. Instead, each Gurkha regiment had its 'home Station' where one of the battalions was, notionally, always stationed, the other battalion being on service on the Frontier or elsewhere. Each Gurkha battalion trained its own recruits and an extra major was authorised to command the training company. After the outbreak of war in 1939, regimental centres were formed on the home station in order to muster reservists, train recruits and raise new battalions.

The Gurkha Brigade was alone until 1947 in not having Indian officers. During the 1939–45 War, Indians had been commissioned into all the other regiments, the arms and services. In theory, there was no reason why the Gurkha regiments should not also have them but the Nepalese Durbar (government) was not in favour and it had been agreed that only British and Gurkha officers should serve in those ten regiments. The Willcox Committee in 1945, however, pointed out the anomaly of a part of the Indian Army into which Indians might not be commissioned and recommended that negotiations be opened with Nepal to persuade them to accept the change. It was felt that if, perhaps, the continued recruitment of Gurkhas into the Indian Army depended upon the decision, they would be prepared to concede. As a reciprocal gesture, commissions might be granted to Nepalese subjects. With the coming of Partition, of course, the six Gurkha regiments which went to India in 1947, soon had their British Officers replaced by Indians, a move clearly accepted by Nepal.

During the Second World War, all ten regiments raised 3rd and 4th Battalions whilst the 1st 2nd and 9th each raised a 5th Battalion to replace their 2nd Battalions captured in Singapore. In addition, two garrison battalions and two parachute battalions were also raised.

The Willcox Committee on the post war Indian Army proposed that the Gurkha Brigade should consist of eight regiments of two battalions each, the 7th and 10th being disbanded; these latter two were the junior in the Brigade, of course, but Partition put paid to most of that Committee's recommendations.

Another suggestion was that permanent centres be established for the enlistment and training of recruits as under:

Centre	*Regiments*	*Class Composition*
14th	1 and 4 GR	⅔ Magars, Gurungs, ⅓ Limbus, Rais, Sunwars
29th	2 and 9 GR	Thakurs, Chettris
38th	3 and 8 GR	⅔ Magars, Gurungs ⅓ Limbus, Rais, Sunwars
56th	5 and 6 GR	⅔ Magars, Gurungs ⅓ Limbus, Rais, Sunwars

(an independent India subsequently implemented a similar proposal)

The Indian Army List, with admirable simplicity, always showed class composition as 'Gurkhas' but each regiment had its own rules as to which of the Nepal clans it enlisted. The 9th Gurkhas enlisted Thakurs and Chettris, mainly from Western Nepal, the 7th and 10th, Limbus, Rais and Sunwars from the east and the remaining seven regiments Magars and Gurungs from the West.

Limbus and Rais were thought to be better in the attack whilst the solid Magars and Gurungs were possibly better when things were going wrong in a retreat. The 9th, with its Thakurs and Chettris, both privileged clans in Nepal's social order, was to maintain its exemplary record.

In the two world wars the Nepalese Durbar willingly extended British recruiting rights within their country. Some 110,000 Gurkhas were recruited during 1939–45 and the equivalent of forty battalions maintained. In addition, Nepalese Army battalions were offered – and accepted – for service in India in the two world wars for internal security duties to release British, Indian and British Gurkha battalions for service abroad in theatres of war.

1st KING GEORGE V'S OWN GURKHA RIFLES (THE MALAUN REGIMENT)

Home Station: **1923 DHARAMSALA, Punjab**
1947 DHARAMSALA

Towards the end of the Nepal War in 1815, parties of captured enemy troops transferred their allegiance to General Ochterlony after the defeat of the Nepalese chieftain Amarsing and the collapse of the fortress of Malaun.

Four battalions were authorised initially, the first two to be known as the 1st and 2nd Nusseree (or Nasiri) Battalions, the title meaning 'friendly'. In 1830, the 2nd was reduced, those men with more than six years service being drafted in equal proportions to the 1st Nusseree and the Sirmoor Battalions: the remainder had the option of transferring to the Kemaoon Battalion or taking their discharge. It was as the 1st Nusseree that the Regiment earned its first battle honour at Bhurtpore in 1826 and the subsequent honours of Aliwal and Sobraon in the First Sikh War. However, in 1849, the 66th Bengal Native Infantry mutinied at Fort Govindgarh at Amritsar and the Nusseree Battalion was ordered to Ambala where it rendezvoused with the 66th. The latter were informed that they were to disband and hand over to the Gurkhas their colours, arms, stores, etc. whereupon the latter would assume these and also the title of the 66th BNI. The new 66th, now a redcoat regiment, marched for Peshawar, beginning almost a century of Gurkha service on the Frontier. Somewhat surprisingly, they did not earn any honours for the Mutiny. However, in February 1858, Lieut J A Tytler earned a Victoria Cross for a single-handed attack on insurgent gunners.

When the 1861 reorganisation took place, the 66th were briefly re-numbered the 11th Bengal Native Infantry but, in October of that year, were placed first in a new Gurkha Line as the 1st Gurkha Regiment. They were also allotted Dharamsala in the Kangra Valley of the Punjab as their home station.

In 1875 when the Malay states were being put into order, the British Resident in Perak was murdered. The Governor in Singapore sought help from India and the 1st became the first Gurkhas to serve overseas. By the time they reached Malaya, the rising had been suppressed and no battle-honour was to be granted although Captain G N Channer received a Victoria Cross and two sepoys the Order of Merit for their gallantry in storming the enemy emplacement at Bukit Putoos.

During the Second Afghan War, the Regiment did not have much opportunity to distinguish itself and more casualties were sustained from disease than from the Afghan enemy.

The new, friendly Amir of Afghanistan – Abdur Rahman – was subsequently invited to India and, at the great review of the army in his honour, it was realised that the 1st Gurkhas, alone of the Gurkha Line, wore scarlet – and were proud of the fact. The Lal Kurti paltan (or red-coat regiment) enjoyed considerable prestige in Nepal, and was reluctant to relinquish its distinctive dress. A second battalion was to be recruited and it came into being in February 1886, wearing the rifle-green of the other Gurkha regiments. Finally, the 1st Bn gave up its scarlet in 1888 and the only relic of this remained in the scarlet facings on green full-dress. The regimental colours on which all recruits were attested continued to be carried for another three years until 1891 when all Gurkha regiments were styled 'Rifles'.

The 1st Battalion was engaged in Waziristan in 1894 and the 2nd took part in the great Frontier campaigns of 1897–98.

The 1903 changes for the rest of the Indian Army left the Gurkhas almost unaffected but the Regiment was granted the subsidiary title of 'The Malaun Regiment' that year, recalling its origins. In 1906, they became the 1st Prince of Wales' Own Gurkha Rifles (The Malaun Regiment) and, in 1910, the 1st King George's Own Gurkha Rifles (The Malaun Regiment). Finally, in 1937, when HM King George VI acceded to the throne, a further change of title made them the 1st King George V's Own Gurkha Rifles (The Malaun Regiment).

FIRST WORLD WAR

In August 1914, the start of the Great War, the 1st Bn was sent at once in the Sirhind Brigade to France but was held with the rest of the brigade in Egypt until December. However, they rejoined the Lahore Division and served through until the Indian Corps was transferred to the Middle East.

1st Battalion – India, France, Mesopotamia, Egypt
2nd Battalion – India
3rd Battalion – (raised in 1917) – India. Disbanded 31 Mar 21

BETWEEN THE WARS

As in the 1903 changes, the post-war reforms of 1922–23 did not much affect the Gurkhas except that the war-raised 3rd Battalion was disbanded. The new regimental badge was to be the formal crossed kukris, cutting edges down; beneath the intersection, the figure '1' appears above a stringed bugle-horn whilst, above, the Prince of Wales' plumes record the grant of the title 'Prince of Wales' Own' in 1906 when the then heir to the throne visited India.

SECOND WORLD WAR

1st Battalion – India, Egypt, Burma, Indo-China
2nd Battalion – India, Malaya. Captured on Singapore Island by the Japanese in February 1942. Reconstituted at midnight 24/25 Aug 46 by redesignation of the 3rd Battalion
3rd Battalion – re-raised 1 Oct 40. India, Burma, Indo-China. Disbanded at midnight 24/25 Aug 46 and reconstituted as the 2nd Battalion
4th Battalion – raised 15 Mar 41 at Dharamsala. India, Burma, Siam. Disbanded 30 Nov 46
5th Battalion – raised 1 Jan 42 at Dharamsala. India. Disbanded 30 Oct 46

PARTITION
The 1st was one of the six regiments of Gurkhas to remain as part of the Indian Army and the regular battalions on transfer of power in August 1947 were the 1st and 2nd.

BATTLE HONOURS
Bhurtpore, Aliwal, Sobraon, Afghanistan 1878–80, Tirah, Punjab Frontier, Givenchy 1914, Neuve Chapelle, Ypres 1915, St. Julien, Festubert 1915, Loos, France & Flanders 1914–15, Megiddo, Sharon, Palestine 1918, Tigris 1916, Kut-al-Amara 1917, Baghdad, Mesopotamia 1916–18, North-West Frontier, India 1915–17, Afghanistan 1919, Jitra, Kampar, Malaya 1941–42, Shenam Pass, Bishenpur, Ukhrul, Myinmu Bridgehead, Kyaukse 1945, Burma 1942–45.

BOOKS
'The 1st King George's Own Gurkha Rifles (The Malaun Regiment) 1815–1921' by F. Loraine Petrie OBE (Pub. Butler & Tanner Ltd. London 1925)
'The History of the 1st King George V's Own Gurkha Rifles (The Malaun Regiment Vol. II, 1920–47' by Brigadier E V R Bellers (Pub. Gale & Polden Ltd., Aldershot, 1956)

2nd KING EDWARD VII's OWN GURKHA RIFLES (THE SIRMOOR RIFLES)

Home Station: **1923 DEHRA DUN**
1947 DEHRA DUN

Another of the four original battalions raised from prisoners after the Nepal War in 1815, the 2nd began life at Nahan in Sirmoor – hence their subsidiary title. Sirmoor was found to be unhealthy and they moved to Dehra Dun where they were to stay until 1947.

The Sirmoor Battalion first attracted attention and their first battle-honour at Bhurtpore in 1825. Twenty years later, they force-marched to Ludhiana to fight the forces of the Khalsa in the First Sikh War but it was the Great Mutiny in May 1857 which established the Sirmoor Battalion in the eyes of the British Army. Ordered to march on Delhi on the 14 May, they were the first unit of the company's army to oppose the mutineers in Red Fort. Together with the 60th Rifles, Britain's King's Royal Rifle Corps, and the Guides Infantry, they held the main picquet at Hindu Rao's house until the end of the siege. Under constant fire for three months, they were never once relieved and they withstood twenty-six attacks on their position. Mutual admiration ensured that the Gurkhas were permitted to wear on their green uniform the same red facings worn by the 60th Rifles. In khaki now, officers of the Regiment and those of the Guides continue to wear red piping to their collars. A less agreeable distinction was that they suffered more casualties during the Mutiny campaign than any other unit. In recognition of their services, after the custom of the time, the Sirmoor Battalion was granted the honour of carrying an additional colour. Despite their green-clad status, their colours were still in use – but not for much longer. Their title was changed in 1858 to the Sirmoor Rifle Regiment which meant an end to the carrying of colours, even the honorary one. To ensure that this mark of her favour should not vanish, Queen Victoria devised a unique symbol – the Truncheon. It is a bronze staff, some six feet high, surmounted by three figures of Gurkha soldiers of the period, supporting a silver crown. Beneath the figures on a silver band, are the words 'Main Picquet, Hindoo Rao's House, Delhi 1857'. Below this is a bronze representation of the Delhi Gate with two kukris under it in silver. Another silver ring below the Gate bears the words 'Sirmoor Rifles' whilst another below that, carries the words 'Main Picquet, Hindoo Rao's House, Delhi 1857', this time in Nagri characters. Finally, a fourth silver ring, this time a plain one, connects the bronze staff with the symbolic upper part of the Truncheon.

The Truncheon was to receive all the normal honours paid to a Queen's Colour and recruits were to swear their allegiance to the British crown by touching the Truncheon as they still do. In due course, the 1st Battalion was to be allowed an extra Indian Officer on its establishment to carry the Truncheon and, although jemadar is no longer a rank in either British or Indian Gurkha regiments, the additional Gurkha Lieutenant authorised is still known as the Truncheon Jemadar.

Briefly, in 1861, during the reorganisation of the army following its take-over by the Crown, the Sirmoor Rifle Regiment became the 17th Regiment, Bengal Native Infantry. However, the concept of the separate Gurkha Line was pursued and, in October that year, the 17th became the 2nd Goorkha (The Sirmoor Rifle) Regiment. In 1876, the then Prince of Wales, later King Edward VII, became their Colonel and it was as the 2nd (Prince of Wales' Own) Gurkha Regiment (The Sirmoor Rifles) that they were sent to Malta during the Russo-Turkish War of 1878, the first Gurkhas to serve in Europe. Returning to India, they were in time for the Second Afghan War and distinction with the relief force from Kabul to Kandahar.

The 2nd Battalion, formed in 1886, went first to Burma in 1888 and then matched the record of their senior battalion when they partnered the Gordon Highlanders in the storming of the Dargai Heights in the Pujab Frontier campaign of 1897.

In Waziristan in 1901, the 1st Battalion tried out the broad-brimmed felt hat as protection from the sun and it found favour: the pagri worn by the rest of the Indian Army had never been popular with Gurkhas. The hat was worn frequently with the side buttoned up as can be seen in photographs of the Great War period and it was not until after that war that the now-familiar double-hat was adopted (one hat has its lining removed, the smaller is pushed inside it and the pair are then machine-stitched together around the brim) and turned into the 'hat, felt Gurkha' which is now one of the uniform trade-marks of the Gurkha soldier although it has been copied by Garhwalis, Burma Rifles and others.

The changes of 1903 did not greatly affect the regiments of the Gurkha Line but in October 1906, the Regiment was restyled the 2nd King Edward's Own Gurkha Rifles (The Sirmoor Rifles).

The 2nd Gurkha Rifles always affect the nineteenth-century spelling unofficially, referring to themselves as the 2nd Goorkhas, despite what it says in the Army List. They also enjoy the distinction of coloured dicing on the Kilmarnock cap and on officers' forage caps. Paradoxically, given this Caledonian dress-distinction, introduced by Sir Hubert MacPherson (comanding 1862–76), the Regiment does not have pipes and drums. The hat, felt, Gurkha bears a piece of red-and-black diced material on the side of the pagri, the precise permutation of red to black squares enabling the informed viewer to identify the battalion of the wearer. Another dress distinction of the regiment is the ram's head boss on the pouch-belt in place of the more familar lion's head worn by other regiments: this dates from the capture of Koonja Fort, near Roorkee in 1824.

THE GREAT WAR

The outbreak of the Great War in August 1914, found the 2nd Battalion with the Meerut Division bound for France the following month where they remained until the Indian Corps withdrew, after which the battalion returned to India for Frontier service. The 1st Battalion, busy fighting against bow-and-arrows-armed tribesmen in Upper Assam, did not leave India until February 1916 when it was summoned to Mesopotamia, serving there and up as far as the Caspian Sea until 1921 when it returned home.

1st Battalion – India, Mesopotamia
2nd Battalion – India, France, Egypt
3rd Battalion – (raised in 1917) – India, Disbanded 3 Oct 20

BETWEEN THE WARS

The 1922–23 post-war reforms had little visible effect on the regiments of the Gurkha Brigade. However, in 1936, another Edward acceded to the throne, albeit briefly and another change of title specified the Regiment as 'King Edward VII's Own'.

SECOND WORLD WAR

1st Battalion – India, Iraq, Iran, Egypt, North Africa, Italy, Greece
2nd Battalion – India, Malaya. Captured by the Japanese on Singapore Island Feb 42. Reconstituted at midnight 14/15 May 46 by redesignation of the 3rd Battalion
3rd Battalion – (re-raised Oct 40 at Dehra Dun) – India, Burma, Malaya, Siam. Disbanded at midnight 14/15 May 46 and reconstituted as the 2nd Battalion
4th Battalion – (raised 3 Mar 41 at Dehra Dun) –India, Burma, Indo-China, North Borneo
Became 5/8 Gurkha Rifles 1 Jan 48
5th Battalion – (raised 18 Mar 42 at Dehra Dun) – India. Disbanded Jan 47

The Prince of Wales' plumes had been authorised as a regimental badge since the appointment of the royal heir to the colonelcy in 1876. Gurkha other ranks had worn the plumes – first splayed but, later, upright – in black on the diced Kilmarnock cap. However, when worn on the coloured field-service cap, the cap GS or the beret, a red backing is worn to the badge.

PARTITION
The 2nd was one of the four Gurkha infantry regiments to be transferred to the British Army and its later history is recorded in the chapter on Britain's Brigade of Gurkhas. The 1st and 2nd Battalions went with the Regiment and 4th Bn became 5/8 GR.

BATTLE HONOURS
Bhurtpore, Aliwal, Sobraon, Delhi 1857, Kabul 1879, Kandahar 1880, Afghanistan 1878–80, Tirah, Punjab Frontier, La Bassee 1914, Festubert 1914–15, Givenchy 1914, Neuve Chapelle, Aubers, Loos, France and Flanders 1914–15, Egypt 1915, Tigris 1916, Kut-al-Amara 1917, Baghdad, Mesopotamis 1916–18, Persia 1918, Baluchistan 1918, Afghanistan 1919, El Alamein, Mareth, Akarit, Djebel el Meida, Enfidaville, Tunis, North Africa 1942–43, Cassino I, Monastery Hill, Pian di Maggio, Gothic Line, Coriano, Poggio San Giovanni, Monte Reggiano, Italy 1944–45, Greece 1944–45, North Malaya, Jitra, Central Malaya, Kampar, Slim River, Johore, Singapore Island, Malaya 1941–42, North Arakan, Irrawaddy, Magwe, Sittang 1945, Point 1433, Arakan Beaches, Myebon, Tamandu, Chindits 1943, Burma 1942–45.

BOOKS
'History of the 2nd King Edward's Own Goorkhas, The Sirmoor Rifles' Vol I 1815–1910 by Col L W Shakespear (Pub. Gale & Polden Ltd., Aldershot 1912)
Vol II 1911–1920 by Col L W Shakespear CB CIE (Pub. Gale & Polden Ltd., Aldershot 1924)
Vol III 1921–1948 by Col G R Stevens OBE (Pub. Gale & Polden Ltd., Aldershot 1952)
'A pride of Gurkhas' – the 2nd King Edward VII's Own Goorkhas (The Sirmoor Rifles) 1948–1971 by Harold James and Denis Sheil-Small (Pub. Leo Cooper, London 1975)

3rd QUEEN ALEXANDRA'S OWN GURKHA RIFLES

Home Station:	**1923**	**1st Bn ALMORA**
		2nd Bn LANSDOWNE
	1947	**1st Bn ALMORA**
		2nd Bn LANSDOWNE

The last of the four Gurkha battalions raised in 1815 was known as the Kemaoon Battalion: its personnel were not all pure Gurkhas but men from Nepal's feudatory districts such as Kumaon and Garhwal who had lost heart in the Gurkha cause. The battalion was to police the Nepalese border for four decades before the Great Mutiny summoned it to Delhi. Ariving there on the 1st August, it was to assault the Kashmir Gate after it had been breached by the Bengal Sappers and Miners. Thereafter, it went down into Oudh where pacification took until February 1859.

Like the other Gurkha battalions, the Kemaoon Battalion was placed in the Bengal Line briefly in 1861, in its case as the 18th Regiment Bengal Native Infantry. In October, however, it became the 3rd Goorkha (The Kemaoon) Regiment.

Just a few years later, in 1865, the battalion was sent to Bhutan for a year to engage in a campaign which brought it no honours.

The Second Afghan War saw the 3rd in the entry to Afghanistan via Quetta. Such was the terrain that the gun-bullocks broke down and the Gurkhas were left to manhandle the guns on their way to Kandahar. A fanatical horde of Afghans attempted to bar their way to Kabul and it was only by Colonel H H Lyster's ordering his men to form square that the attack was thwarted and the honour 'Ahmed Khel' awarded. The battalion next saw action in the Shan States in Burma during the Third Burma War.

In 1887, a second battalion was raised, made up, on the specific order of the then Commander-in-Chief – later Lord Roberts – of Garhwalis who were posted in from other Gurkha units. The following year, there being insufficient space at Almora, the 2nd Battalion moved to a new cantonment in Garhwal, called

Kalananda, the name of which was later changed to 'Lansdowne' after the then Viceroy.

Intelligence reports in 1889 indicated Tibetan incursions and the possible erection of fortifications on the Indian side of the border: as relations with Lhasa at that time were not too cordial, a composite double-company – some 100 rifles from each battalion – was sent to investigate. The march to Bara Hoti took the troops over the Mirchauk Pass to a height of some 18,000 feet, probably the greatest height ever reached at that time by a body of organized troops on the march. No fortifications were found, just a shelter-wall to a camping-ground.

The next year, the 2nd Battalion was redesignated the 39th (The Garhwali) Regiment of Bengal Infantry, later to become the 39th Garhwal Rifles. In January 1891, a new 2nd Battalion was raised at Lansdowne and it moved back to Almora and set about building its own barracks on Sitoli Ridge: difficulties arose about sanitation and, in 1894, the battalion returned to Lansdowne.

Both battalions were, shortly afterwards, engaged in the Tirah and the Punjab Frontier campaigns of 1897, gaining three significant battle-honours.

HM King Edward VII conferred his appreciation of the 3rd Gurkhas by making them in 1907 the 3rd Queen's Own Gurkha Rifles. His queen, however, felt this to be too impersonal an honour and so the change was made to the 3rd Queen Alexandra's Own Gurkha Rifles.

FIRST WORLD WAR

In the initial planning for an Indian expeditionary force in the event of a major war, it was ruled that both regular battalions of a Gurkha regiment were not to leave India since limitations on recruitment would make it hard to replace casualities and other wastage.

1st Battalion – India, Mesopotamia
2nd Battalion – India, France, Egypt, Palestine
3rd Battalion – (raised 3 Feb 17 in Egypt) – Egypt, India. Disbanded September 1920
4th Battalion – (raised 1 Oct 16 at Rawalpindi as the 1st Reserve Bn. Gurkha Rifles: complete companies came from 2/2 GR, 2/3 GR, 1/5 GR and 1/6 GR. Redesignated 4/3 GR at Kohat 9 Jun 17). India. Disbanded 16 Mar 22.

In fact, the 1st Reserve Battalion should not have been assigned to the 3rd Gurkhas as their 4th Battalion. However, because of a clerical error, 3/4 was transcribed as 4/3 and the 4th Gurkhas never received a 3rd Battalion during the Great War.

BETWEEN THE WARS

In February 1928, approval was given for the pipers of the Regiment to wear tartan pipe-bags and ribbons of Clan Colquhoun tartan to commemorate the raising of the 1st battalion by a Colquhoun in 1815. Another dress distinction of the 3rd Gurkhas was the wearing of green cloth triangles on the pagri of the Gurkha hat, one on each side. This is said to have originated with a pre-1914 rugby-football playing colonel who, to illustrate his inspiration for a unique regimental distinction, cut the first two triangles from his international rugby cap.

The badge of the 3rd Gurkhas incorporated the royal cypher of Queen Alexandra, the linked letters 'A' above the figure '3' and crossed kukris, cutting-edges inwards, beneath a crown.

SECOND WORLD WAR
1st Battalion – India, Burma
2nd Battalion – India, Iraq, Egypt, Cyprus, Palestine, Italy
3rd Battalion – re-raised 1 Oct 40, India, Burma, Malaya, Dutch East Indies
4th Battalion – re-raised 15 Mar 41 at Dehra Dun. India. Disbanded 20 Apr 47

PARTITION
On Partition in August 1947, the 3rd Queen Alexandra's Own Gurkha Rifles were allotted to India. Battalions in being at the time were the 1st, 2nd and 3rd.

BATTLE HONOURS
Delhi 1857, Ahmed Khel, Afghanistan 1878–80, Burma 1885–87, Chitral, Tirah, Punjab Frontier, La Bassee 1914, Armentieres 1914, Festubert 1914–15, Givenchy 1914, Neuve Chapelle, Aubers, France and Flanders 1914–15, Egypt 1915–16, Gaza, El Mughar, Nebi Samwil, Jerusalem, Tell-Asur, Megiddo, Sharon, Palestine 1917–18, Sharqat, Mesopotamia 1917–18, Afghanistan 1919, Deir el Shein, North Africa 1940–43, Monte della Gorgace, Il Castello, Monte Farneto, Monte Cavallo, Italy 1943–45, Sittang 1942, Kyaukse 1942, Imphal, Tuitum, Sakawng, Shenam Pass, Bishenpur, Tengnoupal, Meiktila, Defence of Meiktila, Rangoon Road, Pyawbwe, Pegu 1945, Burma 1942–455.

BOOKS
'History of the 3rd Queen Alexandra's Own Gurkha Rifles' (from April 1815 to December 1927) by Major General N G Woodyatt (Pub. Philip Allan and Co Ltd, London 1929)
'The Regimental history of the 3rd Queen Alexandra's Own Gurkha Rifles Vol II 1927 to 1947' by Brig. C N Barclay CBE DSO (Pub. Wm Clowes and Sons Ltd, London 1953)

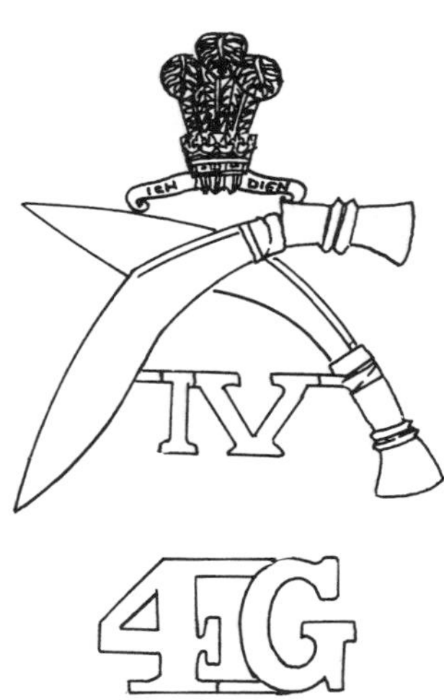

4th PRINCE OF WALES'S OWN GURKHA RIFLES

Home Station: **1923 BAKLOH**
1947 BAKLOH

The three senior Gurkha regiments had had forty years of service with John Company before the Extra Gurkha Regiment was raised on 1 Jul 1857 with the task of holding the Kumaon Hills after the outbreak of the Great Mutiny in May that year. The cadre for this came from the 1st Nusseree Battalion (later 1/1 GR).

The transfer of the Honourable East India Company's army brought the Extra Regiment into the Bengal Line briefly as the 19th Regiment Bengal Native Infantry from May to October 1861 and, in the latter month, they joined the Gurkha Line as the 4th Goorkha Regiment.

Less than two years later, the 4th were in the Ambeyla Expedition in late 1863, a bloody venture in the North West. No battle-honour was awarded but seven British and more than a dozen Indian battalions were engaged. A criterion of its fierceness which always appealed to the man in the ranks was evinced when the Commander, General Sir Neville Chamberlain was, himself, wounded in action. Another action with no apparent recognition was the Lushai operation in 1871–72, more than a thousand miles to the east.

In the Second Afghan war, the 4th were well-used: they were with Sam Browne at Ali Masjid and on the Khyber line: they fought in the operations around Jellalabad and, in the second phase, they were engaged in the actions in the vicinity of Kabul. Finally, they marched, 10,000 soldiers and 8,000 followers, the 320 miles to relieve Kandahar.

A second battalion was raised at Bakloh on 10 Apr 1886 and they were soon despatched to the inhospitable North East, again with no regimental honour being granted.

The last decade of the nineteenth century saw both battalions back in the North-West, this time with due recognition. The same General Gaselee who had had the 2/4th under his command in the Tirah campaign of 1897 was to take the 1/4th to China with him in 1900 to counter the Boxer Rising. They were the only

Gurkhas in the British element of the multi-national force (American, British, French, German, Italian, Japanese, and Russian) and earned a unique Gurkha honour – China 1900.

The 1st Battalion reached France in time for the fighting at Givenchy in December 1914 and, after gaining several other honours in France, was in time to earn an honour for Gallipoli before the evacuation and a return to the North West Frontier after a spell in Egypt.

The 2nd Battalion went to Mesopotamia in early 1915 and, after taking Baghdad, was transferred to Salonika and finished its immediate post-war service in Turkey.

Until the Second World War, the 4th Gurkhas had the record for being the most-travelled regiment of the Gurkha Brigade.

THE GREAT WAR

1st Battalion – India, France, Gallipoli, Egypt

2nd Battalion – India, Mesopotamia, Salonika, Turkey

The 3rd Battalion raised by the other Gurkha regiments was, as explained, not implemented for the 4th Gurkhas. Following a clerical error, a 4/3rd was raised instead of the 3/4th.

BETWEEN THE WARS

It was on 13 Aug 24 that the 4th became the 4th Prince of Wales's Own Gurkha Rifles. Their badge had previously been crossed kukris, cutting-edges outwards with a figure '4' above the intersection. After 1924, the Prince of Wales's plumes replaced the '4' and the Roman numerals 'IV' appeared below the intersection. Shortly before the Second World War, the badge changed again, and the kukris were crossed in an exclusively regimental fashion which almost baffles description but which can be seen in the illustration. The kukris are still crossed but the cutting-edges are down and both handles are to the right. In the hat, felt, Gurkha, a large, black, metal 'IV' was worn on the left side of the pagri.

SECOND WORLD WAR

1st Battalion – India, Burma

2nd Battalion – India, Iran, Iraq, Egypt, Italy

3rd Battalion – (raised 1 Oct 40 at Bakloh) – India, Burma, Dutch East Indies, Malaya

4th Battalion – (raised 5 Mar 41 at Bakloh) – India, Burma. Disbanded 18 Oct 46

PARTITION

In August 1947, the 4th Prince of Wales's Own Gurkha Rifles were transferred to Indian command, the regular battalions being the 1st, 2nd and 3rd.

BATTLE HONOURS

Ali Masjid, Kabul 1879, Kandahar 1880, Afghanistan 1878–80, Waziristan 1895, Chitral, Tirah, Punjab Frontier, China 1900, Givenchy 1914, Neuve Chapelle, Ypres 1915, St. Julien, Aubers, Festubert 1915, France and Flanders 1914–15, Gallipoli 1915, Egypt 1916, Tigris 1916, Kut-al-Amara 1917, Baghdad, Mesopotamia 1916–18, North-West Frontier, India 1917, Baluchistan 1918, Afghanistan 1919, Iraq 1941, Syria 1941, The Cauldron, North Africa 1940–43, Trestina, Monte Cedrone, Italy 1943–45, Pegu 1942, Chindits 1944, Mandalay, Burma 1942–45.

BOOKS

'A history of the 4th Prince of Wales's Own Gurkha Rifles 1857–1937 Vols I and II' by Ranald Macdonnell and Marcus Macaulay (Pub. William Blackwood and Sons Ltd, Edinburgh 1940)

A history of the 4th Prince of Wales's Own Gurkha Rifles 1938–1948 Vol III' by Colonel J M Macaulay DSO (Pub. William Blackwood and Sons Ltd, London, 1952)

5th ROYAL GURKHA RIFLES (FRONTIER FORCE)

Home Station: **1923 ABBOTTABAD**
1947 ABBOTTABAD

The 5th Gurkhas did not evolve via the Bengal Army. The 25th Punjab Infantry, or Huzara Goorkha Battalion, was raised at Abbottabad to hold the Hazara frontier on 22 May 1858 by transferring men borne as Gurkhas on the rolls of the Seikh Infantry, the Corps of Guides Infantry, the 24th Punjab Infantry and the 5th Punjab Police Battalion. The new battalion was located at Abbottabad where it remained for almost ninety years.

In 1861, they joined the new Gurkha Line as the 5th Goorkha Regiment or Hazara Goorkha Battalion, attached to the Punjab Irregular Force which became the Punjab Frontier Force four years later.

Their first major campaign was the Second Afghan War which provided their first battle-honour – Peiwar Kotal and their first Victoria Cross, to Captain John Cook. In Roberts' column, they established a reputation for themselves, working with the 72nd Highlanders, later the 1st Bn Seaforth Highlanders. Years later, when Roberts was elevated to the peerage, he chose as supporters for his new coat of arms, two hillmen – a Seaforth Highlander and a 5th Gurkha.

A second battalion was raised on 20 October 1886 from a cadre of the 1st Battalion and from the 42nd, 43rd and 44th Regiments Goorkha (Light)

Infantry, not more than 100 volunteers per regiment. Their first significant action was in the Hazara Black Mountain Expedition of 1891. That same year, the 1st Battalion was engaged in an action against the Hunzas in northern Kashmir, unrecognised with an honour but sufficiently savage to enable the 5th to gain two more Victoria Crosses, to Lieut G Boisragon and J Manners-Smith.

During the Tirah campaign of 1897–98, the Regimental Scouts of the 1st Battalion combined with those of the 2nd and the 1/3rd to form the Gurkha Scouts, a body of three British officers and some 120 rifles, intended to exploit the well-known performance of Gurkhas in hill-work and their skill as marksmen. Experimentally, the Scouts wore shorts but several years were to elapse before these were universally adopted as part of the Indian Army's uniform.

In 1903, the Punjab Frontier Force ceased to exist when its regiments became part of Kitchener's single Indian Army and it was, thenceforth, to survive only as a name incorporated in the title of those units whose deeds had brought it fame. Thus, on 2 October 1903, the 5th Gurkha Rifles became the 5th Gurkha Rifles (Frontier Force).

In 1907, the two distinctive green folds in the pagri of the Gurkha hat were adopted as a unique dress-feature of the 5th Gurkhas. Another distinction, born of its Frontier Force past, was the wearing by the 1st Bn only of brown boots and belts by all ranks, in line with former Frontier Force practice.

THE GREAT WAR

1st Battalion – India, Egypt, Gallipoli

2nd Battalion – India, Mesopotamia

3rd Battalion – raised 28 Nov 16 at Ferozepore as the 2nd Reserve Battalion, Gurkha Rifles: complete companies came from 1/4 GR, 1/9 GR, 2/1 GR and 2/10 GR. Redesignated 3/5 GR, on 29 May 17 (subsidiary title 'Frontier Force' added 9 Oct 17) India, Mesopotamia. Disbanded July 1921

BETWEEN THE WARS

Indian Army Order 821 of 26 Jul 21 proclaimed, somewhat unnecessarily, perhaps, that, with effect from 15 Feb 21, the 5th Gurkha Rifles (Frontier Force) had become the 5th Royal Gurkha Rifles (Frontier Force), news which had been broken to both battalions at the review held at Rawalpindi in February that year in recognition of the distinguished service by Gurkhas in the recent war. A red shoulder-cord accompanies this distinction and it replaced the current green-and-black cord, to be worn on the right shoulder. Recruits received it personally from the hands of their commanding officer on the day that they were sworn in and no man serving a sentence for any military crime was permitted to wear what came to be called 'The Royal'. The regimental badge also changed: the previous badge had been crossed kukris, points uppermost, cutting-edges inwards, with a figure '5' above the intersection. The new badge had a crown above the numeral. Later, it was realised that half the regiments of the Indian Army, royal or otherwise, bore the same crown. Permission was sought to replace the crown with the Royal Crest – a lion above the Crown – and this was approved in August 1927.

Some measure of the 5th's employment during the decade preceding the Second World War can be judged by the fact that they were the only regiment to receive the between-wars North-West Frontier battle-honours. Twenty British battalions and more than twenty Indian battalions also claimed one or more of these honours but none was awarded, not even to the 5/12th Frontier Force

Regiment (the Guides Infantry) whose adjutant received a posthumous Victoria Cross in 1935 on the Frontier.

SECOND WORLD WAR

1st Battalion – India, Iran, Iraq, Egypt, Italy
2nd Battalion – India, Burma, Japan
3rd Battalion – (re-raised 1 Oct 40) – India, Burma, Malaya, Dutch East Indies
4th Battalion – (raised 15 Mar 41) – India, Burma. Disbanded December 1946

In August 1944, the 2/5th was sent back to India from Burma. It was to serve briefly on the North West Frontier before being nominated to join 1/1 Punjab and 1/5 Mahratta Light Infantry in 268 Indian Infantry Brigade. This brigade was to join Brindiv, a two brigade British Indian formation forming BCOF, the British Commonwealth Occupation Force in Japan. They finally reached Kure in Japan on 15 May 46, spending just over a year there before leaving Kure on 18 Jul 47, in time to be home for the Partition celebrations.

PARTITION

In August 1947, the 5th Royal Gurkha Rifles (Frontier Force) were transferred to Indian command. The serving battalions were the 1st, 2nd and 3rd.

BATTLE HONOURS

Peiwar Kotal, Charasiah, Kabul 1879, Kandshar 1880, Afghanistan 1878–80, Punjab Frontier, Helles, Krithia, Suvla, Sari Bair, Gallipoli 1915, Suez Canal, Egypt 1915–16, Khan Baghdadi, Mesopotamia 1916–18, North-West Frontier, India 1917, Afghanistan 1919, North West Frontier 1930, North West Frontier 1936–39, The Sangro, Caldari, Cassino II, Sant' Angelo in Teodice, Rocca d'Arce, Rippa Ridge, Femmina Morte, Monte San Bartolo, Italy 1943–45, Sittang 1942, 1945, Kyaukse 1942, Yenangyaung 1942, Stockades, Buthidaung, Imphal, Sakawng, Bishenpur, Shenam Pass, The Irrawaddy, Burma 1942–45.

BOOKS

'History of the 5th Royal Gurkha Rifles (Frontier Force) Vol I: 1858–1928. Anon (Pub. Gale and Polden Ltd, Aldershot c. 1928)
Vol II 1919–1947 Anon. (Pub. Gale and Polden Ltd, Aldershot 1956)
'Desperate Encounters' by Lieut Col R M Maxwell (Pub. Pentland Press, Edinburgh 1986)

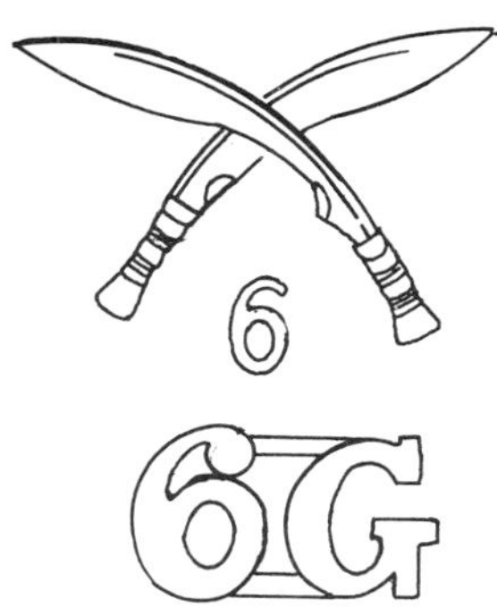

6th GURKHA RIFLES

Home Station: **1923 ABBOTTABAD**
1947 ABBOTTABAD

The 6th is the first one of the ten Gurkha regiments to have started out as a body of plainsmen. The Cuttack Legion was raised in 1817 in Orissa but moved to Northern Bengal in 1823 as the Rungpoor Light Infantry. This title was equally short-lived and, in 1818, they became the Assam Light Infantry. It was at this stage that the first Gurkhas were enlisted, in two of the twelve companies and this proportion increased until, by 1886, only Gurkhas and kindred Himalayan tribes were recruited.

The post-Mutiny reforms saw the Assam Light Infantry become, first the 46th and then the 42nd Regiment of the Bengal Line but it was not until 1886 that the title bore a reference to the Regiment's ethnic content: it became the 42nd Regiment, Goorkha (Light) Infantry. The first regimental battle-honour was Burma 1885–87, really an extension of their service over the previous sixty years against Nagas, Chins, Lushais, and Manipuris. The North East Frontier was no less demanding or strenuous than the North West but, somehow, it did not have the same glamour. The North Eastern tribes fought from behind dense cover, using unpleasant poisoned weapons and did not seem to display the occasional sporting spirit of the Pathans. British and Indian soldiers were to fight over the same ground in the next century and found it no more agreeable.

In 1899, the 42nd were transferred to the other border and, in 1901, became the 42nd Gurkha Rifles. From there, it was a short step to the Gurkha Line where they became the 6th in 1903, the year of the Kitchener reforms.

The 2nd Battalion materialised the following year when the 65th Carnatic Light Infantry, now a redundant Madras unit, was mustered out and reborn as 2/6 GR. The 65th's antecedents were older than the Cuttack Legion, originating in 1759, but although 2/6 GR took over the 65th's funds, band and mess property, they did not take its four hard-earned honours of Carnatic, Sholinghur, Mysore and Pegu.

THE GREAT WAR

1st Battalion – India, Egypt, Gallipoli, Mesopotamia

2nd Battalion – India, Mesopotamia, Greece, Russia

3rd Battalion – (raised 5 Feb 17 at Rawalpindi as the 3rd Reserve Battalion, Gurkha Rifles: drafts came from 1/2 and 2/2 GR, 1/4 and 2/4 GR, 1/9 and 2/9 GR, 1/10 and 2/10 GR and 2/6 GR. Redesignated 3/6 GR later in 1917. India. Disbanded 1 Feb 21.

The 1st Battalion served with distinction in Gallipoli. They put the Turks to flight, were the only battalion to reach the heights and to see the Dardanelles: then tragedy struck, the ridge they held was shelled by the Navy and the Turks regrouped and counter-attacked, driving 1/6 off the summit. At that stage, the survivors of the battalion were under the command of their medical officer. A certain Captain W J Slim, at that time commanding a company of the 9th Royal Warwicks, witnessed the action and decided that these were men with whom he could serve. If he managed to get off the peninsula alive, he would join the 6th Gurkhas. He did both and served with them until 1937. By the end of the Second World War he had commanded the 14th Army, the largest Allied army of the war. After the war, he became Colonel of what became the 7th Duke of Edinburgh's Own Gurkha Rifles.

BETWEEN THE WARS

The badge of the 6th Gurkhas had, since the Regiment's designation as such in 1903, been crossed kukris, but not in the familiar, saltire fashion: the kukri-handles were close together and almost parallel and the blades were crossed, cutting-edges inwards. No numeral was either attached to or co-located with the kukris. It was not until the 1930s that a new badge appeared: the kukris were still crossed but the handles had been parted to admit the entry of a figure '6'.

SECOND WORLD WAR

1st Battalion – India, Burma
2nd Battalion – India, Iraq, Persia, Syria, Lebanon, Egypt, Italy
3rd Battalion – re-raised 1 Oct 40, India, Burma, Siam. Became 5/5 RGR (FF) 31 Dec 47
4th Battalion – raised 15 Mar 41. India, Burma. Disbanded 28 Feb 47

PARTITION

The 6th Gurkhas were one of the four regiments which went to the British Army, taking its 1st and 2nd Battalions only. The 1st Battalion was the last one to sail from Rangoon for Malaya on 28 Jan 48. The Regiment's later history is recorded in the chapter on Britain's Brigade of Gurkhas.

BATTLE HONOURS

Burma 1885–87, Helles, Krithia, Suvla, Sari Bair, Gallipoli 1915, Suez Canal, Egypt 1915–16, Khan Baghdadi, Mesopotamia 1916–18, Persia 1918, North West Frontier, India 1915, Afghanistan 1919, Coriano, Santarcangelo, Monte Chicco, Lamone Crossing, Senio Floodbank, Medicina, Gaiana Crossing, Italy 1944–45, Shwebo, Kyaukmyaung Bridgehead, Mandalay, Fort Dufferin, Maymyo, Rangoon Road, Toungoo, Sittang 1945, Chindits 1944, Burma 1942–45.

BOOKS

'Historical records of the 6th Gurkha Rifles' Vol I 1817–1919 by Major D G J Ryan DSO, Major G C Strachan OBE and Captain J K Jones (Pub. Gale and Polden Ltd, Aldershot 1925)
'Historical Record of the 6th Gurkha Rifles' 1919–1948' by Lieut Col H K R Gibbs (Pub. Gale and Polden Ltd, Aldershot 1955)

'The Happy Warriors – the Gurkha soldier in Malaya 1948–58' by Brig. A E C Bredin DSO MC (Pub. The Blackmore Press, Gillingham, Dorset 1961)
'The Steadfast Gurkha' – historical records of the 6th Queen Elizabeth's Own Gurkha Rifles 1948–82' by Charles Messenger (Pub. Leo Cooper, London 1985)

7th GURKHA RIFLES

Home Station: **1923 QUETTA**
1947 PALAMPUR

The evolution of the 7th Gurkhas was a complex one.

In 1902, it was decided to raise a Gurkha regiment for local service in Burma and it was to become the 8th Gurkha Rifles, taking the funds, band and mess of the 8th Madras Infantry, just disbanded.

It was formed in Thayetmyo, in Central Burma from 400 men of the 10th Gurkha Rifles (another Burma local unit), 100 men from the Burma Military Police and transfers from other Indian Army Gurkha regiments. It was granted the use of 42nd tartan for its pipers and its date of raising was 16 May 02.

In February 1903, it was re-styled the 2nd Bn 10th Gurkha Rifles but, in 1905, the battalion was de-localized and moved to Lansdowne. As compensation, the men of the battalion were given twenty months payment of their Burma Allowance.

The Nepal Durbar agreed in April 1907 to the number of Gurkha units in the Indian Army being increased and it was decided that two of the Gurkha regiments would be entirely composed of men enlisted from Eastern Nepal. A new battalion was to be formed and so the 2nd Bn 10th Gurkha rifles was split into two: the Right Wing became the 1st Bn 7th Gurkha Rifles whilst the Left Wing became the 2nd Bn 7th Gurkha Rifles.

Opportunely, at about this time, the 78th Moplah Rifles was being disbanded in 1907 and a number of the Moplahs' officers were to join the 7th Gurkhas, bringing some of the 78th's mess silver and the band fund and instruments for the new 2/7th.

A replacement second battalion for the 10th Gurkha Rifles was raised in September 1907 in Quetta with a cadre from the 1st Battalion.

Slightly to confuse the picture, the 43rd Gurkha Rifles was re-designated the 7th Gurkha Rifles in 1903 but, in 1907, it changed its name to become the 2nd

Bn 8th Gurkha Rifles. It has no connection with the 7th Gurkha Rifles under review.

Both battalions made their home in Quetta until the outbreak of the Great War, the 1st in Stewart Lines and the 2nd in Kandahar Lines.

THE GREAT WAR

1st Battalion – India, Mesopotamia

2nd Battalion – India, Egypt, Mesopotamia

3rd Battalion – (raised June 1917) – India. Disbanded March 1921.

The 2nd Battalion was forced to surrender at Kut-al-Amara but a replacement battalion was raised at once in 1916 in Mesopotamia. In commemoration of their having served together in 30 Indian Infantry Brigade in the defence of Kut, officers of the 24th Punjabis (later 4/14 Punjab) and the 76th Punjabis (later 3/1 Punjab) became permanent honorary members of the 7GR Officers' Mess.

BETWEEN THE WARS

On 31 May 35, occurred the famous Quetta earthquake in which some 15,000 were thought to have died. The 7th Gurkhas did not suffer any losses but all the 1st Bn Training Company who were on the station were employed in rescue and salvage work.

In March 1936 the 1st Bn moved to Shillong, followed by the 2nd in March 1938. Shillong was to be the new home station for the 7th Gurkhas.

The badge was crossed kukris, the cutting-edge inwards, with a figure '7' between the blades.

SECOND WORLD WAR

1st Battalion – India, Burma

2nd Battalion – India, Iran, Iraq, Egypt, Palestine, Italy, Greece. Captured by the Germans at Tobruk in June 1942. Re-raised in Egypt.

3rd Battalion – (re-raised in Karachi on 1 Oct 40) – India, Burma. Merged temporarily with the survivors of the 1st Battalion after the Sittang crossing in Burma in February 1942 but reconstituted in May that year in Amritsar. In December 1942, they became a parachute battalion, designated 154 (Gurkha) Parachute Battalion in June 1943 and, in November 1945, 3 (Gurkha) Bn Indian Parachute Regiment. Their badge then was a rifle-green rectangle bearing white embroidered crossed kukris, an opened parachute between the blades. On 26 Oct 46, they reverted to their regimental title. Disbanded November 1946.

4th Battalion – (raised 15 Mar 41 at Abbottabad). India. Disbanded 30 May 46.

The Japanese advance on India in early 1942 prompted a move by the regimental centre from Shillong in Assam to Palampur, in the Kangra Valley of the Punjab.

When Major General J H F Lakin, the Colonel of the Regiment died in February 1943, he was succeeded by the then Lieutenant General Sir William Slim, once a 6th Gurkha but who had commanded 1/7 GR in 1938–39.

PARTITION

On Partition in August 1947, the 7th Gurkha Rifles was one of the four Gurkha infantry regiments to transfer to the British Army, taking its 1st and 2nd Battalions. The 1st Bn sailed from Rangoon for Malaya on 8 Jan 48. The Regiment's later history is recorded in the chapter on Britain's Brigade of Gurkhas.

BATTLE HONOURS
Suez Canal, Egypt 1915, Megiddo, Sharon, Palestine 1918, Shaiba, Kut-al-Amara 1915, 1917, Ctesiphon, Baghdad, Sharqat, Mesopotamia 1915–18, Afghanistan 1919, Tobruk 1942, North Africa 1942, Cassino I, Campriano, Poggio del Grillo, Tavoleto, Montebello-Scorticata Ridge, Italy 1944, Pegu 1942, Kyaukse 1942, Shwegyin, Imphal, Bishenpur, Meiktila, Capture of Meiktila, Defence of Meiktila, Rangoon Road, Pyawbwe, Burma 1942–45.

BOOKS
'The Seventh Gurkha Rifles' by Anon (Pub. Gale and Polden Ltd, Aldershot, 1954)
'History of the 7th Duke of Edinburgh's Own Gurkha Rifles' by Colonel J N Mackay DSO (Pub. Wm Blackwood, Edinburgh, 1962)
'East of Katmandu' by Brigadier E D Smith DSO OBE (Pub. Leo Cooper, London, 1976)

8th GURKHA RIFLES

Home Station: **1923 1st Bn QUETTA**
2nd Bn SHILLONG
1947 DEHRA DUN

The two regiments forming the 8th Gurkha Rifles spent their formative years on the North-East Frontier: both, in fact, were born there. The 16th or Sylhet Local Battalion was raised in February 1824 but only joined the Bengal Line in 1861 as the 48th (Sylhet) Light Infantry. This number, like so many of the other Gurkha regiments, lasted only a few months and they then became the 44th. Twenty-five years later, after a permutation of titles, they were styled the 44th Goorkha (Light) Infantry although Gurkhas had long been an essential element in their personnel. In 1901, they were made simply the 44th Gurkha Rifles and, two years later, with the Kitchener reforms, the 8th Gurkha Rifles.

The second battalion-to-be also originated in the North East as the Lower Assam Sebundy Corps in 1839 and they continued to retain the Assam in their title until 1886. After the Great Mutiny, they were taken into the Bengal Line as the 47th (2nd Assam) Light Infantry, changing to the 43rd after only a few months. It was only in June 1886, that they assumed a Gurkha title as the 43rd

Regiment Goorkha (Light) Infantry. The turn of the century saw them simply as the 43rd Gurkha Rifles, being inducted in 1903 into the Gurkha Line as the 7th Gurkha Rifles.

Shortly after this came the decision by the Government to increase the number of Gurkha battalions and the Nepal Durbar was willing to allow the increased recruitment, but not of the Magar and Gurung tribesmen of which the 7th and 8th Gurkhas were composed. However, the Government had ordained that, in the future, all regiments in the Gurkha line were to be of two battalions, one to be at the home station and the other in the field and, since, in the light of the Durbar's strictures, it would not be permitted to recruit second battalions for the 7th and 8th, the 7th was, in September 1907, made the second battalion of the 8th.

The sparseness of nineteenth century honours, is not to suggest a perpetually peaceful patrolling of the North Eastern marches by the old 43rd and 44th. Some twenty-five small campaigns were endured and, in one of them in 1879 against the Nagas, Lieutenant R K Ridgeway of the 43rd won a Victoria Cross. It was also the 43rd which brought the Burma battle-honour for the suppression of Upper Burma after its annexation.

Another Cross was earned at Thobal against the Manipuris in 1891 when Lieutenant C J W Grant, with a small party of the 43rd and fifty men of the 16th Madras Infantry, fought off several thousand armed enemy.

Barely more than a decade later, in 1903, the 1/8th were sent to Tibet. The government in Lhasa had been dallying with Russia, a flirtation which was anathema to the Government of the time in India, Russian arms began to appear and Indian territory was encroached upon. A political officer was despatched to the frontier to treat, but after four months, nobody responsible was forthcoming so that an advance, initially to Gyantse, was ordered and the 1/8th was in the British force escorting the political officer. Gyantse was occupied and the fort stormed, during which operation, another Lieutenant Grant, J.D. this time, won a Victoria Cross before the final advance to Lhasa, the 'Forbidden City'. The treaty following this campaign resulted in a company of Indian infantry being stationed in Gyantse for the next fifty years, nominally as escort to the British and, later, Indian Trade Agent.

THE GREAT WAR

1st Battalion – India, Mesopotamia, Egypt
2nd Battalion – India, France, Egypt
3rd Battalion – (raised June 1917 at Lansdowne) – India. Disbanded 15 Jun 21

BETWEEN THE WARS

Political pressures followed the Great War throughout the world and India was no exception. The two regiments of Moplah Rifles, the 77th and the 78th had been disbanded in 1907 for disaffection and 1921 saw trouble in the Moplah homeland in Malabar, on the west coast of South India. The hill-country was close and movement was difficult so hill-soldiers were called for. After a seven-day journey from Lansdowne to the Kotdwara railhead, the 2/8th reached Tirur, ready to meet the insurgents who may not have heard of the Gurkha reputation. On 26 Nov 21, some two thousand Moplahs attacked the 'C' Company post and, by sheer weight of numbers, about sixty of the rebels broke through the perimeter. With bayonet and kukri, 'C' Company disposed of 234 rebels killed and many were subsequently found who had died of their wounds. Home losses were one British officer and three Gurkha other ranks.

For return to Lansdowne, the 2/8th reached Kotdwara, leaving Tirur on 20 Jan 22, only to find themselves detailed for ceremonial duties in Delhi on the occasion of the visit of HRH The Prince of Wales. Eight days later, in new khaki-drill and with full-dress accoutrements brought down from Lansdowne, they performed the necessary royal duties in the capital.

Before the Great War, and until 1922, the 1st Battalion wore a red pompom on the left side of the Gurkha hat above the red patch with black regimental badge (crossed kukris, points upwards, cutting-edges outwards, a figure '8' above the intersection) on the pagri. In 1922, the red feather-hackle replaced the red pompom, commemorating the wartime association with The Black Watch (Royal Highland Regiment) who traditionally wore that embellishment in their bonnets. The 2nd Battalion also wore a red pompom of a different pattern, in use since 1885.

20 Apr 29 saw an important event in regimental history. The 1st Battalion had been in Shillong when the 2nd Battalion joined them there, the first time that the two battalions of the 8th Gurkha Rifles had ever met as members of the same family.

Men of both battalions were also on duty in Quetta when the great earthquake took place there in May 1935 but they sustained very few casualties. Following this, the 1st Battalion was to move to the 2nd's home station at Shillong.

THE SECOND WORLD WAR

1st Battalion – India, Burma, Dutch East Indies

2nd Battalion – India, Iraq, Egypt, Italy

3rd Battalion – (re-raised 1 Oct 40 at Shillong) – India, Ceylon, Burma, French Indo-China, North Borneo. Disbanded April 1946.

4th Battalion – (raised 15 Mar 41 at Shillong) – India, Burma, Siam, Malaya, Dutch East Indies

In April 1942, the Japanese advance into India prompted a move by the regimental centre from Shillong back to Quetta. This relocation was relatively shortlived: in March/April 1947, the centre moved again, this time to Dehra Dun, there to join with the 2 GR centre.

PARTITION

August 1947 brought Partition and the 8th Gurkha Rifles were to remain in India. The battalions transferred were the 1st, 2nd and 4th.

BATTLE HONOURS

Burma 1885–87, La Bassee 1914, Festubert 1914, 1915, Givenchy 1914, Neuve Chapelle, Aubers, France and Flanders 1914–15, Egypt 1915–16, Megiddo, Sharon, Palestine 1918, Tigris 1916, Kut-al-Amara 1917, Baghdad, Mesopotamia 1916–17, Afghanistan 1919, Iraq 1941, North Africa 1940–43, Gothic Line, Coriano, Santarcangelo, Gaiana Crossing, Point 551, Imphal, Tamu Road, Bishenpur, Kanglatongbi, Mandalay, Myinmu Bridgehead, Singhu, Shandatgyi, Sittang 1945, Burma 1942–45.

BOOKS

'History of the 8th Gurkha Rifles' by Lieut Col H J Huxford OBE (Pub. Gale and Polden Ltd, 1952)

9th GURKHA RIFLES

Home Station **1923 DEHRA DUN**
1947 DEHRA DUN

It must now be apparent to the reader that the number in the regimental title in the case of the Gurkha regiments does not give a very accurate indication of precedence. Thus, the 9th is the senior regiment of the Gurkha Line although the regiment from which it was formed was only raised in 1823, after the creation of the 1st, 2nd and 3rd Gurkha Rifles. However, the last three, although born in 1816, were not considered part of the Bengal Line until after the Great Mutiny. The 9th, of course, was not a Gurkha corps from its inception. Its origins were in the Fatehgarh Levy in 1817, becoming the Mynpoory Levy in 1818. In 1823, they became the 1st Bn 32nd Bengal Native Infantry, changing the next year to the 63rd. After the Great Mutiny, the regiment was retained and the disbandments in the Bengal Line meant that the 63rd advanced to become the 9th BNI with an amended establishment to permit the recruitment of one of the eight companies as Gurkhas or other hillmen. They were then the only infantry, other than the five Gurkha regiments then in being, permitted to enlist that class.

The old 63rd had secured Bhurtpore as their first battle-honour in 1826 and, twenty years later, captured a Sikh standard at Sobraon. The campaign in Bhutan in 1864–66 brought them no honours and the Second Afghan War brought them little action. In 1893, it was announced that sixteen mixed-class Bengal regiments were to be converted to single-class units and the 9th was selected, to be composed principally of Khas Gurkhas. The latter were more strictly Hindu than the other Gurkha clans enlisted who incline more towards Buddhism but the 9th gave observers no reason to doubt their military performance in the Tirah campaign of 1897–98. Finally, in 1901, the regiment became, formally, the 9th Gurkha Rifles.

A second battalion was raised from the first in 1904, replacing the 71st Coorgs, disbanded that year.

THE GREAT WAR
1st Battalion – India, France, Mesopotamia
2nd Battalion – India, Mesopotamia
3rd Battalion – (raised June 1917). India. Disbanded 28 Feb 21.

BETWEEN THE WARS
The 1st and 2nd Battalions had returned to Dehra Dun by mid-1920 and were engaged for some time on ceremonial duties. However, down in South India, the Moplahs, a fanatical Muslim community, of Arab descent had rebelled in July 1921 on the Malabar coast. Competent troops were called for by the Madras Government to clear the rebels from the twelve hundred square miles of hill-country covered in thick jungle to the south-east of Calicut. The 2nd Battalion was sent, together with 2/8 GR, 1/39 Garhwal Rifles and 3/70 Kachins in November and, by February 1922, the rebellion was put down and the troops ready to withdraw. No honours were awarded for this campaign but those engaged received a clasp 'Malabar' to their India General Service Medal 1908. The regimental badge had been crossed kukris, the cutting-edge downwards with a figure '9' between the hafts but, during the 1920s, a crown was added above the intersection. The 2nd Battalion wore a black astrakhan diamond-shaped patch on the pagri of the Gurkha hat to recall its Mesopotamia service after the Great War.

SECOND WORLD WAR
1st Battalion – India, Iraq, Iran, Egypt, North Africa, Italy, Greece.
2nd Battalion – India, Malaya. Captured by Japanese on Singapore Island February 1941. Reconstituted at midnight 31 May/1 Jun 46 at Wana by redesignation of the 5th Battalion
3rd Battalion – (re-raised 1 Oct 40 at Dehra Dun). India, Burma, Malaya, Dutch East Indies
4th Battalion – (raised 1 Nov 40 at Dehra Dun). India, Burma. Disbanded 10 Mar 47
5th Battalion – (raised 1 Jul 42). India. Redesignated 2nd Battalion at midnight 31 May/1 Jun 46 at Wana.

PARTITION
The 9th was one of the six Gurkha regiments being retained by India and the battalions at Partition in August 1947, were the 1st, 2nd and 3rd.

BATTLE HONOURS
Bhurtpore, Sobraon, Afghanistan 1879–80, Punjab Frontier, La Bassee 1914, Armentieres 1914, Festubert 1914, 1915, Givenchy 1914, Neuve Chapelle, Aubers, Loos, France and Flanders 1914–5, Tigris 1916, Kut-al-Amara 1917, Baghdad, Mesopotamia 1916–18, Afghanistan 1919, Djebel el Meida, Djebel Garci, Ragoubet Souissi, North Africa 1940–43, Cassino I, Hangman's Hill, Tavoleto, San Marino, Italy 1943–45, Greece 1944–45, Malaya 1941–42, Chindits 1944, Burma 1942–45.

BOOKS
'The 9th Gurkha Rifles, Vol I: 1817–1936' by Lieut Col F S Poynder MVO, OBE MC (Pub. Butler and Tanner, London, 1937)
'The 9th Gurkha Rifles, Vol II 1937–47' by Lieut Col G R Stevens OBE (Pub. Butler and Tanner, London, 1953)
'9th Gurka Rifles – a regimental history 1817 to 1947' by Lieut Col P Chaudhuri (Pub. Vision Books (Pvt) Ltd, New Delhi, 1984)

10G

10th GURKHA RIFLES

Home Station: **1923 QUETTA**
1947 ALHILAL, Punjab

Among the Madras regiments which were to change their class composition in the last decade of the last century was the 10th Madras Infantry. The South Indian soldiers were mustered out on posting or pension in 1890 and replaced by Gurkhas and Assamese from the Kubo Valley Military Police Battalion, to be known then as the 10th (Burma) Regiment of Madras Infantry.

The Kubo Valley unit had only been formed in 1887 to police what became known as the Kabaw Valley in western Burma to thousands of Gurkhas just over fifty years later. By 1895, the Assamese had gone and the regiment was entirely Gurkha. However, the Madrassi traditions were to live on and much mess silver was retained as well as the regimental colours, still preserved in the officers' mess. The title changed twice more before 1895 when it became the 10th Regiment (1st Burma Gurkha Rifles) Madras Infantry, finally entering the Gurkha Line in September 1901 as the 10th Gurkha Rifles, a happy coincidence whereby they retained their old number.

In 1891, the Regiment was posted to Maymyo for the first time and, six years later, that popular hill-station became its official permanent home until 1921 when the 10th Gurkhas moved to Quetta.

In 1903, for what the Regiment's Centenary Book refers to as 'short-term reasons', the old battle-honours ceased to be carried. More probably, it was a conscious attempt to sever its links with unfashionable South India which had become a sort of military Siberia, shunned by ambitious officers seeking the bubble reputation of Northern India. As will be seen, these honours were later to be repossessed with the result that the 10th Gurkhas might now lay claim to be the senior Gurkha regiment.

Notwithstanding, in two world wars, the 10th went on to amass an impressive array of honours of their own.

In 1902, two British officers, four Gurkha officers, and 200 men were transferred to form the nucleus of the new 8th Gurkha Rifles forming at Thayetmyo and, the following year, the 8th became the 2nd Bn 10th Gurkha Rifles.

The 2nd Battalion moved from Maymyo to Lansdowne in May 1905 and, then again, in April 1907 to Quetta where it was split into two battalions to become the 1st and 2nd Bns 7th Gurkha Rifles.

It was not until September 1908 that another second battalion was raised in Fatehgarh, when 401 Gurkha ranks from the 1st Bn were despatched from Maymyo as the cadre.

THE GREAT WAR

1st Battalion – Burma, Mesopotamia

2nd Battalion – Burma, Egypt, Gallipoli, Mesopotamia

The 10th was one of the two regiments in the Gurkha Line which did not raise a third battalion during the Great War. The 4th, of course, should have had one but, due to a clerical error, the proposed 3/4th became the 4/3rd.

At one point in the Middle East, the 1/10th was down to two companies strong and they combined with the two surviving companies of the 116th Mahrattas to serve as the 126th Gorattas. Their four-and-a-half years in the old Turkish Empire resulted in self-bestowal of an unofficial motto 'Per arida ad astra'.

BETWEEN THE WARS

These years saw the two battalions serving on the North-West and North-East Frontiers of India but they were destined for no more major active service until 1940. The regimental badge had been crossed kukris, cutting-edges downwards with the figure '10' above the intersection. In the mid-1930s, a stringed bugle-horn, long-used on the officers' pouch-belts, was introduced, with a single kukri entwined, below the figures '10'. The badge was worn on a rifle-green patch on the right side of the pagri of the Gurkha-hat.

SECOND WORLD WAR

1st Battalion – India, Burma

2nd Battalion – India, Iraq, Syria, Iran, Italy

3rd Battalion – (raised 1 Oct 40 at Dehra Dun). India, Burma, Malaya, Dutch East Indies. Disbanded 30 Apr 47

4th Battalion – (raised 15 Mar 41 at Abbottabad). India, Burma, French Indo-China, Cambodia

The Regiment's four battalions spent more time in action and won more gallantry awards than any other regiment in the Indian Army. Casualties amounted to more than 1,000 dead and almost 2,000 wounded.

PARTITION

The 10th Gurkhas was the last of the four Gurkha infantry regiments to be transferred to the British Army following Partition in August 1947. Only the 1st and 2nd Battalions were to be taken. The Regiment's later service is recorded in the chapter on Britain's Brigade of Gurkhas.

BATTLE HONOURS

Suez Canal, Egypt 1915, Megiddo, Sharon, Palestine 1918, Shaiba, Kut-al-Amara 1915, 1917, Ctesiphon, Defence of Kut-al-Amara, Baghdad, Sharqat, Mesopotamia 1915–18, Afghanistan 1919, Tobruk 1942, North Africa 1942, Cassino I, Campriano, Poggio del Grillo, Tavoleto, Montebello-Scorticata Ridge, Italy 1944, Sittang 1942, 1945, Pegu 1942, Kyaukse 1942, Shwegyin, Imphal, Bishenpur, Meiktila, Capture of Meiktila, Defence of Meiktila, Rangoon Road, Pyawbwe, Burma 1942–45.

BOOKS

'History of the 10th Gurkha Rifles – The First Battalion 1890–1921' by Captain B R Mullaly (Pub. Gale and Polden Ltd, Aldershot 1924)

'Bugle and Kukri. The story of the 10th Princess Mary's Own Gurkha Rifles' by Colonel B R Mullaly (Pub. Wm Blackwood and Sons Ltd, Edinburgh 1957)

11th GURKHA RIFLES

The 11th did not have an Indian home-station. Their raising was effected overseas and they were not popular with British officers of the other Gurkha regiments who could not see the need to create yet another regiment when more battalions could have been created for existing regiments.

The four battalions of the new regiment were raised in the Middle East in May 1918 to permit the transfer of every possible British battalion to France for the conclusion of the war in Europe.

1st Battalion – raised 18 May 18 at Kut-al-Amara by transfer of one company each from 1/5GR, 2/5GR, 1/6GR and 2/6GR. Disbanded 20 Jul 21 at Abbottabad, men going to 2/5GR

2nd Battalion – raised 24 May 18 at Baghdad by transfer of one company each from 1/2GR, 1/3GR, 1/7GR and 2/4GR. Disbanded 15 Jul 21 at Abbottabad, men going to 2/4GR and 1/7GR

3rd Battalion – raised 25 May 1918 at Baghdad by transfer of one company each from 2/9GR and 1/10GR, 1/39 and 2/39 Garhwal Rifles. Drafts from 1/7GR, 1/9GR and 2/10GR to replace Garhwalis transferred out. Disbanded 12 Mar 22, men going to 2/5GR, 1/7GR and 1/10GR

4th Battalion – raised 24 May 18 in Palestine by transfer of one company each from 1/1GR, 2/3GR, 3/3GR and 2/7GR. Disbanded in India in late 1919, having sent drafts to reinforce 1st, 2nd and 3rd Bns.

The badge chosen was crossed kukris, points upwards, cutting-edges inwards, with 'XI' above the intersection. The 11th Gurkha Rifles raised in 1948 by India, following Partition, utilised the same badge but there was no intention to claim descent from the Great War-raised regiment.

BATTLE HONOURS

Afghanistan 1919.

SUNDRY 1939–45 GURKHA UNITS

153 (GURKHA) PARACHUTE BATTALION
Raised in Delhi in October 1941 from volunteers from all the Gurkha regiments, the largest number coming from 2GR. It became the 2nd (Gurkha) Bn, Indian Parachute Regiment in November 1945 and was disbanded in November 1947.

154 (GURKHA) PARACHUTE BATTALION
Raised in May 1942 by conversion of 3/7 GR, becoming 154 (Gurkha) Parachute Battalion in January 1943. In November 1945, they were re-designated 3rd (Gurkha) Bn, Indian Parachute Regiment but converted back to 3/7GR in October 1946. Finally disbanded November 1946.

5/3rd GURKHA RIFLES
The 3rd Queen Alexandra's Own Gurkha Rifles was not one of the three Gurkha regiments which raised a fifth battalion during the Second World War. However, reference is sometimes found to the 5/3rd. The explanation is that 1/3GR and 2/5RGR both sustained heavy losses in the Sittang battle in Burma in February 1942, being reduced to 107 and 227 men respectively. After withdrawal to India, both battalions were refitted and 5/3GR was no more.

25th GURKHA RIFLES
26th GURKHA RIFLES
The regiments of the Indian Line raised Garrison Battalions during the Second World War, numbered beginning with the 25th Bn. It was, of course, not possible to do this with the Gurkha Line but two new single-battalion regiments were raised from pensioners, graded soldiers and surplus recruits in late 1942 at Jhelum and late 1943 at Kala Base, north Punjab respectively. They were used for guard duties and as protection troops in Burma forward areas. Both were disbanded in May 1946.

The badge of the 25th was crossed kukris, cutting-edges downwards over the Roman numerals 'XXV'. That of the 26th was a single kukri, pointing to the left, cutting-edge uppermost, superimposed on it the numerals '26'. Both were in black.

14TH GURKHA RIFLES – Mohan, near Saharanpur
29th GURKHA RIFLES – Dehra Dun
38th GURKHA RIFLES – Dehra Dun
56th GURKHA RIFLES – Mohan, near Saharanpur
710th GURKHA RIFLES – Alhilal

The five 'regiments' above were, in fact, training battalions. Again, the Indian Line regiments simply detached an existing battalion for training duties but the Gurkha regiments had too few battalions for that so they were paired off and, thus, the 14th Gurkha Rifles served both 1GR and 4GR whilst the 29th served the 2nd and the 9th, etc. These battalions were formed in August/September 1943 and disbanded in May 1946.

9. CORPS AND SERVICES

The Royal Indian Army Service Corps was responsible for two main services – transport and supply. The former was something of a novel concept in the army in India. It had been customary to hire transport contractors when necessary, a notoriously unreliable resort. To be cherished was the remark of the Commander-in-Chief of the Bombay Army in 1879 when giving evidence to the Eden Commission, charged with planning reforms within India's land forces after the first phase of the Second Afghan War; asked about transport, the general observed

'I am not aware that there is any organised system of transport in the Bombay Army.'

Not only was animal transport abysmally slow but the net carrying capacity was low since each animal was required to carry its own forage which represented a high proportion of its carrying capacity. Clearly, animal-drawn wheeled transport would be more economical but India's terrain did not always permit this and 'pack transport' required animals in 'telephone-number' figures. The Eden Commission found that during the first phase of the Afghan campaign some 60,000 camels had died and that operations had come to a standstill after four months for lack of transport.

Draught-animals were usually bullocks, camels, horses, ponies, mules and, at times, elephants and even yaks. Animal transport prevailed within the Indian Army until well into the Great War when motor-ambulances made their appearance and units officially known as Ford Van Companies operated in Palestine and Mesopotamia. Heavier trucks were purchased – Leylands and Thornycrofts – and Mechanical Transport Companies raised, largely with driver-volunteers from the various British Territorial battalions then serving in India as replacement for regular battalions sent to France. Many of the men had pre-war driving experience whereas no Indian soldiers had had such training – nor many British regular soldiers. Supply, the other part of the Corps' duties, suffered a radical change after the Great War. Before 1914, Indian regiments had been largely self-sustaining – for both men and animals – but the exceptional circumstances of that war had made this impracticable, and the Indian Corps took over responsibility for supply of food, fodder and fuel as was the practice of the ASC in the British Army.

The Commissariat Departments of the three Presidencies were merged in 1887 with the three Transport Departments as three Commissariat-Transport Departments. Two years later, the three united as one Commissariat-Transport Department, being restyled the Supply and Transport Corps in 1901. After the Great War, being more closely modelled upon the ASC, it was logical that it should become the Indian Army Service Corps, being made 'Royal' in the Jubilee honours of 1935.

The Second World War saw the RIASC – referred to, irreverently, as the 'Rice-Corps' – expanding dramatically. Its first personnel to experience active service were the mule companies sent to France in 1939 who were evacuated to the UK in May 1940 following Hitler's blitzkrieg. New skills were developed, new experiences were thrust upon them. Notably, in the first category, air-supply to columns operating in a long-range penetration role in Burma and, in the second, on supply convoys to Russia. RIASC GPT (General Purpose Transport) Companies in Paiforce, delivering stores to the Russian railheads at Tabriz in North Persia in December 1942, experienced a fall in temperature during the first four days of the 700-mile trip from 106°F to 19°F. A high proportion of these drivers was of South Indian origin. Partition, in August 1947, brought the fragmentation of the RIASC and the withdrawal of its School from Chaklala, now to be in Pakistan. On 26 Jan 50, India's Republic Day, the RIASC became simply the Army Service Corps as did the Royal Pakistan Army Service Corps in 1956 when Pakistan became a republic. The short-lived Indian Catering Corps was absorbed into the RIASC on 1 Sep 48 and the rather older Indian Army Corps of Clerks was taken over on 1 Feb 49.

The medical structure within the Indian Army was complex. On formation of the Indian Army Medical Corps on 3 Apr 43 (AI 114/43), three elements were combined – the Indian Medical Service, the Indian Medical Department and the Indian Hospital Corps. The first-named was born on 6 Mar 1896, the combination of the Medical Services of the Bengal, Madras and Bombay Presidencies dating back to 1764. The IMS was overwhelmingly British in composition, serving not only the military population of India but also the civil, specialising in many cases in medical research and the skills and problems peculiar to the country. Indianisation came early to the IMS. Many Indian battalions in the Great War had Indian Medical Officers before Indians were commissioned to the 'teeth-arms'. The IMD was mainly made up of natives of India, including Anglo-Indians: the Assistant-Surgeons served the British troops and could be commissioned or warrant-officers. The Sub-Assistant Surgeons, of VCO rank, treated Indian troops. The Indian Hospital Corps dated only from 1 Jul 20 when it amalgamated the Army Hospital Corps and the Army Bearer Corps (the dooli-, or stretcher-bearers). Thus, the IHC embraced hospital staffs, clerical, stores personnel, male-nurses, ambulance-men, servants and domestics. Five Victoria Crosses were won by India's medical men – all Europeans. The Indian Military Nursing Service was established on 1 Oct 26 as the Indian Troops Nursing Service, consisting of India-trained nurses responsible for the supervision and training of Indian nursing orderlies in hospitals for Indian troops, (British troops were under the care of the Royal Army Medical Corps and Queen Alexandra's Imperial Military Nursing Service for India). Before 1914, hospital care for Indian trooops had been a regimental responsibility with widely-varying standards. As with the RIASC after Partition, the two Medical Corps of India and Pakistan dropped their national style when republican status was assumed and both became the Army Medical Corps.

Before the Second World War, there was no dental service for Indian troops but a Dental Branch of the Indian Medical Service was formed in 1940 and a separate Indian Army Dental Corps in March 1943 at the same time as the IAMC. The post-Partition Indian badge of the now Army Dental Corps shows a gentle sense of humour: it depicts crossed elephant tusks within a laurel wreath, surmounted by the lions of Ashoka. In fact, after Partition, the IADC had been absorbed by the IAMC and was only separated again in 1950. The same occurred to the Pakistani share of the IADC which vanished into the PAMC only to emerge a few years later in its own right.

The Remount and Veterinary Service was one of the earliest concerns of John Company. Local breeeds of horse were found to be unsuitable, being small, sickly and of poor physique. Studs were established in each of the three Presidencies in 1793 but as there were then no veterinary surgeons in India as we know them, the experiments in breeding ended in expensive failure. The Madras and Bombay Studs were closed down and the Bengal Stud was only saved by the engagement of William Moorcroft, the joint head of what is now the Royal College of Veterinary Surgeons, to superintend breeding operations in Bengal.

His arrival in 1808 signalled an improvement in India's equine stock and the suppression of contagious disease. The first Army Veterinary officer was appointed to the Governor General's Bodyguard in 1821 with instructions to train Assistant Apothecaries of the Medical Department as veterinary surgeons. The Army Remount Department was responsible for purchasing, rearing and issuing horses required for regiments in India although, in the old, silladar days, the regiments, except for the three Madras units, had bought their own. It also looked after the breeding of horses, mules and donkeys in Northern India. The Army Remount Department at Saharanpur came into being after the Abyssinian campaign in 1875 and is still in use today by India.

Veterinary officers, of course, went with their regiments on active service and, in 1857, in the operations in Persia, at Khushab, the 3rd Bombay Light Cavalry's veterinary officer captured the enemy standard.

In broad terms, artillery and British cavalry soldiers were mounted on heavier Australian horses whilst the slimmer Indian sowars rode 'country-bred', or Indian horses. The Australian horses mostly came from New South Wales and so, they all came to be known as 'Walers'. Two of the large remount depots were at Sargodha and Mona, both now in Pakistan. Although an Army Veterinary Department had been established in 1884 to oversee military veterinary matters, it was not until after the Great War that the Army Veterinary Corps, India, was raised on 14 Dec 20. This was rationalised into the Indian Army Veterinary Corps in 1925 and Indianised a decade later. The Willcox Committee Report of 1945 seemed inclined to the concept of remounts being the responsibility of the RIASC who would command the Animal Tranport companies but, on 15 Apr 47, in the last few months of British India, the ARD and IAVC were amalgamated to form the Indian Remount and Veterinary Corps. The Report also argued that the Military Farms Department might be regarded as a civilian body with a small military hierarchy. 'Farms' as their shoulder-title proclaimed them, had originated as part of the Commissariat Department on 7 Jun 1884, becoming a separate department in 1912. Initially responsible for ensuring adequate supplies of fodder for army animals and dairy products for military personnel, the MFD had come to serve Indian agriculture and animal-husbandry in general. Nevertheless, shortly after the Indian Remount and Veterinary Corps was formed, Partition occurred. Independent India formed the Indian Remount, Veterinary and Farms Corps and, in parallel, the Pakistan Remount, Veterinary and Farms Corps was also formed. As with other regiments and corps, both lost their national designations after republics were declared. In India, in May 1960, the MFD broke away leaving the Remount and Veterinary Corps. Like their parent corps in the UK, both Indian and Pakistan corps faced a declining equine military population but a rapidly-growing canine clientele in the light of the greater demand for guard-dogs within the armed forces.

The responsibility of the Ordnance Services is for the supply of, broadly, munitions, weapons and clothing. Initially, as with the Commissariat-Transport Services, it began as three separate Presidency departments, plus a fourth in the case of ordnance, designed for the supply to the Hyderabad Contingent. This was a miniature organisation attached to and supplied from Madras Ordnance. The development of arsenals, magazines, and supply depots had been haphazard, constructed to meet the needs of the moment. India had been occupied on no pre-arranged plan and communications were poor. In 1875, it was found that, taking India as a whole entity, there were thirty-four ordnance arsenals, magazines and depots. Factories had been established in the same way, based on the needs of each Presidency establishment and ten factories were found to be devoted to the manufacture of guns, gun-carriages and other vehicles and gun-ammunition and powder. Small-arms and their ammunition were either obtained from England or manufactured in the arsenals. The special Ordnance commision in 1875, not surprisingly, recommended drastic reductions in the number of establishments, concentrating storage and distribution services in a minimum number of large centres. Hard on the heels of the one, specialist commission came the 'Army in India Commission' of 1879 – more frequently known as the Eden Commission. This proposed the merger of the several ordnance departments into one and this was implemented in 1884 when they became the Indian Ordnance Department. Having had its distant origins in the artillery arm, the ordnance services had been staffed by John Company's artillery and, after the Great Mutiny, by the Royal Artillery. Officers served a tour in an arsenal or a factory and then returned to their battery. NCOs, also from the Royal Artillery, made up the subordinate staff together with Indians. In 1890, a change was made whereby officers served continuously in the Ordnance Department and this continued for the next thirty years when other officers were admitted to the ordnance service and the Royal Artillery monopoly came to an end.

The prodigalities of the Great War meant a profound reappraisal of many of the Indian Army's services and the ordnance was no exception. Central supply in the future rather than 'by regimental arrangement' and the abolition of silladar service meant more work for the Ordnance Department and there was an obvious need for closer contact with the user. Out of this was born, on 18 Jul 22, the Indian Army Ordnance Corps, intended to furnish troops in barracks and in the field with arms, equipment, clothing and boots.

The 'back-room' role of the ordnance service did not prevent its soldiers winning Britain's supreme award for gallantry. Nine Europeans of the Bengal Ordnance Establishment, on 11 May 1857, defended the Delhi Magazine against the mutineers until, with all hope of relief gone, they set fire to the ammunition stocks, creating an explosion in which they expected to die. Thousands of the mutineers died but four of the defenders survivived, three officers and one warrant-officer. One of the officers was later killed but the remaining three were awarded the Victoria Cross. Later, on 28 Oct 1857, another warrant officer earned the Cross for rescuing a wounded officer.

Like the RIASC and the IAMC, the IAOC split up in August 1947, both Indian and Pakistani elements becoming Army Ordnance Corps in their own armies after their respective assumptions of republican status.

The increasing sophistication of military weapons, transport and equipment during the Second World War brought into being on 1 May 43 the Corps of Indian Electrical and Mechanical Engineers in line with the formation of its parent corps in the United Kingdom. It was, of course, made up of officers, both British and Indian and other ranks, also British and Indian, from the Indian Engineers, the RIASC and IAOC. After Partition, both Indian and Pakistan EME carried those titles until republican changes rendered them simply EME – Electrical and Mechanical Engineers – within their own countries, sharing the common badge – a rearing horse, chained to indicate controlled horsepower and the lightning flash suggestive of the electrical element of their trades.

Education within the Indian Army had been the military responsibility of the Army Educational Corps, dispensed by British officers, warrant officers and

NCOs. It was proposed in the Willcox Committee Report that an Indian Army Educational Corps be formed although the medium of instruction, however, was still to be English. The new IAEC was raised on 1 Jun 47. On Partition, two months later, although India maintained the Corps, the Pakistan Army allowed it to lapse, only reviving it on 1 May 48. As with the other corps, when the two dominions became republics, their military educational bodies became simply the AEC.

The Intelligence Corps (India) was formed in November 1942 and the Centre was at Karachi. The Willcox Committee Report was rather less than enthusiastic as to its future but finally conceded that the Corps might find a place in the post-war Indian Army. However, when Partition took place, there was virtually no hand-over of documentation and the Corps ceased to exist. It was re-raised in 1958 in India but there is, apparently, none in Pakistan's Army. Formation of one is, however, under active consideration.

Provost duties within India were normally performed by British NCOs of the Corps of Military Police. Indian troops, all volunteers, were subject only to regimental policemen. Notwithstanding, the Corps of Military Police (India) was formed on 20 Jul 42, with its centre at Secunderabad. The CMP(I) was destined to form part of the post-war Indian Army and, indeed, did so in independent India. Before Partition, it became the Corps of Indian Military Police and, after August 1947, its Pakistani partner was the Corps of Pakistan Military Police. In March 1948, the CPMP was disbanded as uneconomical and provost duties were run from the Military Police Wing at the School of Infantry but unspecified difficulties arose and the CPMP was re-raised on 1 Feb 49. Following republican status, both Corps are now simply CMP.

The Willcox Committee was strongly in favour of the formation of an Indian Army Physical Training Corps. Until then, Physical Training Instructors had been regimental NCOs and PT specialisation had meant that they frequently forfeited promotion. A separate corps would ensure a career-structure. Accordingly, the IAPTC was formed on 1 Jul 46. After partition, the Corps continued in India, becoming the APTC after Republic Day in January 1950 but no such counterpart appears to have survived in Pakistan.

An Indian Pioneer Corps was raised during the Second World War and amounted to some 400 pioneer companies, a total of about 175,000 men and 1,500,000 civilian labourers employed directly under the War Department, and a part was organised into civil labour units. The officers, VCOs and NCOs of the Corps were purely non-technical supervisors and disciplinarians. The Corps survives in today's army in India as the Pioneer Corps but not, apparently, in Pakistan.

Mention was made earlier in connection with the RIASC of the Indian Catering Corps. This was created in May 1945 in order to improve and standardise the levels of military cooking. The Willcox Committee Report understates the case thus

'. . . has long deserved more attention in the Army in India than it has received.'

Bearing in mind the ready market for good cooks in the country, the report saw no problems in recruitment. It did, however, foresee problems of clawing them back from civilian life in the event of reservist-recall so recommended a fifteen-year regular engagement with no reserve liability! The short-lived ICC was absorbed into the RIASC on 1 Sep 48 and it had no counterpart in the Army of Pakistan.

The well-known Indian Army Corps of Clerks was actually born on 1 Feb 24

(AI(I)352/23) as the Indian Corps of Clerks but was subsequently restyled to stress its military role. Originally, it consisted of British military clerks and Indian civilian clerks. The latter remained thus until 1942 'when optional militarisation was introduced'. The total combined pre-war strength was about 700, to be increased ten-fold during the 1939–45 War. After Partition, the Corps was split, the IACC being absorbed into the RIASC on 1 Feb 49 and the PACC continuing its independence.

The Pakistan Army's corps trained military clerks who, once in their appointed unit, then became part of that unit, badged accordingly. An Army Clerical Corps was later raised to supply senior secretarial and Personal Assistant staff to formation and static headquarters, the ACC personnel wearing the new Corps' badge. The ACC still continues to train the subordinate unit-clerks before their appointments.

No postal service normally existed for the Indian Army in peacetime but emergency facilities were set up to meet specific needs in times of war when censorship was imposed or postal concessions granted. During the 1939–45 war, the Army's postal service was staffed by some 4,300 men, the majority of them from the Indian Posts and Telegraphs, the balance, although trained by the army, to be employed by Posts and Telegraphs after demobilisation. They were enlisted into the Indian General Service Corps (formed in 1939 to parent mostly the non-combatant personnel on the army's strength) but the Willcox Committee Report, which saw no logic in having postal affairs parented to the sappers – as in the British Army – recommended that they be part of the RIASC. Post-Partition, India raised the Army Postal Service, still composed of volunteers from the Posts and Telegraphs but now combatants, trained by the Army. Pakistan has no such service and its Army's postal services in times of war, are managed by the Army Educational Corps.

Finally, a creation of the 1939–45 War was the Woman's Auxiliary Corps (India), generally abbreviated to WAC(I), rendered 'Wack-eye' in conversation. By 1945, its strength had risen to 1,160 officers and 8,900 other ranks. It was not exclusively an Army auxiliary but also served to a lesser extent the Royal Indian Navy and the Royal Indian Air Force. The Corps' responsibilities covered clerical and secretarial duties in static headquarters and extended to cipher and signals duties in rear areas. Recruitment was markedly restricted by the peculiarities of female society in India and out of every eight auxiliaries, one was European, three Anglo-Indian, three Indian Christian, and only one a non-Christian Indian. The Willcox Committee Report could see no future for the Corps in a post-war Indian Army but suggested the retention of a Territorial Army element as a cadre for wartime expansion.

10. INDIA'S ARMY AFTER PARTITION

As a result of Partition in August 1947, the unthinkable decision to split the Indian Army between the two new dominions of India and Pakistan had to be thought of and plans had to be made quickly. In broad terms, the army was to be divided in a 2:1 ratio. Clearly, no solution could be ideal and there were complaints that Pakistan had been given all the training-areas and the traditional cantonments whilst India had the arms and equipment-manufacturers. This however, was a situation dictated by geography and could only be remedied by time.

Shortly after Partition, the remaining British officers in Indian service were removed from active commands, Indian officers were promoted and the Britons moved to staff posts. This was not only good for young Indian officers who, in many cases, received accelerated promotion, but when Indian units were later engaged with Pakistan troops, the prospect of British-officered units in conflict was removed. It was bad enough that senior Indian and Pakistan officers had probably been on the same commissioning course at Dehra Dun in the 1930's, a situation which occurred as late as 1971 in the Bangladesh action.

President's Bodyguard

Headquarters: NEW DELHI

The old Governor-General's (Viceroy's) Bodyguard became, on India's attaining republican status, the President's Bodyguard. The Sikh element remaining after Partition had been reinforced and, after the fashion of its viceregal predecessor, its' personnel underwent parachute training in 1960 and the Bodyguard became an airborne reconnaissance squadron. It's new badge was crossed lances, a winged parachute across the intersection, the lions of Ashoka above and the letters PBG below.

Cavalry/Armour

Centre: AHMADNAGAR, Maharashtra (formerly Bombay Presidency)

Of the twenty-one cavalry regiments in the Indian Army, India received fourteen, as follows:

Skinner's Horse (1st Duke of York's Own Cavalry)
2nd Royal Lancers (Gardner's Horse)
3rd Cavalry
Hodson's Horse (4th Duke of Cambridge's Own Lancers)
7th Light Cavalry
8th King George V's Own Light Cavalry
Royal Deccan Horse (9th Horse)
Scinde Horse (14th Prince of Wales's Own Cavalry)

15th Lancers
16th Light Cavalry
Poona Horse (17th Queen Victoria's Own Cavalry
18th King Edward VII's Own Cavalry
20th Lancers
Central India Horse

The Willcox Committee which submitted its report in 1945, making plans and recommendations for a post-war Indian Army, had indicated that some reductions should take place, especially in the cavalry line. The 3rd Cavalry, the 19th King George V's Own Lancers and the Central India Horse had been nominated for disbandment. Partition, of course, took place and few of the projected reforms were implemented. The 19th Lancers went to Pakistan and the 20th Lancers, a training-regiment since 1937, was promptly activated by India as a field force unit.

In January 1950, India became a republic and a number of regimental titles were changed with the removal of the names of British royalty: badges which embodied the crown or the Garter or the royal patron's name also had to be changed. The new titles became:

1st Horse
2nd Lancers
3rd Cavalry
4th Horse
7th Light Cavalry
8th Light Cavalry
9th Horse
14th Horse
15th Lancers
16th Light Cavalry
17th Horse
18th Cavalry
20th Lancers
Central India Horse

The old titles such as Skinner's , Gardner's, Hodson's, etc are still in common currency, however.

Skinner's Horse forsook the crown on their badge and replaced it with a mounted figure: their unique motto remained, as did the white rose, an uncontroversial reminder of a previous royal link. A Skinner commanded the Regiment as late as the 1960's. The 2nd Lancers (Gardner's Horse) substituted an annalus for the Garter and replaced the crown with the lions of Ashoka. The annalus bears the title 'Second Lancers G.H.'. The 3rd Cavalry, returned from Japanese hands, was reconstituted and its badge remains as before except for the substitution of the lions of Ashoka for the crown. The 4th Horse did the same, retaining the title scroll 'Hodson's Horse'. The old 7th Light Cavalry had a crown on the intersection of their crossed lances and this was simply replaced by the lions of Ashoka but the 8th had been King George V's Own so that the letters 'KGO' had to be removed. In place of the crown, there appeared the mailed fist of the Armoured Corps whilst the scroll below the numeral read 'Light Cavalry'. The Garter had been the principal feature of the Royal Deccan Horse's badge and this was replaced by a circle bearing an inscription in Hindi: the crown gave way to the lions of Ashoka and the central 'RDH' monogram was discarded in favour of the numeral '9'. The title-scroll below reads 'The Deccan Horse'. Socialised India has not yet evolved an overt way to reward its favoured regiments and one Indian military adviser in London used always to refer to his regiment with its 'Royal' prefix although he only joined it after January 1950. In the light of its title perhaps it was surprising that The Scinde Horse did not go to Pakistan in 1947: however, they were a Prince of Wales' Own regiment so the letters 'PWO' on their badge had to go. Notwithstanding, a senior officer of the Regiment, on a course in the UK in 1966, received an invitation to the installation of HRH The Prince Charles as Prince of Wales at Caernarvon Castle.

The 16th Light Cavalry simply traded their crown for the lions of Ashoka. Queen Victoria's Royal Cypher and Garter had to be given up by The Poona Horse but they were fortunate in having the Hand of God, captured almost a century before in Persia and this fitted into an oval bearing a Hindi inscription: the new, shortened title appeared on the scroll below and the familiar lions of Ashoka above. King Edward VII's Own had been the title of the 18th Cavalry but the badge bore the plumes from his period as Prince of Wales and these were removed, yielding place to the lions of Ashoka. However, although the plumes and the associated coronet were removed, the two flanking 'Ich dien' scrolls were left behind with the result that these now flank the lions. Both the 20th Lancers and the Central India Horse simply replaced the crown on their badges with the lions of Ashoka.

The remaining states forces' horsed cavalry units were reorganised in 1951 as under:

(a) Gwalior Lancers – formed by amalgamation of the 1st and 2nd Gwalior Lancers
(b) Jodhpur/Kachhawa Horse, formed by amalgamation of the Jodhpur Lancers, the Kachhawa Horse, Dungar Lancers, Mangal Lancers, Mewar Lancers and Rajendra Lancers
(c) Mysore Lancers
(d) B Sqn 2nd Patiala Lancers
(e) Saurashtra Horsed Cavalry Squadron

During May 1953, Army Headquarters decided to disband all the above and to raise one new horsed regiment instead at Gwalior on 1 Aug 53. Subsequently, the unit location was changed to Jaipur and the regiment has remained there since, the squadrons patrolling the deserts of Rajasthan. The first commanding officer was Lieut. Colonel Phulel Singh (ex-Jammu & Kashmir State forces) and he assumed command of the New Horsed Cavalry Regiment on 19 Nov 53. This frankly uninspired title was, fortunately, short-lived and they became 61 Cavalry in Jan 54. The double-headed eagle of their badge derives from their Mysore past.

The 62nd Cavalry was raised in Jul 56 and the 63rd on 2 Jan 57. At the time of the 1965 War, the 45th Cavalry was being re-raised for the third time. It had first been raised in 1918 and disbanded the following year. It was raised again in 1941 and disbanded on 31 May 46. The 65th and 66th Cavalry were both raised on 1 Sep 66 but were redesignated 65th and 66th Armoured Regiments in Jan 67: thereafter, all new raisings were to be styled 'armoured regiments' although many of their badges were to be in the traditional cavalry style. The next five years saw seven more regiments formed, reaching into the seventies. Subsequently the 80th Armoured Regiment heralded the 'eighties' series and, more recently the familiar 'forties' series was resuscitated yet again.

The 'missing numbers' in the cavalry line after Partition were left vacant but, in the last few years, India has re-raised her own 5th, 6th, 10th, 11th, 12th and 19th Armoured Regiments to fill the gaps left by Probyn's Horse, 6th DCO Lancers, Guides Cavalry, PAVO, Sam Browne's Cavalry and 19 KGO Lancers who all went to Pakistan.

The 1990–91 copy of the International Insititute of Strategic Studies, publication 'The Military Balance' records India as having 56 tank regiments.

BATTLE HONOURS – (POST 1947)

1 Horse	Harar Kalan, Punjab 1971
2 Lancers	Punjab 1965
3 Cavalry	Asal Uttar, Punjab 1965, Shahjra, Punjab 1971
4 Horse	Phillora, Punjab 1965, Basantar River. Punjab 1971
7 Light Cavalry	Naushera, Jhanger, Zoji La, Jammu & Kashmir 1947–48. Punjab 1965. Mian Bazar, Punjab 1971, East Pakistan 1971
8 Light Cavalry	Punjab 1965
9 Horse	Asal Uttar, Punjab 1965
14 Horse	Dograi, Punjab 1965, Malakpur, Punjab 1971
16 Light Cavalry	Punjab 1965
17 Horse	Phillora, Buttur Dograndi, Punjab 1965. Basantar River, Punjab 1971
18 Cavalry	Tilakpur-Mahadipur, Punjab 1965, Jammu & Kashmir, 1965
20 Lancers	Jammu & Kashmir 1965
Central India Horse	Rajauri, Jammu & Kashmir 1947–47, Burki, Punjab 1965
45 Cavalry	Darsana, East Pakistan 1971
63 Cavalry	Bogra, East Pakistan 1971
66 Armoured Regt	Punjab 1971
69 Armoured Regt	Bogra, East Pakistan 1971
72 Armoured Regt	Chhamb, Jammu & Kashmir 1971
75 Armoured Regt	Jammu & Kashmir 1971

BOOKS

'Sworn to die' by Lieut. Colonel M A R Skinner (Pub. Lancer International, New Delhi, 1984) (Skinner's Horse)

'A squire of Hindoostan' by Major Narindar Saroop OBE (Pub. Nottingham Court Press London 1983) (2nd Lancers)

'Indian Armour' by Major General Gurcharn Singh Sandhu PVSM (Pub. Vision Books, New Delhi 1987)

'We lead – 7th Light Cavalry 1784–1990' by Lieut Col. C L Proudfoot (Pub. Lancer International, Delhi 1991)

'I serve – The Eighteenth Cavalry' by Maj Gen Gurcharn Singh Sandhu PVSM (Pub. Lancer International, Delhi 1991)

Infantry

One of the few implementations of the report by the Willcox Committee in October 1945 was the removal of the numbers from the titles of the infantry regiments, except, of course, in the cases of the Punjab Regiments and the re-styling of the Bombay Grenadiers as the Indian Grenadiers.

Of the nineteen pre-war line infantry regiments, India received eleven: she also retained six of the ten regiments of Gurkha Rifles plus four war-raised regiments.

Thus, her infantry line-up on Partition was as under:

Punjab Regiment (previously the 2nd Punjab Regt)
Madras Regiment
Indian Grenadiers
Mahratta Light Infantry
Rajputana Rifles
Rajput Regiment
Jat Regiment
Sikh Regiment
Dogra Regiment
Royal Garhwal Rifles
Kumaon Regiment (previously the 19th Hyderabad Regt)
Sikh Light Infantry } War-raised
Assam Regiment } War-raised
Bihar Regiment } War-raised
Mahar Regiment } War-raised
1st King George V's Own Gurkha Rifles
3rd Queen Alexandra's Own Gurkha Rifles
4th Prince of Wales' Own Gurkha Rifles
5th Royal Gurkha Rifles (Frontier Force)
8th Gurkha Rifles
9th Gurkha Rifles

Raised subsequently were the following:

Brigade of Guards
Parachute Regiment
Mechanised Infantry Regiment
Jammu & Kashmir Rifles
Naga Regiment
Jammu & Kashmir Light Infantry
11th Gurkha Rifles

The first three were raised by conversion of existing battalions as will be seen subsequently but this experience has dictated that any such future raising be done by direct recruitment. Officers and men in, say, 1st Bn Rajputana Rifles found themselves suddenly 3rd Bn Guards in 1949 and, thus, had a tendency towards divided loyalties. Four senior battalions were shanghaied to form The Brigade of the Guards initially and these battalions have not always been replaced by their own regiments. Despite what it may say in their regimental histories about its being an honour to lose their 1st Battalion to the Guards, Para or Mech Inf, that is not the regiment's true feeling. During operations in

Bangladesh in 1971, older Indian officers with Frontier Force origins were secretly amused to see an uppity Guards battalion suffer a setback at the hands of Pakistani Piffers.

The Brigade of The Guards

Centre: KAMPTEE, Madhya Pradesh (formerly Central Provinces)

Within two years after Partition, on 27 Apr 49, the first public announcement was made that the Indian Army was to have a Guards Brigade, modelled on the British Brigade of Guards, and which was to be considered as the cream of the army. It was to be an 'all class mixed' regiment, open to all nationals of India plus Gorkhas. Credit for the creation of the new regiment was attributed to General KM Cariappa OBE, the then Commander-in-Chief who felt that India should have something akin to similar bodies elsewhere and he is reported to have selected the first officers himself.

The training wing was first located in Delhi Cantonment, on 6 Jun 50, sharing the Rajputana Rifles Regimental Centre until 11 Jun 56 when, in its own right as a regimental centre, it moved to Kota where it remained for twenty years, until it moved to its present location at Kamptee (near Nagpur) in November 1976.

The uniform for the new regiment was to be distinctive and all ranks were identified by embroidered gold on red cloth titles 'The Guards' worn on the upper arm. Officers have a special blue cloth peaked cap, almost indistinguishable from that worn by officers of the Welsh Guards together with a scarlet cravat. Initially, special Guards drill was evolved but, in 1956, this was abandoned 'for the sake of simplicity' and the Brigade reverted to normal infantry drill.

The first four battalions accredited to the new Brigade of the Guards were old battalions from line infantry regiments – 2 Punjab, 1 Grenadiers, 1 Rajputana Rifles and 1 Rajput. All of them had had fine service records in the Second World War, thereby conferring on the new regiment an impressive collection of instant battle honours. It was, after all, to be the senior infantry regiment. Two subsequent raisings, The Parachute Regiment and The Mechanised Infantry Regiment were to follow, pushing the old regiments further down the precedence-ladder.

The badge chosen was Garuda, the King of Birds, a figure from Hindu mythology. Garuda, reputedly an inhabitant of the mountains, was said to have been ridden by the gods and his figure, with outstretched wings, stands above a title-scroll.

The first battalion to become Guards was 1 Raj Rif and they were designated 3 Guards on 10 Aug 49. The second was 1 Rajput, who became 4 Guards on 25 Jan 50.

The post of senior battalion in the senior regiment in the army was filled on 1 Apr 51 when 2 Punjab took the post of honour, their first battalion having already gone to The Parachute Regiment. Finally, on 1 Aug 52, 1 Grenadiers became 2 Guards.

Succeeding battalions after the fourth were raised from direct recruitment and not by conversion of entire existing battalions.

By the time of the Indo-Pakistan War in 1971, there were fourteen battalions in existence and eight of them saw active service in that campaign.

Mechanisation is under way and those battalions now converted are appropriately styled: thus, the fourth battalion is known cryptically as 4 Guards (1 Rajput) (Mech).

Current regimental strength rests at nineteen battalions, the latest one 19 Guards (ATGM) – an anti-tank guided missile regiment.

BATTLE HONOURS

Afghanistan 1879–80, China 1900, France and Flanders 1915, Egypt 1915. Megiddo, Mesopotamia 1914–18, Keren, Donbaik, Kangaw, Burma 1942–45, Castle Hill, Cassino, Italy 1943–45.

Post 1947

Naushera, Gurais, Jammu & Kashmir 1947–48, Burki, Punjab 1965, Gadra Road, Shingo River Valley Rajasthan 1965, Sylhet, Hilli, Akhawra, Ganga Sagar, Jammu & Kashmir 1971, East Pakistan 1971.

BOOKS

'The Invincible Garuda – Brigade of the Guards 1949–90' by Col R D Palsokar MC (Regtl Centre 1990)

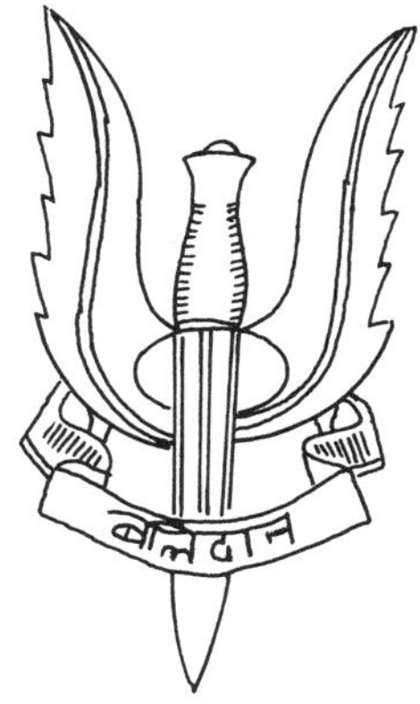

The Parachute Regiment

Centre: **AGRA, Uttar Pradesh** (formerly United Provinces)

Partition left India with an airborne division headquarters, two parachute brigade headquarters, and six parachute battalions, all the latter converted battalions of established old regiments.

Action against Pakistan's ambitions in Jammu and Kashmir in 1947 left India little time to reorganise and, indeed, interior economy was called for to reconstitute three of those battalions. Three of them, 2 (Para) Madras, 3 (Para) Mahratta LI and 1 (Para) Kumaon were class battalions and, thus, effectively intact but 1 (Para) Punjab (late 1/2nd Punjab Regt), 4 (Para) Raj Rif and 3 (Para) Rajput had all had Muslim companies which had gone to Pakistan.

After the cease-fire in Kashmir, at midnight on 1 Jan 49, HQ 50 Parachute Brigade moved to Ranchi. The Parachute Training School before Partition had been at Chaklala, now in Pakistan and it was not until November 1949 that a start was made on establishing a new Training School at Agra. As a measure of the parachuting potential of 50 Para Bde, after its consolidation at Ranchi, it had 2,554 men who had not jumped. At this time, the Brigade was part of 5 Infantry Division but in August 1949 it became an independent command. In 1950, the Brigade commander, Brigadier K. Bhagwati Singh went to the UK to study the post-war structure of British airborne forces. After five months at Aldershot, the home then of 16 Indep Para Bde of the British Army and still the headquarters of Airborne Forces, the Brigadier submitted a report in April 1951, establishing his requirements to set up a Parachute Regiment and an Airborne Forces Depot on the same lines as the British pattern. Made up of mixed classes, it would accept infantry volunteers from any regiment in the army. India would use the C119, Fairchild Packet for parachuting but parachutes would be produced indigenously. A parachute brigade group was envisaged with an armoured squadron and this would contain 1 (Para) Punjab, 3 (Para) Maratha LI and 1 (Para) Kumaon. It had already been decided that 2 (Para) Madras, 4 (Para) Raj Rif and 3 (Para) Rajput would revert to a normal infantry role as would 77 Para Bde HQ.

The formation of the Parachute Regiment was approved in June 1951 but the birth of the new regiment did not take place until 15 Apr 52. On that day, the three existing infantry battalions were restyled: 1 (Para) Punjab became 1st Bn Parachute Regiment, 3 (Para) Maratha LI became 2nd Bn Parachute Regiment and 1 (Para) Kumaon became the 3rd Bn Parachute Regiment. The maroon beret continued to be worn as did the previous regimental dress distinctions, the latter until specifically Parachute Regiment items should be devised to replace them.

The 1st Bn was actually the most senior battalion in the entire army and not disposed to yield the honour. Such was its pride and that of the other two battalions that suffixes were permitted to battalion titles, indicating their origins. Thus, the first bore '(Punjab)' after its title, the second '(Maratha)' and the third '(Kumaon)'.

However, as the new Regiment was to be of mixed classes, the first new recruit intake was to consist of classes other than those already serving. Jats went to the 1st, Gorkhas to the 2nd, and Garhwalis to the 3rd.

At this stage, the new regimental badge was devised, the spread wings flanking an open parachute with an upright bayonet between the wings, all in white metal. Also to be replaced was the formation-sign, instead of the old, British wartime blue Pegasus, the winged horse with Bellerophon, his rider, on a maroon square – chosen as being the first airborne warrior. Hindu mythology was plumbed and Shatrujeet was found. This winged figure, half-horse half-man, the latter part holding a bow, its string fully stretched, ready to fire his arrow seemed suitable. King Shatrujeet, a Puranic monarch and his favourite mount, Kuvalaya were inseparable and the King was said to have slain a fearsome demon with a divinely gifted arrow whilst riding Kuvalaya. Legend combined them into one being, a happy chance for the committee of colonels looking for a new and appropriate device. Worn in maroon and blue, it is easily mistaken for the sign that it replaced!

British parachute-qualification pattern wings continued to be worn and are still in use.

The policy on mixed classes adopted in 1952 had not proved wholly successful and, in 1957, recruitment changed to a zonal basis, thus:

1 Para – All North India classes, excluding hill-tribes
2 Para – All South India classes and Bengalis
3 Para – Hill tribes

In June 1961, the make-up was changed yet again, to safeguard the interests of the older classes and minimum quotas were laid down as under:

1 Para – 25% Dogras
25% Sikhs
50% other plains classes

2 Para – 50% Marathas
50% { Mahars
South Indians
Bengalis }

3 Para – 50% Kumaonis
50% remaining hill classes

The parent regiment distinctions had continued until 1960 and, finally, in January 1963, the distinctive suffixes were removed.

In the meantime, 1 Aug 61 saw the birth of the 4th Bn at Agra, to be made up of class companies 25% each Gorkhas, Dogras, Garhwalis and South Indians.

The China War in 1961 prompted more new raising, the 5th Bn at Kota on 1 Jan 63 (one company each of Rajputs, Marathas, Ahirs and Kumaonis) and the 6th Bn at Agra on 1 Feb 63 (one company each of Sikhs [other than Mazhbis and Ramdassias], Gujars, Rajputs and Dogras).

The 7th was raised on 1 Oct 64 at Agra (one company each Bengalis, Oriyas, Rajputs and Jats) and, three months later, on 1 Jan 65, also at Agra, the 8th Bn came into being with one company each of Mazhbi and Ramdassia Sikhs, Gujars, Garhwalis and Gorkhas.

During operations against Pakistan in September 1965, a volunteer commando was raised under a Brigade of Guards officer and, in July 1966, a nucleus from this unit was used as a basis on which to raise 9th Bn as a para-commando at Gwalior. Less than a year later, also at Gwalior, the 10th Bn was raised, composed of Rajasthanis. The 9th eventually came to be made up of men from Jammu and Kashmir, Himachal, Punjab, Haryana and Delhi. They officially became 9th and 10th Para Commandos in 1969. Personnel of the Para-Commandos wear on the breast pocket a metal badge depicting the winged sword, identical in format to the badge of the British Special Air Service but the motto scroll in Hindi translates as 'The Bold'. Subsequently, the 1st Bn also became a para-commando.

The question of class-composition within battalions had long been a subject for partisan discussion and the British had chosen to establish the class-company system in 1858 after the Great Mutiny.

After a seven-year trial of that system within the new regiment, a battalion commanders' conference in October 1970 opted to revert to mixed composition within companies from 1 Jan 71 without disturbing the overall ratio of classes in the battalions, a seemingly acceptable compromise.

77 Bde was not to be re-activated in a parachute role when the time came to raise another brigade headquarters. In 1965, the 51st Independent Para Bde was created to embrace 1, 7 and 8 Para as first formed.

Somewhat unusually, on 16 Nov 75, 8 Para was transferred as a battalion, becoming the 16th Bn The Mahar Regiment. Subsequently, on 2 Apr 79, 16 Mahar was transferred to become 12 Mech Inf Regt. (16 Mahar).

Bandsmen of the Regiment are parachute-trained, unlike the British Parachute Regiment where they are not required to jump: only the British battalions' Corps of Drums are trained parachutists.

In almost all other respects, a visitor to Agra from Aldershot would find few differences.

BATTLE HONOURS

Keren, Berbera, Abyssinia 1940–41, British Somaliland 1940, Mersa Matruh, North Africa 1940–43, Monte della Gordace, Il Castello, Pratelle Pass, San Martino Sogliano, Monte Farneto, Monte Cavallo, Idice Bridgehead, Italy 1943–45, The Shweli, Magwe, Kama, Sittang 1945, Burma 1942–45.

Post 1947

Srinagar, Naushera, Jhanger, Punch, Jammu & Kashmir 1947–48, Hajipur, Jammu & Kashmir 1965, Defence of Punch, Chachro, Poongli Bridge, Sindh 1971, East Pakistan 1971.

The Second World War honours, of course, were gained by battalions of the old line infantry regiments which later went to form the Parachute Regiment. The honour 'Sangshak', for an action in Upper Burma in March 1944 in which 50 Indian Parachute Brigade earned particular distinction, was awarded to 4 Maratha LI which was under command of the brigade at that time but has not been granted to The Parachute Regiment. The argument has been put forward that the Indian Parachute Regiment which made up 50 Ind Para Bde is not the same regiment as was formed in April 1952 and thus the honour is not appropriate. However, there would seem to be ample precedent for such a grant: the Sikh Light Infantry was awarded the honours of the old Sikh Pioneers and one feels that most of today's Parachute Regiment would be very pleased to carry the honour gained by India's first parachute soldiers in such a significant action.

BOOKS

'India's Paratroopers' by Major K C Praval (Leo Cooper, London, 1975)

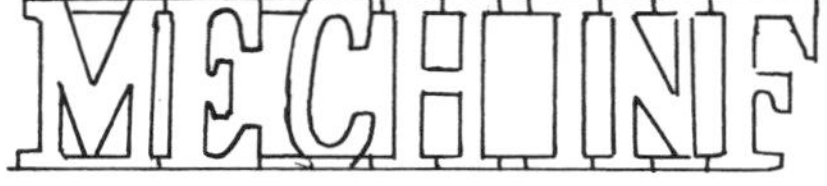

The Mechanised Infantry Regiment

Centre: **AHMADNAGAR, Maharashtra (formerly Bombay Presidency)**

India's most recently-created regiment takes third place in the Infantry of the Line after the Brigade of Guards and the Parachute Regiment.

Armoured Personnel Carriers were introduced into the Indian Army in the late 1960's and some of the oldest regiments had battalions equipped with these Russian vehicles. These units served as APC battalions in the Indo-Pakistan war of 1971 but it was not until 1 Apr 79 that The Mechanised Infantry Regiment was formed initially with fourteen battalions, including six 1st Battalions of historic regiments.

With its regimental centre at Ahmadnagar, the home also of the Armoured Corps, the Regiment went on to raise nine more battalions – now pure Mech Inf battalions with no other loyalties – and it was on 24 Feb 88 that the President of India presented twenty-four regimental colours, one to each battalion and one to the centre, surely a Commonwealth record.

Equipped with BMP (Boyowaya Machina Products), Russian infantry combat vehicles, the regiment claims these to be superior to the similar range of M113 series of combat vehicles developed by the USA and supplied to Pakistan. They are fitted with first and second-generation anti-tank guided missiles with ranges of more than three kilometres. A 30mm cannon is also carried. Besides the commander and crew, the vehicle carries eight infantrymen. The vehicle is amphibious and has an angle of climb of 40 degrees. Both BMP1 and BMP2 are to be produced in Indian under licence.

The badge chosen for the new regiment is an APC surmounted by an upward-pointing bayonet with title-scroll below.

Details of the battalions of the regiment are as follows:

1 Mech Inf (1 Madras)
2 Mech Inf (1 Jat Light Infantry)
3 Mech Inf (1/8 Gorkha Rifles)
4 Mech Inf (1 Sikh)
5 Mech Inf (14 Kumaon)
6 Mech Inf (1 Garhwal Rif)
7 Mech Inf (1 Dogra)
8 Mech Inf (7 Punjab)
9 Mech Inf (7 Grenadiers)
10 Mech Inf (20 Maratha LI)
11 Mech Inf (18 Raj Rif)
12 Mech Inf (16 Mahar)
13 Mech Inf (18 Rajput)
14 Mech Inf (16 Jammu & Kashmir Rif)
15 – 23 Mech Inf (inclusive) are newly-raised battalions originating after the birth of the new regiment as under:
15 Bn – raised 15 Dec 81 at Ahmadnagar
16 Bn – raised 1 Jan 82 at Aurangabad
17 Bn (Reconnaissance & Support) – raised 15 Nov 82 at Aurangabad
18 Bn – raised 1 Mar 83 at Ahmadnagar
19 Bn (Reconnaissance & Support) – raised 15 Sep 83
20 Bn – raised 1 Mar 84 at Ahmadnagar
21 Bn – raised 1 Mar 84 at Nowgong
22 Bn – raised 1 Mar 84 at Nowgong
23 Bn (Reconnaissance & Support) at Akhnoor

The old regiments which contributed battalions were not always, it must be confessed, disposed to regard this as an honour and the missing battalions have not all been re-raised.

BATTLE HONOURS
None.

BOOKS
None known.

The Punjab Regiment

Centre: **RAMGARH, Bihar**

The only one of the six Punjab Regiments to go to India in August 1947 on Partition was not destined to remain as India's senior infantry regiment for long.

The Brigade of Guards, raised in 1949, was given precedence; in 1952, The Parachute Regiment was created and placed second to The Guards. Finally, in 1979, The Mechanised Infantry Regiment was created and ranked after The Parachute Regiment. Not only did these raisings put The Punjab Regiment into fourth place but, to add insult to injury, its two senior battalions were taken for the Paras and Guards respectively whilst the war-raised 7th Battalion became the 8th Bn Mechanised Infantry Regiment (7 Punjab).

On Partition, the badge of the old 2nd Punjab Regiment had only to change its title scroll. The galley of the old 69th Punjabis now sits above a scroll reading 'Punjab Regiment'. In January 1950, no change was necessary since no crown or imperial devices were borne.

1st Battalion (old 67th Punjabis) – redesignated 1st Bn Parachute Regiment (Punjab) 15 Apr 52
2nd Battalion (old 69th Punjabis) – redesignated 1st Bn Brigade of Guards 1 Apr 51
3rd Battalion (old 72nd Punjabis)
The 4th Bn, disbanded by the British in 1938 when a Muslim soldier ran amok, was not re-raised by an independent India.
7th Battalion – raised 5 May 41. Redesignated 8th Bn Mechanised Infantry Regiment (7 Punjab) on 2 Apr 81
8th Battalion – raised 15 Jan 42. Disbanded 28 Aug 46. Re-raised.
9th Battalion – raised 16 Jan 48
13th (Jind) Battalion – Jind Infantry (a State Forces unit raised in 1887) absorbed and redesignated 13th (Jind) Bn The Punjab Regiment 26 Jan 54
14th (Nabha) Battalion – Nabha Akal Infantry (a State Forces unit raised in 1757) absorbed and redesignated 14th (Nabha) Bn The Punjab Regiment 26 Jun 54
15th (Patiala) Battalion – 1st Patiala Infantry (a state Forces unit raised in

1783) absorbed and redesignated 15th (Patiala) Bn. The Punjab Regiment 25 Jun 54

16th (Patiala) Battalion – 2nd Patiala Infantry (a State Forces unit raised in 1710) absorbed and redesignated 16th (Patiala) Bn The Punjab Regiment 26 Jan 54

The 17th and subsequently-numbered battalions were all new raisings from 1962.

BATTLE HONOURS (Post 1947)

Naushera, Jhanger, Zoji La, Punch, Jammu & Kashmir 1947–48, Dograi, Tilakpur-Mahadipur, Burki, Haji Pir, Kalidhar, Punjab 1965, Jammu & Kashmir 1965, Longanewala, Nanga Tekri, Brachil Pass and Wali Malik, Punjab 1971, Sindh 1971, East Pakistan 1971.

BOOKS

'By land and sea. The post-Independence history of The Punjab Regiment' by Brig V R Raghavan AVSM (Regimental Centre – 1986).

The Madras Regiment

Centre: **WELLINGTON, Tamil Nadu.** (previously Madras Presidency)

The Madras Regiment, reformed in 1942 from its Territorial battalions, was destined to remain in the order of battle of independent India. Its battalions had been granted the traditions of previous Madras regiments and a black pom-pom once worn by the old Coast Army, is now worn both in the beret and in the full-dress pagri adopted in 1979. The badge is the pattern approved by HM the King-Emperor in 1946 but the crown has been replaced by the lions of Ashoka. The

Centre is located in what are now known as Shrinagesh Barracks although street-signs still point the way to Wellington Barracks.

1st Battalion (old 73rd Carnatic Infantry) – redesignated 1st Bn Mechanised Infantry Regiment (1 Madras) in 1979
2nd Battalion (old 75th Carnatic Infantry)
3rd Battalion (old 79th Carnatic Infantry) – disbanded 18 May 50. Re-raised 1 Mar 62
4th Battalion (old 83rd Wallajahbad Light Infantry)
5th Battalion – raised 15 May 43. Disbanded Jan 47. Re-raised 1 Jan 63
6th Battalion – raised 15 May 43. Disbanded Feb 47. Re-raised 1 Oct 63
7th Battalion – raised 15 May 43. Disbanded 1950. Re-raised 1 Apr 64
8th Battalion – raised 20 Aug 48
9th (Travancore) Battalion – 1st Bn Travancore Infantry (a State Forces unit raised in 1819) absorbed and redesignated 9th (Travancore) Bn The Madras Regiment May 54
11th Battalion (old Territorial battalion) – re-raised 1 Jul 80.
12th Battalion (old Territorial Battalion) – re-raised 1 Jan 81.
16th (Travancore) Battalion – 2nd Bn Travancore Infantry (a State Forces unit raised in 1901) absorbed and redesignated 16th (Travancore) Bn The Madras Regiment May 54
17th (Cochin) Battalion – 1st Bn Cochin Infantry (a State Forces unit raised in 1900) absorbed and redesignated 17th (Cochin) Bn The Madras Regiment May 54
18th (Mysore) Battalion – 1st Bn Mysore Infantry (a State Forces unit) absorbed and redesignated 18th (Mysore) Bn The Madras Regiment May 54
19th Battalion – raised 15 Jan 66
25th Battalion (old garrison battalion) – raised 15 Sep 42. Disbanded. Re-raised 1 Oct 66
26th Battalion (old garrison battalion) – raised 15 Sep 42. Disbanded. Re-raised 1 Jan 67. Took over the lineage of the old 86th Carnatic Infantry
27th Battalion (old garrison battalion) – raised in 1943. Disbanded. Re-raised 1 Jun 71
28th Battalion (old Coast defence battalion) – raised Feb 42. Disbanded 1946. Re-raised 1976

BATTLE HONOURS – POST 1947

Punch, Tithwal, Jammu & Kashmir 1947–48, Kalidhar, Maharajke, Punjab 1965, Jammu & Kashmir 1965, Basantar River, Siramani, Punjab 1971, Sindh 1971, East Pakistan 1971.

BOOKS

'The Black pom-poms' by Lieut.Colonel JR Daniel (Pub. Madras Regimental Centre 1986)

The Grenadiers

Centre: **JABALPUR, Madhya Pradesh,** (formerly Central Provinces)

In the report of the Willcox Committee in 1945, it was recommended that the old 4th Bombay Grenadiers, in addition to losing their numeral, be restyled The Indian Grenadiers. This title was made effective in November 1945 but, on India's declaring republican status, they became simply The Grenadiers, known still by their old nickname of 'The Grinders'.

The badge prescribed in Indian Army Dress Regulations 1931 was a grenade with a figure '4' on the body but this appears only to have been worn by the re-raised and war-raised battalions. The 1st and 2nd largely continued to wear the badges of the old 101st and 102nd Grenadiers. However, a brass grenade bearing the White Horse of Hanover, a traditional Grenadier emblem, was brought into use in July 1945, and this did not require to be changed in January 1950 since it was not too obviously linked with the imperial past – and even had its place in Hindu mythology. The badge is currently worn with a white hackle.

1st Battalion (old 101st Grenadiers) – redesignated 2nd Bn Brigade of Guards 1 Apr 51
2nd Battalion (old 102nd KEO Grenadiers)
3rd Battalion (old 108th Infantry) – raised 1768. Disbanded 31 Mar 30. Re-raised 1 Nov 40
4th Battalion (old 109th Infantry – raised 1788. Disbanded 31 Mar 30. Re-raised 1 Feb 41
5th Battalion (old 112th Infantry) – raised 1798. Disbanded 18 Nov 23. Re-raised 15 Oct 41. Disbanded Sep 46. Re-raised 1 Sep 60
6th Battalion – raised 1 Jul 42. Disbanded 30 Apr 43. Re-raised 1 Mar 62
7th Battalion – raised 1 Apr 49 from personnel of the Kutch and Saurashtra State Forces in camel-mounted role. Reorganised as normal infantry 29 Mar 57. Redesignated 9th Bn Mechanised Infantry Regiment (7 Grenadiers) 2 Apr 79

8th Battalion – raised 1 Apr 49 from personnel of the state forces of Lunavada, Rajpipla, Baria and Idar. Disbanded 20 Dec 49, personnel being absorbed into 7 Bn. Re-raised 1 Jan 63
9th Battalion (Mewar) – Mewar Infantry (a State Forces unit) absorbed and redesignated 9th (Mewar) Bn The Grenadiers 26 Jun 54
11th Battalion (old Territorial battalion) – redesignated 1st Bn Ajmer Regiment. Re-raised 1 Oct 63
12th Battalion – raised 1 Apr 64
13th Battalion (Ganga Jaisalmer) – redesignated 13th (Ganga Jaisalmer) Bn. The Grenadiers 5 Mar 55
14th Battalion – raised 14 Oct 43. Disbanded 1 Apr 46. Re-raised 1 Jan 65
15th Battalion – raised 1 Jan 66
16th Battalion – raised 1 Jun 66
17th Battalion (Motorised) – raised 10 Nov 66 at Bikanir, originally as a camel-mounted battalion
18th Battalion – raised 1 Mar 76
19th Battalion – raised 1 Jul 79
25th Battalion (old garrison battalion) raised 15 Aug 41. Disbanded 20 Mar 51

BATTLE HONOURS – (POST 1947)
Gurais, Asal Uttar, Punjab 1965, Jammu & Kashmir 1965, Rajasthan 1965, Jarpal, Chakra, Punjab 1971

BOOKS
'The Grenadiers – a tradition of valour' by Colonel R D Palsokar MC (Pub. Grenadiers Regimental Centre, 1980)

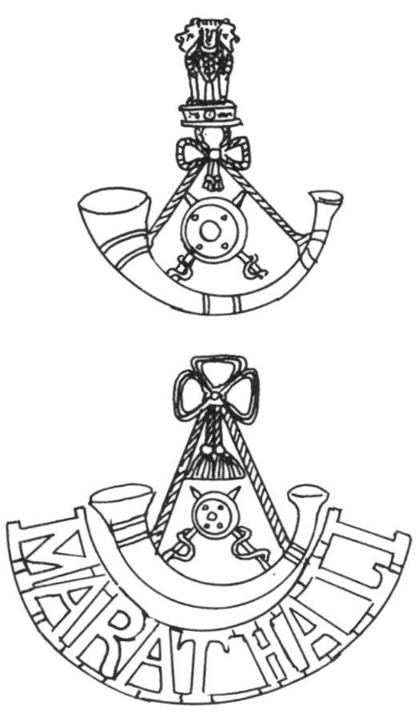

The Maratha Light Infantry

Centre: **BELGAUM, Maharashtra** (formerly Bombay Presidency)

The British-preferred spelling of Mahratta was abandoned shortly after Partition but the Regiment was one of the few to retain its old regimental centre. The old badge had to lose both the numeral '5' and the crown on India's declaring republican status: the traditional light infantry stringed bugle-horn of British Commonwealth light troops was retained, with the addition of a Maratha shield and crossed swords between the strings and the lions of Ashoka above.

1st Battalion (old 103rd Mahratta LI)
2nd Battalion (old 105th Mahratta LI) – captured at Singapore Feb 42. Re-raised 1946 by redesignation of 18 Bn
3rd Battalion (old 110th Mahratta LI) – redesignated 2 Bn Parachute Regiment (Mahratta) 15 Apr 52. Re-raised 7 Jun 69 by redesignation of 8 Bn
4th Battalion (old 116th Mahrattas)
5th Battalion (old 117th Mahrattas and a Royal battalion)
6th Battalion – raised 20 Jun 40. Disbanded. Re-raised 1 Feb 62
7th Battalion – raised 1 Aug 40. Redesignated 51 Regt Indian Armoured Corps 1 Aug 42. Re-raised 1 Jan 63
8th Battalion – raised 1 Feb 41. Redesignated 4th (Mahratta) Anti-Tank Regiment, Indian Artillery 1 Jan 42. Re-raised 1 Oct 63. Redesignated 3rd Battalion 7 Jun 69
9th Battalion – raised 1 Feb 41. Redesignated 5th (Mahratta) Anti-Tank Regiment, Indian Artillery 1 Jan 42. Re-raised 1 Oct 64
11th Battalion (old Territorial battalion) – re-raised 1 Jul 79
12th Battalion (old Territorial battalion) – re-raised late 1979
14th Battalion – raised 1 Feb 41. Disbanded. Re-raised 1 Jun 71
15th Battalion – raised 14 Sep 41 by redesignation of the 11th Bn, a Territorial battalion. Disbanded. Re-raised 1 Jun 66

16th Battalion – raised Sept 41 by redesignation of the 12 Bn, a Territorial battalion. Disbanded. Re-raised 1 Oct 66
17th Battalion – raised 15 Oct 41. Disbanded. Re-raised 15 Nov 62
18th Battalion –
19th (Kolhapur) Battalion – Kolhapur Infantry (a State Forces unit raised in 1844) absorbed and redesignated 19th (Kolhapur) Bn The Maratha Light Infantry 1957
20th (Baroda) Battalion – 1st Baroda Infantry (a State Forces unit raised in 1860) absorbed and redesignated 20th (Baroda) Bn The Maratha Light Infantry May 49. 2nd Baroda Infantry (raised in 1860) absorbed and redesignated 21st Bn May 49. Both 20th and 21st Bns merged Dec 49 to form 20th Bn. Redesignated 10th Bn Mechanised Infantry Regiment (20 Maratha LI) on 2 Apr 81
21st (Baroda) Battalion – see previous entry
22nd (Hyderabad) Battalion – 2nd Hyderabad Infantry (a State Forces unit raised in 1853) absorbed and redesignated 22nd (Hyderabad) Bn The Maratha Light Infantry 1957

BATTLE HONOURS (POST 1947)
Srinagar, Jhanger, Burki, Hussainiwala Bridge, Punjab 1965, Rajasthan 1965, Burj, Jamalpur, Suadih, Punjab 1971, East Paksitan 1971.

BOOKS
'Valour enshrined' Vol II – a history of The Maratha LI 1947–79' by C L Proudfoot (Pub. Regtl Centre, Belgaum 1980)

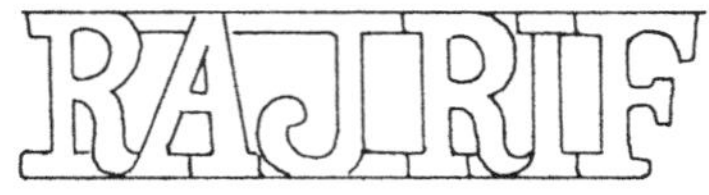

The Rajputana Rifles

Centre: **NEW DELHI, Uttar Pradesh** (formerly United Provinces)

India's senior Rifle regiment is located in Nicholson Lines in the capital and retains all the distinctive 'black-button' embellishments and characteristics of Britain's own Royal Green Jackets. There is even a suggestion, not too veiled, that there exists the same 'Black Mafia' reputation. Not long ago, eight ex-Raj Rif general officers and twelve brigadiers were in the service at the same time. Proximity to the national centre has also meant that nationalism has to be seen to be practised but 5 Bn (Napier's) still rejoices in a set of silver drums presented in 1931; the same battalion's military band has 'Marching through Georgia' for its march-past whilst the pipes and drums play 'Miss Forbes' farewell to Banff'. 4 Bn (Outram's), meanwhile, uses the Rifle Brigade's 'I'm Ninety-five' for both bands. Again, as in Britain the Regiment's officers, when promoted out to staff rank continue to wear their black belts, buttons, badges of rank etc. Following republican status, the badge was changed but only slightly: the stringed bugle-horn with the letters 'RR' within the strings lost the crown but this was replaced by crossed Rajput knives. Also retained has been the traditional use of Urquhart tartan, first approved in 1903 for wear by pipers. The traditional old Indian Army nickname of 'Large Banana Trifles' has not yet died!

1st Battalion (Wellesley's) (old 104th Wellesley's Rifles) – redesignated 3rd Bn Brigade of Guards 10 Aug 49
2nd Battalion (old 120th Rajputana Inf)
3rd Battalion (old 122nd Rajputana Inf)
4th Battalion (Outram's) (old 123rd Outram's Rifles)
5th Battalion (Napier's) (old 125th Napier's Rifles)
6th Battalion – raised 15 Jul 40
7th Battalion – raised 1 Feb 41. Captured at Singapore Feb 42. Re-raised 26 Feb 62
8th Battalion – raised 1 Feb 41. Disbanded Jul 47. Re-raised 1 Jan 63
9th Battalion – raised 1 Feb 41. Redesignated 9th (Rajputana) Light Anti-Aircraft Regiment, Indian Artillery. Re-raised 1 Apr 64
11th Battalion (old Territorial battalion) – redesignated 14 Bn 15 Sep 41. Re-raised 1 Oct 64
12th Battalion (old Territorial battalion) – redesignated 15 Bn 15 Sep 41. Re-raised by redesignation of 31 Bn 10 Feb 71
13th Battalion – raised 15 Jan 66
14th Battalion – raised Sep 41 by redesignation of 11 Bn. Disbanded Mar 47. Re-raised 1 Oct 66
15th Battalion – raised 15 Sep 41 by redesignation of 12 Bn. Disbanded Dec 46. Re-raised 15 Mar 76
16th Battalion – raised 15 Jul 42. Disbanded May 47. Re-raised 1 Jul 79
17th (Sawai Man) Battalion – The Jaipur Sawai Man Guards (a State Forces unit raised in the mid-16th Century) absorbed and redesignated the 17th (Sawai Man Guards) Bn The Rajputana Rifles 1954
18th (Saurashtra) Battalion – 1st and 2nd Bn Saurashtra State Forces absorbed and redesignated 18th (Saurashtra) Bn The Rajputana Rifles 1954 (1st Bn raised 1876: 2nd Bn raised Dec 48 by amalgamation of Bhavnagar Lancers, Bhavnagar Infantry, Dhrangadra Infantry and Porbandar Infantry). Redesignated 11th Bn The Mechanised Infantry Regiment (18 [Saurashtra] Raj Rif) 1981
19th Battalion – raised 1 Sep 62
20th Battalion – raised 1 Jan 81
31st Battalion raised 15th Jan 68. Redesignated 12 Bn 10 Feb 71

BATTLE HONOURS (POST 1947)
Punch, Jammu & Kashmir 1947–48, Asal Uttar, Charwa, Punjab 1965, Jammu & Kashmir 1965, Basantar River, Mynamati, Punjab 1971, East Pakistan 1971

BOOKS
'Traditions of a regiment' by Lieut. General AM Sethna PVSM, AVSM, and Lieut.Colonel V. Katju (Pub. Lancer International 1983)

The Rajput Regiment

Centre: **FATEHGARH, Uttar Pradesh** (formerly United Provinces)

The Rajput Regiment shares its location in Fatehgarh with the Sikh Light Infantry although, having been in the cantonment for almost seventy years, is by far the senior partner. In January 1950 it became necessary to change the regimental badge: the central Roman numbers 'VII' were replaced by crossed Rajput knives and the crown by the lions of Ashoka. The 1st Battalion, awarded an extra colour for service under Lord Lake, continues to bear an additional JCO on establishment.

1st Battalion (old 2nd QVO Rajput LI) – re-designated 4th Bn Brigade of Guards 20 Jan 50
2nd Battalion (old 4th Prince Albert Victor's Rajputs)
3rd Battalion (old 7th DCO Rajputs)
4th Battalion (old 8th Rajputs)
5th Battalion (old 11th Rajputs) – captured at Hong Kong Dec 41. Re-raised Sep 61
6th Battalion – raised 15 Jul 40. Disbanded 20 Dec 46. Re-raised 1 Jan 63
9th Battalion – formed by re-designation of the 11th – a Territorial battalion. Redesignated an Indian Artillery regiment. Re-raised
14th Battalion – formed Sep 41 by redesignation of the 12th – a Territorial battalion. Disbanded. Re-raised
15th Battalion – raised 15 Oct 41. Disbanded 15 Sep 46. Re-raised 1 Oct 63
16th Battalion – raised 15 Apr 42. Disbanded 10 Jul 46. Re-raised 1 Apr 64
17th Battalion – formed Sep 42 by re-designation of 52 Regt Indian Armoured Corps
18th Battalion (old garrison battalion) – raised 15 Aug 41. Disbanded 27 Oct 45. Re-raised 1 Jan 65. Re-designated 13th Bn Mechanised Infantry Regt (18th Rajput) 1 Mar 83
19th Battalion – Bikanir Sadul Light Infantry (a State Forces unit raised in 1461) absorbed and re-designated 19th (Bikanir) Bn The Rajput Regiment 1954
20th Battalion (Motorised) – Jodhpur Infantry (a State Forces unit raised in 1922) absorbed and re-designated 20th (Jodhpur) Bn The Rajput Regiment 1954

Subsequent raisings were prompted initially by the 'China Incident' in 1962. The 26th and 27th Battalions received their colours in Feb 91

BATTLE HONOURS (POST 1947)
Zoji La, Jammu & Kashmir 1947–48, Punjab 1965, Jammu & Kashmir 1965, Akhawra, Khinsar, Madhumati River, Belonia, Khansama, Sindh 1971, East Pakistan 1971

BOOKS
'Heritage – the Story of The Rajput Regiment 1778–1947' by Mustafad Ahmad (Pub. Regtl Centre 1989)

The Jat Regiment

Centre: **BAREILLY, Uttar Pradesh** (formerly United Provinces)

The Regiment is one of the few to remain in the first cantonment allotted in 1923. Bareilly has always been its home. They also continue to wear the same basic badge. The original badge consisted of the Roman 'IX' surmounted by the crown, above a title scroll. Despite republican status for India in January 1950, the Jats continued to wear the same badge until July 1955 when the lions of Ashoka replaced the crown. Although the numerals are now meaningless except to the regimental historian, they are a triumph to the traditionalist. Later, a minor addition was made: to recognise the 1st Bn's previous light infantry status, a bugle-horn was inserted above the scroll but below the numerals. Sadly, this is barely visible even if one knows that it is there.

1st Battalion (Light Infantry) (old 6th Jat LI) – redesignated 2nd Bn Mechanised Infantry regiment (1 Jat LI) 2 Apr 79
2nd Battalion (Mooltan) (old 119th Infantry) – captured in Singapore Feb 42. Re-raised 1 Jul 45 by redesignation of 15th Bn
3rd Battalion (old 10th Jats)
4th Battalion (old 18th Infantry) – disbanded 1923. Re-raised 15 Jul 40. Captured in Singapore Feb 42. Re-raised 15 Jan 62
5th Battalion – raised 1 Feb 41

6th Battalion – raised 1 Feb 41

7th Battalion – formed 15 Sep 41 by redesignation of the 11th, a Territorial battalion. Disbanded 20 Mar 46. Re-raised 15 Mar 62

8th Battalion – formed 15 Sep 41 by redesignation of the 12th a Territorial battalion. Disbanded 30 Nov 46. Re-raised 14 Dec 59

9th Battalion – formed 15 Sep 41 by redesignation of 11/14th Punjab Regiment, a Territorial battalion. Disbanded 30 Dec 46. Re-raised 1 Jan 63

11th Battalion (old Territorial battalion) – redesignated 7th Bn 15 Sep 41. Re-raised 1 Apr 64

12th Battalion (old Territorial battalion) – redesignated 8th Bn 15 Sep 41. Re-raised 1 Jan 70 as 31st Bn. Redesignated 12th Bn 15 Jun 72

14th Battalion – formed 15 Sep 41 by redesignation of 12/14th Punjab Regiment, a Territorial battalion. Disbanded 30 Apr 47. Re-raised 1 Oct 63

15th Battalion – formed 15 Aug 43 by redesignation of 25th Garrison Bn. Redesignated 2nd Bn 1 Jul 46

16th Battalion – raised 1 Oct 64

17th Battalion – raised 1 Jan 66

18th Battalion – raised 1 Oct 66

31st Battalion – raised 1 Jan 70. Redesignated 12th Bn 15 Jun 72

BATTLE HONOURS (POST 1947)

Zoji La, Rajauri, Jammu & Kashmir 1947–48, Ladakh 1962, Phillora, Dograi, Punjab 1965, Jammu & Kashmir 1971, East Pakistan 1971

BOOKS

'History of the Jat Regiment, Vol. III' by Lieut. Colonel Gautam Sharma (Pub. Allied Publishers Private Ltd. New Delhi 1979)

The Sikh Regiment

Centre: **RAMGARH, Bihar**

The Sikhs' pre-Partition centre was in Nowshera in North West Frontier Province and, clearly, they had to move on Partition in August 1947. Initially, they transferred to Ambala and then, in March 1952, to Meerut but, in line with the policy that dictated that regimental centres should not be located in forward areas, the final move was to Ramgarh. Before Partition, only the 1st, 2nd, and 3rd Bns were wholly composed of Jat Sikhs; the others also had Punjabi Mussalman companies. These latter went to Pakistan in August 1947 and the Regiment absorbed eighteen Sikh companies in exchange. The new badge was to be the traditional chakra, with a lion in the centre, surmounted by the lions of Ashoka. Of all the regiments in the Indian Army now, perhaps the Sikh Regiment is most prone to advertise its past. The 3rd Bn still uses the 45th Rattray's Sikhs' silver bugles whilst the 4th appears to avoid using that numeral when they can use the old XXXVI Sikhs' devices. Sadly, after Operation Blue Star, the assault on the Golden Temple in Amritsar in 1984, elements of three battalions and the centre mutinied. As a result of this, there was a move to disperse personnel of the disaffected units and 10 Madras was the first 'receiving unit'. Another measure was to make 13, 20, 21 & 22 Bns into mixed-class units.

1st Battalion (old 14th KGO Ferozepore Sikhs) – redesignated 4th Bn Mechanised Infantry Regiment (1 Sikh) 2 Apr 81
2nd Battalion (old 15th Ludhiana Sikhs)
3rd Battalion (old 45th Rattray's Sikhs)
4th Battalion (old 36th Sikhs)
5th Battalion (old 47th DCO Sikhs) – captured at Singapore Feb 42. Re-raised 22 Mar 60 by redesignation of 7th Bn
6th Battalion – raised 7 Aug 40. Disbanded 5 Aug 46. Re-raised 9 Feb 62
7th Battalion – raised 7 Aug 40. Redesignated 5th Bn 22 Mar 60. Re-raised 1 Jan 63
8th Battalion – raised 1 May 41. Redesignated 8th Light Anti-Aircraft Regt, Indian Artillery 31 Mar 42. Re-raised 1 Jan 63
9th Battalion – raised 1 May 41. Redesignated 7th Light Anti Aircraft Regt, Indian Artillery Mar 42. Re-raised 1 Apr 64
10th Battalion (old 35th Sikhs) – became regimental centre 1923. Re-raised 1 Jun 66
11th Battalion – raised Aug 66. Re-designated 19th Bn Sep 66
13th Battalion –
16th Battalion – raised 26 Jan 48 }
17th Battalion – raised 1 Feb 48 } formed from Sikh companies of 8 Punjab, FF Regt and FF Rifles
18th Battalion – raised 1 Jul 48 }
19th Battalion – formed Sep 66 by redesignation of 11th Bn
21st Battalion – raised 5 Apr 77
22nd Battalion –

BATTLE HONOURS (POST 1947)

Srinagar, Tithwal, Jammu & Kashmir 1947–48, Burki, Punjab 1965, Jammu & Kashmir 1965, Defence of Punch, Siramani, Parbat Ali, Punjab 1971, Sindh 1971, East Pakistan 1971

BOOKS

'Saragarhi Battalion: Ashes to glory' by Colonel Kanwaljit Singh and Major H S Ahluwalia (Pub. Lancer International, New Delhi 1987)

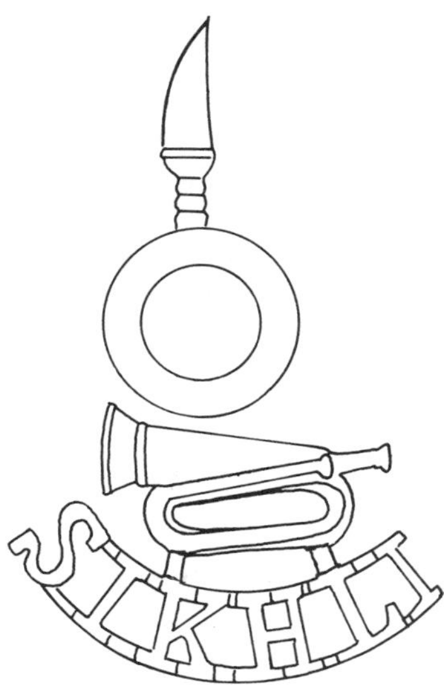

The Sikh Light Infantry

Centre: **FATEHGARH, Uttar Pradesh** (formerly United Provinces)

Despite being created only in 1941 as the Mazhbi and Ramdassia Sikh Regiment, the new regiment takes precedence after the Sikh Regiment since it was accorded the traditions and honours of the old Sikh Pioneer units which were born of the Great Mutiny in 1857. The title Sikh Light Infantry was granted on 23 Jun 44. The end of the Second World War found their regimental centre at Lahore but Partition meant a move to Ferozepore on 27 Sep 47: four years later the centre moved to Meerut where it shared with The Punjab Regiment. In 1963, the regiment formed its own centre once more and, in May 1976, it moved to its present location at Fatehgarh where it shares the cantonment with The Rajput Regiment.

The present regimental badge is the same as was worn before Partition, the Sikh chakra with a kirpan above. Also the same is the distinctive old gold pagri.

On Partition, there were three regular battalions: at least a dozen more have been created since. Following Operation Blue Star, there was no hint of disruption in any of the Sikh LI battalions.

BATTLE HONOURS (POST 1947)
Kalidhar, OP Hill, Punjab 1965, Jammu & Kashmir 1965 Parbat Ali, Fatehpur, Punjab 1971, Sindh 1971, East Pakistan 1971

BOOKS
None Known.

The Dogra Regiment

Centre: **FAIZABAD, Uttar Pradesh** (formerly United Provinces)

The Dogras' traditional home since 1923 had been Jullundur but this was deemed to be too far 'forward' and, in line with the new policy, the regimental centre was moved to its present location at Faizabad. Their old regimental badge carried the number '17' and as they did not wish to retain this link with the past, they decided to incorporate a tiger: not only was this a suitably Indian device but it was also an animal much found in Dogra country. It is posed upon a title-scroll and sometimes worn on their distinctive regimental cap, known as the kisti namuna, a close-fitting cap of dark green worsted material but sometimes seen in Second World War photographs made of khaki-drill. The badge for this cap is the smaller, collar-size, mounted on a diamond-shaped patch of orange felt.

1st Battalion (old 37th Dogras) – redesignated 7th Bn Mechanised Infantry Regt (1 Dogra) in 1981
2nd Battalion (old 38th Dogras) – captured in Singapore Feb 42. Re-formed by redesignation of 6th Bn 15 Apr 46
3rd Battalion (old 41st Dogras) – captured in Singapore Feb 42. Reformed by redesignation of 7th Bn 21 May 46
4th Battalion – raised 1 Oct 40
5th Battalion – raised 1 Jan 63
6th Battalion – formed 15 Sep 41 by redesignation of the 11th, a Territorial Bn. Re-designated 2nd Bn 15 Apr 46. Re-raised 1 Oct 64
7th Battalion – formed 15 Sep 41 by redesignation of the 12th a Territorial Bn. Re-designated 3rd Bn 21 May 46. Re-raised 15 Jan 66
8th Battalion – raised 22 Feb 48
9th Battalion – raised Jan 48
10th Battalion (old 2/41st Dogras) – raised 15 Oct 17. Became regimental centre 1923. Re-raised 1 Jun 66
11th Battalion – raised 16 Aug 22 as a Territorial battalion. Redesignated 6th Bn 15 Sep 41. Re-raised 7 Jun 70 from 2nd Bn Border Scouts

The 2nd Bn Border Scouts, raised 8 Aug 64, were to guard the Indo-Tibetan border from Ladakh to Bara Hoti in the northern Himalayas. It was made up of two wings – redolent of the old British structure in the Frontier Corps – of four companies each. In May 1970, this large battalion was split into two: half became 11 Dogra and the other half became The Scouts Wing, made up of two rifle companies and a support company.

12th Battalion – raised 14 Nov 39 as a territorial battalion. Re-designated 7th Bn 15 Sep 41. Re-raised 1 Jul 76

The 13th to 15th Bns were all raised in 1948–49, the numbers 10th 11th, and 12th Bns having been by-passed due to their previous roles as regimental centre and territorial battalions. No doubt, with the passing of some two decades, it was felt that the numbers could safely be used once more. The 16th was raised on 15 Apr 48, to embody state force units from Sirmoor, Mandi, Suket and Chamba. 17th and 18th Battalions were raised in the 1980's.

BATTLE HONOURS (POST 1947)

Jhanger, Rajauri, Uri, Jammu & Kashmir 1947–48, Asal Uttar, Dograi, Haji Pir, Raja Picquet, OP Hill, Punjab 1965, Jammu & Kashmir 1965, Siramani, Suadih, Derababa Nanak, Chanddagram, Punjab 1971, East Pakistan 1971

BOOKS

'The Dogra Regiment – a saga of gallantry and valour' by Colonel RD Palsokar MC (Pub. Dogra Regimental Centre 1982)

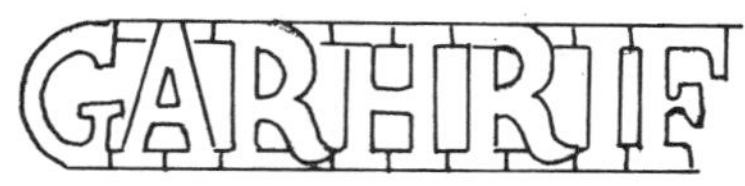

The Garhwal Rifles

Centre: **LANSDOWNE, Uttar Pradesh** (formerly United Provinces)

The Regimental centre of the Garhwalis is still at Lansdowne as it was in 1923 for the 18th Royal Garhwal Rifles. However, in 1950 it became necessary to drop the 'Royal' part of their old title, a distinction so hard-won in the Great War. With republican status for India, the crown was removed from the regimental badge, the lions of Ashoka assumed in its place and the 'Royal' removed from the central circle.

1st Battalion (old 39th Garhwalis) – redesignated 6th Bn Mechanised Infantry Regt (1 Garhwal) 1981

2nd Battalion (old 2/39th Garhwalis) – captured at Singapore Feb 42. Reformed 11 May 46 by re-designation of 4th Bn

3rd Battalion (old 3/39th Garhwalis)

4th Battalion – raised 20 Jun 40. Re-designated 2nd Bn 11 May 46. Re-raised 7 Dec 59
5th Battalion – raised 1 Feb 41. Captured at Singapore Feb 42. Re-raised 1 Feb 62
6th Battalion – formed 15 Sep 41 by redesignation of the 11th, a Territorial battalion. Disbanded 10 Jul 46. Re-raised 1 Jan 63
7th Battalion – raised 1 Jul 42. Disbanded 31 Mar 46. Re-raised 1 Oct 64
8th Battalion – raised 1 Jul 48
9th Battalion – raised 1 Jan 65
10th Battalion – (old 4/39th Garhwalis) – became regimental centre 1923. Re-raised 1 Oct 65
11th Battalion – (old Territorial battalion) – redesignated 6th Bn 15 Sep 41. Re-raised 1 Jan 67
There have been several battalions raised since.
3rd Scout Battalion – an independent battalion affiliated to the Regiment.

BATTLE HONOURS (POST 1947)
Tithwal, Jammu & Kashmir 1947–48, Ladakh 1962, Nuranang, Buttar-Dograndi, Gadra Road, Punjab 1965, Rajasthan 1965, Hilli, East Pakistan 1971

BOOKS
None known.

The Kumaon Regiment

Centre: **RANIKHET, Uttar Pradesh** (formerly United Provinces)

One of the first post-Partition non-operational events was the move of the Kumaon Regimental Centre to Ranikhet in May 1948. The previous 19th Hyderabad/Kumaon centre at Agra had been home to the Regiment for 25 years but the move pleased everyone. The new location was closer to traditional Kumaoni recruiting areas and the centre was privileged to have a commanding view of the eternal snows of the Himalayas. The new badge for The Kumaon Regiment, approved in February 1946, was acceptable to a newly-republican army and so remains as the Russell demi-lion above a 'Kumaon' Scroll. In 1970, it was decided that the Naga Regiment should be formed, on a one-battalion basis and would be under the Kumaoni umbrella.

1st Battalion (old 94th Russell's Infantry) – redesignated 3rd Bn. The Parachute Regiment (Kumaon) 15 Apr 52
2nd Battalion (old 96th Berar Infantry)
3rd Battalion (Rifles) – formed by redesignation of the 1st Kumaon Rifles March 1950 to fill the vacancy which had existed since 1931
4th Battalion (old 98th Infantry) – captured in Singapore Feb 42. Reformed 1 Jun 46 by redesignation of 8th Bn
5th Battalion (old 99th Deccan Infantry) – disbanded 7 Apr 24. Re-raised 15 Jul 40. Disbanded 7 Mar 46. Re-raised 1 Mar 62
6th Battalion – raised 1 Feb 41
7th Battalion – raised 1 Feb 41. Disbanded 20 Dec 46. Re-raised 1 Sep 62
8th Battalion – raised 15 Aug 41. Redesignated 4th Bn 1 Jan 46. Re-raised 1 Jan 63
9th Battalion – raised 15 Apr 42. Disbanded 16 Jul 46. Re-raised 1 Jan 63
11th Battalion (old Territorial battalion) – redesignated 1st Bn. The Bihar Regiment 15 Sep 41. Re-raised 1 Apr 64
12th Battalion – raised 15 Jan 66
13th Battalion – raised 5 Aug 48
14th (Gwalior) Battalion – 4th Gwalior Infantry (a State Forces unit raised in 1852) absorbed and redesignated 14th (Gwalior) Bn The Kumaon Regiment Feb 53. Redesignated 5th Bn. Mechanised Infantry Regt (14 Kumaon) 2 Apr 81
15th (Indore) Battalion – 1st Indore Infantry (a State Forces unit raised in 1730) absorbed and redesignated 15th (Indore) Bn The Kumaon Regiment Feb 53
16th Battalion – raised 1 Jan 66
17th Battalion – formed by redesignation of the 31st Bn 1 Apr 71
26th Battalion – raised 1 Mar 42. Disbanded 25 Mar 51
31st Battalion – raised 15 Jan 68. Redesignated 17th Bn 1 Apr 71
1st Kumaon Rifles – raised Oct 17. Redesignated 3rd (Rifles) Bn The Kumaon Regiment Mar 50

To 4 Kumaon fell the sad but proud distinction of having the first Param Vir Chakra, independent India's supreme decoration for gallantry. Major Som Nath Sharma was awarded the honour posthumously following action in Kashmir in 1947.

It was sad to see, several years ago, when the 3rd (Rifles) Bn was garrison battalion at the Red Fort, in Delhi, a trophy in front of the guardroom, a Chinese weapon – taken from a Frontier Force Regiment unit in an earlier engagement.

BATTLE HONOURS (POST 1947)

Srinagar, Jammu & Kashmir 1947–48, Rezang La, Ladakh 1962, Sanjoi Mirpur, Punjab 1965, Jammu & Kashmir 1965, Gadra City, Shamshernagar, Bhaduria, Punjab 1971, Sindh 1971, East Pakistan 1971.

BOOKS

'Valour Triumphs' by Major K C Praval (Pub. Thomson Press (India) Ltd., Faridabad 1976)

The Assam Regiment

Centre: **SHILLONG, Meghalaya** (formerly part of Assam)

Located at what was a popular hill station of British India, the Regiment has more than doubled its size since Partition. Their badge remains, as before, the rhinoceros above a scroll 'Assam Regt'. When The Naga Regiment was formed in 1970, it was based on Ranikhet, the home of the Kumaon Regt but the JCOs and specialists were provided by The Assam Regiment.

1st Battalion – raised 15 Jun 41
2nd Battalion – raised 15 Apr 42. Disbanded post-Partition for mutiny. Re-raised 1 Oct 63
3rd Battalion – raised 1 Nov 45
4th Battalion – raised 19 Aug 60
5th Battalion – raised 1 Jan 63
6th Battalion – raised 1 Apr 64
7th Battalion – raised 1 Jan 76
8th Battalion – raised 1 Mar 78
9th Battalion – raised 1 Aug 80
10th Battalion – raised 1 Mar 81
12th Battalion – raised 11 Feb 85
14th Battalion – raised 15 Oct 85
15th Battalion – raised 18 Jul 87

BATTLE HONOURS (POST 1947)
Jammu & Kashmir 1947–48, Chhamb, Jammu & Kashmir 1971.

BOOKS
None known.

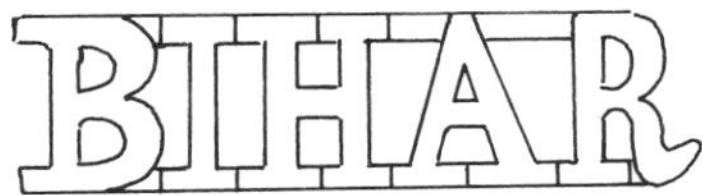

The Bihar Regiment

Centre: **DINAPORE, Bihar**

The choice of Dinapore for the regimental centre for the Biharis was no accident. Aside from the obvious fact that it is in the centre of their recruiting-area, it was the location of the 11th Bn 19th Hyderabad Regiment, the Territorial battalion, from which the 1st Bn Bihar Regiment was formed in 1941. Their badge remains as it was first granted, fifty years ago–the lions of Ashoka above a scroll 'Bihar'.

1st Battalion – formed by redesignation of the Territorial battalion, the 11/19th Hyderabad Regt 15 Sep 41
2nd Battalion – raised 1 Dec 42
3rd Battalion – raised 1 Nov 45
4th Battalion – raised 1 Oct 60
5th Battalion – raised 1 Jan 63
6th Battalion – raised 1 Oct 63
7th Battalion – raised 1 Apr 64
8th Battalion – raised 1 Jan 65
9th Battalion – raised 15 Oct 65

Several additional battalions were raised following the action in East Pakistan in 1971.

BATTLE HONOURS (POST 1947)
None

BOOKS
None known.

The Mahar Regiment

Centre: **SAUGOR, Madhya Pradesh** (formerly Central Provinces)

At Partition in August 1947, the Mahar Regimental Centre was at Arangaon, in Maharashtra but the next year it moved to Saugor. The badge designed in 1946 for wear by the new Machine-Gun regiment was found to be unacceptable. The obelisk commemorating the action at Koregaon in 1818 had to go since it celebrated the action between British-officered Indians and an Indian ruler's troops: the obelisk was removed and its place taken on the badge by a katar, or dagger whilst the offensive honour 'Koregaon' on the upper scroll was removed to give way to a pious exhortation in Hindi – 'Success and Atttainment'. Finally, in 1964, a normal infantry role was resumed and the letters 'M.G.' removed from the title-scrolls: the crossed Vickers machine-guns, however, remain as a reminder of a former role.

1st Battalion – raised 1 Oct 41
2nd Battalion – raised 1 Jun 42
3rd Battalion – raised 1 Nov 43
4th Battalion – 1st Border Scouts Bn re-organised as 4th (Border) MG Bn 15 May 56. Present designation 22 Mar 58
5th Battalion – 2nd Border Scouts Bn reorganised as 5th (Border) MG Bn 15 May 56. Present designation 22 Mar 58
6th Battalion – 3rd Border Scouts Bn re-organised as 6th (Border) MG Bn 15 May 56. Present designation 22 Mar 58
7th Batalion – raised 10 Dec 59
8th Battalion – raised 1 Mar 62
9th Battalion – raised 1 Oct 62
10th Battalion – raised 15 Nov 62
11th Battalion – raised 1 Oct 64

12th Battalion – raised 1 Jan 65
13th Battalion – raised 15 Jan 66
14th Battalion – formed by redesignation of 31st Bn 1 Apr 71
15th Battalion – formed by redesignation of 32nd Bn Jun 72
16th Battalion – formed by redesignation of 8th Bn The Parachute Regiment 16 Nov 75. Redesignated 12th Bn Mechanised Infantry Regt (16 Mahar) 2 Apr 79
17th Battalion – raised 1 Jul 79
18th Battalion – raised 1 Jan 81
31st Battalion – raised 15 Jan 68. Redesignated 14th Bn 1 Apr 71
32nd Battalion – raised 8 Jan 70. Redesignated 15th Bn Jun 72

BATTLE HONOURS (POST 1947)
Jammu & Kashmir 1947–48, Ladakh 1962, Asal Uttar, Kalidhar, Jaurian Kalit, Punjab 1965, Jammu & Kashmir 1965, Shahjra, Harar Kalan, Parbat Ali, Gadra City, Thanpir, Punjab 1971, Sindh 1971, Jammu & Kashmir 1971, East Pakistan 1971.

BOOKS
'History of the Mahar Regiment' by Major B N Mittra (Pub. The Statesman Press, New Delhi 1972)
'Forefront for ever' by Col V Longer (Pub Allied Publisher Pte Ltd., New Delhi 1981)

The Jammu & Kashmir Rifles

Centre: **JABALPUR, Madhya Pradesh** (formerly Central Provinces)

The pre-Partition state forces of Jammu & Kashmir were principally Hindu/Sikh in their composition, owing allegiance to a Hindu ruler in a Muslim-majority state. The earliest-raised battalion was the 4th which claimed 1837 as its birthdate. The 1st, 2nd, and 3rd saw action in the service of the Queen-Empress in the 1890's, some saw service abroad in the two World Wars but it was a nominally nine-battalion force which went over to India after Partition. In line with Indian government policy, the states' forces were integrated into the Indian Army but, in this particular case, a whole new regiment was created. The 1st, 2nd, 3rd, 4th, 7th and 9th Battalions became the Jammu & Kashmir Regiment in 1957 (the 5th, 6th, and 8th had been disbanded in 1951 following the 1947–48 operations). The title became The Jammu & Kashmir Rifles in 1963, the then junior regiment of the Indian Line. The process of integration might now be considered complete since the 16th Bn was accepted by The Mechanised Infantry Regiment as its 14th Bn in 1981.

The badge shows an oval embracing the Sun, the State emblem, surrounded by a Sanskrit insription, translatable as 'Ever victorious in war', the lions of Ashoka above and title-scroll below. The original strength has by now been virtually doubled: the centre has been withdrawn from its natural recruiting-areas down to Central India. They are referred to within the Indian Army as the Jak Rifles.

1st Battalion – raised 13 Apr 1873
2nd Battalion – raised 25 Apr 1869
3rd Battalion – raised 15 Apr 1856
4th Battalion – raised 1837
5th Battalion – raised 1849. Disbanded 1951. Re-raised Sep 62
6th Battalion – raised 1923. Disbanded 1951. Re-raised 1 Jan 63
7th Battalion – raised 1932. Disbanded Jan 45. Re-raised May 47
8th Battalion – raised 13 Mar 40. Disbanded 1951. Re-raised Oct 63.
9th Battalion – raised Mar 40
10th Battalion – raised 1 Oct 64
11th Battalion – raised 1 Jan 65
12th Battalion – raised 15 Jan 66
13th Battalion – raised 1 Oct 66
14th Battalion – raised 1 Jan 67
15th Battalion – raised
16th Battalion – raised. Redesignated 14th Bn Mechanised Infantry Regiment (16 J & K Rifles) 1 Jun 81

In 1989, there were nineteen battalions on strength.

BATTLE HONOURS (POST 1947)
Punch, Skardu, Jammu & Kashmir 1947–48, Asal Uttar, Punjab 1965, Syamganj, East Pakistan 1971.

BOOKS
'History of the Jammu & Kashmir Rifles 1820–1956' by Major Brahma Singh (Pub. Lancer Group, 1990)
'Jammu & Kashmir Arms (History of the J & K Rifles)' by Major General D K Palit (Pub. Palit & Dutt, Dehra Dun 1972)

The Ladakh Scouts

Centre: **LEH, Jammu & Kashmir**

The 1st Battalion Ladakh Scouts was raised on 1 Jun 63 by Lieut. Colonel Bannon from elements of 7 and 14 Bns Jammu & Kashmir Militia.

It was the intention to form a body of para-military frontier scouts such as existed in NWFP of British India but the new unit was to become part of the regular army, recruited and officered in the conventional way. However as a specialist unit, it was to be based in and permanently serving in the Himalayas.

A second battalion was subsequently raised by direct recruitment.

The Naga Regiment

Centre: **RANIKHET, Uttar Pradesh** (formerly United Provinces)
(shared with the Kumaon Regiment)

After the actions taken in 1968–70 to achieve harmony in Nagaland, the moderates among the Naga leaders pressed for the creation of a regiment of their own. Central government agreed to a one-battalion regiment initially and Lieut Colonel R N Mahajan VSM, of 14 Kumaon, was selected to raise and command it. Nagas were to make up 50% of its strength, the other 50% made up of Kumaonis, Garhwalis and Gorkhas (from 3GR) in equal proportions. The Assam Regiment was to supply JCOs and specialists: it already had Nagas in its ranks. Raising-day was 1 Nov 70. Erstwhile hostiles were encouraged to join but many potential recruits were rejected on medical examination. Language presented a problem: all Nagas do not speak the same language and this, combined with the elements of the four contributing regiments, meant that it could only be resolved by all Nagas learning Hindi. To foster competition, A and

C companies were made wholly Naga whilst the remaining companies were on a mixed class basis. The centre was to be at Ranikhet, under the care of the Kumaon Regt. but the badge was to be clearly Naga. Crossed Naga spears and a dah – the cutting weapon of Burma and Nagaland – carry a shield on their intersection bearing a mithun (deer) head, all over a title-scroll in Hindi.

A second battalion was formed in 1988.

The Jammu and Kashmir Light Infantry

Centre: **SRINAGAR, Jammu & Kashmir**

In October 1947, when Pakistani raiders invaded Jammu & Kashmir, there was a popular rising to oppose them. Bodies of Home Guards were formed in the Valley, Militia and Nubra Scouts in Ladakh, Border Defence Scouts in Jammu and Punch Scouts in Punch were all raised and, in recognition of the great services rendered, these volunteers were formed into the Jammu & Kashmir Militia on 15 Apr 48. On 1 Jun 63, elements of 7 & 14 Bns were taken to form the 1st Bn The Ladakh Scouts. In further recognition of the Militia's service during the Chinese aggression in 1962 and the two Pakistani wars of 1965 and 1971, it was reorganised in 1972 and brought on to the same basis as the Indian Army. On 27 Apr 76, it was redesignated The Jammu and Kashmir Light Infantry.

The Militia's badge was crossed muskets over a three-part title-scroll with, between the butts of the weapons, a wooden plough, the sign of the Peasant Party, an indication of the Militia's origins. Bearing in mind the non-political status of the Indian Army, when the time came to choose a badge for the Light Infantry, the wooden plough was consigned to history and the current badge shows simply the crossed muskets above a three-part scroll reading 'J & K Light Infantry'. No traditional bugle-horn was adopted but the traditional 'Rifles' or 'Light Infantry' status of British-Indian hill-corps was maintained.

More than twelve battalions have been raised.

BATTLE HONOURS

Shingo River Valley, Laleali/Picquet 707, Gutrian, Jammu & Kashmir 1971.

BOOKS

'History of the Jammu & Kashmir Militia' by Major Sita Ram Johri (Pub. Broca's Artistic Press, Srinagar 1972)

The Gorkhas

The post-Partition routine for dealing with the Gurkha regiments differed a little from that used for regiments of the normal Indian Line. Most of the men were nominally Hindu and so the regiments were not going to be split on a religious basis. Theirs was a different problem: four of the ten regiments were allotted to Britain and six were to remain in the Indian Army. They had always been entirely British-officered and there was a widely-held belief that the Gurkhas would not serve under Indian Officers. Even if this obstacle would be overcome, then there would surely be competition to follow their sahibs into British service. This was not the case: like many British troops, the Gurkha riflemen had been away from home for almost six years and did not savour the prospect of continuing exile in the proposed centre in Malaya. During the war, each of the ten regiments had raised at least two and sometimes more additional battalions: the four regiments going to the British Army were to revert to pre-1939 two-battalion strengths. British commanding officers, not unnaturally perhaps, felt that the four senior regiments would go to set up the new British Gurkha base in Malaya whilst the 5th, 6th 7th, 8th, 9th and 10th would remain in India: but surely, the 5th, the Royal Gurkhas, would go to Britain? The choice, the final decision, to send the 2nd, 6th, 7th and 10th to Malaya was said to have been based on the fact that most of the eight battalions affected were out of India at decision-time. Independence was set for 15 Aug 47 but, up until a week beforehand, no announcement was made on the future of the regiments of the Gurkha Brigade. When this came, it was to specify which regiments were to be chosen for Britain and which to remain in India. Finally, on 14 Aug 47, a letter from the Adjutant-General in New Delhi declared that every Gurkha officer and soldier in all ten regiments was to be given the choice of which of the two armies he wished to serve in or to serve in neither, take his discharge and return to Nepal. This became known as 'the opt'. In the event, only the men of the four regiments going to Malaya were given the opt. By the time that the new terms of service for the British Gurkhas were declared, many of the pre-war regular and wartime officers had either retired or gone on UK leave. Thus, there were few officers whom the men knew who might advise them as to their decisions. Moreover, those few had been strictly forbidden to talk to the men about anything to do with the opt. This was interpreted by the Gurkhas as a lack of interest, in effect, an erosion of the 130 year old mutual trust.

The eight British Gurkha battalions, after the final count, found themselves with an average strength of about 300 men each, roughly a third of their establishment. Indian propaganda had been directed towards persuading Gurkhas to remain in India and it was interesting to note that the numbers of men opting for British service varied in direct ratio to their unit's proximity to Delhi. Two battalions, 2/6 GR and 2/7 GR came across to the British Army with about one hundred men each whilst 1/6 GR 1/7 GR and 1/10 GR, still in Burma until January 1948, presented very much better figures. The opt however, was not the end. Some men in units detailed for Indian service took home leave in 1948, did not rejoin their battalions but joined the British Army as recruits, some of them forming the nucleus of the Gurkha Engineers, raised in 1948.

It was in February 1949, that the Indian Army ordered that Gurkhas should become Gorkhas, a change in the cause of linguistic purity but the full titles retained the names of their royal patrons as before. Like the rest of the teeth-arms in the Indian Army, however, the Gorkhas shed these honorifics in 1950 when a republic was declared.

Dress distinctions were maintained for the most part and many of the pre-Partition traditional Gurkha centres continued to be used. The 14th Gorkha Rifles Regimental Centre embraced the 1st and 4th at Sabathu in Himachal Pradesh; the 39th Gorkha Rifles Regimental Centre served the 3rd and the 9th at Dehra Dun and 58th Gorkha Rifles Regimental Centre, located at Varanasi (Benares), housed the 5th Gorkha Rifles (Frontier Force) and the 8th. The 'new' 11th Gorkha Rifles, created in January 1948 to accommodate surplus Gurkhas from the regiments which went to Malaya, now has its own centre at Lucknow after several moves.

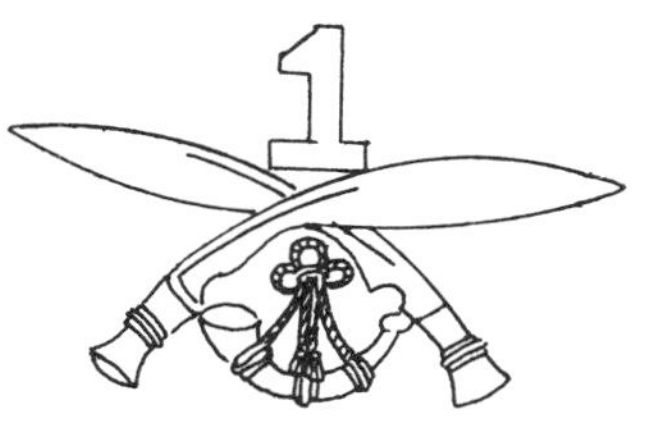

1st Gorkha Rifles (The Malaun Regiment)

Centre: **SABATHU, Himachal Pradesh** (formerly part of the Punjab)

After January 1950, the Regiment ceased to be the 1st King George V's Own Gorkha Rifles and their badge had to lose the Prince of Wales's plumes. The figure '1' was taken from below the crossed kukris and took the place of the plumes above the intersection. The top fold of the khaki pagri on the Gurkha hat is scarlet.

1st Battalion – raised 24 Apr 1815
2nd Battalion – raised Feb 1886
3rd Battalion – redesignated 2nd Bn 15 Aug 46. Re-raised 21 Dec 59
4th Battalion – raised 15 Mar 41. Disbanded 30 Nov 46. Re-raised 1 Jan 63
5th Battalion – raised 1 Jan 42. Disbanded 31 Oct 46. Re-raised 1 Jan 65

BATTLE HONOURS (POST 1947)
Jammu & Kashmir 1965, Darsana, Jammu & Kashmir 1971, East Pakistan 1971.

BOOKS
None known.

3rd Gorkha Rifles

Centre: **VARANASI, Uttar Pradesh** (formerly United Provinces)

The 3rd had been Queen Alexandra's Own before republican status brought about a shortening of their title and had borne her royal cypher – the two, linked letters 'A' – and this had to go but not before one of the first Indian commanding officers had suggested, tongue in cheek, that the letter 'A' must surely have stood for Almora, the pre-1939 centre of the 3rd and was worthy of retention. Authority took scant heed of this piece of whimsy and the royal cypher was replaced by a sort of Star of David which, by a considerable effort of will and adequate pre-briefing, can almost be seen as a double-A. The crown, of course, was replaced by the lions of Ashoka. More easily recognisable at a distance are the twin rifle-green cloth triangles, one worn on each side of the pagri of the Gurkha hat: these are still a cherished part of 3GR's dress. The top fold of the pagri on the Gurkha hat is rifle-green.

1st Battalion – raised 24 Apr 1815
2nd Battalion – raised 1891
3rd Battalion – raised 1 Oct 40
4th Battalion – raised 15 Mar 41. Disbanded 30 Apr 47. Re-raised 20 Feb 62
5th Battalion – raised 1 Oct 63

BATTLE HONOURS (POST 1947)
Uri, Jammu & Kashmir 1947–48, Shingo River Valley, Jammu & Kashmir 1971

BOOKS
'Flash of the Khukri – history of the 3rd Gorkha Rifles 1947–80' by Colonel C L Proudfoot (Pub. Vision Books Pvt Ltd., New Delhi 1984)

4th Gorkha Rifles

Centre: **SABATHU, Himachal Pradesh** (formerly part of the Punjab)

The 4th share their centre with the 1st Gorkha Rifles. Before January 1950, they had been the Prince of Wales' Own but, in that year, their badge lost its Prince of Wales' plumes. It continued that way for almost forty years but they have recently been granted the addition of the lions of Ashoka as recognition of the courage of the 3rd battalion of the Regiment in an action in 1984 on the Siachen Glacier, a ridge in north-eastern Kashmir, 19,000 feet above sea-level where death from the forces of nature is normally ten times more likely than death from the forces of Pakistan.

During the Second World War, the 3rd Battalion served with Wingate in the Chindits in Burma and is now permitted to wear a special badge to commemorate this on the left breast-pocket. Also worn are two black folds in the khaki pagri of the Gurkha hat.

1st Battalion – raised 1857
2nd Battalion raised 10 Apr 1886
3rd Battalion – raised 1 Oct 40
4th Battalion – raised 15 Mar 41. Disbanded 18 Oct 46. Re-raised 1 Mar 62
5th Battalion – raised 1 Jan 63
6th Battalion – raised Sep 70

BATTLE HONOURS (POST 1947)
Gurais, Punch, Jammu & Kashmir 1947–48, Punjab 1965, Jammu & Kashmir 1971

BOOKS
'History of the 4th Gorkha Rifles', Vol IV (1947–71) by Brig H S Sodhi & Brig P K Gupta AVSM (Pub. Vanity Books, New Delhi 1985)

5th Gorkha Rifles (Frontier Force)

Centre: **SHILLONG, Meghalaya,** (formerly part of Assam)

The 5th, once the Royal Gurkhas, were compelled to relinquish the Royal Crest on their badge after January 1950 but the Indian government replaced this with the lions of Ashoka. As a regiment with Frontier Force origins, still evident in their title, they had been accustomed to wear brown leather boots and equipment rather than the black leather of the Gurkha Brigade. This distinction, much cherished by the Regiment, was abolished by a colonel-in-chief without a Gorkha past but later restored for officers and JCOs. Finally, however, wef 1 Nov 90, 'blacks' were assumed once more and 5 GR(FF) brought into line. The two rifle-green folds continue to be worn in the khaki pagri of the Gurkha hat, as does the 'Royal' red lanyard on the right shoulder, whilst the 5th Battalion, with Second World War service with Wingate (as 3/6 GR), wears a distinctive badge commemorating this on the left breast-pocket.

1st Battalion – raised 1858
2nd Battalion – raised 20 Oct 1886
3rd Battalion – raised 1 Oct 40
4th Battalion – raised 15 Mar 41. Disbanded Dec 46. Re-raise 1 Jan 63
5th Battalion (Chindits) – formed by redesignation of 3/6 Gurkha Rifles 1 Jan 48
6th Battalion – formed by redesignation of 3/7 Gurkha Rifles 4 Feb 48

BATTLE HONOURS (POST 1947)
Zoji La, Kargal, Jammu & Kashmir 1947–48, Charwa, Punjab 1965, Shahjra, Sybhat, Punjab 1971, Jammu & Kashmir 1971, East Pakistan 1971

BOOKS
'History of the 5th Gorkha Rifles (Frontier Force) by Col R D Palsokar MC (Pub: Regtl Centre 1991)

8th Gorkha Rifles

Centre: **SHILLONG, Meghalaya** (formerly part of Assam)

The 8th had not had a Royal patron before Partition so that they sustained no change of title following India's change to republic status in 1950. Nor, of course, was any change in their badge necessary. The 1st Battalion had been accustomed to wear a small red hackle on the left side of the Gurkha hat whilst the others wore a red pom-pom. Since the conversion of the 1st Bn to a Mechanised Infantry unit in 1979, all battalions have worn the red pom-pom. In addition, the metal shoulder-title no longer reads '8G' but is actually a smaller, black regimental badge on a red patch. The 5th Battalion, born of 4/2 Gurkha Rifles, continues to wear the diced cap of the 2nd Goorkhas.

1st Battalion – raised 19 Feb 1824. Redesignated 3rd Bn Mechanised Infantry Regiment (1/8 Gorkha Rifles) 2 Apr 81
2nd Battalion – raised 13 Apr 1835
3rd Battalion – raised 1 Oct 40. Disbanded Apr 46. Re-raised 1 Jan 63
4th Battalion – raised 15 Mar 41
5th Battalion – formed by redesignation of the 4/2 Gurkha Rifles 17 Feb 48
6th Battalion – raised 4 Feb 48

BATTLE HONOURS (POST 1947)
Punch, Jammu & Kashmir 1947–48, Chushul, Ladakh 1962, Sanjoi Mirpur, Punjab 1965, Jammu & Kashmir 1965

BOOKS
None known.

9th Gorkha Rifles

Centre: **VARANASI, Uttar Pradesh** (formerly United Provinces)

Like the 8th, the 9th Gorkhas had not had a royal patron but their badge bore the crown and that, obviously, had to go after 1950. It was replaced by the lions of Ashoka. All battalions now wear a black top fold to the khaki pagri on the Gurkha hat and a black diamond-shaped patch on the left of the pagri.

During the Second World War, the 3rd and 4th Battalions served in Burma with Wingate and a distinctive badge to commemorate this service is worn on the left breast-pocket.

1st Battalion – raised 1817
2nd Battalion – raised 1904
3rd Battalion – raised Jun 17. Disbanded. Re-raised 1 Oct 40
4th Battalion – raised 1 Nov 40. Disbanded 10 Mar 47. Re-raised 9 Sep 61
5th Battalion – raised 1 Jul 42. Disbanded 1 Jun 46. Re-raised 1 Jan 63

BATTLE HONOURS (POST 1947)
Phillora, Punjab 1965, Derababas Nanak, Kumar Khali, Punjab 1971, Jammu & Kashmir 1971, East Pakistan 1971.

BOOKS
'9 Gurkha Rifles 1817–1947' by Lieut. Colonel P. Chaudhuri (Pub. Vision Books 1984) (covers immediate post-Partition activities)

11th Gorkha Rifles

Centre: **LUCKNOW, Madhya Pradesh** (formerly Central Provinces)

The present regiment has no connection with the British-raised 11th Gurkha Rifles which came into being during the Great War and was disbanded shortly afterwards. In December 1947, Gurkha soldiers from the 7th and 10th Gurkha Rifles who did not opt for British service were collected together into what was at first known as the Indian Gurkha Detachment. In January 1948, they became the 11th Gurkha Rifles, and in January 1949, the 11th Gorkha Rifles. The top fold of the khaki pagri on the Gurkha hat is crimson and the badge, crossed kukris with the Roman figures 'XI' above the intersection, is worn on a crimson square on the left side of the pagri.

1st Battalion – raised Jan 48
2nd Battalion – raised Jan 48
3rd Battalion – raised Jan 48
4th Battalion – raised 1948 from men of 1/10GR. Disbanded 1952 for mutiny. Re-raised.
5th Battalion – raised 8 May 52
6th Battalion – raised 1964
7th Battalion – raised 1964

BATTLE HONOURS (POST 1947)
Bogra, Shingo River Valley, Jammu & Kashmir 1971, East Pakistan 1971.

BOOKS
'The path of glory – exploits of the 11th Gorkha Rifles' by Lieut Colonel Gautam Sharma (Pub. Allied Publishing Pte Ltd., New Delhi 1988)

11. PAKISTAN'S ARMY AFTER PARTITION

Partition, in August 1947, gave Pakistan six of the old cavalry regiments and eight infantry regiments. Artillery, engineers, signals and the various corps and departments were allocated on the agreed 2:1 basis although, naturally, there were anomalies and inequalities which were unavoidable.

President's Bodyguard

Headquarters: **ISLAMABAD**

The Muslim element of the old Governor-General's (Viceroy's) Bodyguard was built up to full strength and retained largely for ceremonial duties in the capital. Their badge is crossed lances with the Star and Crescent above and the letters 'PBG' below the intersection.

Armour/Cavalry

Centre: NOWSHERA, NWFP.

The six cavalry regiments allocated to Pakistan were as follows:

Probyn's Horse (5th King Edward VII's Own Horse)
6th Duke of Connaught's Own Lancers
Guides Cavalry (10th Queen Victoria's Own Cavalry)
 (Frontier Force)
11th Prince Albert Victor's Own Cavalry (Frontier Force)
13th Duke of Connaught's Own Lancers
19th King George V's Own Lancers

In addition, Sam Browne's Cavalry (Frontier Force) and the 15th Lancers were subsequently reactivated. Both had been cavalry/armoured training regiments since 1937.

There were no all-Muslim units in the Indian Army in 1947 and, in the six regiments initially allocated, there were only eight Muslim squadrons, although there were actually nineteen Muslim squadrons in the entire Indian Armoured Corps. Consequently, ten non-Muslim squadrons had to be transferred to Indian regiments and, eleven Muslim squadrons accepted in exchange. In most cases, one-to-one exchanges were effected and several of the squadrons actually exchanged cap badges.

When Pakistan opted to become a republic in 1956, the names and titles of British royalty associated with the various regiments were set aside and the new titles became:

5th Horse
6th Lancers
Guides Cavalry (Frontier Force)
11th Cavalry (Frontier Force)

12th Cavalry (Frontier Force)
13th Lancers
15th Lancers
19th Lancers

Badges also required to be changed where either a crown or the Garter was borne or the royal patron's title featured on the badge.

The 5th Horse relinquished the crown on their badge, also the Prince of Wales' plumes, replacing the latter with a wheatsheaf: the title-scroll 'Probyn's Horse' remained. The 6th Lancers simply dropped the scroll reading 'Duke of Connaught's Own' but later replaced it with a Persian inscription. The Guides Cavalry kept their distinctive small silver format but replaced the central 'VR' Royal Cypher with the letters 'F.F.'. The Garter device scrolls now read 'The Corps of Guides Cavalry'. They also replaced the crown with a rather indeterminate device. Reluctant to abandon their traditional Kandahar Star, the 11th Cavalry (FF) first dropped the crown and replaced the central 'PAVO' with the number '11' and added a scroll below, 'Frontier Force'. Subsequently, the scroll was dispensed with and the central numerals amended to Arabic figures: the 'Kabul to Kandahar' circlet was translated into Urdu whilst a light infantry bugle with 'F.F.' between the strings surmounted the star. The mounted figure on the old 12th's badge disappeared, the whole design being replaced by crossed lances with '12' above and a monogram 'CAV' on the inter-section. Crossed lances were retained by the 13th Lancers who simply discarded the crown. The 15th Lancers' badge did not need to be changed but the 19th had to abandon both crown and the 'GRI' Royal Cypher.

There would appear to have been initially a tacit agreement that the 'missing numbers' in both India's and Pakistan's cavalry line would not be filled but this has since been disregarded. Pakistan now has a 4th Cavalry of its own as well as a 7th, 8th, 9th and 20th Lancers.

Far from reducing the toal number of armoured cavalry regiments as had been recommended in the Willcox Committee's report in 1945, both countries began raising more and Pakistan, starting at the 22nd Cavalry, worked through to the 33rd and thereafter, with breaks in the numerical sequence, through to the 58th, some two dozen new regiments being created in addition to the initial 1947 share-out. The 23rd, a Frontier Force regiment before 1923, was, once again, designated 23rd Cavalry (Frontier Force).

Pakistan currently has 38 armoured-cavalry regiments.

Infantry

The infantry regiments of the old Indian Army lost their numerical designations in most cases in October 1945 with the exception, of course, of the six Punjab Regiments.

Partition saw Pakistan receiving eight of the old regiments as follows:

1st Punjab Regiment
8th Punjab Regiment
Baluch Regiment
Frontier Force Regiment
Frontier Force Rifles
14th Punjab Regiment
15th Punjab Regiment
16th Punjab Regiment

The following four regiments were created shortly after Partition:

> Bahawalpur Regiment – four battalions strong, formed from the Bahawalpur State Forces
> Pathan Regiment (Frontier Force)
> East Bengal Regiment
> Azad Kashmir Regiment

but the Sind Regiment had to wait for more than another 30 years.

The Bahawalpur Regiment whose badge was the coat of arms of the princely House of Bahawalpur was absorbed into the new Baluch Regiment in 1956, the year not only of republican status but also that of the major infantry restructuring. The Bahawalpur Centre had been at Dera Nawab Sahib.

The Pathan Regiment, three battalions strong, was based at Kohat. Its battalions originated shortly after Partition as units of the old Frontier Force Regiment, being promptly hived off to form the Pathan Regiment. (Frontier Force), its badge being broadly similar to that of the old 40th Pathans, a circular shield bearing the letters 'F.F.', backed by crossed swords above a title scroll. In 1956, 1, 2 and 3 PATHAN were transformed into 11, 12 and 15 FFR.

The East Bengal Regiment was to have its Centre at Chittagong and to consist of some ten battalions, the 10th somewhat optimistically raised in 1971, the year when East Pakistan broke away from the more militarily motivated West to become Bangladesh. Its badge was a Bengal tiger above a title scroll.

The Azad Kashmir Regiment – the Free Kashmir Regiment – had been formed initially from Muslim personnel of the old Jammu and Kashmir State Forces who had re-assessed their loyalties when the Hindu Maharajah opted for India in 1947. The force had been made up predominantly of Hindus and Sikhs.

Pakistan elected to become a republic within the commonwealth in 1956 and it was in that year that sweeping and unpopular changes were made in the infantry regimental system. 'Big regiments' were created in much the same way as happened in the British army shortly afterwards but on a vastly greater scale. Some of the eight original regiments allocated to Pakistan had re-activated battalions which had been disbanded or stood down in 1946–47.

The Punjab Regiment

Centre: **MARDAN, NWFP.**

The 1st, 14th, 15th and 16th Punjab Regiments were merged into one Punjab Regiment in Apr 56.

1st Battalion – ex 1/1 PUNJAB
2nd Battalion – ex 2/1 PUNJAB
3rd Battalion – ex 3/1 PUNJAB
4th Battalion – ex 5/1 PUNJAB
5th Battalion – ex 1/14 PUNJAB
6th Battalion – ex 2/14 PUNJAB
7th Battalion – ex 3/14 PUNJAB
8th Battalion – ex 4/14 PUNJAB
9th Battalion – ex 1/15 PUNJAB
10th Battalion – ex 2/15 PUNJAB
11th Battalion – ex 3/15 PUNJAB
12th Battalion – ex 4/15 PUNJAB
13th Battalion – ex 1/16 PUNJAB
14th Battalion – ex 2/16 PUNJAB
15th Battalion – ex 3/16 PUNJAB (33 MOHAMMADIS)
16th Battalion (PATHANS) – ex 5/14 PUNJAB (PATHANS) (lost in Malaya Feb 42 – re-raised 9 Sep 52)
17th Battalion – ex 4/16 PUNJAB
18th Battalion – ex 7/1 PUNJAB
19th Battalion (SHER SHAH) – ex 7/16 PUNJAB (the subsidiary title was the name of 7/16 PUNJAB'S Victoria Cross winner in 1945)
20th Battalion – ex 14/1 PUNJAB

Subsequently-numbered battalions were new raisings and the Regiment at one time had more than sixty battalions. However, on 1 Jul 80, The Sind Regiment was raised and eleven battalions of The Punjab Regiment were transferred to form the nucleus of the new regiment (44, 45, 46, 47, 48, 49, 50, 51, 52, 53, and 58 Bns).

It being impossible to blend the badges of the four consituent regiments into one acceptable whole, a new design was sought. This now shows a bird, with outstretched wings, standing on a rock within a Crescent, a Star above and title scroll below.

BOOKS

'Veteran campaigners – a history of the Punjab Regiment 1759–1981' by Brig S Haider Abbas Rizvi (pub. Wajidalis, Lahore, 1984)

The Baluch Regiment

Centre: **ABBOTTABAD, NWFP.**

In Apr 56, the 8th Punjab Regiment, the old Baluch Regiment and the Bahawalpur Regiment were merged to form the present Baluch Regiment. Curiously, however, the first battalion of the old Baluch Regiment found itself the sixth battalion of the new regiment since precedence had to be granted to the battalions of the senior 8th Punjab Regiment.

1st Battalion	–	ex 1/8 PUNJAB
2nd Battalion	–	ex 2/8 PUNJAB
3rd Battalion	–	ex 3/8 PUNJAB
4th Battalion	–	ex 4/8 PUNJAB
5th Battalion	–	ex 5/8 PUNJAB
6th Battalion	–	ex 1 BALUCH
7th Battalion	–	ex 2 BALUCH
8th Battalion	–	ex 1 BAHAWALPUR
9th Battalion	–	ex 2 BAHAWALPUR
10th Battalion	–	ex 3 BALUCH
11th Battalion	–	ex 4 BALUCH
12th Battalion	–	ex 5 BALUCH
13th Battalion	–	ex 6/8 PUNJAB

14th Battalion – ex 6 BALUCH
15th Battalion – ex 7 BALUCH
16th Battalion – ex 8 BALUCH
17th Battalion – ex 8/8 PUNJAB
18th Battalion – ex 9/8 PUNJAB
19th Battalion – ex 17 BALUCH (transferred to Special Service Group 11 Apr 59 but later re-raised
20th Battalion – ex 3 BAHAWALPUR
21st Battalion – ex 4 BAHAWALPUR

Successive battalions were new raisings and the Regiment had at one time more than fifty battalions (I noted evidence of 59 Baluch from military graffiti in the Malakand Pass in 1980 but this, of course, is not proof that all the intervening numbers were filled).

The badge of the old 10th Baluch Regiment – the Roman 'X' within the crescent, with crown above – gave way after Partition to an uninspired letter 'B' with star above, encircled by a wreath, over a title-scroll. Happily, a change was made and the present badge is now broadly similar to the old Indian Army badge but with crossed swords replacing the 'X' and a Muslim star instead of the crown. The beret is rifle-green and the badge has a cherry-coloured backing, a look-back to the old full-dress colours of the Bombay Army's Baluch Infantry.

The Frontier Force Regiment

Centre: **ABBOTTABAD, NWFP.**

Although both Baluch and Frontier Force Regiments share Abbottabad with the Pakistan Military Academy, the visitor might be forgiven for thinking it predominantly a Frontier Force Regiment station. The old designation of 'Piffer' – derived originally from the title Punjab Irregular Force – has been adopted by the Pakistanis as if it were their own and the military signwriter has worked overtime to suggest their ascendancy in the garrison. Their distinctive black webbing and buttons lead one to suspect a 'Black Mafia' such as is alleged to exist within Britain's own Royal Green Jackets.

Created in April 1956 from The Frontier Force Regiment, The Frontier Force Rifles and The Pathan Regiment, the battalions of the new Frontier Force Regiment were as follows:

1st Battalion – ex 6 FFRIF
2nd (Guides) Battalion – ex 5 (Guides) FFREGT
3rd Battalion – ex 1 FFREGT
4th Battalion – ex 2 FFREGT
5th Battalion – ex 3 FFREGT
6th Battalion – ex 5 FFREGT
7th (Coke's) Battalion – ex 1 (COKE'S) FFRIF
8th Battalion – ex 2 FFRIF
9th (Wilde's) Battalion – ex 4 (WILDE'S) FFRIF
10th Battalion – ex 5 FFRIF
11th Battalion – ex 1 PATHAN
12th Battalion – ex 3 PATHAN
13th Battalion – ex 8 FFREGT
14th Battalion – ex 9 FFREGT
15th Battalion – ex 2 PATHAN

Subsequently-numbered battalions were later raisings prompted largely by the Indo-Pakistan campaign of 1956.

The position of honour of the 1st Battalion of the new Regiment had been granted to the old, 6th Royal Bn Frontier Force Rifles (Scinde) whilst the Guides Infantry (previously 5th Bn Frontier Force Regiment) became the 2nd Bn, recognition of the fact that they had earlier yielded place to the other battalions of the old 12th Frontier Force Regiment in 1922 so that the latter might retain their earlier numbers.

The badge chosen was not too different from the old badge of the Frontier Force Regiment. The traditional stringed bugle-horn of the light infantry regiments of the British Commonwealth has the script letters 'FF' within the strings whilst two flanking scrolls read 'The' – 'Regt'. This is worn on a rifle-green beret and, as already mentioned, belts and anklets are black.

BOOKS

'The Wardens of the Marches – a History of the Piffers 1947–71' by Lt Gen M Attiqur Rahman MC (pub. Wajidalis, Lahore 1980)

The Azad Kashmir Regiment

Centre: **MANSOR, Punjab**

The Azad Kashmir Regiment was born officially in 1971 but it had existed previously as a para-military force within Azad Kashmir (known in India as POK – Pakistan Occupied Kashmir). Made up of ex-soldiers from many regiments plus some of the 'freedom-fighters' who invaded Kashmir in 1947, the force was regularised as a normal regiment of the Pakistan Army in 1971 and now serves anywhere in the country. More than two dozen battalions exist and the highest number noted is the 38th.

The badge now worn is a brass Star and Crescent, with a scroll below, reading 'A.K. Regt': within the crescent is a leaf of the chinar tree, indigenous to Kashmir but now an endangered botanical species.

The Sind Regiment

Regimental Centre: **HYDERABAD, Sind.**

The Sind Regiment was raised on 1 Jul 80, with the intention of meeting the military aspirations of the Sindhis. Prior to this date, there had been no logical regiment to accept them and the initial idea had been backed by Zulfikar Ali Bhutto. Despite the subsequent death of its motivator, the Regiment was created by the transfer of eleven battalions of The Punjab Regiment and ten battalions of The Baluch Regiment who became instant Sindhis.

1st Battalion	–	ex 13 BALUCH
2nd Battalion	–	ex 17 BALUCH
3rd Battalion	–	ex 18 BALUCH
4th Battalion	–	ex 44 PUNJAB
5th Battalion	–	ex 45 PUNJAB
6th Battalion	–	ex 44 BALUCH
7th Battalion	–	ex 46 PUNJAB
8th Battalion	–	ex 47 PUNJAB
9th Battalion	–	ex 48 PUNJAB
10th Battalion	–	ex 48 BALUCH
11th Battalion	–	ex 49 BALUCH
12th Battalion	–	ex 50 BALUCH
13th Battalion	–	ex 49 PUNJAB
14th Battalion	–	ex 50 PUNJAB
15th Battalion	–	ex 51 PUNJAB
16th Battalion	–	ex 51 BALUCH
17th Battalion	–	ex 52 PUNJAB
18th Battalion	–	ex 53 PUNJAB
19th Battalion	–	ex 52 BALUCH
20th Battalion	–	ex 53 BALUCH
21st Battalion	–	ex 58 PUNJAB

The badge chosen depicts crossed Sindhi axes, an instrument at once a traditional Sindhi weapon and an agricultural implement always carried by Sindhi labourers in the same way as the kukri is both the weapon and the tool of the Gurkha cultivator.

The axes, surmounted by the star and crescent appear above a title scroll in Urdu reading 'SIND REGIMENT'.

All ranks wear the maroon beret with a red feather hackle.

SSG

The Special Service Group

Centre: **ATTOCK, Punjab**

In April 1959, 19 Baluch was removed from normal regimental duties and became the cadre for the new Special Service Group. Naturally, not all its personnel were considered suitable or fit enough for the demanding standards laid down and a programme of postings in and out ultimately achieved the primary objective of a parachute commando-type battalion.

The initial success encouraged army-wide recruitment for subsequent battalions although the SSG is still a very compact force. Wearing disruptively-patterned uniforms and the maroon beret which Britain made traditional wear for parachute-trained troops, men of the Special Service Group are required to double past the saluting-base on ceremonial occasions with their machine-carbines at the high-port, a very tiring procedure when other troops on parade are marching past in normal quick-time.

The regimental badge is the Star and Crescent in white-metal above a scroll bearing the title in English: within the Crescent, a fist is holding a dagger point-upwards.

12. THE FRONTIER CORPS

The Frontier. But which one? To the soldiers, both British and Indian, in the last century of British rule over the sub-continent, the only frontier was that in the North-West. For every red-blooded schoolboy brought up, as I was, in the 1920's and '30's, the North-West Frontier was the setting for a thousand adventure stories. It was also possible for Victoria Crosses to be won on the Frontier in peacetime, as witness, Captain Godfrey Meynell of the Guides Infantry (5/12th Frontier Force Regiment) in 1935.

The First Afghan War resulted in the debacle when the British column withdrawing via Jellalabad to India was harried and massacred. Remaining British-Indian forces in Afghanistan were relieved by a column under Major General George Pollock – the Army of Retribution – which assembled in Peshawar and marched via Jamrud and the Khyber Pass, through Jellalabad to Kabul. They withdrew by the same route and this was the British soldier's first view of the Khyber. He did not much like what he saw. Nothwithstanding, it was to be his destiny to serve in that area for the next century and the military graffiti still to be seen on rockfaces in the pass are enduring evidence of his passage.

Although regular troops fought in the frontier areas, the day-to-day peace was to be kept by local levies, recruited from local tribesmen responsible under their tribal chiefs for law and order in their area. Initially, they were paid for by the Government of India. This system was established by Colonel Sir Robert Sandeman and he recommended that Indian Army officers be seconded to provide the necessary leadership and discipline. The first such secondment-designate in 1878 was assassinated on his way to join the levies and no replacement was sent but, by 1883, tribal levy strength had reached 1,800 men, replacing the regular army in the Bolan Pass area and the upper Sind frontier but Sandeman never got his British Officer.

However, in 1890, the Zhob and Bori Rifles was raised, changing its title quickly to the Zhob Levy Corps and a Punjab Frontier Force cavalryman, Captain W A D O'Mealy, was appointed to its command. The Zhob bordered South Waziristan and Afghanistan and, if secured, would make a very defensible border if the Russians were to attack through Afghanistan. Sandeman recommended that the area be annexed into Baluchistan and this was done in 1889, being initially garrisoned by the army. Five hundred strong, the Zhob Levy Corps was recruited only 50% from local Pathans, the balance being Brahuis and refugee Ghilzais to make a force less susceptible to local politics. The name changed once more, now to become the Zhob Militia.

In the Kurram Valley, the local Turi tribesmen were being organised in 1892–93 by Captains G O Roos-Keppel and E W S K Maconchey into an irregular unit to be known as the Kurram Militia whilst, further north, Robert Warburton was finally successful in his bid to secure a British officer in 1896 for his native-commanded Khyber Rifles.

Towards the end of 1898, Lord Curzon arrived in India as Viceroy at the age of 39. He was not without experience having, a decade earlier, visited Quetta and toured the Khojak Pass with Sandeman. At about the same time, he had also visited Russian Turkestan and noted the success of a few Russian officers who had enlisted the barbarous tribes of Turkestan in their own administration and defence. He had visited the Khyber in 1894 when he met Robert Warburton and was impressed by the Khyber Rifles. Indian officers, of course, would be retained in subordinate ranks.

After the Chitral campaign in 1895, Curzon wrote to The Times stressing the value of para-military tribal irregulars under British officers. It was his view that the territories of the Frontier states would then be controlled by British officers, new recruiting-material would become available to the Government of India, roads would be opened up, the entire Frontier be made militarily accessible and the flow of trade between settled India and the remote valleys of the Hindu Kush created.

Following his appointment as Viceroy, Curzon launched his new Frontier policy. The army was to be withdrawn from tribal territory, being replaced by disciplined tribal irregulars under British officers, seconded to temporary appointments in the Indian Political Service. The army would be regrouped and concentrated near the Indus which would also strengthen the defence of the Frontier against Russian attack.

Tribal leaders would continue to receive allowances from the Government for their levies whilst the Zhob, Kurram and Khyber militiamen would receive direct payment individually.

Thus, the entire Frontier, from Chitral to Baluchistan, would, with the exception of Waziristan, be covered by British-officered tribal irregulars. The Waziristan Militia Committee, set up to examine the problem advised that four battalions of militia be formed, two for North and two for South Waziristan, totalling 3,200 men plus construction of a number of new forts: only 50% of the men were to be locals, the rest from British territory.

Curzon immediately set out to tour the area once more and, on his return, announced in May 1900, the formation of the North and South Waziristan Militias of 850 men each. Each battalion was to have three British officers, a commandant, a 2 i/c and an adjutant/quartermaster. Major R Harman, 53rd Sikhs, was to command the SWM and Captain A Ferguson-Davies, 54th Sikhs the NWM. Government had emphasized that the local Political Officer would always take precedence over the two commandants.

The South Waziristan Militia was to have its HQ at Wana and the HQ North Waziristan Militia was eventually to be located at Miranshah. As the militia took over the frontier posts, the army was withdrawn, leaving only a movable column, based at Bannu.

Some of the best officers of the Indian Army were finding their way to the militias, the general feeling being that service with the Pathans 'might mean a short life if an exciting one'. If the Indian Army was a refuge for impecunious British Army officers then the Militia was a refuge for Indian army officers with financial problems. It offered an independent command at an early age, far from senior headquarters with narrow, textbook constraints and almost no chance to spend any money. Mounted infantry companies existed but most work was done on foot, patrols at platoon-strength often covering more than forty miles in a twenty-four hours period over the harshest terrain in the world.

Curzon, unique among viceroys and senior administrators, had actually trekked the borders through the Pamirs and the Hindu Kush and, in 1900 accepted the suggestion of the local Political Officer in Chitral that a part-time militia from that area be created as the Chitral Scouts. Armed with modern rifles, they would train for one month each year. In 1913, the Gilgit Scouts were to be raised on similar lines: they were not required to patrol, as did the South Waziristan Militia and others, tactically, in anticipation of hostile neighbours.

Gilgit housed no local hostiles and, so, the Gilgit Scouts were not required to restrict their speed to forty miles in twenty-four hours. They expected to cover sixty.

The Great War brought the British Empire into conflict with the Turkish Ottoman Empire and the Frontier tribes, always ready to seize upon an excuse for action, rose in religious indignation but the Frontier Corps remained loyal throughout despite external pressures.

However, the third Afghan War in 1919 saw the eclipse of the Khyber Rifles. The main Afghan attack was launched against them but their loyalty had been undermined by the preaching of the Mullahs summoning all Muslims to a Jehad, or Holy War and by the rumour that the government of India was intent upon the destruction of the Afridi nation by putting the Khyber Rifles into the forefront of the action and then decimating them with artillery. After a number of desertions, the army took over the Khyber posts and the men of the Khyber Rifles were offered their discharge: some 1,180 took up the offer, 146 were transferred to the military police battalion and 200 were formed into the un-uniformed Khyber Levy Corps, armed with their own rifles. No Indian Officers opted for discharge. The Khyber Rifles were not to be re-raised until 1946 when the men of the 1st Afridi Battalion, returning from the Middle East, were offered the chance of their being reconstituted once more with their HQ at Landi Kotal.

The Chitral Scouts, occupying a frontier state, were mobilized by the Assistant Political Agent, Major Reilly and, 1,000 rifles strong, combined with 450 rifles of the 1/11th Rajputs and some 2,000 men of the Mehtar's bodyguard to drive out some six Afghan battalions – with five more in support. Two attacks were repulsed with no losses to the Scouts. The Gilgit Scouts, with no 'external' frontier, were not affected, of course.

On the central front – Waziristan and the Kurram Valley – the Afghans deployed fourteen regular battalions and forty-eight guns. The Government had decided that Waziristan could not be held and should be evacuated but, in the Kurram, things were different. A regular brigade held the defences in the valley whilst the Kurram Militia (1,450 rifles and 80 mounted infantry), with two regular battalions, conducted a guerilla campaign. On 3 Jan 19, they invaded Afghanistan, wreaking havoc amidst disillusioned and distressed Afghans and, on 8 Aug 19, peace was signed.

The North Waziristan Militia was ordered to pull out of all its forward posts. The army was unable to support them and the move was militarily correct although hardly a morale-raiser. This, said the Frontier, was clear evidence that the Sarkar (commonly used in reference to the Government of India – Raj is a term which has largely gained ground since Partition) was on the run and that, before long, Kabul would be in control of the whole land of the Pathans, down to the Indus. Numbers of the men deserted or just drifted away in the confusion, including several Indian officers.

Major G H Russell, commanding the South Waziristan Militia, organised a tactical withdrawal from Wana at the end of May, losing some 200 of his original party of 350, not only from enemy fire but also from desertion-wastage. They were saved by a patrol of the Zhob Militia. At no time during the 1919 troubles were British officers killed or attacked by Militia mutineers or deserters.

In the subsequent reorganisations the two Waziristan Militias were reconstituted and renamed the Tochi Scouts and the South Waziristan Scouts, with predominantly non-local recruitment and both earned good reputations in the next two decades. The Zhob Militia, briefly re-named again the Zhob Levy

Corps, the Chitral Scouts and the Kurram Militia remained loyal because they recruited the local tribes who were the hereditary enemies of their attackers.

During the late 1930's the first King's commissioned Indian Officers reached the Scouts and it was one of them, Sharif Khan, the first Kuki-Khel Afridi to be so honoured, who came to command the re-raised Khyber Rifles in 1946.

The Second World War saw no let-up in operations on the Frontier and, with so many battalions held down in the Middle East, the Scouts bore the brunt of the tribesmen's aggressive activities.

Dress for the Scouts ranged widely from the immaculate starched khaki-drill of the quarter-guard with polished leather and burnished brass to the informal patrol-order khaki pagri, shirt in khaki or Mazri (stout blue-grey cotton flecked with black), khaki shorts in summer, baggy Pathan pyjamas in winter: on the feet, heavy leather, studded chaplis. In the Chitral and Gilgit Scouts, the pagri gave way to the Pathan Pukhol, a flat, coarse woollen, circular khaki hat, worn widely by almost everyone in the Hindu Kush. For formal parades, a white Pukhol was often worn.

The term Indian officer has been used for the ranks which, in the regular Indian Army, would have been called Viceroy's Commissioned Officers (VCO). In the Frontier Corps, these commissions were granted by the Governor-General of the North West Frontier Province. Other ranks were the same as those in use in the Indian army, cavalry terms being favoured for Mounted Infantry personnel.

In August 1947, on Partition, all the Frontier Corps units naturally went to Pakistan. From north to south, the eight units were the Gilgit Scouts, Chitral Scouts, Khyber Rifles, Kurram Militia, Tochi Scouts, South Waziristan Scouts, Zhob Militia and the new Pishin Scouts, raised only in 1946 for the Pishin-Chaman sector of the Frontier.

BOOKS

'The Pathans' by Olaf Caroe (Pub. MacMillan London, 1965)
'The Frontier 1839–1947' by Maj General J G Elliot (Pub. Cassell, London, 1968)
'Frontier Scouts' by Colonel HRC Pettigrew (Privately published Selsey, Sussex 1965)
'Frontier Scouts' by Charles Chevenix Trench (Pub. Cape, London, 1985)

13. POST-PARTITION RESERVES AND PARAMILITARIES

Para-military bodies within the sub-continent had always abounded and Partition was not to see the end of these.

British India's Auxiliary Force, the Territorial Army for its exiled white sons came to an abrupt end in August 1947. Neither India nor Pakistan would care to sponsor British armed bodies in its midst and, moreover, surely the civil unrest which the AFI had been intended to cope with would now be a thing of the past. All such units were stood down at midnight 14/15 Aug 47.

The battalions of the Indian Territorial Force had, almost all, been promoted during the war to active status and had either remained as such, available for transfer to either of the new dominions in the share-out of the Indian Army or had been disbanded in the heady days of peace in 1946. It was in October 1949 that the new Indian Territorial Army was born. Artillery, Engineers, Signals, infantry, medical and EME units were formed. The conditions of and liability for service were more or less the same as those for the TA in Britain, except that there were two categories of unit.

The provincial units recruited in the rural areas and carried out training for two calendar months in a year whilst the urban units trained at week-ends and in the evenings. The infantry battalions were attached to regular regiments, wearing their uniforms and badges, observing their regimental days, etc., but recognisable by their distinctive shoulder-titles. Battalion numbers began at 101. The 105th, based in Delhi, is a Raj Rif battalion, (black titles, of course), the 108th, in Saugor, is a Mahar battalion whilst the 123rd, a Grenadiers battalion, is in Jaipur. Some regiments, like the Jats, had more than one battalion (114th in Dehra Dun and 121st in Calcutta).

Many such TA battalions have been mobilised in India's wars, either to perform Lines of Communications duties or, in a minority of instances, to take their place in the line.

In Pakistan, no such sub-regimental structure exists. Mujahid battalions form the first category of auxiliary infantry but they are simply numbered battalions with no regimental affiliations whatsoever albeit their terms of service are much as in India. The second-line category is made up of Janbaz battalions, less well trained, less well armed and placed lower in mobilisation liability.

One of Pakistan's prized legacies from British India was the Frontier Corps, charged with the task of looking North West. The eight separate units transferred on Partition were soon augmented by others. The Mekran Militia and Chagai Militia were formed in 1948, the Northern Scouts and Thal Scouts in 1949, the Bajaur Scouts were raised in 1961 for the Bajaur, Swat and Dir tribal areas, the Karakoram Scouts in 1964 and the Kalat Scouts in 1965 for duty in Brahui country between Quetta and Karachi. The last to be raised was based on Razmak, in 1973, to be known as the Shawal Scouts. So much for the peace that was expected to prevail in the frontier areas under the newly-appointed Muslim suzerainty. Kabul and Moscow both stirred tribal feelings, urging self-rule for minorities within Baluchistan. All the 'old' corps sent willing volunteers to fight in Kashmir in 1948 and, rather more surprisingly, Khyber Rifles and others were found in East Pakistan in 1971.

In East Pakistan, after Partition, the East Pakistan Rifles was formed as the para-military counterpart of the Frontier Corps in the West. In 1971, most of the EPR deserted to the embryonic Bangladeshi army.

Back in West Pakistan, a force was required to man the frontier facing east into India and this was formed and designated the Pakistan Rangers. These, too, served in East Pakistan in 1971.

In 1977, the Northern Scouts (which had already absorbed the Gilgit Scouts) and the Karakoram Scouts were merged to form the Northern Light Infantry, wearing the white woollen pukhol with a Himalayan pheasant feather in place of the more familiar beret. The NLI is a force which is neither regular army nor Frontier Corps. It is permanently based in what Pakistan calls the Northern Areas with its centre at Gilgit and it confronts the Indian Army in the area of Skardu.

The Frontier Corps is now divided into two bodies, the Frontier Corps

(NWFP) with its HQ in the Bala Hissar in Peshawar and the Frontier Corps (Baluchistan), based in Quetta.

India, deprived in 1947 of the Frontier Corps, was compelled to raise another para-military force to replace them to watch another, rather nearer, North-West frontier with West Pakistan plus the new Chinese threat from the north. This became the Border Security Force, now numbering some one hundred battalions but perhaps best known to the Indian public for its picturesque, ceremonial, camel-mounted sowars seen in the capital every January. In the east, India already had the Assam Rifles, long a source of recruits for Indian Army units in two world wars and the cadre for the raising of the Assam Regiment in 1941. They were expanded and now number more than thirty battalions whilst the Eastern Frontier Rifles, a pre-Partition unit based on Midnapore is still in existence. Both the latter units depend heavily on the recruitment of domiciled Gurkhas.

The requirements of security in both countries make it difficult to be sure that information on new units is up to date. If anything, information on para-military units is often harder to find than on regular regiments whose doings are chronicled in regimental journals and regimental histories.

14. AN HISTORICAL OVERVIEW

Indian soldiers had seen active service beyond India long before 1903's changes had provided for overseas forays by constructing field formations. The ready supply of tropically-acclimatised troops made the Madras Army the ideal manpower-reservoir for service in Burma following the Third Burma War, a 'subaltern's war' then no less than it was sixty years later for the XIVth Army.

Even further afield, Indian troops had served in China in 1857–62, in Malaya in 1875, Malta – as garrison troops – in 1878, in Egypt in 1882, the Sudan in 1885 and Somaliland in 1901–04. These were all, however, ad hoc bodies, regiments cobbled together for the occasion. The Kitchener reforms, begun in 1903, resulted in a field army of more than nine divisions, notionally ready to take the field in an emergency by 1908.

When war came in August 1914, 155,000 men were in these formations and their statistics make interesting reading against comparable logistics seventy-five years afterwards: some 25,000 were cavalry, 121,000 were infantry whilst the modest balance of 9,000 covered the other arms and services – sappers, signals, transport, medical, supply, etc. – no artillery, of course, as that was exclusively a British arm. The 3rd (Lahore) Division, the 7th (Meerut) Division and the 4th (Secunderabad) Cavalry Brigade were despatched to what was then known as the Near East. However, things were not going too well for British arms in Europe and the men of the Indian Corps were re-routed to Marseilles where they landed in late September (the Lahore Division was less the Sirhind Brigade which remained in Egypt and only rejoined the Division in December). By that time, only four British regular divisions had reached France, so that India's contribution represented a significant proportion of Britain's share of the allied war effort. Orders were received at sea on 20 Sep 14 that only the regional titles were to be used in France to avoid confusion with existing British divisions. A fortnight after landing, Indian troops were in the line where they were used to advantage in the early actions. Much has been made of their service in north-western Europe, still in light khaki-drill uniforms, this being represented as some sort of ordnance blunder. Some historians have chosen to ignore that the Indian Corps' intended destination had been Egypt as garrison troops and that the many thousands of khaki service-dress uniforms necessary were not immediately available in the smaller sizes required for some Indian troops. Infantry brigades were made up of one British and three Indian battalions, all having sailed from Karachi and Bombay.

The order of battle for the Lahore Division in September 1914 is shown below: the brigades were the old, 'square' type with four battalions each.

Ferozepore Brigade	*Jullundur Brigade*	*Sirhind Brigade*
1 CONNAUGHT RANGERS	1 MANCHESTER	1 HLI
57 RIFLES	15 SIKHS	1/1 GR
9 BHOPAL	47 SIKHS	1/4 GR
129 BALUCHIS	59 RIFLES	125 RIFLES

Div Mounted Troops	*Div Pioneers*
15 LANCERS (CURETON'S MULTANIS)	34 SIKHS
Artillery	*Engineers*
V,XI and XVIII Brigades RA (64, 73, 81, 83, 84, 85, 59, 93, 94 Batteries)	20 and 21 Coys 3rd. Sappers & Miners
Signals	*Medical*
32 Div Signal Coy	7th and 8th Brit. Field Ambulances 111th, 112th and 113th Ind Field Ambulances

The bloody actions of La Bassée, First Ypres, Neuve Chapelle, Festubert and Loos in 1914 and 1915 meant heavy casualties, especially among British officers. The reinforcement system for Indian ranks had not anticipated such pressures and many units required replacements numbering more than their original strengths. Battalions were frequently taken individually and rushed into the line with previously unknown British flanking units and none of the infantry was too disappointed when the arrival in France in 1915 of newly-raised British divisions meant that the bulk of the Indian troops could be withdrawn and sent to Egypt, leaving the Secunderabad and Sialkot Cavalry Brigades in France. Indian cavalry strength there later grew to two divisions which remained there until November 1918. Those troops who were sent to Egypt met there the troops withdrawn from Gallipoli: the inspired plan to force the Dardanelles and compel the Turks to surrender foundered badly. The only troops actually to get to the top of the ridge and see the Dardanelles were men of 1/6th Gurkha Rifles.

Closer to home, in October, 1914, the 6th (Poona) Division was sent to Iraq to capture Basra and protect British oil interests. This force, augmented by another division and a cavalry brigade advanced up the line of the Euphrates and took Kut-al-Amara in September 1915. Major General Townshend, commanding, facing an overwhelmingly stronger Turkish force, pressed on towards Baghdad but was stopped by the Turks at Ctesiphon and driven back to Kut-al-Amara where, after a siege lasting until April 1916, he was forced to surrender. The general retired to a not-too-rigorous imprisonment in Constantinople whilst his soldiers, British and Indian, marched across the desert in the Mesopotamian summer under savage Turkish guards into prison camps from which few returned. An avenging force under General Sir Stanley Maude, 160,000 strong, advanced up the Tigris, capturing Kut in February 1917 and Baghdad in March. Sadly, the general was to die before the year was out from all-too-prevalent disease and most of his forces were transferred to General Allenby, then building up his force which was to fight its way through Palestine against Turkish resistance. The Lahore and Meerut Divisions and two independent infantry brigades formed part of this force. Jerusalem fell on 9 Dec 17, Allenby entering on foot through the Jaffa Gate, the first Christian commander to enter the city, holy to three major religions, since the First Crusade. The campaign continued, to inflict total defeat upon a Turkish enemy originally almost three million strong, reduced by October 1918 to fewer than half a million.

On another continent, Indian troops found themselves in action against the Germans. Some 18,000 troops were committed to German East Africa where, together with about the same number of British, African and South African troops,they were kept engaged by some 3,000 European and 12,000 locally-enlisted native soldiers intermittently for four years. Of the Indian force, several thousands were Imperial Service troops raised from the princely states: in fact, only 6,369 IS troops were sent overseas of the 22,000 available, and most of those went to East Africa. The campaign rated as something of a sideshow when compared with the major actions in Europe and the Middle East but there was plenty of old-fashioned soldiering there for which the Indian Army was well-suited. The final German surrender took place in Mozambique on 25 Nov 18, a fortnight after the Armistice in Europe.

At that time, the strength of the Indian Army was 573,484 men: 36,000 had been killed and more than 70,000 wounded during the course of the war. Eleven Victoria Crosses had been awarded to Indian soldiers, the first war in which they had had the opportunity to earn the supreme award for gallantry since they had been declared eligible in 1912.

Many changes were to follow the Great War as they always did after a major war and these are outlined elsewhere.

However, before these could be implemented, the new Amir of Afghanistan declared a holy war against India in 1919 and attacked the frontier in several places. There was no lack of troops on hand in India and a force advanced into the Khyber Pass, inflicting a heavy defeat on Afghan irregulars. The Amir sued for peace and the six-month war came to an end. Nineteen Indian cavalry regiments, fifty infantry battalions and all eleven Gurkha regiments received the honour 'Afghanistan 1919' for something of an 'overkill' campaign.

Before the outbreak of the Second World War in September 1939, units of the 4th Indian Division were already on their way to Egypt as Indian troops had been twenty-five years earlier. This time, however, they were to stay in the Middle East, the only Indian troops going to Europe being the mule companies of the RIASC which were duly evacuated from France in May 1940.

Thereafter, 4th Indian Division, joined in 1940 by 5th Indian Division, featured in most Middle East and East African actions. In addition to campaigns in British Somaliland, Abyssinia, Syria, Iraq and North Africa, Indian troops formed the bulk of what became known as Paiforce (Persia and Iraq Force – pronounced pie-force). Once again, British oil interests in the Persian Gulf had to be protected as did the southern supply route to the Soviet Union with the result that two divisions were tied down in garrison and lines-of-communication roles.

Three Indian divisions, the 4th, 8th, and the 10th, served in Italy from 1943 and in Greece during 1944–45.

The small Indian garrison in Malaya in 1941 was nominally reinforced but mainly by battalions which had already been 'milked' to form new Indian Army battalions authorised earlier that year. The campaign following the Japanese invasion in December 1941 lasted a bare two months and virtually the entire force went into Japanese hands in February 1942 in Singapore.

The next step for the Japanese that same month was into Burma where they met 17th Indian Division, also containing 'milked' battalions and it was a tactical masterstroke to have managed to contain the Japanese attacks and to evacuate as many personnel to India as was done. For the next three years, Indian troops were to make up the bulk of the infantry force in Burma. The 5th Indian Division had been sent back from the Middle East and, by August, 1945, at the conclusion of the campaign in Burma, almost a hundred Indian battalions had gained the honour 'Burma 1942–45'. One of the formations created was officially styled 3rd Indian Division and popularly known as the Chindits, intended for long-range penetration of Japanese lines. Its commander, the eccentric Orde Wingate, felt that Indian troops were not suited for that particular type of campaigning and chose only to have British, Gurkha and African troops in his force.

Shown below is the order of battle for 17th Indian Division towards the end of the campaign:

48 Ind Inf Bde
1 WEST YORKS
4/12 FF REGT
1/7 GR

63 Ind Inf Bde
9 BORDER
7/10 BALUCH
1/10 GR

99 Ind Inf Bde
6/15 PUNJAB
1 SIKH LI
1/3 GR

Div Recce Bn
6/7 RAJPUT

Div Defence Bn
6/9 JAT

Div MG Bn
9/13 FF RIF

Artillery
129 Field Regt RA
1 Ind Field Regt IA
21 Ind Mtn Regt IA
82 A Tk Regt RA

Engineers
60 Coy (Madras)
70 Coy (Bengal)
Tehri Garhwal Coy
414 Ind Field Park (Bengal)

RIASC
902 GT Coy
906 GT Coy
42 AT Coy
50 Gwalior Pony Coy

Medical
23 Field Ambulance
37 Field Ambulance
50 Field Ambulance
22 Hygiene Section

IEME
1, 59 and 123 Workshops
17 Recovery Coy

Ordance
117 Ord Field Park
2 Workshop Coys

Under Command: 255 Ind. Tank Bde (5 Probyn's Horse, 9 Royal Deccan Horse, 16 Light Cavalry, squadron 11 PAVO Cavalry), 247 Med. Bty RA, 189 HAA Bty and 250 LAA Bty.

After the war, the far-flung battalions lingered on, much as they had after that earlier conflict. Indian troops were represented in the British Commonwealth Occupation Force in Japan: they served on in the Middle East and they held the ring in the Dutch East Indies until such time as the Dutch could re-establish control. In Burma,in 1947, a task-force of divisional strength was mustered to fight a mixture of opportunist dacoits, a traditional feature of Burmese country-life, and political guerrillas. Some of these battalions returned home to an independent India after August 1947 whilst companies from others went direct to Karachi to their new country, Pakistan.

To cover the potentially explosive Punjab through which hundreds of thousands of civilian refugees would flow in both directions on Partition, the Punjab Boundary Force was formed, almost two divisions strong under that formidable Welshman, Major-General 'Pete' Rees, lately GOC 19th 'Dagger' Division. Indian and Gurkha battalions comprised most of this force and its reputation was impeccable. Sikh soldiers protected Muslim refugees from Sikh bandits whilst Muslim soldiers escorted Hindu columns from Pathan and Afridi predators. By this time, of course, most of the British officers with long experience of Indian service had either gone home on leave or on repatriation and Rees was compelled to ask that the PBF be disbanded and its component battalions be permitted to revert to their new countries. Punjabi Mussalman companies left Sikh battalions to go to Pakistan whilst Dogra companies of Frontier Force battalions left for India. All parted with every evidence of affection for, after all, were they not all soldiers, with an honourable past. In many cases, companies were actually escorted to the border to ensure their safety from marauding parties of the opposing persuasion.

In October 1947, armed Muslim tribesmen 'spontaneously' invaded Jammu and Kashmir in the name of Islam and Pakistan. The state population was more than 70% Muslim and the Hindu maharajah had indicated his intention to cede to India. The state's army was unable to deal with the sheer volume of the attack and the invaders reached Baramula, a resort only 35 miles from Srinagar, the state capital. Under proper discipline, they could have taken Srinagar but the burden of loot was such that they had to return home with it and, by the time that they got back, India had acted. A single battalion, 1 Sikh, had been flown into Srinagar and a further three thousand men in a Brigade-group followed them. By early 1948, the regular Pakistan Army had become involved and sporadic fighting followed. Finally the United Nations Organisation took heed of the situation and, on 1 Jan 49, a sort of peace descended on J & K. Five thousand casualties had been sustained by India, with eleven hundred dead. No comparable figures are to be had for Pakistan: officially, their army had not been involved until Spring 1948 although it is known that the earlier attacks had been orchestrated by army officers.

During the 1950's India appeared to lose interest in its army which kept a low profile until 1961 when it achieved a brief spell of fame as 17th Infantry Division took the Portuguese colony of Goa.

In the meantime, in September 1959, the Chinese occupied several thousand square kilometers of Indian territory in Ladakh and there followed three years of diplomatic wrangling. The 4th Infantry Division, the heroes of the Western Desert twenty years earlier, was moved into the North East Frontier Agency (NEFA), a Sino-Indian area of dispute, Indian politicians, generally even less cognizant of military affairs than British politicians, urged in September 1962 that the Chinese be thrown out. The latter had some four well-equipped divisions on the border with good roads and easy logistical support whereas India, with an under-funded army, had long and tortuous supply lines. On 20 Oct 62, the Chinese launched three major attacks. The 4th Infantry Division ceased to be an effective battle-formation albeit, before it dissolved, heavy casualties were inflicted on the Chinese. Whilst western strategists were hourly expecting the Chinese hordes to debouch on to the plains of Assam, the Chinese high command announced on 21 Nov 62 a unilateral ceasefire and withdrawal to as position twenty kilometers 'behind the line of actual control as of 7 November 1959'. The Indian Defence Minister and a number of senior generals were removed from office. Lavish help was forthcoming from the West: the defence services were expanded and special mountain divisions created but only five infantry regiments received battle-honours for the 1962 actions.

As Kipling had said of an earlier incident, 'The papers 'id it 'andsome, but you know the Army knows'.

Military popularity followed military growth but this did not please Pakistan: nor did the apparent integration of Jammu & Kashmir into the Indian Union. However, Sino-Pakistan links were being forged, Chinese arms were within reach and Chinese support was reassuring. The Rann of Kutch, a stretch of salt-covered desert in Western India, was a perennial area of dispute: one day in January 1965, the Indian Army awoke to find that this insanitary stretch of land, under water for six months each year, had spawned Pakistani soldiers. The Indian reaction was such as to please Pakistan's then military ruler, Field Marshal Ayub Khan – a minimum of military action but much political posturing and ready acceptance of international arbitration to resolve this very local problem. Pakistan was also well-pleased with its American armour, even although the Americans, who made a token protest, had supplied it under CENTO and SEATO agreements for use against Communist aggression. (CENTO was the Central Powers Treaty Organisation made up of Turkey, Iran, Iraq, Pakistan and the UK which lasted from 1955 to 1979, Iraq dropping out in 1957. The South East Asia Treaty Organisation – SEATO – consisted of Australia, France, New Zealand, Pakistan, Philippines, Thailand, UK and the USA and lasted from 1955 to 1977).

The time now appeared ripe for Pakistan to introduce a force of well-armed guerrillas into Jammu and Kashmir as it was felt unlikely that India would wish to attempt a large scale military offensive against Azad Kashmir territory. The guerrillas were to have raised a revolt but they failed: Indian Kashmiri Muslims were suspicious of strangers offering liberation and reported them to the authorities who promptly advanced into POK (Pakistan Occupied Kashmir) with signal success. At this juncture, Ayub Khan felt that it was Pakistan's duty to support such spontaneous freedom fighters and an armoured thrust of about a hundred tanks was launched in an attempt to cut Kashmir off from the rest of India. To relieve the pressure on the Kashmir front, the Indians embarked on operations against Lahore, Sialkot and in Sind. Neither city was reached and the Sind venture was regarded as little more than a diversionary gesture. The forces employed by each side approached parity: Pakistan had two armoured divisions and four infantry divisions whilst India had an armoured division, an independent armoured brigade, four infantry divisions and two mountain divisions.

International reaction had been effective in the imposition of both military and economic strictures by Britain and the USA. A ceasefire was mediated and enforced by the United Nations Organisation on 23 Sep 65. India had taken 1,528 square kilometers of Pakistan territory for the loss of 544 of her own. Her losses in killed were 3,261, of whom 177 were officers including one brigadier and ten commanding officers. Details of Pakistan's losses, of course, are not available.

It was Mountbatten, the last Viceroy of India, who was convinced that Pakistan, the two halves separated by a thousand miles of India, could not last more than twenty-five years. Events were to prove him not too far wrong. Although East Pakistan, carved out of Bengal, was more populous than West Pakistan, it was from the West that the country was governed. Parliamentary elections in 1970 gave the Awami League, the East Pakistan local party, an absolute majority and the main plank in their platform had been that of provincial autonomy. Visions of outright secession prompted alarm in the West so that the strength of the Pakistan Army was reinforced in the East. The National Assembly was to open in Dacca on 25 Mar 71 and, on that day, Sheik Mujib-ur-Rahman, president of the Awami League, declared the independence of Bangladesh – Free Bengal. He was promptly arrested and, within a couple of weeks, West Pakistani sovereignty over the East was re-established. By the end of the month, one million refugees had left for India, a figure which was to rise to nine million. It was not until December 1971 that India appeared to act. On 3 Dec 71, the Pakistani Air Force launched pre-emptive strikes on nine major Indian airfields. However, the attacks had been expected and aircraft dispersed so that immediate reprisals could be undertaken. In the months prior to this, the Indians had not been idle and had massed eight divisions around East Pakistan with an abundance of river-crossing and bridging equipment. The Bengali elements of the Pakistan Army had long since gone over to Bangladesh and the total effective strength available to the Army was little more than two divisions.

Attacks were made from the west, the north and the east and despite strong resistance from Pakistan, the campaign in East Pakistan was over by 15 Dec 71.

In the West, armoured battles took place in the Punjab and, inevitably, activity in Kashmir. It was, however, little more than a holding action by the army whilst Bangladesh was being created but the Navy shelled Karachi and the Air Force established superiority over Pakistan armour in the desert. Casualties for Pakistan were about 8,000 men lost against India's 3,000: India lost 83 tanks against Pakistan's 220. The success of operations brought promotion for General Sam Manekshaw, making him independent India's first field marshal. Ironically, he had been first commissioned into 4/12th Frontier Force Regiment. Somewhat Wellingtonian, he had scant respect for politicians and did not succumb to flattery. He was well aware that his forces outnumbered those of the enemy but he was also not inclined to underrate the quality of the Pakistani soldier.

Since 1971, twenty years of overt peace between the two major countries of the sub-continent have followed.

India has not been slow to identify herself with United Nations operations. In Korea, in 1950, when Britain was forming the Commonwealth Division, India declined to send teeth-arms but furnished 60 Parachute Field Ambulance, a unit first raised in 1942 and converted to a parachute role in 1945. It performed to the total satisfaction of everyone treated and spent longer in Korea than any other unit in the division.

After the cease-fire in Korea on 27 Jul 53, the Neutral Nations Repatriation Committee set up to facilitate the return of some 23,000 prisoners to their respective homelands, ordered 190 Infantry Brigade to Korea. The Indians were to supervise the procedures and the US Army Engineers were to construct the camps. The Brigade was enlarged to form a brigade group and it became known as the Custodian Force, India (CFI). It was made up of 5 Raj Rif, 6 Jat, 3 Dogra and 3 Garhwal Rif, to be joined later by 2 Para and 3 Mahar. India's first foray into the UN arena took the CFI away from home for about six months and established its name internationally. Subsequently, Indian soldiers served the UNEF in the Gaza Strip and in the Congo where real soldiering took place in the aftermath of Belgium's withdrawal from Central Africa in 1961–62.

Some of India's other ventures on to the international stage were in Sri Lanka and in the Maldives, the latter in November 1988. Although the Maldives was little more than a sabre-rattling exercise, the Indian Peace Keeping Force in Sri Lanka was a substantial campaign: about 60 battalions were rotated through the IPKF from July 1987 to March 1990, involving those old campaigners, 4th Infantry Division, the old 'Red Eagles' of the Western desert, 36th 54th and 57th Infantry Divisions plus two independent brigades, the 89th and the 340th. In support were 65th Armoured Regt and 13th Mech. Inf. Regt. At its peak, the Force reached a strength of almost 100,000 men, India's largest expeditionary force. Casualties were higher than was first revealed, being some 6,000 in total, of whom 2,000 were killed. The latter included the commanding officers of 11 Madras, 4/5 GR, 6/8 GR and 7/8 GR. The IPKF left Sri Lanka in March 1990 after an inconclusive thirty-two months.

Indian officers served in Nambia and are taking part in the UNO operations in Cambodia whilst Major General Satish Nambiar, once his country's Defence Adviser in London, was appointed to command the UN Forces in Yugoslavia in March 1992.

Pakistan has also become involved in United Nations operations in both the Congo and also in Western New Guinea. At home, a succession of military rulers gave way in January 1989 to Benazir Bhutto whose civilian administration lasted a bare twenty months before being deposed in favour of the military-backed faction in August 1990. Notwithstanding, Pakistani soldiers are in great demand in the Persian Gulf and have been able to sell their swords to the rulers of the Gulf states. Their familiarity with modern weapons, their discipline and their devotion to Islam have made them welcome mercenaries in an area where expatriate and shifting populations are all too common – and none too dependable. There were, in fact, reports of complete Pakistan Army battalions serving Arab rulers who felt them more reliable than their own household troops for their personal protection.

This would appear to have been substantiated by events in August 1990 following the Iraqi invasion of Kuwait. A brigade was promised by Pakistan to join the Arab forces in Saudi Arabia and it materialised in a flash!

Finally, India's longest-standing international commitment came to an end in 1954. After the Tibet campaign in 1903–04, an Indian infantry company was maintained at Gyantse, in Tibet, with a detachment at Yatung: these were to act as escorts to the British Trade Agents. These posts were maintained by an independent India after Partition, the same Trade agent, Mr Hugh Richardson, remaining in post until 1953. Needless to say, the Chinese invasion of Tibet in 1954 removed the purpose of the company which was, in the final days of British rule, furnished by one of the battalions engaged in aid-to-the-civil-power duties in Bengal.

15. BRITAIN'S BRIGADE OF GURKHAS

Although Partition took place on the 15 Aug 47, it was not until the first week in August that it became known that His Majesty's Government was negotiating to transfer some of the Gurkha regiments to the British Army. In the spring of 1946, the then viceroy, Lord Wavell, had warned HMG that the future Government of India would not be able to continue to employ all ten Gurkha regiments and that the best forecast was for four two-battalion regiments only. His recommendation was that the residue be transferred to British command on independence but no action was taken until the following March when the deadline for independence had been set. In that month, the Executive Committee of the Army Council considered the problem. A large British wartime army was being demobilised and a number of regular battalions of famous British infantry regiments were to be placed in suspended animation. Taking Gurkhas on to British Army strength might mean complete disbandment. However, the wish existed to maintain strong links with Nepal and the military connection was already well-established. Gurkhas in Malaya, their new home-station, would constitute a reserve for South-East Asia and at that time, national service in Britain was for one year only, so that, after training, the young conscripts could not conceivably be sent to Malaya with yet a further six weeks taken from their effective service-time by sea-trooping, standard practice at that time. A division of Gurkhas in Malaya would solve several problems.

The Tripartite Agreement for the employment of Gurkhas in the British and Indian Armies was not ratified until 9 Nov 47 but the decision to take the 2nd, 6th, 7th and 10th Gurkhas was made on 8 Aug. In his letter to the commanding officers of all Gurkha battalions, the Adjutant General in India, Sir Reginald Savory, explained some of the background.

'I know the decision as to which regiments of Gurkhas are to go to the War Office must have been a surprise to you and that you must be wondering how on earth the decision was made. I am, therefore writing this letter that I may try to explain what may appear to you to be inexplicable.

The future of the Gurkhas has been the subject of prolonged negotiations at a very high level in which many were involved – the Foreign Office, the India Office, the War Office, the Government of India, the Government of Nepal, the High Commissioner in India for the United Kingdom, and last but not least, GHQ India. The negotiations have not only been very slow but also very delicate and were of a nature which made it quite impossible for me to give you a hint as to what was going on, because to have done so might have prejudiced the whole question whether or not any Gurkhas were to go to the War Office.

This delay has allowed us very little time between the date of the final decision and the 15th August. The War Office, when stating which particular regiments they would like, said that they wished the *units to be spread as widely as possible over the recruiting area of Nepal. They specified the 7th or 10th Gurkhas and two regiments of Magars and Gurungs.* Among the last-named they particularly specified the 2nd Gurkhas owing to their close relationship with the 60th Rifles. The selection of the second regiment of Magars and Gurungs they left to us.*

In making the final decision we had to be influenced by pressing problems of time and shipping.

Both the 7th and 10th Gurkhas have regular battalions in Burma. The 6th Gurkhas also have a regular battalion in Burma and we, therefore, chose them as our free choice for Magars and Gurungs. All these battalions were serving under the War Office (SEALF) [South-East Asia Land Forces] and their transfer from Burma to their ultimate home in Malaya would be a matter of arrangement by HQ SEALF.

The 2nd Gurkhas were the only Regiment which had no regular battalion overseas, but they were specially nominated by the War Office.'

When the move to Malaya had been completed, some 8,000 Gurkhas were found to be on British strength, more than 25% of them recruits. They were to be collectively known as The Gurkha Regiment and were to be responsible for finding their own men for the support arms and services in the proposed, new Gurkha Division. This was to be the 17th Division, a familiar formation to the many Gurkha soldiers who had served in its ranks in the 1939–45 War.

May 1948 saw 1/7 and 2/7 GR converted to an artillery role, being redesignated respectively the 101 and 102 Field Regiments, Royal Artillery (7th Gurkha Rifles). Gunner commanding officers were posted in and training with 26th Field Regiment RA, stationed at Tampin began. It was intended that thereafter, 103 Field, 104 Anti-Aircraft and 105 Anti-Tank Regiments would be formed.

The future of the regiment as part of the Royal Artillery, however, came to an abrupt end. The Emergency in Malaya began on 15 Jan 48 and it was soon realised that the two battalions of the 7th would be better employed as infantrymen than as none-too-eager gunners. Notwithstanding, it was not until June 1949 that the Regiment reverted to an infantry role.

The first Gurkhas to be granted King's Commissions were gazetted in November 1948 when their official designation became Gurkha Commissioned Officers (GCOs): the former viceroy's Commissioned Officers (VCOs), known as Gurkha Officers, were henceforth, to be styled King's Gurkha Officers (KGOs) and all non-commissioned ranks were to be styled as in the British Army.

Of the four regiments, only the 2nd King Edward VII's Own Gurkha Rifles bore a royal style but, in October, 1949, the 10th Gurkha Rifles became the 10th Princess Mary's Own Gurkha Rifles as a form of recognition of their outstanding service in the Second World War. Their badge was altered to include a title scroll below the stringed bugle-horn whilst the personal cypher of HRH The Princess Royal appeared above the blade of the kukri, displacing the numerals '10' which were placed below the blade. By a happy chance, HRH The Princess Royal, the sister of the then King, HM King George VI, was also Colonel-in-Chief of The

*Those from western Nepal. The 7th and the 10th recruited from Eastern Nepal.

Royal Scots (The Royal Regiment) who had been responsible in India a half-century earlier, for training the pipes and drums of both 1/10 and 2/10 GR. Her appointment formalised the alliance between the two regiments and a patch of Hunting Stuart tartan is now worn behind the badge on the right side of the Gurkha hat.

The 2nd Goorkhas, of course, who still prefer the older spelling, continue to wear the black Prince of Wales's plumes in the beret and the Kilmarnock whilst the black and red diced patch on the pagri of the Gurkha hat serves to identify them.

The emergency in Malaya continued for twelve years. British infantry battalions came and went but the eight Gurkha battalions remained there, being rotated only for a tour in Hong Kong or Brunei. Finally, with the end in sight, the 6th and 7th Gurkha Rifles were rewarded in January 1959 by becoming respectively the 6th Queen Elizabeth's Own Gurkha Rifles and the 7th Duke of Edinburgh's Own Gurkha Rifles. The badge of the 6th had a crown added above the crossed kukris whilst the 7th added not only a ducal coronet but also HRH The Prince Philip's cypher to their badge.

The 6th had previously enjoyed an alliance with the Rifle Brigade and this was later formalised into one with The Royal Green Jackets into which the Rifle Brigade had been absorbed. The link between the 2nd Battalion and the 14/20 The King's Hussars, established at Medicina in Italy in April 1945 was to be extended to the 1st Battalion in 1966 and both battalions came to wear the Hussars' Prussian Eagle badge on their right sleeve.

The 7th had long enjoyed an association with The Cameronians (Scottish Rifles) which was formalised in 1949 and, the Scots regiment having been disbanded in 1969, the 7th Duke of Edinburgh's Own Gurkha Rifles are now the only regular soldiers still to wear the Douglas tartan, in their case as a badge-backing on the Gurkha hat.

The Malayan Emergency resolved, the only victory recorded over communist insurgency, the Brigade of Gurkhas were naturals to face confrontation between Malaysia and Indonesia – usually referred to as the 'Borneo Campaign' – when it began in 1963.

The title 'Brigade of Gurkhas' had been granted in 23 Sep 48 as a replacement for the unpopular Gurkha Regiment title in use since 1 Jan 48. The wider title was intended to embrace the other arms and services which were to be formed as part of the new 17 Gurkha Division.

Engineers were first mustered in late 1948 to form the Gurkha Training Squadron Engineer Training Squadron. Two Gurkha Field Squadrons RE were formed in the two successive years, the title Gurkha Engineers was formalised in 1955 and, the following year, 50 (Gurkha) Field Engineer Regiment was formed with one HQ and three field squadrons. June 1977 saw them granted the title the Queen's Gurkha Engineers. Their badge consists of the familiar crossed kukris, cutting-edges downwards, a scroll 'Ubique' below, with a sapper grenade above the intersection.

The signals unit was first formed in October 1948 as a cadre attached to Malaya District Signal Regiment. Squadrons were formed in successive years until Oct 53 when 17 Gurkha Division Signal Regiment was fully established. The title Gurkha Signals was authorised on 28 Sep 55 (Army Order 102/55) and Queen's Gurkha Signals on 20 Apr 77. Their badge is the familiar Royal Signals' Mercury, or 'Jimmy' between crossed kukris, cutting-edges inwards.

The Gurkha Army Service Corps was not raised until 1 Jul 58 in Singapore but recruiting was fast and, in 1965, in line with the change of title of the Royal

Army Service Corps to the Royal Corps of Transport, the Gurkha Corps became the Gurkha Transport Regiment. Its badge is similar to that of the RCT – an eight-pointed star bearing the Royal Cypher in the centre – but has additionally, crossed kukris.

The last of the Gurkha corps to reach maturity was the provost unit. A divisional provost company was raised on 1 Jul 49 which became 17 Gurkha Divisional Provost Company, Gurkha Military Police, embodying both British and Gurkha NCOs, in Jan 57. Some eight years later, in Jan 65, the provost aspects of the company lapsed and it became 5 (Gurkha) Dog Company, Gurkha Military Police, only to be disbanded in October that year. Their badge was similar to that of the Royal Military Police, the Royal Cypher within a wreath of laurel, surmounted by a crown, all over a title scroll but with the addition of crossed kukris within the wreath.

In 1950, 99 recruits to the Royal Army Ordance Corps were enlisted and trained but posted to regiments afterwards. No Gurkha Ordnance unit was formed.

The same year, 48 recruits to the Royal Electrical and Mechanical Engineers were enlisted and trained but no Gurkha EME unit was formed and the men were posted to regiments.

April 1950 saw 275 Army Catering Corps recruits enlisted and trained for a year. These, too, were posted to the regiments and no Gurkha ACC unit was formed.

The Staff Band, The Brigade of Gurkhas was formed in 1955 at Sungei Patani, then HQ Brigade of Gurkhas in Malaya. Their badge was simply crossed kukris, the cutting-edge downwards. In 1970, the band was combined with the regimental band of the 2nd Gurkha Rifles, to be re-badged as the 2nd Gurkha Rifles to form The Staff Band, The Brigade of Gurkhas (2nd Gurkha Rifles). The 2nd had been the only one of the four regiments which came from India in 1947 to have a regimental band. The others had pipes and drums whereas the 2nd had not.

In 1960, regimental medical assistants were trained at the British Military Hospital, Kekrara with a view to raising a Gurkha element of the Royal Army Medical Corps. The soldiers were posted back to their units after training.

The last Gurkha minor unit to be raised was the Gurkha Independent Parachute Company at Johore Bahru in 1961, initially from a platoon of 1/10 GR and, later, from a platoon each from 1/7 GR and 2/10 GR. The company disbanded on 2 Dec 71. Their badge was that of the Parachute Regiment worn on a rifle-green patch bordered on each side by a strip of Brigade of Gurkhas ribbon.

One of the earliest units to be raised when the Gurkhas reached Malaya was the Boys Training Company in Apr 48 but it was disbanded twenty years later on 1 Nov 68. Their badge was crossed kukris above a scroll reading simply, 'Boys'.

The Borneo Campaign lasted until 1966 whereupon the Brigade found itself controlling border disturbances in Hong Kong in the wake of China's cultural revolution.

Britain's withdrawal as much as possible from East of Suez argued a reduction in the strength of the Brigade of Gurkhas and the second battalions of the 6th, 7th and 10th had to go in 1969–70. Had it not been for the Sultan of Brunei who agreed to pay for a Gurkha battalion to be stationed permanently in his country, the 2/2nd Goorkhas would also have faced amalgamation with the 1/2nd. The new deployment was to be three battalions plus the supporting arms and services in Hong Kong, one battalion in Brunei and one in Church Crookham, in the heart of Hampshire's military belt. Hong Kong was now to be Training Depot, Brigade of Gurkhas in place of Sungei Patani in Malaysia.

During a spell of bureaucratic benevolence, the 2nd Battalion of the 7th Duke of Edinburgh's Own Gurkha Rifles was raised once more in October 1981 but this lasted for a couple of years only, reducing the Brigade's infantry strength to five battalions once more.

The long service in Malaya followed by the Confrontation with Indonesia did not result in any battle-honours but 1/7th were fortunate in securing 'Falkland Islands 1982' for their service in the South Atlantic. They barely made contact with the Argentinians, in fact, whose soldiers in the field had been thoroughly convinced by the propaganda of their political masters back in Buenos Aires, pronouncing that Gurkhas were invincible, unforgiving and only just short of cannibals. Argentine conscripts made haste to surrender to the Scots Guards, not often noted for their humanity in action.

Service with the British crown since 1947 has meant service in Malaya, Hong Kong, Brunei, Borneo, Belize, Cyprus, West Germany, New Zealand, Hawaii, Australia, Canada, the UK and the South Atlantic.

More historically, 10GR decided that they might profitably attempt to claw back the honours gained by their forebears, the old 10th Madras Infantry which they had eschewed back in 1903. In consequence, in 1988, they petitioned for the restitution of the honours 'Amboor', 'Carnatic', 'Mysore', 'Assaye', 'Ava', 'Burma 1885–87' and these were granted by Her Majesty, together with the right to wear a badge combining the symbolic Elephant for Assaye (1803) and the Rockfort for Amboor (1767). This badge is worn on the left upper arm and was displayed for the first time on 1 May 90 at their Centenary Parade in Brunei.

APPENDIX 'A'

CAVALRY AND INFANTRY UNIFORMS AND BADGES

When Kitchener reached India and began his far-reaching changes, the soldier was still being dressed regimentally. The second Afghan War had brought khaki to stay and it became the working-dress for the whole army in India – British and Indian.

Khaki-drill was available and, as it was made up regimentally, patterns varied considerably. Some wore jackets and others blouses: collars, cuffs, pockets, cartridge-loops, number of buttons, etc. were never the same in any two regiments. Loose knickerbockers were much favoured, some such as the 20th and 26th Punjab Infantry having voluminous garments. Khaki shorts and felt hats had been introduced in the closing years of the nineteenth century.

Brass numerals – simply numbers – some 3/4″ high were supplied universally and a very few regimental badges were purchased regimentally by pioneers and infantry for wear in the front of the pagri or fixed to a coloured or fringed pagri-end at the side. These badges were either die-struck in the UK or hand-made by either the regimental 'mistri' or by a bazaar metal-worker. The pagri badges were not worn by cavalry, artillery or transport: most units were content to be identified by their distinctively-coloured pagri or its coloured fringe.

A short description of some of those badges in use when the Great War broke out is of interest, as several of the regiments disappeared following that war.

1st S & M	The Prince of Wales' plumes, adopted at the time when it was a 'P of W' regiment
1st Brahmans	In brass, two carp (crest of Oudh) upon a tablet bearing '1776' the date this regiment was raised.
2nd Rajput LI	Brass bugle with 2 between strings
4th Rajputs	Brass 'Khanjar' (dagger)
6th Jat LI	Brass bugle with 6 below
7th Rajputs	Brass cypher of Duke of Connaught with Roman number and title
8th Rajputs	Brass circle bearing title, surrounded by laurels, and surmounted by Crown. Numeral in centre
14th Sikhs	The Prince of Wales' plumes, adopted at the time when it was a 'P of W' regiment
15th Sikhs	Black steel quoit (worn in Khaki only)
16th Rajputs	Brass 'Gateway of Lucknow' surmounted by numeral, and scroll 'Defence of Lucknow'
17th Infantry	Large crescent in aluminium
18th Infantry	Crescent and five-pointed star.
28th Punjabis	White-metal crescent and quoit below a crown
30th Punjabis	Brass Roman numerals within a laurel wreath, surmounted by a crown
31st Punjabis	White-metal circle bearing title, surmounted by crown, within circle a star of eight points, numeral in centre

32nd Sikh Pioneers	White-metal quoit bearing Roman numeral and title, surmounted by a crown and crossed axes. Below quoit the motto 'Aut viam inveniam aut faciam'
34h Sikh Pioneers	Upon a brass 'Star of India' a white-metal crowned garter, bearing the title and containing the number. Below, crossed axes
45th Sikhs	White-metal quoit with 'Kirpan' (Sikh dagger) above
48th Pioneers	Brass crossed axes upon a white-metal star of six points.
61st Pioneers	(i) Crowned circle bearing title, LXI inside (brass) (ii) P of W Plumes over oval, LXI inside title-scroll 'Prince of Wales' Own') (iii) P of W Plumes over cirlce, LXI inside, title-scroll 'King George's Own') (iv) P of W Plumes over Garter GRI within, numeral and title scroll below) [(ii)–(iv):] Brass & w/m
63rd Palamcottah LI	Brass French-horn with number in the curl and crown above
64th Pioneers	The number 64 over crossed axes in Brass
72nd Punjabis	White-metal peacock and title
74th Punjabis	Brass Chinese dragon
79th Carnatic Infantry	Brass circle bearing the title and containing the numbers, surrounded by laurels and surmounted by a crown
80th Infantry	Brass numerals within a laurel wreath
81st Pioneers	Brass circle bearing the title and containing the number, surmounted by a crown and surrounded by laurels
83rd Wallajahbad LI	Brass bugle with number between the strings
86th Carnatic Infantry	Brass circle bearing the title and containing the number, upon a crowned star of eight points
88th Carnatic Infantry	Solid brass circle, containing the title and number, surmounted by a crown and surrounded by laurels
90th Punjabis	White-metal Burmese 'Chinthe' with number and title below
91st Punjabis	White-metal crossed 'Dahs'
97th Infantry	Numeral within crowned circle, title scroll & Nagpur (w/m)
101st Grenadiers	Brass grenade with white-metal horse on ball
102nd Grenadiers	Brass grenade with white-metal Prince of Wales' plumes on flame and 'Sphinx' on ball
104th Rifles	A black crowned bugle with numeral between the strings
107th Pioneers	Brass garter bearing the number and title. Within the garter crossed axes
108th Infantry	Numeral on brass rising sun: title scroll below (brass)
110th Mahratta LI	Brass bugle with strings
125th Rifles	A black crowned bugle with numeral between the strings
128th Pioneers	Brass garter bearing the number and title. Within the garter crossed axes. Crown above

The cap-badge of the 2nd Goorkhas was Prince of Wales' plumes in black. All other Gurkhas wore a device of crossed kukris in white-metal. The 1st, 6th, 8th, 9th and 10th crossed the kukris back-upwards while the 3rd, 5th and 7th crossed them blade-up. All wore the numeral above the kukri except the 6th, who wore no numeral, and the 9th who kept it between the handles. The later pattern badges of the 1st and 3rd had, respectively, the Prince's plumes and the cypher of Queen Alexandra over the numeral. The 1st GR wore this badge also in bronze upon their service hat. The 4th wore no badge.

Following the formation of a single Indian Army in 1903 from the components of the three old Presidency armies and other contingents, there came a considerable change in the full-dress of the infantry. A long, loose blouse was introduced, made of scarlet, green or drab serge with shoulder straps and piping of the regimental facing-colour on the cuffs, collar and breast-opening. A similar garment had been worn previously by the cavalry and the 32nd Sikh Pioneers and also, in khaki-drill, by certain regiments. It had been found very popular but the Frontier Force regiments (except for Coke's Rifles) and the Gurkhas preferred to wear tunics cut similar to the British pattern. The Carnatic regiments continued to wear their Zouave-jackets and many of them never received red blouses before full-dress disappeared in 1915.

Full-dress blouses or tunics and knickerbockers were the only items issued by the clothing-factories. Coloured pagris, kullahs (the conical cap on which certain regiments rolled their pagri, thus facilitating its removal), puttees or spats, cummerbunds, badges, buttons and titles were all down to regimental purchase.

Ammunition boots, or boots, ankle as the army prefers to call them, were also introduced at about this time, replacing the sandals or slippers previously worn by Indian troops. Pathan soldiers, of course, preferred to wear the heavy, studded chapli for hill-work as did their British officers.

Before and during the Second Afghan War, most regiments had worn circular pill-box (Kilmarnock) caps with a brass numeral on the front but, with the coming of Khaki, the option was either to supply a khaki cap-cover or a khaki pagri and the economic advantage of the latter proved irresistible. Most regiments wore a coloured end-piece (or a dummy one, tucked in) and this was arranged to fall to one side and this formed an easy distinguishing mark between regiments.

Exceptions to this, of course, were the Gurkhas who continued to wear the pill-box caps and the 'hat, felt Gurkha' and some of the South Indian regiments. Buglers of Madras regiments had worn the black glengarry bonnet and the Carnatic pioneers and infantry continued to do so. The experimentally-raised and soon to be disbanded regiments of Coorg and Moplah Rifles wore a red fez whilst the 18th (Mussalman) Infantry appeared in a khaki fez shortly before the Great War.

Cavalry, of course, had long favoured the coloured blouse but theirs was usually improved by 'shoulder-chains' which were unusual in that they were entirely a British Indian concept and had not been lifted from one of the continental armies. They would, in fact, appear to have been adopted during the Great Mutiny. With the coloured kurta or blouse, white breeches were worn, with boots for officers whilst the men wore coloured puttees. By 1915, when full-dress was abolished, blue kurtas were in use by all except the following regiments.

1st	Yellow
4th, 5th, 7th, 18th and 22nd	Scarlet

20th, 25th, 29th and 30th	Green
26th, 27th and 28th	French-Grey
37th, 38th, 39th and Guides	Drab

During the years of the Great War, Indian troops in Europe wore khaki serge service-dress but, on their return, new regiments were created and new uniforms produced. A new pattern long jacket was issued in a greenish-khaki cotton, with two breast pockets and epaulettes. These were usually seen worn with shorts, boots, hose-tops and puttees or with chaplis.

Also, much favoured during this period was the grey, collarless flannel shirt, usually worn in operations and on training. IORs tucked the neck-band inside whilst officers frequently sacrificed the shirt-tail to make a collar.

Brass shoulder-titles, or numerals were issued officially for the first time and these were often worn within the new infantry regiments, mounted on a coloured cloth-backing to distinguish the different battalions.

The shoulder-title, although the least ornamental was the most important badge of the Indian Army. It was the only badge universally worn on service and the only one worn by most of the army. The numerals once issued by the clothing-factories came to be abandoned in the 1890's when most regiments adopted unofficial variations of their own. In 1903, most of these had to be discarded in their turn and, in 1923, the 1903 variants had themselves to be replaced.

The Second World War meant the disappearance for the most part of the metal shoulder-title. It was replaced by cloth, slip-on titles printed or embroidered in black on khaki-drill or olive-green for the new jungle uniforms which came into use in 1942.

The 1908 web-equipment was replaced by 1937 pattern and the pagri slowly disappeared. Not only did it require a lot of material but it took time to teach the young recruit how to roll it. Mechanised cavalry discarded their breeches and spurs and changed into the common wartime uniform of the Imperial armies – battle-dress in temperate areas, KD or OG in the tropics and the universal tank-suit – and the black beret. Infantry, except for Sikhs, wore OG jungle-hats, felt hats, the beret or the cap GS, even less attractive in its OC version than in the original khaki gaberdine pattern.

The wearing of these forms of headdress meant a need for badges and these were usually base-metal copies of silver or gilt badges previously worn only by officers on their service-drsss caps. The copies were usually sand-cast and finished by hand in the bazaar and the quality varied greatly. Titles for wear on battle-dress were worn on the upper sleeve curving with the shoulder-seam, embroidered in colours as were those worn by British troops.

In 1946, orders were issued that Indian infantry would henceforth wear battle-dress and caps in OG serge or the beret in cold weather and OG drill uniforms, caps GS or the beret in summer. Sikhs would wear the pagri in OG whilst Gurkha, Garhwali, Kumaoni and Assam regiments would wear felt hats. For ceremonial and walking-out, berets were to be worn as follows:

8 Punjab and FF Regt	Drab
Baluch and Rifle Regts	Rifle-green
Other Infantry	Scarlet
Gurkhas to wear Kilmarnock caps	

Perhaps the last dress distinction to be ordered for the Indian Army before

Partition was that which authorised the 1st Punjab Regiment to wear a feather-hackle of grass-green above the badge on beret, cap GS or pagri.

In the years since 1947, the Indian Army has kept to its OG uniforms but the Pakistan Army has reverted to KD. Both armies, however, have adopted the cravat and the cummerbund in regimental colours. A British officer returning to his old regiment on either side of the frontier now will find the familiar stripes of his regimental tie around the waist and at the throat of his temporary orderly. Sadly, the 5th Gurkhas (Frontier Force) in India and the Frontier Force Regiment in Pakistan both appear to be wearing the old Piffer colours.

The familiar 'woolly-pully' order in the British Army has also been widely adopted in the armies of the sub-continent although they do not appear to have spread to the same wide range of colours.

As the contemporary photographs will show, Pakistani and Indian soldiers look very much alike. Residual British uniform characteristics are shared, as is their regard for traditions built on more than two centuries of shared history. An enduring alliance would present a massive, reliable, outward-looking power-bloc in South Asia: sadly, many resources are being devoted to looking at each other.

APPENDIX 'B'

RANK STRUCTURE

Whilst the rank-structure within the Indian Army adhered very faithfully to the British model, there was a 'band' of ranks which had no British counterpart. These were latterly to be known as Viceroy's Commissioned Officers (VCOs).

They were originally known as Indian Officers and that was a self-evident classification until 1918 when the first King's Commissioned Indian Officers (KCIOs) emerged from the Indore Cadet School and, later, from the Royal Military College at Sandhurst (KCIOs), and the Indian Military Academy at Dehra Dun (Indian Commissioned Officers – ICOs).

Indian Officers – in the pre-1918 sense – were senior soldiers, promoted NCOs, with a lifetime of military experience, commanding respect from Indian ranks below them and British ranks above them. Their educational standard, however, generally precluded their promotion to KCIO/ICO rank. There were three steps in the IO's promotion ladder and the senior step, to Risaldar-Major (cavalry) or Subadar-Major (infantry and other arms), meant that the holder was the senior Indian soldier in the unit and qualified to give advice on Indian matters to the commanding officer. Indian officers wore stars and crowns on their shoulders, carried a sword and were saluted and addressed as 'Sahib' by Indian soldiers. They did not have authority over British soldiers who, nevertheless, addressed them as 'Jemadar-Sahib', 'Subadar-Sahib', etc. The only visible difference between an IO and a KCIO/ICO was that, before the Second World War, the IO's uniform-jacket had a closed, stand-up collar whilst BO's, KCIOs and ICOs all wore collars and ties in cold weather dress. The IO also wore a pagri or other native headdress: the subadar-major wore a crown on the shoulder, a subadar two stars and a jemadar one star.

During the 1930's when KCIOs and ICOs were becoming more numerous it was deemed expedient to find another name for the Indian Officer and it was decided to call them Viceroy's Commissioned Officers in 1935. At about the same time, it was realised that, on Frontier operations, in shirt-sleeve order, with British Officers wearing the pagri to prevent their identification by the tribesmen, it was not possible to distinguish a BO/KCIO/ICO subaltern from a VCO.

Nothwithstanding the realisation, it was not until 1941 that an Indian Army Order (IAO 922/41) laid down details of new badges of rank. Jemadars were to wear one silver star, risaldars/subadars two silver stars and the risaldar/subadar-major three silver crowns: each badge was to be mounted on a transverse strip of red-yellow-red braid. The order mentioned that these were for wear only in shirt-sleeve order, the older badges being permissible on the jacket provided that it had a stand-up collar.

The 1941 changes were not popular. VCOs felt that the silver badges cut across regimental tradition and lessened their status as they had previously worn the same badges as British Officers. They may also have felt that three crowns looked somewhat Ruritanian.

Finally, in September 1945, IAO 1827/45 cancelled IAO 922/41 on the grounds that the silver badges were 'unsatisfactory'. VCOs were 'to revert to the pre-war badges with a single strip of braid (red-yellow-red)'. The Order mentioned that the badges were to be embroidered but that metal badges 'black where already authorised', would be worn on the jacket on ceremonial occasions. The strip of braid was to be worn beneath the badge nearest to the sleeve-seam.

The Willcox Committee Report in 1945 foresaw a great increase in ICOs in the post-war British-Indian Army with the inevitable conclusion that VCOs would be phased out. Both India and Pakistan changed the title from VCO to Junior Commissioned Officer (JCO) although the lowest rank, previously Jemadar, was changed to Naib-Subadar. JCOs are still being used in both armies and, in 1992, do not seem to be disappearing. Whilst India continues to use the red-yellow-red braid, Pakistan's JCOs use braid of red-Pakistan green-red.

Present badges of rank are similar to those before republican status was declared except that the stars are now of a different pattern whilst the British crown has been replaced, for India, by the Lions of Ashoka and, for Pakistan, by the Star and Crescent.

Thus, it will be apparent that IOs/VCOs/ICOs do not have a counterpart in any Western army except in the case of the British Brigade of Gurkhas.

	Indian Army	
British Army	*Cavalry*	*Infantry*
Private/Trooper	Sowar	Sepoy
Lance-Corporal	Acting Lance Daffadar	Lance-Naik
Corporal	Lance-Daffadar	Naik
Sergeant	Daffadar	Havildar

The variants on NCO rank, of course, can all be compounded – thus one finds squadron-daffadar-majors (SDM) company quartermaster havildars (CQMH) etc. Badges of rank again are similar to the British pattern except where a crown is required in which case the national device mentioned above in connection with JCOs takes its place.

In the British Brigade of Gurkhas, the VCO continues, in effect, to exist.

Before Partition, these were known as Gurkha Officers (GOs) but, after 1 Jan 48 came to be referred to as King's Gurkha Officers (KGOs), progressing, after Her Majesty's accession, to Queen's Gurkha Officers (QGOs). They are found in three grades:

Lieutenant (Queen's Gurkha Officer) – Lt (QGO) – two black stars
Captain (Queen's Gurkha Officer) – Capt (QGO) – three black stars
Major (Queen's Gurkha Officer) – Major (QGO) – one black crown

The badges of rank are mounted on a strip of Brigade red, black and green ribbon, stitched vertically on the epaulette. Unofficially, QGOs are referred to as Gurkha Lieutenant, Gurkha Captain and Gurkha Major.

APPENDIX C

TABLE OF UNITS 1903–22

List of cavalry, pioneer and infantry units showing the titles in use prior to the Kitchener Reforms of 1903 and those after, the titles under which they served in the Great War and their titles after the 1922 changes. Shortened titles have been used but the full titles are to be found in the text of the regimental entries.

Previous title	1903 title	1914–18 title	1922 title
1 Bengal Lancers (Skinner's Horse)	DYO Lancers (Skinner's Horse)	1 DYO Lancers (Skinner's Horse)	1 DYO Skinner's Horse
3 Bengal Cavalry (Skinner's Horse)	3 Skinner's Horse	3 Skinner's Horse	
2 Bengal Lancers	2 Lancers (Gardner's Horse)	2 Lancers (Gardner's Horse)	2 Lancers (Gardner's Horse)
4 Bengal Lancers	4 Lancers	4 Cavalry	
5 Bengal Cavalry	5 Cavalry	5 Cavalry	3 Cavalry
8 Bengal Lancers	8 Lancers	8 Cavalry	
9 Bengal Lancers (Hodson's Horse)	9 Hodson's Horse	9 Hodson's Horse	4 DCO Hodson's Horse
10 Bengal Lancers (Hodson's Horse)	10 Lancers (Hodson's Horse)	10 Lancers (Hodson's Horse)	
11 Bengal Lancers	11 PWO Lancers	11 (KEO) Lancers (Probyn's Horse)	5 KEO Probyn's Horse
12 Bengal Cavalry	12 Cavalry	12 Cavalry	

Previous title	1903 title	1914–18 title	1922 title
13 Bengal Lancers	13 DCO Lancers	13 DCO Lancers (Watson's Horse)	6 DCO Lancers
16 Bengal Lancers	16 Cavalry	16 Cavalry	
3 Madras Lancers	28 Light Cavalry	28 Light Cavalry	7 Light Cavalry
1 Madras Lancers	26 Light Cavalry	26 KGO Light Cavalry	8 KGO Light Cavalry
4 Lancers (Hyd. Cont.)	30 Lancers (Gordon's Horse)	30 Lancers (Gordon's Horse)	
1 Lancers (Hyd. Cont.)	20 Deccan Horse	20 Deccan Horse	9 Royal Deccan Horse
2 Lancers (Hyd. Cont.)	29 Lancers, Deccan Horse	29 Lancers (Deccan Horse)	
QO Corps of Guides	QO Corps of Guides	QO Corps of Guides Cavalry	10 QVO Corps of Guides Cavalry
1 Punjab Cavalry	21 PAVO Cavalry	21 PAVO Cavalry (Daly's Horse)	11 PAVO Cavalry
3 Punjab Cavalry	23 Cavalry	23 Cavalry	
2 Punjab Cavalry	22 Cavalry	22 Sam Browne's Cavalry	12 Cavalry
5 Punjab Cavalry	25 Cavalry	25 Cavalry	
1 Bombay Lancers	31 DCO Lancers	31 DCO Lancers	13 DCO Bombay Lancers
2 Bombay Lancers	32 Lancers	32 Lancers	

5 Bombay Cav (Scinde Horse)	35 Scinde Horse	35 Scinde Horse	14 PWO Scinde Horse
6 Bombay Cav (Jacob's Horse)	36 Jacob's Horse	36 Jacob's Horse	
17 Bengal Lancers	17 Cavalry	17 Cavalry	15 Lancers
7 Bombay Lancers (Baluch Horse)	37 Lancers (Baluch Horse)	37 Lancers (Baluch Horse)	
2 Madras Lancers	27 Light Cavalry	27 Light Cavalry	16 Light Cavalry
3 Bombay Light Cavalry	33 QO Light Cavalry	33 QVO Light Cavalry	17 QVO Poona Horse
4 Bombay Cavalry (Poona Horse)	34 PAVO Poona Horse	34 PAVO Poona Horse	
6 Bengal Cavalry	6 Prince of Wales's Cavalry	6 KEO Cavalry	18 KEO Cavalry
7 Bengal Lancers	7 Lancers	7 Hariana Lancers	
18 Bengal Lancers	18 Tiwana Lancers	18 KGO Lancers	19 KGO Lancers
19 Bengal Lancers (Fane's Horse)	19 Lancers (Fane's Horse)	19 Lancers (Fane's Horse)	
14 Bengal Lancers (Murray's Jat Horse)	14 Murray's Jat Lancers	14 Murray's Jat Lancers	20 Lancers
15 (Cureton's Multani) Bengal Lancers	15 Lancers (Cureton's Multanis)	15 Lancers (Cureton's Multanis)	
1 Central India Horse	38 Central India Horse	38 KGO Central India Horse	21 KGO Central India Horse
2 Central India Horse	39 Central India Horse	39 KGO Central India Horse	

Previous title	1903 title	1914–18 title	1922 title
		40 Cavalry	Disbanded 1921
		41 Cavalry	Disbanded 1921
		42 Cavalry	Disbanded 1921
		43 Cavalry	Disbanded 1919
		44 Cavalry	Disbanded 1919
		45 Cavalry	Disbanded 1919
		46 Cavalry	Disbanded 1919
1 Brahman Infantry	1 Brahmans	1 Bn 1 Brahmans	4 Bn 1 Punjab Regt
		2 Bn 1 Brahmans	Disbanded Nov 1920
2 (QO) Rajput Light Infantry	2 QO Rajput Light Infantry	1 Bn 2 QVO Rajput Light Inf	1 Bn 7 Rajput Regt
		2 Bn 2 QVO Rajput Light Inf	Disbanded 2 Sep 21
		3 Bn 2 QVO Rajput Light Inf	Disbanded 1919
3 Brahman Infantry	3 Brahmans	1 Bn 3 Brahmans	Disbanded 6 May 22
		2 Bn 3 Gaur Brahmans	Disbanded 1920
4 (PAV) Rajput Infantry	4 PAV Rajputs	1 Bn 4 PAV Rajputs	2 Bn 7 Rajput Regt
		2 Bn 4 PAV Rajputs	Disbanded 11 Mar 22
5 Bengal (Light) Infantry	5 Light Infantry	1 Bn 5 Light Infantry	Disbanded 12 Jan 22
		2 Bn 5 Light Infantry	Disbanded 1919
6 Jat Light Infantry	6 Jat Light Infantry	1 Bn 6 Jat Light Infantry	1 Royal Bn 9 Jat Regt
		2 Bn 6 Jat Light Infantry	10 Bn 9 Jat Regt
7 (DCO) Rajput Infantry	7 DCO Rajputs	1 Bn 7 DCO Rajputs	3 Bn 7 Rajput Regt
		2 Bn 7 DCO Rajputs	Disbanded 20 Aug 21
8 Rajput Infantry	8 Rajputs	1 Bn 8 Rajputs	4 Bn 7 Rajput Regt
		2 Bn 8 Rajputs	Disbanded 1919
Bhopal Battalion	9 Bhopal Infantry	1 Bn 9 Bhopal Infantry	4 Bn 16 Punjab Regt
		2 Bn 9 (Delhi) Infantry	Disbanded 1 Aug 21
		3 Bn 9 Bhopal Infantry	Disbanded Aug 21
		4 Bn 9 Bhopal Infantry	Disbanded 20 Mar 21

10 Jat Infantry	10 Jats	1 Bn 10 Jats 2 Bn 10 Jats	3 Bn 9 Jat Regt Disbanded 27 Sep 21
11 Rajput Infantry	11 Rajputs	1 Bn 11 Rajputs 2 Bn 11 Rajputs	5 Bn 7 Rajput Regt Disbanded 31 May 20
12 Bengal Pioneers	12 Pioneers	1 Bn 12 Pioneers 2 Bn 12 Pioneers	2 Bn 2 Bombay Pioneers Disbanded 24 Dec 21
13 Rajput Infantry	13 Rajputs	13 Rajputs	10 Bn 6 Rajputana Rifles
14 Sikh Infantry	14 Ferozepore Sikhs	14 KGO Ferozepore Sikhs	1 Bn 11 Sikh Regt
15 Sikh Infantry	15 Ludhiana Sikhs	1 Bn 15 Ludhiana Sikhs 2 Bn 15 Ludhiana Sikhs	2 Bn 11 Sikh Regt Disbanded 3 Nov 21
16 Rajput Infantry	16 Rajputs	16 Rajputs	10 Bn 7 Rajput Regt
17 Mussalman Rajput Infantry	17 Infantry	1 Bn 17 Infantry 2 Bn 17 Infantry	Disbanded 20 Dec 21 Disbanded 1 Jun 21
18 Mussalman Rajput Infantry	18 Infantry	1 Bn 18 Infantry 2 Bn 18 Infantry	4Bn 9 Jat Regt Disbanded 15 Nov 20
19 Punjab Infantry	19 Punjabis	1 Bn 19 Punjabis 2 Bn 19 Punjabis	1 Bn 14 Punjab Regt Disbanded 24 Aug 22
20 (DCO) Punjab Infantry	20 DCO Punjabis	20 DCO Infantry	2 Bn 14 Punjab Regt
21 Punjab Infantry	21 Punjabis	1 Bn 21 Punjabis 2 Bn 21 Punjabis	10 Bn 14 Punjab Regt Disbanded 1 Apr 22
22 Punjab Infantry	22 Punjabis	1 Bn 22 Punjabis 2 Bn 22 Punjabis	3 Bn 14 Punjab Regt Disbanded 15 Jun 22
23 Punjab Pioneers	23 Sikh Pioneers	1 Bn 23 Sikh Pioneers 2 Bn 23 Sikh Pioneers 3 Bn 23 Sikh Infantry	1 Bn 3 Sikh Pioneers 10 Bn 3 Sikh Pioneers Disbanded 30 Apr 22

Previous title	1903 title	1914–18 title	1922 title
24 Punjab Infantry	24 Punjabis	24 Punjabis	4 Bn 14 Punjab Regt
25 Punjab Infantry	25 Punjabis	1 Bn 25 Punjabis	1 Bn 15 Punjab Regt
		2 Bn 25 Punjabis	Disbanded 21 Mar 22
26 Punjab Infantry	26 Punjabis	1 Bn 26 Punjabis	2 Bn 15 Punjab Regt
		2 Bn 26 Punjabis	Disbanded 29 Jan 22
27 Punjab Infantry	27 Punjabis	1 Bn 27 Punjabis	3 Bn 15 Punjab Regt
		2 Bn 27 Punjabis	Disbanded 15 Apr 21
28 Punjab Infantry	28 Punjabis	1 Bn 28 Punjabis	4 Bn 15 Punjab Regt
		2 Bn 28 Punjabis	Disbanded 1919
29 Punjab Infantry	29 Punjabis	29 Punjabis	10 Bn 15 Punjab Regt
30 Punjab Infantry	30 Punjabis	1 Bn 30 Punjabis	Bn 16 Punjab Regt
		2 Bn 30 Punjabis	Disbanded 15 Mar 22
		3 Bn 30 Punjabis	Disbanded 1919
		4 Bn 30 Punjabis	Disbanded 1919
31 Punjab Infantry	31 Punjabis	31 Punjabis	2 Bn 16 Punjab Regt
32 Punjab Pioneers	32 Sikh Pioneers	1 Bn 32 Sikh Pioneers	2 Bn 3 Sikh Pioneers
		2 Bn 32 Sikh Pioneers	Disbanded 18 Aug 21
		3 Bn 32 Sikh Pioneers	Disbanded 1919
33 Punjab Infantry	33 Punjabis	1 Bn 33 Punjabis	3 Bn 16 Punjab Regt
		2 Bn 33 Punjabis	Disbanded 15 Mar 21
34 Punjab Pioneers	34 Sikh Pioneers	1 Bn 34 Sikh Pioneers	3 Royal Bn 3 Sikh Pioneers
		2 Bn 34 Sikh Pioneers	Disbanded 31 Jan 21
		3 Bn 34 Sikh Pioneers	Disbanded 1 Jul 21
35 Sikh Infantry	35 Sikhs	1 Bn 35 Sikhs	10 Bn 11 Sikh Regt
		2 Bn 35 Sikhs	Disbanded 25 Aug 21

36 Sikh Infantry	36 Sikhs	36 Sikhs	4 Bn 11 Sikh Regt
37 Dogra Infantry	37 Dogras	37 Dogras	1 Bn 17 Dogra Regt
38 Dogra Infantry	38 Dogras	38 Dogras	2nd Bn 17 Dogra Regt
1 Bn 39 Garhwal Rifles	1 Bn 39 Garhwal Rifles	1 Bn 39 Garhwal Rifles	1 Bn 18 Royal Garhwal Rifles
2 Bn 39 Garhwal Rifles	2 Bn 39 Garhwal Rifles	2 Bn 39 Garhwal Rifles	2 Bn 18 Royal Garhwal Rifles
		3 Bn 39 Garhwal Rifles	3 Bn 18 Royal Garhwal Rifles
		4 Bn 39 Garhwal Rifles	10 Bn 18 Royal Garhwal Rifles
40 Punjab Infantry	40 Pathans	1 Bn 40 Pathans	5 Bn 14 Punjab Regt
		2 Bn 40 Pathans	Disbanded 1921
41 Dogra Infantry	41 Dogras	1 Bn 41 Dogras	3 Bn 17 Dogra Regt
		2 Bn 41 Dogras	10 Bn 17 Dogra Regt
Deoli Irregular Force	42 Deoli Regt	1 Bn 42 Deoli Regt	Disbanded 10 Dec 21
		2 Bn 42 Deoli Regt	Disbanded 20 Jul 21
Erinpura Irregular Force	43 Erinpura Regt	1 Bn 43 Erinpura Regt	Disbanded 15 Oct 21
		2 Bn 43 Erinpura Regt	Disbanded 20 Jul 20
Merwara Bn	44 Merwara Infantry	1 Bn 44 Merwara Infantry	Disbanded 22 Jun 21
		2 Bn 44 Merwara Infantry	Disbanded 1918
45 Sikh Infantry	45 Rattray's Sikhs	45 Rattray's Sikhs	3 Bn 11 Sikh Regt
46 Punjab Infantry	46 Punjabis	46 Punjabis	10 Bn 16 Punjab Regt
47 Sikh Infantry	47 Sikhs	47 Sikhs	5 Bn 11 Sikh Regt
48 Bengal Pioneers	48 Pioneers	1 Bn 48 Pioneers	4 Bn Bombay Pioneers
		2 Bn 48 Pioneers	Disbanded 15 Jul 20
		49 Bengalis	Disbanded 30 Aug 20

Previous title	1903 title	1914–18 title	1922 title
		1 Bn 50 Kumaon Rifles 2 Bn 50 Kumaon Rifles	1 Bn Kumaon Rifles 2 Bn Kumaon Rifles (Disbanded March 1923)
1 Sikh Infantry	51 Sikhs	51 Sikhs	1 Bn 12 Frontier Force Regt
2 Sikh Infantry	52 Sikhs	52 Sikhs	2 Bn 12 Frontier Force Regt
3 Sikh Infantry	53 Sikhs	53 Sikhs	3 Bn 12 Frontier Force Regt
4 Sikh Infantry	54 Sikhs	1 Bn 54 Sikhs 2 Bn 54 Sikhs	4 Bn 12 Frontier Force Regt Disbanded 17 Oct 21
QO Corps of Guides	QO Corps of Guides	QVO Corps of Guides 2 Bn QVO Corps of Guides 3 Bn QVO Corps of Guides	5 Bn 12 Frontier Force Regt 10 Bn 12 Frontier Force Regt Disbanded 2 Aug 21
1 Punjab Infantry	55 Coke's Rifles	1 Bn 55 Coke's Rifles 2 Bn 55 Coke's Rifles	1 Bn 13 Frontier Force Rifles Disbanded
2 Punjab Infantry	56 Infantry	1 Bn 56 Punjabi Rifles 2 Bn 56 Punjabi Rifles	2 Bn 13 Frontier Force Rifles 10 Bn 13 Frontier Force Rifles
4 Punjab Infantry	57 Wilde's Rifles	1 Bn 57 Wilde's Rifles 2 Bn 57 Wilde's Rifles	4 Bn 13 Frontier Force Rifles Disbanded 1918
5 Punjab Infantry	58 Vaughan's Rifles	58 Vaughan's Rifles	5 Bn 13 Frontier Force Rifles
6 Punjab Infantry	59 Scinde Rifles	59 Scinde Rifles	6 Royal Bn 13 Frontier Force Rifles
1 Madras Pioneers	61 Pioneers	1 Bn 61 KGO Pioneers 2 Bn 61 KGO Pioneers	1 Bn 1 Madras Pioneers Disbanded 30 Sep 21
2 Madras Infantry	62 Punjabis	62 Punjabis	1 Bn 1 Punjab Regt

3 Madras Light Infantry	63 Palamcottah Light Infantry	1 Bn 63 Palamcottah Light Inf. 2 Bn 63 Palamcottah Light Inf.	Disbanded 13 Sep 22 Disbanded 1919
4 Madras Pioneers	64 Pioneers	64 Pioneers	2 Bn 1 Madras Pioneers
5 Madras Infantry	65 Carnatic Light Infantry	Disbanded 1904	–
6 Madras Infantry	66 Punjabis	1 Bn 66 Punjabis 2 Bn 66 Punjabis	2 Bn 1 Punjab Regt Disbanded 22 Jul 22
7 Madras Infantry	67 Punjabis	1 Bn 67 Punjabis 2 Bn 67 Punjabis	1 Bn 2 Punjab Regt 10 Bn 2 Punjab Regt
9 Madras Infantry	69 Punjabis	1 Bn 69 Punjabis 2 Bn 69 Punjabis	2 Bn 2 Punjab Regt Disbanded 23 Apr 22
		1 Bn 70 Burma Rifles 2 Bn 70 Burma Rifles 3 Bn 70 Burma Rifles 4 Bn 70 Burma Rifles	1 Bn 20 Burma Rifles 2 Bn 20 Burma Rifles 10 Bn 20 Burma Rifles 4 Bn 20 Burma Rifles
11 Coorg Infantry	71 Coorg Rifles (Disbanded 1904)	71 Punjabis (Transferred to 111 Mahars 1920)	–
12 Burma Infantry	72 Punjabis	1 Bn 72 Punjabis 2 Bn 72 Punjabis	3 Bn 2 Punjab Regt Disbanded 15 May 21
13 Madras Infantry	73 Carnatic Infantry	1 Bn 73 Carnatic Infantry 2 Bn 73 Carnatic Infantry	1 Bn 3 Madras Regt Disbanded 8 Oct 21
14 Madras Infantry	74 Punjabis	74 Punjabis	4 Bn 2 Punjab Regt
15 Madras Infantry	75 Carnatic Infantry	1 Bn 75 Carnatic Infantry 2 Bn 75 Carnatic Infantry	2 Bn 3 Madras Regt Disbanded 5 Dec 20
16 Madras Infantry	76 Punjabis	1 Bn 76 Punjabis 2 Bn 76 Punjabis	3 Bn 1 Punjab Regt Disbanded 4 Aug 22
	77 Moplah Rifles	Disbanded 1907	–

Previous title	1903 title	1914–18 title	1922 title
	78 Moplah Rifles	Disbanded 1907	–
19 Madras Infantry	79 Carnatic Infantry	79 Carnatic Infantry	3 Bn 3 Madras Regt
20 Madras Infantry	80 Carnatic Infantry	1 Bn 80 Carnatic Infantry 2 Bn 80 Carnatic Infantry	Disbanded 10 Sep 21 Disbanded 31 Jan 21
21 Madras Pioneers	81 Pioneers	1 Bn 81 Pioneers 2 Bn 81 Pioneers	10 Bn 1 Madras Pioneers Disbanded 15 Feb 21
22 Madras Infantry	82 Punjabis	82 Punjabis	5 Bn 1 Punjab Regt
23 Madras Light Infantry	83 Wallajahbad Light Infantry	83 Wallajahbad Light Infantry	4 Bn 3 Madras Regt
24 Madras Infantry	84 Punjabis	84 Punjabis	10 Bn 1 Punjab Regt
		85 Burman Rifles	3 Bn 20 Burma Rifles
26 Madras Infantry	86 Carnatic Infantry	86 Carnatic Infantry	10 Bn 3 Madras Regt
27 Madras Infantry	87 Punjabis	87 Punjabis	5 Bn 2 Punjab Regt
28 Madras Infantry	88 Carnatic Infantry	1 Bn 88 Carnatic Infantry 2 Bn 88 Carnatic Infantry	Disbanded 10 Jan 21 Disbanded 1920
29 Burma Infantry	89 Punjabis	1 Bn 89 Punjabis 2 Bn 89 Punjabis	1 Bn 8 Punjab Regt 10 Bn 8 Punjab Regt
30 Burma Infantry	90 Punjabis	1 Bn 90 Punjabis 2 Bn 90 Punjabis	2 Bn 8 Punjab Regt Disbanded 15 May 22
31 Burma Light Infantry	91 Punjabis	1 Bn 91 Punjabis (Light Inf.) 2 Bn 91 Punjabis (Light Inf.)	3 Bn 8 Punjab Regt Disbanded 1 Jun 21
32 Burma Infantry	92 Punjabis	92 Punjabis	4 Bn 8 Punjab Regt

33 Burma Infantry	93 Burma Infantry	93 Burma Infantry	5 Bn 8 Punjab Regt
1 Infantry, Hyderabad Cont.	94 Russell's Infantry	1 Bn 94 Russell's Infantry 2 Bn 94 Russell's Infantry	1 Bn 19 Hyderabad Regt Disbanded 31 Dec 20
2 Infantry, Hyderabad Cont.	95 Russell's Infantry	1 Bn 95 Russell's Infantry 2 Bn 95 Russell's Infantry	10 Bn 19 Hyderabad Regt Disbanded 15 Feb 21
3 Infantry, Hyderabad Cont.	96 Berar Infantry	1 Bn 96 Berar Infantry 2 Bn 96 Berar Infantry	2 Bn 19 Hyderabad Regt Disbanded 28 Jan 22
4 Infantry, Hyderabad Cont.	97 Deccan Infantry	1 Bn 97 Deccan infantry 2 Bn 97 Deccan Infantry	3 Bn 19 Hyderabad Regt Disbanded 30 August 1922
5 Infantry, Hyderabad Cont.	98 Infantry	1 Bn 98 Infantry 2 Bn 98 Infantry	4 Bn 19 Hyderabad Regt Disbanded 15 Mar 21
6 Infantry, Hyderabad Cont.	99 Deccan Infantry	1 Bn 99 Deccan Infantry 2 Bn 99 Deccan Infantry	5 Bn 19 Hyderabad Regt Disbanded 1919
1 Bombay Grenadiers	101 Grenadiers	1 Bn 101 Grenadiers 2 Bn 101 Grenadiers	1 Bn 4 Bombay Grenadiers Disbanded 31 Jan 21
2 (PWO) Bombay Grenadiers	102 PWO Grenadiers	1 Bn 102 KEO Grenadiers 2 Bn 102 KEO Grenadiers	2 Bn 4 Bombay Grenadiers Disbanded 24 Jan 22
3 Bombay Light Infantry	103 Mahratta Light Infantry	1 Bn 103 Mahratta Light Inf. 2 Bn 103 Mahratta Light Inf. 3 Bn 103 Mahratta Light Inf.	1 Bn 5 Mahratta Light Infantry Disbanded 8 Mar 21 Disbanded 1919
4 Bombay Rifles	104 Wellesley's Rifles	104 Wellesley's Rifles	1 Bn 6 Rajputana Rifles
5 Bombay Light Infantry	105 Mahratta Light Infantry	1 Bn 105 Mahratta Light Inf. 2 Bn 105 Mahratta Light Inf.	2 Bn 5 Mahratta Light Infantry Disbanded 1918
	106 Hazara Pioneers (raised 1904)	106 Hazara Pioneers	1 Bn 4 Hazara Pioneers

Previous title	1903 title	1914–18 title	1922 title
7 Bombay Pioneers	107 Pioneers	1 Bn 107 Pioneers 2 Bn 107 Pioneers	1 Bn 2 Bombay Pioneers Disbanded 15 Jun 21
8 Bombay Infantry	108 Infantry	108 Infantry	3 Bn 4 Bombay Grenadiers
9 Bombay Infantry	109 Infantry	1 Bn 109 Infantry 2 Bn 109 Infantry	4 Bn 4 Bombay Grenadiers Disbanded 5 Apr 20
10 Bombay Light Infantry	110 Mahratta Light Infantry	110 Mahratta Light Inf.	3 Bn 5 Mahratta light Infantry
		111 Mahars	Disbanded 1922
12 Bombay Infantry	112 Infantry	1 Bn 112 Infantry	5 Bn 4 Bombay Grenadiers 2 Bn 112 Infantry Disbanded May 1922
13 Bombay Infantry	113 Infantry	1 Bn 113 Infantry 2 Bn 113 Infantry	10 Bn 4 Bombay Grenadiers Disbanded January 1922
14 Bombay Infantry	114 Mahrattas	114 Mahrattas	10 Bn 5 Mahratta Light Infantry
16 Bombay Infantry	116 Mahrattas	1 Bn 116 Mahrattas 2 Bn 116 Mahrattas	4 Bn 5 Mahratta Light Infantry Disbanded 25 Oct 21
17 Bombay Infantry	117 Mahrattas	1 Bn 117 Mahrattas 2 Bn 117 Mahrattas	5 Royal Bn 5 Mahratta LI Disbanded 25 Aug 21
19 Bombay Infantry	119 Infantry	1 Bn 119 Infantry 2 Bn 119 Infantry	2 Bn 9 Jat Regt Disbanded 1 Aug 21
20 Bombay Infantry	120 Rajputana Infantry	120 Rajputana Infantry	2 Bn 6 Rajputana Rifles
21 Bombay Infantry	121 Pioneers	121 Pioneers	10 Bn 2 Bombay Pioneers
22 Bombay Infantry	122 Rajputana Infantry	122 Rajputana Infantry	3 Bn 6 Rajputana Rifles

23 Bombay Rifles	123 Outram's Rifles	1 Bn 123 Outram's Rifles	4 Bn 6 Rajputana Rifles
		2 Bn 123 Outram's Rifles	Disbanded 12 Aug 21
24 (DCO) Baluchistan Infantry	124 DCO Baluchistan Infantry	1 Bn 124 DCO Baluchistan Inf.	1 Bn 10 Baluch Regt
		2 Bn 124 DCO Baluchistan Inf.	10 Bn 10 Baluch Regt
		3 Bn 124 DCO Baluchistan Inf.	Disbanded 20 Jul 21
25 Bombay Rifles	125 Napier's Rifles	1 Bn 125 Napier's Rifles	5 Bn 6 Rajputana Rifles
		2 Bn 125 Napier's Rifles	Disbanded 20 Jun 22
26 Baluchistan Infantry	126 Baluchistan Infantry	126 Baluchistan Infantry	2 Bn 10 Baluch Regt
27 Baluch Light Infantry	127 Baluch Light Infantry	1 Bn 127 Baluch Light Infantry	3 Bn 10 Baluch Regt
		2 Bn 127 Baluch Light Infantry	Disbanded 15 Jun 21
28 Bombay Pioneers	128 Pioneers	1 Bn 128 Pioneers	3 Bn 2 Bombay Pioneers
		2 Bn 128 Pioneers	Disbanded 28 Aug 22
29 (DCO) Baluch Infantry	129 DCO Baluchis	1 Bn 129 DCO Baluchis	4 Bn 10 Baluch Regt
		2 Bn 129 DCO Baluchis	Disbanded 16 Mar 22
30 Baluch Infantry	130 Baluchis	1 Bn 130 Baluchis	5 Bn 10 Baluch Regt
		2 Bn 130 Baluchis	Disbanded 15 Jun 20
		1 Bn 131 U P Regt	Disbanded 1919
		2 Bn 131 U P Regt	Disbanded 1919
		1 Bn 132 (Punjab Police) Regt	Disbanded 1918
		2 Bn 132 (Punjab Police) Regt	Disbanded 1918
		1 Bn 133 Regt	Disbanded 1919
		1 Bn 140 Patiala Infantry	Disbanded 1919
		1 Bn 141 Bikanir Infantry	Disbanded 1919
		1 Bn 142 Jodhpur Infantry	Disbanded 1919

Previous title	1903 title	1914–18 title	1922 title
		1 Bn 143 Narsingh (Dholpur) Inf.	Disbanded 1919
		1 Bn 144 Bharatpur Infantry	Disbanded 1919
		1 Bn 145 Alwar (Jai Paltan) Inf.	Disbanded 1919
		1 Bn 150 Indian Infantry	Disbanded 15 Apr 21
		2 Bn 150 Indian Infantry	Disbanded 15 Jun 21
		3 Bn 150 Indian Infantry	Disbanded 30 Nov 20
		1 Bn 151 Sikh Infantry	Disbanded 15 May 21
		2 Bn 151 Indian Infantry	Disbanded 31 Jul 20
		3 Bn 151 Punjabi Rifles	Disbanded 15 May 21
		1 Bn 152 Punjabis	Disbanded 1920
		2 Bn 152 Punjabis	Disbanded 4 Sep 21
		3 Bn 152 Punjabis	Disbanded 30 Apr 21
		1 Bn 153 Punjabis	Disbanded 15 Jun 21
		2 Bn 153 Punjabis	Disbanded 15 Jun 21
		3 Bn 153 Rifles	Disbanded 24 Jun 1922
		1 Bn 154 Indian Infantry	Disbanded 1919
		2 Bn 154 Indian Infantry	Disbanded 15 May 21
		3 Bn 154 Indian Infantry	Disbanded 1919
		1 Bn 155 Indian Pioneers	Disbanded 1920
		2 Bn 155 Indian Infantry	Disbanded 1920
		1 Bn 156 Indian Infantry	Disbanded 1919
1 Bn 1 Gurkha Rifles	1 Bn 1 Gurkha Rifles	1 Bn 1 Gurkha Rifles	1 Bn 1 Gurkha Rifles
2 Bn 1 Gurkha Rifles	2 Bn 1 Gurkha Rifles	2 Bn 1 Gurkha Rifles	2 Bn 1 Gurkha Rifles
		3 Bn 1 Gurkha Rifles	Disbanded 30 Apr 21
1 Bn 2 Gurkha Rifles	1 Bn 2 Gurkha Rifles	1 Bn 2 Gurkha Rifles	1 Bn 2 Gurkha Rifles
2 Bn 2 Gurkha Rifles	2 Bn 2 Gurkha Rifles	2 Bn 2 Gurkha Rifles	2 Bn 2 Gurkha Rifles
		3 Bn 2 Gurkha Rifles	Disbanded 30 Sep 20

1 Bn 3 Gurkha Rifles 2 Bn 3 Gurkha Rifles	1 Bn 3 Gurkha Rifles 2 Bn 3 Gurkha Rifles	1 Bn 3 Gurkha Rifles 2 Bn 3 Gurkha Rifles 3 Bn 3 Gurkha Rifles 4 Bn 3 Gurkha Rifles	1 Bn 3 Gurkha Rifles 2 Bn 3 Gurkha Rifles Disbanded 31 Jul 20 Disbanded 16 Mar 22
1 Bn 4 Gurkha Rifles 2 Bn 4 Gurkha Rifles	1 Bn 4 Gurkha Rifles 2 Bn 4 Gurkha Rifles	1 Bn 4 Gurkha Rifles 2 Bn 4 Gurkha Rifles	1 Bn 4 Gurkha Rifles 2 Bn 4 Gurkha Rifles
1 Bn 5 Gurkha Rifles 2 Bn 5 Gurkha Rifles	1 Bn 5 Gurkha Rifles 2 Bn 5 Gurkha Rifles	1 Bn 5 Gurkha Rifles 2 Bn 5 Gurkha Rifles 3 Bn 5 Gurkha Rifles	1 Bn 5 Royal Gurkha Rifles 2 Bn 5 Royal Gurkha Rifles Disbanded 15 Jul 21
42 Gurkha Rifles	6 Gurkha Rifles 2 Bn 6 Gurkha Rifles (raised 1904)	1 Bn 6 Gurkha Rifles 2 Bn 6 Gurkha Rifles 3 Bn 6 Gurkha Rifles	1 Bn 6 Gurkha Rifles 2 Bn 6 Gurkha Rifles Disbanded 31 Jan 21
8 Gurkha Rifles	2 Bn 10 Gurkha Rifles (until 1907) 2 Bn 7 Gurkha Rifles (raised 1907)	1 Bn 7 Gurkha Rifles 2 Bn 7 Gurkha Rifles 3 Bn 7 Gurkha Rifles	1 Bn 7 Gurkha Rifles 2 Bn 7 Gurkha Rifles Disbanded 31 Mar 21
44 Gurkha Rifles	8 Gurkha Rifles	1 Bn 8 Gurkha Rifles	1 Bn 8 Gurkha Rifles
43 Gurkha Rifles	7 Gurkha Rifles	2 Bn 8 Gurkha Rifles 3 Bn 8 Gurkha Rifles	2 Bn 8 Gurkha Rifles Disbanded 15 Jul 21
9 Gurkha Rifles	1 Bn 9 Gurkha Rifles 2 Bn 9 Gurkha Rifles (raised 1904)	1 Bn 9 Gurkha Rifles 2 Bn 9 Gurkha Rifles 3 Bn 9 Gurkha Rifles	1 Bn 9 Gurkha Rifles 2 Bn 9 Gurkha Rifles Disbanded 28 Feb 21
10 Gurkha Rifles	1 Bn 10 Gurkha Rifles 2 Bn 10 Gurkha Rifles (raised 1908)	1 Bn 10 Gurkha Rifles 2 Bn 10 Gurkha Rifles	1 Bn 10 Gurkha Rifles 2 Bn 10 Gurkha Rifles
		1 Bn 11 Gurkha Rifles 2 Bn 11 Gurkha Rifles 3 Bn 11 Gurkha Rifles 4 Bn 11 Gurkha Rifles	Disbanded 20 Aug 21 Disbanded 15 Aug 21 Disbanded 12 Apr 22 Disbanded 1 Aug 20

APPENDIX D

TABLE OF UNITS 1922–91

List of cavalry, pioneer and infantry units showing the titles allotted in 1922, the unit allocation in 1947 and present titles. As in the preceding table, shortened titles have been used but the full titles are, of course, in the text in the regimental entries. **Post-Partition raisings are not included in this table.**

1922 title	1939–45 title	Partition 1947	India or Pakistan	Current title
1 DYO Skinner's Horse	Skinner's Horse (1 DYO Cav)	Skinner's Horse (1 DYO Cav)	I	Skinner's Horse
2 Lancers (Gardner's Horse)	2 Royal Lancers (Gardner's Horse)	2 Royal Lancers (Gardner's Horse)	I	2 Lancers (Gardner's Horse)
3 Cavalry	3 Cavalry	3 Cavalry	I	3 Cavalry
4 DCO Hodson's Horse	Hodson's Horse (4 DCO Lancers)	Hodson's Horse (4 DCO Lancers)	I	Hodson's Horse
5 KEO Probyn's Horse	Probyn's Horse (5 KE VII's O Lancers)	Probyn's Horse (5 KE VII's O Lancers)	P	5 Lancers
6 DCO Lancers	6 DCO Lancers (Watson's Horse)	6 DCO Lancers (Watson's Horse)	P	6 Lancers
7 Light Cavalry	7 Light Cavalry	7 Light Cavalry	I	7 Light Cavalry
8 KGO Light Cavalry	8 KG V's O Light Cavalry	8 KG V's O Light Cavalry	I	8 Light Cavalry
9 Royal Deccan Horse	Royal Deccan Horse (9 Horse)	Royal Deccan Horse (9 Horse)	I	Deccan Horse (9 Horse)
10 QVO Guides Cavalry (FF)	Guides Cavalry (10 QVO Frontier Force)	Guides Cavalry (FF)	P	Guides Cavalry (FF)
11 PAVO Cavalry (FF)	PAVO Cavalry (11 FF)	PAVO Cavalry (1 FF)	P	11 Cavalry (FF)
12 Cavalry (FF)	2 IAC Training Centre	IAC Training Centre	P	12 Cavalry (FF)*
13 DCO Bombay Lancers	13 DCO Lancers	13 DCO Lancers	P	13 Lancers

14 PWO Scinde Horse	Scinde Horse (14 PWO Cav)	Scinde Horse (14 PWO Cav)	I	Scinde Horse
15 Lancers	1 IAC Training Centre	IAC Training Centre	I	15 Lancers*
16 Light Cavalry	16 Light Cavalry	16 Light Cavalry	I	16 Light Cavalry
17 QVO Poona Horse	Poona Horse (17 QVO Cavalry)	Poona Horse (17 QVO Cavalry)	I	Poona Horse
18 KEO Cavalry	18 KE VII's O Cavalry	18 KE VII's O Cavalry	I	18 Cavalry
19 KGO Lancers	19 KG V's O Lancers	19 KG V's O Lancers	P	19 Lancers
20 Lancers	3 IAC Training Centre	IAC Training Centre	I	20 Lancers*
21 KGO's Central India Horse	Central India Horse (21 KG V's O Horse)	Central India Horse (21 KG V's O Horse)	I	Central India Horse
	42 Cavalry	Disbanded December 1943		
	43 Cavalry	Disbanded December 1946		
	44 Cavalry	Disbanded December 1943		
	45Cavalry	Disbanded 1946		
	46 Cavalry	Disbanded December 1943		
	47 Cavalry	Disbanded December 1943		
	48 Cavalry	Disbanded December 1943		
	51 Cavalry (raised as 7/5 Mahratta LI – became 8 Mahratta A/Tk Regt I Artillery October1942)			
	52 Cavalry (raised as MG Bn 7 Rajput – became 17/7 Rajput September 1942)			
	53 Cavalry (raised as MG Bn 10 Baluch – became 17/10 Baluch November 1942)			
	54 Cavalry (raised as 9/13 FFRIF: Became 54 Regt IAC Aug 42 Reverted to 9/13th Oct 42)			
	65 Cavalry	Disbanded July 1943		
	66 Cavalry	Disbanded July 1943		
	67 Cavalry	Disbanded July 1943		
	75 Cavalry	Disbanded 1946		
	76 Cavalry	Disbanded 1946		

*These regiments have been re-raised since Partition as active units.

1922 title	1939–45 title	Partition 1947	India or Pakistan	Current title
1st Madras Pioneers 1 Bn 2 Bn 10 Bn	Disbanded February 1933			
2nd Bombay Pioneers 1 Bn 2 Bn 3 Bn 4 Bn 10 Bn	Disbanded February 1933			
3rd Sikh Pioneers 1 Bn 2 Bn 3 Bn 10 Bn	Disbanded February 1933			
4th Hazara Pioneers 1 Bn	Disbanded March 1933			

1st Punjab Regiment				
1 Bn	1 Bn 1 Punjab Regt	1 Bn 1 Punjab Regt	P	1 Bn Punjab Regt
2 Bn	2 Bn 1 Punjab Regt	2 Bn 1 Punjab Regt	P	2 Bn Punjab Regt
3 Bn	3 Bn 1 Punjab Regt	3 Bn 1 Punjab Regt	P	3 Bn Punjab Regt
4 Bn	Disbanded December 1931	–		–
5 Bn	5 Bn 1 Punjab Regt	5 Bn 1 Punjab Regt	P	4 Bn Punjab Regt
10 Bn	Regimental Centre	–		–
11 Bn ITF	9 Bn 1 Punjab Regt	–		–
	(to R. Indian Navy March 1943)	–		–
	6 Bn 1 Punjab Regt	–		
	7 Bn 1 Punjab Regt	7 Bn 1 Punjab Regt	P	18 Bn Punjab Regt
	8 Bn 1 Punjab Regt	–		–
	(to I. Artillery December 1941)	–		–
	14 Bn 1 Punjab Regt	–		–
	15 Bn 1 Punjab Regt	–		–
	16 Bn 1 Punjab Regt	–		–
	(raised as 25/1 Punjab)			
	26 Bn 1 Punjab Regt			
2nd Punjab Regiment				
1 Bn	1 Bn 2 Punjab Regt	1 Bn Punjab Regt	I	1 Bn Parachute Regt
2 Bn	2 Bn 2 Punjab Regt	2 Bn Punjab Regt	I	1 Bn Guards
3 Bn	3 Bn 2 Punjab Regt	3 Bn Punjab Regt	I	3 Bn Punjab Regt
4 Bn	Disbanded January 1939	–	I	–
5 Bn	5 Bn 2 Punjab Regt	–		–
10 Bn	Regimental Centre	–		–
	6 Bn 2 Punjab Regt	–		–
	7 Bn 2 Punjab Regt	7 Bn Punjab Regt	I	8 Bn Mech Inf Regt
	8 Bn 2 Punjab Regt	–		–
	25 Bn 2 Punjab Regt	–		–
	26 Bn 2 Punjab Regt	–		–
	27 Bn 2 Punjab Regt	–		–
	(became 1 Chamar February 1943)			

1922 title	1939–45 title	Partition 1947	India or Pakistan	Current title
3rd Madras Regiment				
1 Bn	Disbanded 10 Feb 28	–		–
2 Bn	Disbanded 24 May 26	–		–
3 Bn	Disbanded 10 Nov 23	–		–
4 Bn	Disbanded 30 Jun 23	–		–
10 Bn	Disbanded 24 May 26	–		–
11 Bn ITF	1 Bn 3 Madras Regt	1 Bn Madras Regt	I	1 Bn Mech Inf Regt
12 Bn ITF	2 Bn 3 Madras Regt	2 Bn Madras Regt	I	2 Bn Madras Regt
13 Bn ITF	3 Bn 3 Madras Regt	3 Bn Madras Regt	I	3 Bn Madras Regt
14 Bn ITF	1 Coorg Bn June 1942	–		–
15 Bn ITF (1939)	4 Bn 3 Madras Regt	4 Bn Madras Regt	I	4 Bn Madras Regt
	5 Bn 3 Madras Regt	–		–
	6 Bn 3 Madras Regt	–		–
	7 Bn 3 Madras Regt	–		–
	25 Bn 3 Madras Regt	–		–
	26 Bn 3 Madras Regt	–		–
	27 Bn 3 Madras Regt	–		–
	28 Bn 3 Madras Regt	–		–
4th Bombay Grenadiers				
1 Bn	1 Bn 4 Bombay Grenadiers	1 Bn Indian Grenadiers	I	2 Bn Guards
2 Bn	2 Bn 4 Bombay Grenadiers	2 Bn Indian Grenadiers	I	2 Bn Grenadiers
3 Bn (disbanded 31 Mar 30)	3 Bn 4 Bombay Grenadiers*	3 Bn Indian Grenadiers	I	3 Bn Grenadiers
4 Bn (disbanded 31 Mar 30)	4 Bn 4 Bombay Grenadiers†	4 Bn Indian Grenadiers	I	4 Bn Grenadiers
5 Bn (disbanded 18 Nov 23)	5 Bn 4 Bombay Grenadiers‡	–		–
10 Bn (merged with 10/9 Jat		–		–
1 Oct 30)	Regimental Centre January 1942	–		–
11 Bn ITF	26 Bn 4 Bombay Grenadiers	–		–
	(became 1 Ajmer 1 Jul 42)	–		–
	14 Bn 4 Bombay Grenadiers	–		–
	25 Bn 4 Bombay Grenadiers			
	27 Bn 4 Bombay Grenadiers			
	(became 2 Ajmer 1 Jul 42)			

*(re-raised 1 Nov 40) †(re-raised 1 Feb 41) †(re-raised 15 Oct 41)

5th Mahratta Light Infantry				
1 Bn	1 Bn 5 Mahratta LI	1 Bn Mahratta LI	I	1 Bn Maratha LI
2 Bn	2 Bn 5 Mahratta LI	2 Bn Mahratta LI	I	2 Bn Maratha LI
3 Bn	3 Bn 5 Mahratta LI	3 Bn Mahratta LI	I	2 Bn Parachute Regt
4 Bn	4 Bn 5 Mahratta LI	4 Bn Mahratta LI	I	4 Bn Maratha LI
5 Bn	5 Bn 5 Mahratta LI	5 Bn Mahratta LI	I	5 Bn Maratha LI
10 Bn	Regimental Centre	–		–
11 Bn ITF	15 Bn 5 Mahratta LI	–		–
12 Bn ITF (1939)	16 Bn 5 Mahratta LI	–		–
	6 Bn 5 Mahratta LI	–		–
	7 Bn 5 Mahratta LI	–		–
	(to I Artillery October 1942)	–		–
	8 Bn 5 Mahratta LI	–		–
	(to I Artillery January 1942)	–		–
	9 Bn 5 Mahratta LI	–		–
	(to I Artillery January 1942)	–		–
	14 Bn 5 Mahratta LI	–		–
	17 Bn 5 Mahratta LI	–		–
	18 Bn 5 Mahratta LI	–		–
	(raised as 25/5 Mahratta LI)	–		
	26 Bn 5 Mahratta LI	–		
	27 Bn 5 Mahratta LI			
	28 Bn 5 Mahratta LI			
	29 Bn 5 Mahratta LI			
	30 Bn 5 Mahratta LI			

1922 title	1939–45 title	Partition 1947	India or Pakistan	Current title
6th Rajputana Rifles				
1 Bn	1 Bn 6 Rajputana Rifles	1 Bn Rajputana Rifles	I	3 Bn Guards
2 Bn	2 Bn 6 Rajputana Rifles	2 Bn Rajputana Rifles	I	2 Bn Rajputana Rifles
3 Bn	3 Bn 6 Rajputana Rifles	3 Bn Rajputana Rifles	I	3 Bn Rajputana Rifles
4 Bn	4 Bn 6 Rajputana Rifles	4 Bn Rajputana Rifles	I	4 Bn Rajputana Rifles
5 Bn	5 Bn 6 Rajputana Rifles	5 Bn Rajputana Rifles	I	5 Bn Rajputana Rifles
10 Bn	Regimental Centre	–		–
11 Bn ITF	14 Bn 6 Rajputana Rifles	–		–
12 Bn ITF (1940)	15 Bn 6 Rajputana Rifles	–		–
	6 Bn 6 Rajputana Rifles	6 Bn Rajputana Rifles	I	6 Bn Rajputana Rifles
	7 Bn 6 Rajputana Rifles	–		–
	8 Bn 6 Rajputana Rifles	–		–
	9 Bn 6 Rajputana Rifles	–		–
	(to I Artillery February 1941)	–		–
	16 Bn 6 Rajputana Rifles	–		–
	MG Bn 6 Rajputana Rifles	–		–
	25 Bn 6 Rajputana Rifles	–		–
	26 Bn 6 Rajputana Rifles	–		–
	27 Bn 6 Rajputana Rifles			

7th Rajput Regiment				
1 Bn	1 Bn 7 Rajput Regt	1 Bn Rajput Regt	I	4 Bn Guards
2 Bn	2 Bn 7 Rajput Regt	2 Bn Rajput Regt	I	2 Bn Rajput Regt
3 Bn	3 Bn 7 Rajput Regt	3 Bn Rajput Regt	I	3 Bn Rajput Regt
4 Bn	4 Bn 7 Rajput Regt	4 Bn Rajput Regt	I	4 Bn Rajput Regt
5 Bn	5 Bn 7 Rajput Regt	5 Bn Rajput Regt	I	5 Bn Rajput Regt
10 Bn	Regimental Centre	–		–
11 Bn ITF	9 Bn 7 Rajput Regt	–		–
12 Bn ITF (1940)	14 Bn 7 Rajput Regt	14 Bn Rajput Regt	I	14 Bn Rajput Regt
	6 Bn 7 Rajput Regt	–		–
	7 Bn 7 Rajput Regt (to I Artillery February 1942)	–		–
	8 Bn 7 Rajput Regt (to I Artillery February 1942)	–		–
	15 Bn 7 Rajput Regt	–		–
	16 Bn 7 Rajput Regt	–		–
	17 Bn 7 Rajput Regt (raised as MG Bn)	17 Bn Rajput Regt	I	17 Bn Rajput Regt
	18 Bn 7 Rajput Regt (raised as 25/7 Rajput)	–		–
	26 Bn 7 Rajput Regt	–		–
8th Punjab Regiment				
1 Bn	1 Bn 8 Punjab Regt	1 Bn 8 Punjab Regt	P	1 Bn Baluch Regt
2 Bn	2 Bn 8 Punjab Regt	2 Bn 8 Punjab Regt	P	2 Bn Baluch Regt
3 Bn	3 Bn 8 Punjab Regt	3 Bn 8 Punjab Regt	P	3 Bn Baluch Regt
4 Bn	4 Bn 8 Punjab Regt	4 Bn 8 Punjab Regt	P	4 Bn Baluch Regt
5 Bn	5 Bn 8 Punjab Regt	5 Bn 8 Punjab Regt	P	5 Bn Baluch Regt
10 Bn	Regimental Centre	–		–
	6 Bn 8 Punjab Regt	6 Bn 8 Punjab Regt	P	1 Bn Sind Regt
	7 Bn 8 Punjab Regt	–		–
	8 Bn 8 Punjab Regt	8 Bn 8 Punjab Regt	P	2 Bn Sind Regt
	9 Bn 8 Punjab Regt	–		–
	14 Bn 8 Punjab Regt (to I Artillery June 1942)	–		–
	15 Bn 8 Punjab Regt	–		–
	16 Bn 8 Punjab Regt	–		–
	25 Bn 8 Punjab Regt	–		–
	26 Bn 8 Punjab Regt	–		–

1922 title	1939–45 title	Partition 1947	India or Pakistan	Current title
9th Jat Regiment				
1 Bn	1 Bn 9 Jat Regt	1 Bn Jat Regt	I	2 Bn Mech Inf Regt
2 Bn	2 Bn 9 Jat Regt	2 Bn Jat Regt	I	2 Bn Jat Regt
3 Bn	3 Bn 9 Jat Regt	3 Bn Jat Regt	I	3 Bn Jat Regt
4 Bn	4 Bn 9 Jat Regt	–		–
10 Bn (merged with 10/4 Bo Grenadiers 1 Oct 30)	Regimental Centre January 1942	–		–
11 Bn ITF	7 Bn 9 Jat Regt	–		–
12 Bn ITF (1940)	8 Bn 9 Jat Regt	–		–
	5 Bn 9 Jat Regt	5 Bn Jat Regt	I	5 Bn Jat Regt
	6 Bn 9 Jat Regt	6 Bn Jat Regt	I	6 Bn Jat Regt
	9 Bn 9 Jat Regt (raised as 11/14 Punjab 15 Sep 41)	–		–
	14 Bn 9 Jat Regt (raised as 12/14 Punjab 15 Sep 41)	–		–
	15 Bn 9 Jat Regt (raised as 25/9 Jat)	–		–
	MG Bn 9 Jat Regt	–		–
	26 Bn 9 Jat Regt	–		–
	27 Bn 9 Jat Regt	–		–

10th Baluch Regiment				
1 Bn	1 Bn 10 Baluch Regt	1 Bn Baluch Regt	P	6 Bn Baluch Regt
2 Bn	2 Bn 10 Baluch Regt	2 Bn Baluch Regt	P	7 Bn Baluch Regt
3 Bn	3 Bn 10 Baluch Regt	3 Bn Baluch Regt	P	10 Bn Baluch Regt
4 Bn	4 Bn 10 Baluch Regt	4 Bn Baluch Regt	P	11 Bn Baluch Regt
5 Bn	5 Bn 10 Baluch Regt	5 Bn Baluch Regt	P	12 Bn Baluch Regt
10 Bn	Regimental Centre			–
	6 Bn 10 Baluch Regt	–		
	7 Bn 10 Baluch Regt	7 Bn Baluch Regt	P	15 Bn Baluch Regt
	8 Bn 10 Baluch Regt	–		–
	9 Bn 10 Baluch Regt	–		–
	14 Bn 10 Baluch Regt	–		–
	15 Bn 10 Baluch Regt	–		–
	16 Bn 10 Baluch Regt	–		–
	17 Bn 10 Baluch Regt (raised as MG Bn)	17 Bn Baluch Regt	P	19 Bn Baluch Regt–
	18 Bn 10 Baluch Regt (raised as 25/10 Baluch)	–		–
	26 Bn 10 Baluch Regt	–		–
11th Sikh Regiment				
1 Bn	1 Bn 11 Sikh Regt	1 Bn Sikh Regt	I	4 Bn Mech Inf Regt
2 Bn	2 Bn 11 Sikh Regt	2 Bn Sikh Regt	I	2 Bn Sikh Regt
3 Bn	3 Bn 11 Sikh Regt	3 Bn Sikh Regt	I	3 Bn Sikh Regt
4 Bn	4 Bn 11 Sikh Regt	4 Bn Sikh Regt	I	4 Bn Sikh Regt
5 Bn	5 Bn 11 Sikh Regt	–		–
10 Bn	Regimental Centre	–		–
	6 Bn 11 Sikh Regt	–		–
	7 Bn 11 Sikh Regt	7 Bn Sikh Regt	I	5 Bn Sikh Regt
	8 Bn 11 Sikh Regt (to I Artillery March 1942)	–		–
	9 Bn 11 Sikh Regt (to I Artillery March 1942)	–		–
	14 Bn 11 Sikh Regt	–		–
	15 Bn 11 Sikh Regt (raised as 25/11 Sikh)	–		–
	MG Bn 11 Sikh Regt	–		–
	26 Bn 11 Sikh Regt	–		–

1922 title	1939–45 title	Partition 1947	India or Pakistan	Current title
12th Frontier Force Regiment				
1 Bn	1 Bn 12 Frontier Force Regt	1 Bn Frontier Force Regt	P	3 Bn Frontier Force Regt
2 Bn	2 Bn 12 Frontier Force Regt	2 Bn Frontier Force Regt	P	4 Bn Frontier Force Regt
3 Bn	3 Bn 12 Frontier Force Regt	3 Bn Frontier Force Regt	P	5 Bn Frontier Force Regt
4 Bn	4 Bn 12 Frontier Force Regt	4 Bn Frontier Force Regt	P	6 Bn Frontier Force Regt
5 Bn	5 Bn 12 Frontier Force Regt	5 Bn Frontier Force Regt	P	2 Bn Frontier Force Regt
10 Bn	Regimental Centre			–
11 Bn ITF	14 Bn 12 Frontier Force Regt	–		–
	6 Bn 12 Frontier Force Regt	–		–
	7 Bn 12 Frontier Force Regt	–		–
	8 Bn 12 Frontier Force Regt	8 Bn Frontier Force Regt	P	13th Bn Frontier Force Regt
	9 Bn 12 Frontier Force Regt	–		–
	MG Bn 12 Frontier Force Regt	–		–
	25 Bn 12 Frontier Force Regt	–		–
	26 Bn 12 Frontier Force Regt	–		–
13th Frontier Force Rifles				
1 Bn	1 Bn 13 Frontier Force Rifles	1 Bn Frontier Force Rifles	P	7 Bn Frontier Force Regt
2 Bn	2 Bn 13 Frontier Force Rifles	2 Bn Frontier Force Rifles	P	8 Bn Frontier Force Regt
4 Bn	4 Bn 13 Frontier Force Rifles	4 Bn Frontier Force Rifles	P	9 Bn Frontier Force Regt
5 Bn	5 Bn 13 Frontier Force Rifles	5 Bn Frontier Force Rifles	P	10 Bn Frontier Force Regt
6 Bn	6 Bn 13 Frontier Force Rifles	6 Bn Frontier Force Rifles	P	1 Bn Frontier Force Regt
10 Bn	Regimental Centre			
11 Bn ITF	15 Bn 13 Frontier Force Rifles (to Royal Indian Navy February 1943)	–		–
	7 Bn 13 Frontier Force Rifles	–		–
	8 Bn 13 Frontier Force Rifles	–		–
	9 Bn 13 Frontier Force Rifles	–		–
	14 Bn 13 Frontier Force Rifles	–		–
	16 Bn 13 Frontier Force Rifles	–		–
	17 Bn 13 Frontier Force Rifles	–		–
	MG Bn 13 Frontier Force Rifles	–		–
	26 Bn 13 Frontier Force Rifles	–		–
	27 Bn 13 Frontier Force Rifles	–		–

14th Punjab Regiment				
1 Bn	1 Bn 14 Punjab Regt	1 Bn 14 Punjab Regt	P	5 Bn Punjab Regt
2 Bn	2 Bn 14 Punjab Regt	2 Bn 14 Punjab Regt	P	6 Bn Punjab Regt
3 Bn	3 Bn 14 Punjab Regt	3 Bn 14 Punjab Regt	P	7 Bn Punjab Regt
4 Bn	4 Bn 14 Punjab Regt	4 Bn 14 Punjab Regt	P	8 Bn Punjab Regt
5 Bn	5 Bn 14 Punjab Regt	–		–
10 Bn	Regimental Centre			
11 Bn ITF	11 Bn 14 Punjab Regt	–		–
	(became 9/9 Jat 15 Sep 41)			
12 Bn ITF (1940)	12 Bn 14 Punjab Regt	–		–
	(became 14/9 Jat 15 Sep 41)			
	6 Bn 14 Punjab Regt	–		–
	7 Bn 14 Punjab Regt	–		–
	8 Bn 14 Punjab Regt	–		–
	9 Bn 14 Punjab Regt	–		–
	14 Bn 14 Punjab Regt	–		–
	15 Bn 14 Punjab Regt	–		–
	(raised as MG Bn)			
	16 Bn 14 Punjab Regt	–		–
	(raised as 25/14 Punjab)			–
	26 Bn 14 Punjab Regt	–		

1922 title	1939–45 title	Partition 1947	India or Pakistan	Current title
15th Punjab Regiment				
1 Bn	1 Bn 15 Punjab Regt	1 Bn 15 Punjab Regt	P	9 Bn Punjab Regt
2 Bn	2 Bn 15 Punjab Regt	2 Bn 15 Punjab Regt	P	10 Bn Punjab Regt
3 Bn	3 Bn 15 Punjab Regt	3 Bn 15 Punjab Regt	P	11 Bn Punjab Regt
4 Bn	4 Bn 15 Punjab Regt	4 Bn 15 Punjab Regt	P	12 Bn Punjab Regt
10 Bn	Regimental Centre			
11 Bn ITF	8 Bn 15 Punjab Regt	–		–
12 Bn ITF (1940)	9 Bn 15 Punjab Regt	–		–
	5 Bn 15 Punjab Regt	–		–
	6 Bn 15 Punjab Regt	–		–
	7 Bn 15 Punjab Regt	–		–
	14 Bn 15 Punjab Regt (to CMP (I) September 1943)	–		–
	15 Bn 15 Punjab Regt (converted to Garrison Coys)	–		–
	16 Bn 15 Punjab Regt (raised as 25/15 Punjab)	–		–
	MG Bn 15 Punjab Regt (to I Artillery August 1942)	–		– –
	26 Bn 15 Punjab Regt	–		
	27 Bn 15 Punjab Regt	–		
16th Punjab Regiment				
1 Bn	1 Bn 16 Punjab Regt	1 Bn 16 Punjab Regt	P	13 Bn Punjab Regt
2 Bn	2 Bn 16 Punjab Regt	2 Bn 16 Punjab Regt	P	14 Bn Punjab Regt
3 Bn	3 Bn 16 Punjab Regt	3 Bn 16 Punjab Regt	P	15 Bn Punjab Regt
4 Bn	4 Bn 16 Punjab Regt	4 Bn 16 Punjab Regt	P	17 Bn Punjab Regt
10 Bn	Regimental Centre			
	5 Bn 16 Punjab Regt	–		–
	6 Bn 16 Punjab Regt	–		–
	7 Bn 16 Punjab Regt	7 Bn 16 Punjab Regt	P	19 Bn Punjab Regt
	9 Bn 16 Punjab Regt (raised as 25/16 Punjab)	–		–
	MG Bn 16 Punjab Regt (to I Artillery August 1942)	–		–
	26 Bn 16 Punjab Regt	–		–

17th Dogra Regiment				
1 Bn	1 Bn 17 Dogra Regt	1 Bn Dogra Regt	I	7 Bn Mech Inf Regt
2 Bn	2 Bn 17 Dogra Regt	2 Bn Dogra Regt	I	2 Bn Dogra Regt
3 Bn	3 Bn 17 Dogra Regt	3 Bn Dogra Regt	I	3 Bn Dogra Regt
10 Bn	Regimental Centre	–		–
11 Bn ITF	6 Bn 17 Dogra Regt	–		–
12 Bn ITF (1940)	7 Bn 17 Dogra Regt	–		–
	4 Bn 17 Dogra Regt	4 Bn Dogra Regt	I	4 Bn Dogra Regt
	5 Bn 17 Dogra Regt	–		–
	MG Bn 17 Dogra Regt	–		–
	25 Bn 17 Dogra Regt	–		–
	26 Bn 17 Dogra Regt	–		–
18th Royal Garhwal Rifles				
1 Bn	1 Bn 18 R Garhwal Rifles	1 Bn R Garhwal Rifles	I	6 Bn Mech Inf Regt
2 Bn	2 Bn 18 R Garhwal Rifles	2 Bn R Garhwal Rifles	I	2 Bn Garhwal Rifles
3 Bn	3 Bn 18 R Garhwal Rifles	3 Bn R Garhwal Rifles	I	3 Bn Garhwal Rifles
10 Bn	Regimental Centre	–		–
11 Bn ITF	6 Bn 18 R Garhwal Rifles	–		–
	4 Bn 18 R Garhwal Rifles	–		–
	5 Bn 18 R Garhwal Rifles	–		–
	7 Bn 18 R Garhwal Rifles (to 17/18 Trg Unit)	–		–
	25 Bn 18 R Garhwal Rifles	–		–

1922 title	1939–45 title	Partition 1947	India or Pakistan	Current title
19th Hyderabad Regiment				
1 Bn	1 Bn 19 Hyderabad Regt	1 Bn Kumaon Regt	I	3 Bn Parachute Regt
2 Bn	2 Bn 19 Hyderabad Regt	2 Bn Kumaon Regt	I	2 Bn Kumaon Regt
3 Bn	Disbanded 15 Dec 31	–		–
4 Bn	4 Bn 19 Hyderabad Regt	4 Bn Kumaon Regt	I	4 Bn Kumaon Regt
5 Bn (disbanded 7 Apr 24)	5 Bn 19 Hyderabad Regt (re-raised 1940)	–		–
1 Kumaon Rifles	1 Kumaon Rifles	1 Kumaon Rifles	I	3 Bn Kumaon Regt (Rifles)
10 Bn	Regimental Centre	–		–
11 Bn ITF	11 Bn 19 Hyderabad Regt (became 1 Bihar September 1941)	–		–
	6 Bn 19 Hyderabad Regt	6 Bn Kumaon Regt	I	6 Bn Kumaon Regt
	7 Bn 19 Hyderabad Regt	–		–
	8 Bn 19 Hyderabad Regt	–		–
	9 Bn 19 Hyderabad Regt	–		–
	25 Bn 19 Hyderabad Regt	–		–
	26 Bn 19 Hyderabad Regt	26 Bn Kumaon Regt		–
20th Burma Rifles				
1 Bn	Transferred to Burma Service 1937			
2 Bn				
3 Bn (disbanded 1923)				
4 Bn				
10 Bn				
11 Bn ITF				
	Indian Parachute Regt			
	1 Bn (raised as 152 Para Bn)	–		–
	2 Bn (raised as 153 Para Bn)	–		–
	3 Bn (raised as 154 Para Bn) previously 3/7 Gurkha Rifles)	–		–
	4 Bn (raised as 152 Para Bn)	–		–

(raised as 11/19 Hyderabad)	1 Bn Bihar Regt	I	1 Bn Bihar Regt
2 Bn Bihar Regt	2 Bn Bihar Regt	I	2 Bn Bihar Regt
3 Bn Bihar Regt	3 Bn Bihar Regt	I	3 Bn Bihar Regt
Regimental Centre			
1 Bn Assam Regt	1 Bn Assam Regt	I	1 Bn Assam Regt
2 Bn Assam Regt	2 Bn Assam Regt	I	2 Bn Assam Regt
3 Bn Assam Regt	3 Bn Assam Regt	I	3 Bn Assam Regt
Regimental Centre			
1 Bn Sikh LI	1 Bn Sikh LI	I	1 Bn Sikh LI
2 Bn Sikh LI	2 Bn Sikh LI	I	2 Bn Sikh LI
3 Bn Sikh LI	3 Bn Sikh LI	I	3 Bn Sikh LI
25 Bn Sikh LI	–		–
26 Bn Sikh LI	–		–
(raised as 1,2,3,25,26 Bns Mazhbi & Ramdassia Sikhs)			
Regimental Centre			
1 Bn Mahar Regt	1 Bn Mahar MG Regt	I	1 Bn Mahar Regt
2 Bn Mahar Regt	2 Bn Mahar MG Regt	I	2 Bn Mahar Regt
3 Bn Mahar Regt	3 Bn Mahar MG Regt	I	3 Bn Mahar Regt
25 Bn Mahar Regt	–		–
Regimental Centre	–		–
1 Afridi Bn	Khyber Rifles	P	Khyber Rifles
1 Bn Ajmer Regt	–		–
(raised as 11/4 Bo Grenadiers)			
2 Bn Ajmer Regt	–		–
(raised as 27/4 Bo Grenadiers)			
3 Bn Ajmer Regt	–		–
25 Bn Ajmer Regt			
Training Bn	–		

1922 title	1939–45 title	Partition 1947	India or Pakistan	Current title
	1 Bn Chamar Regt (raised as 27/2 Punjab)	–		–
	1 Lingayat Bn (to RI Artillery June 1946)	35 (Lingayat) A/Tk Regt RIA	I	35 (Lingayat) Heavy Mortar Regt Artillery
	1 Coorg Bn (raised as 15/3 Madras – to RI Artillery 1946)	37 (Coorg) A/Tk Regt RIA	I	37 (Coorg) Regt Artillery
1st Gurkha Rifles				
1 Bn	1 Bn 1 Gurkha Rifles	1 Bn 1 Gurkha Rifles	I	1 Bn 1 Gorkha Rifles
2 Bn	2 Bn 1 Gurkha Rifles	2 Bn 1 Gurkha Rifles	I	2 Bn 1 Gorkha Rifles
	3 Bn 1 Gurkha Rifles	–		–
	4 Bn 1 Gurkha Rifles	–		–
	5 Bn 1 Gurkha Rifles	–		–
2nd Gurkha Rifles				
1 Bn	1 Bn 2 Gurkha Rifles	1 Bn 2 Gurkha Rifles	UK	1 Bn 2 Gurkha Rifles
2 Bn	2 Bn 2 Gurkha Rifles	2 Bn 2 Gurkha Rifles	UK	2 Bn 2 Gurkha Rifles
	3 Bn 2 Gurkha Rifles	–		–
	4 Bn 2 Gurkha Rifles	4 Bn 2 Gurkha Rifles	I	5 Bn 8 Gorkha Rifles
	5 Bn 2 Gurkha Rifles	–		–
3rd Gurkha Rifles				
1 Bn	1 Bn 3 Gurkha Rifles	1 Bn 3 Gurkha Rifles	I	1 Bn 3 Gorkha Rifles
2 Bn	2 Bn 3 Gurkha Rifles	2 Bn 3 Gurkha Rifles	I	2 Bn 3 Gorkha Rifles
	3 Bn 3 Gurkha Rifle	3 Bn 3 Gurkha Rifles	I	3 Bn 3 Gorkha Rifles
	4 Bn 3 Gurkha Rifles	–		–

4th Gurkha Rifles				
1 Bn	1 Bn 4 Gurkha Rifles	1 Bn 4 Gurkha Rifles	I	1 Bn 4 Gorkha Rifles
2 Bn	2 Bn 4 Gurkha Rifles	2 Bn 4 Gurkha Rifles	I	2 Bn 4 Gorkha Rifles
	3 Bn 4 Gurkha Rifles	3 Bn 4 Gurkha Rifles	I	3 Bn 4 Gorkha Rifles
	4 Bn 4 Gurkha Rifles	–		–
5th Royal Gurkha Rifles (Frontier Force)				
1 Bn	1 Bn 5 R Gurkha Rifles	1 Bn 5 R Gurkha Rifles	I	1 Bn 5 Gorkha Rif (FF)
2 Bn	2 Bn 5 R Gurkha Rifles	2 Bn 5 R Gurkha Rifles	I	2 Bn 5 Gorkha Rif (FF)
	3 Bn 5 R Gurkha Rifles	3 Bn 5 R Gurkha Rifles	I	3 Bn 5 Gorkha Rif (FF)
	4 Bn 5 R Gurkha Rifles	–		—
6th Gurkha Rifles				
1 Bn	1 Bn 6 Gurkha Rifles	1 Bn 6 Gurkha Rifles	UK	1 Bn 6 Gurkha Rifles
2 Bn	2 Bn 6 Gurkha Rifles	2 Bn 6 Gurkha Rifles	UK	–
	3 Bn 6 Gurkha Rifles	3 Bn 6 Gurkha Rifles	I	5 Bn 5 Gorkha Rif (FF)
	4 Bn 6 Gurkha Rifles	–		–
7th Gurkha Rifles				
1 Bn	1 Bn 7 Gurkha Rifles	1 Bn 7 Gurkha Rifles	UK	1 Bn 7 Gurkha Rifles
2 Bn	2 Bn 7 Gurkha Rifles	2 Bn 7 Gurkha Rifles	UK	–
	3 Bn 7 Gurkha Rifles (to 154(Gurkha) Para Bn June 1943, redesignated 3 Bn Indian Para Regt November 1945. Reverted to 3/7 GR November 1946)	–		–
	4 Bn 7 Gurkha Rifles	–		–
8th Gurkha Rifles				
1 Bn	1 Bn 8 Gurkha Rifles	1 Bn 8 Gurkha Rifles	I	3 Bn Mech Inf Regt
2 Bn	2 Bn 8 Gurkha Rifles	2 Bn 8 Gurkha Rifles	I	2 Bn 8 Gorkha Rifles
	3 Bn 8 Gurkha Rifles	–		–
	4 Bn 8 Gurkha Rifles	4 Bn 8 Gurkha Rifles	I	4 Bn 8 Gorkha Rifles

1922 title	1939–45 title	Partition 1947	India or Pakistan	Current title
9th Gurkha Rifles				
1 Bn	1 Bn 9 Gurkha Rifles	1 Bn 9 Gurkha Rifles	I	1 Bn 9 Gorkha Rifles
2 Bn	2 Bn 9 Gurkha Rifles	2 Bn 9 Gurkha Rifles	I	2 Bn 9 Gorkha Rifles
	3 Bn 9 Gurkha Rifles	3 Bn 9 Gurkha Rifles	I	3 Bn 9 Gorkha Rifles
	4 Bn 9 Gurkha Rifles	–		–
	5 Bn 9 Gurkha Rifles	–		–
10th Gurkha Rifles				
1 Bn	1 Bn 10 Gurkha Rifles	1 Bn 10 Gurkha Rifles	UK	1 Bn 10 Gurkha Rifles
2 Bn	2 Bn 10 Gurkha Rifles	2 Bn 10 Gurkha Rifles	UK	–
	3 Bn 10 Gurkha Rifles			–
	4 Bn 10 Gurkha Rifles			–
	25 Gurkha Rifles (late 1942)	–		–
	26 Gurkha Rifles (November 1943)	–		–
	14 Gurkha Rifles (September 1943)	–		–
	29 Gurkha Rifles (August 1943)	–		–

38 Gurkha Rifles (August 1943)		–	–
56 Gurkha Rifles (1943)		–	–
710 Gurkha Rifles (August 1943)	–		–

APPENDIX 'E'

THE ANGLO-INDIAN FORCE 1916

It was on 15 Mar 16, almost two years into the Great War, that sanction was granted to raise an Anglo-Indian Force. The pay, privileges, concessions, allowances, etc were to be identical with those of British troops serving in India.

This was, of course, not the first movement that had been made towards Anglo-Indian recruitment. On the 5 Aug 14, the day after the outbreak of war, the Hon JH Abbott, the then Anglo-Indian Representative on the Imperial Legislative Council and the accredited head of the community, at once wired the Commander-in-Chief, India, offering to raise an Anglo-Indian Regiment for service abroad, as well as a corps of women nurses.

> *'Scarcely had the dread tocsin been sounded when back from the 'outposts of the Empire' came the eager response of loyal sons answering the mother-call. Class and creed distinction were alike forgotten in the hour of threatened danger. Forgotten also were former disabilities. Fancied or real all were relegated to the realms of the immaterial, and nothing deemed worthy of consideration save the call 'Your King and country need you''.*
>
> *(The Anglo-Indian Force 1916 – Published 1919)*

Little information has appeared on this body and I am indebted to Tony Farrington of the India Office Library and Records who located a copy of the locally-produced book quoted above.

The offer made on the outbreak of war was not taken up but Mr Abbott continued to press for the formation of the force until March 1916. Notwithstanding, in the meantime, almost eight thousand members of the Domiciled European and Anglo-Indian Community had been accepted for service or were already in uniform.

The tardy acceptance of Abbott's offer meant that many of the leaders of the Community were minded to decline the military authorities' request: many of its best men had already volunteered and their services lost to the new Force. The ranks of the British regiments were opened to members of the Community in January 1916, in particular The Dorsetshire Regiment and it was lamented that their identity became lost and their value to the Community made of no effect.

Other more attractive offers were available to tempt the potential recruits away from the new Force. The Community was proverbially a poor one and monetary considerations had to be paramount; moreover, the men married young and it is surprising that the AIF recruited as well as it did. The monthly twenty-five rupees for a private soldier had to be set against the attractions of a nursing-orderly corps paid Rs70/- per month and demanding lower physical standards and the Supply and Transport Corps paid Rs168/- per month, supposedly only to Europeans, although several hundreds of the fairer Anglo-Indians had already enlisted.

In addition to these, opportunities existed for employment on railways in East Africa and Mesopotamia, regular and well-paid work already familiar to the majority of Anglo-Indians of military age.

In the first instance, two troops of cavalry were authorised, each troop consisting of one subaltern and thirty NCOs and men. Initially, they were attached to the 7th Queen's Own Hussars, then stationed at Meerut but, on 4 May 17, it was decreed that the two troops would be better employed as signal troops and they became 4 Cavalry Brigade Signal Troop and the Secunderabad Cavalry Brigade Signal Troop.

The artillery element was to be one section of field artillery and this was located at Jhansi, made up of one subaltern and seventy NCOs and men, attached to 77 Battery RFA. The gunners regarded themselves as the élite of the Anglo-Indian Force and they were expanded to a strength of three subalterns and more than two hundred NCOs and men, having moved to Rawalpindi. On 23 Oct 16, the members of the Anglo-Indian Empire League in Karachi bade godspeed to the first sons of the Community to go to the front as Anglo-Indian soldiers. The first battery was to see action in Mesopotamia.

The proposed infantry establishment was laid down as sixteen platoons, each of one subaltern and forty NCOs and men. There was no mention of other officers and it is assumed that the company commanders and the battalion commander would be British Service officers since it was Major H M Bowers of The Hampshire Regiment who took No 1 Company to Mesopotamia on 12 Jan 17.

Training of the infantry was at Sialkot, attached to The Duke of Wellington's Regiment but the intended strength was never realised, only 601 men being enlisted. The recruits from North India were deemed to be of better calibre than those from the South and not all those from the existing Indian Volunteers were acceptable. Among the officers, one had been in the UK at the outbreak of war and had enlisted in The Artists' Rifles, serving subsequently in Salonika with the 2/13 London Regiment. Somewhat surprisingly, he was not in the company which went to Mesopotamia but served out the war in Malabar with No 2 Company under Captain F E D Campbell of The South Lancashire Regiment.

It was, apparently, not the intention to use the infantry as an integral battalion. Indian Army Order 203/16 announced that 'after completion of training, any of the above units or any portion of them will be liable to be sent to any British unit of the same arm, regular or Territorial, serving in India on active service'. The cavalry and field artillery were to be recruited throughout India: infantry was to be raised as follows:

4 platoons from Bengal, Orissa, Bihar and Assam
2 platoons from Burma
4 platoons from Madras (incl Mysore and Hyderabad)
2 platoons from Bombay, Scinde and Baluchistan
2 platoons from United Provinces
1 platoon from Punjab, NWFP and Kashmir
1 platoon from Central Provinces, Central India and Rajputana

Little information appeared on uniform but for officers it was to be khaki, as for British cavalry, RFA or British Infantry of the Line (other than Highland, Scottish or Rifle regiments). On the shoulders, instead of the titles of the corps to which they were attached, the letters 'AIF' were to be worn below and of the same material as the badges of rank. Buttons were to be plain full dome. Other rank uniform was to be as for ORs in British cavalry, RFA or Line infantry, brass letters 'AIF' on the shoulder and universal pattern buttons.

Following the return after the war of those units of the AIF which served out of India, the Government of India sanctioned the formation of a permanent Anglo-Indian Battery to be styled Anglo-Indian Battery No1, armed with 18 pdr QF guns, to be stationed initially at Trimulgherry, South Indian. No trace of this remains.

BIBLIOGRAPHY

The following list does not include those specific regimental histories which are already included at the end of each of the regimental entries.

Govt. of India	'The Army in India and its evolution' (1924)
Govt. of India	'The Tiger Strikes' (1942)
HMSO	'The Tiger Kills' (1944)
HMSO	'The Tiger Triumphs' (1945)
Mohamed Amin	'Defenders of Pakistan' (Midland Counties Publications, Leicester, 1988)
Major Anthony Baker	'Battle honours of the British and Commonwealth Armies' (Ian Allan, London, 1987)
Major Shankar Bhaduri	'The Indian Army' (Lancer International, New Delhi, 1990)
Victor Bayley	'Permanent way through the Khyber' (Jarrolds, London, 1939)
W Y Carman	'Indian Army Uniforms – Cavalry' (Morgan Grampian, London, 1968)
W Y Carman	'Indian Army Uniforms – Artillery, Engineers and Infantry' (Morgan Grampian, 1969)
Charles Chevenix-Trench	'The Indian Army and the King's Enemies 1900–1947' (Thames & Hudson, London, 1988)
Stephen P Cohen	'The Indian Army' (OUP Bombay, 1971)
Lt Col J P Cross	'In Gurkha Company' (Arms & Armour Press, London 1986)
Maj Gen Chand N Das	Traditions & Customs of the Indian Armed Forces' (Vision Books, New Delhi, 1984)
Lt Col A A David	'Know your armed forces' (Army Educational Stores, New Delhi, 1969)
Maj Gen S Shahid Hamid	'So they rode and fought' (Midas Books, Tunbridge Wells, 1983)
Major F G Harden	Sepoy Uniforms (unpublished, 1958)
Major F G Harden	Sepoy Insignia (unpublished, 1959)
T A Heathcote	'The Indian Army' (David & Charles, Newton Abbot, 1974)
Edward H Hilton	'The Mutiny Records, Oudh and Lucknow – (1856–57)' (Lucknow, 1911)
Major Donovan Jackson	'India's Army' (Sampson Low, Marston & Co London, 1940)
Rajesh Kadian	'India and its Army' (Vision Books, New Delhi, 1990)
Maj Gen James Lunt	'Imperial Sunset' (Macdonald, London, 1981)
Compton Mackenzie	'Eastern Epic – Vol I' (Chatto & Windus, London, 1951)

Major G F MacMunn — 'The Armies of India' (A & C Black, London, 1911)

Lieut Gen Sir George MacMunn — The Martial races of India', (Sampson Low, Marston & Co Ltd London, n.d.)

Philip Mason — 'A matter of honour' (Jonathan Cape, London 1974)

John Masters — 'Bugles and a tiger' (Michael Joseph Ltd, London, 1956)

Leigh Maxwell — 'My God, Maiwand!' (Leo Cooper, London, 1979)

C P Mills — 'A strange war' (Alan Sutton, Gloucester, 1988)

Boris Mollo — 'The Indian Army' (Blandford Press, Poole, 1981)

Geoffrey Moorhouse — 'To the Fontier' (Hodder & Stoughton, London, 1984)

Geoffrey Moorhouse — 'India Britannica' (Harvill Press, London, 1983)

Gen Mohammad Musa H J — 'Jawan to General' (ABC Publishing House, New Delhi, 1985)

Roger Perkins — 'Regiments of the Empire' (Perkins, Newton Abbot, 1989)

Major K C Praval — 'Indian Army after Independence' (Lancer International, New Delhi, 1987)

Earl Roberts — 'Forty-one years in India' (Macmillan, London, 1914)

Brian Robson — 'The Road to Kabul' (Arms & Armour Press, 1986)

Victoria Schofield — 'Every rock, every hill' (Buchan & Enright, London, 1984)

Len Whittaker — 'Some talk of private armies' (Albanium Publishing, Harpenden, 1984)

Nigel Woodyatt — 'Under ten viceroys' (Herbert Jenkins, London, 1922)

The Regiment — 'Calcutta Light Horse' (Gale & Polden Ltd Aldershot, 1955)

Regimental Index

The index has been constructed in seven separate parts; three represent specific periods of time since 1903 and deal with cavalry, pioneer and infantry units whilst the fourth covers the Gurkhas in the period 1903–47 as they remained virtually unaffected by the 1923 renumbering. The fifth, sixth and seventh parts deal with particular categories of unit. Artillery, Engineers and Signals are not included since they are clearly identified in Chapter 7 whilst the corps and services are all within Chapter 9.

- (i) 1903–23
- (ii) 1923–47
- (iii) 1947–91
- (iv) Gurkhas 1903–47
- (v) Indian Volunteers, Indian Defence Force and Auxiliary Force, India units
- (vi) Frontier Corps, Scouts and para-military units
- (vii) Indian State Force units

Part (i)

1903–23

Cavalry

Infantry

Part (ii)

1923–47

Cavalry

Pioneers

Infantry

War–raised Units

Part (iii)

1947–91

INDIA

Cavalry

Infantry

PAKISTAN

Infantry

Part (iv)

1903–47

Gurkhas

Part (v)

Indian Volunteers, Indian Defence Force and Auxiliary Force, India units are not listed individually except in the case of the railway regiments. The others are all localised under geographical locations: thus, 'Bombay' will embrace light horse, artillery, engineer and infantry units within the Presidency

Railway Units

Part (vi)

Frontier Corps, Scouts and para–military units

Part (vii)

Indian State Forces